Cisco CCNA in 60 Days

Study Guide

Paul Browning (LLB Hons) CCNP, MCSE
Farai Tafa dual CCIE
Daniel Gheorghe CCIE
Dario Barinic dual CCIE

ISBN-13: 978-1548378738
ISBN-10: 1548378739

Published by:
Reality Press Ltd.
Midsummer Court
314 Midsummer Blvd.
Milton Keynes
UK
MK9 2UB

LEGAL NOTICE

The advice in this book is designed to help you achieve the standard of the Cisco Certified Network Associate (CCNA) exam, which is Cisco's foundation internetworking examination. A CCNA is able to carry out basic router and switch installations and troubleshooting. Before you carry out more complex operations, it is advisable to seek the advice of experts or Cisco Systems, Inc.

The practical scenarios in this book are meant to illustrate a technical point only and should be used only on your privately owned equipment, never on a live network.

Also From Reality Press

101 Labs for the Cisco CCNA Exam

Cisco CCNA Simplified

Subnetting Secrets

About the Authors

Paul Browning

I worked in the police force in the UK from 1988 to 2000. I was always on active duty and spent time both as a detective and as a sergeant. I got involved in IT in 1995 when I bought my first computer and had to get a friend to help me sort out the autoexec.bat file to get DOS working. Then I had to fix something inside the computer when it broke. I sort of enjoyed that so I paid to go on an A+ PC assembly course.

I volunteered to teach e-mail in the police station when that came in, around 1995, and that was fun too. I left the police force to work on a helpdesk in 2000 but quickly grew tired of the monotony of fixing the same problems. I studied hard and in a few months passed my MCSE and CCNA exams. I got a job with Cisco Systems in the UK in late 2000, where I was on the WAN support team.

We were all made redundant in 2002 because the IT bubble had burst by then and I found myself out of work. Frightened and desperate, I offered to teach a Cisco course at a local IT training center and, to my surprise, they agreed. I quickly had to write some notes and labs, which became a book I called *Cisco CCNA Simplified*. That book has now been replaced by the one you are reading now.

The book gave readers all the information they needed to pass the CCNA exam, as well as the ability to apply everything they had learned to the real world of Cisco networking. The book sold many thousands of copies all over the world, and eventually it turned into an online course at www.howtonetwork.com, which now offers video based IT certification training.

With the notes I had written, I started my own Cisco training company, which taught CCNA and CCNP boot camps in the UK for a few years. I sold the company to a friend in 2008 so I could work on online training, which gave me more time with my family.

Farai Tafa

Farai Tafa, CCIE 14811 RS/SP, is an internetwork engineer with over 15 years of experience in core IP routing, LAN and WAN switching, IP telephony, and wireless LAN implementation. He currently holds two Cisco CCIE certifications in the Routing and Switching and the Service Provider tracks. His other certifications include CCVP, JNCIA, JNCIS, and ITILv3 Foundation.

Farai lives in Dallas, Texas, with his wife and two daughters.

Daniel Gheorghe

Daniel Gheorghe is a CCIE in Routing and Switching. He is currently preparing for his second CCIE certification (in Security) and he is developing his skills in system penetration testing. He also holds numerous certifications in networking and security, from Cisco and other vendors, including CCNA, CCDA, CCNA Security, CCNP, CCDP, CCIP, FCNSA, FCNSP, and CEH. He took an interest in IT at an early age and soon developed a passion for computer networking, which made him study hard in order to reach an expert level.

Daniel has worked for different Cisco Partners and System Integrators in Romania in system design, implementation, and troubleshooting for enterprise-level networks. He is also involved in several international freelance consulting projects in his areas of expertise. Daniel is a very dynamic person, and in his spare time he likes to travel and to participate in all kinds of sports.

Dario Barinic

Dario Barinic is a network expert (dual CCIE #25071—Routing and Switching, and Service Provider) with a Master of Engineering degree and 12 years of experience in the networking field. He also holds other certifications, such as Cisco CCNA and CCNP, HP AIS, ASE, MASE, and various Cisco specializations.

Dario is specialized in the area of routing and switching (designing, implementing, troubleshooting, and operating service provider and large enterprise WAN and LAN networks). His major fields of interest are service provider/large enterprise networks (core routing and switching), network security, and passing on knowledge to enthusiastic individuals who are at the start of their networking career.

Dario works as a regional systems integrator for a Cisco Gold Partner in Zagreb, Croatia, where he lives. He is also involved in various international freelance consulting projects, primarily in the area of routing and switching.

Table of Contents

Preface i

Day 1: Networks, Cables, OSI, and TCP Models 1
    Day 1 Tasks 1
    Network Devices 2
    Firewalls 11
    Wireless Networking and Components 16
    Campus LAN Topologies 21
    OSI and TCP Models 25
    TCP/IP 32
    Cables and Media 42
    Connecting to a Router 51
    Day 1 Lab 67

Day 2: IP Addressing and VLSM 69
    Day 2 Tasks 69
    Network Traffic Types 70
    IP Addressing 72
    Address Classes 76
    Using IP Addresses 78
    Subnetting 79
    Route Summarization 88
    Variable Length Subnet Masking 92
    Troubleshooting IP Addressing Issues 94
    Day 2 Lab 97

Day 3: IPv6 Concepts 99
    Day 3 Tasks 99
    History of IPv6 100
    IPv6 Addressing 102
    IPv6 Address Representation 105
    The Different IPv6 Address Types 107
    IPv6 Protocols and Mechanisms 115
    Subnetting with IPv6 128
    IPv6 Compared to IPv4 131
    Day 3 Lab 135

Day 4: Review 137
    Day 4 Tasks 137

Day 5: Switching Concepts 139
    Day 5 Tasks 139
    Switching Basics 140
    Switching Concepts 146
    Initial Switch Configuration 150
    Virtual Local Area Networks (VLANs) 153
    Basic Switching Troubleshooting 162
    Basic VLAN Troubleshooting 166
    Day 5 Labs 172

Day 6: Trunking and DTP 177
    Day 6 Tasks 177
    Configuring and Verifying Trunk Links 177
    Dynamic Trunking Protocol (DTP) 180
    VTP 183
    Troubleshooting Trunking and VTP 187
    Day 6 Labs 188

Day 7: CDP and LLDP 191
    Day 7 Tasks 191
    Cisco Discovery Protocol (CDP) 191
    Link Layer Discovery Protocol (LLDP) 193
    Day 7 Lab 195

Day 8: Review 198
    Day 8 Tasks 198

Day 9: Switch Security 201
    Day 9 Tasks 201
    Securing the Switch 202
    Switch Port Security 211
    Day 9 Labs 227

Day 10: Routing Concepts 230
    Day 10 Tasks 230
    Basic Routing 231
    Classful and Classless Protocols 243
    Passive Interfaces 243
    Routing Protocol Classes 244
    The Objectives of Routing Protocols 247
    Routing Problems Avoidance Mechanisms 248
    Troubleshooting Routing Issues 249
    Inter-VLAN Routing 253
    Troubleshooting Inter-VLAN Routing 257
    Day 10 Lab 259

Day 11: Static Routing 262
    Day 11 Tasks 262
    Configuring Static Routes 263

Configuring Static IPv6 Routes..274
Troubleshooting Static Routes..275
Day 11 Labs..276

Day 12: Routing Information Protocol..280
Day 12 Tasks..280
Routing Information Protocol..281
Troubleshooting RIP..285
Day 12 Lab..286

Day 13: Review...288
Day 13 Tasks..288

Day 14: DHCP, DNS and NTP..292
Day 14 Tasks..292
DHCP Functionality..293
Configuring DHCP..298
Troubleshooting DHCP Issues..302
DNS Operations...303
Troubleshooting DNS Issues..303
Network Time Protocol..304
Day 14 Labs...306

Day 15: IPv4 Access Lists...308
Day 15 Tasks..308
ACL Basics...309
Port Numbers..309
Access Control List Rules..310
Wildcard Masks...314
Configuring Access Control Lists...315
ACL Sequence Numbers..320
ACL Logging..321
Using ACLs to Limit Telnet and SSH Access...322
Troubleshooting and Verifying ACLs...323
Day 15 Labs...325

Day 16: Network Address Translation.......................................329
Day 16 Tasks..329
NAT Basics...329
Configuring and Verifying NAT...332
Troubleshooting NAT...337
Day 16 Labs...338

Day 17: Review...346
Day 17 Tasks..346

Day 18: Syslog and IOS...350
Day 18 Tasks..350
Router Memory and Files...351

Managing the IOS......354
Cisco Password Recovery......357
File System Management......358
IOS Licensing......362
Syslog Logging......366
Day 18 Labs......372

Day 19: Router Security......375
Day 19 Tasks......375
Securing the Router......376
Day 19 Lab......382

Day 20: Review......385
Day 20 Tasks......385

Day 21: Troubleshooting Layers 1 and 2......386
Day 21 Tasks......386
Troubleshooting at the Physical Layer......387
Using the Command Line Interface to Troubleshoot Link Issues......392
Troubleshooting Port Configuration......397
Troubleshooting VLANs and Trunking......398
Ping, Traceroute, and Their Extended Options......411
Terminal Monitor......417
Logging Events......418
Day 21 Labs......420

Day 22: Review......421
Day 22 Tasks......421

Day 23: Review......425
Day 23 Tasks......425

Day 24: Review......428
Day 24 Tasks......428

Day 25: Review......431
Day 25 Tasks......431

Day 26: Review......433
Day 26 Tasks......433

Day 27: Review......436
Day 27 Tasks......436

Day 28: Review......437
Day 28 Tasks......437

Day 29: Review......438
Day 29 Tasks......438

Day 30: Review......439
Day 30 Tasks......439

Day X: Exam Day......440

Day 31: Spanning Tree Protocol 441
    Day 31 Tasks 441
    The Need for STP 442
    IEEE 802.1D Configuration BPDUs 443
    Spanning Tree Port States 445
    Spanning Tree Bridge ID 447
    Spanning Tree Root Bridge Election 448
    Spanning Tree Cost and Priority 451
    Spanning Tree Root and Designated Ports 452
    Cisco Spanning Tree Enhancements 456
    Troubleshooting STP 464
    The Need for RSTP 465
    Configuring RSTP 468
    Extended VLANs 468
    Day 31 Lab 471

Day 32: EtherChannels and Link Aggregation Protocols 475
    Day 32 Tasks 475
    Understanding EtherChannels 475
    Port Aggregation Protocol Overview 477
    Link Aggregation Control Protocol Overview 481
    EtherChannel Load-Distribution Methods 482
    EtherChannel Configuration Guidelines 483
    Day 32 Lab 498

Day 33: Switch Stacking and Layer 2 Mitigation Techniques 499
    Day 33 Tasks 499
    Switch Stacking and Chassis Aggregation 500
    Common Access Layer Threat Mitigation Techniques 501

Day 34: Review 506
    Day 34 Tasks 506

Day 35: InterVLAN Routing—Switched Virtual Interfaces 509
    Day 35 Tasks 509
    Inter-VLAN Routing Using Switched Virtual Interfaces 509
    Day 35 Lab 512

Day 36: EIGRP 515
    Day 36 Tasks 515
    Cisco EIGRP Overview and Fundamentals 516
    EIGRP Configuration Fundamentals 517
    EIGRP Messages 524
    EIGRP Neighbor Discovery and Maintenance 528
    Metrics, DUAL, and the Topology Table 537
    Equal Cost and Unequal Cost Load Sharing 548
    Default Routing Using EIGRP 554
    Split Horizon in EIGRP Networks 558

EIGRP Route Summarization..562
Understanding Passive Interfaces...573
Understanding the Use of the EIGRP Router ID...576
Troubleshooting EIGRP..578
Day 36 Lab..593

Day 37: EIGRP For IPv6...596
Day 37 Tasks..596
Cisco IOS Software EIGRPv4 and EIGRPv6 Configuration Differences........597
Configuring and Verifying EIGRPv6 in Cisco IOS Software..........................598
Day 37 Lab..602

Day 38: Review...603
Day 38 Tasks..603

Day 39: OSPF...606
Day 39 Tasks..606
OSPF Overview and Fundamentals...607
OSPF Configuration...613
Designated and Backup Designated Routers...619
Additional Router Types...626
OSPF Packet Types...627
Establishing Adjacencies...636
OSPF LSAs and the Link State Database (LSDB)..638
OSPF Areas..641
Route Metrics and Best Route Selection..643
OSPF Default Routing..646
Configuring OSPF..646
Troubleshooting OSPF...647
Day 39 Labs..657

Day 40: OSPFv3...660
Day 40 Tasks..660
OSPF Version 3...660
OSPFv2 and OSPFv3 Configuration Differences...662
Configuring and Verifying OSPFv3 in Cisco IOS Software............................663
Day 40 Labs..665

Day 41: Review...668
Day 41 Tasks..668

Day 42: Wide Area Networking Services...670
Day 42 Tasks..670
WAN Overview...671
NBMA Technologies...673
WAN Components...675
WAN Protocols...675
WAN Services...676

VPN Technologies...683
MPLS...685
Basic Serial Line Configuration...686
PPPoE..686
PPP Operations...689
Troubleshooting PPP...691
Configuring and Verifying PPP and MLPPP on WAN Interfaces Using Local Authentication...691
Troubleshooting WAN Connections..692
Day 42 Labs..694

Day 43: Generic Routing Encapsulation...699
Day 43 Tasks..699
GRE Tunnel Connectivity..699
Configuring GRE Tunnels..700
Troubleshooting GRE Tunnels..701
Day 43 Lab..703

Day 44: eBGP...705
Day 44 Tasks..705
Single-homed Branch eBGP Connectivity...705
eBGP Configuration...709
Day 44 Lab..714

Day 45: Review..716
Day 45 Tasks..716

Day 46: Cloud Computing..718
Day 46 Tasks..718
Cloud Computing...718
Virtualization...721

Day 47: Hot Standby Router Protocol...729
Day 47 Tasks..729
Hot Standby Router Protocol..729
Configuring HSRP...746
Day 47 Lab..751

Day 48: Quality of Service..752
Day 48 Tasks..752
Basic QoS Concepts...753
QoS Models..755
Catalyst Ingress QoS Mechanisms..758

Day 49: Review..764
Day 49 Tasks..764

Day 50: IPv6 Access Lists..765
Day 50 Tasks..765
Configuring IPv6 Access Control Lists..765
Day 50 Lab..770

Day 51: Cisco APIC-EM Path Trace ACL Analysis Application 772
   Day 51 Tasks 772
   Cisco APIC-EM Path Trace Tool 772

Day 52: IP SLA and Simple Network Managment Protocol 774
   Day 52 Tasks 774
   Cisco IOS IP Service Level Agreement 775
   Simple Network Management Protocol 780

Day 53: Switched Port Analyzer and AAA 783
   Day 53 Tasks 783
   Monitoring and Capturing Packets Using SPAN 783
   Authentication, Authorization, and Accounting 787

Day 54: Network Programmability 796
   Day 54 Tasks 796
   Software Defined Networking 796

Day 55: Review 799
   Day 55 Tasks 799

Day 56: Review 801
   Day 56 Tasks 801

Day 57: Review 803
   Day 57 Tasks 803

Day 58: Review 805
   Day 58 Tasks 805

Day 59: Review 807
   Day 59 Tasks 807

Day 60: Review 808
   Day 60 Tasks 808

Preface

My name is Paul Browning and, along with Farai, Dario, and Daniel, my job is to get you through your CCNA (or ICND1 and ICND2) exam(s) in the next 60 days. Your job is to do what I tell you to do, when I tell you to do it. If you can do that, then in 60 days' time you will be a qualified Cisco CCNA engineer. If you skip days or try to play catch-up by doing two or three days' work when you have time, you will fail—badly. Trust me, I've been teaching a long time and I know what I'm talking about.

Do any of the following problems sound familiar to you?

> *"I just don't know where to start studying. I feel overwhelmed by the information."*
> *"I've bought all the CBT-style videos and books, and have even been on a course, but I don't feel ready to take the exam and I don't know if I ever will."*
> *"I've been studying for a long time now, but I haven't booked the exam yet because I just don't feel ready."*

I hear these comments every day from Cisco students on forums and via e-mails to my office. I've come to realize that the problem isn't the lack of quality training materials; that used to be the case in the late '90s, but now there are too many training manuals. The problem isn't the lack of desire to pass the exam. The problem is a lack of two things which mean the difference between success and obscurity—a plan and structure.

This is why personal trainers do so well. We can all exercise every day, go for a run, do push ups, and eat healthy food, but having a trainer means you don't have to think about it. You just turn up and do what he tells you to do and you get the results (unless you cheat). This is where I come in—you turn up at the time you agree to each day and do what I ask you to do. Don't argue with me, don't complain, and don't make excuses as to why you can't do something. Just do it, as the Nike slogan goes.

READ THIS FIRST!

I've learned a lot and have had some great feedback from the first version of this book, so I thought I'd add this bit to save you and me some time.

1. In order to pass the exam, you need both this book and access to either Packet Tracer/ GNS3 or a live rack of Cisco equipment. Although I do own other training websites for IT certifications and I do refer to them sometimes, there is <u>absolutely no need to join them</u> in order to pass.

2. If Cisco make any exam changes after this book is printed, I will add notes/videos or exams to **https://www.in60days.com/free/ccnain60days/** so you aren't disadvantaged in any way. I've also added your daily exams and other bonus resources here to save space. You must use this free bonus URL in order to prepare for the exam.

3. You must dedicate two hours per day for 60 days in order to pass the exam. More is better if you can manage it. It's only for two months. I've done my best to balance the book out but some days will be longer than two hours whilst others will be shorter, so please do extra study to fill up the time if you finish a module early.

4. Some days are really tough such as EIGRP but it balances out because EIGRP for IPv6 is a very short section you can complete in about 30 minutes so don't get stressed out if you can't finish the days tasks at the exact time frame I allocate. The important thing is getting in two hours of quality study time per day with no excuses. If it takes you 70 or 80 days to become exam ready it's okay. Others get it done in 30 days but we are all different.

5. This course is modular and flexible. We repeat subjects several times to you really learn the material but you can swap or move lessons as you see fit. Only you will know where your strong and weak areas are so feel free to follow my plan exactly or make changes.

GETTING HANDS-ON TIME

You have a few options when it comes to doing the labs. Each option has benefits and drawbacks.

Packet Tracer (PT) is a router and switch simulator created for Cisco Academy students but now available for free download from Cisco (once you register online). I've completed many of the labs and examples in this book using PT purely for convenience. Bear in mind that PT is not live equipment so it will never act in exactly the same way live equipment does. Some students become confused when they can't see certain commands or get the same results they would have gotten when using live equipment. I've had many frustrated students contact me trying to get labs working properly only for me to find out they were using PT. In my opinion, it's enough for CCNA-level study but not beyond that; and remember that for job interviews, you need to have some hands-on time using live equipment.

Next option is a router emulator. This is running actual Cisco IOS code on your computer. GNS3 is a free tool used by many thousands of Cisco engineers, from CCNA to CCIE, to create virtual networks for lab work. The major weakness of GNS3 is that it cannot emulate Cisco switches (this may change soon) because they use hardware to forward frames. You can prepare around 70% towards the exam using GNS3, but then you need to revert to either PT or live switches for lab work. This may change in the near future if Cisco agree to release some of their code to the public to allow students to study for exams.

I've created my version of GNS3 with a network topology created at **www.howtonetwork. com/vRack**. It's free but I don't offer any support and you need to have a valid IOS to add in order for it to work.

Live equipment is another choice. You can buy reasonably priced racks bundled on eBay. You will need at least two 2960 switches and three or four routers in order to do all the labs. I've tried to keep it simple with the minimum amount of labs in this book. You will need to have the correct cables and interface cards, which is why many people turn to racks on eBay. Just double check the price because many racks can be overpriced.

Cisco do test you on 15.x IOS in the exam; however, at the moment, it is a tiny part of the syllabus so anything running 12.3 onwards will do everything you need. If you plan to take the CCNP exam, then you may prefer to choose higher-end models.

Your last option is renting remote racks. Cisco offer a rack rental service (although it's an emulator) which will cover all your CCNA needs and beyond. I have a live rack on **www. howtonetwork.com** but it's for members only.

DOES *CCNA IN 60 DAYS* WORK?

My idea for the program came whilst following a keep fit program provided by a special forces soldier. He wrote a get fit guide where every day you ate certain foods at certain times and did prescribed workouts. The results for me were amazing. I put it down to not having to think; each day I did what he told me to do and I saw my body literally transform from flabby to fit.

It then struck me. If a step-by-step fitness program (which is now all the rage) works for many tens of thousands of normal people, surely it would work for pretty much anything else—like learning guitar, speaking Spanish, or even passing Cisco exams. *Cisco CCNA in 60 Days* was born. The results have been astounding. I started to receive e-mails and forum posts every week from people who had been stuck, sometimes for years, and who were now passing their exams.

I'm not sure why I was surprised, but I had my critics of course. Most hid behind usernames and posted negative reviews on Amazon. When I read them I realized they hadn't actually read what I wrote or even followed the program at all. They were looking for reasons to hate my program. But it all boils down to this, I suppose: If you follow the 60-day program, will it work for YOU?

Well, please don't take my word for it. The program has been around for over 6 years now, and here is a very small sample of the results.

I have a ton of reviews on Amazon from people who have passed the exam and forum posts also. There are no secrets or tricks, they just put 2 hours work in every day and followed the plan I set out in this guide. If you do the same you will get the same result. If you fall behind then don't sweat, just pick up where you left off and carry on.

INTRODUCTION TO THE THIRD EDITION

Updates to the Cisco CCNA exam have always made it harder but the newest changes have made it pretty tough to pass now. So many CCNP level subjects have now dropped into the syllabus including BGP, DHCP snooping, EIGRP for IPv6 as well as new topics including cloud computing and network programmability. You certainly have your work cut out for you I'm afraid.

The exam updates are both good and bad news for you. Good that when you pass, you will be admired and respected by colleagues and employers, but bad in that you have a very difficult task ahead of you. You have a huge amount of information to digest and understand, as well as complex configuration tasks to configure and troubleshoot, with the clock ticking whilst under exam conditions.

In order to help you pass the new-style CCNA exam, I've completely rewritten this book. Some parts of the earlier editions have stayed because they teach you exactly what you need to know and they have been battle tested by thousands of students who came before you. Other parts have been improved or updated as a result of feedback. Entirely new sections have been added due to changes to the syllabus.

I've used several tools this time, including my personal experience in the exams, dual CCIE Farai Tafa's CCNP study guides, real-world experience, RFCs, and what I've learned since 2000, when I left the police force in the UK and started my career in Cisco networking. I've also hired CCIE Daniel Gheorghe and dual CCIE Dario Barinic, who have added sections, updated others, and trimmed other bits out. Bear in mind that all three CCIEs are full-time network architects I hired to improve this guide. None of them teach internetworking, they DO internetworking. Bear that in mind when you are checking out other books and training materials!

FREE STUFF

Unlike Sybex and Cisco Press, Reality Press is a tiny publishing operation. In fact, to be honest, it's just me! I sit in my little office writing and working on my training websites and hire freelancers when I need them. In fact, here is me taking a break from editing this book:

I'm telling you this because I need a small favor from you.

I need your help to promote this book and get the word out by posting a review on Amazon. I do my best to give you great value-for-money and your review will really help. When you've done that, please fill in the form on www.in60days.com/reviews, attach a screenshot, and I'll send you access to a CCNA exam to help you prepare for the real thing. I'll do this no matter what the review says.

FAQS

Q. Is this book the same as your other CCNA book, *Cisco CCNA Simplified*?
A. Nope. I do have a tiny bit of the text from that book and some from my CCNP books in here, but most of it is new. I wanted to include other stuff and some more of my own comments and observations, so this book is an improvement on the others in many ways.

Q. Do I need to take the video course at www.in60days.com?
A. No. Check out https://www.in60days.com/free/ccnain60days/, which complements this book and has all the free exams and other materials.

Q. Is there a discount if I want to do the video course which matches this course?
A. Yes. I want to be clear that I'm not promoting the paid course but I do need to make a charge in order to cover streaming video and production costs. Just use the coupon code '60book' when you visit - https://www.in60days.com/products/ and it drops to $17 from $67.

Q. Does the book cover network foundations for beginners?
A. It used to but because the new exam subjects have added over 300 pages to this book, it's now impossible to fit in many of the basics. If you are a novice, I recommend reading a good Network+ book first.

Q. Why is some stuff in your cram guide/exams but not in the theory?
A. Some stuff I just want to give you in the cram guide or exams, but if I want to cover it in more detail, it will be in the book. I cover all the syllabus stuff in the book but sometimes Cisco sneak in other stuff into the exam so I'll cover it in the crams or practice exams.

Q. Should I do the one-exam route or the two-exam route?
A. You can do either with this program. At the 30-day mark, you can take the ICND1 exam, or you can continue on to the ICND2 module and at the end take the CCNA exam.

Q. Which is best?
A. There is no best. It is cheaper to take one exam and get it over with, but there is more to cover. The two-exam route gives you more breathing space and you get a qualification after the first exam. Personally, I'd take the two-exam route, as it lets you focus on less topics per exam.

Q. How much time do I need to study each day?
A. Set aside two hours per day. Bear in mind that the average person watches five hours of TV every day and more on weekends.

Q. What if I miss a day?

A. You'll want to avoid that at all costs. Find a time when you can study every day. If you have to miss a day, then just pick up where you left off the next day.

Q. What if I have a question?

A. It's impossible for me to support everybody because this book sells thousands of copies.

Q. Can a person really pass in just 60 days? Cisco Academy teaches the CCNA course over two years.

A. They do, but it is usually only one evening per week for two hours, with 20 to 30 students per class. The poor results speak for themselves on that program. My method is more intensive but it is also of very high quality.

Q. Do I need to buy anything else?

A. Not really. You need this book and some Cisco equipment. If you really want extra stuff, then please check out the video course I mention above.

Q. I have more than two hours per day to spend on studying, so can I study more?

A. Sure. Study the same stuff again or do more labs. Don't study what you already know.

Q. What if I can't do two hours per day?

A. You will find it hard to pass if you put less in unless you have previous experience.

Q. I didn't get today's lesson finished. What do I do now?

A. Don't sweat it. Just continue where you left off. Some days are pretty easy so you will actually catch up to where you should be.

HOW THE PROGRAM WORKS

The 60-day study program offers a combination of learning techniques, including reading, reviewing, cramming, testing, and hands-on labs. You will take in new information for the first few sessions and then start to review each module each day, as well as implement the lessons on live Cisco equipment. You will then begin to employ the theory to exam-style questions and eventually apply your knowledge in the real exam.

You need to factor in two hours of study per day spread amongst the theory, labs, exams, and review. I've also built in free sessions for you to choose what you want to study. You start off with mainly theory and then build up to mainly labs and exams, plus review. You will review every lesson the next day and then come back to it again on other review days, as well as in labs and exams. Take NAT, for example:

> Day 16—NAT
> Day 16—NAT labs
> Day 17—NAT review
> Days 23 through 30—Free study and NAT labs
> All days—NAT in the cram guide

In addition, there are NAT challenge labs and you study NAT every day in the cram guide. The same goes for many other subjects. Minor subjects such as CSMA/CD I refer to twice, but that is all. There is little chance these will come up in the exam, so there is little incentive to remember them. There will be ample time to cover everything, as well as free study sessions where you can go over any weak areas. You should keep working on your weak areas until there are none left.

I have included some bonus labs on in60days.com, so if you want to test your hands-on skills further, then please follow those. If you're looking for some other review materials, please check out **https://www.in60days.com/free/ccnain60days/**.

ARE YOU READY?

I've split your study into ICND1 and ICND2. When you book your exam(s), the exam titles are 100-105 for ICND1 and 200-105 for ICND2. You can also take both exams at the same time in the 200-125 CCNAX composite exam. I would recommend that you take the two-exam route because you can concentrate on specific topics and there is less chance of becoming overwhelmed. The downside, of course, is having to pay for two exams, which is more expensive. Please print out the CCNA/ICND1/ICND2 exam syllabus before you take the exam to ensure you have covered everything. Mark each subject out of 10 and ensure you work on the weak areas well before exam day.

EXAM QUESTIONS

Cisco exams are recognized as amongst the toughest in the IT industry. You have not only a large amount of theory to learn for every exam, but you also need to know how to apply your knowledge under exam conditions whilst the clock is ticking.

The CCNA exams are broken down into theory questions and hands-on labs using a router or switch emulator which responds in much the same way as a live one will. Theory questions can be multiple choice or drag-and-drop, where you have to drop answers into the correct place. You can also be shown a network diagram or router output and then be asked to answer a question about it. Additionally, questions can entail multiple parts, for example, four different questions pertaining to the same issue.

The hands-on simulation questions can ask you to configure or troubleshoot routing or switching issues. You may have to connect to multiple devices in order to complete the task. You could also be asked to log in to one specific device and issue various "show" commands in order to answer questions. Cisco may even block you from using certain commands to test your knowledge of more specific IOS commands.

So I think we can agree that the exam is tough, but every day, hundreds of people just like you pass. I was working on a helpdesk when I passed my CCNA exam and I had very limited networking knowledge at the outset.

Now, let's get started.

Networks, Cables, OSI, and TCP Models

DAY 1 TASKS

- Read today's lesson notes (below)
- Read the ICND1 cram guide (download from https://www.in60days.com/free/ccnain60days/)
- Take the day 1 exam
- Do today's lab

Welcome to day 1. Each day you will read the theory notes, review the previous days theory notes (apart from today of course), take a practice exam and do a lab. Some subjects have no lab requirements in the syllabus such as Cloud computing. As the lessons progress you will complete challenge labs.

Some days will be very challenging such as EIGRP and OSPF and may take more than two hours to complete but the following days lessons (EIGRP for IPv6 and OSPFv3) are very short so it balances out.

Today should be a refresher for most of you because it's all basic networking. If it's all new then please stop and read a Network+ study guide before you progress. The CCNA is no longer suitable for complete beginners. There is simply too much to cover.

Today you will learn about the following:

- Network devices
- Firewalls
- Wireless networking
- Campus LAN topologies
- The OSI and TCP models
- TCP/IP
- Cables and media
- Connecting to a router

This module maps to the following ICND1 syllabus requirements:

- 1.0 Network Fundamentals
- 1.1 Compare and contrast OSI and TCP/IP models
- 1.2 Compare and contrast TCP and UDP protocols
- 1.3 Describe the impact of infrastructure components in an enterprise network
- 1.3.a Firewalls
- 1.3.b Access points
- 1.3.c Wireless controllers
- 1.4 Compare and contrast collapsed core and three-tier architectures
- 1.5 Compare and contrast network topologies
- 1.5.a Star
- 1.5.b Mesh
- 1.5.c Hybrid
- 1.6 Select the appropriate cabling type based on implementation requirements
- 5.2.f Loopback
- 5.3 Configure and verify initial device configuration
- 3.4 Describe WAN topology options [ICND2]
- 3.4.a Point-to-point
- 3.4.b Hub and spoke
- 3.4.c Full mesh

NETWORK DEVICES

As a network engineer, you will be using a range of network cables and other media. You need to know which cables will work with which devices and interfaces for WAN, LAN, and management ports and how each devices fits into the overall network infrastructure.

Common Network Devices

Network Switches

Only a few years ago, due to costs, networks were still pretty small. This meant that you could simply plug all devices into a hub or a number of hubs. The hub's job was to boost the signal on the network cable, if required, and then pass out the data on the wire to every other device plugged in. The problem with this, of course, is that the message was intended for only one network host, but it would be sent to all of the other hosts connected to other hubs on the network. (Hubs and switching technology will be covered in more detail in the next module.)

Network switches are a more intelligent version of hubs. Switches use Content Addressable Memory (CAM) and therefore have the ability to remember which device is plugged into which port. Cisco manufactures switch models which are designed to work in small offices and all the way up to large enterprise networks consisting of thousands of devices. We will explore this in more detail later, but, basically, switches operate by using the device's MAC addresses (known as Layer 2 address) and IP addresses (known as Layer 3 address), or they can perform more complex tasks, such as processing lists of permit/deny traffic or protocols and port numbers (known as Layer 4 traffic), or a combination of all these layers and more. We will cover what comprises these layers and their functions later in this module.

Early versions of switches were referred to as network bridges. Bridges examined the source ports and MAC addresses of frames in order to build a table and make forwarding decisions. The tables were typically accessed via software, whereas switches used hardware (i.e., Application Specific Integrated Chips, or ASICs) to access a CAM table (more on this later). Therefore, a switch can be thought of as a multi-port bridge.

Using a switch (see Figure 1.1) allows you to divide your network into smaller, more manageable sections (known as segments). This in turn allows the teams who work inside your company, such as human resources, finance, legal, etc., to work on the same section of the network at the same time, which is useful because the devices will spend most of their time communicating with each other.

Figure 1.1—Cisco 2960 Switch

Each device will connect to an interface on the switch, which is referred to as a port. Common network port speeds are 100Mbps and 1000Mbps (usually referred to as 1Gbps). There are often fiber ports you can use to connect a switch to another switch. Each switch features management ports, which you can connect to in order to perform an initial configuration and gain general access for maintenance over the network.

Figure 1.2 below shows a close-up of ports on a Cisco 2960 switch. Several models of the 2960 are available to meet the needs of a small- to medium-sized business. Please check Cisco release notes for more information on port functions and model differences.

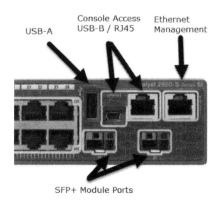

Figure 1.2—Switch Interface Types

You can also use IP telephones with the switches and, even better, the switch ports can provide power to these telephones (using power over Ethernet (PoE) interfaces). The basic network switch will be used to:

- Connect network devices such as printers and PCs
- Give access to network servers and routers
- Segment the network with VLANs

VLANs are virtual Local Area Networks. We will cover these in detail in Day 5.

Routers

As a Cisco engineer, you will spend a lot of time installing, configuring, and troubleshooting routers. For this reason, over half of the CCNA syllabus is dedicated to learning all about router configuration.

A router (see Figure 1.3) is a device used for networking. While network switches involve devices on the same network communicating with each other, the router communicates with devices on different networks. Older models of routers only had ports, which were physically built into them and soldered to the motherboard. This is still sometimes the case, but modern networks now require a router to perform functions for IP telephony, switching, and security, and to connect to several types of telecoms companies. For this reason, routers are also modular, which means you have the router chassis and empty slots into which you can connect a variety of routing or switching modules.

Figure 1.3—Modular Cisco Router with a Blank Slot to the Right

The Cisco website has a lot of advice and information available to explain which router model will suit your business needs. There are also tools which will help you select the correct model and operating system. It's well worth your time learning how to navigate the support and configuration pages and bookmarking them for quick reference.

How Networks Are Represented in Diagrams

All network engineers need a common method to communicate, despite which vendor and telecoms provider they are using. If I had to describe my network topology to you for design or security recommendations, it would work much better if it were in an agreed format as opposed to something I had drawn by hand from memory. The Cisco Certified Design Associate (CCDA) exam is where you will learn about network topologies in far more detail. As for the CCNA exam, you will need a basic understanding of these topologies because the exam may present network issues and ask where you think the problem lies.

Here are the common symbols for network devices you will encounter in your work as a network engineer. You can download these icons from the Cisco website if you type "Cisco icons" in your browser's search engine. We use either plain blue or color (for the Kindle version). I've used a mix of the most common router and switch symbols throughout the book so get used to the types you will see in network diagrams in the real world.

Routers

Switch (Layer 2)

Router with Firewall

Wireless Router

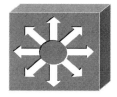

Multilayer Switch

The Cloud—Equipment Owned by the Telecoms Provider

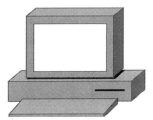

End Device—a PC

Serial Line

Ethernet Link

IP Telephone

Firewall

LAN and WAN Topologies

Topology refers to how network equipment is arranged in order to communicate. How this is done could be limited by the communication protocols the equipment uses, cost, geography, or other factors, such as the need for redundancy should the main link fail.

You should also note that there is often a difference between physical and logical topology. Physical topology is how the network appears when you look at it, whereas logical topology is how the network sees itself. The most common topologies are described in the following sections.

Point-to-Point

This topology is used mainly for WAN links. A point-to-point link is simply one in which one device has one connection to another device. You could add a secondary link connecting each device for redundancy but if the device itself fails, then you lose all connectivity.

Figure 1.4—Point-to-Point Topology

Bus

This topology was created with the first Ethernet networks, where all devices had to be connected to a thick cable referred to as the backbone. If the backbone cable fails, then the network goes down. If a cable linking the device to the backbone cable fails, then only that device will lose connection.

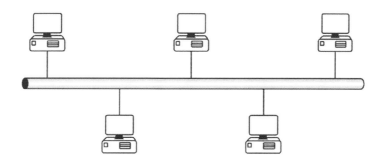

Figure 1.5—Bus Topology

Star

This is probably the most common topology you will encounter. Each network device is connected to a central hub or switch. If one of the cables to the devices fails, then only that device becomes disconnected.

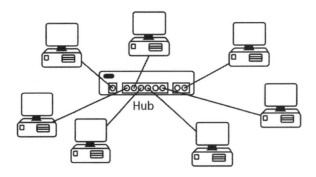

Figure 1.6—Star Topology

Ring

A ring topology is used by token ring networks and Fiber Distributed Data Interface (FDDI) networks, both of which were retired several years ago.

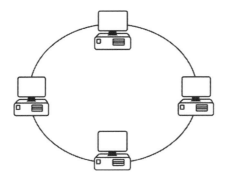

Figure 1.7—Token Ring Topology

A ring topology that is used with FDDI networks employs a dual-ring connection to provide redundancy should one ring fail.

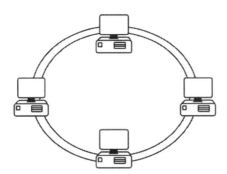

Figure 1.8—Dual-Ring Topology

Mesh

When downtime is not an option, a mesh topology can be considered. Full-mesh networks provide a connection to each device from every other device. This solution is often used with WAN connections.

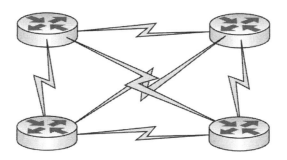

Figure 1.9—Full-Mesh Topology

Typically, this type of solution will prove very costly. For this reason, partial-mesh topologies can be considered. This means that there may be one or more "hops," or routers, to get to each device. A mixture of topologies can be referred to as a hybrid design.

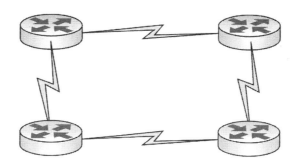

Figure 1.10—Partial-Mesh Topology

Hub-and-Spoke

Due to the cost of equipment and WAN connections and bandwidth, companies often use a hub-and-spoke design. A powerful router is in the center (hub), usually at a company's HQ, while the spokes represent remote offices, which require less powerful routers. There are obviously issues with this type of topology; however, it is still widely used.

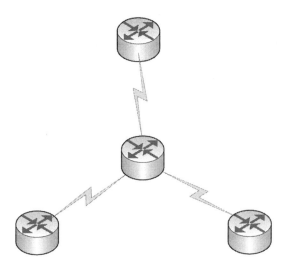

Figure 1.11—Hub-and-Spoke Topology

Physical versus Logical

When you can see the network equipment, you are looking at the physical topology. This can be misleading because, although the network appears to be wired in a star fashion, it could in fact be working logically as a ring. A classic example of this is a ring network. Although the traffic circulates around the ring in a circular fashion, all of the devices plug into a hub. The ring is actually inside the token ring hub, so you can't see it from the outside, as illustrated in Figure 1.12 below:

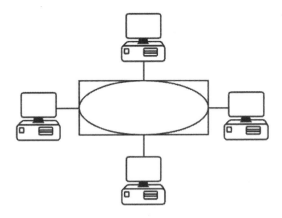

Figure 1.12—The Ring Is Inside the Hub

You may be asked to identify the different types of networks, both physically and logically. It is a good idea to remember that the physical topology is what you can see and the logical topology is what the network can see (i.e., how the data flows). This is summarized in Table 1.1 below:

Table 1.1—Physical versus Logical Topologies

Topology	Physical	Logical
Bus	Bus	Bus
Star	Star	Bus
Token Ring	Star	Ring
Point-to-Point	Bus	Bus
FDDI	Ring	Ring

FIREWALLS

Firewalls have always been on the periphery of the CCNA syllabus but only inasmuch as knowing what they do in general terms. A deep understanding of firewall technology is expected for the security track of CCNA, CCNP, and CCIE.

In order to reflect the role of modern CCNA engineers, you are now expected to know a little more about how they do their job. However, configuration and troubleshooting is outside the syllabus. Bear in mind that the firewall could be the cause of network issues and, in particular, packet loss because its job is to filter packets. If ICMP is blocked by your firewalls, it will prevent you from using the ping command as part of your troubleshooting.

Purpose of Firewalls

We will cover access control lists (ACLs) later, but you may already know that they are a series of configuration lines permitting or denying traffic based on IP address, source, destination, protocol, port number, etc. Once you understand this, you will easily understand the concept of firewalls.

A firewall protects the network by analyzing and taking action on traffic that flows through it. Desired traffic (typically HTTP, FTP, etc.) is allowed through the firewall and undesired traffic is blocked. Just like with ACLs, you specify which traffic you want to traverse the firewall and which traffic you want to block. This is where the comparison with ACLs ends though. Firewalls can do much more, as they are designed to provide robust and intelligent network packet-filtering solutions. We will dig deeper into these nuances a little later in this section.

Location of Firewalls

Typically, a firewall will be placed at the edge of a network that it is supposed to protect. For example, a firewall is often placed between a core and edge router (i.e., one that is connected to an external provider), such as an Internet Service Provider. These aspects and terms are covered in more detail in the Cisco Certified Design Associate (CCDA) exam, which I strongly recommend that you take.

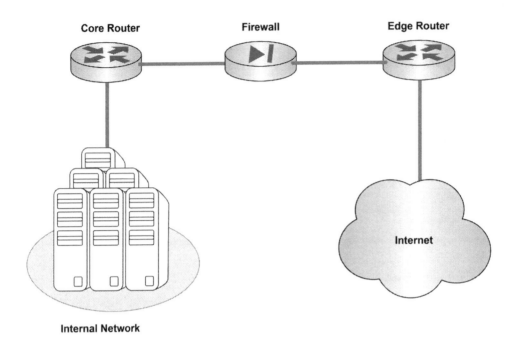

Figure 1.13—Standard Firewall Placement

In Figure 1.13 above, the firewall is protecting the inside network from the Internet. This is a very high-level but common firewall design. The firewall is protecting the internal network from unwanted traffic sourced from the Internet. A good metaphor may be to think of the firewall as acting as a security guard standing at the door of an elite nightclub. He sees every person (packet) trying to get into the door (interface) but is only permitting entry to people (packets) who are on the guest list (firewall rules). Packets allowed by firewall rules may proceed through the firewall. All other packets will be discarded by the firewall.

Of course, you can have internal firewalls separating various departments in your company or facing out to employees who work from home. This would all be decided in the design phase of your network.

Security Zones

Firewalls use the concept of security zones when defining which areas of the network they are protecting versus which areas of the network they are offering protection from. They provide protection by using rules that specifically define which network host can initiate a connection from one security zone to another. The rules are programmed into the application and saved on the firewall. Generally speaking, the smaller the network that is being protected, the fewer the rules, while the larger the network, the more rules that are required. With large enterprise networks, firewalls can actually have hundreds of rules and can be very complex to administer.

In a basic deployment of a firewall, it separates two zones but will allow hosts from one zone to initiate connections to hosts in another zone. In Figure 1.14 below, the firewall is allowing hosts in the corporate network to initiate HTTP (Port 80) requests to the Internet so that users can browse traffic as seen by the top flow (indicated by a dashed arrow). An IP flow is based on (most or all of) the following list of packet attributes:

- Source address
- Destination address
- Source port
- Destination port
- Layer 3 protocol type
- Class of Service
- Router or switch interface

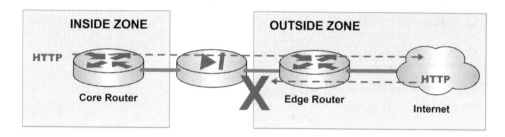

Figure 1.14—Security Zones

Do you think the corporate firewall should allow Internet users to initiate HTTP requests back to the internal network? No, you would not want to invite that type of traffic, so you would block that traffic as seen by the bottom flow.

What if you did want Internet users to access the company Web server to learn about the company and submit orders? In that case, you would create a new security zone so that any traffic coming from the Internet goes to the Web server, which is isolated from the internal network. This is often called a DMZ, or demilitarized zone. In the military, this is an area that doesn't belong to either party and it fits for use in networking. Even though the company owns and operates the DMZ, it understands that with so many Internet users, this zone is compromised in some way and is really a shared space.

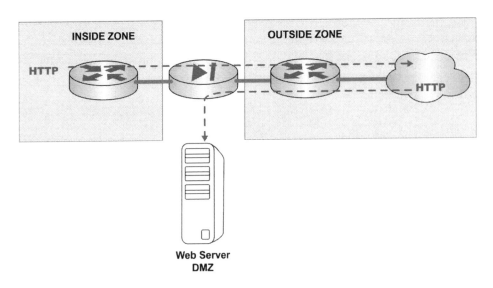

Figure 1.15—DMZ Security Zone

Security zones can be created for databases, Web servers, classified information, or even for teams of people who require their own secure network with limited access in or out of their zone. Regardless of what type of security zone is created, a firewall is the ideal solution to create it.

Advanced Features of Firewalls

If all firewalls did was allow or deny traffic between security zones, they could easily be replaced by routers that can do that already using ACLs or prefix lists. What makes firewalls invaluable is that they provide advanced security features that require the software, processing power, and network placement of an individual and a specialized security device leaving the router to do what it was designed to do (i.e., route packets).

Here are some tasks that a firewall can perform that would be difficult or impossible for a router to perform:

- Compare packets to thousands of rules that are based on criteria from multiple layers of the OSI model
- Monitor and allow detailed analysis of Application Layer (Layer 7) flows to make filtering decisions
- Make decisions on filtering future packets based on the information of previous packets received

By sharing just a few examples, you can hopefully understand that dedicated processing and memory resources are needed for these types of complex transactions. Routers and switches, on the other hand, need to move traffic as efficiently as possible so that traffic moves as quickly as possible from the source to the destination. It's not that a router cannot do complex filtering or traffic analysis, but ideally it shouldn't.

Stateful versus Stateless Firewalls

A stateful firewall can track, for example, the number of connections to a Web server per second to understand what is typical (e.g., five to six connections per second). Then, if the state changes, that is, if the connections go to 100 per second, the stateful firewall will notice this and then analyze what is happening. It can determine whether it's a Denial of Service attack, and if that's the case, it would start dropping those packets so that the Web server is not negatively impacted by the attack. A router would not be able to perform that type of task because it would not be able to analyze historical data and make a decision based on the data.

Stateful firewalls operate at Layers 3, 4, and 5 of the OSI model. They are ubiquitous on modern networks. All traffic flows are kept in a state table that is used by the firewall to check for attacks, permit or deny packets, and for inspection by the network administrator.

In the following example, the stateful firewall allows FTP traffic to enter the network only if the request has come from an internal source. The firewall tracks the outgoing FTP session requests and blocks any FTP responses from the Internet if they weren't requested from the internal network.

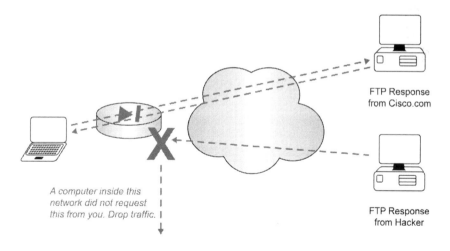

FTP Response
from Cisco.com

A computer inside this
network did not request
this from you. Drop traffic.

FTP Response
from Hacker

Figure 1.16—Stateful Firewall

A stateless firewall doesn't have the enhanced capability to make decisions based on historical data (i.e., it isn't aware of whether the packet is part of an existing connection or a new one). Stateless firewalls watch real-time network traffic and block traffic based on static values, such as source or destination address. They do not take into account traffic patterns or the history of data flows. They perform simple and static comparisons between the traffic and check it against its defined rule. Because of these factors, stateless firewalls are less commonly used.

WIRELESS NETWORKING AND COMPONENTS

Cisco all but removed wireless from the previous version of the CCNA exam after they created CCNA Wireless certification. However, there has been a shift in thinking for the current CCNA syllabus, with Cisco customers (who influence the syllabus) saying that they expect their CCNA-level engineers to understand wireless basics as part of their day-to-day role. The same goes for many of the new CCNA syllabus items, such as Layer 2 security, firewalls, BGP, etc.

The IEEE defines both (wired) Ethernet LANs (IEEE 802.3) and Wireless LANs (IEEE 802.11). While this section will focus on enterprise wireless infrastructure components, in order to understand how wireless components work in the enterprise, you should build foundational knowledge first. A good place to start is in the small office/home office (SOHO) network. Just as important, you are expected to know SOHO as well as enterprise wireless networking concepts for the ICND1 exam.

SOHO Wireless Solutions

At first glance, a SOHO wireless router may not look like a very impressive piece of network equipment. While it certainly lacks the size, complexity, and cost of some of Cisco's core routers (which can run into tens of thousands of dollars), there is a lot going on inside that you need to be aware of. First, the router typically has an Ethernet switch that provides wired Ethernet connectivity. This allows for wired LAN connectivity for devices that may not support Wi-Fi or for devices that won't be moving and warrant a dedicated physical connection.

The router features a wireless access point (WAP or just AP) to communicate with any wireless devices on the network and forward frames to/from the wireless router to the endpoints. Finally, a router can forward traffic received from the wireless or wired devices out of the WAN (Internet) interface based on the IP address.

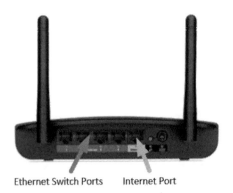

Ethernet Switch Ports   Internet Port

Figure 1.17—Linksys N300+ SOHO Wireless Router

Before we go any further, let's explore the concept of WAPs because they play a key role in both home and enterprise wireless solutions.

Wireless Access Points

Whether you are in someone's home, visiting a small office, or staying at a hotel, wireless connectivity will likely be available for you to use. A WAP is what allows wireless access and wireless-enabled devices to connect to a network. APs work with other wireless or wired devices to provide access to the local network or Internet, but they play the important role of being the wireless "entrance" onto the network "freeway."

Wireless networks use carrier sense multiple access with collision avoidance (CSMA/CA) to prevent frames from colliding. This means that wireless nodes will attempt to avoid collisions by transmitting only when they sense that the channel they are on is idle. One way to think of this is how we behave when participating in a group conversation. Typically, you would wait until someone has stopped talking before sharing your thoughts. The same concept applies to CSMA/CA—wireless devices wait for silence before beginning their transmission.

WAPs are the moderators who help make group conversations happen, and they can support hundreds of users at the same time, although, for obvious reasons, the fewer the better from a performance perspective.

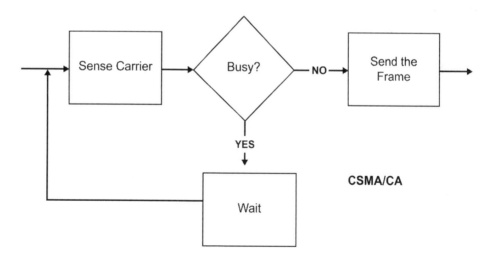

Figure 1.18—CSMA/CA High-level Process Map

Enterprise Wireless Solutions

A single wireless router may work fine for a few users in a limited area, but what if you want to offer wireless to hundreds or thousands of people over an area of a few acres of land or in a high-rise building? In this scenario, you need a wireless solution that can span multiple floors or allow people to roam from one building to another without losing their wireless connectivity. You will need a robust wireless deployment that includes not just routing, switching, and WAPs, but further intelligence to help manage the wireless network.

Each AP has a limited area that it can service due to signal strength and limitations of technology. The size of an AP's coverage area can be affected by many different factors, including the materials of the building, the wireless standard chosen, interference from electronic devices, the shape of the antenna on the WAP, and even the weather! There are a large number of conditions that can affect wireless coverage for an AP, but it's a fair estimate to state that a single AP can provide about 150 feet of coverage in diameter.

Determining how many APs are required in a specific location is done via a site survey by professional wireless engineers using specialist equipment. The survey of a building or campus prior to a rollout of the wireless solution is critical to a successful wireless deployment. If the building or campus has not been built yet, you can use software simulators to determine your future wireless needs.

Now that you have determined the number of APs that you require, you need to connect them to a local area network; otherwise, your end-users will have wireless connectivity to talk with each other, but nothing more (no Internet or access to local servers).

Let's say you are the Network Manager for a large hotel that wants to offer a seamless wireless solution to its customers. The goal is for the customers to walk anywhere in the building (roam) without losing their wireless connection. Simply deploying APs throughout the hotel will not be sufficient to solve this challenge. This is because the APs operate as individual devices and users would be forced to manually connect, disconnect, and reconnect to a new AP every time they roamed.

You can overcome this hurdle by allowing the APs to communicate as a group, so if users access the wireless network in the conference center, and then they walk a few hundred feet to the restaurant, the APs are aware of what the users are doing and adapt to ensure that the customers don't lose wireless connectivity. This concept is referred to as roaming.

The solution is a centralized "brain" that can receive and send endpoint information to and from all wireless APs. This centralized administration hub is called a Wireless LAN Controller (WLC), as shown in Figure 1.19 below. User A is on a wireless laptop or mobile device and is moving around the building, but is experiencing a seamless connection.

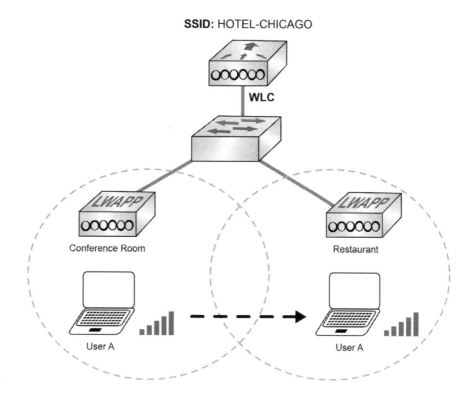

Figure 1.19—Enterprise Wireless Roaming

Wireless LAN Controllers

With WLCs, the APs no longer act as individual devices that store information on endpoints; rather, they become "lightweight" (morphing from APs to lightweight WAPs, or LWAPs) and forward everything they learn, such as WLAN (SSID) information, roaming, or authentication, to the centralized WLC. The WLC then takes over the role of the AP by managing the wireless network with all of the information it learns from the LWAPs. LWAPs typically use a protocol called CAPWAP (Control and Provisioning of Wireless Access Points) to accomplish this task. Figure 1.20 below shows a typical WLC provided by Cisco Systems:

Figure 1.20—Wireless LAN Controller

A Cisco AP is shown below in Figure 1.21. It becomes "lightweight" by simply forwarding traffic to the WLC.

Figure 1.21—Access Point

Every mobile device will join a wireless network identified by a Service Set ID (SSID). Once joined, the device will usually ignore other SSIDs. Multiple APs servicing the same SSID are referred to as an Extended Service Set (ESS). A single AP is referred to as a Basic Service Set (BSS). You can see a range of available SSIDs in Figure 1.22 below. You will have seen this on your mobile device already I'm sure.

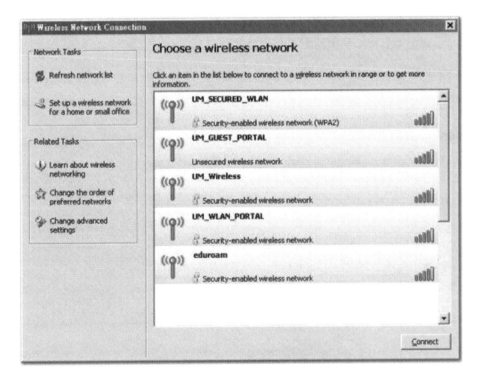

Figure 1.22—Available SSIDs

CAMPUS LAN TOPOLOGIES

Cisco has always alluded to its three-layer design model in the CCNA syllabus. It's now been officially added so you will need a deeper understanding than you would have previously. Before we go into that though, you need to understand the concept of campus LAN.

The term campus LAN can refer to devices in one or multiple buildings that service business, university, or government departments that are located next to one another, typically within line of sight. For example, if a business has expanded their office space from one to three buildings in the same geographical location, they will have also expanded their LAN to ensure high-speed connectivity between all three buildings. Typically, high-speed Ethernet trunks will connect each building so that a user in Building A can communicate with a user in Building C with nearly the same level of network performance had they been in the same building.

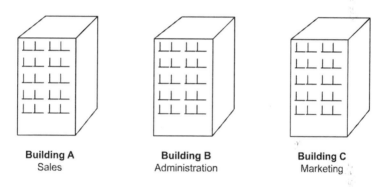

Building A
Sales

Building B
Administration

Building C
Marketing

Figure 1.23—Multi-building Campus LAN

Cisco has laid down design recommendations for the campus LAN. After all, if you want to build a network that can scale as the business grows, you need to carefully consider the short-term and long-term goals of the company. Understanding these goals will help you choose the appropriate network topologies when building the campus LAN.

In a perfect world, you would design the campus LAN from scratch, but since we don't live in a perfect world, you likely will have to begin designing from the network that is already in place, and it will be your job to create the vision as to what the network should look like in the future. This is much more difficult but will be easier if you understand key concepts and terms that translate to a quality design for the campus network.

Layers of the Campus LAN

Cisco uses three distinct layers to describe the role of each switch in a campus design: access, distribution, and core. It's critical that you understand each layer in order to design scalable solutions.

Access switches provide connectivity for nodes on the network. This is the "on ramp" for systems that typically do not require a lot of bandwidth and that normally host one user at a time. A few examples of such nodes include workstations, mobile devices, printers, and IP phones. The primary purpose of an access layer switch is to provide network connectivity. For this reason, you will see more emphasis on port density (i.e., providing a lot of ports to plug into) and less emphasis on manipulating the frames. Figure 1.24 below illustrates access layer switch models from the 2960.X range:

Figure 1.24—2960.X range of Cisco switches (Image ©Cisco Systems)

Distribution layer switches act as the intelligent intermediary between access and core layer switches. Many Quality of Service (QoS) parameters and filtering (e.g., ACLs, prefix lists) are programmed on distribution layer switches because they typically have the features and hardware, as well as the proper network location, to appropriately handle or filter voice, video, and data traffic. Typically, they provide redundant connectivity for each access layer switch connected to two different distribution layer switches (see Figure 1.25 below). This way, if a distribution layer switch failed, the end-users would not be impacted.

Figure 1.25 below demonstrates the three layers of the Cisco design model. Note that Layer 3 switches are at the distribution and core layers.

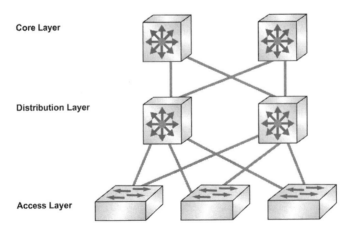

Figure 1.25—Three Layers of the Campus LAN

Core layer switches have a primary goal of forwarding traffic as quickly as possible. They do this while also shouldering the heaviest loads of traffic, since all of the distribution layer switches connect into the core. Needless to say, the core must have a redundant high-speed infrastructure that is tuned to forward large amounts of traffic to any and usually every single zone in the network (e.g., Internet, DMZ, Server Farm, Workgroups, etc.).

Any programming that requires additional processor speed or memory should be avoided in the core. You would not want to add ACLs, QoS, or any other programming that delays the forwarding of traffic unless you have no other choice.

So far, you have learned that:

- Access switches send and receive traffic from endpoints;
- Distribution switches are the intelligence of the network, providing redundancy, QoS, and filtering; and
- Core switches aggregate all traffic and provide high bandwidth and speed in order to forward traffic as quickly as possible.

Let's put what you have learned to use and develop a high-level campus LAN. As you will see in Figure 1.26 below, there are three buildings on the property, with the main data center in the Headquarters (Building B).

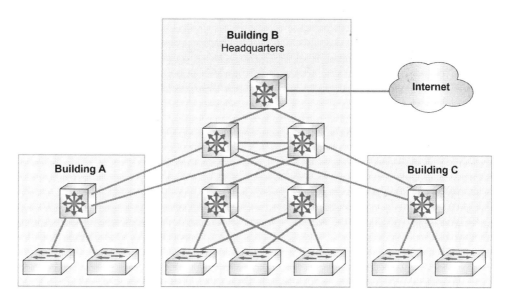

Figure 1.26—High-level Three-tier Campus LAN Design

In the Headquarters, there are three high-end switches in the core layer (the top three), and there are two distribution layer switches in the same building that service three access layer switches. The company expanded to two additional buildings nearby and was able to easily expand the network because they already built a proper core layer. They installed distribution layer switches in Buildings B and C with high-speed Ethernet redundant connectivity between the buildings. End-users at all locations are serviced by access layer switches, but you will notice that, since there is only one distribution layer switch in Buildings B and C, the access layer switches do not have redundant connectivity in those buildings.

In this design, the core layer of the network is full mesh, but that doesn't always have to be the case, as a partial mesh is sometimes deployed. In addition, there is redundant connectivity everywhere, but that also isn't always possible depending on the availability of cabling between the buildings or budget. In other words, connectivity between the buildings can vary depending on budget and the environment.

Assuming that the budget allows it, a typical install would be fiber cabling between the core and distribution layer switches in two separate buildings. Other options, depending on the distance between buildings, could be copper or wireless connectivity. For example, two office buildings that are a mile away from each other could communicate via wireless bridges. Regardless, if you are creating connectivity between buildings, it's going to be more expensive than creating connectivity within a building.

Cisco designers will typically provide you with expert design advice based on your specific needs and budget.

Two-Tier Campus Design—The Collapsed Core

Not every campus design requires a three-tiered approach. For example, if you have a campus with 200 PCs that simply need network access for e-mail, printing, occasional file-sharing, and the Internet, then there really is no need to deploy a three-tier model because your distribution layer switches can easily handle the amount of traffic traversing the network.

As you can see in Figure 1.27 below, the two-tier design allows end-users to connect to the network, and then, using a reasonable number of cables, allows all access layer switches redundant connectivity to two distribution layer switches. In this type of design, centralized servers and printers can also be connected into the distribution layer switches. In addition, the edge routing and security infrastructure facing the Internet would also connect into the distribution layer switches.

This design is also referred to as a collapsed core, with the distribution layer providing both distribution and core functions (as listed in the Cisco design model).

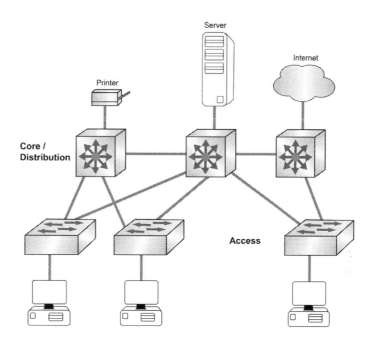

Figure 1.27—Two-Tier Design

OSI AND TCP MODELS

The OSI Model

Open Standards Interconnection (OSI) was created by the International Organization for Standardization (ISO). With the 1980s technology boom came the rise of several giants in the fields of networking devices and software, including Cisco, Microsoft, Novell, IBM, HP, Apple, and others. Each vendor had their own cable types and ports and ran their own communication protocols. This caused major problems if you wanted to buy routers from one company, switches from another, and servers from yet another.

There were workarounds for these problems, such as deploying gateways on the network that could translate between protocols, but such solutions created bottlenecks (i.e., slow portions of the network) and made troubleshooting very difficult and time-consuming. Eventually, vendors had to agree on a common standard which worked for everyone, and the free suite of protocols called Transmission Control Protocol/Internet Protocol (TCP/IP) was ultimately adopted by most. In the end, those vendors who failed to adopt TCP/IP lost market share and went bust.

The ISO created the OSI model to help vendors agree on a set of common standards with which they could all work. This involved dividing network functions into a set of logical levels or layers. Each layer would perform a specific set of functions, so, for example, if your company wanted to focus on network firewalls, they would work with other vendors' equipment.

The advantage was that each device was designed to perform a specific role well, rather than several roles inadequately. Customers could choose the best device for their solution without being tied to one vendor. Troubleshooting became much easier because certain errors could be traced to a certain OSI layer.

The OSI model divides all network functions into seven distinct layers. The layered model starts at Layer 7 and goes all the way down to Layer 1. The more complex functions, which are closer to the user, are at the top, moving down to network cable specifications at the bottom layer, as illustrated in Table 1.2 below:

Table 1.2—The OSI Model

Layer #	Layer Name
7	Application
6	Presentation
5	Session
4	Transport
3	Network
2	Data Link
1	Physical

You can easily remember the names of the layers with the mnemonic "**A**ll **P**eople **S**eem **T**o **N**eed **D**ata **P**rocessing." I would certainly get used to referring to each layer by its number because this is how real-world network technicians use the OSI.

As data is passed down from the top layers to the bottom for transportation across the physical network media, the data is placed into different types of logical data boxes. Although we often call these data boxes "packets," they have different names depending upon the OSI layer. The process of data moving down the OSI model is referred to as encapsulation (see Figure 1.28). Moving back up and having these boxes stripped of their data is called de-encapsulation.

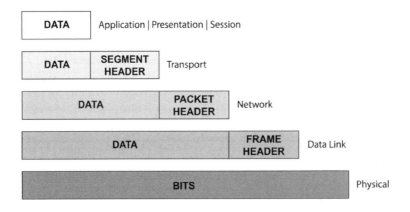

Figure 1.28—Encapsulation

For the CCNA exam, you will be expected to understand the OSI model and which applications and protocols fit in which layer. You may also have to apply your troubleshooting knowledge using the OSI layered approach. Let's examine each layer of the OSI, starting with Layer 7.

Layer 7—Application Layer

This layer is the closest layer to the end-user, you and me. The Application Layer isn't the operating system of the devices but usually provides services such as e-mail (SNMP and POP3), web browsing (using HTTP), and file transfer services (using FTP). The Application Layer determines resource availability.

Layer 6—Presentation Layer

The Presentation Layer presents data to the Application Layer. Multimedia works here, so think MP4, JPEG, GIF, etc. Encryption, decryption, and data compression also take place at this layer.

Layer 5—Session Layer

The role of the Session Layer is to set up, manage, and terminate sessions or dialogues between devices. These take place over logical links, and what is really happening is the joining of two software applications. SQL, RPC, and NFS all work at the Session Layer.

Layer 4—Transport Layer

The role of the Transport Layer is to break down the data from the higher layers into smaller parts, which are referred to as segments (at this layer). Virtual circuits are set up here, which are required before devices can communicate.

Before the data can be passed across the network, the Transport Layer needs to establish how much data can be sent to the remote device. This will depend upon the speed and reliability of the link from end to end. If you have a high-speed link but the end-user has a low-speed link, then the data will need to be sent in smaller chunks.

The three methods used to control data flow are as follows:

- Flow control
- Windowing
- Acknowledgements

Flow Control

If the receiving system is being sent more information than it can process, it will ask the sending system to stop for a short time. This normally happens when one side uses broadband and the other uses a dial-up modem. The packet sent telling the other device to stop is known as a source quench message.

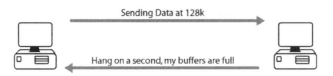

Figure 1.29—Flow Control

Windowing

With windowing, each system agrees upon how much data is to be sent before an acknowledgment is required. This "window" opens and closes as data moves along in order to maintain a constant flow.

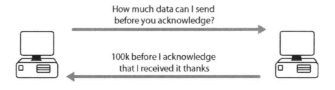

Figure 1.30—Windowing

Acknowledgements

When a certain amount of segments is received, the fact that they all arrived safely and in the correct order needs to be communicated to the sending system.

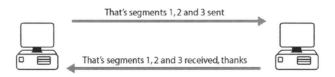

Figure 1.31—Acknowledgements

All of this is agreed upon during a process known as a three-way handshake (see Figure 1.32). This is where you send a packet to establish the session. This first packet is called a synchronize (SYN) packet. Then the remote device responds with a synchronize acknowledgment (SYN-ACK) packet. The session is established in the third phase when an acknowledgment (ACK) packet is sent. This is all done via the TCP service.

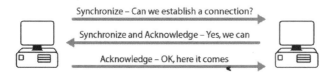

Figure 1.32—Three-Way Handshake

The Transport Layer includes several protocols, and the most widely known are Transmission Control Protocol (TCP) and User Datagram Protocol (UDP), which are part of the TCP/IP suite of protocols. This suite is well known because it is the standard used on the Internet. TCP is known as a reliable connection-oriented protocol. It uses the three-way handshake, windowing, and other techniques to guarantee that the data gets to its destination safely. Many protocols use TCP, including Telnet, HTTPS, and FTP (although it sits at the Application Layer, it does use TCP).

UDP, on the other hand, is known as a connectionless protocol. It numbers each packet and then sends them to their destination. It never checks to see whether they arrived safely and will never set up a connection before sending the packet. Sometimes data is not that important and the application developer decides that the information can always be sent again if it fails to arrive at its destination.

Why is UDP used at all? TCP uses a lot of bandwidth on the network and there is a lot of traffic sent back and forth to set up the connection, even before the data is sent. This all takes up valuable time and network resources. UDP packets are a lot smaller than TCP packets and they are very useful if a really reliable connection is not that necessary. Protocols that use UDP include TFTP.

Layer 3—Network Layer

The Network Layer takes the segments from the Transport Layer and breaks them down into smaller units called packets. Most network engineers refer to data as packets, no matter what the OSI layer, which is fine; however, just remember that they are technically packets at the Network Layer.

The Network Layer must determine the best path to take from one network to another; for this reason, routers work at this layer. Routers use logical addressing here, and TCP/IP addressing is called IP addressing, which will be covered in detail later.

Layer 2—Data Link Layer

The Data Link Layer chops down packets into smaller units referred to as frames. Layer 2 switches work at this layer and use hardware or MAC addresses, so they can switch traffic much faster because there is no need to check IP addresses and routing tables. WAN protocols operate at Layer 2, including HDLC, ISDN, and PPP, as does Ethernet.

In order to interface with the upper and lower levels, the Data Link Layer is further subdivided into the Logical Link Control (LLC) Sublayer and the Media Access Control (MAC) Sublayer. The LLC Sublayer interfaces with the Network Layer and the MAC Sublayer interfaces with the Physical Layer.

Layer 1—Physical Layer

At this layer, frames are converted into bits for placing on the wire. These bits consist of electrical pulses, which are read as "on" and "off" bits, or in binary 1s and 0s, respectively. Hubs work at this layer, and here is where you will find cable specifications, such as RJ45.

OSI Troubleshooting

Using a layered approach can be very effective when you're troubleshooting your network. The only decision from this point onwards is to determine which way you want to use the OSI stack—top-down, bottom-up, or divide-and-conquer method, which involves focusing on sections of the network in turn.

I recommend using the bottom-up method at the beginning so you don't waste time looking at applications when the cause can often be found at the lower layers, such as loose or broken cables or incorrect IP addressing. As you gain more experience, using the divide-and-conquer method will probably be faster, depending on the symptoms. If you start at the bottom layer and work your way up, you would do something like this:

Layer 1—Are all the cables inserted into the ports correctly, or have they come loose? Are the cable ends bent or worn out? If cables are the problem, you will usually see an amber light showing on the device when it should be green. Has somebody forgotten to add the correct speed to the interface? Has the speed of the Ethernet port been set correctly? Has the interface been opened for use by the network administrator?

Layer 2—Has the correct protocol been applied to the interface so it agrees with the other side, such as Ethernet/PPP/HDLC, etc.?

Layer 3—Is the interface using the correct IP address and subnet mask?

Layer 4—Is the correct routing protocol being used, and is the correct network being advertised from the router?

You will see how to apply these steps as you complete the labs in this book. Experts may argue that some Layer 4 issues are at Layer 3, some Layer 2 issues are actually at Layer 1, and so on. I prefer to focus on the fact that we are applying a layered troubleshooting method rather than debating about whether the correct issue is at the correct layer.

The TCP/IP, or DoD, Model

The TCP/IP model is another framework and an alternative to the OSI model. The TCP/IP model is a four or five-layered model created by an association known as DARPA. It is also known as the Department of Defense (DoD) model. The four layers from the top down are as follows:

> 4—Application [Telnet/FTP/DNS/RIP]
> 3—Transport/Host-to-Host [UDP/TCP/ICMP]
> 2—Internet or Internetwork [IPSec/IP]
> 1—Link/Network Interface [Frame Relay/Ethernet/ATM]

The TCP/IP model has been updated from four to five layers, so you may be asked questions about a five-layered TCP model in the exam. The upper layers are closer to the end-user and the lower layers describe how the technology or protocols interact with other systems. The five-layered TCP model is as follows:

> 5—Application [Telnet/FTP/DNS/RIP/HTTP]
> 4—Transport/Host-to-Host [UDP/TCP/ICMP]
> 3—Network [IPSec/IP]
> 2—Data Link [Ethernet/Frame Relay/PPP]
> 1—Link/Network Interface/Physical [Bits on the wire]

A five-layered TCP model allows for more granularity and it more accurately represents what actually occurs before data is put onto the wire. For example, at Layer 2 encapsulation of data occurs and addressing takes place (i.e., Data Link addressing). Cisco seem to prefer the five-layered model when it comes to exam questions.

Data is encapsulated as it travels down from the Application Layer to the Physical Layer in exactly the same way as demonstrated in the OSI model, as illustrated in Table 1.3 below:

Table 1.3—The Five-Layered TCP Model

Application	Data, but not encapsulated yet	
Transport	TCP header added to the data	Segment
Network	IP header added (including IP address)	Packet
Data Link	Data Link header added (Data Link address)	Frame
Physical	Turned into electrical signals	Bits on the wire

You may be asked how the TCP/IP model maps to the OSI model. This is illustrated below in Table 1.4:

Table 1.4—Mapping the TCP/IP Model to the OSI Model

Layer #	OSI	Data
7	Application	Application
6	Presentation	Application
5	Session	
4	Transport	Host to Host
3	Network	Internetwork
2	Data Link	Network Interface
1	Physical	

Cisco now prefer the (new) TCP model over the OSI model as a network framework, but they still expect you to understand the OSI model and thus have left it in the syllabus for now.

Table 1.5—Old versus New TCP Model

Old TCP Model	Layer	New TCP Model
	5	Application
Application	4	Transport/Host-to-Host
Transport/Host-to-Host	3	Network
Internet	2	Data Link
Link/Network Interface	1	Link/Network Interface

TCP/IP

TCP/IP is a complete suite of protocols and services which enable communication to take place over networks. Earlier competitors to TCP/IP, such as IPX/SPX, have all but died out due to their lack of adoption and ongoing development.

TCP/IP is a freely available and free to use set of standards maintained by the Internet Engineering Task Force (IETF), and it is used for end-to-end device connectivity. It has been developed and improved upon through submission of Requests for Comments (RFCs), which are documents submitted by engineers to convey new concepts or for peer review. One example is Network Address Translation (NAT) discussed in RFC 2663. The IETF adopted some of these RFCs as Internet standards. You can learn more about the IETF and RFCs at the link below:

www.ietf.org/rfc.html

TCP/IP offers many services but many are outside the scope of the CCNA exam and will not be covered. I will also omit those covered in later sections, such as DNS and DHCP. The following sections outline the basics of TCP/IP. Because the CCNA isn't a basic networking exam, it is expected that you already have a good grasp of networking concepts such as those learned in the Network+ exam from CompTIA.

Transmission Control Protocol (TCP)

TCP operates at the Transport Layer of the OSI model. It provides a connection-oriented service for reliable transfer of data between network devices. TCP also provides flow control, sequencing, windowing, and error detection. It attaches a 32-bit header to the Application Layer data, which is in turn encapsulated in an IP header. TCP is described in RFC 793. Common TCP ports include the following:

- FTP Data—20
- FTP Control—21
- SSH—22
- Telnet—23
- SMTP—25

- DNS—53 (also uses UDP)
- HTTP—80
- POP3—110
- NNTP—119
- NTP—123
- TLS/SSL—443

Internet Protocol (IP)

IP operates at the Network Layer of the OSI model. It is connectionless and is responsible for transporting data over the network. IP addressing is a function of Internet Protocol. IP examines the Network Layer address of every packet and determines the best path for that packet to take to reach its destination. IP is discussed in detail in RFC 791.

User Datagram Protocol (UDP)

UDP also operates at the Transport Layer of the OSI model. It transports information between network devices but, unlike TCP, no connection is established first. UDP is connectionless, gives best-effort delivery, and gives no guarantee that the data will reach its destination. UDP is much like sending a letter with no return address. You know it was sent, but you never know if the letter got there.

UDP consumes less bandwidth than TCP does and is suitable for applications in which low latency is preferred over reliability or guarantees. Both TCP and UDP are carried over IP. UDP is described in RFC 768. Common UDP port numbers include the following:

- DNS—53
- TFTP—69
- SNMP—161/162

File Transfer Protocol (FTP)

FTP operates at the Application Layer and is responsible for reliably transporting data across a remote link. Because it has to be reliable, FTP uses TCP for data transfer.

You can debug FTP traffic with the `debug ip ftp` command. Debugging is a troubleshooting tool we will cover in detail later.

FTP uses ports 20 and 21. Usually, a first connection is made to the FTP server from the client on port 21. A second data connection is then made either leaving the FTP server on port 20 or from a random port on the client to port 20 on the FTP server. You may wish to read more about active versus passive FTP for your own information, but it is unlikely that this will be covered in CCNA-level exams.

Trivial File Transfer Protocol (TFTP)

For less reliable transfer of data, TFTP provides a good alternative. TFTP provides a connectionless transfer by using UDP port 69. TFTP can be difficult to use because you have to specify exactly the directory in which the file is located.

To use TFTP, you need to have a client (the router, in your case) and a TFTP server, which could be a router or a PC, or a server on the network (preferably on the same subnet). You need to have TFTP software on the server so the files can be pulled off it and forwarded on to the client.

> **IN THE REAL WORLD:** Having a server on a network containing backup copies of the startup configuration and IOS is a very good idea indeed.

TFTP is used extensively on Cisco routers to back up configurations and upgrade the router. The following command will carry out these functions:

```
RouterA#copy tftp flash:
```

You will be prompted to enter the IP address of the other host in which the new flash file is located:

```
Address or name of remote host []? 10.10.10.1
```

You will then have to enter the name of the flash image on the other router:

```
Source filename []? / c2500-js-1.121-17.bin
Destination filename [c2500-js-1.121-17.bin]?
```

If you have an older version of IOS, you may be prompted to erase the flash on your router before copying, and then the file will be transferred. When the router reloads, your new flash image should be available for use.

Other optional commands are `copy flash tftp` if you want to store a backup copy or `copy running config tftp` if you want to back up your running configuration file.

You can run a debug on TFTP traffic with the `debug tftp` command.

Simple Mail Transfer Protocol (SMTP)

SMTP defines how e-mails are sent to the e-mail server from the client. It uses TCP to ensure a reliable connection. SMTP emails are pulled off the SMTP server in different ways, and SMTP is used as an e-mail delivery service by most networks. POP3 is another popular way to do this. POP3 is a protocol that transfers the e-mail from the server to the client. SMTP uses TCP port 25.

Hyper Text Transfer Protocol (HTTP)

HTTP uses TCP (port 80) to send text, graphics, and other multimedia files from a web server to clients. This protocol allows you to view web pages, and it sits at the Application Layer of the OSI model. HTTPS is a secure version of HTTP that uses Secure Sockets Layer (SSL) or Transport Layer Security (TLS) to encrypt the data before it is sent.

You can debug HTTP traffic with the `debug ip http` command.

Telnet

Telnet uses TCP (port 23) to allow a remote connection to network devices. You will learn more about Telnet in the labs. Telnet is not secure so many administrators are now using Secure Shell (SSH), which uses TCP port 22, as an alternative to ensure a secure connection. Telnet is the only utility that can check all seven layers of the OSI model, so if you Telnet to an address, then all seven layers are working properly. If you can't Telnet to another device, it doesn't necessarily indicate a network problem. There could be a firewall or an access control list blocking the connection purposely, or Telnet may not be enabled on the device.

In order to connect remotely to a Cisco router or switch, there must be an authentication method for VTY lines configured on the router. If you are trying to Telnet to another device but cannot connect to it, you can hold down the Ctrl+Shift+6 at the same time, and then release them and hit the X key to quit. To quit an active Telnet session, you can simply type `exit` or `disconnect`.

You can debug Telnet with the `debug telnet` command.

Internet Control Message Protocol (ICMP)

ICMP is a protocol used to report problems or issues with IP packets (or datagrams) on a network. ICMP is a requirement for any vendor who wishes to use IP on their network. When a problem is experienced with an IP packet, the IP packet is destroyed and an ICMP message is generated and sent to the host that originated the packet.

As defined in RFC 792, ICMP delivers messages inside IP packets. The most popular use of ICMP is to send ping packets to test the network connectivity of remote hosts. A ping command issued from a network device generates an echo request packet that is sent to the destination device. Upon receiving the echo request, the destination device generates an echo reply.

Because pings also have a Time to Live (TTL) field, they give a good indication of network latency (delay). The ping output below is from a desktop PC:

```
C:\>ping cisco.com
Pinging cisco.com [198.133.219.25] with 32 bytes of data:
Reply from 198.133.219.25: bytes=32 time=460ms TTL=237
Reply from 198.133.219.25: bytes=32 time=160ms TTL=237
```

```
Reply from 198.133.219.25: bytes=32 time=160ms TTL=237
Reply from 198.133.219.25: bytes=32 time=180ms TTL=237
Ping statistics for 198.133.219.25:
    Packets: Sent = 4, Received = 4, Lost = 0 (0% loss),
Approximate round trip times in milli-seconds:
Minimum = 160ms, Maximum = 460ms, Average = 240ms
```

In the output above, the ping packet is 32 bytes long, the Time field reports how many milliseconds the response took, and the TTL is the Time to Live field (i.e., how many milliseconds before the packet expires).

The ping command on a Cisco router has a verbose facility that provides more granularity from which you can specify the source you are pinging, how many pings, and what size you are sending, along with other parameters. This feature is referred to as an extended ping and is very useful for testing. In fact, it is used several times in the accompanying lab scenarios, as illustrated in the output below. Any output in squared brackets is the default which you can either change or hit the enter key to use:

```
Router#ping   ← press Enter here
Protocol [ip]:
Target IP address: 172.16.1.5
Repeat count [5]:
Datagram size [100]: 1200
Timeout in seconds [2]:
Extended commands [n]: yes
Source address: ← you can specify a source address or interface here
Type of service [0]:
Set DF bit in IP header? [no]: yes
Data pattern [0xABCD]:
Loose, Strict, Record, Timestamp, Verbose[none]:
Type escape sequence to abort.
Sending 5, 1000-byte ICMP Echos to 131.108.2.27, timeout is 2 seconds:
U U U U U
Success rate is 0% percent, round-trip min/avg/max = 4/6/12 ms
```

Several notations represent the response the ping packet receives, as follows:

- !—One exclamation mark per response
- .—One period for each timeout
- U—Destination unreachable message
- N—Network unreachable message
- P—Protocol unreachable message
- Q—Source quench message
- M—Could not fragment
- ?—Unknown packet type

You can terminate a ping session by holding down the Ctrl+Shift+6 keys (all together) and then the X key (on its own).

ICMP packet types are defined in RFC 1700. Learning all the code numbers and names is outside the scope of the CCNA syllabus.

Many junior network engineers misuse the ping facility when it comes to troubleshooting. A failed ping could indicate a network issue or that ICMP traffic is blocked on the network. Because ping attacks are a common way to attack a network, ICMP is often blocked.

Traceroute

Traceroute is a very widely used facility which can test network connectivity and is a handy tool for measurement and management. Traceroute follows the destination IP packets by sending UDP packets with a small maximum TTL field, and then listens for an ICMP time-exceeded response. As the Traceroute packet progresses, the records are displayed hop by hop. Each hop is measured three times. An asterisk [*] indicates that a hop has exceeded its time limit.

Cisco routers use the `traceroute` command, whereas Windows PCs use `tracert`, as illustrated in the output below:

```
C:\Documents and Settings\pc>tracert hello.com
Tracing route to hello.com [63.146.123.17]
over a maximum of 30 hops:
1 81 ms 70 ms 80 ms imsnet-c110-hg2-berks.ba.net [213.140.212.45]
2 70 ms 80 ms 70 ms 192.168.254.61
3 70 ms 70 ms 80 ms 172.16.93.29
4 60 ms 81 ms 70 ms 213.120.62.177
5 70 ms 70 ms 80 ms core1-pos4-2.berks.ukore.ba.net [65.6.197.133]
6 70 ms 80 ms 80 ms core1-pos13-0.ealng.core.ba.net [65.6.196.245]
7 70 ms 70 ms 80 ms transit2-pos3-0.eang.ore.ba.net [194.72.17.82]
8 70 ms 80 ms 70 ms t2c2-p8-0.uk-eal.eu.ba.net [165.49.168.33]
9 151 ms 150 ms 150 ms t2c2-p5-0.us-ash.ba.net [165.49.164.22]
10 151 ms 150 ms 150 ms dcp-brdr-01.inet.qwest.net [205.171.1.37]
11 140 ms 140 ms 150 ms 205.171.251.25
12 150 ms 160 ms 150 ms dca-core-02.inet.qwest.net [205.171.8.221]
13 190 ms 191 ms 190 ms atl-core-02.inet.qwest.net [205.171.8.153]
14 191 ms 180 ms 200 ms atl-core-01.inet.net [205.171.21.149]
15 220 ms 230 ms 231 ms iah-core-03.inet.net [205.171.8.145]
16 210 ms 211 ms 210 ms iah-core-02.inet.net [205.171.31.41]
17 261 ms 250 ms 261 ms bur-core-01.inet.net [205.171.205.25]
18 230 ms 231 ms 230 ms bur-core-02.inet.net [205.171.13.2]
19 211 ms 220 ms 220 ms buc-cntr-01.inet.net [205.171.13.158]
20 220 ms 221 ms 220 ms msfc-24.buc.qwest.net [66.77.125.66]
21 221 ms 230 ms 220 ms www.hello.com [63.146.123.17]
Trace complete.
```

The fields in the Traceroute output are as follows:

- ...—Timeout
- U—Port unreachable message
- H—Host unreachable message
- P—Protocol unreachable message

- N—Network unreachable message
- ?—Unknown packet type
- Q—Source quench received

Traceroute is a very useful command when you want to troubleshoot network connectivity issues. Although it is outside the scope of the CCNA syllabus, here is a more detailed explanation of how it operates.

Traceroute works by sequentially incrementing the TTL field of UDP packets (only used in Cisco and Linux; Microsoft Windows tracert command uses ICMP echo request datagrams instead of UDP datagrams as probes) destined for a host and recording the replies received from intermediate routers.

Every packet has a TTL value associated with it and each time the packet reaches a hop, its TTL value is decreased by 1. The first packet is sent to the destination with TTL=1, which reaches Router 1, but because its TTL value has dropped to 0, the router sends an error message (TTL exceeded in transit). Then a second packet is sent with TTL=2. This reaches Router 2, which also sends the same error message that Router 1 sent. This is continued until the destination is reached.

All hops, except for the last one, should return a "TTL exceeded in transit" message, whereas the last hop should return a "destination unreachable/port unreachable" message, indicating that it cannot handle the received traffic (UDP Traceroute packets are typically addressed to a pseudorandom high port on which the end host is not likely to be listening).

Address Resolution Protocol (ARP)

Two types of addressing are used to identify network hosts—the IP (or Layer 3) address and the local (or Data Link Layer 2) address. The Data Link Layer address is also commonly referred to as the MAC address. Address resolution, as defined in RFC 826, is the process in which the IOS determines the Data Link Layer address from the Network Layer (or IP) address.

ARP resolves a known IP address to a MAC address. When a host needs to transfer data across the network, it needs to know the other host's MAC address. The host checks its ARP cache and if the MAC address is not there, it sends out an ARP broadcast message to find the host, as illustrated in Figure 1.33 below:

Figure 1.33—One Host Broadcasts for Another Host's MAC Address

You can debug ARP with the debug arp command.

An ARP entry is required for communication across the network. You can see that a broadcast has taken place if there is no ARP entry. It is also important to understand that ARP tables on routers and switches are flushed after a certain amount of time (four hours by default) to conserve resources and prevent inaccurate entries.

On the router below, it has an ARP entry only for its own FastEthernet interface until its neighbor is pinged, so the first of five ping (ICMP) packets fails, as shown by the period followed by four exclamation marks:

```
Router#show arp
Protocol  Address    Age (min)  Hardware Addr   Type   Interface
Internet  192.168.1.1    -       0002.4A4C.6801  ARPA   FastEthernet0/0

Router#ping 192.168.1.2

Type escape sequence to abort.
Sending 5, 100-byte ICMP Echos to 192.168.1.2, timeout is 2 seconds:
.!!!! ← first packet fails due to ARP request
Success rate is 80 percent(4/5),round-trip min/avg/max = 31/31/31 ms

Router#show arp
Protocol  Address    Age (min)  Hardware Addr   Type   Interface
Internet  192.168.1.1            0002.4A4C.6801  ARPA   FastEthernet0/0
Internet  192.168.1.2     0      0001.97BC.1601  ARPA   FastEthernet0/0
Router#
```

Proxy ARP

Proxy ARP (see Figure 1.34 below) is defined in RFC 1027. Proxy ARP enables hosts on an Ethernet network to communicate with hosts on other subnets or networks, even though they have no knowledge of routing.

If an ARP broadcast reaches a router, it will not forward it (by default). Routers do not forward broadcasts, but if they do know how to find the host (i.e., they have a route to it), they will send their own MAC address to the host. This process is called proxy ARP and it allows the host to send the data thinking it is going straight to the remote host. The router swaps the MAC address and then forwards the packet to the correct next hop.

The ip proxy-arp command is enabled on Cisco routers by default.

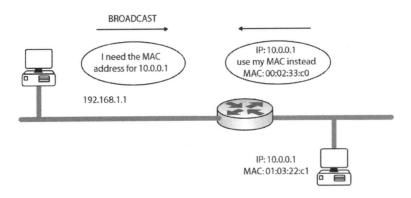

Figure 1.34—Router Uses Proxy ARP to Allow the Hosts to Connect

Expanding upon the previous point, part of the exam requirements is understanding how addressing changes as packets traverse the network. As the packet traverses the network, there must be a way for each end device to communicate, but also a way for intermediary devices to be able to exchange the next-hop address for the packet to traverse. Proxy ARP provides the answer again. The source and destination IP address never change but in order for the packet to be passed to a next-hop address, the MAC address (in the frame) changes between devices.

In Figure 1.35 below, the frame will leave HOST A with the source IP address 192.168.1.1, the destination IP address 172.16.1.2, the source MAC address AAAA:AAAA:AAAA, and the destination MAC address AAAA: AAAA:BBBB. R1 will retain the IP addresses but change the source address to AAAA:AAAA:CCCC. By the time the packet leaves R2 for HOST B, the IP addresses will not have changed but the source MAC address is now AAAA:AAAA:DDDD and the destination MAC address is AAAA:AAAA:EEEE.

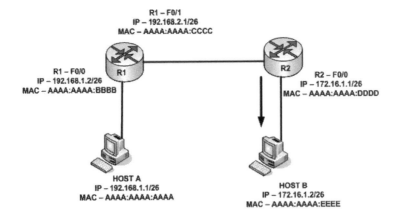

Figure 1.35—MAC Address Changes as the Packet Traverses Network Devices

Reverse Address Resolution Protocol (RARP)

RARP maps a known MAC address to an IP address. Hosts such as diskless workstations (also known as thin clients) know their MAC address when they boot. They use RARP to discover their IP address from a server on the network.

Gratuitous Address Resolution Protocol (GARP)

GARP is a special ARP packet. A normal host will always send out a GARP request after the link goes up or the interface is enabled. Gratuitous in this case means a request/reply that is not normally needed according to the ARP RFC specification but could be used in some cases. A gratuitous ARP request is an ARP request packet where the source MAC, the source IP, and the destination IP addresses are all set to the IP address of the machine issuing the packet, and the destination MAC is the broadcast address FFFF: FFFF: FFFF. Ordinarily, no reply packet will occur.

A GARP reply is one to which no request has been made (if you see a GARP reply, that means another computer on the network has the same IP address as you have). GARP is used when a change of state happens in FHRP protocols (e.g., HSRP; this will be covered later), with the objective of updating the Layer2 CAM table. We will discuss GARP again in the IPv6 section.

Simple Network Management Protocol (SNMP)

SNMP is used for network management services. An SNMP management system allows network devices to send messages called traps to a management station. This informs the network administrator of any faults on the network (such as faulty interfaces), high CPU utilization on servers, etc.

You can debug SNMP traffic with the `debug snmp` command. SNMP uses UDP ports 161 and 162.

Hyper Text Transfer Protocol Secure (HTTPS)

TLS, and the older protocol SSL, is used for secure communication over the Internet, which is carried out by means of cryptography. You will also find these used for e-mail and Voice over IP (VoIP), and when surfing sites which begin with the URL https://. HTTP with TLS/SSL (HTTPS) uses port 443.

IP Configuration Command

This is not actually a Cisco tool but it's part of your troubleshooting toolkit. The `ipconfig` command used at a Windows command prompt allows you to use several switches, but perhaps the most commonly used command is `ipconfig /all`, as shown in the screenshot below:

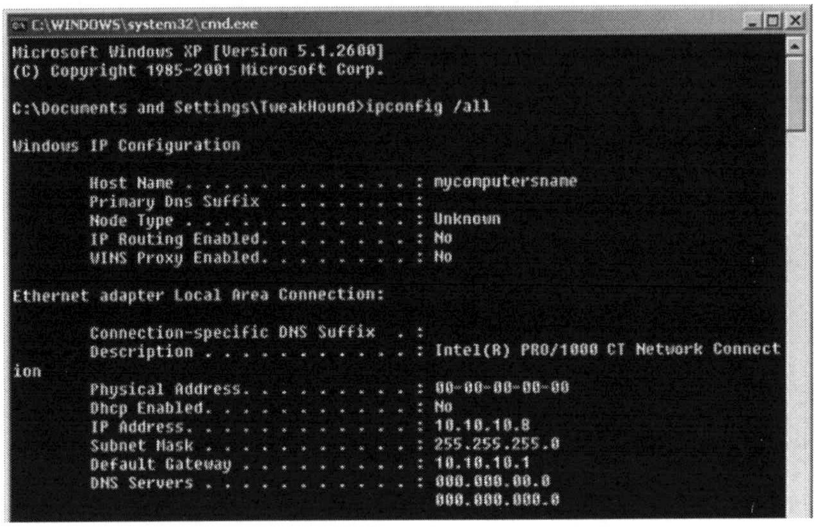

```
C:\WINDOWS\system32\cmd.exe
Microsoft Windows XP [Version 5.1.2600]
(C) Copyright 1985-2001 Microsoft Corp.

C:\Documents and Settings\TweakHound>ipconfig /all

Windows IP Configuration

        Host Name . . . . . . . . . . . . : mycomputersname
        Primary Dns Suffix  . . . . . . . :
        Node Type . . . . . . . . . . . . : Unknown
        IP Routing Enabled. . . . . . . . : No
        WINS Proxy Enabled. . . . . . . . : No

Ethernet adapter Local Area Connection:

        Connection-specific DNS Suffix  . :
        Description . . . . . . . . . . . : Intel(R) PRO/1000 CT Network Connect
ion
        Physical Address. . . . . . . . . : 00-00-00-00-00
        Dhcp Enabled. . . . . . . . . . . : No
        IP Address. . . . . . . . . . . . : 10.10.10.8
        Subnet Mask . . . . . . . . . . . : 255.255.255.0
        Default Gateway . . . . . . . . . : 10.10.10.1
        DNS Servers . . . . . . . . . . . : 000.000.00.0
                                            000.000.000.0
```

Figure 1.36—The `ipconfig /all` **Command Output**

Other switches you can use with the `ipconfig` command are as follows:

```
/?           Display this help message
/all         Display full configuration information
/release     Release the IP address for the specified adapter
/renew       Renew the IP address for the specified adapter
/flushdns    Purges the DNS Resolver cache
/registerdns Refreshes all DHCP leases and re-registers DNS names
```

CABLES AND MEDIA

Cabling and cable-related issues will become part of your day-to-day routine as a network engineer. You will need to know which cables plug into which devices, the industry limitations, and how to configure equipment for use with the correct cable type.

LAN Cables

Ethernet Cables

Most cable-related network problems will occur on the Local Area Network (LAN) side rather than on the Wide Area Network (WAN) side due to the sheer volume of cables and connectors, and the higher frequency of reseating (unplugging and plugging in) the cables for device moves and testing.

Ethernet cables are used to connect workstations to the switch, switch-to-switch, and switch-to-router. The specifications and speeds have been revised and improved many times in recent years, which means you can soon expect today's standard speeds to be left behind for new and improved high-speed links right to your desktop. The current standard Ethernet cable still uses eight wires twisted into pairs to prevent electromagnetic interference (EMI), as well as crosstalk, which is a signal from one wire spilling over into a neighboring cable.

Cable categories, as defined by ANSI/TIA/EIA-568-A, include Categories 3, 5, 5e, and 6. Each one gives standards, specifications, and achievable data throughput rates, which can be achieved if you comply with distance limitations. Category 3 cabling can carry data up to 10Mbps. Category 5 cabling is primarily used for faster Ethernet networks, such as 100BASE-TX and 1000BASE-T. Category 5e cabling uses 100-MHz-enhanced pairs of wires for running GigabitEthernet (1000Base-T). Finally, with Category 6 cabling, each pair runs 250 MHz for improved 1000Base-T performance. ("1000" refers to the speed of data in Mbps, "Base" stands for baseband, and "T" stands for twisted pair.) Table 1.6 below demonstrates some common Ethernet standards you should be familiar with:

Table 1.6.—Common Ethernet Standards

Speed	Name	IEEE Name	IEEE Standard	Cable/Length
10Mbps	Ethernet	10BASE-T	802.3	Copper/100 m
100Mbps	FastEthernet	100BASE-T	802.3u	Copper/100 m
1000Mbps	GigabitEthernet	1000BASE-LX	802.3z	Fiber/5000 m
1000Mbps	GigabitEthernet	1000BASE-T	802.3ab	Copper/100 m
10Gbps	TenGigabitEthernet	10GBASE-T	802.3an	Copper/100 m

Cisco like to sneak cable specification questions into the exam from time to time, so make sure you memorize the table above.

Duplex

When Ethernet networking was first used, data was able to pass on the wire in only one direction at a time. This is because of the limitations of the cables used at that time. The sending device had to wait until the wire was clear before sending data on it, without a guarantee that there wouldn't be a collision. This is no longer an issue because a different set of wires is used for sending and receiving signals.

Half duplex means that data can pass in only one direction at a time, while full duplex means that data can pass in both directions on the wire at the same time (see Figure 1.37). This is achieved by using spare wires inside the Ethernet cable. All devices now run at full duplex unless configured otherwise.

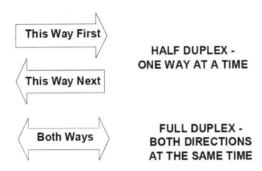

Figure 1.37—Duplex Topology

You will still be expected to understand and troubleshoot duplex issues in the exam; we will cover troubleshooting Layer 1 and Layer 2 issues later in this guide. You can easily check an interface's duplex settings with the show interface X command.

```
Switch#show interface FastEthernet0/1
FastEthernet0/1 is down, line protocol is down (disabled)
  Hardware is Lance, address is 0030.a388.8401 (bia 0030.a388.8401)
  BW 100000 Kbit, DLY 1000 usec,
      reliability 255/255, txload 1/255, rxload 1/255
  Encapsulation ARPA, Loopback not set
  Keepalive set (10 sec)
  Half-duplex, 100Mb/s
```

If this interface was connected to a full duplex device, you would see interface errors immediately and experience slow traffic on the link. You can also issue the show interfaces status command on a live switch, although this command may not work in the exam because a router simulator has limited commands (same for Packet Tracer). You can see possible issues with interface Fast Ethernet 1/0/2 below:

```
Switch#show interfaces status

Port Name        Status       Vlan      Duplex  Speed  Type
Fa1/0/1          notconnect   1         auto    auto   10/100BaseTX
Fa1/0/2          notconnect   1         half     10    10/100BaseTX
Fa1/0/3          notconnect   1         auto    auto   10/100BaseTX
Fa1/0/4          notconnect   1         auto    auto   10/100BaseTX
Fa1/0/5          notconnect   1         auto    auto   10/100BaseTX
```

And of course you can fix this issue easily, as shown below:

```
Switch(config)#int f1/0/2
Switch(config-if)#duplex ?
  auto  Enable AUTO duplex configuration
  full  Force full duplex operation
  half  Force half-duplex operation

Switch(config-if)#duplex full
```

Please do try this and all the other commands on live Cisco equipment, GNS3, or at least Packet Tracer in order to remember them! We will cover the speed setting next.

Speed

You can leave the speed of the Ethernet port on your routers or switches as auto-negotiate, or you can hard set them to 10Mbps, 100Mbps, or 1000Mbps.

To set the speed manually, you would configure the router as follows:

```
Router#config t
Router(config)#interface GigabitEthernet 0/0
Router(config-if)#speed ?
  10     Force 10 Mbps operation
  100    Force 100 Mbps operation
  1000   Force 1000 Mbps operation
  auto   Enable AUTO speed configuration
```

The following commands would allow you to view the router Ethernet interface settings:

```
Router#show interface FastEthernet0
FastEthernet0 is up, line protocol is up
  Hardware is DEC21140AD, address is 00e0.1e3e.c179 (bia 00e0.1e3e.c179)
  Internet address is 1.17.30.4/16
  MTU 1500 bytes, BW 10000 Kbit, DLY 1000 usec, rely 255/255, load 1/255
  Encapsulation ARPA, Loopback not set, keepalive set (10 sec)
  Half-duplex, 10Mb/s, 100BaseTX/FX
```

Specifications for Ethernet cables by EIA/TIA dictate that the end of the cable presentation should be RJ45 male (see Figure 1.38; Figure 1.39 shows the female end), which will allow you to insert the cable into the Ethernet port on your router/switch/PC.

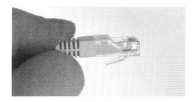

Figure 1.38—RJ45 Male End

Figure 1.39—RJ45 Female End

Straight Cables

Each Ethernet cable contains eight wires and each wire connects to a pin at the end. The position of these wires when they meet the pin determines what the cable can be used for. If each pin on one end matches the other side, then this is known as a straight-through cable. These cables can be used to connect an end device to an Ethernet port on a switch, and a switch to a router. You can easily check whether the wires match by comparing one side of the cable to the other, as shown in Figures 1.40 and 1.41 below:

Figure 1.40—Comparing Cable Ends

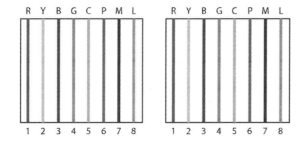

Figure 1.41—Cable Ends Match

Crossover Cables

By swapping two of the wires on the cable, it can now be used to connect a PC to a PC (without the use of a switch or a hub, although Auto-MDIX ports on newer network interfaces detect whether the connection requires a crossover, and automatically chooses the MDI or MDIX configuration to properly match the other end of the link) or a switch to a switch. The wire on pin 1 on one end needs to connect to pin 3 on the other end, and pin 2 needs to connect to pin 6 on the other end (see Figure 1.42). I have created my own color scheme for the cables purely to illustrate my point—red, yellow, blue, green, cyan, pink, magenta, and lilac.

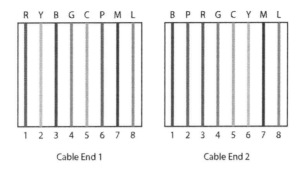

Figure 1.42—Pin 1 to Pin 3 and Pin 2 to Pin 6

Rollover/Console Cables

All Cisco routers and switches have physical ports to connect to for initial set up and disaster recovery or access. These ports are referred to as console ports and you will regularly use these as a Cisco engineer. In order to connect to this port, you need a special type of cable called a rollover or console cable (see Figure 1.43). It can sometimes be referred to as a flat cable because, as opposed to most round-bodied Ethernet cables, it is often flat along its body.

A rollover cable swaps all pins (see Figure 1.44), so pin 1 on one end goes to pin 8 on the other end, pin 2 goes to pin 7, and so on.

Figure 1.43—A Typical Rollover Cable

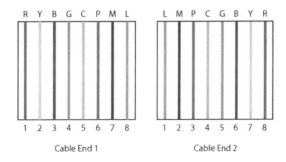

Figure 1.44—All Pins Swapped

Rollover cables usually have an RJ45 connection on one end and a 9-pin D-shaped connection on the other end, which is designed to connect to the COM port on a PC or laptop. The trouble is that devices no longer come with these ports, as they were so rarely used. You can now buy a DB9-to-USB converter cable (see Figure 1.45) from many electrical stores or online. They come with software drivers which allow you to connect a logical COM port on your PC via a terminal program, such as PuTTY or HyperTerminal.

Cisco have started to put mini-USB ports (in addition to RJ45 ports) on their devices to allow for console port connectivity using the USB Type A to 5-pin mini-Type B cable. If both console cables are plugged in at the same time, the mini-USB cable takes precedence and becomes active. Figures 1.46 and 1.47 below show the different connection types.

Figure 1.45—A COM-to-USB Converter Cable

Figure 1.46—Connecting to the USB Console Port (Image © 51sec.org)

Figure 1.47—Connecting to the Router RJ45 Console Port

WAN Cables

Used for Wide Area Network connections, serial cables can come in several shapes, sizes, and specifications, depending upon the interface on the router and connection type. ISDN uses different cables than Frame Relay or ADSL do, for example.

One common type of WAN cable you will use, especially if you have a home network to practice on, is a DB60. For this type of cable, you will have a data terminal equipment (DTE) end, which plugs into the customer equipment, and a data communication equipment (DCE) end, which determines the speed of the connection from the ISP. Figure 1.48 below shows a DB60 serial interface on a WIC-1T card.

Figure 1.48—A DB60 Cable

Figure 1.49—The DB60 Serial Interface on a WIC-1T Card

There is another common presentation type for Cisco WAN Interface Cards (WICs) known as a smart serial cable:

Figure 1.50—Smart Serial Cable

Of course, you will need the correct interface card in the router if you use this cable type, as shown below in Figure 1.51:

Figure 1.51—WIC-2T Smart Serial Card

The smart serial WIC card gives you two connections for one slot on the router, as opposed to only one connection you would get with a standard WIC-1T card. Each serial connection can use a different encapsulation type, such as PPP for one and Frame Relay for the other.

The most important thing to remember about DCE and DTE cables is that you need to apply a clock rate to the DCE end in order for the line to come up. Normally, your ISP would do this because they own the DCE end, but on a home lab or live rack, you own the DCE end, which makes you the customer on one router and the ISP on the other router. The command you would enter is `clock rate 64000` (or whatever speed you like from the available options in bits per second). You can type `clock rate ?` to see your options.

Please ensure that you understand the following commands before typing them out on a router. Firstly, to establish which router has the DCE cable attached, you need to type the `show controllers` command, followed by the interface number. This is a very useful command to know for troubleshooting problems in the actual exam (and in the real world). You can see which interfaces you have on your router with the `show ip interface brief` command.

You can actually shorten most Cisco IOS commands, which is demonstrated in the output below. The shortened versions may not work in the exam, though, because the exam uses a router simulator (i.e., not a live router).

```
Router#sh ip int brie
Interface        IP-Address    OK? Method Status Protocol
FastEthernet0/0 unassigned     YES unset  administratively down down
FastEthernet0/1 unassigned     YES unset  administratively down down
Serial0/1/0     unassigned     YES unset  administratively down down
Vlan1           unassigned     YES unset  administratively down down
Router#show controllers s0/1/0
Interface Serial0/1/0
Hardware is PowerQUICC MPC860
DCE V.35, no clock
Router(config-if)#clock rate ?
Speed (bits per second)
  1200
```

```
2400
4800
9600
19200
38400
56000
64000

[Truncated Output]
```

CONNECTING TO A ROUTER

The first time you connect to a router or a switch, it can seem a little daunting. We have covered console connections above, so once you connect the cable, you will need to use a terminal emulation program on your PC or laptop. This will allow you to see router output and type in the configuration commands.

HyperTerminal has been the default for many years, and you may need to use this still if you need to perform disaster recovery; however, for now you can stick to Putty, which is very widely used. You can download Putty from www.putty.org. An old-fashioned connection using the COM port on a PC almost always uses a logical port on it labeled COM1 or COM2. You can see the facility of using this on Putty, which actually calls this a serial connection, as shown in Figure 1.52 below:

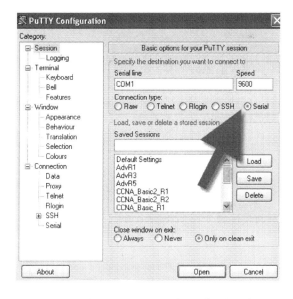

Figure 1.52—PuTTY Uses COM Ports for Serial Access

If you are using a USB-to-rollover cable, then you will have received a driver CD, which, when run, will give you a COM port number to use. You can find this port number in the Device Manager if you are using Windows, as shown in Figure 1.53 below:

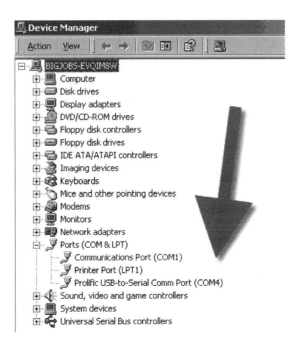

Figure 1.53—The Driver Has Assigned COM4 for Console Connection

If you are using HyperTerminal, you will also need to select more connection parameters, such as baud rate. You should choose the following, which is illustrated in Figure 1.54:

- Bits per second: 9600
- Data bits: 8 is the default
- Parity: None is the default
- Stop bits: 1 is the default
- Flow control: must be None

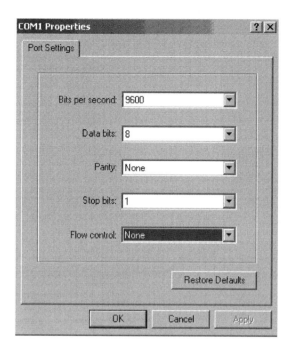

Figure 1.54—Setting Your HyperTerminal Settings

When you turn on the router, if you have selected the correct COM port AND plugged the rollover cable into the console port (instead of a different port by accident), you should see the router boot-up text (see Figure 1.55). If you can't see any text, hit the Enter key a few times and then double-check your settings.

```
00:00:08: %LINK-3-UPDOWN: Interface Serial1, changed state to down
00:00:24: %LINEPROTO-5-UPDOWN: Line protocol on Interface Ethernet0, changed sta
te to down
00:00:24: %LINEPROTO-5-UPDOWN: Line protocol on Interface Ethernet1, changed sta
te to down
01:15:56: %LINK-5-CHANGED: Interface Ethernet0, changed state to administrativel
y down
01:15:56: %LINK-5-CHANGED: Interface Ethernet1, changed state to administrativel
y down
01:15:56: %LINK-5-CHANGED: Interface Serial0, changed state to administratively
down
01:15:56: %LINK-5-CHANGED: Interface Serial1, changed state to administratively
down
01:15:59: %LINEPROTO-5-UPDOWN: Line protocol on Interface Serial0, changed state
 to down
01:15:59: %LINEPROTO-5-UPDOWN: Line protocol on Interface Serial1, changed state
 to down
01:16:37: %SYS-5-RESTART: System restarted --
Cisco Internetwork Operating System Software
IOS (tm) 2500 Software (C2500-JS-L), Version 12.1(17), RELEASE SOFTWARE (fc1)
Copyright (c) 1986-2002 by cisco Systems, Inc.
Compiled Wed 04-Sep-02 03:08 by kellythw
Router>enable
Router#_
```

Figure 1.55—The Router Boot-up Text

The router may ask whether you want to enter Initial Configuration mode. This happens when it can't find a startup configuration file in NVRAM (covered later) or if the configuration register is set to ignore the startup configuration file (usually 0x2142). Always type "n" or "no" because, otherwise, you will enter setup mode, which you don't want to do:

```
Would you like to enter the initial configuration dialog? [yes/no]:
% Please answer 'yes' or 'no'.
Would you like to enter the initial configuration dialog? [yes/no]: no
Press RETURN to get started!
Router>
```

With a different router model, you would see the following output:

```
Technical Support: www.cisco.com/techsupport
Copyright (c) 1986-2007 by Cisco Systems, Inc.
Compiled Wed 18-Jul-07 04:52 by pt_team
        --- System Configuration Dialog ---
Continue with configuration dialog? [yes/no]: no
Press RETURN to get started!
Router>
```

Router Modes

In order to pass the CCNA exam, you will need to understand which router prompt you should start from to perform various actions. Whatever function you wish to perform, you will have to be in the correct mode (signified by the router prompt). This is the biggest mistake novice students make when they are having problems configuring the router and cannot find the right command to use. Make sure you are in the correct mode!

User Mode

The first mode you will be presented with when the router boots is known as User mode or User Exec mode. User mode has a very limited set of commands that can be used, but it can be useful for looking at basic router elements. The default name of the router is "Router" but this can be changed, as you will see later.

```
Router>
```

Privileged Mode

Typing enable at the User prompt takes you into the next mode, known as Privileged mode or Privileged Exec mode. To get back to User mode, you simply type disable. To quit the session altogether, type logout or exit.

```
Router>enable
Router#
Router#disable
Router>
```

Privileged mode is very useful for looking at the entire configuration of the router, the statistics about how it is performing, and even which modules you have connected to the router. At this prompt, you would type show commands and troubleshoot with debug commands.

Global Configuration Mode

In order to configure the router, you have to be in Global Configuration mode. To get to Global Configuration mode, you simply type `configure terminal`, or `config t` for short, at the Privileged Exec prompt. Alternatively, just type `config` and the router will ask you which mode you would like to enter. The default is `terminal` (the default options will be shown inside the square brackets [ ]). If you press Enter, the command inside the brackets will be accepted.

```
Router#config
Configuring from terminal, memory, or network[terminal]? ← press Enter
Enter configuration commands, one per line. End with CNTL/Z.
Router(config)#
```

Interface Configuration Mode

Interface Configuration mode allows you to enter commands for individual router interfaces, such as FastEthernet, Serial, etc. On a new router, all of the interfaces will be shut down by default, with no configuration present.

```
Router>enable
Router#config t
Enter configuration commands, one per line. End with CNTL/Z.
Router(config)#interface Serial0/0
Router(config-if)#
```

It is okay to read through this the first time, but it will make far more sense if you try out all the commands on a real router as you read them. Remember to issue the `show ip interface brief` command to see which interfaces you have available.

Line Configuration Mode

Line Configuration mode is used to make any changes to the console, Telnet, or auxiliary ports (if your router has these). You can control who can access the router via these ports, as well as put passwords or a security feature called "access control lists" on them.

```
Router#config t
Enter configuration commands, one per line. End with CNTL/Z.
Router(config)#line console 0
Router(config-line)#
```

You can also configure baud rates, exec levels, and more in Line Configuration mode.

Router Configuration Mode

In order to configure a routing protocol onto the router so it can dynamically build a picture of the network, you will need to be in Router Configuration mode.

```
Router#config t
Enter configuration commands, one per line. End with CNTL/Z.
Router(config)#router rip
Router(config-router)#
```

VLAN Configuration Mode

This mode actually only applies to switches but it's worth mentioning it here while we are discussing modes. You will spend a lot of time in this mode when configuring the switching labs in this book.

```
Switch#conf t
Enter configuration commands, one per line.  End with CNTL/Z.
Switch(config)#vlan 10
Switch(config-vlan)#
```

Routers equipped with Ethernet switch cards use VLAN Database Configuration mode (this mode is deprecated on switches), which is similar to VLAN Configuration mode:

```
Router#vlan database
Router(vlan)#vlan 10
VLAN 10 added:
    Name: VLAN0010
Router(vlan)#exit
APPLY completed.
Exiting....
Router#
```

Configuring a Router

There are no menus available on a router, and you cannot use a mouse to navigate between the different modes, as it is all done via the command line interface (CLI). There is, however, some context-sensitive help in the form of the ?. If you type a question mark at the router prompt, you will be presented with a list of all the available commands.

Please note that you will only see the commands available for your mode. If you want to see interface configuration commands, you must be at the interface prompt.

```
Router#?
Exec commands:
access-enable    Create a temporary Access-List entry
access-profile   Apply user-profile to interface
access-template  Create a temporary Access-List entry
alps       ALPS exec commands
archive    manage archive files
bfe        For manual emergency modes setting
cd Change current directory
clear      Reset functions
clock      Manage the system clock
cns        CNS subsystem
configure  Enter configuration mode
connect    Open a terminal connection
copy       Copy from one file to another
debug      Debugging functions (see also 'undebug')
delete     Delete a file
dir        List files on a directory
disable    Turn off privileged commands
```

```
disconnect        Disconnect an existing network connection
enable      Turn on privileged commands
erase       Erase a file
exit        Exit from the EXEC mode
help        Description of the interactive help system
-- More -
```

If there is too much information to display on the screen, you will see the -- More -- tab. If you want to see the next page, press the space bar. If not, hold down the Ctrl+Z keys together or press "Q" to get back to the router prompt.

In addition, if you have started to type a command but forget what else you need to type in, using the question mark will give you a list of options available. The ? WILL work in the CCNA exam, but if you are using it, you didn't follow all my labs!

```
Router#cl?
clear clock
```

If you begin to type out a command, as long as there is only one possible word or command available with that syntax, you can press the Tab key to have it completed for you.

```
Router#copy ru      ← press the Tab key here
Router#copy running-config
```

The router has several modes from which to choose. This is to ensure that you do not make changes to parts of the router configuration you do not intend to change. You can recognize which mode you are in by looking at the command prompt. For example, if you wanted to make some changes to one of the FastEthernet interfaces, you would need to be in Interface Configuration mode.

First, go into Global Configuration mode:

```
Router#config t
Router(config)#
```

Next, tell the router which interface you want to configure:

```
Router(config)#interface FastEthernet0
Router(config-if)#exit
Router(config)#
```

If you are not sure which way to enter the interface number, then use the ?. Do not worry about all of the choices you will be given. Most people only use the FastEthernet, Serial, and Loopback interfaces.

```
Router(config)#interface ?
Async       Async interface
BRI         ISDN Basic Rate Interface
BVI         Bridge-Group Virtual Interface
CTunnel     CTunnel interface
```

```
Dialer      Dialer interface
FastEthernet      IEEE 802.3u
Group-Async      Async Group interface
Lex      Lex interface
Loopback  Loopback interface
Multilink Multilink-group interface
Null      Null interface
Serial    Serial interface
Tunnel    Tunnel interface
Vif       PGM Multicast Host interface
Virtual-Template Virtual Template interface
Virtual-TokenRing      Virtual TokenRing interface
range     interface range command

Router(config)#interface FastEthernet?
<0-0> FastEthernet interface number
Router(config)#interface FastEthernet0
```

Finally, the router drops into Interface Configuration mode:

```
Router(config-if)#
```

From here, you can put an IP address on the interface, set the bandwidth, apply an access control list, and do a lot of other things. Please note that your router and switch may well have different interface numbers from mine, so use the ? or show ip interface brief commands to see your options.

If you ever need to exit out of a configuration mode, simply type exit. This takes you back to the next-highest level. To quit any sort of configuration mode, simply press Ctrl+Z together (or type end).

```
Router(config-if)#exit
Router(config)#
```

Or, if using the Ctrl+Z option:

```
Router(config-if)#^z
Router#
```

Loopback Interfaces

Loopback interfaces are not normally covered in the CCNA syllabus, but they are very useful in the real world and for practice labs. A Loopback interface is a virtual or logical interface that you configure, but it does not physically exist (so you will never see it on the router panel). The router will let you ping this interface, though, which will save you from having to connect devices to the FastEthernet interfaces in the labs.

An advantage of using Loopback interfaces is that they always remain up, if the router is powered up, because they are logical, meaning they can never go down. However, you cannot put a network cable into the Loopback interface because it is a virtual interface.

```
Router#config t
```

```
Router#(config)#interface Loopback0
Router#(config-if)#ip address 192.168.20.1 255.255.255.0
Router#(config-if)#^z  ← press Ctrl+Z

Router#
Router#show ip interface brief
Interface  IP-Address    OK?  Method Status Protocol
Loopback0  192.168.20.1  YES  manual up     up
```

Your output for this command will show all of the available interfaces on your router.

> **IN THE REAL WORLD:** If you need to, you can shut down a Loopback interface with the shutdown command in Interface Configuration mode.

Loopback interfaces have to be given a valid IP address. You can then use them for routing protocols or for testing your router to see whether it is permitting certain traffic. You will be using these interfaces a lot throughout the course.

Editing Commands

It is possible to navigate your way around a line of configuration you have typed rather than deleting the whole line. The keystrokes shown in Table 1.7 below will move the cursor to various places in the line:

Table 1.7—Keystrokes and Resulting Actions

Keystroke	Action
Ctrl+A	Moves to the beginning of the command line
Ctrl+E	Moves to the end of the command line
Ctrl+B	Moves back one character
Ctrl+F	Moves forward one character
Esc+B	Moves back one word
Esc+F	Moves forward one word
Ctrl+P or up arrow	Recalls the previous command
Ctrl+N or down arrow	Recalls the next command
Ctrl+U	Deletes a line
Ctrl+W	Deletes a word
Tab	Finishes typing a command for you
Show history	Shows the last 10 commands entered by default
Backspace	Deletes a single character

It is fairly common to have a question on the above in the exam.

Configuring a Router Interface

In order to address a specific router interface and to enter Interface Configuration mode to configure specific parameters, you must know the interface notation. This can vary based on the router manufacturer, but the interface notation is usually made up of two parts:

- Interface type (Ethernet, FastEthernet, etc.)
- Interface slot/module and port number

For example, common interface notations include the following:

- Ethernet1/0 (slot 1, port 0)
- FastEthernet0/3 (slot 0, port 3)
- GigabitEthernet0/1/1 (module 0, slot 1, port 1)

NOTE: Slot 0 usually represents the built-in ports, and the other slots represent extension slots that can be added at any time. Slot and port numbering usually starts at 0.

In order for a router interface to have basic functionality, you must configure the following parameters (unless they already have defaults set by the manufacturer):

- Speed
- Duplex
- IP address

You can exemplify these basic configuration settings on a Cisco router, as they are commonly used in modern enterprise networks. To see the available interfaces and their current state, you can issue the following command:

```
Router#show ip interface brief
Interface       IP-Address   OK? Method Status                Protocol
FastEthernet0/0 unassigned   YES unset  administratively down down
FastEthernet0/1 unassigned   YES unset  administratively down down
```

From the output above, you can see that the router has two FastEthernet (100 Mbps) interfaces on slot 0, both unconfigured (i.e., no IP address) and administratively disabled (i.e., status: administratively down).

Before starting to configure interface parameters, you must enter Router Configuration mode using the `configure terminal` command on Cisco devices, and then Interface Configuration mode using the `interface <interface name>` command. The first step in the interface configuration process is enabling the interface. For example, the interface FastEthernet0/0 can be enabled using the `no shutdown` command:

```
Router#configure terminal
Enter configuration commands, one per line.  End with CNTL/Z.
Router(config)#interface FastEthernet0/0
Router(config-if)#no shutdown
```

```
*Mar  1 00:32:05.199: %LINK-3-UPDOWN: Interface FastEthernet0/0, changed
state to up
*Mar  1 00:32:06.199: %LINEPROTO-5-UPDOWN: Line protocol on Interface
FastEthernet0/0, changed state to up
```

The next configuration step involves setting up speed and duplex settings and we have already covered these.

Configuring an IP Address on an Interface

In order for a router to communicate with other devices, it will need to have an address on the connected interface. Configuring an IP address on an interface is very straightforward, although you have to remember to go into Interface Configuration mode first.

Don't worry about where to find the IP address at the moment, as we will look at that later on.

```
Router>enable    ← takes you from User mode to Privileged mode
Router#config t    ← from Privileged mode to Configuration mode
Router(config)#interface Serial0    ← and then into Interface Configuration mode
Router(config-if)#ip address 192.168.1.1 255.255.255.0
Router(config-if)#no shutdown    ← the interface is opened for traffic
Router(config-if)#exit    ← you could also hold down the Ctrl+Z keys together to exit
Router(config)#exit
Router#
```

A description can also be added to the interface, as shown in the following output:

```
RouterA(config)#interface Serial0
RouterA(config-if)#description To_Headquarters
RouterA(config-if)#^Z ← press Ctrl+Z to exit
```

After the router interface configuration is complete, you can verify the setting by inspecting the full interface-configured parameters using the commands below on Cisco routers:

```
RouterA#show interface Serial0
Serial0 is up, line protocol is up
Hardware is HD64570
Description: To_Headquarters
Internet address is 12.0.0.2/24
MTU 1500 bytes, BW 1544 Kbit, DLY 20000 usec,
reliability 255/255, txload 1/255, rxload 1/255
Encapsulation HDLC, loopback not set
Keepalive set (10 sec)
Last input 00:00:02, output 00:00:03, output hang never [Output
Truncated]
```

Show Commands

You can look at most of the settings on the router simply by using the show x command from Privileged mode, with x being the next command, as illustrated in the following output:

```
Router#show ?
access-expression       List access expression
```

```
access-lists    List access lists
accounting        Accounting data for active sessions
adjacency  Adjacent nodes
aliases    Display alias commands
alps       Alps information
apollo     Apollo network information
appletalk  AppleTalk information
arap       Show AppleTalk Remote Access statistics
arp        ARP table
async      Information on terminal lines used as router interfaces
backup     Backup status
bridge     Bridge Forwarding/Filtering Database [verbose]
bsc        BSC interface information
bstun      BSTUN interface information
buffers    Buffer pool statistics
cca        CCA information
cdapi      CDAPI information
cdp        CDP information
cef        Cisco Express Forwarding
class-map  Show QoS Class Map
clns       CLNS network information
--More--
```

Some of the more common show commands and their meanings, along with an example, are listed below in Table 1.8:

Table 1.8—Common show Commands and Their Meanings

Command	Meaning
show running-configuration	Shows configuration in DRAM
show startup-configuration	Shows configuration in NVRAM
show flash:	Shows which IOS is in flash
show ip interface brief	Shows brief summary of all interfaces
show interface Serial0	Shows Serial interface statistics
show history	Shows last 10 commands entered

```
Router#show ip interface brief
Interface  Address     OK?   Method Status Protocol
Ethernet0  10.0.0.1    YES   manual up      up
Ethernet1  unassigned  YES   unset  administratively down      down
Loopback0  172.16.1.1  YES   manual up      up
Serial0    192.168.1.1 YES   manual down    down
Serial1    unassigned  YES   unset  administratively down      down
```

The method tag indicates how the address has been assigned. It can state unset, manual, NVRAM, IPCP, or DHCP.

Routers can recall commands previously entered at the router prompt (the default is 10 commands), which can be recalled by using the up arrow. Using this feature can save a lot of time and effort, as it prevents you from having to re-enter a long line. The show history command shows the buffer of the last 10 commands.

```
Router#show history
show ip interface brief
show history
show version
show flash:
conf t
show access-lists
show process cpu
show buffers
show logging
show memory
```

You can increase the history buffer with the terminal history size command:

```
Router#terminal history ?
size Set history buffer size
<cr>
Router#terminal history size ?
<0-256> Size of history buffer
Router#terminal history size 20
```

Verifying Basic Router Configuration and Network Connectivity

The most useful commands that help verify basic router configuration are explained in the following sections.

Show Version

The show version command provides useful information that might represent a starting point in verifying most of the router operations. This information includes the following:

- Type of router (another useful command for listing the router hardware is show inventory)
- IOS version
- Memory capacity
- Memory usage
- CPU type
- Flash capacity
- Other hardware parameters
- Reason for last reload

Here is a shortened output of the show version command. Please try it out for yourself.

```
Router#show version
Cisco 1841 (revision 5.0) with 114688K/16384K bytes of memory.
Processor board ID FTX0947Z18E
M860 processor: part number 0, mask 49
2 FastEthernet/IEEE 802.3 interface(s)
```

```
2 Low-speed Serial(sync/async) network interface(s)
191K bytes of NVRAM.
63488K bytes of ATA CompactFlash (Read/Write)

Configuration register is 0x2102
```

Show Running-config

The show running-config command provides full configuration on the router, and it can be used to verify that the device is configured with the proper features. The output for this command is too extensive so it will not be presented here.

Show IP Interface Brief

The show ip interface brief command, as mentioned in a previous section, lists the router interfaces and their state, including:

- Interface name and number
- IP address
- Link status
- Protocol status

```
Router#show ip interface brief
Interface       IP-Address OK? Method Status             Protocol
FastEthernet0/0 unassigned YES unset  administratively down down
FastEthernet0/1 unassigned YES unset  administratively down down
Serial0/0/0     unassigned YES unset  administratively down down
Serial0/1/0     unassigned YES unset  administratively down down
Vlan1           unassigned YES unset  administratively down down
Router#
```

Show IP Route

The show ip route command provides deep information regarding the routing capabilities of the device. It lists all the networks the router can reach and information about the way they can be reached, including:

- Network
- Routing protocol
- Next hop
- Outgoing interface

```
R1#show ip route
Codes: C - connected, S - static, R - RIP, M - mobile, B - BGP
       D - EIGRP, EX - EIGRP external, O - OSPF, IA - OSPF inter
       area, N1 - OSPF NSSA external type 1, N2 - OSPF NSSA external
       type 2, E1 - OSPF external type 1, E2 - OSPF external type 2,
       i - IS-IS, L1 - IS-IS level-1, L2 - IS-IS level-2, ia - IS-IS
       inter area, * - candidate default, U - per-user static route,
       o—ODR, P - periodic downloaded static route

Gateway of last resort is not set
```

```
R        80.1.1.0/24 [120/1] via 10.1.1.2, 00:00:04, Ethernet0/0.1
D        80.0.0.0/8 [90/281600] via 10.1.1.2, 00:02:02, Ethernet0/0.1
O E2     80.1.0.0/16 [110/20] via 10.1.1.2, 00:00:14, Ethernet0/0.1
```

In addition to the show commands presented above, other useful methods of verifying router connectivity include using the ping and traceroute commands.

Ping

The ping command provides a basic connectivity test to a specific destination. This way you can test whether the router can reach a network or not. Ping works (using ICMP) by sending echo requests to a machine to verify whether it is up and running. If a specific machine is operating, it will send an ICMP echo reply message back to the source, confirming its availability. A sample ping is presented below:

```
Router#ping 10.10.10.2
Type escape sequence to abort.
Sending 5, 100-byte ICMP Echos to 10.10.10.2, timeout is 2 seconds:
.!!!!
Success rate is 80 percent (4/5), round-trip min/avg/max = 20/40/76 ms
```

A standard ping command sends five ICMP packets to the destination. When looking at the ping output, a dot (.) represents a failure and an exclamation mark (!) represents a successfully received packet. The ping command output also shows the round-trip time to the destination network (minimum, average, and maximum).

If you need to manipulate ping-related parameters, you can issue an extended ping from a Cisco router. This is done by typing ping and pressing Enter in the console. The router will prompt you with an interactive menu where you can specify the desired parameters, including:

- Number of ICMP packets
- Packet size
- Timeout
- Source interface
- Type of service

We looked at the extended ping output earlier and will do so several times throughout this guide.

Traceroute

The traceroute command is another useful tool that allows you to see the hops a packet passes until it reaches its destination. The output below shows that the packet has to cross a single hop until it reaches its destination:

```
R2#traceroute 192.168.1.1
Type escape sequence to abort.
Tracing the route to 192.168.1.1
  1 10.10.10.1 60 msec *   64 msec
```

Just like with ping, Cisco routers allow you to perform an extended traceroute command that can define a number of associated parameters, most of them similar to the ping-related parameters:

```
Router#traceroute
Protocol [ip]:
Target IP address: 192.168.1.1
Source address: 10.10.10.2
Numeric display [n]:
Timeout in seconds [3]:
Probe count [3]:
Minimum Time to Live [1]:
Maximum Time to Live [30]:
Port Number [33434]:
Loose, Strict, Record, Timestamp, Verbose[none]:
Type escape sequence to abort.
Tracing the route to 192.168.1.1
  1 10.10.10.1 76 msec *  56 msec
```

Now please take the Day 1 exam at **https://www.in60days.com/free/ccnain60days/**

DAY 1 LAB

IOS Command Navigation Lab

Topology

Purpose

Learn how to connect to a router via the console port and try out some commands.

Walkthrough

1. Use a console cable, along with PuTTY (free online; search for "PuTTY"), to connect to a router console port.

2. From the Router> prompt, enter the commands below, exploring various router modes and commands. If you are asked to enter Setup mode, type "no" and hit Enter. Please bear in mind that you will have a different router model from mine, so some output will differ.

```
Cisco IOS Software, 1841 Software (C1841-ADVIPSERVICESK9-M), Version
12.4(15)T1, RELEASE SOFTWARE (fc2)
Technical Support: www.cisco.com/techsupport
Copyright (c) 1986-2007 by Cisco Systems, Inc.
Compiled Wed 18-Jul-07 04:52 by pt_team

        --- System Configuration Dialog ---

Continue with configuration dialog? [yes/no]:no
Press RETURN to get started!

Router>enable
Router#show version
Cisco 1841 (revision 5.0) with 114688K/16384K bytes of memory.
Processor board ID FTX0947Z18E
M860 processor: part number 0, mask 49
2 FastEthernet/IEEE 802.3 interface(s)
2 Low-speed Serial(sync/async) network interface(s)
191K bytes of NVRAM.
63488K bytes of ATA CompactFlash (Read/Write)

Configuration register is 0x2102

Router#show ip interface brief
Interface       IP-Address  OK? Method Status                 Protocol
FastEthernet0/0 unassigned  YES unset  administratively down  down
FastEthernet0/1 unassigned  YES unset  administratively down  down
```

```
Serial0/0/0        unassigned YES unset  administratively down down
Serial0/1/0        unassigned YES unset  administratively down down
Vlan1              unassigned YES unset  administratively down down
Router#

Router#conf t
Enter configuration commands, one per line.  End with CNTL/Z.
Router(config)#interface Serial0/1/0 ← put your serial # here
Router(config-if)#ip address 192.168.1.1 255.255.255.0
Router(config-if)#interface Loopback0

Router(config-if)#ip address 10.1.1.1 255.0.0.0
Router(config-if)#^Z ← press Ctrl+Z keys together
Router#
Router#show ip interface brief
Interface       IP-Address  OK? Method Status                Protocol
FastEthernet0/0 unassigned  YES unset  administratively down down
FastEthernet0/1 unassigned  YES unset  administratively down down
Serial0/0/0     unassigned  YES unset  administratively down down
Serial0/1/0     192.168.1.1 YES manual administratively down down
Loopback0       10.1.1.1    YES manual up                    up
Vlan1           unassigned  YES unset  administratively down down

Router#show history
Router(config)#hostname My_Router
My_Router(config)#line vty 0 ?
  <1-15>  Last Line number
  <cr>
My_Router(config)#line vty 0 15 ← enter 0 ? to find out how many lines you
have
My_Router(config-line)#
My_Router(config-line)#exit
My_Router(config)#router rip
My_Router(config-router)#network 10.0.0.0
My_Router(config-router)#
```

IP Addressing and VLSM

DAY 2 TASKS

- Read today's lesson notes (below)
- Review yesterday's lesson notes
- Read the ICND1 cram guide
- Take the day 2 exam
- Complete today's lab

Welcome to what many people find to be one of the hardest areas of the CCNA syllabus to understand. In order to understand IP addressing for the CCNA exam, we must cover binary mathematics and the hexadecimal numbering system, classes of addresses, powers of two and rules such as subnet zero, and broadcast and network addresses, as well as formulas to work out subnets and host addresses.

Don't worry, though; this is a process, not a one-off event, so follow my notes and then feel assured that we will be coming back to review these concepts many times.

Today you will learn about the following:

- Network traffic types
- IP addressing (using binary and hexadecimal)
- Address classes
- Using IP addresses
- Subnetting
- Easy subnetting
- Route summarization
- VLSM
- Troubleshooting IP addressing issues

This module maps to the following ICND1 syllabus requirements:

- 1.8 Configure, verify, and troubleshoot IPv4 addressing and subnetting
- 1.9 Compare and contrast IPv4 address types
- 1.9.a Unicast
- 1.9.b Broadcast

- 1.9.c Multicast
- 1.10 Describe the need for private IPv4 addressing

NETWORK TRAFFIC TYPES

You should already be familiar with basic networking concepts but as a refresher, when describing various network devices, the following terminology is often used:

- **Domain:** a specific part of a network
- **Bandwidth:** the amount of data that can be carried on a link in a given time period
- **Unicast data:** data sent to one device
- **Multicast data:** data sent to a group of devices
- **Broadcast data:** data sent to all devices
- **Collision domain:** includes all devices that share the same bandwidth; collision domains are separated by switch ports
- **Broadcast domain:** includes all devices that receive broadcast messages; broadcast domains are separated by routers (and VLANs)

We will cover multicast and broadcast traffic throughout the guide, in particular, how routing protocols use these traffic types. We will also look into collision domains.

If you use GNS3 for any of your labs, you can easily use a network sniffer such as Wireshark to check the type of traffic being forwarded. Figure 2.1 below shows a unicast packet capture. You can see that a single source (Src:) is contacting a single destination (Dst:), in this case, 192.168.1.1 to host 192.168.1.2.

```
        Address: c2:00:06:fa:00:00 (c2:00:06:fa:00:00)
        .... ..1. .... .... .... .... = LG bit: Locally administered address (this is NOT the factory defa
        .... ...0 .... .... .... .... = IG bit: Individual address (unicast)
      Type: IP (0x0800)
  ▽ Internet Protocol Version 4, Src: 192.168.1.1 (192.168.1.1), Dst: 192.168.1.2 (192.168.1.2)
      Version: 4
      Header length: 20 bytes
    ▷ Differentiated Services Field: 0x00 (DSCP 0x00: Default; ECN: 0x00: Not-ECT (Not ECN-Capable Transpo
      Total Length: 100
      Identification: 0x0006 (6)
    ▷ Flags: 0x00
      Fragment offset: 0
```

Figure 2.1—Unicast Packet Capture

Figure 2.2 below is a capture of a broadcast packet. RIPv1 routing protocol is broadcasting to the entire LAN. We know it's a broadcast packet because the destination address is 255.255.255.255. This means that every device receiving the packet must accept and process it in case it's one of the intended recipients.

```
   Address: c2:00:06:fa:00:00 (c2:00:06:fa:00:00)
      ....1.              = LG bit: Locally administered address (this is NOT the factory defau
      .... ...0 .... .... .... .... = IG bit: Individual address (unicast)
   Type: IP (0x0800)
▽ Internet Protocol Version 4, Src: 192.168.1.1 (192.168.1.1), Dst: 255.255.255.255 (255.255.255.255)
      Version: 4
      Header length: 20 bytes
   ▷ Differentiated Services Field: 0xc0 (DSCP 0x30: Class Selector 6; ECN: 0x00: Not-ECT (Not ECN-Capable
      Total Length: 52
      Identification: 0x0000 (0)
   ▷ Flags: 0x00
      Fragment offset: 0
```

Figure 2.2—Broadcast Packet Capture

If you were to check the Ethernet frame, you would see the broadcast address in hexadecimal, which is the Destination field filled with Fs in Figure 2.3 below:

```
▷ Frame 121: 66 bytes on wire (528 bits), 66 bytes captured (528 bits)
▽ Ethernet II, Src: c2:00:06:fa:00:00 (c2:00:06:fa:00:00), Dst: Broadcast (ff:ff:ff:ff:ff:ff)
   ▽ Destination: Broadcast (ff:ff:ff:ff:ff:ff)
      Address: Broadcast (ff:ff:ff:ff:ff:ff)
      .... ..1. .... .... .... .... = LG bit: Locally administered address (this is NOT the factory
      .... ...1 .... .... .... .... = IG bit: Group address (multicast/broadcast)
   ▽ Source: c2:00:06:fa:00:00 (c2:00:06:fa:00:00)
      Address: c2:00:06:fa:00:00 (c2:00:06:fa:00:00)
      .... ..1. .... .... .... .... = LG bit: Locally administered address (this is NOT the factory
```

Figure 2.3—Broadcast Frame Capture

Figure 2.4 below shows a multicast packet capture. Multicast addresses cannot be used for hosts on a network. You will usually see multicast addresses used by routing protocols to send updates to devices configured as part of the routing domain that needs to receive routes. They can also be used by streaming video events such as concerts. Multicast addresses range from 224.0.0.0 to 239.255.255.255 and are referred to as Class D addresses. We will cover address classes later.

```
   ▽ Source. c2:00:06:fa:00:00 (c2:00:06:fa:00:00)
      Address: c2:00:06:fa:00:00 (c2:00:06:fa:00:00)
      .... ..1. .... .... .... .... = LG bit: Locally administered address (this is NOT th
      .... ...0 .... .... .... .... = IG bit: Individual address (unicast)
   Type: IP (0x0800)
▽ Internet Protocol Version 4, Src: 192.168.1.1 (192.168.1.1), Dst: 224.0.0.9 (224.0.0.9)
      Version: 4
      Header length: 20 bytes
   ▷ Differentiated Services Field: 0xc0 (DSCP 0x30: Class Selector 6; ECN: 0x00: Not-ECT (
      Total Length: 52
      Identification: 0x0000 (0)
   ▷ Flags: 0x00
```

Figure 2.4—Multicast Packet Capture

IP ADDRESSING

All devices on a network need some way to identify themselves as a specific host. Early networks simply used a naming format, and a server on the network kept a map of MAC addresses to host names. Tables quickly grew very large and with this grew issues such as consistency and accuracy (see Figure 2.5 below). IP addressing effectively resolved this issue.

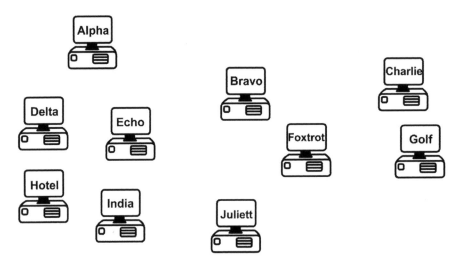

Figure 2.5—Device Naming Tables Became Too Cumbersome

IP Version 4

IP version 4 (IPv4) was devised to resolve the device naming issue. IPv4 uses binary to apply an address to network devices. IPv4 addresses use 32 binary bits divided into four groups of eight (octets). The following is an example of an IPv4 address in binary:

11000000.10100011.11110000.10101011 which you would see in decimal as 192.163.240.171.

Each binary bit represents a decimal number, and you can use or not use the number by placing a 1 or a 0, respectively, in the relevant column. The eight columns are as follows:

128	64	32	16	8	4	2	1
1	1	0	0	0	0	0	0

In the chart above, you can see that only the first two decimal numbers are used (those with 1s beneath them), which produces the value 128 + 64 = 192.

Binary

In order to understand how IP addressing works, you need to understand binary mathematics (sorry). Computers and networking equipment do not understand decimal. We use decimal because it is a numbering system using 10 digits, invented by a caveman millennia ago when he realized he had 10 digits on his hands that could be used for counting things.

Computers and networking equipment can only understand electrical signals. Since an electrical signal is either on or off, the only numbering system that will work is binary. Binary uses only two numbers, a 0 or a 1. A 0 means there is no electrical pulse on the wire and a 1 means that there is a pulse on the wire.

Any number can be made up using binary values. The more binary values you add, the larger the number becomes. For every binary value you add, you double the next number (e.g., 1 to 2 to 4 to 8 to 16, and so on into infinity), starting at the right and moving left. With two binary digits, you can count up to 3. Just place a 0 or a 1 in the column to decide whether you want to use that value.

Let's start with only two binary values in columns 1 and 2:

2	1
0	0

$0 + 0 = 0$

2	1
0	1

$0 + 1 = 1$

2	1
1	0

$2 + 0 = 2$

2	1
1	1

$2 + 1 = 3$

If you use eight binary bit places (an octet), you can get any number from 0 up to 255. You can see that the numbers start from the right and move across to the left doubling in value each step:

128	64	32	16	8	4	2	1

If you add a 0 to each of these columns, you have a value of 0 in decimal:

128	64	32	16	8	4	2	1
0	0	0	0	0	0	0	0

If you add a 1 to each of these columns, you have a value of 255 in decimal:

128	64	32	16	8	4	2	1
1	1	1	1	1	1	1	1

Don't believe me?

128 + 64 + 32 + 16 + 8 + 4 + 2 + 1 = 255

So logic dictates that you can actually make any number from 0 to 255 inclusive by placing a 0 or a 1 in various columns, for example:

128	64	32	16	8	4	2	1
0	0	1	0	1	1	0	0

32 + 8 + 4 = 44

IP addressing and subnetting are based on the fundamentals above. Table 2.1 below summarizes what you know so far. Pay special attention to this table because the values can be used for any subnet mask (more on that later).

Table 2.1—Binary Values

Binary	Decimal
10000000	128
11000000	192
11100000	224
11110000	240
11111000	248
11111100	252
11111110	254
11111111	255

Make up some of your own binary numbers to ensure that you understand this concept fully.

Hexadecimal

Hexadecimal (or hex) is an alternative numbering system. Rather than counting in 2s or by 10, 16 numbers or characters are used. Hex starts at 0 and goes all the way up to F, as illustrated below:

0 1 2 3 4 5 6 7 8 9 A B C D E F

Each hexadecimal digit actually represents four binary digits, as shown below in Table 2.2:

Table 2.2—Decimal, Hex, and Binary Digits

Decimal	0	1	2	3	4	5	6	7
Hex	0	1	2	3	4	5	6	7
Binary	0000	0001	0010	0011	0100	0101	0110	0111

Decimal	8	9	10	11	12	13	14	15
Hex	8	9	A	B	C	D	E	F
Binary	1000	1001	1010	1011	1100	1101	1110	1111

Converting from binary to hex to decimal is fairly simple, as shown in Table 2.3 below:

Table 2.3—Conversion of Binary to Hex to Decimal

Decimal	13	6	2	12
Hex	D	6	2	C
Binary	1101	0110	0010	1100

Hex is a more manageable counting system for humans than binary, but it's close enough to binary to be used by computers and networking equipment. Any number can be made using hex, as it can use binary or decimal; just count in multiples of 16 instead, for example:

1 x 16 = 16
16 x 16 = 256
256 x 16 = 4096
...and so on.

Hex	4096	256	16	1
			1	A

Counting in hex, therefore, goes 0 1 2 3 4 5 6 7 8 9 A B C D E F 10 11 12 13 14 15 16 17 18 19 1A 1B 1C 1D 1E 1F 20 21 22, etc., to infinity. 1A (above), for example, is an A in the 1 column and a 1 in the 16 column: A = 10 + 16 = 26.

When converting binary to hex, it makes the task easier if you break the octet into two groups of four bits. So 11110011 becomes 1111 0011. 1111 is 8 + 4 + 2 + 1 = 15, and 0011 is 2 + 1 = 3. 15 is F in hex and 3 is 3 in hex, giving us the answer F3. You can check Table 5.2 to confirm this.

Hex to binary is carried out using the same process. For example, 7C can be split into 7, which is 0111 in binary, and C (12 in decimal), which is 1100 in binary. The answer, then, is 01111100.

Converting Exercise

Here are some examples for you to try. Write out the charts above for working out hex and binary (i.e., for hex, a 1 column, then a 16 column, then a 256 column, and so on):

1. Convert 1111 to hex and decimal.
2. Convert 11010 to hex and decimal.
3. Convert 10000 to hex and decimal.
4. Convert 20 to binary and hex.
5. Convert 32 to binary and hex.
6. Convert 101 to binary and hex.
7. Convert A6 from hex to binary and decimal.
8. Convert 15 from hex to binary and decimal
9. Convert B5 from hex to binary and decimal.

It would be useful in the exam to write out Table 2.2 to help you work out any binary to hex to decimal conversions.

The rule for using IP addressing is that each address on the network must be unique to that host (i.e., it can't be shared). Some addresses can't be used for hosts. This will be covered in more detail later, but for now, know that you can't use an address which is reserved for the entire network, a broadcast address, or addresses reserved for testing. In addition, three groups are reserved for use on internal networks to save addresses.

Because of the rapid growth of network sizes, each IP address must be used in conjunction with a subnet mask. The subnet mask is there to tell the network devices how to use the numbers in the IP address. The reason for this is that some of the addresses available for hosts on your network can actually be used to chop down the network into smaller chunks or subnets.

An example of an IP address with a subnet mask is 192.168.1.1 255.255.255.240.

ADDRESS CLASSES

You need to know this and you don't! I know, I'm not helping much, but address classes are actually only significant historically, so as a new Cisco engineer, you might become confused when you look at the old rules and try to apply them to new methods of network design.

We still refer to groups of IP addresses as classes, but with the introduction of subnet masking and VLSM, they are actually no longer applicable to network design. Address classes are useful to know, though, because they show us which parts of the IP address we can and can't use for our mini-networks (subnets).

When IPv4 was first invented, addresses were divided into classes. The classes of addresses were then allocated to companies on an as-needed basis. The bigger the company, the bigger the address class. The address classes were assigned letters, A through E. A Class A address was reserved for the biggest networks. A Class A address can be numbered from 1 to 126 in the first octet. The reason for this is that the first bit on the first octet must be 0. If you have 0 in the first octet, then the remaining values can only go from 1 to 126, for example:

00000001 = 1
01111111= 126

You can't have an address of all 0s on a network. If you actually add the other three octets, then you can see Class A addresses in full, for example:

10.1.1.1
120.2.3.4
126.200.133.1

These are all Class A addresses because they are within the range of 1 to 126. 127 is not a permitted number for IP addresses; 127.0.0.1 is actually an address used to test whether TCP/IP is working on your device.

A Class B address must have the first two bits of the first octet set to 10. This means that the first octet can only use the numbers 128 to 191, for example:

10000000 = 128
10111111 = 191

For Class C addresses, the first three bits on the first octet must be set to 110, giving us addresses 192 to 223, for example:

11000000 = 192
11011111 = 223

Class D addresses range from 224.0.0.0 to 239.255.255.255 and are used for multicasting (directed broadcasts). Class E addresses range from 240.0.0.0 to 255.255.255.254 and are for experimental use only.

Subnet Mask Primer

I mentioned earlier that part of the address identifies the network and part of it identifies the host on the network. Subnet masks establish which parts are which. The difficulty is that it isn't always easy to establish which is which by just looking at the subnet mask. This requires practice, and for the more difficult addresses, you must work them out by hand (or cheat by using a subnet calculator).

Even if you are not chopping your network into smaller parts, you must still apply a subnet mask to every address used. Each network class comes with a default subnet mask, for example:

Class A = 255.0.0.0
Class B = 255.255.0.0
Class C = 255.255.255.0

When the binary bits are turned on, the network knows that this number is to be used for the network, not for a host on the network, as illustrated below:

192	168	12	2
255	255	255	0
Network	Network	Network	Host

The address above means that 192.168.12 is the network and 2 is a host on that network. Furthermore, any address starting with 192.168.12 is on the same network. You can see from the number in the first octet and the default subnet mask that this is a Class C network.

Remember the rule I mentioned earlier: You can't use the network numbers for hosts, so the numbers below cannot be used on devices:

10.0.0.0
192.168.2.0
174.12.0.0

The other rule is that you can't use the broadcast address on each network or subnet. A broadcast address goes to all devices on the network, so, logically, it can't be used for devices. A broadcast address is one in which all the host bits are active, or turned on:

10.255.255.255
192.168.1.255

In the examples above, each binary bit is turned on for the host portion.

USING IP ADDRESSES

Next up, the practicalities of using IP addresses—which ones can be used and which ones can't be used?

You know that there has been a huge explosion in the use of computers over the past three decades. A PC used to be a very expensive item which few people could afford; therefore, they were reserved for use by well-funded companies only. Today, nearly every house contains one or more computers.

The problem, of course, is that IPv4 was devised when only a limited number of devices were being used and there was no anticipation of this situation changing. As addresses were being allocated, it was realized that at the current rate of growth, we would quickly run out of available addresses.

Private IP Addresses

One of several solutions was to reserve some classes of addresses for anybody to use, as long as that address wasn't used over the Internet. This range of addresses is known as private IP addresses, and this solution was created by two RFCs, 1918 and 4193. As a refresher, RFC stands for Request for Comments and is a means for engineers to submit ideas for networking methods, protocols, and technology advancements.

The ranges of private addresses are as follows:

> 10.x.x.x—any address starting with a 10
> 172.16.x.x to 172.31.x.x—any address starting with 172.16 to 172.31, inclusive
> 192.168.x.x—any address starting with 192.168

SUBNETTING

Subnetting allows you to steal bits of an IP address which were traditionally used for hosts on the network. You can now carve smaller networks from your larger network space, and these smaller networks are referred to as subnetworks, or subnets for short.

If you apply the default subnet masks to the three usable address classes, you will see the portions (octets) of the address you can't use for carving out subnets, as illustrated in the chart below:

A—255	0	0	0
Can't Use	Can Use	Can Use	Can Use
B—255	255	0	0
Can't Use	Can't Use	Can Use	Can Use
C—255	255	255	0
Can't Use	Can't Use	Can't Use	Can Use

For example, if you take a Class C network with the default subnet mask

IP Address	192	168	1	0
Subnet Mask	255	255	255	0
In Binary	11111111	11111111	11111111	00000000

and steal some of the available host bits on the last octet,

IP Address	192	168	1	0
Subnet Mask	255	255	255	192
In Binary	11111111	11111111	11111111	11000000

you get two stolen bits on the last octet. This gives you the following subnets, each with 62 hosts:

Network	Network	Network	Subnet	Hosts	Broadcast Address
192	168	1	0	1–62	63
192	168	1	64	65–126	127
192	168	1	128	129–190	191
192	168	1	192	193–254	255

With a bigger network, you could have used host numbers 1 to 254, so you have less available host numbers to use here but the trade-off is more networks. The chart below shows how the four subnets were determined:

128	64	32	16	8	4	2	1	Subnet
0	0	0	0	0	0	0	0	0
0	1	0	0	0	0	0	0	64
1	0	0	0	0	0	0	0	128
1	1	0	0	0	0	0	0	192

Delving into binary math, you can see that using the first two bits of the host address lets you use the binary combinations 00, 01, 10, and 11, and writing these out in full, as you see in the subnets column, gives you the subnets 0, 64, 128, and 192. To clarify this further, the first two rows in gray are subnet numbers and the remaining six rows are for use by host numbers on each subnet.

If you feel your head spinning right about now, this is normal. It takes a while for all of this to finally click, I'm afraid.

Easy Subnetting

Come exam day, or when troubleshooting a subnetting issue on a live network, you will want to get to your answer quickly and accurately. For these reasons, I devised an easy way to subnet, which is the subject of my Subnetting Secrets Amazon Kindle book. You won't need to read it though to be honest, because I cover what you need to know in this book.

A very useful resource I've created is www.subnetting.org, which gives you free challenge questions to solve around subnetting and network design.

Classless Inter-Domain Routing

Classless Inter-Domain Routing (CIDR) was created by the Internet Engineering Task Force as a method to allocate blocks of IP addresses and to route IP packets. The main feature of CIDR we will examine here is using slash address notation to represent subnet masks. This is important because it saves time, it is used in the real world, and, if that isn't enough, you will be given exam questions involving CIDR addresses.

With CIDR, instead of using the full subnet mask, you write down the number of binary bits used. For 255.255.0.0, for example, there are two lots of eight binary bits used, so this would be represented with a /16. For 255.255.240.0, there are 8 + 8 + 4 bits used, giving you /20.

When you refer to subnet masks or network masks in the context of internetworking, you would say "slash sixteen" or "slash twenty" to work colleagues and they would know that you are referring to a CIDR mask.

The Subnetting Secrets Chart

I'm about to save you many weeks of subnetting frustration. My Subnetting Secrets cheat chart has been used by thousands of CCNA and CCNP students all over the world to pass exams and ace technical interviews for networking roles.

Seriously. Until I stumbled across the easy way while studying for my CCNA several years ago, students were forced to write out network addresses in binary or go through painful calculations in order to get to the correct answer.

In order to write out the Subnetting Secrets chart, you will need a pencil and paper. You need to be able to write it out from memory because in your exam you will be given a whiteboard to use for any working out. You can also use pen and paper in any technical interviews.

On the top right side of your paper, write the number 1, and then to the left of that double it to 2, then 4, then 8, and keep doubling up to number 128. This is one binary octet:

128	64	32	16	8	4	2	1

Under the 128 and going down, write out the number you would get if you put a tick in the first box (the 128 box). Then the next number below that will be what you would get if you ticked the next box (64), and the next (32), and the next (16), and so on until you had ticked all eight boxes:

128
192
224
240
248
252
254
255

If you put together both parts, you will have the upper portion of the Subnetting Secrets cheat sheet:

Bits	128	64	32	16	8	4	2	1
Subnets								
128								
192								
224								
240								
248								
252								
254								
255								

The top row represents your subnet increment and the left column your subnet mask. Using this part of the chart, you could answer any subnetting question in a few seconds. If you want to add the part of the chart which tells you how to answer any design question, such as "How many subnets and hosts will subnet mask 'X' give you," just add a "powers of two" section.

One column will be "powers of two" and another will be "powers of two minus two." The minus two is meant to cover the two addresses you can't use, which are the subnet (subnetwork) and the broadcast addresses on the subnet. You start with the number 2 and double it as many times as you need to in order to answer the question.

Bits	128	64	32	16	8	4	2	1
Subnets								
128								
192								
224								
240				For working out which subnet a host is in				
248								
252								
254								
255								
	Subnets	Hosts -2						
2								
4			For working out how many subnets and how many hosts per subnet					
8								
16								
32								
64								

You will probably learn best by jumping straight into an exam-style question:

Which subnet is host 192.168.1.100/26 in?

Well, you know that this is a Class C address and the default mask is 24 binary bits, or 255.255.255.0. You can see that instead of 24 there are 26 bits, so 2 bits have been stolen to make the subnet. Simply write down your Subnetting Secrets cheat sheet and tick two places (from the left) along the top row. This will reveal in what amount your subnets go up. You can then tick down two places in the subnets column to reveal the actual subnet mask.

Bits	128	64	32	16	8	4	2	1
Subnets	✔	✔						
128	✔							
192	✔							
224								
240								
248								
252								
254								
255								
	Subnets	Hosts -2						
2								
4								
8								
16								
32								
64								

Now you know two things: subnets will go up in increments of 64 (you can use 0 as the first subnet value) and your subnet mask for /26 ends in 192, so, in full, it is 255.255.255.192:

    192.168.100.0 is your first subnet
    192.168.100.64 is your second subnet
    192.168.100.128 is your third subnet
    192.168.100.192 is your last subnet

You can't go any further than your actual subnet value, which is 192 in this example. But remember that the question is asking you to find host 100. You can easily see that the subnet ending in 64 is where host 100 would lie because the next subnet is 128, which is too high.

Just for completeness, I will add the host addresses and the broadcast addresses. You can quickly work out the broadcast address by taking the next subnet value and subtracting 1:

Subnet	First Host	Last Host	Broadcast
192.168.100.0	192.168.100.1	192.168.100.62	192.168.100.63
192.168.100.64	192.168.100.65	192.168.100.126	192.168.100.127
192.168.100.128	192.168.100.129	192.168.100.190	192.168.100.191
192.168.100.192	192.168.100.193	192.168.100.254	192.168.100.255

Consider the IP addresses to be values of anything from 0 to 255. Much like an odometer in a car, each number rolls up until it rolls back to 0 again, but the next box rolls over 1. Below are two sample octets. I jump up when we get to 0 2 to save space:

Octet 1	Octet 2
0	0
0	1
0	2 (jump up)
0	255
1	0
1	1
1	2

If you wanted to use the design part of the chart, you could. There is no need to for this question, but to see how it works, you just tick down two places in the subnets column because you stole 2 bits. From 8 bits in the last octet, that leaves you 6 bits for hosts, so tick down six places in the Hosts -2 column to reveal that you get 64 minus 2 bits per subnet, or 4 subnets, and 62 hosts per subnet:

Bits	128	64	32	16	8	4	2	1
Subnets	✔	✔						
128	✔							
192	✔							
224								
240								
248								
252								
254								
255								
	Subnets	Hosts -2						
2	✔	✔						
4	✔	✔						
8		✔						
16		✔						
32		✔						
64		✔						

Ready for another question? Of course you are.

Which subnet is host 200.100.2.210/25 in?

Same drill as before. You know this is a Class C address, and that to get from 24 to 25 bits, you need to steal 1 bit. Tick one across in the top row and then one down in the left column:

Bits	128	64	32	16	8	4	2	1
Subnets	✔							
128	✔							
192								
224								
240								
248								
252								
254								
255								

Therefore, your mask will be 255.255.255.128, and your subnets will go up in increments of 128. You can't actually steal less than 1 bit for a Class C address; this will give you only two subnets:

200.100.2.0
and
200.100.2.128

You can already answer the question because you can see that host 210 will be in the second subnet. Just to demonstrate, I will write out the host and broadcast addresses again:

Subnet	First Host	Last Host	Broadcast
200.100.2.0	200.100.2.1	200.100.2.126	200.100.2.127
200.100.2.128	200.100.2.129	200.100.2.254	200.100.2.255

Next question: Which subnet is 172.16.100.11/19 in?

You need to add 3 to 16 (the default Class B mask) to get to 19. Tick across three places in the top row of the chart to get the subnet increment, and then down three in the left column to get the subnet mask. You don't need the lower portion of the chart for these types of questions.

Bits	128	64	32	16	8	4	2	1
Subnets	✔	✔	✔					
128	✔							
192	✔							
224	✔							
240								
248								
252								
254								
255								

Your subnet mask is 255.255.224.0, and you are subnetting on the third octet because the first two are reserved for the network address/default subnet mask.

Your subnets will be as follows:

172.16.0.0
172.16.32.0
172.16.64.0
172.16.96.0*
172.16.128.0
172.16.160.0
172.16.192.0
172.16.224.0

In the exam, please stop once you get to one subnet past the one your host is in, because going one past will make sure you have the right subnet. You are looking for host 100.11 on the 172.16 network; the asterisk in the list of subnets above denotes the subnet that the host number resides in.

If, for some reason, in the exam they asked you to identify the host addresses and broadcast address (for extra points), you can easily add these. I will put them in for the first few subnets:

Subnet	First Host	Last Host	Broadcast
172.16.0.0	172.16.0.1	172.16.31.254	172.16.31.255
172.16.32.0	172.16.32.1	172.16.63.254	172.16.63.255
172.16.64.0	172.16.64.1	172.16.95.254	172.16.95.255
172.16.96.0	172.16.96.1	172.16.127.254	172.16.127.255

In the exam, they may well try to trick you by adding broadcast addresses as options for host addresses, or even subnet addresses for host addresses. This is why you need to be able to identify which is which. You will also come across the same issue on live networks, where other engineers have tried to add the wrong address to an interface.

Next question: Which subnet is host 172.16.100.11/29 in?

As you can see by now, you can use any mask you wish with most any subnet. I could have asked you about the address 10.100.100.1/29, so don't let the fact that you have a Class A address with subnet bits going into the second, third, or fourth octet put you off.

You need to steal 13 bits for the subnet mask but the subnetting chart has only eight places. Since you are looking at the easy way to subnet, just focus on the part of the chart which the remaining numbers spill over into. If you drew another chart next to the one you had just filled up, you would have five places filled up (8 + 5 = 13 bits):

Bits	128	64	32	16	8	4	2	1
Subnets	✔	✔	✔	✔	✔			
128	✔							
192	✔							
224	✔							
240	✔							
248	✔							
252								
254								
255								

From the chart above, you can see that the subnet mask is 255.255.255.248. The 255 in the third octet is there because you filled it up whilst moving over into the fourth octet. The subnets are also going up in increments of 8.

You could start off with 172.16.0.0, but the problem with that is it would take quite some time to count up in multiples of 8 before you got to 172.16.100.11 this way, and the exam is a timed one. Therefore, you need to fast track the counting process.

If you start counting up in increments of 8, you would get the following:

> 172.16.0.0
> 172.16.0.8
> 172.16.0.16, and you could keep counting up to
> 172.16.1.0
> 172.16.1.8, and keep counting up to
> 172.16.20.0
> 172.16.20.8

This would take a very long time because there are over 8000 subnets (2 to the power of 13 gives you 8192, and you can check this using the design section of the Subnetting Secrets cheat sheet).

Let's presume that each third octet is going up one digit at a time (which it is). Why not jump up to 172.16.100.x to start with?

172.16.100.0
172.16.100.8*
172.16.100.16

From the above, you can see which subnet host 11 is in, and if you were asked to work out the broadcast address, it would look like the chart below:

Subnet	First Host	Last Host	Broadcast
172.16.100.0	172.16.100.1	172.16.100.6	172.16.100.7
172.16.100.8	172.16.100.9	172.16.100.14	172.16.100.15
172.16.100.16	172.16.100.17	172.16.100.22	172.16.100.23

That is enough subnetting for now. We will revisit this subject many times over. For some network design examples using the lower part of the chart, please check out resources on https://www.in60days.com/free/ccnain60days.

Remember also that there are a few subnetting resources available for you to use:

www.subnetting.org—subnetting question generator
www.youtube.com/user/paulwbrowning—my YouTube channel with free videos including subnetting.

ROUTE SUMMARIZATION

There are many millions of routes on the Internet. If these routes all had to be stored individually, the Internet would have come to a stop many years ago. Route summarization, also known as supernetting, was proposed in RFC 1338, which you can read online by clicking on the RFC—www.faqs.org/rfcs/rfc1338.html.

If you want to read a very comprehensive guide to route summarization, then please grab a hold of Jeff Doyle's excelling Cisco book *Routing TCP/IP Volume 1*, which is now in its second edition.

ZIP Codes

ZIP codes are used by the United States Postal Service to improve routing of letters to addresses within the USA (see Figure 2.6). The first digit represents a group of US states, and the second and third digits represent a region inside that group. The idea is that letters and parcels can be quickly routed by machine or by hand into the correct state and then forwarded to that state. When it reaches the state, it can be routed to the correct region. From there, it can be routed to the correct city and so on, until it is sorted into the correct mailbag for the local postal delivery person.

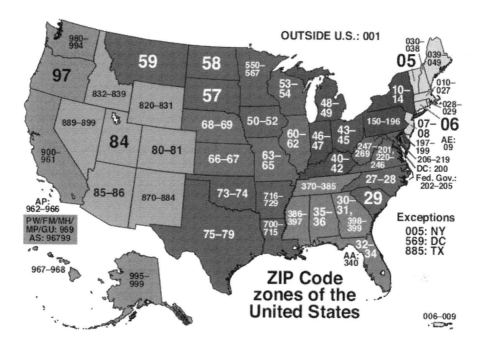

Figure 2.6—US ZIP Codes

The ZIP code system was devised to make the routing of mail more accurate and efficient. For example, the sorting office in Atlanta doesn't need to know which street in San Francisco the packet is destined for. Having to store that information would make the sorting process unworkable.

Route Summarization Prerequisites

In order to use route summarization on your network, you need to use a classless protocol (covered later), such as RIPv2, EIGRP, or OSPF. You also need to design your network in a hierarchical order, which will require careful planning and design. This means that you can't randomly assign networks to various routers or LANs within your network.

Applying Route Summarization

Let's move on to an example of a network and what the problem will look like on your network if you don't use route summarization. In this example, this is how summarization would work with a range of IP addresses on a network. The router in Figure 2.7 below has several networks attached. The first choice is to advertise all of these networks to the next-hop router. The alternative is to summarize these eight networks down to one route and send that summary to the next-hop router, which will cut down on bandwidth, CPU, and memory requirements.

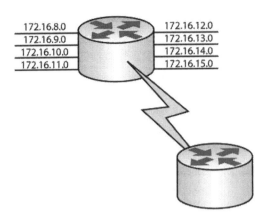

Figure 2.7—An Example of Route Summarization

The only way to work out a summary route is by converting the IP address into binary (sorry). If you don't do this, then you will have no way of knowing whether you are advertising the correct summary route, which will lead to problems on your network.

Firstly, write out all of the network addresses in full and then the binary versions to the right of that, as illustrated below:

172.16.8.0	*10101100.00010000.00001*000.00000000
172.16.9.0	*10101100.00010000.00001*001.00000000
172.16.10.0	*10101100.00010000.00001*010.00000000
172.16.11.0	*10101100.00010000.00001*011.00000000
172.16.12.0	*10101100.00010000.00001*100.00000000
172.16.13.0	*10101100.00010000.00001*101.00000000
172.16.14.0	*10101100.00010000.00001*110.00000000
172.16.15.0	*10101100.00010000.00001*111.00000000
Matching Bits	*10101100.00010000.00001* = 21 bits

I have italicized and underlined the bits in each address that match. You can see that the first 21 bits match in every address, so your summarized route can reflect the following 21 bits:

172.16.8.0 255.255.248.0

One other significant advantage of using route summarization is that if a local network on your router goes down, the summary network will still be advertised out. This means that the rest of the network will not need to update its routing tables or, worse still, have to deal with a flapping route (rapidly going up and down). I have chosen two exercises dealing with route summarization for you to work out.

Exercise 1: Write out the binary equivalents for the addresses below, and then determine which bits match. I have written the first two octets for you to save time.

172.16.50.0	*10101100.00010000.*
172.16.60.0	*10101100.00010000.*
172.16.70.0	*10101100.00010000.*
172.16.80.0	*10101100.00010000.*
172.16.90.0	*10101100.00010000.*
172.16.100.0	*10101100.00010000.*
172.16.110.0	*10101100.00010000.*
172.16.120.0	*10101100.00010000.*

What summarized address would you advertise? Answer at the end of the chapter.

Exercise 2: The company below has three routers connected to their HQ router. They need to summarize the routes advertised from London 1, 2, and 3:

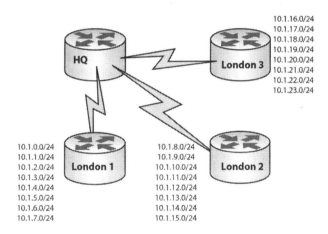

Figure 2.8—Summarised Routes Advertised from London 1, 2, and 3

Let's start with London 1:

10.1.0.0	*00001010.00000001.00000000.00000000*
10.1.1.0	*00001010.00000001.00000001.00000000*
10.1.2.0	*00001010.00000001.00000010.00000000*
10.1.3.0	*00001010.00000001.00000011.00000000*
10.1.4.0	*00001010.00000001.00000100.00000000*
10.1.5.0	*00001010.00000001.00000101.00000000*
10.1.6.0	*00001010.00000001.00000110.00000000*
10.1.7.0	*00001010.00000001.00000111.00000000*

And for London 2:

10.1.8.0	*00001010.00000001.00001000.00000000*
10.1.9.0	*00001010.00000001.00001001.00000000*
10.1.10.0	*00001010.00000001.00001010.00000000*
10.1.11.0	*00001010.00000001.00001011.00000000*
10.1.12.0	*00001010.00000001.00001100.00000000*
10.1.13.0	*00001010.00000001.00001101.00000000*
10.1.14.0	*00001010.00000001.00001110.00000000*
10.1.15.0	*00001010.00000001.00001111.00000000*

And on to London 3:

10.1.16.0	*00001010.00000001.00010000.00000000*
10.1.17.0	*00001010.00000001.00010001.00000000*
10.1.18.0	*00001010.00000001.00010010.00000000*
10.1.19.0	*00001010.00000001.00010011.00000000*
10.1.20.0	*00001010.00000001.00010100.00000000*
10.1.21.0	*00001010.00000001.00010101.00000000*
10.1.22.0	*00001010.00000001.00010110.00000000*
10.1.23.0	*00001010.00000001.00010111.00000000*

You will be expected to understand route summarization for the CCNA exam. If you can quickly work out the common bits, then you should be able to answer the questions quickly and accurately.

VARIABLE LENGTH SUBNET MASKING

Using VLSM

Look at the following network:

- 192.168.1.0/24 = 1 network with 254 hosts

While this may work fine, what if your network requires more than one subnet? What if your subnets have less than 254 hosts in them? Either situation requires some changes to be made. If you applied a /26 mask to your network instead, you would get this:

- 192.168.1.0/26 = 4 subnets with 62 hosts

If that wasn't suitable, what about a /28 mask?

- 192.168.1.0/28 = 16 subnets with 14 hosts

You can refer back to the Subnetting Secrets cheat sheet design section to help you work out how to apply VLSM to your network or to an exam question. With the /26 mask, you can see how many subnets and hosts you will get:

Bits	128	64	32	16	8	4	2	1
Subnets	✔	✔						
128	✔							
192	✔							
224								
240								
248								
252								
254								
255								
	Subnets	Hosts -2						
2	✔	✔						
4	✔	✔						
8		✔						
16		✔						
32		✔						
64		✔						

You have to take away 2 bits for the hosts, so you get four subnets, each with 62 hosts.

Slicing Down Networks

The point of VLSM is to take your network block and make it work for your particular network needs. Taking the typical network address of 192.168.1.0/24, with VLSM, you can use a /26 mask and now do this:

192.168.1.0/26	Subnet	Hosts
192.168.1.0	1	62
192.168.1.64—IN USE	2	62
192.168.1.128—IN USE	3	62
192.168.1.192—IN USE	4	62

This may work fine until you realize that you have two smaller networks on your infrastructure which require 30 hosts each. What if three of your smaller subnets are taken (marked as IN USE above) and you have only one left (i.e., 192.168.1.0)? VLSM lets you take any of your chopped down subnets and chop them down even further. The only rule is that any IP address can be used only once, no matter which mask it has.

If you use the design section of the Subnetting Secrets cheat sheet, you will see which mask gives you 30 hosts:

	Subnets	Hosts -2					
2	✔	✔					
4	✔	✔					
8	✔	✔					
16		✔					
32		✔					
64							

The upper section of the chart (not shown here) tells us that three ticks down in the left column gives you a mask of 224 or /27 (3 stolen bits).

192.168.1.0/27	Subnet	Hosts
192.168.1.0	1	30
192.168.1.32	2	30
192.168.1.64	CAN'T USE	CAN'T USE

You can't use the .64 subnet because this is already in use. You are now free to use either of the other two subnets. If you needed only one, you could chop down the remaining one to give you more subnets, each with fewer hosts.

Please also read bonus stuff on VLSM on the in60days.com website.

TROUBLESHOOTING IP ADDRESSING ISSUES

Troubleshooting Subnet Mask and Gateway Issues

You may see a number of symptoms occurring whenever you have a problem with IP addressing, the subnet mask, or gateway issues. Some of the problems that might occur include the following:

- Network devices can communicate within their local subnet but are unable to communicate with devices outside the local network. This usually indicates that you have some type of issue with the gateway configuration or operation.
- Not having any type of IP communication, either internally or remote. This usually points to a major issue which might involve a lack of functionality on certain devices.
- Situations in which you can communicate with some IP addresses but not all of those that are available. This is usually the most difficult problem to troubleshoot because it has many possible causes.

One of the first things you should always do during the troubleshooting process for such situations is double-check the IP address, the subnet mask, and the default gateway configuration on your devices. You should also check the documentation in order to verify this information. A great many issues stem from misconfigurations.

If you are installing network devices for the first time, very often you will manually type in the IP address information, along with the subnet mask and the default gateway. The recommendation is to verify this information before submitting it because human errors are rife in this area. Most enterprise networks have procedures for introducing new devices to the network, including testing the gateway and SNMP server reachability.

If you need to gather information during the troubleshooting process, you might want to perform some packet capturing to see exactly which packets are sent between devices. If you see packets from hosts that are not on your network, you may have some kind of VLAN misconfiguration issue. If you suspect that your subnet mask is incorrect, you should check the parameters of other devices on your network. If the other machines work properly, you should use the same subnet mask on the device that is not working as expected and start testing again.

When using dynamic IP addressing (DHCP) to allocate IP address information to devices in your network, including the subnet mask and the default gateway, you should investigate the DHCP server configuration because that might be another area where problems may occur. Perhaps the DHCP server is misconfigured or the DHCP service is jammed, so you should include this step in your troubleshooting process. You must also remember to exclude reserved addresses from the DHCP pool because these addresses will usually be allocated to servers and router interfaces.

Other useful troubleshooting tools that will help you identify the point in the network where problems occur are traceroute and ping. We will cover these throughout the book and in labs.

Please take today's exam at https://www.in60days.com/free/ccnain60days/

Answers for the conversion exercises

1. Convert 1111 to hex and decimal
Hex = F
Decimal = 15

2. Convert 11010 to hex and decimal
Hex = 1A
Decimal = 26

3. Convert 10000 to hex and decimal
Hex = 10
Decimal = 16

4. Convert 20 to binary and hex
Binary = 10100
Hex = 14

5. Convert 32 to binary and hex
Binary = 100000
Hex = 20

6. Convert 101 to binary and hex
Binary = 1100101
Hex = 65

7. Convert A6 from hex to binary and decimal
Binary = 10100110
Decimal = 166

8. Convert 15 from hex to binary and decimal
Binary = 10101
Decimal = 21

9. Convert B5 from hex to binary and decimal
Binary = 10110101
Decimal = 181

Answers to Summarization

Here is the answer to Exercise 1:

00110010.00000000
00111100.00000000
01000110.00000000
01010000.00000000
01011010.00000000
01100100.00000000
01101110.00000000
01111000.00000000

I would make it 172.16.50.0 255.255.128.0, or /17.

London 1—There are 21 common bits, so London 1 can advertise 10.1.0.0/21 to the HQ router.

London 2—London 2 also has 21 common bits, so it can advertise 10.1.8.0/21 to the HQ router.

London 3 has 21 common bits also, so it can advertise 10.1.16.0/21 upstream to the HQ router.

DAY 2 LAB

IP Addressing on Routers Lab

Topology

Purpose

Learn how to get used to configuring IP addresses on routers and pinging across a Serial interface.

Walkthrough

1. Start off by establishing your Serial interface numbers, as they may differ from mine in the diagram above. Also, please establish which side has the DCE cable attached because this side will require the `clock rate` command.

    ```
    Router>en
    Router#sh ip interface brief
    Interface       IP-Address  OK? Method Status                Protocol
    FastEthernet0/0 unassigned  YES unset  administratively down down
    FastEthernet0/1 unassigned  YES unset  administratively down down
    Serial0/1/0     unassigned  YES unset  administratively down down
    Vlan1           unassigned  YES unset  administratively down down
    Router#
    Router#show controllers Serial0/1/0

    M1T-E3 pa: show controller:
    PAS unit 0, subunit 0, f/w version 2-55, rev ID 0x2800001, version 2
    idb = 0x6080D54C, ds = 0x6080F304, ssb=0x6080F4F4
    Clock mux=0x30, ucmd_ctrl=0x0, port_status=0x1
    line state: down
    DCE cable, no clock rate
    ```

2. Add a hostname and IP address to one side. If this side is the DCE, add the clock rate.

    ```
    Router#conf t
    Enter configuration commands, one per line.  End with CNTL/Z.
    Router(config)#hostname RouterA
    RouterA(config)#interface s0/1/0
    RouterA(config-if)#ip add 192.168.1.1 255.255.255.0
    RouterA(config-if)#clock rate 64000
    RouterA(config-if)#no shut
    %LINK-5-CHANGED: Interface Serial0/1/0, changed state to down
    RouterA(config-if)#
    ```

3. Add an IP address and hostname to the other router. Also, bring the interface up with the no shut command.

```
Router>en
Router#conf t
Enter configuration commands, one per line.  End with CNTL/Z.
Router(config)#hostname RouterB
RouterB(config)#int s0/1/0
RouterB(config-if)#ip address 192.168.1.2 255.255.255.0
RouterB(config-if)#no shut
%LINK-5-CHANGED: Interface Serial0/1/0, changed state to down
RouterB(config-if)#^Z
RouterB#
%LINK-5-CHANGED: Interface Serial0/1/0, changed state to up
```

4. Test the connection with a ping.

```
RouterB#ping 192.168.1.1

Type escape sequence to abort.
Sending 5, 100-byte ICMP Echos to 192.168.1.1, timeout is 2 seconds:
!!!!!
Success rate is 100 percent (5/5), round-trip min/avg/max = 31/31/32
ms
```

NOTE: If the ping doesn't work, then double-check to make sure that you have added the clock rate command to the correct router. Ensure that the cable is inserted correctly and use the show controllers serial x/x/x command, inputting your own interface number.

Binary Conversion and Subnetting Practice

Please spend the rest of this day's lesson practicing these critical topics:

- Conversion from decimal to binary (random numbers)
- Conversion from binary to decimal (random numbers)
- Subnetting IPv4 (random networks and scenarios)

IPv6 Concepts

DAY 3 TASKS

- Read today's lesson notes (below)
- Review yesterday's lesson notes
- Complete today's lab
- Complete today's exam
- Read the ICND1 cram guide
- Spent 10 minutes on subnetting.org answering questions

IPv6 has been in development for several years and has actually been implemented on networks all over the world (in conjunction with IPv4). Many network engineers have expressed their fear about having to learn a new addressing method, and I've even heard many say that they hope to retire before it becomes a requirement.

This fear, however, is unfounded. IPv6 is a user-friendly format, and once you become used to it, you will see that it is an improvement on IPv4 and you may actually come to prefer it. IPv6 is heavily tested in the CCNA exam; for this reason, you need to feel comfortable understanding how it works, as well as how to configure addresses, understand the standard, and apply IPv6 addresses to address network requirements.

Today you will learn about the following:

- History of IPv6
- IPv6 addressing
- IPv6 addressing representation
- Different IPv6 address types
- IPv6 protocols and mechanisms
- Subnetting with IPv6
- IPv6 vs IPv4

This module maps to the following ICND1 syllabus requirements:

- 1.11 Identify the appropriate IPv6 addressing scheme to satisfy addressing requirements in a LAN/WAN environment
- 1.12 Configure, verify, and troubleshoot IPv6 addressing

- 1.13 Configure and verify IPv6 Stateless Address Auto Configuration
- 1.14 Compare and contrast IPv6 address types
- 1.14.a Global unicast
- 1.14.b Unique local
- 1.14.c Link local
- 1.14.d Multicast
- 1.14.e Modified EUI 64
- 1.14.f Autoconfiguration
- 1.14.g Anycast

HISTORY OF IPV6

Fit for Purpose?

When Sir Tim Berners-Lee devised the World Wide Web in 1989, there was no way he could have predicted the huge impact it was to have on the world. Personal computers were prohibitively expensive and there was no easy way to communicate over long distances unless you could afford expensive WAN connections. Even then, there was no agreed communication model for all to follow.

Something needed to change and change came in the form of a new addressing standard for IP. Learning from mistakes made and responding to changes in business requirements, the Internet Engineering Task Force (IETF) published the first of many IPv6 standards as far back as 1998.

There will be no switch-over date; instead, networks will gradually transition to running both IPv4 and IPv6, and then eventually IPv4 will be phased out of existence. When I wrote the last version of this book in 2014, approximately 1% of all Internet traffic was running on IPv6. It's now at 20%. You can see why you must understand it if you wish to remain working in IT.

Why Migrate?

I've already said that when IPv4 was devised, the Internet wasn't used by the general public, and why would they? There were no websites, no e-commerce, no mobile networks, and no social media. Even if you could afford a PC, there wasn't much you could do with it. Now, of course, almost everybody is online. We carry out most of our day-to-day tasks using the Internet, and businesses rely on it to exist. Soon we will be using mobile devices to manage our cars and home security, to turn the coffee maker on, to set the heating level, and to set the TV to record our favorite show.

Some of this is already taking place, not only in Europe and the Americas but also in fast-developing countries such as India and China where billions of people live. IPv4 simply isn't up to the job and even if it was, there aren't enough addresses to cater for demand.

Here are a few benefits to changing to IPv6:

- The simplified IPv6 Packet header
- Larger address space
- IPv6 addressing hierarchy
- IPv6 extensibility
- IPv6 broadcast elimination
- Stateless autoconfiguration
- Integrated mobility
- Integrated enhanced security

I'd like to delve into packet layer analysis of IPv6, as well as the many types of headers available, but there isn't space here to do so, and since it isn't tested in the exam there is no need to include it. Instead, I will focus on what you need to know for the exam and your role as a Cisco engineer.

Hex Numbering

It may be well worthwhile to have a short memory jogger on hex numbering.

You know that decimal numbers consist of 10 digits ranging from 0 to 9. Binary consists of two digits ranging from 0 to 1. Hex numbering ranges from 0 to F and has 16 digits. These addresses are also referred to as base 10, base 2, and base 16, respectively.

You can see that each numbering system starts with a zero, so:

Decimal—0,1,2,3,4,5,6,7,8,9
Binary—0,1
Hex—0,1,2,3,4,5,6,7,8,9,A,B,C,D,E,F

When you write these addresses, you may not realize it but you are using columns from right to left; the rightmost is the one column and the next column is the base number times the preceding column, so:

Numbering Base	N to 3rd power	N to 2nd power	N to 1st power	N
10—Decimal	1000	100	10	1
2—Binary	8	4	2	1
16—Hex	4096	256	16	1

You can see that each successive column from the right increases in value. For decimal numbering it is 10 multiplied by 1. For binary it is 1 and then 1 multiplied by the numbering system of 2. If you compare the three numbering systems up to the last hex digit, you can begin to see why hex is the preferred format for IPv6 addressing.

Decimal	Binary	Hex
0	0000	0
1	0001	1
2	0010	2
3	0011	3
4	0100	4
5	0101	5
6	0110	6
7	0111	7
8	1000	8
9	1001	9
10	1010	A
11	1011	B
12	1100	C
13	1101	D
14	1110	E
15	1111	F

In order to provide enough addresses for our needs many years into the future, IPv6 has been designed to provide many trillions of available addresses. In order to do this, the numbering range has been expanded from 32 binary bits to 128 bits. Every 4 bits can be represented as one hex digit (as can be seen from the chart above). Logic then dictates that two hex digits will give us 8 bits, which is a single byte, or octet.

An IPv6 address is 128 bits in length and this is broken down into eight sets of 16 bits each separated by a colon when written in full format. Every 4 hex bits can range from 0000 to FFFF, with F being the highest digit available in hex numbering:

0000	0000	0000	0000	0000	0000	0000	0000
to	to	to	to	to	to	to	to
FFFF	FFFF	FFFF	FFFF	FFFF	FFFF	FFFF	FFFF

IPV6 ADDRESSING

As we already know, IPv6 uses 128-bit addresses. Because the address format is different from the IPv4 address format that we are all accustomed to, it is often confusing at first glance. However, once understood, the logic and structure is all very simple. The 128-bit IPv6 addresses use hexadecimal values (i.e., numbers 0 through 9 and letters A through F). While in IPv4 the subnet mask can be represented in either CIDR notation (e.g., /16 or /32) or in dotted-decimal notation (e.g., 255.255.0.0 or 255.255.255.255), IPv6 subnet masks are represented only in CIDR notation due to the length of the IPv6 address. Global 128-bit IPv6 addresses are divided into the following three sections:

- The provider-assigned prefix
- The site prefix
- The interface or host ID

The provider-assigned prefix, which is also referred to as the global address space, is a 48-bit prefix that is divided into the following three distinct parts:

- The 16-bit reserved IPv6 global prefix
- The 16-bit provider-owned prefix
- The 16-bit provider-assigned prefix

The IPv6 global prefix is used to represent the IPv6 global address space. All IPv6 global Internet addresses fall within the 2000::/16 to 3FFF::/16 range. The 16-bit provider-owned IPv6 prefix is assigned to and owned by the provider. The assignment of these prefixes follows the same rules as prefix assignment in IPv4. The provider-owned prefix falls within the 0000::/32 to FFFF::/32 range.

The next 16-bits represent an IPv6 prefix assigned to an organization by the actual provider from within the provider-assigned prefix address space. This prefix falls within the 0000::/48 to FFFF::/48 range. Collectively, these first 48-bits are referred to as the provider-assigned prefix, which is illustrated in Figure 3.1 below:

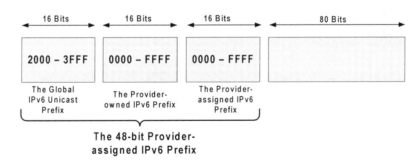

Figure 3.1—The 48-bit Provider-Assigned IPv6 Prefix

The site prefix is the next 16 bits following the 48-bit provider-assigned prefix. The subnet mask length for a site prefix is /64, which includes the 48-bit provider-assigned prefix. This prefix length allows for 264 addresses within each site prefix. Figure 3.2 below illustrates the 16-bit site prefix:

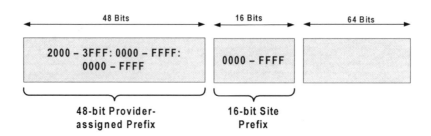

Figure 3.2—The 16-bit IPv6 Site Prefix

Following the site prefix, the next 64 bits are used for interface or host addressing. The interface or host ID portion of an IPv6 address represents the network device or host on the IPv6 subnet. The different ways in which the interface or host address is determined will be described in detail later in this module. Figure 3.3 below illustrates how IPv6 prefixes are assigned:

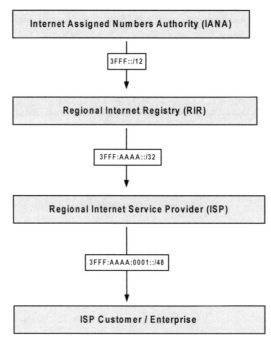

Figure 3.3—Assigning IPv6 Prefixes

Referencing Figure 3.3, once customers have been assigned the /48 prefix by the ISP, they are then free to assign and use whatever site prefixes and host or interface addresses they want within that 48-bit provider-assigned prefix. The sheer amount of address space available makes it impossible for any single enterprise customer to require more than a single provider-assigned prefix, while still allowing all devices within the enterprise network to be allocated a unique IPv6 global address. NAT, therefore, will never be required for IPv6.

IPV6 ADDRESS REPRESENTATION

The three ways in which IPv6 addresses can be represented are as follows:

- The preferred or complete address representation or form
- Compressed representation
- IPv6 addresses with an embedded IPv4 address

While the preferred form or representation is the most commonly used method for representing the 128-bit IPv6 address in text format, it is also important to be familiar with the other two methods of IPv6 address representation. These methods are described in the following sections.

The Preferred Form

The preferred representation for an IPv6 address is the longest format, also referred to as the complete form of an IPv6 address. This format represents all 32 hexadecimal characters that are used to form an IPv6 address. This is performed by writing the address as a series of eight 16-bit hexadecimal fields, separated by a colon (e.g., 3FFF:1234:ABCD:5678:020C:CEFF:FE A7:F3A0).

Each 16-bit field is represented by four hexadecimal characters and each character represents 4 bits. Each 16-bit hexadecimal field can have a value of between 0x0000 and 0xFFFF, although, as will be described later in this module, different values have been reserved for use in the first 16 bits, so all possible values are not used. When writing IPv6 addresses, hexadecimal characters are not case sensitive. In other words, 2001:ABCD:0000 and 2001:abcd:0000 are the exact same thing. The complete form for IPv6 address representation is illustrated in Figure 3.4 below:

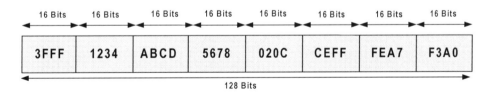

Figure 3.4—The Preferred Form for IPv6 Address Representation

The following IPv6 addresses are examples of valid IPv6 addresses in the preferred form:

- 0000:0000:0000:0000:0000:0000:0000:0001
- 2001:0000:0000:1234:0000:5678:af23:bcd5
- 3FFF:0000:0000:1010:1A2B:5000:0B00:DE0F
- fec0:2004:ab10:00cd:1234:0000:0000:6789
- 0000:0000:0000:0000:0000:0000:0000:0000

Compressed Representation

Compressed representation allows for IPv6 addresses to be compressed in one of two ways. The first method allows a double colon (::) to be used to compress consecutive zero values in a valid IPv6 address for successive 16-bit fields comprised of zeros or for leading zeros in the IPv6 address. When using this method, it is important to remember that the double colon can be used only once in an IPv6 address.

When the compressed format is used, each node and router is responsible for counting the number of bits on either side of the double colon to determine the exact number of zeros it represents. Table 3.1 below shows IPv6 addresses in the preferred form and the compressed representation of those addresses:

Table 3.1—Complete IPv6 Addresses in the Preferred Compressed Form

Complete IPv6 Address Representation	Compressed IPv6 Address Representation
0000:0000:0000:0000:0000:0000:0000:0001	::0001
2001:0000:0000:1234:0000:5678:af23:bcd5	2001::1234:0000:5678:af23:bcd5
3FFF:0000:0000:1010:1A2B:5000:0B00:DE0F	3FFF::1010:1A2B:5000:0B00:DE0F
FEC0:2004:AB10:00CD:1234:0000:0000:6789	FEC0:2004:AB10:00CD:1234::6789
0000:0000:0000:0000:0000:FFFF:172.16.255.1	::FFFF:172.16.255.1
0000:0000:0000:0000:0000:0000:172.16.255.1	::172.16.255.1
0000:0000:0000:0000:0000:0000:0000:0000	::

As previously stated, the double colon cannot be used more than once in a single IPv6 address. If, for example, you wanted to represent the complete IPv6 address for 2001:0000:0000:1234:0000:0000:af23:bcd5 in compressed form, you could use the double colon only once, even though there are two consecutive strings of zeros within the address. Therefore, attempting to compress the address to 2001::1234::af23:bcd5 would be considered illegal; however, the same IPv6 address could be compressed to either 2001::1234:0000:0000:af23:bcd5 or 2001:0000:0000:1234::af23:bcd5, depending upon preference.

The second method of IPv6 compressed address representation is applicable to each 16-bit field and allows leading zeros to be omitted from the IPv6 address. When using this method, if every bit in the 16-bit field is set to 0, then one zero must be used to represent this field. In this case, not all of the zero values can be omitted. Table 3.2 below shows IPv6 addresses in the preferred form and how they can be compressed using the second method of IPv6 compressed form representation.

Table 3.2—Complete IPv6 Addresses in the Alternative Compressed Form

Complete IPv6 Address Representation	Compressed IPv6 Address Representation
0000:0123:0abc:0000:04b0:0678:f000:0001	0:123:abc:0:4b0:678:f000:1
2001:0000:0000:1234:0000:5678:af23:bcd5	2001:0:0:1234:0:5678:af23:bcd5
3FFF:0000:0000:1010:1A2B:5000:0B00:DE0F	3FFF:0:0:1010:1A2B:5000:B00:DE0F
fec0:2004:ab10:00cd:1234:0000:0000:6789	fec0:2004:ab10:cd:1234:0:0:6789
0000:0000:0000:0000:0000:FFFF:172.16.255.1	0:0:0:0:0:FFFF:172.16.255.1
0000:0000:0000:0000:0000:0000:172.16.255.1	0:0:0:0:0:0:172.16.255.1
0000:0000:0000:0000:0000:0000:0000:0000	0:0:0:0:0:0:0:0

While there are two methods of representing the complete IPv6 address in compressed form, it is important to remember that both methods are not mutually exclusive. In other words, these methods can be used at the same time to represent the same IPv6 address. This is commonly used when the complete IPv6 address contains both consecutive strings of zeros and leading zeros in other fields within the address. Table 3.3 below shows IPv6 addresses in the complete form that include both consecutive strings of zeros and leading zeros, and how these addresses are represented in the compressed form:

Table 3.3 –Complete IPv6 Addresses Using Both Compressed Form Methods

Complete IPv6 Address Representation	Compressed IPv6 Address Representation
0000:0000:0000:0000:1a2b:000c:f123:4567	::1a2b:c:f123:4567
FEC0:0004:AB10:00CD:1234:0000:0000:6789	FEC0:4:AB10:CD:1234::6789
3FFF:0c00:0000:1010:1A2B:0000:0000:DE0F	3FFF:c00:0:1010:1A2B::DE0F
2001:0000:0000:1234:0000:5678:af23:00d5	2001::1234:0:5678:af23:d5

IPv6 Addresses with an Embedded IPv4 Address

The third representation of an IPv6 address is to use an embedded IPv4 address within the IPv6 address. While valid, it is important to keep in mind that this method is being deprecated and is considered obsolete because it is applicable only in the transition of IPv4 to IPv6.

THE DIFFERENT IPV6 ADDRESS TYPES

IPv4 supports four different classes of addresses, which are Anycast, Broadcast, Multicast, and Unicast. While the term Anycast has not been used in previous modules in this guide, it is important to remember that Anycast addresses are not special types of addresses. Instead, an Anycast address is simply an IP address that is assigned to multiple interfaces. Common examples of technologies that use Anycast addressing include IP Multicast implementations and 6to4 relay implementation.

> **NOTE:** 6to4 is a transition mechanism for migrating from IPv4 to IPv6. For the CCNA exam, you only need to know that it exists.

With Anycast addressing, devices use the common address that is closest to them based on the routing protocol metric. The next closest address is then used in the event that the primary address is no longer reachable. This concept is illustrated in Figure 3.5 below:

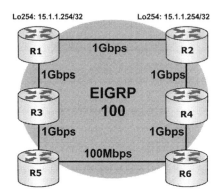

Figure 3.5—Understanding Anycast Addressing

Referencing Figure 3.5, both R1 and R2 have a Loopback 254 interface that is configured using a common address: 15.1.1.254/32. This prefix is then advertised dynamically via EIGRP. By default, both R1 and R2 will prefer the 15.1.1.254/32 prefix via their respective Loopback interfaces, as that is a directly connected subnet. Therefore, the common address used will never result in a conflict on either router.

Assuming normal EIGRP metric calculation, R3 and R5 will prefer the Anycast address advertised by R1 due to the lower IGP metric (we cover metrics later). Similarly, R4 and R6 will prefer the Anycast address advertised by R2 due to the lower IGP metric. In the event that either R1 or R2 fails, the remaining routers in the network will use the Anycast address advertised by the remaining router. When using Anycast addressing, organizations can use a Unicast address either in the RFC 1918 address space or within their public block.

> **NOTE:** You are not expected to implement any Anycast addressing or solutions in the current CCNA exam. However, it is important to be familiar with the concept. It will make more sense after you have reviewed the routing chapters.

At this level, IPv4 Broadcast, Multicast, and Unicast addresses require no further explanation and will not be described in any additional detail in this module or in the remainder of this guide. While IPv4 supports these four different types of addresses, IPv6 does away with Broadcast addresses and instead supports only the following types of addresses:

- Link-Local addresses
- Site-Local addresses

- Aggregate Global Unicast addresses
- Multicast addresses
- Anycast addresses
- Loopback addresses
- Unspecified addresses

Link-Local Addresses

IPv6 Link-Local addresses can be used only on the local link (i.e., a shared segment between devices), and are automatically assigned to each interface when IPv6 is enabled on that interface. These addresses are assigned from the Link-Local prefix FE80::/10. Keep in mind that FE80::/10 is the equivalent of FE80:0:0:0:0:0:0:0/10, which can also be represented as FE80:0000:0000:0000:0000:0000:0000:0000/10. To complete the address, bits 11 through 64 are set to 0 and the interface Extended Unique Identifier 64 (EUI-64) is appended to the Link-Local address as the low-order 64 bits. The EUI-64 is comprised of the 24-bit manufacturer ID assigned by the IEEE and the 40-bit value assigned by that manufacturer to its products. EUI-64 addressing is described in greater detail later in this module. The format for a Link-Local address is illustrated in Figure 3.6 below:

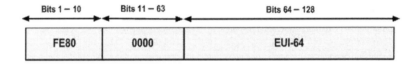

Figure 3.6—IPv6 Link-Local Addressing

Link-local addresses are unique in that they do not change once assigned to an interface. This means that if an interface is assigned a public IPv6 address (e.g., 2001:1000::1/64) and the public IPv6 prefix was changed (i.e., 2001:2000::1/64), the Link-Local address would not change. This allows the host or router to remain reachable by its neighbor, while IPv6 global Internet addresses change. IPv6 routers should not forward packets that have Link-Local source or destination addresses to other IPv6 routers.

Site-Local Addresses

Site-Local addresses are Unicast addresses that are used only within a site. Unlike Link-Local addresses, Site-Local addresses must be configured manually on network devices. These addresses are the IPv6 equivalent of the private IPv4 address space defined in RFC 1918 and can be used by organizations that do not have globally routable IPv6 address space. These addresses are not routable on the IPv6 Internet.

While it is possible to perform NAT for IPv6, it is not recommended; hence, the reason for the much larger IPv6 addresses. Site-Local addresses are comprised of the FEC0::/10 prefix, a 54-bit subnet ID, and an interface identifier in the EUI-64 format used by Link-Local addresses. While the 54 bits in a Link-Local address are set to a value of 0, the same 54 bits in

Site-Local addresses are used to create different IPv6 prefixes (up to 254). The format for the Site-Local address is illustrated in Figure 3.7 below:

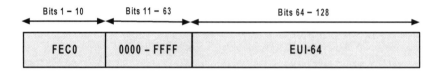

Figure 3.7—IPv6 Site-Local Addressing

While IPv6 Site-Local addresses are described in this section and are still supported in Cisco IOS software, it is important to know that these addresses are deprecated by RFC 3879 (Deprecating Site Local Addresses). Moreover, RFC 4193 (Unique Local IPv6 Unicast Addresses) describes Unique-Local addresses (ULAs), which serve the same function as Site-Local addresses but they are not routable on the IPv6 global Internet, only within a site.

Unique-Local addresses are assigned from the FC00::/7 IPv6 address block, which is then further divided into two /8 address groups referred to as the assigned and random groups. These two groups are the FC00::/8 and the FD00::/8 IPv6 address blocks. The FC00::/8 block is managed by an allocation authority for /48s in use, while the FD00::/8 block is formed by appending a randomly generated 40-bit string to derive a valid /48 block.

Aggregate Global Unicast Addresses

Aggregate Global Unicast addresses are the IPv6 addresses used for generic IPv6 traffic, as well as for the IPv6 Internet. These are similar to the public addresses used in IPv4. From a network addressing point of view, each IPv6 Global Unicast address is comprised of three main sections: the prefix received from the provider (48 bits in length), the site prefix (16 bits in length), and the host portion (64 bits in length). This makes up the 128-bit address used in IPv6.

As we learned earlier in this module, the provider-assigned prefix is assigned to an organization by an IPv6 provider. By default, these prefixes use /48 prefix lengths. In addition, these prefixes are assigned from the IPv6 address spaces (i.e., the /32 prefix lengths) that are owned by the provider. Each provider will own its own IPv6 address space, and the IPv6 prefix assigned by one provider cannot be used on the network of another provider.

Within a site, administrators can then subnet the provider-assigned 48-bit prefix into 64-bit site prefixes by using bits 49 through 64 for subnetting, allowing for 65,535 different subnets for use within their network. The host portion of an IPv6 address represents the network device or host on the IPv6 subnet. This is represented by the low-order 64 bits of the IPv6 address.

Aggregate Global Unicast addresses for IPv6 are assigned by the Internet Assigned Numbers Authority (IANA) and fall within the IPv6 prefix 2000::/3. This allows for a range of Aggregate Global Unicast addresses from 2000 to 3FFF, as illustrated in Table 3.4 below:

Table 3.4—IPv6 Aggregate Global Unicast Addresses

Description	Address
First Address in Range	2000:0000:0000:0000:0000:0000:0000:0000
Last Address in Range	3FFF:FFFF:FFFF:FFFF:FFFF:FFFF:FFFF:FFFF
Binary Notation	The three high-order bits are set to 001

From the 2000::/3 IPv6 block, only three subnets have been allocated for use at the time this module was written. These allocations are illustrated in Table 3.5 below:

Table 3.5—Assigned IPv6 Aggregate Global Unicast Addresses

IPv6 Global Prefix	Binary Representation	Description
2001::/16	0010 0000 0000 0001	Global IPv6 Internet (Unicast)
2002::/16	0010 0000 0000 0010	6to4 Transition Prefix
3FFE::/16	0110 1111 1111 1110	6bone Prefix

NOTE: The 6to4 transition addresses and the 6bone prefix are not described in this guide in any detail.

Within the range of IPv6 Global Aggregate Unicast addresses, a special experimental range is reserved called ORCHID (an acronym for Overlay Routable Cryptographic Hash Identifiers defined in RFC 4843). ORCHID addresses are non-routed IPv6 addresses used for cryptographic hash identifiers. These addresses use the IPv6 prefix 2001:10::/28. Going into detail on ORCHID addresses is beyond the scope of the current CCNA exam requirements and will not be included in this module or in the remainder of this guide.

Multicast Addresses

The Multicast addresses used in IPv6 are derived from the FF00::/8 IPv6 prefix. In IPv6, Multicast operates in a different manner than that of Multicast in IPv4. IP Multicast is used extensively in IPv6 and replaces IPv4 protocols, such as the Address Resolution Protocol (ARP). In addition, Multicast is used in IPv6 for prefix advertisements and renumbering, as well as for Duplicate Address Detection (DAD). These concepts are all described later in this module.

Multicast packets in IPv6 do not use the TTL value to restrict such packets to the local network segment. Instead, the scoping is defined within the Multicast address itself via the use of the Scope field. IPv6 nodes on a network segment listen to Multicast and may even send Multicast packets to exchange information. This allows all nodes on an IPv6 segment to know about all the other neighbors on that same segment. The format for Multicast addresses used in IPv6 networks is illustrated in Figure 3.8 below:

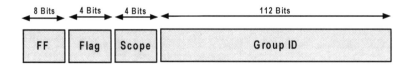

Figure 3.8—IPv6 Multicast Addressing

As illustrated in Figure 3.8, the format of the IPv6 Multicast address is slightly different from the formats of the other IPv6 addresses you have learned about up until this point. The first 8 bits of the IPv6 Multicast address represent the Multicast prefix FF::/8. The Flag field in the IPv6 Multicast address is used to indicate the type of Multicast address, either permanent or temporary.

Permanent IPv6 Multicast addresses are assigned by IANA, while temporary IPv6 Multicast addresses can be used in pre-deployment Multicast testing. The Flag field may contain one of the two possible values illustrated in Table 3.6 below:

Table 3.6—IPv6 Permanent and Temporary Multicast Addresses

Type of Multicast Address	Binary Representation	Hexadecimal Value
Permanent	0000	0
Temporary	0001	1

The next 4 bits in the Multicast address represent the scope. In IPv6 Multicasting, this field is a mandatory field that restricts Multicast packets from being sent to other areas in the network. This field essentially provides the same function as the TTL field that is used in IPv4. However, with IPv6, there are several types of scopes, which are listed in Table 3.7 below:

Table 3.7—IPv6 Multicast Address Scopes

Scope Type	Binary Representation	Hexadecimal Value
Interface-Local	0001	1
Link-Local	0010	2
Subnet-Local	0011	3
Admin-Local	0100	4
Site-Local	0101	5
Organization	1000	8
Global	1110	E

Within the IPv6 Multicast prefix, certain addresses are reserved. These reserved addresses are referred to as Multicast Assigned addresses, which are presented in Table 3.8 below:

Table 3.8—IPv6 Reserved Multicast Addresses

Address	Scope	Description
FF01::1	Hosts	All hosts on the Interface-Local scope
FF01::2	Hosts	All routers on the Interface-Local scope
FF02::1	Link-Local	All hosts on the Link-Local scope
FF02::2	Link-Local	All routers on the Link-Local scope
FF05::2	Site	All routers on the Site scope

In addition to these addresses, a Solicited-Node Multicast address is enabled automatically for each Unicast and Anycast address configured on a router interface or network host. This address has a Link-Local scope, which means that it will never traverse farther than the local network segment. Solicited-Node Multicast addresses are used for the following two reasons: the replacement of IPv4 ARP and DAD.

Because IPv6 does not use ARP, Solicited-Node Multicast addresses are used by network hosts and routers to learn the Data Link addresses of neighboring devices. This allows for the conversion and sending of IPv6 packets to IPv6 hosts and routers as frames. DAD is part of the IPv6 Neighbor Discovery Protocol (NDP), which will be described in detail later in this module. DAD simply allows a device to validate whether an IPv6 address is already in use on the local segment before it configures the address as its own using autoconfiguration. In essence, it provides a similar function to Gratuitous ARP used in IPv4. Solicited-Node Multicast addresses are defined by the IPv6 prefix FF02::1:FF00:0000/104. These addresses are comprised of the FF02::1:FF00:0000/104 prefix in conjunction with the low-order 24 bits of the Unicast or Anycast address. Figure 3.9 below illustrates the format of these IPv6 addresses:

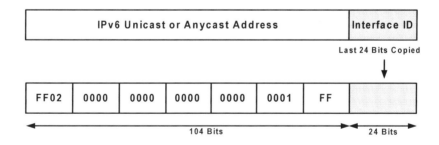

Figure 3.9—IPv6 Solicited-Node Multicast Addresses

In a manner similar to IPv4 Multicast mapping for Ethernet, IPv6 also uses a unique means to map Layer 3 IPv6 Multicast addresses to Layer 2 Multicast addresses. Multicast mapping in IPv6 is enabled by appending the low-order 32 bits of a Multicast address to the 16-bit prefix 33:33, which is the defined Multicast Ethernet prefix for IPv6 networks. This is illustrated in Figure 3.10 below for all the routers on the Interface-Local scope prefix FF02::2:

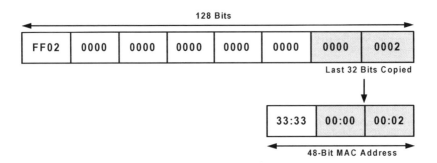

Figure 3.10—IPv6 Multicast Addresses

Anycast Addresses

Anycast, which was introduced earlier in this section, can be described simply as one-to-nearest communication, because the nearest common address, based on routing protocol metrics, will always be preferred by the local device. In IPv6 there is no specially allocated range for Anycast, as Anycast addresses use Global Unicast, Site-Local, or even Link-Local addresses. However, there is an Anycast address reserved for special use. This special address is referred to as the Subnet-Router Anycast address and is formed with the subnet's 64-bit Unicast prefix, with the remaining 64 bits set to zero (e.g., 2001:1a2b:1111:d7e5:0000:0000:000:0000). Anycast addresses must not be used as the source address of an IPv6 packet. These addresses are typically used by protocols such as Mobile IPv6, which is outside the scope of the CCNA.

Loopback Addresses

Loopback addresses in IPv6 are used in the same manner as in IPv4. Each device has one IPv6 Loopback address, which is comparable to the 127.0.0.1 Loopback address used in IPv4, and this address is used by the device itself. IPv6 Loopback addresses use the prefix ::1, which can be represented as 0000:0000:0000:0000:0000:0000:0000:0001 in the preferred address format. This means that in Loopback addresses, all bits are set to 0, except for the last bit, which is always set to 1. These addresses are always assigned automatically when IPv6 is enabled on a device and they can never be changed.

Unspecified Addresses

In IPv6 addressing, unspecified addresses are simply Unicast addresses that are not assigned to any interface. These addresses indicate the absence of an IPv6 address and are used for special purposes that include IPv6 DHCP and DAD. Unspecified addresses are represented by all 0 values in the IPv6 address and can be written using the :: prefix. In the preferred format, these addresses are represented as 0000:0000:0000:0000:0000:0000:0000:0000.

IPV6 PROTOCOLS AND MECHANISMS

While version 6 of the Internet Protocol is similar to version 4, there are significant differences in the operation of the former compared to the latter. The following IPv6 protocols and mechanisms are described in this section:

- ICMP for IPv6
- The IPv6 Neighbor Discovery Protocol (NDP)
- IPv6 stateful autoconfiguration
- IPv6 stateless autoconfiguration

ICMP for IPv6

ICMP is used to report errors and other information to the source hosts regarding the delivery of IP packets to the intended destination. ICMPv6, which is defined in RFC 2463 as protocol number 58, supports messages for ICMPv4 and includes additional messages for ICMPv6. ICMPv6 is used in the Next Header field of the basic IPv6 packet header. Unlike in IPv4, IPv6 views ICMPv6 as an upper-layer protocol, such as TCP, for example, which means that ICMPv6 is placed after all possible extension headers in the IPv6 packet. The fields that are contained within the ICMPv6 packet are illustrated in Figure 3.11 below:

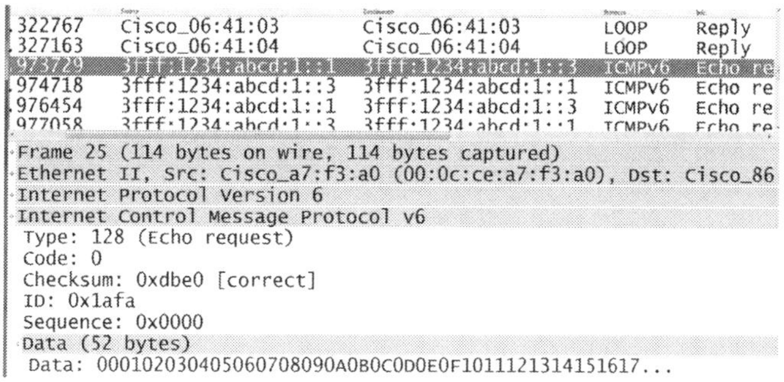

Figure 3.11—The ICMPv6 Packet Header

Within the ICMPv6 packet header, the 8-bit Type field is used to indicate or identify the type of ICMPv6 message. This field is used to provide both error and informational messages. Table 3.9 below lists and describes some common values that can be found within this field:

Table 3.9—ICMPv6 Message Types

ICMPv6 Type	Description
1	Destination Unreachable
2	Packet Too Big
3	Time Exceeded
128	Echo Request
129	Echo Reply

NOTE: These same message types are also used in ICMPv4.

Following the Type field, the 8-bit Code field provides details pertaining to the type of message sent. Table 3.10 below illustrates common values for this field, which are also shared by ICMPv4:

Table 3.10—ICMPv6 Codes

ICMPv6 Code	Description
0	Echo Reply
3	Destination Unreachable
8	Echo
11	Time Exceeded

Following the Code field, the 16-bit Checksum field contains a computed value used to detect data corruption in ICMPv6. Finally, the Message or Data field is an optional, variable-length field that contains the data specific to the message type indicated by the Type and Code fields. When used, this field provides information to the destination host. ICMPv6 is a core component of IPv6. Within IPv6, ICMPv6 is used for the following:

- Duplicate Address Detection (DAD)
- The replacement of ARP
- IPv6 stateless autoconfiguration
- IPv6 prefix renumbering
- Path MTU Discovery (PMTUD)

NOTE: Of the options above, DAD and stateless autoconfiguration will be described later in this section. PMTUD is beyond the scope of the current CCNA exam requirements and will not be described in any additional detail in this module or in the remainder of this guide.

The IPv6 Neighbor Discovery Protocol (NDP)

The IPv6 NDP enables the plug-and-play features of IPv6. It is defined in RFC 2461 and is an integral part of IPv6. NDP operates in the Link Layer and is responsible for the discovery of other nodes on the link, determining the Link Layer addresses of other nodes, finding available routers, and maintaining reachability information about the paths to other active neighbor nodes. NDP performs functions for IPv6 similar to the way ARP (which it replaces) and ICMP Router Discovery and Router Redirect Protocols do for IPv4. However, it is important to remember that NDP provides greater functionality than the mechanisms used in IPv4. Used in conjunction with ICMPv6, NDP allows for the following:

- Dynamic neighbor and router discovery
- The replacement of ARP

- IPv6 stateless autoconfiguration
- Router redirection
- Host parameter discovery
- IPv6 address resolution
- Next-hop router determination
- Neighbor Unreachability Detection (NUD)
- Duplicate Address Detection (DAD)

NOTE: You are not required to delve into specifics on each of the advantages listed above.

Neighbor Discovery Protocol defines five types of ICMPv6 packets, which are listed and described in Table 3.11 below:

Table 3.11—ICMPv6 NDP Message Types

ICMPv6 Type	Message Type Description and IPv6 Usage
133	Used for Router Solicitation (RS) messages
134	Used for Router Advertisement (RA) messages
135	Used for Neighbor Solicitation (NS) messages
136	Used for Neighbor Advertisement (NA) messages
137	Used for Router Redirect messages

Router Solicitation messages are sent by hosts when interfaces are enabled for IPv6. These messages are used to request that routers on the local segment generate RA messages immediately, rather than at the next scheduled RA interval. Figure 3.12 below illustrates a wire capture of an RS message:

```
Frame 529 (70 bytes on wire, 70 bytes captured)
Ethernet II, Src: Dell_f5:7e:a2 (00:24:e8:f5:7e:a2), Dst: IPv
Internet Protocol Version 6
Internet Control Message Protocol v6
 Type: 133 (Router solicitation)
 Code: 0
 Checksum: 0x6e61 [correct]
 ICMPv6 Option (Source link-layer address)
 Type: Source link-layer address (1)
 Length: 8
 Link-layer address: 00:24:e8:f5:7e:a2
```

Figure 3.12—IPv6 Router Solicitation Message

Upon receiving the RS message, routers advertise their presence using RA messages, which typically include prefix information for the local link as well as any additional configuration, such as suggested hop limits. The information contained within the RA is illustrated in Figure 3.13 below:

```
Ethernet II, Src: Cisco_a7.13.a0 (00.0c.ce.a7.13.a0), Dst: 11
Internet Protocol Version 6
Internet Control Message Protocol v6
 Type: 134 (Router advertisement)
 Code: 0
 Checksum: 0x17ed [correct]
 Cur hop limit: 64
 Flags: 0x00
 Router lifetime: 1800
 Reachable time: 0
 Retrans timer: 0
 ICMPv6 Option (Source link-layer address)
 ICMPv6 Option (MTU)
 ICMPv6 Option (Prefix information)
 ICMPv6 Option (Prefix information)
```

Figure 3.13—IPv6 Router Advertisement Message

To reiterate, RS and RA messages are for router-to-host or host-to-router exchanges, as illustrated below:

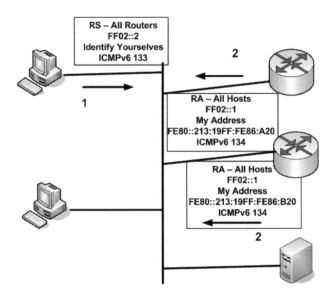

Figure 3.14—IPv6 RS and RA Messages

IPv6 NS messages are Multicast by IPv6 routers on the local network segment and are used to determine the Data Link address of a neighbor or to verify that a neighbor is still reachable (thus replacing the ARP function). These messages are also used for Duplicate Address Detection. While delving into detail on NS messages is beyond the scope of the CCNA exam requirements, Figure 3.15 below illustrates a wire capture of an IPv6 Neighbor Solicitation message:

```
Frame 185 (86 bytes on wire, 86 bytes captured)
Ethernet II, Src: Dell_f5:7e:a2 (00:24:e8:f5:7e:a2), Dst: IPv6mca
Internet Protocol Version 6
Internet Control Message Protocol v6
 Type: 135 (Neighbor solicitation)
 Code: 0
 Checksum: 0x3f71 [correct]
 Target: fe80::213:19ff:fe86:a20
ICMPv6 Option (Source link-layer address)
 Type: Source link-layer address (1)
 Length: 8
 Link-layer address: 00:24:e8:f5:7e:a2
```

Figure 3.15—IPv6 Neighbor Solicitation Message

Neighbor Advertisement messages are typically sent by routers on the local network segment in response to received NS messages. However, if, for example, an IPv6 prefix changes, then routers may also send out unsolicited NS messages advising other devices on the local network segment of the change. As is the case with NA messages, going into detail on the format or fields contained within the NA message is beyond the scope of the CCNA exam requirements. Figures 3.16 and 3.17 below illustrate a wire capture of the Neighbor Advertisement message, which is also sent via IPv6 Multicast:

```
0::coff:fe-7:fff02::16            ICMPv6  Multicast Listener Report Mes
Frame 58 (86 bytes on wire, 86 bytes captured)
Ethernet II, Src: Cisco_a7:f3:a0 (00:0c:ce:a7:f3:a0), Dst: IPv6mcast_00:(
Internet Protocol Version 6
Internet Control Message Protocol v6
 Type: 136 (Neighbor advertisement)
 Code: 0
 Checksum: 0x909f [correct]
Flags: 0xa0000000
  1... .... .... .... .... .... .... .... = Router
  .0.. .... .... .... .... .... .... .... = Not adverted
  ..1. .... .... .... .... .... .... .... = Override
 Target: fe80::20c:ceff:fea7:f3a0
ICMPv6 Option (Target link-layer address)
 Type: Target link-layer address (2)
 Length: 8
 Link-layer address: 00:0c:ce:a7:f3:a0
```

Figure 3.16—IPv6 Neighbor Advertisement Message

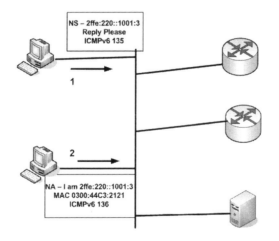

Figure 3.17—IPv6 Neighbor Advertisement Messages

Finally, router redirection uses ICMPv6 Redirect messages, which are defined as message type 137. Router redirection is used to inform network hosts that a router with a better path to the intended destination exists on the network. It works in the same manner as it does for ICMPv4, which redirects traffic in current IPv4 networks.

IPv6 Stateful Autoconfiguration

As previously stated in this module, stateful autoconfiguration allows network hosts to receive their addressing information from a network server (e.g., via DHCP). This method of autoconfiguration is supported by both IPv4 and IPv6. In IPv6 networks, DHCPv6 is used to provide stateful (and stateless) autoconfiguration services for IPv6 hosts. In IPv6 implementations, when an IPv6 host receives RA messages from routers on the local network segment, the host examines these packets to determine whether DHCPv6 can be used. The RA messages provide this information by setting either the M (Managed) or the O (Other) bits to 1.

With DHCP the client is configured to obtain information from the DHCP server. With DHCPv6, the client doesn't know where the information comes from, which could be from SLAAC (covered shortly), stateful DHCPv6, or a combination of both.

The M bit in Router Advertisement messages is the Managed Address Configuration Flag bit. When this bit is set (i.e., it contains a value of 1), it instructs the IPv6 host to obtain a stateful address, which is provided by DHCPv6 servers. The O bit in Router Advertisement messages is the Other Stateful Configuration Flag bit. When this bit is set (i.e., it contains a value of 1), it instructs the IPv6 host to use DHCPv6 to obtain more configuration settings, such as DNS and WINS servers, for example.

If a host has not been configured with an IPv6 address, it can use one of three methods to obtain one, as well as other network settings such as the DNS server address:

- SLAAC—Stateless Autoconfiguration M and O bits set to 0 means that there is no DHCPv6 information. The host receives all necessary information from an RA.
- Stateful DHCPv6—M flag set to 1 tells the host to use DHCPv6 for all address and network information.
- Stateless DHCPv6—M flag set to 0 and O flag set to 1 means that the host will use SLAAC for the address (from an RA) but will also obtain other information from DNS servers.

While one of the advantages of IPv6 is stateless autoconfiguration capability, stateful autoconfiguration still provides several advantages, which include the following:

- Greater controls than those provided by stateless autoconfiguration
- Can be used on networks when stateless autoconfiguration is available
- Provides addressing to network hosts in the absence of routers
- Can be used for network renumbering by assigning new prefixes to hosts
- Can be used to issue entire subnets to customer premise equipment

IPv6 Stateless Autoconfiguration

IPv6 permits interfaces to self-configure an IP address in order for host-to-host communication to take place. Stateful autoconfiguration involves a server allocating address information, and for IPv6 DHCPv6 is used. Stateful refers to the fact that details of an exchange are stored by the server (or router), whereas stateless means they are not. DHCPv6 can either be stateful or stateless.

In IPv6, stateless autoconfiguration allows hosts to configure their Unicast IPv6 addresses by themselves based on prefix advertisements from routers on the local network segment. Other network information can be obtained from the DHCPv6 server (such as the DNS server address). The three mechanisms that allow for stateless autoconfiguration in IPv6 are as follows:

- Prefix advertisement
- Duplicate Address Detection (DAD)
- Prefix renumbering

IPv6 prefix advertisement uses ICMPv6 Router Advertisement messages, which are sent to the all-hosts-on-the-local-link IPv6 Multicast address FF02::1. By design, only routers are allowed to advertise prefixes on the local link. When stateless autoconfiguration is employed, it is imperative to remember that the prefix length used must be 64 bits (e.g., 2001:1a2b::/64).

Following the configuration of the prefix, RA messages used for IPv6 stateless autoconfiguration include the following information:

- The IPv6 prefix
- The lifetime
- Default router information
- Flags and/or Options fields

As previously stated, the IPv6 prefix must be 64 bits. In addition, multiple IPv6 prefixes may be advertised on the local segment. When hosts on the network segment receive the IPv6 prefix, they append their MAC address to the prefix in EUI-64 format, which was described earlier in this module, and automatically configure their IPv6 Unicast address. This provides a unique 128-bit IPv6 address to each host on the network segment.

The lifetime value for each advertised prefix is also provided to the nodes and may contain a value from 0 to infinite. When nodes receive the prefix, they validate the lifetime value and cease using the prefix when the lifetime value reaches 0. Alternatively, if a value of infinite is received for a particular prefix, the network hosts will never cease using that prefix. Each advertised prefix contains two-lifetime values: the valid lifetime value and the preferred lifetime value.

The valid lifetime value is used to determine how long the host address will remain valid. When this value expires (i.e., reaches a value of 0), the host address becomes invalid. The preferred lifetime value is used to determine how long an address configured via stateless autoconfiguration will remain valid. This value must be less than or equal to the value specified in the valid lifetime and is typically used for prefix renumbering.

The default router provides information about the existence and lifetime of its IPv6 address. By default, the address used for default routers is the Link-Local address (FE80::/10). This allows the Global Unicast address to be changed without interrupting network services, as would be the case in IPv4 if a network were renumbered.

Finally, the Flags and Options fields can be used to instruct network hosts to use stateless autoconfiguration or stateful autoconfiguration. These fields are included in the wire capture of the Router Advertisement shown in Figure 3.13.

Duplicate Address Detection is an NDP mechanism used in stateless autoconfiguration when a host on the network segment is booting up. DAD mandates that before a network host permanently configures its own IPv6 address during boot up, it should validate that another network host is not already using the IPv6 address it wants to use.

Duplicate Address Detection performs this validation by using Neighbor Solicitation (ICMPv6 Type 135) and Solicited-Node Multicast addresses. The host sends a Neighbor Solicitation on the local network segment using an unspecified IPv6 address (i.e., the :: address) as its source address and the Solicited-Node Multicast address of the IPv6 Unicast address it wants to use as the destination address. If no other host is using this same address, the host will not automatically configure itself with this address; however, if no other device is using the same address, the host automatically configures itself and begins to use this IPv6 address.

Finally, prefix renumbering allows for the transparent renumbering of network prefixes in IPv6 when changing from one prefix to another. Unlike in IPv4, where the same global IP address can be advertised by multiple providers, the strict aggregation of the IPv6 address space prevents providers from advertising prefixes that do not belong to their organization.

In cases where a transition is made from one IPv6 Internet provider to another, the IPv6 prefix renumbering mechanism provides a smooth and transparent transition from one prefix to another. Prefix renumbering uses the same ICMPv6 messages and Multicast address used in prefix advertisement. Prefix renumbering is made possible by using the time parameters contained within the Router Advertisement messages.

In Cisco IOS software, routers can be configured to advertise current prefixes with the valid and preferred lifetime values decreased to a value closer to zero, which allows those prefixes to become invalid faster. The routers are then configured to advertise the new prefixes on the local network segments. This allows the old and new prefixes to exist on the same network segment.

During this transition period, hosts on the local network segment use two Unicast addresses: one from the old prefix and one from the new prefix. Any current connections using the old prefix are still handled; however, any new connections from these hosts are made using the new prefix. When the old prefix expires, only the new prefix is used.

Configuring Stateless DHCPv6

There are a few simple steps to follow in order to configure stateless DHCPv6 on a router:

- Create the pool name and other parameters
- Enable it on an interface
- Modify Router Advertisement settings

An Identity Association (IA) is a collection of addresses assigned to the client. There must be at least one IA assigned per interface using DHCPv6. We won't go into configuration examples for the CCNA exam.

Enabling IPv6 Routing in Cisco IOS Software

Now that you have a solid understanding of IPv6 fundamentals, the remainder of this module will focus on the configuration of IPv6 in Cisco IOS software. By default, IPv6 routing functionality is disabled in Cisco IOS software. Therefore, IPv6 routing functionality must be enabled manually using the ipv6 unicast-routing global configuration command.

After enabling IPv6 routing globally, the ipv6 address [ipv6-address/prefix-length | prefix-name sub-bits/prefix-length | anycast | autoconfig <default> | dhcp | eui-64 | link-local] interface configuration command can be used to configure interface IPv6 addressing. The [ipv6-address/prefix-length] keyword is used to specify the IPv6 prefix and prefix length assigned to the interface. The following configuration illustrates how to configure a router interface with the first address on the 3FFF:1234:ABCD:5678::/64 subnet:

```
R1(config)#ipv6 unicast-routing
R1(config)#interface FastEthernet0/0
R1(config-if)#ipv6 address 3FFF:1234:ABCD:5678::1/64
R1(config-if)#exit
```

Following this configuration, the show ipv6 interface [name] command can be used to validate the configured IPv6 address subnet, as illustrated below:

```
R1#show ipv6 interface FastEthernet0/0
FastEthernet0/0 is up, line protocol is up
  IPv6 is enabled, link-local address is FE80::20C:CEFF:FEA7:F3A0
  Global unicast address(es):
    3FFF:1234:ABCD:5678::1, subnet is 3FFF:1234:ABCD:5678::/64
  Joined group address(es):
    FF02::1
    FF02::2
    FF02::1:FF00:1
    FF02::1:FFA7:F3A0
[Truncated Output]
```

As was stated earlier in this module, IPv6 allows multiple prefixes to be configured on the same interface. If multiple prefixes have been configured on the same interface, the show `ipv6 interface [name] prefix` command can be used to view all assigned prefixes as well as their valid and preferred lifetime values. The following output displays the information that is printed by this command for a router interface with multiple IPv6 subnets configured:

```
R1#show ipv6 interface FastEthernet0/0 prefix
IPv6 Prefix Advertisements FastEthernet0/0
Codes: A - Address, P - Prefix-Advertisement, O - Pool
       U - Per-user prefix, D - Default
       N - Not advertised, C - Calendar

     default [LA] Valid lifetime 2592000, preferred lifetime 604800
AD   3FFF:1234:ABCD:3456::/64 [LA] Valid lifetime 2592000, preferred
lifetime 604800
AD   3FFF:1234:ABCD:5678::/64 [LA] Valid lifetime 2592000, preferred
lifetime 604800
AD   3FFF:1234:ABCD:7890::/64 [LA] Valid lifetime 2592000, preferred
lifetime 604800
AD   3FFF:1234:ABCD:9012::/64 [LA] Valid lifetime 2592000, preferred
lifetime 604800
```

NOTE: The valid and preferred lifetime values can be adjusted from default values, allowing for a smooth transition when implementing prefix renumbering. This configuration, however, is beyond the scope of the CCNA exam requirements and will not be illustrated in this lesson.

Continuing with the use of the `ipv6 prefix` interface configuration command, the `[prefix-name sub-bits/prefix-length]` keyword is used to configure a general prefix, which specifies the leading bits of the subnet to be configured on the interface. This configuration is beyond the scope of the current CCNA exam requirements and will not be illustrated in this module.

The `[anycast]` keyword is used to configure an IPv6 Anycast address. As was stated earlier, Anycast addressing simply allows the same common address to be assigned to multiple router interfaces. Hosts use the Anycast address that is closest to them based on routing protocol metrics. Anycast configuration is beyond the scope of the CCNA exam requirements and will not be illustrated in this module.

The `[autoconfig <default>]` keyword enables stateless autoconfiguration (SLAAC). If this keyword is used, the router will dynamically learn prefixes on the link and then add EUI-64 addresses for all the learned prefixes. The `<default>` keyword is an optional keyword that allows a default route to be installed. The following configuration example illustrates how to enable stateless autoconfiguration on a router interface and additionally allow the default route to be installed.

```
R2(config)#ipv6 unicast-routing
R2(config)#interface FastEthernet0/0
R2(config-if)#ipv6 address autoconfig default
R2(config-if)#exit
```

Following this configuration, router R2 will listen to Router Advertisement messages on the local segment on which the FastEthernet0/0 interface resides. The router will configure dynamically an EUI-64 address for each learned prefix and then install the default route pointing to the Link-Local address of the advertising router. The dynamic address configuration is validated using the show ipv6 interface [name] command, as illustrated below:

```
R2#show ipv6 interface FastEthernet0/0
FastEthernet0/0 is up, line protocol is up
  IPv6 is enabled, link-local address is FE80::213:19FF:FE86:A20
  Global unicast address(es):
    3FFF:1234:ABCD:3456:213:19FF:FE86:A20, subnet is
3FFF:1234:ABCD:3456::/64 [PRE]
      valid lifetime 2591967 preferred lifetime 604767
    3FFF:1234:ABCD:5678:213:19FF:FE86:A20, subnet is
3FFF:1234:ABCD:5678::/64 [PRE]
      valid lifetime 2591967 preferred lifetime 604767
    3FFF:1234:ABCD:7890:213:19FF:FE86:A20, subnet is
3FFF:1234:ABCD:7890::/64 [PRE]
      valid lifetime 2591967 preferred lifetime 604767
    3FFF:1234:ABCD:9012:213:19FF:FE86:A20, subnet is
3FFF:1234:ABCD:9012::/64 [PRE]
      valid lifetime 2591967 preferred lifetime 604767
    FEC0:1111:1111:E000:213:19FF:FE86:A20, subnet is
FEC0:1111:1111:E000::/64 [PRE]
      valid lifetime 2591967 preferred lifetime 604767
  Joined group address(es):
    FF02::1
    FF02::2
    FF02::1:FF86:A20
  MTU is 1500 bytes
[Truncated Output]
```

In the output above, notice that while no explicit IPv6 addresses were configured on the interface, an EUI-64 address was configured dynamically for the subnet the router discovered by listening to Router Advertisement messages. The timers for each of these prefixes are derived from the router advertising the RA messages. In addition to verifying the stateless autoconfiguration, the show ipv6 route command can be used to validate the default route to the Link-Local address of the preferred advertising router, as illustrated below:

```
R2#show ipv6 route ::/0
IPv6 Routing Table - 13 entries
Codes: C - Connected, L - Local, S - Static, R - RIP, B - BGP
       U - Per-user Static route
       I1 - ISIS L1, I2 - ISIS L2, IA - ISIS inter area, IS - ISIS
summary
       O - OSPF intra, OI - OSPF inter, OE1 - OSPF ext 1, OE2 - OSPF ext
2
       ON1 - OSPF NSSA ext 1, ON2 - OSPF NSSA ext 2
S   ::/0 [1/0]
     via FE80::20C:CEFF:FEA7:F3A0, FastEthernet0/0
```

Continuing with the `ipv6 address` command, the `[dhcp]` keyword is used to configure the router interface to use stateful autoconfiguration (i.e., DHCPv6) to acquire the interface addressing configuration. With this configuration, an additional keyword, `[rapid-commit]`, can also be appended to the end of this command to allow the two-message exchange method for address assignment and other configuration information.

Reverting back to the topic of discussion, with the `ipv6 address` command, the `[eui-64]` keyword is used to configure an IPv6 address for an interface and enables IPv6 processing on the interface using an EUI-64 interface ID in the low-order 64 bits of the address. By default, Link-Local, Site-Local, and IPv6 stateless autoconfiguration all use the EUI-64 format to make their IPv6 addresses. EUI-64 addressing expands the 48-bit MAC address into a 64-bit address. This is performed in two steps, both of which are described in the following section. This process is referred to as stateless autoconfiguration, or SLAAC.

In the first step of creating the EUI-64 address, the value FFFE is inserted into the middle of the MAC address, thereby expanding the MAC address from 48 bits, which is 12 hexadecimal characters, to 64 bits, which is 16 hexadecimal characters. The conversion of the 48-bit MAC address into the 64-bit EUI address is illustrated in Figure 3.18 below:

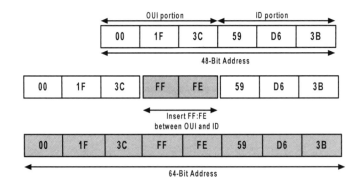

Figure 3.18—Creating the EUI-64 Address

The second step of EUI-64 addressing entails the setting of the seventh bit of the 64-bit address. This seventh bit is used to identify whether the MAC address is unique. If this bit is set to 1, this indicates that the MAC address is a globally managed MAC address—which means that the MAC address has been assigned by a vendor. If this bit is set to 0, this indicates that the MAC address is locally assigned—which means that the MAC address has been added by the administrator, for example. To clarify this statement further, as an example, MAC address 02:1F:3C:59:D6:3B would be considered a globally-assigned MAC address, while MAC address 00:1F:3C:59:D6:3B would be considered a local address. This is illustrated in Figure 3.19 below:

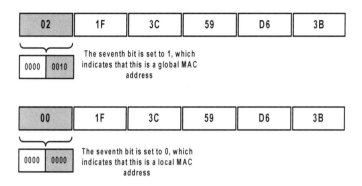

Figure 3.19—Determining Local and Global MAC Addresses

The following configuration example illustrates how to assign an IPv6 prefix to an interface and configure the router to create the interface ID automatically using EUI-64 addressing:

```
R2(config)#interface FastEthernet0/0
R2(config-if)#ipv6 address 3fff:1a2b:3c4d:5e6f::/64 eui-64
R2(config-if)#exit
```

Following this configuration, the show ipv6 interface command can be used to validate the IPv6 interface ID assigned to the FastEthernet0/0 interface, as illustrated below:

```
R2#show ipv6 interface FastEthernet0/0
FastEthernet0/0 is up, line protocol is up
  IPv6 is enabled, link-local address is FE80::213:19FF:FE86:A20
  Global unicast address(es):
    3FFF:1A2B:3C4D:5E6F:213:19FF:FE86:A20, subnet is
3FFF:1A2B:3C4D:5E6F::/64 [EUI]
  Joined group address(es):
    FF02::1
    FF02::2
    FF02::1:FF86:A20
  MTU is 1500 bytes
[Truncated Output]
```

To validate the creation of the EUI-64 address, you can verify the complete IPv6 address by also viewing the MAC address for the specified interface using the show interface command:

```
R2#show interface FastEthernet0/0
FastEthernet0/0 is up, line protocol is up
  Hardware is AmdFE, address is 0013.1986.0a20 (bia 0013.1986.0a20)
    Internet address is 10.0.1.1/30
```

From the output above, you can see that the EUI-64 address is indeed valid and is based on the MAC address of the interface. In addition, the address is global, as the seventh bit has been enabled (i.e., contains a non-zero value).

Finally, the [link-local] keyword is used to assign a Link-Local address to the interface. By default, it is important to remember that an IPv6 prefix does not have to be enabled on the interface in order for a Link-Local address to be created dynamically. Instead, if the ipv6 enable interface configuration command is issued under an interface, a Link-Local address is created automatically for that interface using EUI-64 addressing.

To configure a Link-Local address manually, you must assign an address within the FE80::/10 Link-Local address block. The following configuration example illustrates how to configure a Link-Local address on an interface:

```
R3(config)#interface FastEthernet0/0
R3(config-if)#ipv6 address fe80:1234:abcd:1::3 link-local
R3(config-if)#exit
```

Following this configuration, the show ipv6 interface [name] command can be used to validate the manual configuration of the Link-Local address, as shown in the output below:

```
R3#show ipv6 interface FastEthernet0/0
FastEthernet0/0 is up, line protocol is up
  IPv6 is enabled, link-local address is FE80:1234:ABCD:1::3
  Global unicast address(es):
    2001::1, subnet is 2001::/64
  Joined group address(es):
    FF02::1
    FF02::2
    FF02::1:FF00:1
    FF02::1:FF00:1111
  MTU is 1500 bytes
[Truncated Output]
```

NOTE: When configuring Link-Local addresses manually, if Cisco IOS software detects another host using one of its IPv6 addresses, an error message will be printed on the console and the command will be rejected. Be very careful when configuring Link-Local addressing manually.

SUBNETTING WITH IPV6

As you have already learned, IPv6 addresses are allocated to companies with a prefix. The host part of the address is always 64 bits and the standard prefix is usually 48 bits or /48. This leaves 16 bits free for network administrators to use for subnetting.

Because the same rules apply to both IPv4 and IPv6, as far as network addressing is concerned, you can have only one network per network segment. You can't break the address and use some host bits on one part of the network and some on another.

If you look at the addressing in the chart below, the situation should make more sense:

Global Routing Prefix	Subnet ID	Interface ID
48 bits or /48	16 bits (65,536 possible subnets)	64 bits

You need never concern yourself about running out of host bits per subnet because each subnet has over 18 quintillion hosts. It's unlikely that any organization would ever run out of subnets, but even if this were the case, another global routing prefix could easily be provided by the ISP.

Let's say, for example, that you are allocated the global routing prefix 0:123:abc/48. This address is occupying three sections of a full IPv6 address and each section or quartet is 16 bits, so you have 48 bits used so far. The host portion will require 64 bits, leaving you 16 bits for allocation as subnets.

You would simply start counting up in hex from zero (zero is legal) and keep going. For your hosts you would do the same, unless you wanted to reserve the first few addresses for servers on the segment, for example.

Let me use a simpler prefix for our example—2001:123:abc/48. The first subnet would be all zeros and, of course, the first host on each subnet would be all zeros, which is legal (since you don't reserve the all 0s and all 1s addresses in IPv6). You would represent the all zeros host by using the abbreviated format of ::. Here are the first few subnets and host addresses:

Global Prefix	Subnet	First Address
2001:123:abc	0000	::
2001:123:abc	0001	::
2001:123:abc	0002	::
2001:123:abc	0003	::
2001:123:abc	0004	::
2001:123:abc	0005	::
2001:123:abc	0006	::
2001:123:abc	0007	::
2001:123:abc	0008	::
2001:123:abc	0009	::
2001:123:abc	000A	::
2001:123:abc	000B	::
2001:123:abc	000C	::
2001:123:abc	000D	::
2001:123:abc	000E	::
2001:123:abc	000F	::
2001:123:abc	0010	::
2001:123:abc	0011	::
2001:123:abc	0012	::
2001:123:abc	0013	::
2001:123:abc	0014	::
2001:123:abc	0015	::
2001:123:abc	0016	::
2001:123:abc	0017	::

You have already noticed a difference from IPv4 addressing rules, I'm sure, in that you can use the all zeros subnet and the first subnet address is always all zeros. Looking at a simple network topology, you could allocate the subnets in the fashion below:

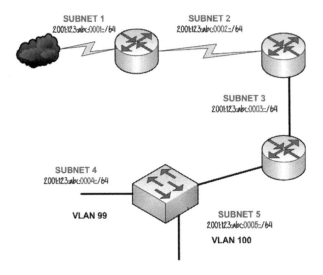

SUBNET 1
2001:123:abc:0001::/64

SUBNET 2
2001:123:abc:0002::/64

SUBNET 3
2001:123:abc:0003::/64

SUBNET 4
2001:123:abc:0004::/64

VLAN 99

SUBNET 5
2001:123:abc:0005::/64

VLAN 100

Figure 3.20—Allocating IPv6 Subnets

Can it really be that easy? If you recall from the IPv4 subnetting section, it can become somewhat of a nightmare to figure that out, as well as having to work out how many hosts and subnets and remembering to exclude certain addresses. IPv6 subnetting is far easier. You may not be allocated a 48-bit prefix, it could be /56 for a home network or smaller, but the principle would be the same.

You can also subnet off the bit boundary, but this would be most unusual and unfair of Cisco to expect you to go into that amount of detail in the short amount of time you have in the exam. Hopefully, the exam won't be a mean attempt to catch you out, but you never know. Just in case, here is an example of a /56 prefix length address:

2001:123:abc:8bbc:1221:cc32:8bcc:4231/56

The prefix is 56 bits, which translates to 14 hex digits (14 x 4 = 56), so you know that the prefix will take you to the middle of a quartet. This is where you could make a mistake in the exam. You must zero hex bits 3 and 4 in the quartet before the prefix breaks:

2001:123:abc:<u>8b00</u>:0000:0000:0000:0000/56

I've underlined the quartet where the bit boundary is broken. In haste and due to time pressures in the exam, you could well miss this important step. Remember that you would also abbreviate this address (the first host on the first subnet) to:

2001:123:abc:<u>8b00</u>::/56

If they do try to catch you out in the exam, it would probably be an attempt to have you remove the trailing zeros from the quartet before the bit boundary is broken:

2001:123:abc:<u>8b</u>::/56

The above abbreviation is illegal.

You can steal bits from the host portion to use for subnets, but there should never be a reason to and it would break the ability to use many of the features IPv6 was invented to utilize, including stateless autoconfiguration.

IPV6 COMPARED TO IPV4

A network engineer should have a very clear picture of the advantages IPv6 brings over IPv4. Looking at the enhancements of IPv6, we can summarize the following:

- IPv6 has an expanded address space, from 32 bits to 128 bits.
- IPv6 uses hexadecimal notation instead of dotted-decimal notation (as in IPv4).
- IPv6 addresses are globally unique due to the extended address space, eliminating the need for NAT.
- IPv6 has a fixed header length (40 bytes), allowing vendors to improve switching efficiency.
- IPv6 supports enhanced options (that offer new features) by placing extension headers between the IPv6 header and the Transport Layer header.
- IPv6 offers address autoconfiguration, providing for dynamic assignment of IP addresses even without a DHCP server.
- IPv6 offers support for labeling traffic flows.
- IPv6 has security capabilities built in, including authentication and privacy via IPSec.
- IPv6 offers MTU path discovery before sending packets to a destination, eliminating the need for fragmentation.
- IPv6 supports site multihoming.
- IPv6 uses the ND (Neighbor Discovery) protocol instead of ARP.
- IPv6 uses AAAA DNS records instead of A records (as in IPv4).
- IPv6 uses Site-Local addressing instead of RFC 1918 (as in IPv4).
- IPv4 and IPv6 use different routing protocols.
- IPv6 provides for Anycast addressing.

Configuring, Verifying, and Troubleshooting IPv6 Addressing

We have already covered the available options to configure IPv6 addressing on an interface. You can manually add your own addresses or just rely on address autoconfiguration to apply one.

As you know, IPv6 interfaces that are directly connected do not need to be in the same subnet in order to communicate, although they may well be in order to comply with whatever network design and addressing policy you have in place where you work.

Troubleshooting Tools for IPv6 Addressing

While troubleshooting IPv6 in a network can vary greatly depending on the routing protocol and transport mechanisms in use, this section is dedicated only to troubleshooting IPv6 addressing. Beyond checking the interface for typos (which is a common reason for IPv6 addressing issues) you should be aware of the following commands in Table 3.12 below that will assist you with troubleshooting the deployment of IPv6 addresses. Please do try them out on any IPv6 lab you complete.

Table 3.12—IPv6 Commands and Actions

Keyword	Description
Router#clear ipv6 route *	Deletes all IPv6 routes from the routing table.
Router#clear ipv6 route 2001:ab8:c1:1::/64	Deletes a specific IPv6 route from the routing table.
Router#clear ipv6 traffic	Resets IPv6 traffic counters.
Router#debug ipv6 packet	Displays debug messages for IPv6 packets.
Router#debug ipv6 routing	Displays debug messages for IPv6 routing table updates and route cache updates.
Router#show ipv6 interface	Displays the status of IPv6 interfaces for IPv6.
Router#show ipv6 interface brief	Displays a summary of IPv6 interfaces.
Router#show ipv6 neighbors	Displays IPv6 neighbor information.
Router#show ipv6 route	Displays the IPv6 routing table.
Router#show ipv6 route summary	Displays a summary of the IPv6 routing table.
Router#show ipv6 static	Displays static IPv6 routes in the routing table.
Router#show ipv6 static 2001:ab8:1:0/16	Displays specific static route information.
Router#show ipv6 static interface serial0/0	Displays static route information with the specified interface as the outgoing interface
Router#show ipv6 static detail	Displays detailed entry for IPv6 static routes
Router#show ipv6 traffic	Displays IPv6 traffic statistics

Most of the commands above are self-explanatory, but some of them may look new to you. It's very important to try these commands out when you do IPv6 labs and note the output. Please also make your own labs up after doing the ones in this book a few times. It's the only way to understand the technology and available outputs. It's also important to note that some of the debug commands and clearing the routes can cause a spike in traffic or the CPU, so you may need to seek permission for a planned outage before issuing them.

Let's do a deeper dive into two of the commands that can help you solve IPv6 issues.

debug ipv6 packet

If you don't have the ability to physically attend the site and perform a packet capture of traffic with dedicated software, you may benefit from the `debug ipv6 packet` command. This command will display all packets received, generated, and forwarded to the device. Needless to say, the amount of data can become overwhelming, so it is strongly encouraged that you specify an ACL at the end of this command so that you are only viewing the packets you intend to review, instead of all IPv6 packets. If you fail to specify an ACL, it is likely you will cause system performance issues, but also you may have too much data to try to analyze.

The following example shows output for the `debug ipv6 packet` command. You can read "Cisco IOS IPv6 Command Reference" for detailed information about the various fields and outputs.

```
*Mar  1 00:03:11.535: IPV6: source :: (FastEthernet0/0)
*Mar  1 00:03:11.535:      dest FF02::1:FFED:0
*Mar  1 00:03:11.535:      traffic class 224, flow 0x0, len 64+14, prot
58, hops 255, forward to ulp
*Mar  1 00:03:12.483: IPV6: source FE80::C001:6FF:FEED:0
(FastEthernet0/0)
*Mar  1 00:03:12.483:      dest FF02::1
*Mar  1 00:03:12.483:      traffic class 224, flow 0x0, len 72+14, prot
58, hops 255, forward to ulp
*Mar  1 00:03:12.507: IPV6: source FE80::C001:6FF:FEED:0
(FastEthernet0/0)
*Mar  1 00:03:12.507:      dest FF02::1
*Mar  1 00:03:12.507:      traffic class 224, flow 0x0, len 72+14, prot
58, hops 255, forward to ulp
```

show ipv6 traffic

The `show ipv6 traffic` command will display important statistics on IPv6 that will help with troubleshooting. For example, let's say that you are experiencing connectivity issues to and from a specific interface on your router. You run the `show ipv6 traffic` command and see the display below. What stands out to you that possibly points to the root cause of the issue?

```
hostname#show ipv6 traffic
IPv6 statistics:
  Rcvd: 545 total, 545 local destination
       0 source-routed, 0 truncated
       0 format errors, 0 hop count exceeded
       0 bad header, 0 unknown option, 0 bad source
       0 unknown protocol, 0 not a router
       218 fragments, 109 total reassembled
       0 reassembly timeouts, 0 reassembly failures
  Sent: 255 generated, 0 forwarded
       1 fragmented into 2 fragments, 0 failed
       0 encapsulation failed, 200 no route, 0 too big
  Mcast: 168 received, 70 sent
  ICMP statistics:
```

```
Rcvd: 116 input, 0 checksum errors, 0 too short
    0 unknown info type, 0 unknown error type
    unreach: 0 routing, 0 admin, 0 neighbor, 0 address, 0 port
    parameter: 0 error, 0 header, 0 option
    0 hopcount expired, 0 reassembly timeout,0 too big
    0 echo request, 0 echo reply
    0 group query, 0 group report, 0 group reduce
    0 router solicit, 60 router advert, 0 redirects
    31 neighbor solicit, 25 neighbor advert
Sent: 85 output, 0 rate-limited
    unreach: 0 routing, 0 admin, 0 neighbor, 0 address, 0 port
    parameter: 0 error, 0 header, 0 option
    0 hopcount expired, 0 reassembly timeout,0 too big
    0 echo request, 0 echo reply
    0 group query, 0 group report, 0 group reduce
    0 router solicit, 18 router advert, 0 redirects
    33 neighbor solicit, 34 neighbor advert
UDP statistics:
  Rcvd: 109 input, 0 checksum errors, 0 length errors
      0 no port, 0 dropped
  Sent: 37 output
TCP statistics:
  Rcvd: 85 input, 0 checksum errors
  Sent: 103 output, 0 retransmitted
```

Notice that under the IPv6 sent statistics there are 255 generated and 200 listed with "no route." This command nicely summarizes IPv6-specific information that will help with any issue you are troubleshooting on the network.

Now please take the day 3 exam at **https://www.in60days.com/free/ccnain60days/**

DAY 3 LAB

IPv6 Ping

Topology

2001:aaaa:bbbb:cccc::/64

Purpose

Learn how to configure IPv6 addresses and ping across the interface.

Walkthrough

1. Enable IPv6 routing on both sides. Here is how to enable it on R1.

    ```
    R1(config)#ipv6 unicast-routing
    ```

2. Add the below IPv6 address to F0/0 on R1. For R2 add the :2 address. Make sure you no shut the interfaces.

    ```
    R1(config)#int f0/0
    R1(config-if)#ipv6 address 2001:aaaa:bbbb:cccc::1/64
    R1(config-if)#no shut
    ```

3. Ping from R2 to R1 or vice versa.

    ```
    R2#ping 2001:aaaa:bbbb:cccc::1

    Type escape sequence to abort.
    Sending 5, 100-byte ICMP Echos to 2001:AAAA:BBBB:CCCC::1, timeout is 2
    seconds:
    !!!!!
    Success rate is 100 percent (5/5), round-trip min/avg/max = 0/0/0 ms
    ```

4. Try out the below commands and note the various outputs. Note how the MAC address is used to create the link local address. The show ipv6 interface brief command will reveal the MAC address to you.

    ```
    R1#show ipv6 interface brief
    R1#show ipv6 interface f0/0
    R1#show ip interface brief
    ```

IPv6 Concepts Lab

Test the IPv6 concepts and commands detailed in this module on a pair of Cisco routers that are directly connected:

- Enable IPv6 Global Unicast routing on both routers
- Manually configure an IPv6 address on each of the connected interfaces. For example:
  - 2001:100::1/64 on R1
  - 2001:100::2/64 on R2
- Verify the configuration using the `show ipv6 interface` and `show ipv6 interface prefix` commands
- Test direct ping connectivity
- Repeat the test using IPv6 stateless autoconfiguration (`ipv6 address autoconfig default`)
- Repeat the test using EUI-64 addresses (IPv6 address 2001::/64 EUI-64)
- Hard code an interface Link-Local address: IPv6 address fe80:1234:abcd:1::3 Link-Local
- Verify the IPv6 routing table

Review

DAY 4 TASKS

- Read today's instructions (below)
- Review days 1-3 lesson notes
- Repeat the labs in days 1-3
- Complete the challenge labs
- Read the ICND1 cram guide
- Take today's exam at **https://www.in60days.com/free/ccnain60days/**
- Spend 15 minutes on subnetting.org

Today is the first of many review days you will have during the 60-day program. It's a chance to reread the theory, do some hands on labs again and consolidate your learning. Don't put yourself under pressure to nail the subjects the first, second or third time around. We will cover all of the subjects many times over in the form of review days, the cram guide, labs and exams and free choice review days.

I will set you tasks during the first few review days but then I will hand this task over to you because only you will know what your weak areas are. At any time you see fit, change or adjust the set tasks. If you are already a subnetting master then swap that task for a weak area such as memorizing administrative distances (for example).

Challenge 1

What are the compressed addresses for the below?

```
0000:0000:0000:0000:01a2b:000c:f123:456
FEC0:0004:AB10:00CD:1234:0000:0000:6789
3FFF:0c00:0000:1010:1A2B:0000:0000:DE0F
2001:0000:0000:1234:0000:5678:af23:00d5
```

Challenge 2

Write out subnets 192.168.16.0/24 through to 192.168.31.0/24. Now write out the supernet address you would advertise out if you owned all these networks.

Challenge 3

Complete this short IP addressing lab. We don't provide the solutions to challenge labs because the answers are in the earlier version of the lab you have already completed.

10.0.0.0/28

Instructions

Choose whichever interfaces you wish (Ethernet or Serial but you need a clockrate on the DCE end). Ensure you have the correct cable types for the devices.

1. Add the IP addresses to the interfaces
2. Apply the appropriate subnet masks
3. Add a clock rate to the DCE end if you are using a serial connection
4. No shut the interfaces with the `no shut` command if requried
5. Ping from Router A to Router B

Challenge 1—Solution

Complete IPv6 Address Representation

0000:0000:0000:0000:01a2b:000c:f123:456
FEC0:0004:AB10:00CD:1234:0000:0000:6789
3FFF:0c00:0000:1010:1A2B:0000:0000:DE0F
2001:0000:0000:1234:0000:5678:af23:00d5

Compressed IPv6 Address Representation

::1a2b:c:f123:456
FEC0:4:AB10:CD:1234::6789
3FFF:c00:0:1010:1A2B::DE0F
2001::1234:0:5678:af23:d5

Challenge 2—Solution

Write out the subnets in binary. You will see that for 20 places, all binary bits match so you advertise a /20 mask.

192.168.16.0 / 20

Switching Concepts

DAY 5 TASKS

- Read today's lesson notes (below)
- Review days 1-3 lesson notes
- Complete today's lab
- Take today's exam
- Read the ICND1 cram guide
- Spend 15 minutes on the subnetting.org website

The bread-and-butter work of any Cisco engineer is installing, configuring, and troubleshooting switches. Strangely enough, this is the weakest area for many of those engineers. Perhaps some people rely on the switches' plug-and-play capabilities, or they try to work through issues as they crop up. This "fly by the seat of your pants" mentality backfires for many engineers when there is a switching-related issue.

We briefly cover some trunking concepts today but will go into more detail in tomorrows lesson.

Today you will learn about the following:

- Switching basics
- Switching concepts
- Initial switch configuration
- VLANs
- Switch troubleshooting
- Troubleshooting VLANs
- Voice and data ports

This module maps to the following CCNA syllabus requirements:

- 2.4 Configure, verify, and troubleshoot VLANs (normal range) spanning multiple switches
- 2.4.a Access ports (data and voice)
- 2.4.b Default VLAN
- 1.7.c Nondefault native VLAN [ICND2]

SWITCHING BASICS

Carrier Sense, Multiple Access with Collision Detection

CSMA/CD can be broken down as follows. Carrier sense means that the wire is listened to in order to determine whether there is a signal passing along it. A frame cannot be transmitted if the wire is in use. Multiple access simply means that more than one device is using the cables on the segment. Finally, collision detection means that the protocol is running an algorithm to determine whether the frames on the wire have become damaged due to hitting another frame. In Figure 5.1 below, you can see the switch port listening to the wire.

Figure 5.1—Port Listening to the Wire

If there is a collision on the wire, the detecting device(s) send a jamming signal informing other network devices that a collision has occurred, so they should not attempt to send data onto the wire. Then, the algorithm runs and generates a random interval to wait before retransmitting. It must still wait for the wire to be clear before sending a frame. Figure 5.2 illustrates the process:

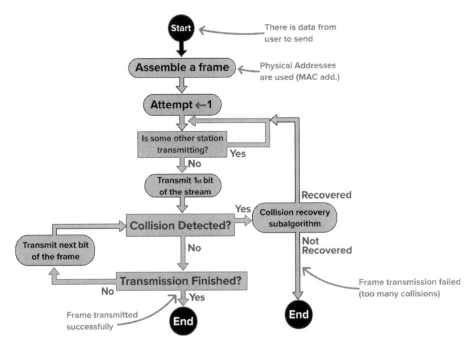

Figure 5.2—CSMA/CD Process

FARAI SAYS—"Please note that modern Ethernet networks using switches with full-duplex connections no longer utilize CSMA/CD. It is still supported, but only for backward compatibility."

Collision and Broadcast Domains

One of the main drawbacks of network hubs is that when there is a collision on the wire, the damaged frame is sent to all connected devices. One of the advantages of modern switches is that each port on the switch is considered to be a collision domain. In the event of a collision (not possible with full duplex) the damaged frame does not pass the interface. Figure 5.3 shows that a switch has been added to a small network using two hubs. The switch breaks the network into two collision domains.

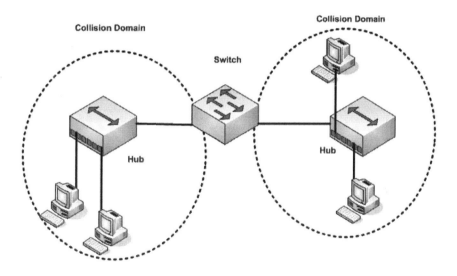

Figure 5.3—A Switch Creates Two Collision Domains

Cisco often try to catch you out in the exam by asking whether switches reduce the amount of collision domains. In haste, you might be tempted to say they do but the opposite is actually the case, and this is a good thing. Switches increase the number of collision domains. It's also worth noting that hubs can only work at half duplex due to the limitations of the technology. In Figure 5.4 below, four PCs are connected to a switch, creating four collision domains. Each PC has full use of 100Mbps bandwidth operating in full duplex.

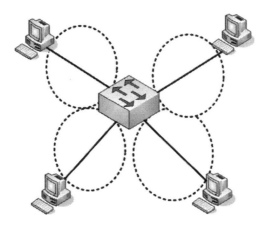

Figure 5.4—Four Collision Domains

Switches (here we are talking about Layer 2 switches) do not separate broadcast domains, routers do. If a switch receives a frame with a broadcast destination address, then it must forward it out of all ports, apart from the port the frame was received on. A router is required to separate broadcast domains. Figure 5.5 represents a small network using switches/bridges and a router to represent how collision domains are separated.

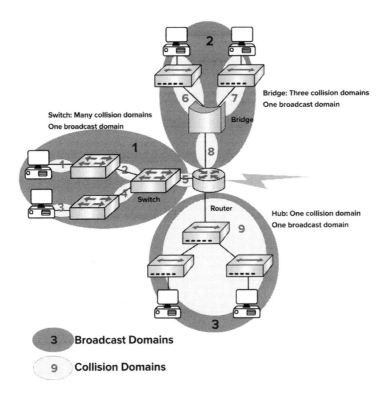

Figure 5.5—Broadcast and Collision Domains

Auto-negotiation

You have already seen that issues can arise when you connect devices with different speeds and duplex settings. You can often upgrade one section of the network but have legacy equipment on another due to budget constraints. This can lead to duplex and speed mismatches, leading to errors and dropped frames. We will cover switch troubleshooting in more detail later.

The IEEE offer a solution to this issue with auto-negotiation, which allows devices to agree on the speed and duplex settings before passing traffic. The speed is set to the speed of the slower device. In the output below, the speed can be set manually to 10Mbps or 100Mbps, or set to auto-negotiate:

```
Switch(config)#int f1/0/1
Switch(config-if)#speed ?
  10    Force 10 Mbps operation
  100   Force 100 Mbps operation
  auto  Enable AUTO speed configuration
```

You can check the settings with the `show interface x` command:

```
Switch#show int f1/0/1
FastEthernet1/0/1 is down, line protocol is down (notconnect)
  Hardware is FastEthernet, address is 001e.13da.c003 (bia 001e.13da.
c003)
  MTU 1600 bytes, BW 10000 Kbit, DLY 1000 usec,
     reliability 255/255, txload 1/255, rxload 1/255
  Encapsulation ARPA, Loopback not set
  Keepalive set (10 sec)
  Auto-duplex, Auto-speed, media type is 10/100BaseTX
```

Bear in mind, though, that auto-negotiation may cause issues. This is why many production networks insist on configuring ports directly as 100/full or 1000/full for GigabitEthernet. According to Cisco:

> *Auto-negotiation issues can result from non-conforming implementation, hardware incapabilities, or software defects. When NICs or vendor switches do not conform exactly to the IEEE specification 802.3u, problems can result. Hardware incompatibility and other issues can also exist as a result of vendor-specific advanced features, such as auto-polarity or cable integrity, which are not described in IEEE 802.3u for 10/100 Mbps auto-negotiation (Cisco.com).*

Switching Frames

Switches exist to switch frames (i.e., transport a frame from an incoming interface to the correct outgoing interface). Broadcast frames are switched out of all interfaces except the interface on which they were received (referred to as frame flooding), as are frames with an unknown destination (not in the MAC table). In order to achieve this function, a switch performs three actions:

- Forwarding (switching) or filtering (dropping) frames based on destination MAC addresses
- Learning MAC addresses from incoming frames
- Using STP to prevent Layer 2 loops (STP will be covered in ICND2 Day 31)

In Figure 5.6 below, the switch filters the frame from leaving interface F0/2 and correctly forwards it out of F0/3 when sourcing from Host A (F0/1) destined for Host C:

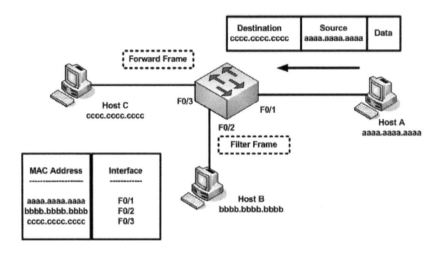

Figure 5.6—Frame Filtering

If the destination address was not in the MAC address table, then the switch would have flooded the frame out of all interfaces, except the interface it was received on. The switch will also store MAC addresses for devices connected to another switch; however, the interface name will remain the same, so multiple MAC addresses will be listed with the same exit interface. This is a useful way to find a device on a network you are not familiar with. Figure 5.7 below illustrates this concept:

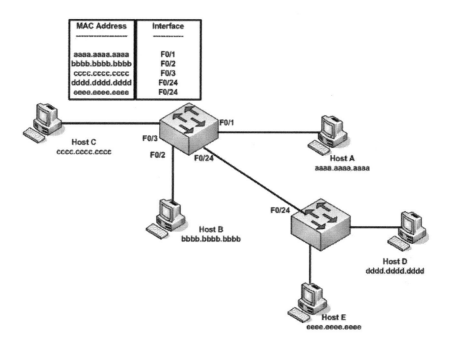

Figure 5.7—Multiple MAC Addresses on the Same Interface

Any delay in passing traffic is known as latency. Cisco switches offer three ways to switch the traffic, depending upon how thoroughly you want the frame to be checked before it is passed on. The more checking performed, the more latency you will introduce to the switch. The three switching modes to choose from are:

- Cut-through
- Store-and-forward (default on modern switches)
- Fragment-free

Cut-through

Cut-through switching is the fastest switching method, meaning it has the lowest latency. The incoming frame is read up to the destination MAC address. Once it reaches the destination MAC address, the switch then checks its CAM table for the correct port to forward the frame out of and sends it on its way. There is no error checking, so this method gives you the lowest latency. The price, however, is that the switch will forward any frames containing errors.

The process of switching modes can best be described by using a metaphor. You are the bouncer at a nightclub and are asked to make sure that everyone who enters has a picture ID—you are not asked to make sure the picture matches the person, only that the ID has a picture. With this method of checking, people are surely going to move quickly to enter the establishment. This is how cut-through switching works.

Store-and-forward

Here, the switch reads the entire frame and copies it into its buffers. A cyclic redundancy check (CRC) takes place to check the frame for any errors. If errors are found, the frame is dropped. Otherwise, the switching table is examined and the frame forwarded. Store-and-forward ensures that the frame is at least 64 bytes but no larger than 1518 bytes. If the frame is smaller than 64 bytes or larger than 1518 bytes, then the switch will discard the frame.

Now imagine that once again you are the bouncer at a nightclub, only this time you have to make sure that the picture matches the person, and you must write down the name and address of everyone before they can enter. Checking IDs this way causes a great deal of delay, and this is how the store-and-forward method of switching works.

Store-and-forward switching has the highest latency of all the switching methods and is the default setting on the 2900 series switches.

Fragment-free (Modified Cut-through/Runt-free)

Since cut-through switching doesn't check for errors and store-and-forward takes too long, we need a method that is both quick and reliable. Using the example of the nightclub bouncer, imagine you are asked to make sure that everyone has an ID and that the picture matches the person. With this method you have made sure everyone is who they say they are, but you do not have to take down all of their information. In switching, this is accomplished by using the fragment-free method of switching, which is the default configuration on lower-level Cisco switches.

Fragment-free switching is a modified variety of cut-through switching. The first 64 bytes of a frame are examined for any errors, and if none are detected, it will pass it on. The reasoning behind this method is that any errors are most likely to be found in the first 64 bytes of a frame.

As mentioned in the previous section, the minimum size of an Ethernet frame is 64 bytes; anything less than 64 bytes is called a "runt" frame. Since every frame must be at least 64 bytes before forwarding, this will eliminate the runts, and that is why this method is also known as "runt-free" switching.

SWITCHING CONCEPTS

The Need for Switches

Before switches were invented, every device on a network would receive data from every other device. Every time a frame was detected on the wire, the PC would have to stop for a moment and check the header to see whether it was the intended recipient. Imagine hundreds of frames going out on the network every minute. Every device would soon grind to a halt. Figure 5.8 below shows all the devices on the network; note that they all have to share the same bandwidth because they are connected by hubs, which only forward frames.

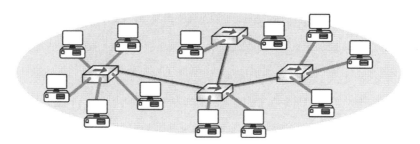

Figure 5.8—Every Device Listens to Every Other Device

The Problem with Hubs

I mentioned before that hubs are simply multi port repeaters (see Figure 5.9). They take the incoming signal, clean it up, and then send it out of every port with a wire connected. They also create one huge collision domain.

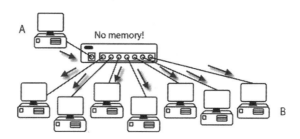

Figure 5.9—Hubs Send the Frame Out of Every Port

Hubs are dumb devices. They have no way of storing MAC addresses, so each time Device A sends a frame to Device B, it is repeated out of every port. Switches, on the other hand, contain a memory chip known as an application-specific integrated circuit (ASIC), which builds a table listing which device is plugged into which port (see Figure 5.10). This table is held in Content Addressable Memory (CAM).

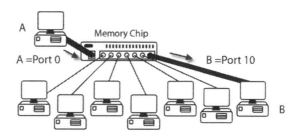

Figure 5.10—Switches Build a Table of MAC Addresses

When first booted, a switch has no addresses stored in its CAM table (Cisco exams also refer to this as the MAC address table.) Once frames start to pass, the table builds. If no frames pass through the port for a specified period of time, then the entry ages out. In the following output, no frames have been sent through the switch yet:

```
Switch#show mac-address-table
          Mac Address Table
-------------------------------------------
Vlan    Mac Address     Type        Ports
----    -----------     --------    -----
Switch#
```

There is no entry in the table, but when you ping from one router to another (both attached to the switch), the table entry is added.

```
Router#ping 192.168.1.2
Type escape sequence to abort.
Sending 5, 100-byte ICMP Echos to 192.168.1.2, timeout is 2 seconds:
.!!!!
Success rate is 80 percent (4/5), round-trip min/avg/max = 62/62/63 ms
Switch#show mac-address-table
          Mac Address Table
-------------------------------------------
Vlan    Mac Address     Type        Ports
----    -----------     --------    -----
   1    0001.c74a.0a01  DYNAMIC     Fa0/1
   1    0060.5c55.da01  DYNAMIC     Fa0/2
```

This entry means that any frames destined for the MAC addresses attached to FastEthernet ports 0/1 or 0/2 on the switch will be sent straight out of the relevant port. Any other frames would mean the switch would have to perform a one-off broadcast (frame flooding) to see whether the destination devices were attached. You can see this with the period in the first of five pings above. The first ping times out whilst waiting for the switch to broadcast and receive a response from the destination router (80% success rate).

Frame flooding is illustrated in Figure 5.11 below.

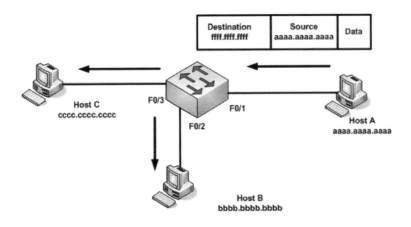

Figure 5.11—Broadcast Frames Will Be Sent out of All Interfaces

The `show mac-address-table` command is a very important one, so be sure to remember this both for the exam and for the real world. You should already be aware of what a MAC address actually is, but as a brief refresher—MAC addresses are assigned to all devices to allow communication to take place at the Data Link Layer. You will see them assigned by vendors of Ethernet NICs, Ethernet interfaces on routers, and wireless devices. Here is the MAC address assigned to the Ethernet card on my laptop:

```
Ethernet adapter Local Area Connection:

        Connection-specific DNS Suffix  . : BigPond
        Description . . . . . . . . . . . : Realtek RTL8168C(P)
igabit Ethernet NIC
        Physical Address. . . . . . . . . : 00-1E-EC-54-85-17
        Dhcp Enabled. . . . . . . . . . . :
        Autoconfiguration Enabled . . . . : Yes
        IP Address. . . . . . . . . . . . : 10.0.0.11
        Subnet Mask . . . . . . . . . . . : 255.255.255.0
        Default Gateway . . . . . . . . . : 10.0.0.138
```

Vendors are assigned an address called an Organizationally Unique Identifier (OUI), which forms the first half of the MAC address. They are then free to create the second half of the address according to their own numbering system. A MAC address is 48 binary bits, so my address above consists of:

OUI	Vendor's Number
24 binary bits	24 binary bits
6 hexadecimal digits	6 hexadecimal digits
00 1E EC	54 85 17

Ethernet Frames

Ethernet has four different frame types available:

- Ethernet 802.3
- Ethernet II
- Ethernet 802.2 SAP
- Ethernet 802.2 SNAP

The first two Ethernet standards deal with the framing used for communication between network cards. They cannot identify the upper-layer protocols, which is where the 802.2 frames come in. You need only concern yourself with the 802.3 frame, which is shown below:

Preamble	SFD	Destination Address	Source Address	Length	Data	FCS

Figure 5.12—Ethernet 802.3 Frame

The IEEE 802.3 Ethernet frame consists of specific fields that have been determined by the IEEE committee:

- Preamble—synchronizes and alerts the network card for the incoming data
- Start-of-frame delimiter (SFD)—indicates the start of the frame
- Destination address—the destination MAC address (can be Unicast, Broadcast, or Multicast)
- Source address—the MAC address of the sending host
- Length—defines the length of the Data field in the frame
- Data—the payload in the frame (this is the data being transferred)
- Frame-check sequence (FCS)—provides a cyclic redundancy check (CRC) on all data in the frame

INITIAL SWITCH CONFIGURATION

You will connect to a new switch via the console port, the same as with any new router, because in order to connect via Telnet or SSH (more on these later), you will need to have at least a line or two of configuration on the switch already. Many of the initial configuration commands for the switch are the same for an initial router configuration.

It's well worth issuing a show version command (see the output below) on any device you connect to for the first time. You will also be expected to know in the exam which show command provides which information.

The show version command provides a lot of useful information, including:

- Switch uptime
- Model
- IOS release
- Reason for last reload
- Interfaces and type
- Memory installed
- Base MAC address

```
Switch>en
Switch#show version
Cisco IOS Software, C2960 Software (C2960-LANBASE-M), Version 12.2(25)FX,
RELEASE SOFTWARE (fc1)
Copyright (c) 1986-2005 by Cisco Systems, Inc.
Compiled Wed 12-Oct-05 22:05 by pt_team

ROM: C2960 Boot Loader (C2960-HBOOT-M) Version 12.2(25r)FX, RELEASE
SOFTWARE (fc4)

System returned to ROM by power-on
```

```
Cisco WS-C2960-24TT (RC32300) processor (revision C0) with 21039K bytes
of memory.

24 FastEthernet/IEEE 802.3 interface(s)
2 GigabitEthernet/IEEE 802.3 interface(s)

63488K bytes of flash-simulated non-volatile configuration memory.
Base Ethernet MAC Address       : 0090.2148.1456
Motherboard assembly number     : 73-9832-06
Power supply part number        : 341-0097-02
Motherboard serial number       : FOC103248MJ
Power supply serial number      : DCA102133JA
Model revision number           : B0
Motherboard revision number     : C0
Model number                    : WS-C2960-24TT
System serial number            : FOC1033Z1EY
Top Assembly Part Number        : 800-26671-02
Top Assembly Revision Number    : B0
Version ID                      : V02
CLEI Code Number                : COM3K00BRA
Hardware Board Revision Number  : 0x01

Switch  Ports  Model          SW Version    SW Image
------  -----  -----          ----------    ----------------
*   1   26     WS-C2960-24TT  12.2          C2960-LANBASE-M

Configuration register is 0xF
```

I know we haven't covered VLANs yet, but for now, consider a VLAN a logical Local Area Network where devices could be anywhere on the network physically but, as far as they are concerned, they are all directly connected to the same switch. In the configuration below, by default, all ports on the switch are left in VLAN 1:

```
Switch#show vlan
VLAN Name            Status   Ports
---- --------        ------   ------------------------------
1    default         active   Fa0/1, Fa0/2, Fa0/3, Fa0/4,
                              Fa0/5, Fa0/6, Fa0/7, Fa0/8,
                              Fa0/9, Fa0/10, Fa0/11, Fa0/12,
                              Fa0/13, Fa0/14, Fa0/15, Fa0/16,
                              Fa0/17, Fa0/18, Fa0/19, Fa0/20,
                              Fa0/21, Fa0/22, Fa0/23, Fa0/24,
```

If you want to add an IP address to the switch in order to connect to it over the network (known as a management address), you simply add an IP address to the VLAN; in this instance, it will be VLAN1:

```
Switch#conf t
Enter configuration commands, one per line.  End with CNTL/Z.
Switch(config)#interface vlan1
Switch(config-if)#ip add 192.168.1.3 255.255.255.0
Switch(config-if)#   ← hold down Ctrl+Z keys now
```

```
Switch#show interface vlan1
Vlan1 is administratively down, line protocol is down
  Hardware is CPU Interface, address is 0010.1127.2388 (bia
0010.1127.2388)
  Internet address is 192.168.1.3/24
```

VLAN1 is shut down by default so you would have to issue a no shut command to open it. You should also tell the switch where to send all IP traffic because a Layer 2 switch has no ability to build a routing table; this is illustrated in the output below:

```
Switch#conf t
Enter configuration commands, one per line.  End with CNTL/Z.
Switch(config)#ip default-gateway 192.168.1.1
Switch(config)#
```

If you have more than one switch on your network, you will want to change the default hostname of your switch so it can be identified more easily when remotely connected (see configuration line below). Imagine trying to troubleshoot five switches from a remote Telnet connection when they are all named "Switch."

```
Switch(config)#hostname Switch1
```

If you would like to Telnet (or SSH) to the switch over the network, you will need to enable this protocol as well. Remote access to the switch is disabled by default:

```
Switch1#conf t
Enter configuration commands, one per line.  End with CNTL/Z.
Switch1(config)#line vty 0 15
Switch1(config-line)#password cisco
Switch1(config-line)#login
```

Please add the commands above to a switch, and then connect to it from another device (on the same subnet) to test your configuration. This is a fundamental CCNA topic.

VTYs are virtual ports on a router or switch used for Telnet or secure Telnet (SSH) access. They are closed until you configure an authentication method for VTY lines (the simplest way is to add a password to them and the login command). You can often see ports 0 to 4, inclusive, or 0 to 15. One way to learn how many you have available is to type a question mark after the number zero, or use the show line command, as illustrated in the output below:

```
Router(config)#line vty 0 ?
  <1-15>  Last Line number
Router#show line
   Tty Typ  Tx/Rx      A Modem  Roty AccO AccI   Uses  Noise  Overruns Int
*   0 CTY              -    -     -    -    -      0      0     0/0
    1 AUX 9600/9600    -    -     -    -    -      0      0     0/0        *
    2 VTY              -    -     -    -    -      2      0     0/0
    3 VTY              -    -     -    -    -      0      0     0/0
    4 VTY              -    -     -    -    -      0      0     0/0
    5 VTY              -    -     -    -    -      0      0     0/0
    6 VTY              -    -     -    -    -      0      0     0/0
```

CTY is the console line, whilst VTY lines are for Telnet connections and AUX is the auxiliary port.

For a more secure access method, you can permit only SSH connections into the switch, which means the traffic will be encrypted. You will need a security image on your switch in order for this to work, as shown in the output below:

```
Switch1(config-line)#transport input ssh
```

Now, Telnet traffic will not be permitted into the VTY ports.

Please configure all of these commands on a switch. Just reading them will not help you recall them come exam day!

VIRTUAL LOCAL AREA NETWORKS (VLANS)

As you have already seen, a switch breaks a collision domain. Taken a step further, a router breaks a Broadcast Domain, which means a network would look something like the following figure:

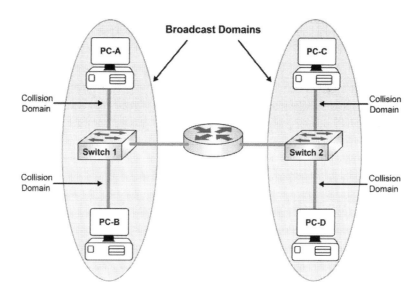

Figure 5.13—Routers Separate Broadcast Domains

Before we continue, let's discuss what a LAN really is. A LAN is essentially a Broadcast Domain. In the network shown in Figure 5.13, if PC-A sends a broadcast packet, it will be received by PC-B but not by PC-C or PC-D. This is because the router breaks the Broadcast Domain. Now you can use virtual LANs (VLANs) to put switch ports into different Broadcast Domains, as illustrated in the figure below:

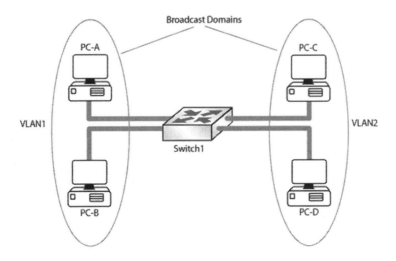

Figure 5.14—Broadcast Domains with VLAN

In Figure 5.14, the Layer 2 network has been divided into two Broadcast Domains using VLANs. Now a broadcast sent by PC-A will be received by PC-B but not by PC-C and PC-D. Without VLANs PC-C and PC-D would have received the broadcasts sent by PC-A. The following are some advantages of VLANs:

- Containing broadcasts within a smaller group of devices will make the network faster.
- Saves resources on devices because they process fewer broadcasts.
- Added security by keeping devices in a certain group (or function) in a separate Broadcast Domain. A group, as implied here, can mean department, security level, etc. For example, devices belonging to a development or testing lab should be kept separate from the production devices.
- Flexibility in expanding a network across a geographical location of any size. For example, it does not matter where in the building a PC is. It thinks it is on the same segment of the network as any other PC configured to be in the same VLAN. In Figure 5.15 below, all hosts in VLAN 1 can talk to each other, even though they are on different floors. The VLAN is transparent or invisible to them.

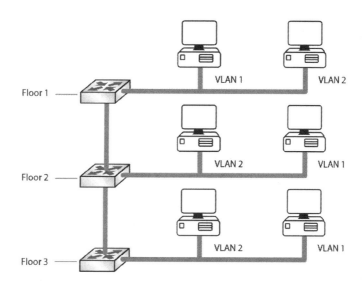

Figure 5.15—VLANs Remove the Physical Boundaries from a LAN

VLAN Marking

Although vendors used individual approaches to create VLANs, a multi-vendor VLAN must be carefully handled to deal with interoperability issues. For example, Cisco developed the ISL standard that operates by adding a new 26-byte header, plus a new 4-byte trailer, encapsulating the original frame as illustrated in Figure 5.16 below. To solve incompatibility problems, IEEE developed 802.1Q, a vendor-independent method to create interoperable VLANs.

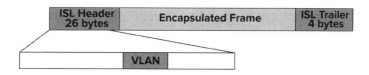

Figure 5.16—ISL Marking Method

802.1Q is often referred to as frame tagging because it inserts a 32-bit header, called a "tag," into the original frame, after the Source Address field, without modifying other fields. The next 2 bytes after the Source Address field hold a registered Ethernet type value of 0x8100, which implies the frame contains an 802.1Q header. The next 3 bits represent the 802.1P User Priority field and are used as Class of Service (CoS) bits in Quality of Service (QoS) techniques. The next subfield is a 1-bit Canonical Format Indicator, followed by the VLAN ID (12 bits). This gives us a total of 4096 VLANs when using 802.1Q.

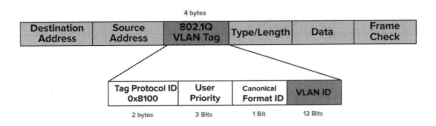

Figure 5.17—802.1Q Marking Method

A port that carries data from multiple VLANs is called a trunk. It can use either the ISL or the 802.1Q protocols. A special concept in the 802.1Q world is "native VLAN." This is a particular type of VLAN in which frames are not tagged. The native VLAN's purpose is to allow a switch to use 802.1Q trunking (multiple VLANs on a single link) on an interface, but if the other device does not support trunking, the traffic for the native VLAN can still be sent over the link. If a switch receives any untagged traffic over a trunk link, it will assume it is destined for the native VLAN. Cisco uses VLAN 1 as the default native VLAN.

VLAN Membership

There are two common ways to associate ports with VLANs—statically or dynamically.

With static VLAN assignment or configuration, the ports on the switch are configured by the network administrator to be in different VLANs, and the relevant device is then connected to the port. If the user needs to move to another part of the building, this will require the administrator to change the configuration on the switch. All switch ports belong to VLAN 1 by default.

Dynamic VLAN assignment allows devices to join a specific VLAN based on the MAC address of the device. This gives the administrator the flexibility to allow users to connect to any switch or move around the building without having to change the configuration on the switch. This is achieved using a VLAN Management Policy Server (VMPS).

FARAI SAYS—"Ports are assigned to VLANs and devices are connected to ports."

Please note that since each VLAN is a different Broadcast Domain, this means:

- Hosts in one VLAN cannot reach hosts in another VLAN, by default
- A Layer 3 device is needed for inter-VLAN communication (this will be covered later)
- Each VLAN needs its own subnet, for example, VLAN 1—192.168.1.0/24, VLAN 2— 192.168.2.0/24
- All hosts in a VLAN should belong to the same subnet

VLAN Links

We know that one switch can have hosts connected to multiple VLANs. But what happens when traffic goes from one host to another? For example, in Figure 5.15 above, when the host in VLAN 1 on Floor 1 tries to reach the host in VLAN 1 on Floor 2, how will the switch on Floor 2 know which VLAN the traffic belongs to?

We already know now that switches use a mechanism called VLAN marking or "frame tagging" to keep traffic on different VLANs separate. The switch adds a header on the frame, which contains the VLAN ID. In Figure 5.15, the switch on Floor 1 will tag the traffic originating from VLAN 2 and pass it to Switch 2, which will see the tag and know that the traffic needs to be kept within that VLAN. Such tagged traffic can only flow across special links called trunk links. VLAN 1 is usually designated as the native VLAN and traffic on the native VLAN is not tagged. We will cover native VLANs in more detail later.

Switch ports (within the scope of the CCNA exam) can be divided into the following:

- Access links or ports
- Trunk links or ports
- Dynamic (this will be discussed shortly)

Access Links
A switch port, which is defined as an access link, can be a member of only one VLAN. The device connected to the access link is not aware of the existence of any other VLANs. The switch will add a tag to a frame as it enters an access link from the host and remove the tag when a frame exits the switch access link towards the host. Access links are used to connect to hosts, but they can also be used to connect to a router. Trunk links are covered in the following section.

Trunking
A switch port usually will connect either to a host on the network or to another network switch, router, or server. If this is the case, then the link may need to carry traffic from several VLANs. In order to do this, each frame needs to identify which VLAN it is from. This identification method is known as frame tagging, and all frames are tagged before passing over the trunk link, apart from the native VLAN. The tag in the frame contains the VLAN ID. When the frame reaches the switch where the destination host resides, the tag is removed.

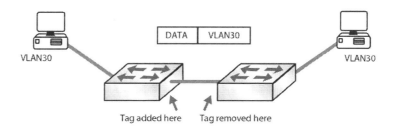

Figure 5.18—VLAN Tagging

VLAN trunks are used to carry data from multiple VLANs. To differentiate one VLAN frame from another, all frames sent across a trunk link are specially tagged so that the destination switch knows which VLAN the frame belongs to. ISL and 802.1Q are the two primary encapsulation methods which we mentioned briefly earlier. They can be used to ensure that VLANs that traverse a switch trunk link can be uniquely identified.

ISL is Cisco proprietary; however, the model tested in the CCNA exam is the 2960 switch, which only recognizes 802.1Q. We cover it here for completeness and in case you have to configure an older switch model.

FARAI SAYS—"All new switches now default to 802.1Q. ISL is being deprecated."

802.1Q differs from ISL in several ways. The first significant difference is that 802.1Q supports up to 4096 VLANs, whereas ISL supports up to 1000. Another significant difference is that of the native VLAN concept used in 802.1Q. By default, all frames from all VLANs are tagged when using 802.1Q. The only exception to this rule is frames that belong to the native VLAN, which are not tagged.

However, keep in mind that it is possible to specify which VLAN will not have frames tagged by specifying that VLAN as the native VLAN on a particular trunk link. For example, to prevent tagging of frames in VLAN 400 when using 802.1Q, you would configure that VLAN as the native VLAN on a particular trunk. IEEE 802.1Q native VLAN configuration will be illustrated in detail later.

The following summarizes some features of 802.1Q:

- Supports up to 4096 VLANs
- Uses an internal tagging mechanism, modifying the original frame
- Open standard protocol developed by the IEEE
- Does not tag frames on the native VLAN; however, all other frames are tagged

The following is a short sample configuration of a switch. I have included the `switchport` command, which tells the switch to act as a switch port for Layer 2, as opposed to Layer 3. This command would be added on a multilayer switch such as a 3660.

```
Sw(config)#interface FastEthernet 0/1
Sw(config-if)#switchport
Sw(config-if)#switchport mode trunk
Sw(config-if)#switchport trunk encapsulation dot1q
Sw(config-if)#exit
```

Of course, on a 2960 switch, the `encapsulation` command won't be recognized because there is only one type available (802.1Q). You will need to set the interface as a trunking interface when connecting to another switch to allow VLANs to be tagged. The same thing goes for the `switchport` command. Again, I cover this because in the real world you may well have to configure a Layer 3 switch, and if we stuck strictly to the 2960 model, you may become confused, which we don't want!

A trunk link on a switch can be in one of five possible modes:

1. On—forces the port into permanent trunking mode. The port becomes a trunk, even if the connected device does not agree to convert the link into a trunk link.
2. Off—the link is not used as a trunk link, even if the connected device is set to "trunk."
3. Auto—the port is willing to become a trunk link. If the other device is set to "on" or "desirable," then the link becomes a trunk link. If both sides are left as "auto," then the link will never become a trunk, as neither side will attempt to convert.
4. Desirable—the port actively tries to convert to a trunk link. If the other device is set to "on," "auto," or "desirable," then the link will become a trunk link.
5. No-negotiate—prevents the port from negotiating a trunk connection. It will be forced into an access or trunk mode as per the configuration.

Configuring VLANs

Now that you understand VLANs and trunk links, let's configure the network shown in Figure 5.19 below. You will need to configure the switches such that the hosts on fa0/1 are in VLAN 5 and the link on port fa0/15 is a trunk link.

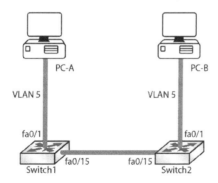

Figure 5.19—Test Network

Before assigning ports to VLANs, the VLAN itself must be created using the `vlan <vlan#>` global configuration command. This will put you into VLAN Configuration mode, where a descriptive name can be given to the VLANs (if you wish). Here is an example:

```
Switch1(config)#vlan 5
Switch1(config-vlan)#name RnD
Switch2(config)vlan 5
Switch2(config-vlan)#name RnD
```

To see which VLANs exist on a switch, use the show vlan command. The output will be similar to the one below:

```
Switch1#show vlan
VLAN      Name          Status       Ports
----      --------      -------      ----------
1         default       active       Fa0/1, Fa0/2, Fa0/3, Fa0/4 Fa0/5,
                                 Fa0/6, Fa0/7, Fa0/8 Fa0/9,
                             Fa0/10, Fa0/11, Fa0/12, Fa0/13
                         Fa0/14, Fa/15, Fa0/16, Fa0/17,
                    Fa0/18

[Truncated Output]

5   RnD    active

[Truncated Output]
```

Let's assign port fa0/1 to VLAN 5 using the switchport access vlan [vlan#] interface configuration command:

```
Switch1(config)#int fa0/1
Switch1(config-if)#switchport access vlan 5

Switch2(config)#int fa0/1
Switch2(config-if)#switchport access vlan 5
```

On a Layer 3-capable switch, such as the 3560, you would have to set the port manually to access it with the switchport mode access command before putting it into a VLAN. Now let's look at the output for the show vlan command:

```
Switch1#show vlan

VLAN      Name          Status       Ports
----      ----          -------      ----------
1         default       active       Fa0/2, Fa0/3, Fa0/4, Fa0/5,
                                 Fa0/6, Fa0/7, Fa0/8, Fa0/9,
                             Fa0/10, Fa0/11, Fa0/12, Fa0/13,
                         Fa0/14, Fa/15, Fa0/16, Fa0/17,
                    Fa0/18

[Truncated Output]

5         RnD    active Fa0/1

[Truncated Output]
```

Note that fa0/1 is now assigned to VLAN 5. Let's configure interface fa0/15 on both switches as trunk links. It should be noted here that the default mode on (the 3550 model) switch ports is desirable (on the 3560 model it's auto, so check your platform notes). Dynamic Trunking Protocol (DTP) will cause fa0/15 on both switches to become ISL trunk links. We will cover

DTP in the next lesson, but I wanted to mention it here briefly. This can be verified using the `show interface trunk` command:

```
Switch1#show interface trunk
Port        Mode        Encapsulation    Status        Native vlan
Fa0/15      desirable   n-isl            trunking      1
```

Note that the mode is desirable and the encapsulation is ISL ("n" stands for negotiated).

The following output shows how to configure the trunk to use ISL trunking:

```
Switch1(config)#interface fa0/15
Switch1(config-if)#switchport trunk encapsulation isl
Switch1(config-if)#switchport mode trunk

Switch2(config)#interface fa0/15
Switch2(config-if)#switchport trunk encapsulation isl
Switch2(config-if)#switchport mode trunk
```

The `switchport trunk encapsulation` command sets the trunking protocol on the port, and the `switchport mode trunk` command sets the port to trunking. The output for the `show interface trunk` command will now look like this:

```
Switch2#show interface trunk
Port        Mode    Encapsulation      Status        Native vlan
Fa0/15      on      isl                trunking      1
```

Note that the encapsulation is now ISL instead of n-ISL. This is because this time the protocol was not negotiated but configured on the interface.

> **IMPORTANT NOTE:** Trunk encapsulation needs to be configured on the switch port before setting it to trunk mode. Please note that this does not apply to switch model 2960 (currently used for the CCNA syllabus), which can only use dot1q (another name for 802.1Q) encapsulation. For this reason, the `switchport trunk encapsulation` command will not work on the 2960 switch.

Similarly, you can configure the switch port to use 802.1Q instead of ISL, as illustrated in the output below:

```
Switch1(config)#interface fa0/15
Switch1(config-if)#switchport trunk encapsulation dot1q
Switch1(config-if)#switchport mode trunk

Switch2(config)#interface fa0/15
Switch2(config-if)#switchport trunk encapsulation dot1q
Switch2(config-if)#switchport mode trunk
```

The `show interface trunk` output now looks like this:

```
Switch2#show interface trunk
```

```
Port      Mode   Encapsulation Status       Native vlan
Fa0/15    on     802.1q        trunking     1
```

Note that the native VLAN is 1. That is the default native VLAN on an 802.1Q trunk and it can be changed using the `switchport trunk native vlan <vlan#>` command. The native VLAN of each port on the trunk must match. This command is part of the CCNA syllabus and is considered a security measure.

> **IMPORTANT NOTE:** Switches remember all VLAN info, even when reloaded. If you want your switch to boot with a blank configuration, then you will need to issue the `delete vlan.dat` command on your switch, as shown in the output below. This applies to live switches only, not switch emulators such as Packet Tracer.

```
SwitchA#dir flash:
Directory of flash:/

    1  -rw-      3058048          <no date>  c2960-i6q412-mz.121-22.EA4.
bin
    2  -rw-          676          <no date>  vlan.dat

64016384 bytes total (60957660 bytes free)
SwitchA#
SwitchA#delete vlan.dat
Delete filename [vlan.dat]?
Delete flash:/vlan.dat? [confirm]

SwitchA#dir flash:
Directory of flash:/

    1  -rw-      3058048          <no date>  c2960-i6q412-mz.121-22.EA4.
bin

64016384 bytes total (60958336 bytes free)
SwitchA#
```

BASIC SWITCHING TROUBLESHOOTING

In theory, once a device is configured and working it should stay that way, but, often, you will be working on a network which you didn't configure, or you will be working on a shift pattern supporting many unfamiliar networks on which changes have been made, causing one or more issues for the company. I suggest you revisit this section after completing a few labs in this guide as the days progress.

Common Switch Issues

Can't Telnet to Switch

The first question is was Telnet ever working? If it was and is no longer, then perhaps somebody has made a change on the switch, reloaded it, and lost the configuration, or a device is now blocking Telnet traffic somewhere on the network:

```
Switch#telnet 192.168.1.1
Trying 192.168.1.1 ...Open

[Connection to 192.168.1.1 closed by foreign host]
```

The first thing to check is whether Telnet has actually been enabled on the switch (see the output below). Around 80% of errors on the network are due to silly mistakes or oversights, so never presume anything, and check out everything personally, rather than relying on other people's opinions.

A simple show run command will reveal the switch configuration. Under the vty lines, you will see whether Telnet has been enabled. Note that you will need to have the login or login local (or configured AAA) command under the vty lines and the password command, as shown below:

```
line vty 0 15
 password cisco
 login

The login local command tells the switch or router to look for a username
and password configured on it, as illustrated in the output below:
Switch1#sh run
Building configuration...
Current configuration : 1091 bytes!
version 12.1
hostname Switch1
username david privilege 1 password 0 football
line vty 0 15
 password cisco
 login local
[Truncated Output]
```

Can't Ping the Switch
Find out why the person wants to ping the switch in the first place. If you do want to ping a switch, there needs to be an IP address configured on it; in addition, the switch needs to know how to get traffic back out (the default gateway).

Can't Ping through the Switch
If a ping through the switch is unsuccessful, then check to ensure that the end devices are in the same VLAN. Each VLAN is considered a network and for this reason must have a different address range from any other VLAN. In order for one VLAN to reach another, a router must route the traffic.

Interface Issues
By default, all router interfaces are closed to traffic and switch interfaces are open. If you find that your switch has had its interfaces administratively shut, to open it, the interface must be set with the no shut interface-level command:

```
Switch1(config)#int FastEthernet0/3
Switch1(config-if)#no shut
```

Layer 2 interfaces can be set in three modes: trunk, access, or dynamic. Trunk mode lets the switch connect to another switch or a server. Access mode is for an end device, such as a PC or a laptop. Dynamic mode lets the switch detect which setting to select.

The default on platforms such as the 3550 model switch is usually dynamic desirable, but please check your model's settings and release notes on Cisco.com. For the CCNA exam, you will be asked to configure a 2960 model switch. It will select the mode dynamically unless you hard set it to trunk or access mode:

```
Switch1#show interfaces switchport
Name: Fa0/1
Switchport: Enabled
Administrative Mode: dynamic auto
```

The default can easily be changed, as shown in the output below:

```
Switch1#conf t
Enter configuration commands, one per line.  End with CNTL/Z.
Switch1(config)#int FastEthernet0/1
Switch1(config-if)#switchport mode ?
  access   Set trunking mode to ACCESS unconditionally
  dynamic  Set trunking mode to dynamically negotiate access or
trunk mode
  trunk    Set trunking mode to TRUNK unconditionally
Switch1(config-if)#switchport mode trunk
%LINEPROTO-5-UPDOWN: Line protocol on Interface FastEthernet0/1, changed
state to down
Switch1(config-if)#^Z
Switch1#
%SYS-5-CONFIG_I: Configured from console by console
Switch1#show interfaces switchport
Name: Fa0/1
Switchport: Enabled
Administrative Mode: trunk
Operational Mode: trunk
```

More Interface Issues

Switch port default settings are auto-detect duplex and auto-detect speed. If you plug a 10Mbps device into a switch running at half duplex (if you could even find such a device), then the port should detect this and work. This isn't always the case, though, so the generic advice is hard set the switch port speed and duplex, as illustrated in the output below:

```
Switch1#show interfaces switchport
Name: Fa0/1
Switchport: Enabled
Administrative Mode: dynamic auto
Switch1#show interface FastEthernet0/2
FastEthernet0/2 is up, line protocol is up (connected)
```

```
   Hardware is Lance, address is 0030.f252.3402 (bia 0030.f252.3402)
   BW 100000 Kbit, DLY 1000 usec,
      reliability 255/255, txload 1/255, rxload 1/255
   Encapsulation ARPA, loopback not set
   Keepalive set (10 sec)
   Full-duplex, 100Mb/s
Switch1(config)#int fast 0/2
Switch1(config-if)#duplex ?
   auto  Enable AUTO duplex configuration
   full  Force full-duplex operation
   half  Force half-duplex operation

Switch1(config-if)#speed ?
   10    Force 10Mbps operation
   100   Force 100Mbps operation
   auto  Enable AUTO speed configuration
```

Signs of duplex mismatches (apart from error messages) include input and CRC errors on the interface, as illustrated in the output below. Please also see the Layer 1 and Layer 2 Troubleshooting sections in Day 21 of the ICND1 section.

```
Switch#show interface f0/1
FastEthernet0/1 is down, line protocol is down (disabled)
   Hardware is Lance, address is 0030.a388.8401 (bia 0030.a388.8401)
   BW 100000 Kbit, DLY 1000 usec,
      reliability 255/255, txload 1/255, rxload 1/255
   Encapsulation ARPA, loopback not set
   Keepalive set (10 sec)
   Half-duplex, 100Mb/s
   input flow-control is off, output flow-control is off
   ARP type: ARPA, ARP Timeout 04:00:00
   Last input 00:00:08, output 00:00:05, output hang never
   Last clearing of "show interface" counters never
   Input queue: 0/75/0/0 (size/max/drops/flushes); Total output drops: 0
   Queueing strategy: fifo
   Output queue :0/40 (size/max)
   5 minute input rate 0 bits/sec, 0 packets/sec
   5 minute output rate 0 bits/sec, 0 packets/sec
      956 packets input, 193351 bytes, 0 no buffer
      Received 956 broadcasts, 0 runts, 0 giants, 0 throttles
      755 input errors, 739 CRC, 0 frame, 0 overrun, 0 ignored, 0 abort
      0 watchdog, 0 multicast, 0 pause input
      0 input packets with dribble condition detected
      2357 packets output, 263570 bytes, 0 underruns
      0 output errors, 0 collisions, 10 interface resets
      0 babbles, 0 late collision, 0 deferred
      0 lost carrier, 0 no carrier
      0 output buffer failures, 0 output buffers swapped out
```

Hardware Issues

As with any electrical device, ports on a switch can fail or work only part of the time, which is harder to troubleshoot. Engineers often test the interface by plugging a known working device into another port on the switch. You can also bounce a port, which means applying the shut command and then the no shut command to it. Swapping the Ethernet cable is also a common troubleshooting step. Other common switch problems and solutions are shown in Figure 5.20 below.

Please check the documentation for your switch because, as well as featuring system and port LEDs, each port can display flashing or solid red, amber, and green, indicating normal function or port/system issues.

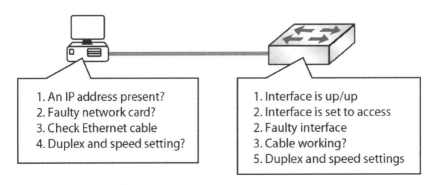

1. An IP address present?
2. Faulty network card?
3. Check Ethernet cable
4. Duplex and speed setting?

1. Interface is up/up
2. Interface is set to access
2. Faulty interface
3. Cable working?
5. Duplex and speed settings

Figure 5.20—Common Switch Problems and Solutions

BASIC VLAN TROUBLESHOOTING

VLANs are a fairly straightforward feature which rarely requires troubleshooting. A few of the problems that you will see are mostly configuration errors. We will cover Layer 2 troubleshooting in detail on Day 15. Common problems include the following:

1. Inter-VLAN routing not working: Check to ensure that the link between the switches and the routers is set up correctly, and the relevant VLANs are allowed and not pruned (see VTP pruning). The show interface trunk command will provide the required information. Also, check to ensure that the router's sub interfaces are configured with correct encapsulation and VLAN, and the sub interface's IP address is the default gateway for the hosts.
2. VLANs cannot be created: Check whether the VTP mode on the switch is set to "client." VLANs cannot be created if the VTP mode is client. Another important factor is the number of VLANs allowed on the switch. The show vtp status command will provide the information required (see the Troubleshooting Trunking and VTP section below).
3. Hosts within the same VLAN cannot reach each other: It is important that hosts in a VLAN have an IP address that belongs to the same subnet. If the subnet is different, then they will not be able to reach each other. Another factor to consider is whether the hosts are connected to the same switch. If they are not connected to the same switch, then ensure that the trunk link(s) between the switches is/are

working correctly and that the VLAN is not excluded/not pruned from the allowed list. The `show interface trunk` command will show needed information regarding the trunk link.

VLAN Assignment Issues

Networks in small environments are relatively easy to manage because a limited number of features need to be implemented in order to achieve the business's goals. However, in an enterprise environment you won't be using small workgroup switches and SOHO devices. Rather, you will use high-end devices that are capable of optimizing the traffic flow by offering a number of advanced functionalities.

One particular feature that might be configured in such an environment is logically separating different network areas using VLANs. Issues can appear when you have configuration issues related to a particular VLAN and this can become difficult to troubleshoot. One way of doing this is analyzing the entire configuration on the switch and trying to identify the problem.

VLAN-related problems are usually detected by observing the lack of connectivity between network hosts (e.g., a user cannot ping a server), even though Layer 1 seems to operate without problems. One important characteristic of VLAN-related problems is that they do not generate any performance degradation on the network. If you misconfigure a VLAN, the connection will simply not work, especially considering that they usually separate IP subnets so that only devices within the same VLAN will be able to communicate with each other.

The first step in troubleshooting VLAN problems is to review the documentation and the logical diagrams developed in the design phase so you can identify the span area for each VLAN, including the associated devices and ports on each switch. The next step is to inspect each switch configuration and try to find the problem by comparing them with the documented solution.

You should also verify the IP addressing scheme. If you are statically assigning IP addresses to devices, you may want to go back and check the device to ensure that it has the proper IP address and subnet mask combination. If there are any mistakes in the IP addressing scheme, like configuring devices on the wrong network or with a wrong subnet mask/default gateway, then you are going to have connectivity problems, even though you have the correct VLAN configured on the switch.

You will also want to confirm that the trunk configuration on the switches is correct. If you have multiple switches, there are usually uplinks between them and VLANs carried across those uplinks. These inter-switch links are often configured as trunks to allow communication across multiple VLANs. The VLAN has to be a member of the trunk group if data is to be sent from one switch to the other, so you also have to make sure that the switch configuration on both sides is set up properly.

Finally, if you move a device to another VLAN, you will have to make changes to both the switch and the client because the client will have a different IP address in a different IP subnet as a result of that move.

If you follow all of these VLAN troubleshooting methods, you can be sure that when plugging in devices for the first time or moving them from VLAN to VLAN, you will have the exact connectivity you desired.

Data and Voice Access Ports

Before the advent of Voice over IP, large companies that wanted their own internal telephone network would employ a voice team that would run phone cabling into a Private Branch Exchange (PBX). The PBX was a big box of ports and software, and each port would be allocated an extension number on which the phone could be reached. There was one set of cables for phones and another for the network.

This, of course, was a costly and cumbersome solution, so it was proposed to use the existing network cabling infrastructure for voice traffic and VoIP was born.

IP telephony refers to a special type of telephone using IP packets to send and receive voice traffic. The phones connect into a switch, just like laptops and desktops. The phones then communicate using the same network as every other networked device in the building. They no longer need to communicate with a PBX for call control; rather, they communicate with an application that resides on a server. You can learn more about voice and video networking in the CCNA Collaboration exam if this area interests you.

So far, all of this sounds ideal until you realize that the existing network cannot possibly support the number of phones that you have because you would instantly need double the amount of ports on your switches (and, of course, you would have to install twice the amount of network cables). Cisco was forward-thinking enough to start offering small switches built inside each IP phone. As you can see below, a Cisco IP telephone has an embedded LAN switch. Typically, one port connects into the local switch to provide network connectivity and another port connects to the local personal computer.

Figure 5.21 below shows an IP phone with some typical connections. The device needs power and ports for a headset but there are also two IP ports, one for the phone to connect to the network switch and one to connect to the desktop PC.

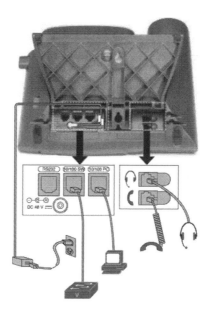

Figure 5.21—Cabling with an IP phone (Image © Cisco Press)

Figure 5.22 below shows network cables physically connected to an IP phone:

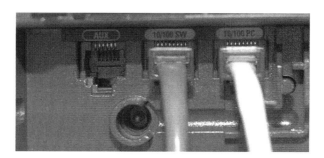

Figure 5.22—Network Cables in an IP Phone (Image © http://www.scsb.org/voip)

This then means that the IP phone is acting as a mini-switch and providing network access for the PC. There is now an issue because IP phones typically operate in a separate VLAN from data devices (if you follow Cisco best practices).

As you can see in Figure 5.23 below, there are two phones in voice VLAN10 and three laptops in data VLAN20. The switchports are capable of sending traffic to either VLAN off of the same port. The phones are also capable of forwarding traffic on the data VLAN to the connected personal computer. This Layer 1 and 2 design allows for IP telephony deployments without extensive purchasing of additional switchports.

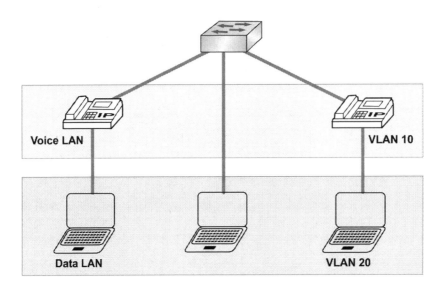

Figure 5.23—Data and Voice VLANs

Data and Voice VLAN Configuration

Configuring a switchport to support IP phones is not as complex as you may think once you understand the full capabilities of what an access port can do. For example, even though a port connected to a phone acts like an access port, the voice frames are tagged with an 802.1Q header so that the switch and the phone will understand what is voice traffic versus data traffic.

In the following example, we programmed switchport F0/6 with a default configuration so that it will support the new data and voice VLANs that we will be adding. You can use the IP phone in Packet Tracer to copy the configuration below. Just make sure that you add the power supply by dragging it to the power socket on the IP phone; otherwise, no interfaces will come up.

```
SW1#configure terminal
Enter configuration commands, one per line. End with CTRL/Z.
SW1(config)#vlan10
SW1(config-vlan)#vlan20
SW1(config-vlan)#interface FastEthernet0/6
SW1(config-if)#switchport mode access
SW1(config-if)#switchport access vlan20
SW1(config-if)#switchport voice vlan10
SW1(config-if)#^Z
```

After we programmed the switch, we verified that it was ready for use. The first command we used was the show interfaces switchport command. This command provides detailed (Layer 2) information regarding the current operating mode of the interface.

```
SW1#show interfaces FastEthernet0/1 switchport
Name: Fa0/6
Switchport: Enabled
Administrative Mode: static access
Operational Mode: static access
Administrative Trunking Encapsulation: dot1q
Operational Trunking Encapsulation: native
Negotiation of Trunking: Off
Access Mode VLAN: 20 (VLAN020)
Trunking Native Mode VLAN: 1 (default)
Administrative Native VLAN tagging: enabled
Voice VLAN: 10 (VLAN010)
[Output Truncated]
```

The switch must be running CDP in order to identify the connected device as an IP phone.

The output above is (hopefully) self-explanatory, but you may have a question about the operational mode of the interface. As you can see, it is static access even though it supports multiple VLANs and 802.1Q trunking is allowed. In case you had any doubt that Cisco does not consider these types of ports trunking ports, if you perform the show interfaces trunk general command, the telephony ports will not show up in that list. That being said, you may need to dig deeper into the multi-VLAN capabilities of the port while troubleshooting. If you issue the show interfaces [interface] trunk command with the interface specified, you will see additional information:

```
SW1#show interfaces trunk

SW1#show interfaces F0/1 trunk

Port         Mode             Encapsulation  Status        Native vlan
Fa0/6        off              802.1q         not-trunking  1

Port         Vlans allowed on trunk
Fa0/6        10, 20

Port         Vlans allowed and active in management domain
Fa0/6        10, 20

Port         Vlans in spanning tree forwarding state and not pruned
Fa0/6        10, 20
```

Please take the day 5 exam at https://www.in60days.com/free/ccnain60days/

DAY 5 LABS

Switching Concepts

Please log on to a Cisco switch and enter the commands explained in this module. This should include:

- Configure different port speeds/auto-negotiation on various switch ports
- Verify the port parameters with the `show run` and the `show interface` commands
- Issue a `show version` command to see the hardware details and IOS version
- Verify the switch MAC address table
- Configure a password on the VTY lines
- Define a couple of VLANs and assign names to them
- Assign a VLAN to a port configured as switchport access
- Configure a port as a trunk (802.1Q) and assign VLANs to the trunk
- Verify VLAN configuration using the `show vlan` command
- Verify interface trunking and VLAN configuration using the `show interface switchport` command and the `show interface trunk` command
- Check for and then delete the "vlan.dat" file

Voice VLANs

Topology

| PC-PT | 7960 | 2960-24TT |
| PC0 | IP Phone0 | Switch0 |

Purpose

Learn how to configure voice VLANs on a Cisco switch.

Unless you have a Cisco IP phone lying around you will want to use Packet Tracer for this lab. Ensure you use a crossover cable between the PC and IP phone and straight between the phone and Switch. You will also need to physically drag the power cable to the power port on the switch.

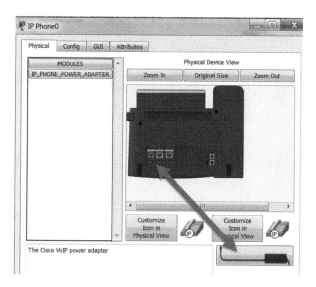

CDP need to be running on the switch but it is enabled by default.

Walkthrough

1. Create VLAN 10 for data and VLAN11 for voice traffic on the switch.

```
Switch#conf t
Enter configuration commands, one per line.  End with CNTL/Z.
Switch(config)#vlan 10
Switch(config-vlan)#name data
Switch(config-vlan)#vlan 11
Switch(config-vlan)#name voice
Switch(config-vlan)#end
Switch#
%SYS-5-CONFIG_I: Configured from console by console
show vlan brief

VLAN Name                 Status    Ports
---- ----------------     --------- ------------------------------
1    default              active    Fa0/1, Fa0/2, Fa0/3, Fa0/4
                                    Fa0/5, Fa0/6, Fa0/7, Fa0/8
                                    Fa0/9, Fa0/10, Fa0/11, Fa0/12
                                    Fa0/13, Fa0/14, Fa0/15, Fa0/16
                                    Fa0/17, Fa0/18, Fa0/19, Fa0/20
                                    Fa0/21, Fa0/22, Fa0/23, Fa0/24
                                    Gig0/1, Gig0/2
10   data                 active
11   voice                active
1002 fddi-default         active
1003 token-ring-default   active
1004 fddinet-default      active
1005 trnet-default        active
```

2. Set the interface on the switch to static access.

```
Switch(config)#int f0/1
Switch(config-if)#switchport mode access
```

3. Configure the interface for VLANs 10 and 11.

```
Switch(config-if)#switchport access vlan 10
Switch(config-if)#switchport voice vlan 11
```

4. Check the Layer 2 settings on the switch.

```
Switch#show int f0/1 switchport
Name: Fa0/1
Switchport: Enabled
Administrative Mode: static access
Operational Mode: static access
Administrative Trunking Encapsulation: dot1q
Operational Trunking Encapsulation: native
Negotiation of Trunking: Off
Access Mode VLAN: 10 (data)
Trunking Native Mode VLAN: 1 (default)
Voice VLAN: 11
```

5. Last step is optional. Check the CDP entry for the switch interface. We won't be testing the actual phone connection.

```
Switch#show cdp neighbors
Capability Codes: R - Router, T - Trans Bridge, B - Source Route
Bridge
                 S - Switch, H - Host, I - IGMP, r - Repeater, P
- Phone
Device ID    Local Intrfce   Holdtme    Capability   Platform    Port
ID
IP Phone     Fas 0/1          147          H P        7960

Switch#show cdp nei detail

Device ID: IP Phone
Entry address(es):
Platform: cisco 7960, Capabilities: Host Phone
Interface: FastEthernet0/1, Port ID (outgoing port): Switch
Holdtime: 143

Version :
P00303020214

advertisement version: 2
Duplex: full
```

VLAN and Trunking

Topology

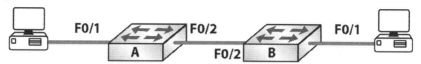

Purpose

Learn how to configure VLANs and trunk links. We cover trunking in far more detail tomorrow.

Walkthrough

1. You will need to add IP addresses on each PC. Feel free to choose your own, as long as they are on the same subnet!

2. On Switch A, set the hostname, create VLAN 2, and put the interface to which your PC is connected into VLAN 2. You can also give the VLAN a name if you wish.

```
Switch>en
Switch#conf t
Enter configuration commands, one per line.  End with CNTL/Z.
Switch(config)#hostname SwitchA
SwitchA(config)#vlan 2
SwitchA(config-vlan)#name 60days
SwitchA(config-vlan)#interface FastEthernet0/1
SwitchA(config-if)#switchport mode access
SwitchA(config-if)#switchport access vlan 2
SwitchA(config-if)#^Z

SwitchA#show vlan brief

VLAN Name                        Status    Ports
---- ----------                  --------------------------------
1    default                     active    Fa0/2, Fa0/3, Fa0/4, Fa0/5,
             Fa0/6, Fa0/7, Fa0/8, Fa0/9,
             Fa0/10, Fa0/11, Fa0/12, Fa0/13,
                                           Fa0/14, Fa0/15, Fa0/16, Fa0/17,
                                           Fa0/18, Fa0/19, Fa0/20, Fa0/21,
                                           Fa0/22, Fa0/23, Fa0/24
2    60days                      active    Fa0/1
1002 fddi-default                active
1003 token-ring-default active
1004 fddinet-default             active
1005 trnet-default               active
SwitchA#
```

3. Set your trunk link to trunk mode.

```
SwitchA#conf t
Enter configuration commands, one per line.  End with CNTL/Z.
SwitchA(config)#int FastEthernet0/2
```

```
SwitchA(config-if)#switchport mode trunk

SwitchA#show interface trunk
Port        Mode        Encapsulation  Status        Native vlan
Fa0/2       on          802.1q         trunking      1

Port        Vlans allowed on trunk
Fa0/2       1-1005
```

4. If you wish, permit only VLAN 2 on the trunk link.

```
SwitchA(config)#int FastEthernet0/2
SwitchA(config-if)#switchport trunk allowed vlan 2
SwitchA(config-if)#^Z
SwitchA#
%SYS-5-CONFIG_I: Configured from console by console

SwitchA#show int trunk
Port        Mode        Encapsulation  Status        Native vlan
Fa0/2       on          802.1q         trunking      1

Port        Vlans allowed on trunk
Fa0/2       2
```

5. At this point, if you ping from one PC to another, it should fail. This is because one side is in VLAN 1 and the other is in VLAN 2.

```
PC>ping 192.168.1.1

Pinging 192.168.1.1 with 32 bytes of data:

Request timed out.

Ping statistics for 192.168.1.1:
    Packets: Sent = 2, Received = 0, Lost = 2 (100% loss)
```

6. Configure the same commands on Switch B now. For VLAN creation, put the PC port into VLAN 2, and set the interface to "access" and the trunk link to "trunk."

7. Now you should be able to ping across the trunk link from PC to PC.

```
PC>ping 192.168.1.1

Pinging 192.168.1.1 with 32 bytes of data:

Reply from 192.168.1.1: bytes=32 time=188ms TTL=128
Reply from 192.168.1.1: bytes=32 time=78ms TTL=128
Reply from 192.168.1.1: bytes=32 time=94ms TTL=128
Reply from 192.168.1.1: bytes=32 time=79ms TTL=128

Ping statistics for 192.168.1.1:
    Packets: Sent = 4, Received = 4, Lost = 0 (0% loss),
Approximate round trip times in milli-seconds:
    Minimum = 78ms, Maximum = 188ms, Average = 109ms
```

Trunking and DTP

DAY 6 TASKS

- Read today's lesson notes (below)
- Review yesterday's lesson notes and labs
- Complete today's labs
- Take today's exam
- Read the ICND1 cram guide
- Spend 15 minutes on the subnetting.org website

You will only encounter networks using one switch in the smallest of offices. You will usually find multiple switches forming part of the network infrastructure. This brings its own set of configuration challenges, which will require a good understanding of trunking and associated issues. Cisco consider the ability to install, configure and troubleshoot multiple switch connections a fundamental CCNA-level topic.

Today you will learn about the following:

- Configuring and verifying trunk links
- Dynamic Trunking Protocol
- Virtual Trunking Protocol
- Troubleshooting trunking and VTP

This module maps to the following ICND1 syllabus requirements:

- 2.5.a Trunk ports
- 2.5.b 802.1Q
- 2.5.c Native VLAN
- 1.2.b DTP and VTP (v1&v2) (ICND2)

CONFIGURING AND VERIFYING TRUNK LINKS

A trunk is a switch port that can carry multiple traffic types, each tagged with a unique VLAN ID. As data is switched across the trunk port or trunk link, it is tagged (or colored) by the egress switch trunk port, which allows the receiving switch to identify that it belongs to a particular VLAN. On the receiving switch ingress port, the tag is removed and the data is forwarded to the intended destination.

The first configuration task when implementing VLAN trunking in Cisco IOS Catalyst switches is to configure the desired interface as a Layer 2 switch port. This is performed by issuing the switchport interface configuration command.

NOTE: This command and the encaplulation command below are required only on Layer 3-capable or multilayer switches. It is not applicable to Layer 2-only switches, such as the Catalyst 2960 series. A switch would need to support the command ip routing in order to be considered Layer 3 capable.

The second configuration task is to specify the encapsulation protocol that the trunk link should use. This is performed by issuing the switchport trunk encapsulation [option] command. The options available with this command are as follows (performed on a multilayer switch):

```
Switch(config)#interface FastEthernet1/1
Switch (config-if)#switchport trunk encapsulation ?
dot1q - Interface uses only 802.1q trunking encapsulation when trunking
isl - Interface uses only ISL trunking encapsulation when trunking
negotiate - Device will negotiate trunking encapsulation with peer on
interface
```

The [dot1q] keyword forces the switch port to use IEEE 802.1Q encapsulation. The [isl] keyword forces the switch port to use Cisco ISL encapsulation. The [negotiate] keyword is used to specify that if the Dynamic Inter-Switch Link Protocol (DISL) and the Dynamic Trunking Protocol (DTP) negotiation fails to successfully agree on the encapsulation format, then ISL is the selected format. DISL simplifies the creation of an ISL trunk from two interconnected Fast Ethernet devices. DISL minimizes VLAN trunk configuration procedures because only one end of a link needs to be configured as a trunk.

DTP is a Cisco proprietary point-to-protocol that negotiates a common trunking mode between two switches. DTP will be described in detail later. The following output illustrates how to configure a switch port to use IEEE 802.1Q encapsulation when establishing a trunk:

```
Switch(config)#interface FastEthernet1/1
Switch(config-if)#switchport
Switch(config-if)#switchport trunk encapsulation dot1q
```

This configuration can be validated via the show interfaces [name] switchport command, as illustrated in the following output:

```
Switch#show interfaces FastEthernet1/1 switchport
Name: Fa0/2
Switchport: Enabled
Administrative Mode: dynamic desirable
Operational Mode: trunk
```

```
Administrative Trunking Encapsulation: dot1q
Operational Trunking Encapsulation: dot1q
Negotiation of Trunking: On
Access Mode VLAN: 1 (default)
Trunking Native Mode VLAN: 1 (default)

[Truncated Output]
```

The third trunk port configuration step is to implement configuration to ensure that the port is designated as a trunk port. This can be done in one of two ways:

- Manual (static) trunk configuration
- Dynamic Trunking Protocol (DTP)

Manual (Static) Trunk Configuration

The manual configuration of a trunk is performed by issuing the switchport mode trunk interface configuration command on the desired switch port. This command forces the port into a permanent (static) trunking mode. The following configuration output shows how to configure a port statically as a trunk port:

```
Switch(config)#interface FastEthernet0/1
Switch(config-if)#switchport
Switch(config-if)#switchport trunk encapsulation dot1q
Switch(config-if)#switchport mode trunk
Switch(config-if)#exit
Switch(config)#
```

Feel free to ignore the switchport command if you are using a lower-end switch (the above output was from a Cat6K switch). This configuration can be validated via the show interfaces [name] switchport command, as illustrated in the following output:

```
Switch#show interfaces FastEthernet0/1 switchport
Name: Fa0/1
Switchport: Enabled
Administrative Mode: trunk
Operational Mode: trunk
Administrative Trunking Encapsulation: dot1q
Operational Trunking Encapsulation: dot1q
Negotiation of Trunking: On
Access Mode VLAN: 1 (default)
Trunking Native Mode VLAN: 1 (default)
[Truncated Output]
```

Although manual (static) configuration of a trunk link forces the switch to establish a trunk, Dynamic ISL and Dynamic Trunking Protocol (DTP) packets will still be sent out of the interface. This is performed so that a statically configured trunk link can establish a trunk with a neighboring switch that is using DTP, as will be described in the following section. This can be validated in the output of the show interfaces [name] switchport command illustrated below:

```
Switch#show interfaces FastEthernet0/1 switchport
Name: Fa0/1
Switchport: Enabled
Administrative Mode: trunk
Operational Mode: trunk
Administrative Trunking Encapsulation: dot1q
Operational Trunking Encapsulation: dot1q
Negotiation of Trunking: On
Access Mode VLAN: 1 (default)
Trunking Native Mode VLAN: 1 (default)

[Truncated Output]
```

In the output above, the text in bold indicates that despite the static configuration of the trunk link, the port is still sending out DTP and DISL packets. In some cases, this is considered undesirable. Therefore, it is considered good practice to disable the sending of DISL and DTP packets on a port statically configured as a trunk link by issuing the `switchport nonegotiate` interface configuration command, as illustrated in the following output:

```
Switch(config)#interface FastEthernet0/1
Switch(config-if)#switchport
Switch(config-if)#switchport trunk encapsulation dot1q
Switch(config-if)#switchport mode trunk
Switch(config-if)#switchport nonegotiate
Switch(config-if)#exit
Switch(config)#
```

Again, the `show interfaces [name] switchport` command can be used to validate the configuration, as follows:

```
Switch#show interfaces FastEthernet0/1 switchport
Name: Fa0/1
Switchport: Enabled
Administrative Mode: trunk
Operational Mode: trunk
Administrative Trunking Encapsulation: dot1q
Operational Trunking Encapsulation: dot1q
Negotiation of Trunking: Off
Access Mode VLAN: 1 (default)
Trunking Native Mode VLAN: 1 (default)

[Truncated Output]
```

DYNAMIC TRUNKING PROTOCOL (DTP)

DTP is a Cisco proprietary point-to-protocol that negotiates a common trunking mode between two switches. This dynamic negotiation can also include trunking encapsulation. The two DTP modes that a switch port can use, depending upon the platform, are as follows:

- Dynamic desirable
- Dynamic auto

When using DTP on two neighboring switches, if the switch port defaults to a dynamic desirable state, the port will actively attempt to become a trunk. If the switch port defaults to a dynamic auto state, the port will revert to being a trunk only if the neighboring switch is set to dynamic desirable mode.

Figure 6.1 below illustrates the DTP mode combinations that will result in a trunk either being established or not being established (in this case they are all established; see note after Figure 6.2) between two Cisco Catalyst switches:

Figure 6.1—DTP Mode Combinations

Figure 6.2 below illustrates the valid combinations that will result in the successful establishment of a trunk link between two neighboring switches—one using DTP and the other statically configured as a trunk port:

Figure 6.2—DTP Mode Combinations, Part 2

NOTE: It is important to know that if the switches are both set to dynamic auto, they will not be able to establish a trunk between them. This is because, unlike dynamic desirable mode, dynamic auto mode is a passive mode that waits for the other side to initiate trunk establishment. Similarly, if a statically configured switch port is also configured with the switchport nonegotiate command, it will never form a trunk with a neighboring switch using DTP because this prevents the sending of DISL and DTP packets out of that port.

When using DTP in a switched LAN, the show dtp [interface <name>] command can be used to display DTP information globally for the switch or for the specified interface. The following output shows the information printed by the show dtp command:

```
Switch#show dtp
Global DTP information
        Sending DTP Hello packets every 30 seconds
        Dynamic Trunk timeout is 300 seconds
        4 interfaces using DTP
```

Based on the output above, the switch is sending DTP packets every 30 seconds. The timeout value for DTP is set to 300 seconds (5 minutes), and 4 interfaces are currently using DTP. The show dtp interface [name] command prints DTP information about the specified interface, which includes the type of interface (trunk or access), the current port DTP configuration, the trunk encapsulation, and DTP packet statistics, as illustrated in the following output:

```
Switch#show dtp interface FastEthernet0/1
DTP information for FastEthernet0/1:
  TOS/TAS/TNS:                            TRUNK/ON/TRUNK
  TOT/TAT/TNT:                            802.1Q/802.1Q/802.1Q
  Neighbor address 1:                     000000000000
  Neighbor address 2:                     000000000000
  Hello timer expiration (sec/state):     7/RUNNING
  Access timer expiration (sec/state):    never/STOPPED
  Negotiation timer expiration (sec/state): never/STOPPED
  Multidrop timer expiration (sec/state):  never/STOPPED
  FSM state:                              S6:TRUNK
  # times multi & trunk                   0
  Enabled:                                yes
  In STP:                                 no

  Statistics
  ----------
  0 packets received (0 good)
  0 packets dropped
      0 nonegotiate, 0 bad version, 0 domain mismatches, 0 bad TLVs, 0
other
  764 packets output (764 good)
      764 native, 0 software encap isl, 0 isl hardware native
  0 output errors
  0 trunk timeouts
  2 link ups, last link up on Mon Mar 01 1993, 00:00:22
  1 link downs, last link down on Mon Mar 01 1993, 00:00:20
```

IEEE 802.1Q Native VLAN

In the previous module, you learned that 802.1Q, or VLAN tagging, inserts a tag into all frames, except those in the native VLAN. The IEEE defined the native VLAN to provide for connectivity to old 802.3 ports that did not understand VLAN tags.

By default, an 802.1Q trunk uses VLAN 1 as the native VLAN. The default native VLAN on an 802.1Q trunk link can be verified by issuing the show interfaces [name] switchport or the show interfaces trunk command, as illustrated in the following output:

```
Switch#show interfaces FastEthernet0/1 switchport
Name: Fa0/1
```

```
Switchport: Enabled
Administrative Mode: trunk
Operational Mode: trunk
Administrative Trunking Encapsulation: dot1q
Operational Trunking Encapsulation: dot1q
Negotiation of Trunking: On
Access Mode VLAN: 1 (default)
Trunking Native Mode VLAN: 1 (default)
Voice VLAN: none
[Truncated Output]
```

VLAN 1 is used by the switch to carry specific protocol traffic, like Cisco Discovery Protocol (CDP), VLAN Trunking Protocol (VTP), Port Aggregation Protocol (PAgP), and Dynamic Trunking Protocol (DTP) information. CDP and PAgP will be described in detail later in this guide. Although the default native VLAN is always VLAN 1, the native VLAN can be manually changed to any valid VLAN number that is not in the reserved range of VLANs.

However, it is important to remember that the native VLAN must be the same on both sides of the trunk link. If there is a native VLAN mismatch, Spanning Tree Protocol (STP) places the port in a port VLAN ID (PVID) inconsistent state and will not forward traffic on the link. Additionally, CDPv2 passes native VLAN information between switches and will print error messages on the switch console if there is a native VLAN mismatch. The default native VLAN can be changed by issuing the `switchport trunk native vlan [number]` interface configuration command on the desired 802.1Q trunk link, as illustrated in the following output:

```
Switch(config)#interface FastEthernet0/1
Switch(config-if)#switchport trunk native vlan ?
  <1-4094>  VLAN ID of the native VLAN when this port is in trunking mode
```

VTP

VLAN Trunking Protocol (VTP) is a Cisco proprietary Layer 2 messaging protocol that manages the addition, deletion, and renaming of VLANs on switches in the same VTP domain. VTP allows VLAN information to propagate through the switched network, which reduces administration overhead in a switched network, whilst enabling switches to exchange and maintain consistent VLAN information. This concept is illustrated in Figure 6.3 below:

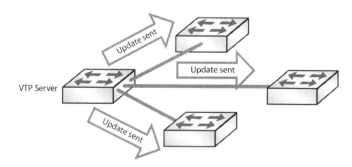

Figure 6.3—VTP Updates

Some benefits to using VTP include the following:

- Accurate monitoring and reporting of VLANs
- VLAN consistency across the network
- Ease of adding and removing VLANs

Configuring VTP

All switches must be configured with the same VTP domain name if they are to exchange VLAN information, as illustrated in the output below:

```
Switch(config)#vtp mode server  ←this is on by default
Switch(config)#vtp domain in60days
Changing VTP domain name from NULL to in60days

Switch#show vtp status
VTP Version                    : 2
Configuration Revision         : 0
Maximum VLANs Supported Locally : 255
Number of Existing VLANs       : 5
VTP Operating Mode             : Server
VTP Domain Name                : in60days
VTP Pruning Mode : Disabled
VTP V2 Mode : Disabled
VTP Traps Generation : Disabled
MD5 digest : 0x7D 0x5A 0xA6 0x0E 0x9A 0x72 0xA0 0x3A
```

If you want to secure your VTP updates, you can add a password, but it must match on each switch in the VTP domain:

```
Switch(config)#vtp password Cisco321
Setting device VLAN database password to Cisco321
```

VTP Versions

There are three versions of VTP, which are versions 1, 2, and 3. As of the time of this writing, the default version used by Cisco Catalyst switches is VTP version 1. This can be validated in the output of the show vtp status command as illustrated above.

The first line in bold text is confusing, as it shows that the VTP version is VTP version 2. However, this line simply indicates that this switch is version 2-capable. To determine whether VTP version 2 is enabled, the VTP V2 Mode line should be referred to. In the output printed above, this shows 'Disabled', meaning that even though the switch is version 2-capable, as is stated in the first line, it is still running the default version (1) and version 2 is disabled.

VTP version 2 is similar in basic operation to version 1 but provides additional capabilities and features over version 1. The first additional feature supported in VTP version 2 is Token Ring support. VTP version 2 supports Token Ring switching and Token Ring Bridge Relay Function (TrBRF) and Token Ring Concentrator Relay Function (TrCRF). Token Ring is beyond the scope of the SWITCH exam requirements and will not be described any further in this guide.

VTP version 3 differs from VTP versions 1 and 2 in that it distributes a list of opaque databases over an administrative domain in situations where VTP version 1 and VTP version 2 interacted with the VLAN process directly. By offering a reliable and efficient transport mechanism for a database, usability can be expanded from just serving the VLAN environment.

VTP Modes

VTP runs in the following three modes:

- Server (default)
- Client
- Transparent

You can see the server mode in the configuration and output above.

Server Mode

In Server mode, the switch is authorized to create, modify, and delete VLAN information for the entire VTP domain. Any changes you make to a server are propagated throughout the whole domain. VLAN configuration is stored in the VLAN database file "vlan.dat" located on the flash memory.

Client Mode

In Client mode, the switch will receive VTP information and apply any changes, but it does not allow adding, removing, or changing VLAN information on the switch. The client will also send the VTP packet received out of its trunk ports. Remember that you cannot add a switch port on a VTP client switch to a VLAN that does not exist on the VTP server. VLAN configuration is stored in the VLAN database file "vlan.dat" located on the flash memory.

Transparent Mode

In Transparent mode, the switch will forward the VTP information received out of its trunk ports, but it will not apply the changes. A VTP Transparent-mode switch can create, modify, and delete VLANs, but the changes are not propagated to other switches. VTP Transparent mode also requires configuration of domain information. A VTP transparent switch is needed when a switch separating a VTP server and client needs to have a different VLAN database. Transparent mode is needed to configure the extended VLAN range (1006 to 4096).

VTP Pruning

There will often be situations where you have VLANs 20 to 50, for example, on one side of your network and 60 to 80 on the other. It doesn't make sense for VLAN information from the switches on one side to be passed to every switch on the other. For this reason, switches can prune unnecessary VLAN information on the switches, thus reducing the broadcast traffic, as shown in Figure 6.4 below:

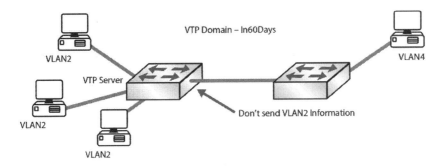

Figure 6.4—VTP Pruning in Operation

The following line of configuration will add VTP pruning to your switch:

```
Switch(config)#vtp pruning
```

It is worth noting that if you have a switch set to transparent mode in-between two other switches, then pruning will not work.

Configuration Revision Number

The configuration revision number is a 32-bit number that indicates the level of revision for a VTP packet (see the show vtp status output above). This information is used to determine whether the received information is more recent than the current version. Each time that you make a VLAN change on a switch in VTP Server mode, the configuration revision is incremented by one and change will be propagated to VTP clients (switches in VTP Transparent mode will have a revision number of 0 and will not increase with database changes). In order to reset the configuration revision of a switch, change the VTP domain name, and then change the name back to the original name.

> **IMPORTANT NOTE:** If a switch configured as VTP Server or VTP Client with a matching domain name and a higher revision number connects to the network, its database will be propagated to all other switches, potentially replacing their existing VTP databases. This can bring the whole LAN network down, so be very careful (always check the VTP status) when connecting a new switch to the LAN network!

TROUBLESHOOTING TRUNKING AND VTP

The following are examples of problems and possible solutions:

Trunk down?

- Interface must be up/up
- Encapsulation must match both sides

```
SwitchA#show interface fa1/1 switchport
Name: Fa1/1
Switchport: Enabled
Administrative Mode: trunk
Operational Mode: trunk
Administrative Trunking Encapsulation: dot1q
Operational Trunking Encapsulation: dot1q
Negotiation of Trunking: Disabled
Access Mode VLAN: 0 ((Inactive))
```

VLAN information not passing?

- Is the VLAN blocked on the trunk?
```
Switch#show interface trunk
```

VTP information not reaching the client?

- Correct domain and VTP password?
```
show vtp status / show vtp password
```

Added a new switch and all VTP information has changed?

- Always add a new switch in Client mode (but check the above note on the configuration revision number)
- Server mode will propagate new information

VTP pruning not working?

- Is there a transparent switch in the middle?
- Is the VLAN allowed across the trunk?

Please take today's exam at https://www.in60days.com/free/ccnain60days/

DAY 6 LABS

DTP

Topology

Gig0/1   Gig0/1

2960-24TT   2960-24TT
Switch0   **Switch1**

Purpose

Learn how to configure DTP settings on Cisco switches.

DTP settings differ from platform to platform so feel free to alter the settings on your switch so you try out the available commands. Please note the results. The below lab was configured on 2960 model switches using Packet Tracer.

For this lab I simply connected two 2960 switches using a crossover cable on port G0/1.

Walkthrough

1. Check the current DTP settings on your switch.

```
Switch#show int g0/1 switchport
Name: Gig0/1
Switchport: Enabled
Administrative Mode: dynamic auto
Operational Mode: static access
Administrative Trunking Encapsulation: dot1q
Operational Trunking Encapsulation: native
Negotiation of Trunking: On
Access Mode VLAN: 1 (default)
Trunking Native Mode VLAN: 1 (default)
Voice VLAN: none
Administrative private-vlan host-association: none
Administrative private-vlan mapping: none
Administrative private-vlan trunk native VLAN: none
Administrative private-vlan trunk encapsulation: dot1q
Administrative private-vlan trunk normal VLANs: none
Administrative private-vlan trunk private VLANs: none
Operational private-vlan: none
Trunking VLANs Enabled: ALL
Pruning VLANs Enabled: 2-1001
Capture Mode Disabled
Capture VLANs Allowed: ALL
Protected: false
Appliance trust: none
```

The settings tell you that the port has dynamically become an access port (as opposed to a manual configuration). It's operating as an access port and DTP is turned on due to the `Negotiation of Trunking: On` output.

2. Change the port setting from dynamic auto (passively becomes a trunk) to dynamic desirable (seeks to actively become a trunk). I've added a question mark so you can see the options available on this platform.

```
Switch(config-if)#switchport mode ?
access Set trunking mode to ACCESS unconditionally
dynamic Set trunking mode to dynamically negotiate access or trunk
mode
trunk Set trunking mode to TRUNK unconditionally
Switch(config-if)#switchport mode dynamic ?
auto Set trunking mode dynamic negotiation parameter to AUTO
desirable Set trunking mode dynamic negotiation parameter to DESIRABLE
Switch(config-if)#switchport mode dynamic desirable
```

3. Ping from R2 to R1 or vice versa.

```
R2#ping 2001:aaaa:bbbb:cccc::2

Type escape sequence to abort.
Sending 5, 100-byte ICMP Echos to 2001:AAAA:BBBB:CCCC::2, timeout is 2
seconds:
!!!!!
Success rate is 100 percent (5/5), round-trip min/avg/max = 0/0/0 ms
```

4. Check the interface settings again. What has changed? I've truncated the output to save space.

```
Switch#show int g0/1 switchport
Name: Gig0/1
Switchport: Enabled
Administrative Mode: dynamic desirable
Operational Mode: trunk
Administrative Trunking Encapsulation: dot1q
Operational Trunking Encapsulation: dot1q
Negotiation of Trunking: On
Access Mode VLAN: 1 (default)
Trunking Native Mode VLAN: 1 (default)
Voice VLAN: none
```

5. Last step is to turn off DTP for the interface. You will see that the command won't be accepted while the port is set to dynamic.

```
Switch(config-if)#switchport nonegotiate
Command rejected: Conflict between 'nonegotiate' and 'dynamic' status.
Switch(config-if)#switchport mode trunk
Switch(config-if)#switchport nonegotiate
Switch(config-if)#
Switch(config-if)#end
```

```
Switch#
%SYS-5-CONFIG_I: Configured from console by console

Switch#show int g0/1 switchport
Name: Gig0/1
Switchport: Enabled
Administrative Mode: trunk
Operational Mode: trunk
Administrative Trunking Encapsulation: dot1q
Operational Trunking Encapsulation: dot1q
Negotiation of Trunking: Off
Access Mode VLAN: 1 (default)
Trunking Native Mode VLAN: 1 (default)
Voice VLAN: none
```

VTP Lab

Test the VTP configuration commands presented in this module in a topology made up of two switches:

- Configure one of the switches as a VTP server
- Configure the other switch as a VTP client
- Configure the same VTP domain and password on both switches
- Create a series of VLANs on the server switch and see how they propagate to each other
- Configure VTP pruning on both switches
- Verify (show) the VTP configuration on both switches
- Configure a different VTP domain name and password and repeat the process; see how the results differ

CDP and LLDP

DAY 7 TASKS

- Read today's lesson notes (below)
- Review yesterday's lesson notes and labs
- Complete today's labs
- Take today's exam
- Read the ICND1 cram guide
- Spend 15 minutes on the subnetting.org website

CDP has always been a popular exam topic because it's both a powerful tool and a potential security risk you need to be aware of. LLDP is a new open standard version and has recently been added to the CCNA syllabus.

Today you will learn about the following:

- CDP
- LLDP

This module maps to the following ICND1 syllabus requirements:

- Configure and verify Layer 2 protocols
- 2.6.a Cisco Discovery Protocol
- 2.6.b LLDP

CISCO DISCOVERY PROTOCOL (CDP)

CDP is a hot exam topic because it provides a means to discover information about network devices before any configuration has been applied. This is a very useful troubleshooting tool; however, it also presents a security risk.

CDP is Cisco proprietary, which means it will only work on Cisco devices. It is a Layer 2 service used by devices to advertise and discover basic information about directly connected neighbors. The IEEE version of CDP is Link Layer Discovery Protocol (LLDP).

Because CDP is a Layer 2 service it does not require IP addresses to be configured in order to exchange information. The interface need only be enabled. If an IP address is configured, then this will be included in the CDP message.

CDP is a very powerful troubleshooting tool and you will be expected to understand how to use it in the exam. Figure 7.1 below shows a small network we can discover using CDP outputs from Router 0. Imagine if you were asked to troubleshoot this network but had no topology diagram to work from.

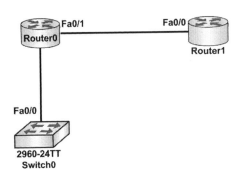

Figure 7.1—CDP Discovery Topology

The following configuration outputs correspond to Figure 7.1:

```
Router0#show cdp neighbors
Capability Codes: R - Router, T - Trans Bridge, B - Source Route Bridge,
S - Switch, H - Host, I - IGMP, r - Repeater, P - Phone
Device ID  Local Interface  Holdtime  Capability  Platform  Port
Switch0    Fas 0/0          165       S           2960      Fas 0/1
Router1    Fas 0/1          169       R           C1841     Fas 0/0
Router0#
```

You can see more information by adding the detail command to the end:

```
Router0#show cdp neighbors detail
Device ID: Switch0
Entry address(es):
Platform: cisco 2960, Capabilities: Switch
Interface: FastEthernet0/0, Port ID (outgoing port): FastEthernet0/1
Holdtime: 178
Version :
Cisco IOS Software, C2960 Software (C2960-LANBASE-M), Version 12.2(25)FX,
RELEASE SOFTWARE (fc1)
Copyright (c) 1986-2005 by Cisco Systems, Inc.
Compiled Wed 12-Oct-05 22:05 by pt_team
advertisement version: 2
Duplex: full
- - - - - - - - - - - - - - - - - - - - - - - - - -
Device ID: Router1
Entry address(es):
   IP address : 192.168.1.2
Platform: cisco C1841, Capabilities: Router
Interface: FastEthernet0/1, Port ID (outgoing port): FastEthernet0/0
Holdtime: 122
Version :
Cisco IOS Software, 1841 Software (C1841-ADVIPSERVICESK9-M), Version
12.4(15)T1, RELEASE SOFTWARE (fc2)
```

```
Technical Support: http://www.cisco.com/techsupport
Copyright (c) 1986-2007 by Cisco Systems, Inc.
Compiled Wed 18-Jul-07 04:52 by pt_team
advertisement version: 2
Duplex: full
```

Now you can see the IOS release, model, IP address, and other information. Remember that you still haven't configured an IP address on Router 0 yet, I added one on Router1 to demonstrate the output.

We will cover how to disable CDP on the device or interface only in the lab. Two other commands are `show cdp`, which displays protocol information for the device, and `show cdp entry <Router>`, which shows information about a specific device by inputting the name. I recommend that you spend some time checking CDP outputs during the labs you will configure in this guide.

```
Router0#show cdp
Global CDP information:
    Sending CDP packets every 60 seconds
    Sending a holdtime value of 180 seconds
    Sending CDPv2 advertisements is enabled
Router0#show cdp ?
  entry      Information for specific neighbor entry
  interface  CDP interface status and configuration
  neighbors  CDP neighbor entries
  traffic    CDP statistics
  |          Output modifiers
  <cr>
```

LINK LAYER DISCOVERY PROTOCOL (LLDP)

Cisco created CDP to address an issue left unresolved by any open standard protocol. Eventually, a standard protocol was released, defined by IEEE standard 802.1AB, and it's called Link Layer Discovery Protocol (LLDP). LLDP provides many of the same features as CDP but the similarities don't end there, because LLDP shares many of the same configurations and show commands as CDP.

Please bear in mind that both your IOS release and platform (router or switch model) must support LLDP if you want to use it. I only bring this up for those of you using a home lab. LLDP is supported in Packet Tracer but the commands are somewhat limited. If you have some out-of-date routers running older IOS versions, then LLDP may not be supported.

Here is an example of some common LLDP commands:

```
R1#show lldp neighbors
Capability codes:  (R) Router, (B) Bridge, (T) Telephone,
                   (C) DOCSIS Cable Device  (W) WLAN Access Point,
                   (P) Repeater, (S) Station, (O) Other
Device ID  Local Intf  Hold-time Capability  Port
IDSW1      Gi0/2       105       B           Gi0/1
R2         Fa0/13      91        R           Gi0/1
```

```
Total entries displayed: 2
SW2#show lldp entry R2
Capability codes: (R) Router, (B) Bridge, (T) Telephone,
                  (C) DOCSIS Cable Device (W) WLAN Access Point,
                  (P) Repeater, (S) Station, (O) Other
Chassis id: 0200.2222.2222
Port id: Gi0/1
Port Description: GigabitEthernet0/1
System Name: R2
System Description:Cisco IOS Software, C2900 Software (C2900-
UNIVERSALK9-M), Version 15.4(3)M3, RELEASE SOFTWARE (fc2)Technical
Support: http://www.cisco.com/techsupportCopyright (c) 1986-2015 by Cisco
Systems, Inc.Compiled Fri 05-Jun-15 13:24 by prod_rel_team
Time remaining: 100 seconds
System Capabilities: B,REnabled Capabilities: R
Management Addresses:  IP: 10.1.1.9
Auto Negotiation - not supported
Physical media capabilities - not advertised
Media Attachment Unit type - not advertised
Vlan ID: - not advertised
Total entries displayed: 1
```

Based on what you know about CDP, the LLDP output should look very familiar. Most importantly, the interface information, such as local and remote port information, is the same between both protocols and is very useful when analyzing or troubleshooting a network. You can enable LLDP globally or per interface.

Enabling and Disabling LLDP

Unlike CDP, LLDP is disabled globally on all supported interfaces, which (of course) means that you must enable LLDP globally to allow a device to send LLDP packets. However, no changes are required at the interface level. The following example shows how to globally enable LLDP:

```
Switch#configure terminal
Switch(config)#lldp run
Switch(config)#end
```

You can configure the interface to selectively not send and receive LLDP packets with the no lldp transmit and no lldp receive commands.

The following example demonstrates how to enable LLDP on an interface:

```
Switch#configure terminal
Switch(config)#interface GigabitEthernet1/1
Switch(config-if)#lldp transmit
Switch(config-if)#lldp receive
Switch(config-if)#end
```

As with CDP, leaving LLDP turned on while on any edge devices represents a security risk. We will cover this in the security notes (and the following lab).

Now please take today's exam at **https://www.in60days.com/free/ccnain60days/**

DAY 7 LAB

CDP/LLDP

Topology

2960-24TT
Switch0

2960-24TT
Switch1

Purpose

Learn how to verify and configure CDP and LLDP settings on Cisco switches.

CDP is enabled by default on Cisco devices. LLDP is disabled.

For this lab I simply connected two 2960 switches using a crossover cable on port G0/1.

Walkthrough

1. Check the current CDP settings on your switch.

```
Switch#show cdp neighbors
Capability Codes: R - Router, T - Trans Bridge, B - Source Route
Bridge
S - Switch, H - Host, I - IGMP, r - Repeater, P - Phone
Device ID Local Intrfce Holdtme Capability Platform Port ID
Switch Gig 0/1 121 S 2960 Gig 0/1

Switch#show cdp neighbors detail

Device ID: Switch
Entry address(es):
Platform: cisco 2960, Capabilities: Switch
Interface: GigabitEthernet0/1, Port ID (outgoing port):
GigabitEthernet0/1
Holdtime: 172

Version :
Cisco IOS Software, C2960 Software (C2960-LANBASE-M), Version 12.2(25)
FX, RELEASE SOFTWARE (fc1)
Copyright (c) 1986-2005 by Cisco Systems, Inc.
Compiled Wed 12-Oct-05 22:05 by pt_team

advertisement version: 2
Duplex:full
```

2. Turn CDP off on the remote interface. Clear the CDP entry on the switch and check the outputs again. The entry should be blank.

```
Switch1(config)#int g0/1
```

```
Switch1(config-if)#no cdp ?
enable Enable CDP on interface
Switch1(config-if)#no cdp enable

Switch#clear cdp table
Switch#show cdp neighbors
Capability Codes: R - Router, T - Trans Bridge, B - Source Route
Bridge
S - Switch, H - Host, I - IGMP, r - Repeater, P - Phone
Device ID Local Intrfce Holdtme Capability Platform Port ID
Switch#
```

3. Check the LLDP entry for Switch1, note that LLDP is disabled and then enable it on both sides.

```
Switch#show lldp neighbors
% LLDP is not enabled
Switch#conf t
Switch(config)#lldp run

Switch1(config)#lldp run
```

4. Check the LLDP entry again. Normal and detailed.

```
Switch#show lldp neighbors
Capability codes:
    (R) Router, (B) Bridge, (T) Telephone, (C) DOCSIS Cable Device
    (W) WLAN Access Point, (P) Repeater, (S) Station, (O) Other
Device ID         Local Intf    Hold-time  Capability    Port ID
Switch1           Gig0/1        120        B             Gig0/1

Total entries displayed: 1
Switch#show lldp neighbors detail
------------------------------------------------
Chassis id: 0001.64EE.CB19
Port id: Gig0/1
Port Description: GigabitEthernet0/1
System Name: Switch1
System Description:
Cisco IOS Software, C2960 Software (C2960-LANBASE-M), Version 12.2(25)
FX, RELEASE SOFTWARE (fc1)
Copyright (c) 1986-2005 by Cisco Systems, Inc.
Compiled Wed 12-Oct-05 22:05 by pt_team
Time remaining: 90 seconds
System Capabilities: B
Enabled Capabilities: B
Management Addresses - not advertised
Auto Negotiation - supported, enabled
Physical media capabilities:
    100baseT(HD)
    1000baseT(FD)
    1000baseT(HD)
Media Attachment Unit type: 10
```

```
Vlan ID: 1

Total entries displayed: 1
Switch#Name: Gig0/1
```

5. Last step are to check the commands to enable LLDP per interface and disable per device.

```
Switch1(config-if)#lldp ?
  receive   Enable LLDP reception on interface
  transmit  Enable LLDP transmission on interface

Switch1(config-if)#exit
Switch1(config)#no lldp ?
  run  Enable LLDP
Switch1(config)#no lldp run
```

DAY 8

Review

DAY 8 TASKS

- Read today's lesson notes (below)
- Re-read notes from days 5-7 and redo the labs
- Complete today's challenge labs
- Take today's exam at **https://www.in60days.com/free/ccnain60days/**
- Read the ICND1 cram guide

We have covered some important ground over the last three days. Ensure you read over the notes again, making your own notes and highlighting important learning points which you will find makeup questions in the actual exam. The challenge labs throughout this book are based on previous labs already configured so we don't provide solutions.

Challenge 1—Configuring VLANs Lab

Topology

VLAN 2

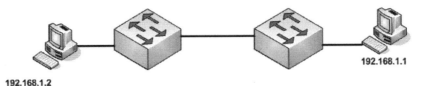

192.168.1.1

192.168.1.2

Instructions

Connect to the switch using a console connection. Connect a PC to each switch or connect the switch to the fast ethernet port on a router.

1. Add IP addresses to the PCs or router Ethernet interfaces.
2. Create VLAN 2 on the switch.
3. Set the ports the PCs connect to as access ports (default but do it anyway).
4. Put the two switch ports into VLAN 2.
5. Configure the link between the switches as trunk ports and no shut them.
6. Wait about 30 seconds at most and then ping from PC to PC.

Challenge 2—Trunking, VLANs and DTP Lab

Topology

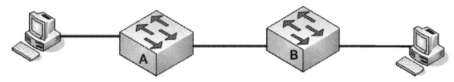

Instructions

Connect to the switch using a console connection. Choose whichever ports you wish. Ensure you have the correct cable types for the devices.

1. Add VLAN2 to the switches.
2. Give VLAN2 an IP address of 192.168.1.1 (SVI) on A and 192.168.1.2 on B.
3. Put two fast Ethernet interfaces into VLAN2 for the hosts and add IP addresses 192.168.1.3 and .4. Set the default gateway to the SVI address of the closest switch.
4. Set the hosts ports on the switches to access ports.
5. Issue the `show vlan brief` command to check the interfaces are in VLAN 2.
6. Set interface to trunk on the left switch.
7. Disable DTP on the right switch and set interface to trunk. Issue a `show interface trunk` command on either switch.
8. Issue a `show interface fast x/x switchport` on the trunk interface and check DTP is off on switch B (replace x/x with the correct interface number).

Challenge 3—CDP Lab

Topology

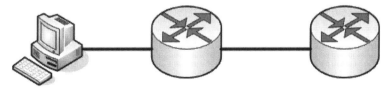

Instructions

Connect to a router with a console cable and Ethernet cable. Connect another router (or just use PT).

1. Configure an IP address on the two routers facing interfaces and ping across.
2. Using CDP commands see what information you can gather about the other router.

Challenge 4—LLDP Lab

Topology

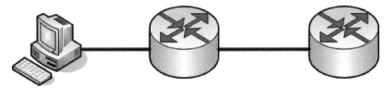

Instructions

Connect to a router with a console cable and Ethernet cable. Connect another router (or just use PT).

1. Configure an IP address on the two routers facing interfaces and ping across.
2. Using LLDP commands see what information you can gather about the other router.
3. On the left router turn LLDP off the interface.
4. On the right router, turn LLDP off the entire device.

Switch Security

DAY 9 TASKS

- Read today's lesson notes (below)
- Complete today's lab
- Read the ICND1 cram guide
- Take today's exam
- Spend 15 minutes on the subnetting.org website

In this section of the guide, we will look at the basic steps you should take on every network to protect your switches. All of these steps equally apply to router security (apart from switch port security of course) so review this section again when you come to router security because I won't repeat the ground already covered.

Today you will learn about the following:

- Securing the switch
- Switch port security

This module maps to the following CCNA syllabus requirements:

- 2.7 Configure, verify, and troubleshoot port security
- 2.7.a Static
- 2.7.b Dynamic
- 2.7.c Sticky
- 2.7.d Max MAC addresses
- 2.7.e Violation actions
- 2.7.f Err-disable recovery
- 5.4.c. (ii) Telnet/SSH
- 5.4.d Login banner

SECURING THE SWITCH

Prevent Telnet Access

Telnet traffic sends the password in clear text, which means that it could easily be read on the configuration or by a network sniffer, if one was attached to your network.

Telnet is actually disabled by default (i.e., you need to set a password and, optionally, a username to get it working). However, if you still want to have remote access to the management ports, you can enable SSH traffic to the switch with the transport input ssh command, which was discussed earlier.

 FARAI SAYS—"The command transport input all is enabled by default for all VTY lines, while transport input none is enabled by default for other lines."

Enable SSH

When possible, you should always use SSH instead of Telnet and SNMP to access your switches. SSH stands for secure shell and allows a secure exchange of information between two devices on a network. SSH uses public-key cryptography to authenticate the connecting device. Telnet and SNMP versions 1 and 2 are unencrypted and susceptible to packet sniffing (SNMP version 3 offers confidentiality—encryption of packets to prevent snooping by an unauthorized source). SSH, on the other hand, is encrypted.

To enable SSH you must have a version of IOS that supports encryption. A quick way to find this out is the show version command. Look for K9 in the file name and/or the security statement of Cisco Systems.

```
Switch#sh version
Cisco IOS Software, C3560 Software (C3560-ADVIPSERVICES K9-M), Version
12.2(35)SE1, RELEASE SOFTWARE (fc1)
Copyright (c) 1986-2006 by Cisco Systems, Inc.
Compiled Tue 19-Dec-06 10:54 by antonio
Image text-base: 0x00003000, data-base: 0x01362CA0
ROM: Bootstrap program is C3560 boot loader
BOOTLDR: C3560 Boot Loader (C3560-HBOOT-M) Version 12.2(25r)SEC, RELEASE
SOFTWARE (fc4)
Switch uptime is 1 hour, 8 minutes
System returned to ROM by power-on
System image file is "flash:/c3560-advipservicek9-mz.122-35.SE1.bin"
This product contains cryptographic features and is subject to United
States and local country laws governing import, export, transfer and
use. Delivery of Cisco cryptographic products does not imply third-party
authority to import, export, distribute or use encryption.
[Output Truncated]
```

NOTE: If you do not have a security version of IOS, you must purchase a license for it.

For an encrypted connection , you will need to create a private/public key on the switch (see below). When you connect, use the public key to encrypt the data and the switch will use its private key to decrypt the data. For authentication, use your chosen username/password combination. Next, set the switch hostname and domain name because the private/public keys will be created using the hostname.domainname nomenclature. Obviously, it makes sense for the key to be named something representing the system.

Firstly, make sure that you have a hostname other than the default one, which is Switch. Next, add your domain name (this typically matches your FQDN in Windows Active Directory). Then, create the crypto key that will be used for encryption. The modulus will be the length of the keys you want to use, in the range from 360 to 2048, with the latter being the most secure; 1024 and above is considered secure. At this point, SSH is enabled on the switch.

There are a few maintenance commands you should enter as well. The `ip ssh time-out 60` will time out any SSH connection that has been idle for 60 seconds. The `ip ssh authentication-retries 2` will reset the initial SSH connection if authentication fails two times. This will not prevent the user from establishing a new connection and retrying authentication. This process is illustrated in the output below:

```
Switch(config)#hostname SwitchOne
SwitchOne(config)#ip domain-name mydomain.com
SwitchOne(config)#crypto key generate rsa
Enter modulus: 1024
SwitchOne(config)#ip ssh time-out 60
SwitchOne(config)#ip ssh authentication-retries 2
```

You can optionally enable SSH version 2 with the `ip ssh version 2` command. Let's take a look at one of the keys. In this example, the key was generated for HTTPS. Because the key was automatically generated when enabling HTTPS, the name will also be auto-generated.

```
firewall#show crypto key mypubkey rsa
Key name: HTTPS_SS_CERT_KEYPAIR.server
Temporary key
Usage: Encryption Key
Key is not exportable.
Key Data:
306C300D 06092A86 4886F70D 01010105 00035B00 30580251 00C41B63 8EF294A1
DC0F7378 7EF410F6 6254750F 475DAD71 4E1CD15E 1D9086A8 BD175433 1302F403
2FD22F82 C311769F 9C75B7D2 1E50D315 EFA0E940 DF44AD5A F717BF17 A3CEDBE1
A6A2D601 45F313B6 6B020301 0001
```

To verify that SSH is enabled on the switch, enter the following command:

```
Switch#show ip ssh
SSH Enabled - version 1.99
Authentication timeout: 120 secs; Authentication retries: 2
Switch#
```

If you have SSH enabled, you should probably disable Telnet and HTTP. When you enter the `transport input` command, any protocol entered after it is allowed. Any protocol not entered is not allowed. In the output below, you can see that only SSH is allowed:

```
line vty 0 15
transport input ssh
```

The following output shows that both SSH and Telnet are allowed:

```
line vty 0 15
transport input ssh telnet
```

You can disable HTTP access with one simple command:

```
Switch(config)#no ip http server
```

To view the status of the HTTP server on the switch:

```
Switch#show ip http server status
HTTP server status: Disabled
HTTP server port: 80
HTTP server authentication method: enable
HTTP server access class: 0
HTTP server base path: flash:html
Maximum number of concurrent server connections allowed: 16
Server idle time-out: 180 seconds
Server life time-out: 180 seconds
Maximum number of requests allowed on a connection: 25
HTTP server active session modules: ALL
HTTP secure server capability: Present
HTTP secure server status: Enabled
HTTP secure server port: 443
HTTP secure server ciphersuite: 3des-ede-cbc-sha des-cbc-sha rc4-128-md5
rc4-12
HTTP secure server client authentication: Disabled
HTTP secure server trustpoint:
HTTP secure server active session modules: ALL
```

You could also apply an access control list to the VTY lines and permit only SSH. We will cover access control lists on Day 15.

Set an Enable Secret Password

Global Configuration mode will permit a user to configure the switch or router and erase configurations, as well as reset passwords. You must protect this mode by setting a password or a secret password (which actually prevents the user from getting past User mode). The secret password will be displayed on the routers running the configuration file, whereas the `enable secret` password will be encrypted.

I've already mentioned that you can actually have both a password and an enable secret password on your router and switch, but this can cause confusion. Just set the enable secret password. The configuration file below illustrates how to issue a command without dropping back to Privileged mode by typing do before the command:

```
Switch1(config)#enable password cisco
Switch1(config)#do show run
Building configuration...
Current configuration: 1144 bytes
hostname Switch1
enable password cisco
```

 FARAI SAYS—"You can encrypt the enable secret password with the service password-encryption command."

You can erase most lines of configuration by issuing it again with the word no before the command. It is also worth noting that, as Farai says, you can issue a service password-encryption command, but this only offers weak (level 7) encryption, whereas below, the secret password has strong (MD5) encryption :

```
Switch1(config)#no enable password
Switch1(config)#enable secret cisco
Switch1(config)#do show run
Building configuration...
Current configuration: 1169 bytes
hostname Switch1
enable secret 5 $1$mERr$hx5rVt7rPNoS4wqbXKX7m0 [strong level 5 password]
```

Services

You should always disable the services you are not going to use. Cisco has done a good job by not enabling insecure or rarely used services/protocols by default; however, you might want to disable them just to make sure. Some services are helpful as well. The majority of services are found under the command service in Global Configuration mode.

```
Switch(config)#service ?
compress-config         Compress the configuration file
config                  TFTP load config files
counters                Control aging of interface counters
dhcp                    Enable DHCP server and relay agent
disable-ip-fast-frag    Disable IP particle-based fast fragmentation
exec-callback           Enable exec callback
exec-wait               Delay EXEC startup on noisy lines
finger                  Allow responses to finger requests
hide-telnet-addresses   Hide destination addresses in telnet command
linenumber              enable line number banner for each exec
nagle                   Enable Nagle's congestion control algorithm
old-slip-prompts        Allow old scripts to operate with slip/ppp
pad                     Enable PAD commands
```

```
password-encryption     Encrypt system passwords
password-recovery       Disable password recovery
prompt                  Enable mode specific prompt
pt-vty-logging          Log significant VTY-Async events
sequence-numbers        Stamp logger messages with a sequence number
slave-log               Enable log capability of slave IPs
tcp-keepalives-in       Generate keepalives on idle incoming network
                        connections
tcp-keepalives-out      Generate keepalives on idle outgoing network
                        connections
tcp-small-servers       Enable small TCP servers (e.g., ECHO)
telnet-zeroidle         Set TCP window 0 when connection is idle
timestamps              Timestamp debug/log messages
udp-small-servers       Enable small UDP servers (e.g., ECHO)
```

Generally speaking, the most common services to enable/disable are listed below with their descriptions in Table 9.1:

Table 9.1—Most Commonly Used Services to Enable/Disable

Service	Description
no service pad	Packet assembler/disassembler, used in asynchronous networking; rarely used
no service config	Prevents the switch from getting its config file from the network
no service finger	Disables the finger server; rarely used
no ip icmp redirect	Prevents ICMP redirects, which can be used for router poisoning
no ip finger	Another way to disable the finger service
no ip gratuitous-arps	Disable to prevent man-in-the-middle attacks
no ip source-route	Disables user-provided hop-by-hop routing to destination
service sequence-numbers	In each log entry, gives it a number and increases sequentially
service tcp-keepalives-in	Prevents the router from keeping hung management sessions open
service tcp-keepalives-out	Same as service tcp-keepalives-in
no service udp-small-servers	Disables echo, chargen, discard, daytime; rarely used
no service tcp-small-servers	Disables echo, chargen, discard; rarely used
service timestamps debug datetime localtime show-timezone	Timestamps each logged packet (in debug mode) with the date and time, using local time, and shows the time zone
service timestamps log datetime localtime show-timezone	Timestamps each logged packet (not in debug mode) with the date and time, using local time, and shows the time zone—very useful for observing the log file (especially if the clock is set up correctly)

Change the Native VLAN

We already know that the native VLAN is used by the switch to carry specific protocol traffic, such as Cisco Discovery Protocol (CDP), VLAN Trunking Protocol (VTP), Port Aggregation Protocol (PAgP), and Dynamic Trunking Protocol (DTP) information. The default native VLAN is always VLAN 1; however, the native VLAN can be manually changed to any valid VLAN number (except for 0 and 4096, because these are in the reserved range of VLANs).

You can verify the native VLAN with the commands (issued per interface) illustrated in the output below:

```
Switch#show interfaces FastEthernet0/1 switchport
Name: Fa0/1
Switchport: Enabled
Administrative Mode: trunk
Operational Mode: trunk
Administrative Trunking Encapsulation: dot1q
Operational Trunking Encapsulation: dot1q
Negotiation of Trunking: On
Access Mode VLAN: 1 (default)Trunking Native Mode VLAN: 1 (default)
Voice VLAN: none
```

NOTE: This is one of the key objectives in the CCNA syllabus, so bear it in mind.

Having ports in VLAN 1 is considered a security vulnerability which allows hackers to gain access to network resources. To mitigate this problem, it is advisable to avoid putting any hosts into VLAN 1. You can also change the native VLAN on all trunk ports to an unused VLAN:

```
Switch(config-if)#switchport trunk native vlan 888
```

You can also prevent native VLAN data from passing on the trunk with the command below:

```
Switch(config-if)#switchport trunk allowed vlan remove 888
```

Change the Management VLAN

You can also add an IP address to the switch to allow you to Telnet to it for management purposes. This is referred to as a Switch Virtual Interface (SVI). It is a wise precaution to have this management access in a VLAN other than VLAN 1, as shown in the output below:

```
Switch(config)#vlan 3
Switch(config-vlan)#interface vlan3

%LINK-5-CHANGED: Interface Vlan3, changed state to up
Switch(config-if)#ip address 192.168.1.1 255.255.255.0
```

Turn Off CDP

Cisco Discovery Protocol (CDP) was covered earlier. It is turned on by default on most routers and switches universally and per interface, and its function is to discover attached Cisco devices. You may not want other Cisco devices to see information about your network devices, so you can turn this off, at least on the devices at the edge of your network which connect to other companies or your ISP.

 FARAI SAYS—"CDP is not enabled by default on all platforms, such as ASR routers, for example."

In the output below, you can see how a router connected to my switch is able to see basic information when I issue the show cdp neighbor detail command:

```
Router#show cdp neighbor detail
Device ID: Switch1
Entry address(es):
Platform: Cisco 2960, Capabilities: Switch
Interface: FastEthernet0/0, Port ID (outgoing port): FastEthernet0/2
Holdtime: 176
Version :
Cisco Internetwork Operating System Software
IOS (tm) C2960 Software (C2960-I6Q4L2-M), Version 12.1(22)EA4, RELEASE
SOFTWARE(fc1)
Copyright (c) 1986-2005 by Cisco Systems, Inc.
Compiled Wed 18-May-05 22:31 by jharirba
advertisement version: 2
Duplex: full
Router#The command below will turn off CDP for the entire device:
Switch1(config)#no cdp run
```

NOTE: The switchport command is not required on Layer 2-only switches, such as the Catalyst 2950 and Catalyst 2960 series. However, it must be used on Multilayer switches, such as the Catalyst 3750, Catalyst 4500, and Catalyst 6500 series.

To turn off CDP for a particular interface, issue the following command:

```
Switch1(config)#int FastEthernet0/2
Switch1(config-if)#no cdp enable
```

Add a Banner Message

A banner message will show when a user logs in to your router or switch. It won't offer any actual security but it will display a warning message of your choice. In the configuration below, I chose the letter Y as my delimiting character, which tells the router that I've finished typing my message:

```
Switch1(config)#banner motd Y
Enter TEXT message.  End with the character 'Y'.

KEEP OUT OR YOU WILL REGRET IT Y

Switch1(config)#
```

When I Telnet to the switch from my router, I can see the banner message. The mistake was choosing Y as the delimiting character because it cuts off my message:

```
Router#telnet 192.168.1.3
Trying 192.168.1.3 ...Open
KEEP OUT OR
```

Banner messages can be:

- MOTD (message of the day)—shown before the user sees the login prompt
- Login— shown before the user sees the login prompt
- Exec— shown to the user after the login prompt (used when you want to hide information from unauthorized users)

I suggest that you learn to configure all three types and test them by logging in to the router. You will have different choices depending upon your platform and IOS:

```
Router(config)#banner ?
  LINE            c banner-text c, where 'c' is a delimiting character
  exec            Set EXEC process creation banner.
  incoming        Set incoming terminal line banner
  login           Set login banner
  motd            Set Message of the Day banner
  prompt-timeout  Set Message for login authentication timeout
  slip-ppp        Set Message for SLIP/PPP
```

Set a VTP Password

VTP ensures that accurate VLAN information is passed between the switches on your network. In order to protect these updates, you should add a VTP password on your switch (it should match on all switches in the VTP domain), as illustrated in the output below:

```
Switch1(config)#vtp domain 60days
Changing VTP domain name from NULL to 60days
Switch1(config)#vtp password cisco
Setting device VLAN database password to cisco
Switch1(config)#
```

Restrict VLAN Information

By default, switches permit all VLANs across the trunk links. You can change this by specifying which VLANs can pass, as illustrated in the following output:

```
Switch1(config)#int FastEthernet0/4
Switch1(config-if)#switchport mode trunk
Switch1(config-if)#switchport trunk allowed vlan ?
  WORD    VLAN IDs of the allowed VLANs when this port is in trunking
mode
  add     add VLANs to the current list
  all     all VLANs
  except  all VLANs except the following
  none    no VLANs
  remove  remove VLANs from the current list
Switch1(config-if)#switchport trunk allowed vlan 7-12

Switch1#show interface trunk
Port        Mode        Encapsulation  Status       Native vlan
Fa0/4       on          802.1q         trunking     1

Port        Vlans allowed on trunk
Fa0/4       7-12
```

Shut Down Unused Ports

Unused or "empty" ports within any network device pose a security risk, as someone might plug a cable into them and connect an unauthorized device to the network. This can lead to a number of issues, including:

- Network not functioning as it should
- Network information vulnerable to outsiders

This is why you should shut down every port that is not used on routers, switches, and other network devices. Depending upon the device, the shutdown state might be the default, but you should always verify this.

Shutting down a port is done with the shutdown command under the Interface Configuration mode:

```
Switch#conf t
Switch(config)#int fa0/0
Switch(config-if)#shutdown
```

You can verify a port is in the shutdown state in multiple ways, one of which is using the show ip interface brief command:

```
Router(config-if)#do show ip interface brief
Interface       IP-Address   OK? Method Status                  Protocol
FastEthernet0/0 unassigned   YES unset  administratively down   down
FastEthernet0/1 unassigned   YES unset  administratively down   down
```

Note that the administratively down status means that the port has been manually shut down.

Another way to verify the shutdown state is using the show interface x command:

```
Router#show interface fa0/0
FastEthernet0/0 is administratively down, line protocol is down
   Hardware is Gt96k FE, address is c200.27c8.0000 (bia c200.27c8.0000)
   MTU 1500 bytes, BW 10000 Kbit/sec, DLY 1000 usec,
```

SWITCH PORT SECURITY

The port security feature is a dynamic Catalyst switch feature that secures switch ports, and ultimately the CAM table, by limiting the number of MAC addresses that can be learned on a particular port or interface. With the port security feature, the switch maintains a table that is used to identify which MAC address (or addresses) can access which local switch port. Additionally, the switch can also be configured to allow only a certain number of MAC addresses to be learned on any given switch port. Port security is illustrated below in Figure 9.1:

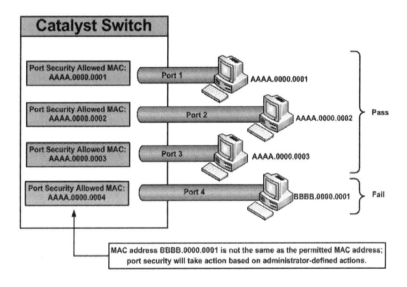

Figure 9.1—Port Security Operation

Figure 9.1 shows four ports on a Catalyst switch configured to allow a single MAC address via the port security feature. Ports 1 through 3 are connected to hosts whose MAC address match the address permitted by port security. Assuming no other filtering is in place, these hosts are able to forward frames through their respective switch ports. Port 4, however, has been configured to allow a host with MAC address AAAA.0000.0004, but instead a host with MAC address BBBB.0000.0001 has been connected to this port. Because the host MAC and the permitted MAC are not the same, port security will take appropriate action on the port as defined by the administrator. The valid port security actions will be described in detail in a subsequent section.

The port security feature is designed to protect the switched LAN from two primary methods of attack. These attack methods, which will be described in the following sections, are:

- CAM table overflow attacks
- MAC spoofing attacks

CAM Table Overflow Attacks

Switch CAM tables are storage locations that contain lists of known MAC addresses on physical ports, as well as their VLAN parameters. Dynamically learned contents of the switch CAM table, or MAC address table, can be viewed by issuing the show mac-address-table dynamic command, as illustrated in the following output:

```
Switch-1#show mac-address-table dynamic
          Mac Address Table
-------------------------------------------

Vlan    Mac Address       Type       Ports
----    -----------       --------   -----
   2    000c.cea7.f3a0    DYNAMIC    Fa0/1
   2    0013.1986.0a20    DYNAMIC    Fa0/2
   6    0004.c16f.8741    DYNAMIC    Fa0/3
   6    0030.803f.ea81    DYNAMIC    Fa0/4
   8    0004.c16f.8742    DYNAMIC    Fa0/5
   8    0030.803f.ea82    DYNAMIC    Fa0/6

Total Mac Addresses for this criterion: 6
```

Switches, like all computing devices, have finite memory resources. This means that the CAM table has a fixed, allocated memory space. CAM table overflow attacks target this limitation by flooding the switch with a large number of randomly generated invalid source and destination MAC addresses until the CAM table fills up and the switch is no longer able to accept new entries. In such situations, the switch effectively turns into a hub and simply begins to broadcast all newly received frames to all ports (within the same VLAN) on the switch, essentially turning the VLAN into one big Broadcast Domain.

CAM table attacks are easy to perform because common tools, such as MACOF and DSNIFF, are readily available to perform these activities. While increasing the number of VLANs (which reduces the size of Broadcast Domains) can assist in reducing the effects of CAM table attacks, the recommended security solution is to configure the port security feature on the switch.

MAC Spoofing Attacks

MAC address spoofing is used to spoof a source MAC address in order to impersonate other hosts or devices on the network. Spoofing is simply a term that means masquerading or pretending to be someone you are not. The primary objective of MAC spoofing is to confuse the switch and cause it to believe that the same host is connected to two ports, which causes the switch to attempt to forward frames destined to the trusted host to the attacker as well. Figure 9.2 below shows the CAM table of a switch connected to four different network hosts:

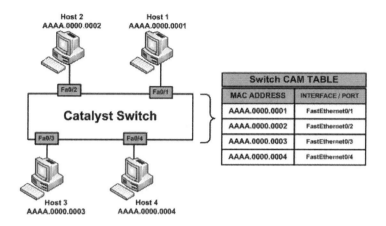

Figure 9.2—Building the Switch CAM Table

In Figure 9.2, the switch is operating normally and, based on the CAM table entries, knows the MAC addresses for all the devices connected to its ports. Based on the current CAM table, if Host 4 wanted to send a frame to Host 2, the switch would simply forward the frame out of its FastEthernet0/2 interface toward Host 2.

Now, assume that Host 1 has been compromised by an attacker who wants to receive all traffic destined for Host 2. By using MAC address spoofing, the attacker crafts an Ethernet frame using the source address of Host 2. When the switch receives this frame, it notes the source MAC address and overwrites the CAM table entry for the MAC address of Host 2, and points it to port FastEthernet0/1 instead of FastEthernet0/2, where the real Host 2 is connected. This concept is illustrated below in Figure 9.3:

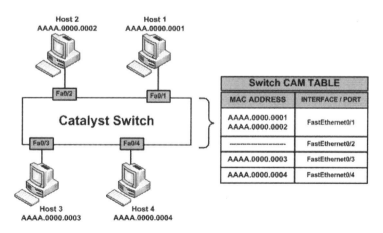

Figure 9.3—MAC Address Spoofing

Referencing Figure 9.3, when Host 3 or Host 4 attempts to send frames to Host 2, the switch will forward them out of FastEthernet0/1 to Host 1 because the CAM table has been poisoned by a MAC spoofing attack. When Host 2 sends another frame, the switch relearns its MAC address from FastEthernet0/2 and rewrites the CAM table entry once again to reflect this change. The result is a tug-of-war between Host 2 and Host 1 as to which host owns this MAC address.

In addition, this confuses the switch and causes repetitive rewrites of MAC address table entries, causing a Denial of Service (DoS) attack on the legitimate host (i.e., Host 2). If the number of spoofed MAC addresses used is high, this attack could have serious performance consequences for the switch that is constantly rewriting its CAM table. MAC address spoofing attacks can be mitigated by implementing port security.

Port Security Secure Addresses

The port security feature can be used to specify which specific MAC address is permitted access to a switch port, as well as to limit the number of MAC addresses that can be supported on a single switch port. The methods of port security implementation described in this section are as follows:

- Static secure MAC addresses
- Dynamic secure MAC addresses
- Sticky secure MAC addresses

Static secure MAC addresses are statically configured by network administrators and are stored in the MAC address table, as well as in the switch configuration. When static secure MAC addresses are assigned to a secure port, the switch will not forward frames that do not have a source MAC address that matches the configured static secure MAC address or addresses.

Dynamic secure MAC addresses are dynamically learned by the switch and are stored in the MAC address table. However, unlike static secure MAC addresses, dynamic secure MAC address entries are removed from the switch when the switch is reloaded or powered down. These addresses must then be relearned by the switch when it boots up again.

Sticky secure MAC addresses are a mix of static secure MAC addresses and dynamic secure MAC addresses. These addresses can be learned dynamically or configured statically and are stored in the MAC address table, as well as in the switch running configuration. This means that when the switch is powered down or rebooted, it will not need to dynamically discover the MAC addresses again because they are already saved in the configuration file (if you save the running configuration).

Port Security Actions

Once port security has been enabled, administrators can define the actions the switch will take in the event of a port security violation. Cisco IOS software allows administrators to specify four different actions to take when a violation occurs, as follows:

- Protect
- Shutdown (default)
- Restrict
- Shutdown VLAN (outside of the CCNA syllabus)

The protect option forces the port into Protected Port mode. In this mode, the switch will simply discard all Unicast or Multicast frames with unknown source MAC addresses. When the switch is configured to protect a port, it will not send out a notification when operating in Protected Port mode, meaning that administrators would never know when any traffic was prevented by the switch port operating in this mode.

The shutdown option places a port in an err-disabled state (covered later) when a port security violation occurs. The corresponding port LED on the switch is also turned off when this configured action mode is used. In Shutdown mode, the switch sends out an SNMP trap and a syslog message, and the violation counter is incremented. This is the default action taken when port security is enabled on an interface.

The restrict option is used to drop packets with unknown MAC addresses when the number of secure MAC addresses reaches the administrator-defined maximum limit for the port. In this mode, the switch will continue to restrict additional MAC addresses from sending frames until a sufficient number of secure MAC addresses is removed, or the number of maximum allowable addresses is increased. As is the case with the shutdown option, the switch sends out an SNMP trap and a syslog message, and the violation counter is incremented.

The shutdown VLAN option is similar to the shutdown option; however, this option shuts down a VLAN instead of the entire switch port. This configuration could be applied to ports that have more than one single VLAN assigned to them, such as a voice VLAN and a data VLAN, as well as to trunk links on the switches.

Configuring Port Security

Before configuring port security, it is recommended that the switch port be statically configured as a Layer 2 access port (it can only be configured on static access or trunk ports, not on dynamic ports). This configuration is illustrated in the following output:

```
Switch-1(config)#interface FastEthernet0/1
Switch-1(config-if)#switchport
Switch-1(config-if)#switchport mode access
```

NOTE: The switchport command is not required on Layer 2-only switches, such as the Catalyst 2950 and Catalyst 2960 series. However, it must be used on Multilayer switches, such as the Catalyst 3750, Catalyst 4500, and Catalyst 6500 series.

By default, port security is disabled; however, this feature can be enabled using the switchport port-security [mac-address {mac-address} [vlan {vlan-id | {access | voice}}] | mac-address {sticky} [mac-address | vlan {vlan-id | {access | voice}}] [maximum {value} [vlan {vlan-list | {access | voice}}]]] interface configuration command. The options that are available with this command are described below in Table 9.2:

Table 9.2—Port Security Configuration Keywords

Keyword	Description
mac-address {mac-address}	This keyword is used to specify a static secure MAC address. You can add additional secure MAC addresses up to the maximum value configured.
vlan {vlan id}	This keyword should be used on a trunk port only to specify the VLAN ID and the MAC address. If no VLAN ID is specified, the native VLAN is used.
vlan {access}	This keyword should be used on an access port only to specify the VLAN as an access VLAN.
vlan {voice}	This keyword should be used on an access port only to specify the VLAN as a voice VLAN. This option is only available if a voice VLAN is configured on the specified port.
mac-address {sticky} [mac-address]	This keyword is used to enable dynamic or sticky learning on the specified interface or to configure a static secure MAC address.
maximum {value}	This keyword is used to specify the maximum number of secure addresses that can be learned on an interface. The default is 1.

Configuring Static Secure MAC Addresses

The following output illustrates how to enable port security on an interface and to configure a static secure MAC address of 001f:3c59:d63b on a switch access port:

```
Switch-1(config)#interface GigabitEthernet0/2
Switch-1(config-if)#switchport
Switch-1(config-if)#switchport mode access
Switch-1(config-if)#switchport port-security
Switch-1(config-if)#switchport port-security mac-address 001f.3c59.d63b
```

The following output illustrates how to enable port security on an interface and to configure a static secure MAC address of 001f:3c59:d63b in VLAN 5 on a switch trunk port:

```
Switch-1(config)#interface GigabitEthernet0/2
Switch-1(config-if)#switchport
Switch-1(config-if)#switchport trunk encapsulation dot1q
Switch-1(config-if)#switchport mode trunk
```

```
Switch-1(config-if)#switchport port-security
Switch-1(config-if)#switchport port-security mac-address 001f.3c59.d63b
vlan 5
```

The following output illustrates how to enable port security on an interface and to configure a static secure MAC address of 001f:3c59:5555 for VLAN 5 (the data VLAN) and a static secure MAC address of 001f:3c59:7777 for VLAN 7 (the voice VLAN) on a switch access port:

```
Switch-1(config)#interface GigabitEthernet0/2
Switch-1(config-if)#switchport
Switch-1(config-if)#switchport mode access
Switch-1(config-if)#switchport access vlan 5
Switch-1(config-if)#switchport voice vlan 7
Switch-1(config-if)#switchport port-security
Switch-1(config-if)#switchport port-security maximum 2
Switch-1(config-if)#switchport port-security mac-address 001f.3c59.5555
vlan access
Switch-1(config-if)#switchport port-security mac-address 001f.3c59.7777
vlan voice
```

It is very important to remember that when enabling port security on an interface that is also configured with a voice VLAN in conjunction with the data VLAN, the maximum allowed secure addresses on the port should be set to 2. This is performed via the switchport port-security maximum 2 interface configuration command, which is included in the output above.

One of the two MAC addresses is used by the IP phone and the switch learns about this address on the voice VLAN. The other MAC address is used by a host (such as a PC) that may be connected to the IP phone. This MAC address will be learned by the switch on the data VLAN.

Verifying Static Secure MAC Address Configuration

Global port security configuration parameters can be validated by issuing the show port-security command. The following shows the output printed by this command based on default values:

```
Switch-1#show port-security
Secure Port MaxSecureAddr  CurrentAddr SecurityViolation  Security Action
            (Count)        (Count)     (Count)
---------------------------------------------------------------------
 Gi0/2        1              1            0                 Shutdown
---------------------------------------------------------------------

Total Addresses in System : 1
Max Addresses limit in System : 1024
```

As seen in the output above, by default, only a single secure MAC address is permitted per port. In addition, the default action in the event of a violation is to shut down the port. The text in bold indicates that only a single secured address is known, which is the static address configured on the interface. The same can also be confirmed by issuing the show port-security interface [name] command, as illustrated in the following output:

```
Switch-1#show port-security interface gi0/2
Port Security : Enabled
Port status : SecureUp
Violation mode : Shutdown
Maximum MAC Addresses : 1
Total MAC Addresses : 1
Configured MAC Addresses : 1
Sticky MAC Addresses : 0
Aging time : 0 mins
Aging type : Absolute
SecureStatic address aging : Disabled
Security Violation count : 0
```

NOTE: The modification of the other default parameters in the output above will be described in detail as we progress through this section.

To see the actual configured static secure MAC address on the port, the show port-security address or the show running-config interface [name] command must be used. The following output illustrates the show port-security address command:

```
Switch-1#show port-security address
         Secure Mac Address Table
------------------------------------------------------------Vlan

Mac Address    Type                  Ports    Remaining Age
                                                  (mins)
----   -----------        ----        -----    -----------
   1   001f.3c59.d63b   SecureConfigured   Gi0/2      -
------------------------------------------------------------
Total Addresses in System : 1
Max Addresses limit in System : 1024
```

Configuring Dynamic Secure MAC Addresses

By default, when port security is enabled on a port, the port will dynamically learn and secure one MAC address without any further configuration from the administrator. To allow the port to learn and secure more than a single MAC address, the switchport port-security maximum [number] command must be used. Keep in mind that the [number] keyword is platform-dependent and will vary on different Cisco Catalyst switch models.

REAL-WORLD IMPLEMENTATION:

In production networks with Cisco Catalyst 3750 switches, it is always a good idea to determine what the switch will be used for, and then select the appropriate Switch Database Management (SDM) template via the `sdm prefer {access | default | dual-ipv4-and-ipv6 {default | routing | vlan} | routing | vlan} [desktop]` global configuration command.

Each template allocates system resources to best support the features being used or that will be used. By default, the switch attempts to provide a balance between all features. However, this may impose a limit on the maximum possible values for other available features and functions. An example would be the maximum possible number of secure MAC addresses that can be learned or configured when using port security.

The following output illustrates how to configure a switch port to dynamically learn and secure up to two MAC addresses on interface GigabitEthernet0/2:

```
Switch-1(config)#interface GigabitEthernet0/2
Switch-1(config-if)#switchport
Switch-1(config-if)#switchport mode access
Switch-1(config-if)#switchport port-security
Switch-1(config-if)#switchport port-security maximum 2
```

Verifying Dynamic Secure MAC Addresses

Dynamic secure MAC address configuration can be verified using the same commands as those illustrated in the static secure address configuration examples, with the exception of the `show running-config` command. This is because, unlike static or sticky secure MAC addresses, all dynamically learned addresses are not saved in the switch configuration and are removed if the port is shut down. These same addresses must then be relearned when the port comes back up. The following output illustrates the `show port-security address` command, which shows an interface configured for secure dynamic MAC address learning:

```
Switch-1#show port-security address
          Secure Mac Address Table
-------------------------------------------------------------------
Vlan    Mac Address       Type            Ports    Remaining Age
                                                      (mins)
----    -----------       ----            -----    ------------
   1    001d.09d4.0238    SecureDynamic   Gi0/2        -
   1    001f.3c59.d63b    SecureDynamic   Gi0/2        -
-------------------------------------------------------------------
Total Addresses in System : 2
Max Addresses limit in System : 1024
```

Configuring Sticky Secure MAC Addresses

The following output illustrates how to configure dynamic sticky learning on a port and restrict the port to dynamically learn up to a maximum of 10 MAC addresses:

```
Switch-1(config)#interface GigabitEthernet0/2
Switch-1(config-if)#switchport
Switch-1(config-if)#switchport mode access
Switch-1(config-if)#switchport port-security
Switch-1(config-if)#switchport port-security mac-address sticky
Switch-1(config-if)#switchport port-security maximum 10
```

Based on the configuration above, by default, up to 10 addresses will be dynamically learned on interface GigabitEthernet0/2 and will be added to the current switch configuration. When sticky address learning is enabled, MAC addresses learned on each port are automatically saved to the current switch configuration and added to the address table. The following output shows the dynamically learned MAC addresses (in bold font) on interface GigabitEthernet0/2:

```
Switch-1#show running-config interface GigabitEthernet0/2
Building configuration...

Current configuration : 550 bytes
!
interface GigabitEthernet0/2
 switchport
 switchport mode access
 switchport port-security
 switchport port-security maximum 10
 switchport port-security mac-address sticky
 switchport port-security mac-address sticky 0004.c16f.8741
 switchport port-security mac-address sticky 000c.cea7.f3a0
 switchport port-security mac-address sticky 0013.1986.0a20
 switchport port-security mac-address sticky 001d.09d4.0238
 switchport port-security mac-address sticky 0030.803f.ea81
```

The MAC addresses in bold text in the output above are dynamically learned and added to the current configuration. No manual administrator configuration is required to add these addresses to the configuration. By default, sticky secure MAC addresses are not automatically added to the startup configuration (NVRAM). To ensure that this information is saved to NVRAM, which means that these addresses are not relearned when the switch is restarted, it is important to remember to issue the copy running-config startup-config command, or the copy system:running-config nvram:startup-config command, depending upon the IOS version of the switch on which this feature is implemented. The following output illustrates the show port-security address command on a port configured for sticky address learning:

```
Switch-1#show port-security address
            Secure Mac Address Table
----------------------------------------------------------------
Vlan    Mac Address     Type                Ports    Remaining Age
```

```
                                                        (mins)
    ----  -----------     ----          -----  ------------
     1    0004.c16f.8741   SecureSticky   Gi0/2    -
     1    000c.cea7.f3a0   SecureSticky   Gi0/2    -
     1    0013.1986.0a20   SecureSticky   Gi0/2    -
     1    001d.09d4.0238   SecureSticky   Gi0/2    -
     1    0030.803f.ea81   SecureSticky   Gi0/2    -
    ----------------------------------------------------------------
Total Addresses in System : 5
Max Addresses limit in System : 1024
```

You can also set an aging time and type on the switch, but this is going beyond the CCNA-level requirements. (Have a try on your own time if you wish.)

Configuring the Port Security Violation Action

As stated earlier, Cisco IOS software allows administrators to specify four different actions to take when a violation occurs, as follows:

- Protect
- Shutdown (default)
- Restrict
- Shutdown VLAN (this is outside the CCNA syllabus)

These options are configured using the `switchport port-security [violation {protect | restrict | shutdown | shutdown vlan}]` interface configuration command. If a port is shut down due to a security violation, it will show as `errdisabled`, and the `shutdown` and then `no shutdown` command will need to be applied to bring it back up.

```
Switch#show interfaces FastEthernet0/1 status
Port    Name         Status        Vlan   Duplex  Speed  Type
Fa0/1                errdisabled   100    full    100    100BaseSX
```

Cisco do want you to know which violation action triggers an SNMP message for the network administrator and a logging message, so here is that information for you in Table 9.3 below:

Table 9.3—Port Security Violation Actions

Mode	Port Action	Traffic	Syslog	Violation Counter
Protect	Protected	Unknown MACs discarded	No	No
Shutdown	Errdisabled	Disabled	Yes and SNMP trap	Incremented
Restrict	Open	# of excess MAC traffic denied	Yes and SNMP trap	Incremented

Make sure that you memorize the table above for the exam!

The following output illustrates how to enable sticky learning on a port for a maximum of 10 MAC addresses. In the event that an unknown MAC address (e.g., an eleventh MAC address) is detected on the port, the port will be configured to drop the received frames:

```
Switch-1(config)#interface GigabitEthernet0/2
Switch-1(config-if)#switchport port-security
Switch-1(config-if)#switchport port-security mac-address sticky
Switch-1(config-if)#switchport port-security maximum 10
Switch-1(config-if)#switchport port-security violation restrict
```

Verifying the Port Security Violation Action

The configured port security violation action is validated via the show port-security command, as shown in the following output:

```
Switch-1#show port-security
Secure Port  MaxSecureAddr CurrentAddr SecurityViolation  Security Action
               (Count)       (Count)     (Count)

Gi0/2           10             5            0             Restrict

Total Addresses in System : 5
Max Addresses limit in System : 1024
```

If logging is enabled and either the Restrict mode or the Shutdown Violation mode is configured on the switch, messages similar to those shown in the following output will be printed on the switch console, logged into the local buffer, or sent to a syslog server (as per Table 9.2 above):

```
Switch-1#show logging
[Truncated Output]
04:23:21: %PORT_SECURITY-2-PSECURE_VIOLATION: Security violation
occurred, caused by MAC address 0013.1986.0a20 on port Gi0/2.
04:23:31: %PORT_SECURITY-2-PSECURE_VIOLATION: Security violation
occurred, caused by MAC address 000c.cea7.f3a0 on port Gi0/2.
04:23:46: %PORT_SECURITY-2-PSECURE_VIOLATION: Security violation
occurred, caused by MAC address 0004.c16f.8741 on port Gi0/2.
```

One final point is that switch security can be configured on Packet Tracer, but many of the commands and show commands don't work.

Troubleshooting Port Security

When troubleshooting port security, it is important to check the configuration that has been implemented by first using the show running-config interface <name> command. Default port security configuration parameters can cause operational issues with other features, such as first hop redundancy protocols which we cover later (i.e., HSRP, VRRP, and GLBP) because only a single MAC address is allowed per port. This can be validated via the show port-security interface <name> command as illustrated below:

```
Switch#show port-security interface FastEthernet0/2
Port Security            : Enabled
Port Status              : Secure-down
Violation Mode           : Shutdown
Aging Time               : 0 mins
Aging Type               : Absolute
SecureStatic Address Aging : Disabled
Maximum MAC Addresses    : 1
Total MAC Addresses      : 0
Configured MAC Addresses : 0
Sticky MAC Addresses     : 0
Last Source Address:Vlan : 0000.0000.0000:0
Security Violation Count : 0
```

When looking at the output of this command, it is important to understand the information that is printed by the switch. The `Port Status` field indicates the operational state of the port (i.e., whether the port is up or down). In the example above, the port is down, which could be due to Layer 1 issues, or because the `shutdown` command was issued under the port, or because the `switchport port-security` command has not been issued under the interface or port.

The `Violation Mode` field indicates the configuration violation mode. The default mode is shutdown. The `Aging Time` and `Aging Type` fields specify the aging time and type parameters. By default, secure MAC addresses will not be aged out and will remain in the switch MAC table until the switch is powered off. However, this default behavior may be adjusted by configuring aging values for dynamic and secure static MAC addresses. The valid aging time range is 0 to 1440 minutes.

The `SecureStatic Address Aging` field specifies how secure addresses are aged. This can be either an absolute value or following a configured period of inactivity. The absolute mechanism causes the secured MAC addresses on the port to age out after a fixed specified time. All references are flushed from the secure address list after the specified time and the address must then be relearned on the switchport. Once relearned, the timer begins again and the process is repeated as often as has been defined in the configured timer values. This is the default aging type for secure MAC addresses.

The inactivity time, also referred to as idle time, causes secured MAC addresses on the port to age out if there is no activity (i.e., frames or data) received from the secure addresses learned on the port for the specified time period.

The `Maximum MAC Addresses` field specifies the number of allowed secure MAC addresses per port. The default is one and the maximum value depends on the switch platform. The `Total MAC Addresses` field indicates the current total MAC addresses learned on the port. The `Configured MAC Addresses` field specifies the number of statically configured secure addresses on the port. The `Sticky MAC Addresses` field specifies the number of sticky secure MAC addresses configured on the port. The `Last Source Address:Vlan` field specifies the

MAC address of the last secure MAC address learned on the port. This is applicable only when port security is configured on a trunk link.

Finally, the Security Violation Count field specifies the number of security violations on the port. To reinforce what has been discussed in this section further, consider the following output:

```
Switch#show port-security interface FastEthernet0/2
Port Security              : Enabled
Port Status                : Secure-up
Violation Mode             : Restrict
Aging Time                 : 10 mins
Aging Type                 : Inactivity
SecureStatic Address Aging : Disabled
Maximum MAC Addresses      : 10
Total MAC Addresses        : 6
Configured MAC Addresses   : 1
Sticky MAC Addresses       : 5
Last Source Address:Vlan   : 0000.0000.0000:0
Security Violation Count   : 0
```

From the port security interface output that is printed above, we can determine the following:

- The interface is up, and the switchport port-security command was issued under the interface. This is reflected in the Secure-up port status.
- The switchport port-security violation restrict command was issued under the interface (the default violation mode is shutdown).
- The switchport port-security aging time 10 and switchport port-security aging type inactivity commands were issued under the interface because the aging time default is 0 minutes and the aging type default is absolute.
- The switchport port-security maximum 10 command was issued under the interface since by default only one MAC address is permitted when port security is enabled.
- Referencing the total MAC addresses, we can determine that the switchport port-security mac-address sticky command was issued and specified five secure sticky addresses, while the switchport port-security mac-address was issued and specified one secure address because, by default, these addresses are not defined.
- Finally, we can determine that no security violations have been detected on the interface or port as the counter still has a value of 0. The last source MAC address will be recorded when traffic hits the interface.

Error Disable Recovery

A series of events can cause Cisco switches to put their ports into a special disabled mode called err-disabled. This basically means that a particular port has been disabled (shut down) due to an error. This error can have multiple causes, one of the most common being a violation of a port security policy. This is a normal behavior when an unauthorized user tries to connect to a switch port and it prevents rogue devices from accessing the network.

An err-disabled port might look something like this:

```
Switch# show interface f0/1
FastEthernet0/1 is down, line protocol is down [err-disabled]
```

NOTE: Please repeat this lab until you understand the commands and can type them without looking at the Walkthrough section (and do the same for all the other labs in this book).

In order to re-activate an err-disabled interface, manual intervention is necessary via issuing the shutdown and no shutdown commands on the interface (referred to a bouncing the port by network engineers). However, some situations might require automatic recovery of the original port state instead of waiting for an administrator to manually enable the port. The err-disable recovery mode functions by configuring the switch to automatically re-enable an err-disabled port after a certain period, based on the event that generated the failure. This provides granularity in deciding which events can be monitored by the err-disable recovery function.

The command to do this is the errdisable recovery cause, entered under Global Router Configuration mode:

```
Switch(config)#errdisable recovery cause ?
  all        Enable timer to recover from all causes
  bpduguard  Enable timer to recover from bpdu-guard error disable state
  dtp-flap   Enable timer to recover from dtp-flap error disable state
  link-flap  Enable timer to recover from link-flap error disable state
  pagp-flap  Enable timer to recover from pagp-flap error disable state
  rootguard  Enable timer to recover from root-guard error disable state
  udld       Enable timer to recover from udld error disable state
```

The errdisable recovery cause command can vary based on the device model, but the most common parameters are:

- all
- arp-inspection
- bpduguard
- dhcp-rate-limit
- link-flap
- psecure-violation
- security-violation
- storm-control
- udld

The time after which the port is automatically restored is 300 seconds by default on most platforms, but this can be manually configured with the `errdisable recovery interval` global configuration command:

```
Switch(config)#errdisable recovery interval ?
  <30-86400>  timer-interval(sec)
```

The `show errdisable recovery` command will provide information about the active features monitored by the err-disable recovery function and about the interfaces being monitored, including the time left until the interface is enabled.

```
Switch#show errdisable recovery
ErrDisable Reason          Timer Status
-----------------          -------------
arp-inspection             Disabled
bpduguard                  Disabled
channel-misconfig          Disabled
dhcp-rate-limit            Disabled
dtp-flap                   Disabled
gbic-invalid               Disabled
inline-power               Disabled
l2ptguard                  Disabled
link-flap                  Disabled
mac-limit                  Disabled
link-monitor-failure       Disabled
loopback                   Disabled
oam-remote-failure         Disabled
pagp-flap                  Disabled
port-mode-failure          Disabled
psecure-violation          Enabled
security-violation         Disabled
sfp-config-mismatch        Disabled
storm-control              Disabled
udld                       Disabled
unicast-flood              Disabled
vmps                       Disabled

Timer interval: 300 seconds

Interfaces that will be enabled at the next timeout:

Interface     Errdisable reason      Time left(sec)
---------     -----------------      -------------
Fa0/0         psecure-violation      193
```

Now please take today's exam at **https://www.in60days.com/free/ccnain60days/**

DAY 9 LABS

Switch and Switchport Security

Topology

Please note that your switch will need to have a security image which permits basic security settings.

Purpose

Learn how to apply basic security settings to a Cisco switch.

Walkthrough

1. Connect a PC or laptop to your switch. In addition, set up a console connection for your configuration. The port to which you connect your PC will be the one you configure security settings on in this lab. I have chosen FastEthernet 0/1 on my switch.

2. Log in to the VTY lines and set up Telnet access referring to a local username and password.

```
Switch#conf t
Enter configuration commands, one per line.  End with CNTL/Z.
Switch(config)#line vty 0 ?
  <1-15>  Last Line number
  <cr>
Switch(config)#line vty 0 15
Switch(config-line)#?
Switch(config-line)#login local
Switch(config-line)#exit
Switch(config)#username in60days password cisco
Switch(config)#
```

3. Add an IP address to VLAN 1 on the switch (all ports are in VLAN 1 automatically). Additionally, add the IP address 192.168.1.1 to your PC's FastEthernet interface.

```
Switch(config)#interface vlan1
Switch(config-if)#ip address 192.168.1.2 255.255.255.0
Switch(config-if)#no shut
%LINK-5-CHANGED: Interface Vlan1, changed state to up
%LINEPROTO-5-UPDOWN: Line protocol on Interface Vlan2, changed state to
up
Switch(config-if)#^Z  ← press Ctrl+Z keys
Switch#
Switch#ping 192.168.1.1  ← test connection from switch to PC
```

```
Type escape sequence to abort.
Sending 5, 100-byte ICMP Echos to 192.168.1.1, timeout is 2 seconds:
.!!!!
Success rate is 80 percent (4/5), round-trip min/avg/max = 31/31/32 ms
Switch#
```

4. Test Telnet by Telnetting from your PC to your switch.

```
Command Prompt
PC>telnet 192.168.1.2
Trying 192.168.1.2 ...Open


User Access Verification

Username: in60days
Password:
Switch>
```

5. Your IT manager changes his mind and wants only SSH access, so change this on your VTY lines. Only certain models and IOS versions will support the SSH command.

```
Switch(config)#line vty 0 15
Switch(config-line)#transport input ssh
```

6. Now Telnet from your PC to the switch. Because only SSH is permitted, the connection should fail.

```
Command Prompt
Packet Tracer PC Command Line 1.0
PC>telnet 192.168.1.2
Trying 192.168.1.2 ...Open

[Connection to 192.168.1.2 closed by foreign host]
PC>
```

7. Set port security on your switch for the FastEthernet port. It will fail if you have not hard set the port to access (as opposed to dynamic or trunk).

```
Switch(config)#interface FastEthernet0/1
Switch(config-if)#switchport port-security
Command rejected: FastEthernet0/1 is a dynamic port.
Switch(config-if)#switchport mode access
Switch(config-if)#switchport port-security
Switch(config-if)#
```

8. Hard set the MAC address from your PC to be permitted on this port. You can check this with the ipconfig/all command on your PC command line. Then check the port security status and settings.

```
Switch(config-if)#switchport port-security mac-address 0001.C7DD.CB18
Switch(config-if)#^Z
Switch#show port-security int FastEthernet0/1
Port Security              : Enabled
Port Status                : Secure-up
```

```
Violation Mode              : Shutdown
Aging Time                  : 0 mins
Aging Type                  : Absolute
SecureStatic Address Aging  : Disabled
Maximum MAC Addresses       : 1
Total MAC Addresses         : 1
Configured MAC Addresses    : 0
Sticky MAC Addresses        : 0
Last Source Address:Vlan    : 0001.C7DD.CB18:1
Security Violation Count    : 0
```

9. Change the MAC address on your PC, or if you can't do this, plug another device into the switch port. This should make the port shut down due to a breach in the security settings. The screenshot below shows where you would change the MAC address in Packet Tracer.

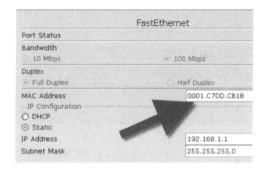

10. You should see your FastEthernet port go down immediately.

```
Switch#
%LINK-5-CHANGED: Interface FastEthernet0/1, changed state to
administratively down
%LINEPROTO-5-UPDOWN: Line protocol on Interface FastEthernet0/1,
changed state to down
%LINEPROTO-5-UPDOWN: Line protocol on Interface Vlan1, changed state
to down
Switch#
%SYS-5-CONFIG_I: Configured from console by console
Switch#show port-security interface FastEthernet0/1
Port Security               : Enabled
Port Status                 : Secure-shutdown
Violation Mode              : Shutdown
Aging Time                  : 0 mins
Aging Type                  : Absolute
SecureStatic Address Aging  : Disabled
Maximum MAC Addresses       : 1
Total MAC Addresses         : 0
Configured MAC Addresses    : 0
Sticky MAC Addresses        : 0
Last Source Address:Vlan    : 0001.C7DD.CB19:1
Security Violation Count    : 1
```

Routing Concepts

DAY 10 TASKS

- Read today's lesson notes (below)
- Review yesterday's lesson notes and lab
- Complete today's lab
- Take today's exam
- Read the ICND1 cram guide
- Spend 15 minutes on the subnetting.org website

Although many network engineers can configure routing protocols, they lack an understanding as to how packets are encapsulated as well as other routing fundamentals. Cisco have addressed this in the new exam syllabus. The ICND1 exam requires you to have an understanding of basic routing and packet flow across a network. We will also take a look at the technology behind routing protocols.

Today you will learn about the following:

- Basic routing
- Classful and classless protocols
- Passive interfaces
- Routing protocol classes
- The objectives of routing protocols
- Routing problems avoidance mechanisms
- Troubleshooting routing issues
- InterVLAN routing
- Troubleshooting inter-VLAN routing

This module maps to the following CCNA syllabus requirements:

- 3.1 Describe the routing concepts
- 3.1.a Packet handling along the path through a network
- 3.1.b Forwarding decision based on route lookup
- 3.1.c Frame rewrite
- 3.2 Interpret the components of routing table

- 3.2.a Prefix
- 3.2.b Network mask
- 3.2.c Next hop
- 3.2.d Routing protocol code
- 3.2.e Administrative distance
- 3.2.f Metric
- 3.2.g Gateway of last resort
- 3.3 Describe how a routing table is populated by different routing information sources
- 3.3.a Admin distance
- 3.4 Configure, verify, and troubleshoot inter-VLAN routing
- 3.4.a Router on a stick
- 3.5 Compare and contrast static routing and dynamic routing
- 3.4.d Single vs dual-homed [ICND2]

BASIC ROUTING

The role of routing protocols is to learn about other networks dynamically, exchange routing information with other devices, and connect internal and/or external networks.

It is important to note that routing protocols DO NOT send packets across the network. Their role is to determine the best path for routing. Routed protocols actually send the data, and the most common example of a routed protocol is IP.

Different routing protocols use different means of determining the best or most optimal path to a network or network node. Some types of routing protocols work best in static environments or environments with few or no changes, but it might take a long time to converge when changes to those environments are made. Other routing protocols, however, respond very quickly to changes in the network and can converge rapidly.

Network convergence occurs when all routers in the network have the same view and agree on optimal routes. When convergence takes a long time to occur, intermittent packet loss and loss of connectivity may be experienced between remote networks. In addition to these problems, slow convergence can result in network routing loops and outright network outages. Convergence is determined by the routing protocol algorithm used.

Because routing protocols have different characteristics, they differ in their scalability and performance. Some routing protocols are suitable only for small networks, while others may be used in small, medium, and large networks.

Packet Forwarding

Packet forwarding involves two processes:

- Determining the best path
- Sending the packet (switching)

When the router receives a packet for a directly connected network, the router checks the routing table and then the packet is forwarded to that network, as shown in Figure 10.1 below:

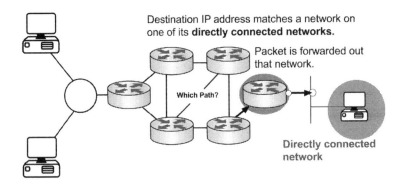

Figure 10.1—Directly Connected Networks

If the packet is destined for a remote network, the routing table is checked and if there is a route or default route, the packet is forwarded to the next-hop router, as shown in Figure 10.2 below:

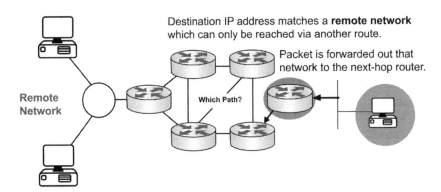

Figure 10.2—Remote Networks

If the packet is destined for a network not in the routing table and no default route exists then it is dropped, as shown in Figure 10.3 below:

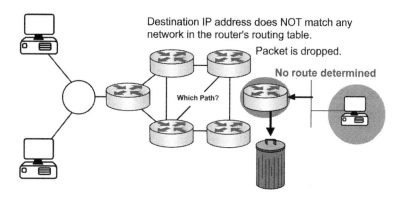

Figure 10.3—No Route

The switching process allows the router to accept the packet via one interface and send it out of another. The router will also encapsulate the packet in the appropriate Data Link frame for the outgoing link.

You may be asked to explain what happens with a packet received from one network and destined for another network. Firstly, the router decapsulates the Layer 3 packet by removing the Layer 2 frame header and trailer. Next, it examines the destination IP address of the IP packet to find the best path in the routing table. Finally, it encapsulates the Layer 3 packet into a new Layer 2 frame and forwards the frame out of the exit interface, so the encapsulation could change from Ethernet to HDLC. This is illustrated in Figure 10.4 below:

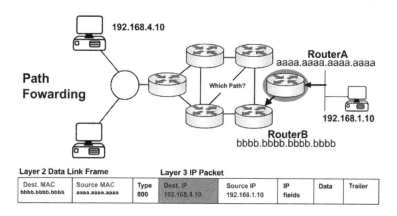

Figure 10.4—Layer 3 Address in a Packet

Remember in an earlier module that the source and destination IP address will never change as the packet traverses towards its final destination. The MAC address, however, will change to permit transport between intermediary devices. This is illustrated in Figure 10.5 below:

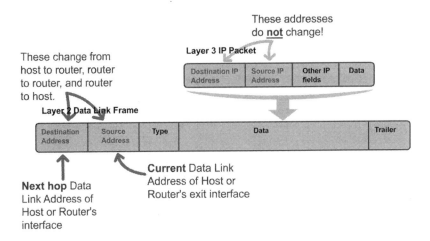

Figure 10.5—Layer 2 Address Changes

Figure 10.6 shows a packet leaving Host X destined for Host Y. Note that the next-hop MAC address belongs to Router A (using proxy ARP); however, the IP address belongs to Host Y. When the frame reaches Router B, the Ethernet header and trailer will be exchanged for the WAN protocol, which you can presume is HDLC here.

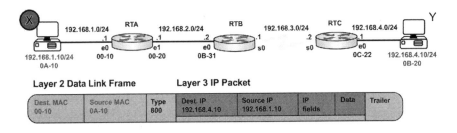

Figure 10.6—Packet Leaving Host X

Figure 10.7 shows the same packet leaving Router A for Router B. There is a route lookup and then the packet is switched out of interface E1. Type 800 indicates that the packet is IPv4.

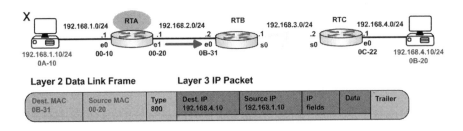

Figure 10.7—Packet Leaving Router A

Figure 10.8 shows that the frame eventually reaches Router C and is forwarded to Host Y:

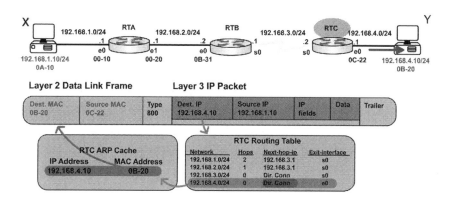

Figure 10.8—Packet Leaving Router C

Internet Protocol Routing Fundamentals

A routing protocol allows a router to learn dynamically how to reach other networks. A routing protocol also allows the router to exchange learned network information with other routers or hosts. Routing protocols may be used for connecting interior (internal) campus networks, as well as for connecting different enterprises or routing domains. Therefore, in addition to understanding the intricacies of routing protocols, it is also important to have a solid understanding of when and in what situation one routing protocol would be used versus another.

Flat and Hierarchical Routing Algorithms

Routing protocol algorithms operate using either a flat routing system or a hierarchical routing system. A hierarchical routing system uses a layered approach wherein routers are placed in logical groupings referred to as domains, areas, or autonomous systems. This allows different routers within the network to perform specific tasks, optimizing the functionality performed at those layers. Some routers in the hierarchical system can communicate with other routers in other domains or areas, while other routers can communicate only with routers in the same domain or area. This reduces the amount of information that routers in the domain or area must process, which allows for faster convergence within the network.

A flat routing system has no hierarchy. In such systems, routers must typically be connected to every other router in the network and each router essentially has the same function. Such algorithms work well in very small networks; however, they are not scalable. In addition, as the network grows, troubleshooting becomes much more difficult because instead of just focusing your efforts on certain areas, for example, you now have to look at the entire network.

The primary advantage afforded by hierarchical routing systems is their scalability. Hierarchical routing systems also allow for easier changes to the network, in much the same way afforded by the traditional hierarchical design comprised of the Core, Distribution, and Access Layers. In addition, hierarchical algorithms can be used to reduce routing update traffic, as well as routing table size, in certain areas of the network while still allowing full network connectivity.

IP Addressing and Address Summarization

An IP address is divided into two parts. The first part designates the network address, while the second part designates the host address. When designing a network, an IP addressing scheme is used to uniquely identify hosts and devices within the network. The IP addressing scheme should be hierarchical and should build on the traditional logical hierarchical model. This allows the addressing scheme to provide designated points in the network where effective route summarization can be performed.

Summarization reduces the amount of information that routers must process, which allows for faster convergence within the network. Summarisation also restricts the size of the area that is affected by network changes by hiding detailed topology information from certain areas within the network. This concept is illustrated in Figure 10.9 below:

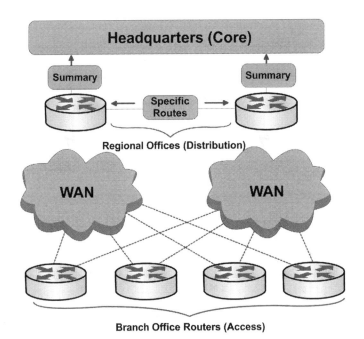

Figure 10.9—Route Summarization Using Cisco Design Model

Referencing Figure 10.9, the branch offices (Access Layer) are dual-homed to the regional office routers (Distribution Layer). Layers are defined using Cisco design models. Using a hierarchical addressing scheme allows the Distribution Layer routers to advertise a summary route for the branch office subnets to the Core Layer. This protects the Core Layer from the effects of any route flapping between the Distribution and the Access Layer routers, because a summary route will not flap until every last one of the more specific prefixes from which it is derived is removed from the routing table. This increases stability within the area. In addition, the routing table size at the Core Layer is further reduced.

Administrative Distance

Administrative distance is used to determine the reliability of one source of routing information from another. Some sources are considered more reliable than others are; therefore, administrative distance can be used to determine the best or preferred path to a destination network or network node when there are two or more different paths to the same destination from two or more different routing protocols.

In Cisco IOS software, all sources of routing information are assigned a default administrative distance value. This default value is an integer between 0 and 255, with a value of 0 assigned to the most reliable source of information and a value of 255 assigned to the least reliable source of information. Any routes that are assigned an administrative distance value of 255 are considered untrusted and will not be placed into the routing table.

The administrative distance is a locally significant value that affects only the local router. This value is not propagated throughout the routing domain. Therefore, manually adjusting the default administrative distance for a routing source or routing sources on a router affects the preference of routing information sources only on that router. Table 10.1 below shows the default administrative values used in Cisco IOS software (you need to learn these for the exam):

Table 10.1—Router Administrative Distances (ADs)

Route Source	AD
Connected Interfaces	0
Static Routes	1
Enhanced Interior Gateway Routing Protocol (EIGRP) Summary Routes	5
External Border Gateway Protocol (eBGP) Routes	20
Internal Enhanced Interior Gateway Routing Protocol (EIGRP) Routes	90
Open Shortest Path First (OSPF) Internal and External Routes	110
Intermediate System-to-Intermediate System (IS-IS) Internal and External Routes	115
Routing Information Protocol (RIP) Routes	120
Exterior Gateway Protocol (EGP) Routes	140
On-Demand Routing (ODR) Routes	160
External Enhanced Interior Gateway Routing Protocol (EIGRP) Routes	170
Internal Border Gateway Protocol (iBGP) Routes	200
Unreachable or Unknown Routes	255

The default route source administrative distance is displayed in the output of the show ip protocols command. This is illustrated in the following output:

```
R1#show ip protocols
Routing Protocol is "isis"
  Invalid after 0 seconds, hold down 0, flushed after 0
  Outgoing update filter list for all interfaces is not set
  Incoming update filter list for all interfaces is not set
  Redistributing: isis
  Address Summarization:
    None
  Maximum path: 4
  Routing for Networks:
    Serial0/0
  Routing Information Sources:
    Gateway          Distance       Last Update
    10.0.0.2              115        00:06:53
  Distance: (default is 115)
```

Routing Metrics

Routing protocol algorithms use metrics, which are numerical values that are associated with specific routes. These values are used to prioritize or prefer routes learned by the routing protocol, from the most preferred to the least preferred. In essence, the lower the route metric, the more preferred the route by the routing protocol. The route with the lowest metric is typically the route with the least cost or the best route to the destination network. This route will be placed into the routing table and will be used to forward packets to the destination network.

Different routing algorithms use different variables to compute the route metric. Some routing algorithms use only a single variable, while other advanced routing protocols may use more than one variable to determine the metric for a particular route. In most cases, the metrics that are computed by one routing protocol are incompatible with those used by other routing protocols. The different routing protocol metrics may be based on one or more of the following:

- Bandwidth
- Cost
- Delay
- Load
- Path length
- Reliability

Bandwidth
The term bandwidth refers to the amount of data that can be carried from one point to another in a given period. Routing algorithms may use bandwidth to determine which link type is preferred over another. For example, a routing algorithm might prefer a GigabitEthernet link to a FastEthernet link because of the increased capacity of the GigabitEthernet link.

In Cisco IOS software, the `bandwidth` interface configuration command can be used to adjust the default bandwidth value for an interface, effectively manipulating the selection of one interface against another by a routing algorithm. For example, if the FastEthernet interface was configured with the `bandwidth 1000000` interface configuration command, both the FastEthernet and the GigabitEthernet links would appear to have the same capacity to the routing algorithm and would be assigned the same metric value. The fact that one of the links is actually a FastEthernet link while the other is actually a GigabitEthernet link is irrelevant to the routing protocol.

From a network administrator's point of view, it is important to understand that the `bandwidth` command does not affect the physical capability of the interface (so it is sometimes referred to as a cosmetic command). In other words, configuring the higher bandwidth on the FastEthernet interface does not mean that it is capable of supporting GigabitEthernet speeds. Open Shortest Path First (OSPF) and Enhanced Interior Gateway Routing Protocol (EIGRP) use bandwidth in metric calculations.

Cost

The cost, as it pertains to routing algorithms, refers to communication cost. The cost may be used when, for example, a company prefers to route across private links rather than public links that include monetary charges for sending data across them or for the usage time. Intermediate System-to-Intermediate System (IS-IS) supports an optional expense metric that measures the monetary cost of link utilization. Configuring cost varies depending upon the protocol.

Delay

There are many types of delay, all of which affect different types of traffic. In general, delay refers to the length of time required to move a packet from its source to its destination through the internetwork. In Cisco IOS software, the interface delay value is in microseconds (μs).

The interface value is configured using the `delay` interface configuration command. When you configure the interface delay value, it is important to remember that this does not affect traffic (another cosmetic command). For example, configuring a delay value of 5000 does not mean that traffic sent out of that interface will have an additional delay of 5000 μs. Table 10.2 below shows the default delay values for common interfaces in Cisco IOS software:

Table 10.2—Interface Delay Values

Interface Type	Delay (μs)
10Mbps Ethernet	1000
FastEthernet	100
GigabitEthernet	10
T1 Serial	20000

EIGRP uses the interface delay value as part of its metric calculation. Manually adjusting the interface delay value results in the recomputation of the EIGRP metric.

Load

The term load means different things to different people. For example, in general computing terminology, load refers to the amount of work a resource, such as the CPU, is performing. Load, as it applies in this context, refers to the degree of use for a particular router interface. The load on the interface is a fraction of 255. For example, a load of 255/255 indicates that the interface is completely saturated, while a load of 128/255 indicates that the interface is 50% saturated. By default, the load is calculated as an average over a period of five minutes (in the real world this is often changed to a minimum of 30 seconds using the `load-interval 30` command). The interface load value can be used by EIGRP in its metric calculation.

Path Length

The path length metric is the total length of the path that is traversed from the local router to the destination network. Different routing algorithms represent this in different forms. For example, Routing Information Protocol (RIP) counts all intermediate routers (hops) between the local router and the destination network and uses the hop count as the metric, while Border Gateway Protocol (BGP) counts the number of traversed autonomous systems between the local router and the destination network and uses the autonomous system count to select the best path.

Reliability

Like load, the term reliability means different things depending upon the context in which it is used. Here, unless stated otherwise, it should always be assumed that reliability refers to the dependability of network links or interfaces. In Cisco IOS software, the reliability of a link or interface is represented as a fraction of 255. For example, a reliability value of 255/255 indicates that the interface is 100% reliable. Similar to the interface load, by default the reliability of an interface is calculated as an average over a period of five minutes.

Prefix Matching

Cisco routers use the longest prefix match rule when determining which of the routes placed into the routing table should be used to forward traffic to a destination network or node. Longer, or more specific, routing table entries are preferred over less specific entries, such as summary addresses, when determining which entry to use to route traffic to the intended destination network or node.

The longest prefix or the most specific route will be used to route traffic to the destination network or node, **regardless of the administrative distance of the route source**, or even the routing protocol metric assigned to the prefix if multiple overlapping prefixes are learned via the same routing protocol. Table 10.3 below illustrates the order of route selection on a router sending packets to the address 1.1.1.1. This order is based on the longest prefix match lookup:

Table 10.3—Matching the Longest Prefix

Routing Table Entry	Order Used
1.1.1.1/32	First
1.1.1.0/24	Second
1.1.0.0/16	Third
1.0.0.0/8	Fourth
0.0.0.0/0	Fifth

NOTE: Although the default route is listed last in the route selection order in Table 10.3, keep in mind that a default route is not always present in the routing table. If that is the case, and no other entries to the address 1.1.1.1 exist, packets to that destination are simply discarded by the router. In most cases, the router will send the source host an ICMP message indicting that the destination is unreachable. A default route is used to direct packets addressed to networks not explicitly listed in the routing table.

Building the IP Routing Table

Without a populated routing table, or Routing Information Base (RIB), that contains entries for remote networks, routers will not be able to forward packets to those remote networks. The routing table may include specific network entries or simply a single default route. The information in the routing table is used by the forwarding process to forward traffic to the destination network or host. The routing table itself does not actually forward traffic.

Cisco routers use the administrative distance, the routing protocol metric, and the prefix length to determine which routes will actually be placed into the routing table, which allows the router to build the routing table. The routing table is built via the following general steps:

1. If the route entry does not currently exist in the routing table, add it to the routing table.
2. If the route entry is more specific than an existing route, add it to the routing table. It should also be noted that the less specific entry is still retained in the routing table.
3. If the route entry is the same as an existing one, but it is received from a more preferred route source, replace the old entry with the new entry.
4. If the route entry is the same as an existing one, and it is received from the same protocol, then:
   a) Discard the new route if the metric is higher than the existing route; or
   b) Replace the existing route if the metric of the new route is lower; or
   c) Use both routes for load balancing if the metric for both routes is the same.

When building the RIB by default, the routing protocol with the lowest administrative distance value will always be chosen when the router is determining which routes to place into the routing table. For example, if a router receives the 10.0.0.0/8 prefix via external

EIGRP, OSPF, and internal BGP, the OSPF route will be placed into the routing table. If that route is removed or is no longer received, the external EIGRP route will be placed into the routing table. Finally, if both the OSPF and the external EIGRP routes are no longer present, the internal BGP route is used.

Once routes have been placed into the routing table, by default the most specific or longest match prefix will always be preferred over less specific routes. This is illustrated in the following example, which shows a routing table that contains entries for the 80.0.0.0/8, 80.1.0.0/16, and 80.1.1.0/24 prefixes. These three route prefixes are received via the EIGRP, OSPF, and RIP routing protocols, respectively.

```
R1#show ip route
Codes: C - connected, S - static, R - RIP, M - mobile, B - BGP
       D - EIGRP, EX - EIGRP external, O - OSPF, IA - OSPF inter area
       N1 - OSPF NSSA external type 1, N2 - OSPF NSSA external type 2
       E1 - OSPF external type 1, E2 - OSPF external type 2
       i - IS-IS, L1 - IS-IS level-1, L2 - IS-IS level-2, ia - IS-IS
inter area
       * - candidate default, U - per-user static route, o - ODR
       P - periodic downloaded static route

Gateway of last resort is not set

R       80.1.1.0/24 [120/1] via 10.1.1.2, 00:00:04, Ethernet0/0.1
D       80.0.0.0/8 [90/281600] via 10.1.1.2, 00:02:02, Ethernet0/0.1
O E2    80.1.0.0/16 [110/20] via 10.1.1.2, 00:00:14, Ethernet0/0.1
```

Referencing the output shown above, the first route is 80.1.1.0/24. This route is learned via RIP and therefore has a default administrative distance value of 120. The second route is 80.0.0.0/8. This route is learned via internal EIGRP and therefore has a default administrative distance value of 90. The third route is 80.1.0.0/16. This route is learned via OSPF and is an external OSPF route that has an administrative distance of 110.

> **NOTE:** Because the routing protocol metrics are different, they are a non-factor in determining the best route to use when routes from multiple protocols are installed into the routing table. The following section will describe how Cisco IOS routers build the routing table.

Based on the contents of this routing table, if the router received a packet destined to 80.1.1.1, it would use the RIP route because this is the most specific entry, even though both EIGRP and OSPF have better administrative distance values and are therefore more preferred route sources. The show ip route 80.1.1.1 command illustrated below can be used to verify this statement:

```
R1#show ip route 80.1.1.1
Routing entry for 80.1.1.0/24
  Known via "rip", distance 120, metric 1
  Redistributing via rip
```

```
Last update from 10.1.1.2 on Ethernet0/0.1, 00:00:15 ago
Routing Descriptor Blocks:
* 10.1.1.2, from 10.1.1.2, 00:00:15 ago, via Ethernet0/0.1
      Route metric is 1, traffic share count is 1
```

CLASSFUL AND CLASSLESS PROTOCOLS

Classful protocols can't use VLSM (i.e., RIPv1 and IGRP, which are no longer in the CCNA syllabus). This is because they don't recognize anything other than default network masks due to being developed prior to VLSM.

```
Router#debug ip rip
RIP protocol debugging is on
01:26:59: RIP: sending v1 update to 255.255.255.255 via Loopback0
192.168.1.1
```

Classless protocols use VLSM (i.e., RIPv2 and EIGRP):

```
Router#debug ip rip
RIP protocol debugging is on
01:29:15: RIP: received v2 update from 172.16.1.2 on Serial0
01:29:15:192.168.2.0/24 via 0.0.0.0
```

PASSIVE INTERFACES

An important routing protocol design and configuration consideration is to limit unnecessary peerings, as shown in Figure 10.10 below. This is done using passive interfaces, which prevents the router from forming routing adjacencies on the specific interface. This functions differently based on the specific routing protocol used but the behavior usually falls within the following two categories:

- The router does not send routing updates on the passive interface
- The router does not send Hello packets on the interface, so neighbor relationships are not formed

Passive interfaces are usually able to receive routing updates or Hello packets but are not allowed to send any kind of routing protocol information outbound.

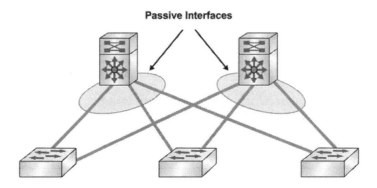

Figure 10.10—Limit Unnecessary Peerings

A use case example for passive interfaces is avoiding routing protocol peerings from the Distribution Layer to the Access Layer, as presented in Figure 10.10 above. By having Layer 3 peering across the different Access Layer switches (i.e., having multiple hosts on different switches across switch blocks) you are basically adding memory load, routing protocol update overhead, and more complexity. Also, if there is a link failure, the traffic may transit through a neighboring Access Layer switch to get to another VLAN member.

Basically, you want to eliminate unnecessary routing peering adjacencies, so you would configure the ports towards the Layer 2 switches as passive interfaces in order to suppress routing updates advertisements. If a Distribution Layer switch does not receive a routing update from a potential peer on one of these interfaces, it will not have to process the updates and will not form a neighbor adjacency across that interface. The command for accomplishing this is usually `passive-interface [interface number]` in the Routing Process Configuration mode.

ROUTING PROTOCOL CLASSES

There are two major classes of routing protocols—

- Distance Vector
- Link State

Distance Vector routing protocols traditionally use a one-dimensional vector when determining the most optimal path(s) through the network, while Link State routing protocols use the Shortest Path First (SPF) when determining the most optimal path(s) through the network. Before delving into the specifics of these two classes of routing protocols, we will first take a look at vectors, as well as at the elusive SPF algorithm.

Understanding Vectors

A one-dimensional vector is a directed quantity. It is simply a quantity (number) in a particular direction or course. The vector concept is illustrated in Figure 10.11 below:

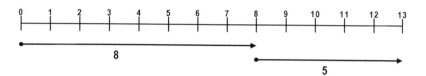

Figure 10.11—Understanding Vectors

Referencing Figure 10.11, the first line starts at 0 and ends at 8, and the second line begins at 8 and ends at 13. The vector for the first line is 8, while the vector for the second line is 5. Using basic math, we know that 8 + 5 = 13. The starting and ending points of the vector are not relevant. Instead, the only thing that actually matters is how long the vector is and how far it travels.

> **NOTE:** Vectors can also travel in the opposite direction (i.e., they represent negative numbers).

The Shortest Path First Algorithm

The SPF algorithm creates a shortest-path tree to all hosts in an area or in the network backbone with the router that is performing the calculation at the root of that tree. In order for the SPF algorithm to work in the correct manner, all routers in the area should have the same database information. In OSPF, this is performed via the database exchange process.

Distance Vector Routing Protocols

Distance Vector uses distance or hop count as its primary metric for determining the best forwarding path. Distance Vector routing protocols are primarily based on the Bellman-Ford algorithm. Distance Vector routing protocols periodically send their neighbor routers copies of their entire routing tables to keep them up to date on the state of the network. While this may be acceptable in a small network, it increases the amount of traffic that is sent across networks as the size of the network grows. All Distance Vector routing protocols share the following characteristics:

- Counting to infinity
- Split horizon
- Poison reverse
- Hold-down timers

Utilizing the counting to infinity characteristic, if a destination network is farther than the maximum number of hops allowed for that routing protocol, the network would be considered unreachable. The network entry would therefore not be installed into the IP routing table.

Split horizon mandates that routing information cannot be sent back out of the same interface through which it was received. This prevents the re-advertising of information back to the source from which it was learned. While this characteristic is a great loop prevention mechanism, it is also a significant drawback, especially in hub-and-spoke networks.

Poison reverse (or route poisoning) expands on split horizon. When used in conjunction with split horizon, poison reverse allows the networks to be advertised back out of the same interface on which they were received. However, poison reverse causes the router to advertise these networks back to the sending router with a metric of "unreachable" so that the router that receives those entries will not add them back into its routing table.

Hold-down timers are used to prevent networks that were previously advertised as down from being placed back into the routing table. When a router receives an update that a network is down, it begins its hold-down timer. This timer tells the router to wait for a specific amount of time before accepting any changes to the status of that network.

During the hold-down period, the router suppresses the network and prevents advertising false information. The router also does not route to the unreachable network, even if it receives information from another router (that may not have received the triggered update) that the network is reachable. This mechanism is designed to prevent black-holing traffic.

The two most common Distance Vector routing protocols are RIP and IGRP. EIGRP is an advanced Distance Vector routing protocol, using features from both Distance Vector and Link State (i.e., it's a hybrid protocol).

Link State Routing Protocols

Link State routing protocols are hierarchical routing protocols that use the concept of areas to logically group routers within a network. This allows Link State protocols to scale better and operate in a more efficient manner than Distance Vector routing protocols. Routers running Link State routing protocols create a database that comprises the complete topology of the network. This allows all routers within the same area to have the same view of the network.

Because all routers in the network have the same view of the network, the most optimal paths are used for forwarding packets between networks and the possibility of routing loops is eliminated. Therefore, techniques such as split horizon and route poisoning do not apply to Link State routing protocols as they do to Distance Vector routing protocols.

Link State routing protocols operate by sending Link State Advertisements or Link State Packets to all other routers within the same area. These packets include information on attached interfaces, metrics, and other variables. As the routers accumulate this information, they run the SPF algorithm and calculate the shortest (best) path to each router and destination network. Using the received Link State information, routers build the Link State Database (LSDB). When the LSDBs of two neighboring routers are synchronized, the routers are said to be adjacent.

Unlike Distance Vector routing protocols, which send their neighbors their entire routing table, Link State routing protocols send incremental updates when a change in the network topology is detected, which makes them more efficient in larger networks. The use of incremental updates also allows Link State routing protocols to respond much faster to network changes and thus converge in a shorter amount of time than Distance Vector routing protocols. Table 10.4 below lists the different Interior Gateway Protocols (IGPs) and their classification:

Table 10.4—IGP Classification

Protocol Name	Classful/Classless	Protocol Classification
RIP (version 1)	Classful	Distance Vector
IGRP	Classful	Distance Vector
RIP (version 2)	Classless	Distance Vector
EIGRP	Classless	Advanced Distance Vector
IS-IS	Classless	Link State
OSPF	Classless	Link State

THE OBJECTIVES OF ROUTING PROTOCOLS

Routing algorithms, while different in nature, all have the same basic objectives. While some algorithms are better suited for certain networks than others are, all routing protocols have their advantages and disadvantages. Routing algorithms are designed with the following objectives and goals:

- Optimal routing
- Stability
- Ease of use
- Flexibility
- Rapid convergence

Optimal Routing

One of the primary goals of all routing protocols is to select the most optimal path through the network from the source subnet or host to the destination subnet or host. The most optimal route depends upon the metrics used by the routing protocols. A route that may be considered the best by one protocol may not necessarily be the most optimal route from the perspective of another protocol. For example, RIP might consider a path that is only two hops long as the most optimal path to a destination network, even though the links were 64Kbps links, while advanced protocols such as OSPF and EIGRP might determine that the most optimal path to that same destination is the one traversing four routers but using 10Gbps links.

Stability

Network stability, or a lack thereof, is another major objective for routing algorithms. Routing algorithms should be stable enough to accommodate unforeseen network events, such as hardware failures and even incorrect implementations. While this is typically a characteristic of all routing algorithms, the manner and time in which they respond to such events makes some better than others and thus more preferred in modern-day networks.

Ease of Use

Routing algorithms are designed to be as simple as possible. In addition to providing the capability to support complex internetwork deployments, routing protocols should take into consideration the resources required to run the algorithm. Some routing algorithms require more hardware or software resources (e.g., CPU and memory) to run than others do; however, they are capable of providing more functionality than alternative simple algorithms.

Flexibility

In addition to providing routing functionality, routing algorithms should also be feature-rich, allowing them to support the different requirements encountered in different networks. It should be noted that this capability typically comes at the expense of other features, such as convergence, which is described next.

Rapid Convergence

Rapid convergence is another primary objective of all routing algorithms. As stated earlier, convergence occurs when all routers in the network have the same view of and agree on optimal routes. When convergence takes a long time to occur, intermittent packet loss and loss of connectivity may be experienced between remote networks. In addition to these problems, slow convergence can result in network routing loops and outright network outages.

ROUTING PROBLEMS AVOIDANCE MECHANISMS

It is a known fact that Distance Vector routing protocols are prone to major problems as a result of their simplistic "routing by rumor" approach. Distance Vector and Link State protocols use different techniques to prevent routing problems. The most important mechanisms include the following (some we have mentioned briefly already):

- **Invalidation timers:** These are used to mark routes as unreachable when updates for those routes are not received for a long time.
- **Hop count limit:** This parameter marks routes as unreachable when they are more than a predefined number of hops away. The hop count limit for RIP is 15, as it is not usually used in large networks. Unreachable routes are not installed in the routing table as best routes. The hop count limit prevents updates from looping in the network, just like the TTL field in the IP header.

- **Triggered updates:** This feature allows the update timer to be bypassed in the case of important updates. For example, the RIP 30-second timer can be ignored if a critical routing update must be propagated through the network.
- **Hold-down timers:** If a metric for a particular route keeps getting worse, updates for that route are not accepted for a delayed period.
- **Asynchronous updates:** Asynchronous updates represent another safety mechanism that prevents the routers from flooding the entire routing information at the same time. As mentioned before, OSPF does this every 30 minutes. The asynchronous updates mechanism generates a small delay for every device so they do not flood the information exactly at the same time. This improves bandwidth utilization and processing capabilities.
- **Route poisoning:** This feature prevents routers from sending packets through a route that has become invalid. Distance Vector protocols use this to indicate that a route is no longer reachable. This is accomplished by setting the route metric to a maximum value.
- **Split horizon:** Split horizon prevents updates from being sent out of the same interface they came from because routers in that area should already know about that specific update.
- **Poison reverse:** This mechanism is an exception to the split horizon rule for the poisoned routes.

TROUBLESHOOTING ROUTING ISSUES

When configuring routing on your network devices, you have to carefully configure static or dynamic routing based on the design. If you have a problem and are not able to send/receive traffic across the network, then you probably have some kind of configuration issue. When you initially set up a router there will most likely be some type of configuration problem that you will have to troubleshoot. If the router has been running for a while and you suddenly have a complete failure of traffic (no communication), you should analyze the situation and figure out whether the routing protocol functions as expected.

Sometimes certain routes might intermittently disappear and appear from the routing table, causing intermittent connectivity to specific destinations. This may be because a certain network area has some kind of communication problem and routers along the path propagate new routing information every time that area becomes accessible. This process is called "route flapping," and the specific routes can be blocked so the entire network is not affected using a feature called "route dampening."

> **NOTE:** When using static routing, the routing table never changes so you will have no idea about problems that occur in different network areas.

When troubleshooting routing issues the standard approach is to follow the routing table for every route along the path. You might perform a traceroute to find out exactly where the packets are going and to see the routers along the path. This way you would know exactly which device might be causing the issues and you can start investigating the routing tables of the specific routers.

A common mistake when performing such a troubleshooting process is investigating the issue in a single direction (for example, source to destination). Instead, you should perform the troubleshooting in both directions because you might come across situations in which packets are blocked in a single direction and you have no return traffic from the destination to the source. The routing tables on devices along the path between two points should correctly point in both directions in order to ensure an optimal traffic flow.

Often you will be using connections provided by third parties, so when you want to troubleshoot issues in a certain area you should communicate with the provider and synchronize the troubleshooting effort. This includes sharing routing table information.

Using dynamic routing protocols makes the troubleshooting process easier because you can inspect the routing updates as they are sent and received by the router. This can be done via packet capture or internal device mechanisms and will help you to see how and when the routing table is populated. Having a topology map and other documentation that lists where every prefix is located in the network would further help your understanding of the routing updates and would shorten the troubleshooting process. The general idea in such a troubleshooting process is deciding which path a specific packet should take, based on the network design, and investigating where exactly it is deviating from this path.

Different tools can be used to monitor network devices. A common network management protocol used by these tools is Simple Network Management Protocol (SNMP), which was designed to query network devices for different parameters from a management station (SNMP is covered in ICND2). Besides the standard "health" parameters checked (e.g., CPU, memory, disk space, etc.), SNMP can also query the router for things like:

- Interface packet counters
- Used bandwidth and throughput
- CRC or other types of errors on device interfaces
- Routing table information

Other types of tools you can use are standard ping and traceroute utilities in order to verify end-to-end connectivity. They can also show relevant output that might help you determine the point in the network where problems occur.

The steps to troubleshooting almost all routing issues include the following:

- Verifying that routing is enabled
- Verifying that the routing table is valid
- Verifying the correct path selection

Verifying That Routing Is Enabled

The first step in troubleshooting routing is verifying that the routing protocol is enabled and properly configured. This can be done either by inspecting the current running configuration (i.e., the show run command) or by using show commands associated with each particular routing protocol. Some of these options are listed below:

```
Router#show ip ospf ?
  <1-65535>             Process ID number
  border-routers       Border and boundary router information
  database             Database summary
  flood-list           Link state flood list
  interface            Interface information
  max-metric           Max-metric origination information
  mpls                 MPLS related information
  neighbor             Neighbor list
  request-list         Link state request list
  retransmission-list  Link state retransmission list
  rib                  Routing information base (RIB)
  sham-links           Sham link information
  statistics           Various OSPF Statistics
  summary-address      Summary-address redistribution information
  timers               OSPF timers information
  traffic              Traffic related statistics
  virtual-links        Virtual link information
  |                    Output modifiers
  <cr>

Router#show ip eigrp ?
  <1-65535>    Autonomous System
  accounting   IP-EIGRP accounting
  interfaces   IP-EIGRP interfaces
  neighbors    IP-EIGRP neighbors
  topology     IP-EIGRP topology table
  traffic      IP-EIGRP traffic statistics
  vrf          Select a VPN routing/forwarding instance

Router#show ip bgp ?
  A.B.C.D              Network in the BGP routing table to display
  A.B.C.D/nn           IP prefix <network>/<length>, e.g., 35.0.0.0/8
  all                  All address families
  cidr-only            Display only routes with non-natural netmasks
  community            Display routes matching the communities
  community-list       Display routes matching the community-list
  dampening            Display detailed information about dampening
  extcommunity-list    Display routes matching the extcommunity-list
  filter-list          Display routes conforming to the filter-list
  inconsistent-as      Display only routes with inconsistent origin ASs
  injected-paths       Display all injected paths
  ipv4                 Address family
  ipv6                 Address family
  labels               Display labels for IPv4 NLRI specific information
  neighbors            Detailed information on TCP and BGP neighbor
connections
  nsap                 Address family
```

```
oer-paths          Display all oer controlled paths
paths              Path information
peer-group         Display information on peer-groups
pending-prefixes   Display prefixes pending deletion
prefix-list        Display routes matching the prefix-list
quote-regexp       Display routes matching the AS path "regular
expression"
regexp             Display routes matching the AS path regular
expression
replication        Display replication status of update-group(s)
rib-failure        Display bgp routes that failed to install in the
routing table (RIB)
route-map          Display routes matching the route-map
summary            Summary of BGP neighbor status
template           Display peer-policy/peer-session templates
update-group       Display information on update-groups
vpnv4              Address family
|                  Output modifiers
<cr>
```

Verifying That the Routing Table Is Valid

After successfully determining that the routing process is enabled, the next step is to analyze the routing table and see whether the information listed there is valid. Some of the points you should focus on include:

- Verifying that the correct prefixes are being learned via the correct routing protocol
- Verifying the number of learned prefixes
- Verifying route metrics and next-hop information

Depending on the routing protocol, you should also verify that the correct prefixes are being advertised outbound from your device.

Verifying the Correct Path Selection

After verifying that the relevant prefixes are indeed present in the routing table, you should carefully analyze their attributes and the path selection method for each of them. This might include:

- Verifying all the routing protocols that advertise that specific prefix (including static routing)
- Comparing and manipulating the AD in order to prefer it over the correct routing protocol
- Verifying and adjusting protocol metrics

By properly configuring the router in your network, documenting each step along the way, and constantly monitoring the path between different points in the network, you will have a solid understanding of exactly how the traffic should traverse all the devices in the network.

INTER-VLAN ROUTING

By default, although VLANs can span the entire Layer 2 switched network, hosts in one VLAN cannot communicate directly with hosts in another VLAN. In order to do so, traffic must be routed between the different VLANs. This is referred to as inter-VLAN routing. The three methods of implementing inter-VLAN routing in switched LANs below, including their advantages and disadvantages, will be described in the following sections:

- Inter-VLAN routing using physical router interfaces
- Inter-VLAN routing using router subinterfaces
- Inter-VLAN routing using switched virtual interfaces (ICND2 topic)

Inter-VLAN Routing Using Physical Router Interfaces

The first method of implementing inter-VLAN routing for communication entails using a router with multiple physical interfaces as the default gateway for each individually configured VLAN. The router can then route packets received from one VLAN to another using these physical LAN interfaces. This method is illustrated below in Figure 10.12:

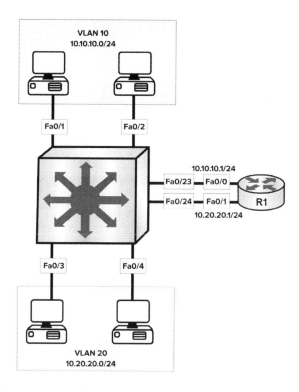

Figure 10.12—Inter-VLAN Routing Using Multiple Physical Router Interfaces

Figure 10.12 illustrates a single switch using two different VLANs, each with an assigned IP subnet. Although the network hosts depicted in the figure are connected to the same physical switch, because they reside in different VLANs, packets between hosts in VLAN 10 and those in VLAN 20 must be routed, while packets within the same VLAN are simply switched.

The primary advantage of using this solution is that it is simple and easy to implement. The primary disadvantage, however, is that it is not scalable. For example, if 5, 10, or even 20 additional VLANs were configured on the switch, the same number of physical interfaces as VLANs would also be needed on the router. In most cases, this is technically not feasible.

When using multiple physical router interfaces, each switch link connected to the router is configured as an access link in the desired VLAN. The physical interfaces on the router are then configured with the appropriate IP addresses, and the network hosts are either statically configured with IP addresses in the appropriate VLAN, using the physical router interface as the default gateway, or dynamically configured using DHCP. The configuration of the switch illustrated in Figure 10.12 is illustrated in the following output:

```
Switch-1(config)#vlan 10
Switch-1(config-vlan)#name Example-VLAN-10
Switch-1(config-vlan)#exit
Switch-1(config)#vlan 20
Switch-1(config-vlan)#name Example-VLAN-20
Switch-1(config-vlan)#exit
Switch-1(config)#interface range FastEthernet0/1-2, 23
Switch-1(config-if-range)#switchport
Switch-1(config-if-range)#switchport access vlan 10
Switch-1(config-if-range)#switchport mode access
Switch-1(config-if-range)#exit
Switch-1(config)#interface range FastEthernet0/3-4, 24
Switch-1(config-if-range)#switchport
Switch-1(config-if-range)#switchport access vlan 20
Switch-1(config-if-range)#switchport mode access
Switch-1(config-if-range)#exit
```

As you know, the switchport command isn't required on the 2960 switch because the interface is already running in Layer 2 mode.

The router illustrated in Figure 10.12 is configured as shown in the following output:

```
R1(config)#interface FastEthernet0/0
R1(config-if)#ip add 10.10.10.1 255.255.255.0
R1(config-if)#exit
R1(config)#interface FastEthernet0/1
R1(config-if)#ip add 10.20.20.1 255.255.255.0
R1(config-if)#exit
```

Inter-VLAN Routing Using Router Sub interfaces

Implementing inter-VLAN routing using sub interfaces addresses the scalability issues that are possible when using multiple physical router interfaces. With sub interfaces, only a single physical interface is required on the router and subsequent subinterfaces are configured off that physical interface. This is illustrated below in Figure 10.13:

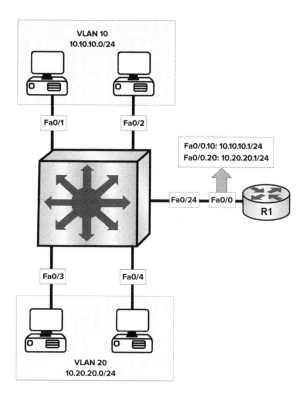

Figure 10.13—Inter-VLAN Routing Using Router Subinterfaces

Figure 10.13 depicts the same LAN illustrated in Figure 10.12. In Figure 10.13, however, only a single physical router interface is being used. In order to implement an inter-VLAN routing solution, subinterfaces are configured off the main physical router interface using the `interface [name].[subinterface number]` global configuration command. Each subinterface is associated with a particular VLAN using the `encapsulation [isl|dot1Q] [vlan]` subinterface configuration command. The final step is to configure the desired IP address on the interface.

On the switch, the single link connected to the router must be configured as a trunk link because routers don't support DTP. If the trunk is configured as an 802.1Q trunk, a native VLAN must be defined if a VLAN other than the default will be used as the native VLAN. This native VLAN must also be configured on the respective router subinterface using the `encapsulation dot1Q [vlan] native` subinterface configuration command.

The following output illustrates the configuration of inter-VLAN routing using a single physical interface (also referred to as "router-on-a-stick"). The two VLANs depicted in Figure 10.13 are shown in the following output, as is an additional VLAN used for Management; this VLAN will be configured as the native VLAN:

```
Switch-1(config)#vlan 10
Switch-1(config-vlan)#name Example-VLAN-10
Switch-1(config-vlan)#exit
Switch-1(config)#vlan 20
Switch-1(config-vlan)#name Example-VLAN-20
Switch-1(config-vlan)#exit
Switch-1(config)#vlan 30
Switch-1(config-vlan)#name Management-VLAN
Switch-1(config-vlan)#exit
Switch-1(config)#interface range FastEthernet0/1–2
Switch-1(config-if-range)#switchport
Switch-1(config-if-range)#switchport access vlan 10
Switch-1(config-if-range)#switchport mode access
Switch-1(config-if-range)#exit
Switch-1(config)#interface range FastEthernet0/3–4
Switch-1(config-if-range)#switchport
Switch-1(config-if-range)#switchport access vlan 20
Switch-1(config-if-range)#switchport mode access
Switch-1(config-if-range)#exit
Switch-1(config)#interface FastEthernet0/24
Switch-1(config-if)#switchport
Switch-1(config-if)#switchport trunk encapsulation dot1q
Switch-1(config-if)#switchport mode trunk
Switch-1(config-if)#switchport trunk native vlan 30
Switch-1(config-if)#exit
Switch-1(config)#interface vlan 30
Switch-1(config-if)#description 'This is the Management Subnet'
Switch-1(config-if)#ip address 10.30.30.2 255.255.255.0
Switch-1(config-if)#no shutdown
Switch-1(config-if)#exit
Switch-1(config)#ip default-gateway 10.30.30.1
```

The router illustrated in Figure 10.13 is configured as shown in the following output:

```
R1(config)#interface FastEthernet0/0
R1(config-if)#no ip address
R1(config-if)#exit
R1(config)#interface FastEthernet0/0.10
R1(config-subitf)#description 'Subinterface For VLAN 10'
R1(config-subif)#encapsulation dot1Q 10
R1(config-subif)#ip add 10.10.10.1 255.255.255.0
R1(config-subif)#exit
R1(config)#interface FastEthernet0/0.20
R1(config-subitf)#description 'Subinterface For VLAN 20'
R1(config-subif)#encapsulation dot1Q 20
R1(config-subif)#ip add 10.20.20.1 255.255.255.0
R1(config-subif)#exit
R1(config)#interface FastEthernet0/0.30
R1(config-subitf)#description 'Subinterface For Management'
R1(config-subif)#encapsulation dot1Q 30 native
R1(config-subif)#ip add 10.30.30.1 255.255.255.0
R1(config-subif)#exit
```

The primary advantage of this solution is that only a single physical interface is required on the router. The primary disadvantage is that the bandwidth of the physical interface is shared between the various configured subinterfaces. Therefore, if there is a lot of inter-VLAN traffic, the router can quickly become a bottleneck in the network.

We cover SVIs in the ICND2 notes.

TROUBLESHOOTING INTER-VLAN ROUTING

Inter-VLAN routing issues can come in many forms, especially considering that multiple devices are involved (switches, routers, etc.) in the process. By following a proper troubleshooting methodology, you should be able to isolate the problem to a particular device and then map it to a specific feature that has been misconfigured.

From a connectivity standpoint, some of the things that need to be checked include:

- Verifying that the end-stations are connected in the proper switch ports
- Verifying that the proper switch ports are connected in the proper router ports (if a router is used for inter-VLAN routing)
- Verifying that each of the ports involved in this process carry the correct VLANs
  - The ports that connect the end-stations are usually access ports allocated to a particular VLAN
  - The ports connecting the switch to the router are usually trunk ports

After confirming that the connectivity between the devices is correct, the next logical step is investigating Layer 2 configuration, starting with the configured encapsulation method on the trunk ports, which is usually 802.1Q, the preferred method. Next, make sure that the same encapsulation is configured on both ends of the trunk link.

Some of the commands that can be used to verify the encapsulation types are as follows:

```
show interface trunk
show interface <number> switchport
```

Here is an example output:

```
Switch#show interfaces trunk

Port        Mode         Encapsulation  Status      Native vlan
Fa0/1       on           802.1q         trunking    1
Fa0/2       on           802.1q         trunking    1

Port        Vlans allowed on trunk
Fa0/1       1,10,20,30,40,50
Fa0/2       1-99,201-4094
```

Another important detail that is offered by the show interface trunk command is the trunk status. This confirms whether the trunk is formed or not and it has to be checked at both ends of the link. If the interface is not in "trunking" mode, one of the most important things that has to be verified is the mode of operation (on, auto, etc.) to see whether it will allow a trunking state to form with the other end of the link.

The native VLAN is another important element that you should verify on the trunk ports. Misconfigured native VLANs can lead to a lack of functionality or security issues. The native VLAN should match at both ends of the trunk links.

If after verifying the Layer 2 verification tasks the inter-VLAN issue is still not resolved, you can proceed to verifying Layer 3 configuration. Depending upon the Layer 3 device used to ensure the actual inter-VLAN routing, this can be configured/verified on one of the following devices:

- Multilayer switch
- Router—physical interfaces
- Router—subinterfaces

On the Layer 3 device, you should verify that the correct subnet is assigned to each interface (or SVI), and you should also verify the routing protocol, if needed. Usually, a different subnet is assigned to each VLAN so you should make sure that you don't misconfigure the interfaces. In order to verify this you can use the show interface command for the specific physical interface, subinterface, or SVI.

Please take today's exam at **https://www.in60days.com/free/ccnain60days/**

DAY 10 LAB

Routing Concepts

Use two directly connected routers and test the basic commands depicted in this module. RIP is covered soon so just copy my commands for now.

- Assign an IPv4 address to the directly connected interfaces (10.10.10.1/24 and 10.10.10.2/24)
- Test direct connectivity using ping
- Configure a Loopback interface on each router and assign addresses from two different ranges (11.11.11.1/24 for R1 and 12.12.12.2/24 for R2)
- Configure RIP and advertise all the local networks

R1:

```
router rip
 version 2
 no auto
 network 10.10.10.0
 network 11.11.11.0
```

R2:

```
router rip
 version 2
 no auto
 network 10.10.10.0
 network 12.12.12.0
```

- Ping R2 Loopback from R1 to test connectivity
- Issue a show ip route command to verify that routes are being received via RIP
- Issue a show ip protocols command to verify that RIP is configured and active on the devices. Check the administrative distance.

Inter-VLAN Router Subinterfaces Lab

Topology

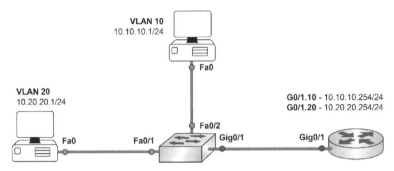

Purpose

Learn how to configure inter-VLAN routing using router subinterfaces.

I've used Packet Tracer for this lab but you can use your own home lab if you have access to all the available equipment. Set the displayed IP address on each PC and put the default gateway to 10.10.10.254 for the top PC and 10.20.20.254 for the bottom PC. Here is the top PC configuration:

Walkthrough

1. Create VLAN 10 and 20 on the switch and set the correct ports for the correct VLANs.

```
Switch#conf t
Enter configuration commands, one per line.  End with CNTL/Z.
Switch(config)#vlan 10
Switch(config-vlan)#vlan 20
Switch(config-vlan)#int f0/2
Switch(config-if)#switchport mode access
Switch(config-if)#switchport access vlan 10
Switch(config-if)#no shut
```

```
Switch(config-if)#int f0/1
Switch(config-if)#switchport mode access
Switch(config-if)#switchport access vlan 20
```

2. Set the router facing interface to trunk.

```
Switch(config-if)#int g0/1
Switch(config-if)#switchport mode trunk
```

3. Configure a sub-interface on the router, one for each VLAN.

```
Router(config)#int g0/1
Router(config-if)#no ip address
Router(config-if)#int g0/1.10
Router(config-subif)#encap dot1Q 10
Router(config-subif)#ip add 10.10.10.254 255.255.255.0
Router(config-subif)#
Router(config-subif)#int g0/1.20
Router(config-subif)#encap dot
Router(config-subif)#encap dot1Q 20
Router(config-subif)#ip add 10.20.20.254 255.255.255.0
Router(config-subif)#int g0/1
Router(config-if)#no shut
```

4. Open a command prompt on the 10.10.10.1 device and ping the default gateway. Then ping the PC in VLAN 20 to prove that the sub-interface configuration is working.

```
Packet Tracer PC Command Line 1.0
C:\>ping 10.10.10.254

Pinging 10.10.10.254 with 32 bytes of data:

Reply from 10.10.10.254: bytes=32 time=1ms TTL=255
Reply from 10.10.10.254: bytes=32 time=1ms TTL=255
Reply from 10.10.10.254: bytes=32 time<1ms TTL=255
Reply from 10.10.10.254: bytes=32 time<1ms TTL=255

Ping statistics for 10.10.10.254:
    Packets: Sent = 4, Received = 4, Lost = 0 (0% loss),
Approximate round trip times in milli-seconds:
    Minimum = 0ms, Maximum = 1ms, Average = 0ms

C:\>ping 10.20.20.1

Pinging 10.20.20.1 with 32 bytes of data:

Request timed out.
Reply from 10.20.20.1: bytes=32 time<1ms TTL=127
Reply from 10.20.20.1: bytes=32 time<1ms TTL=127
Reply from 10.20.20.1: bytes=32 time<1ms TTL=127

Ping statistics for 10.20.20.1:
    Packets: Sent = 4, Received = 3, Lost = 1 (25% loss),
Approximate round trip times in milli-seconds:
    Minimum = 0ms, Maximum = 0ms, Average = 0ms
```

Static Routing

DAY 11 TASKS

- Read today's lesson notes (below)
- Review yesterday's lesson notes and labs
- Complete today's lab
- Take today's exam
- Read the ICND1 cram guide
- Spend 15 minutes on the subnetting.org website

Your choices as a network administrator are to use dynamic routing protocols on your network or static routing, which is where you manually add each route for your network onto each router.

I'm often asked which routing protocol or method is the "best." There is no method which will suit every network, as even a particular company's network requirements will change over time. Static routing will take time and effort to configure, but you will save on network bandwidth and CPU cycles. If a new route is added, then you will have to add this manually to every router. In addition, if a route goes down, static routing has no method to deal with this, so it will continue to send traffic to the down network (reliable static routing is outside the CCNA syllabus).

Today you will learn about the following:

- Configuring static routes
- Configuring IPv6 static routes
- Troubleshooting static routes

This module maps to the following CCNA syllabus requirements:

- 3.6 Configure, verify, and troubleshoot IPv4 and IPv6 static routing
- 3.6.a Default route
- 3.6.b Network route
- 3.6.c Host route
- 3.6.d Floating static

If you look back at the administrative distances table in Day 10, you will see that manually configured networks are preferred over routing protocols. The reason for this is, as a network administrator, you will be expected to know your network better than any protocol can and to understand what you want to achieve. By now, it should be clear that you can use static routing with dynamic routing if your needs require it.

The same command are discussed more than once in this chapter. Firstly by myself but then in a different context by one of our CCIE authors. I decided to do it this way so you can see another perspective.

CONFIGURING STATIC ROUTES

Static routes are a quick and easy way to instruct your router to forward traffic destined for a particular host or network or even to anywhere not listed in your routing table. You can use them as a standalone solution, in conjunction with dynamic routing or as a fail safe in case your main route goes down.

The commands to configure a static route (see Figure 11.1 below) include the following:

- network address/prefix mask
- address or exit interface
- distance (optional)

Here is an example of these commands in use:

```
RouterA(config)#ip route network prefix mask {address | interface}
[distance]
```

Figure 11.1—Sample Network for Static Routes

To add a static route for the network above, you would write the following line of configuration on the router on the left:

```
Router(config)#ip route 192.168.1.0 255.255.255.0 172.16.1.2
```

With static routes, you can specify a next-hop IP address the router needs to go to on the way to the destination address, or you can specify an exit interface. Often, you won't know your next hop because it is your ISP, or your IP address will change over time (see Figure 11.2 below). If this is the case, use an exit interface.

SO/0

Figure 11.2—You Might Not Always Know Your Next-Hop Address

```
Router(config)#ip route 192.168.1.0 255.255.255.0 s0/0
```

The command line above tells the router to send traffic destined for the 192.168.1.0 network out of the Serial interface. The next command tells the router to send all traffic for all networks out of the Serial interface:

```
Router(config)#ip route 0.0.0.0 0.0.0.0 s0/0
```

The route above is actually a default route. Default routes are used to direct packets addressed to networks not explicitly listed in the routing table. We cover these as well as your other options in more detail below.

Static Default Routes

Unlike switches, which broadcast if the destination address is unknown, routers drop such packets. Routers store a table of routes to all of the relevant parts of the network, but as network administrators, we rarely want our routers to simply drop traffic when they receive packets that they don't have a route for. For example, LAN routers don't have every route to the Internet in their routing table, but network administrators still want the LAN router to forward traffic to and from the Internet. This is achieved through default routing.

With default routing, if a router receives a packet and it doesn't have a destination route in its routing table, it can forward the packet to the default route, which is usually a more powerful Internet edge router carrying a larger routing table.

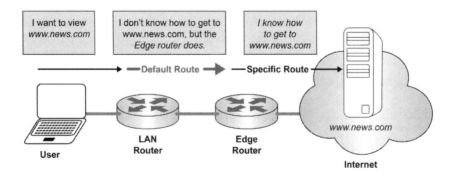

Figure 11.3—Static Default Routing

Default routes can be created statically or learned dynamically. In Figure 11.3 above, the static default route is pointing to the edge router. Now, if you didn't want to keep the entire routing table for the Internet (using BGP) on your edge router and preferred that your Internet Service Provider did this work for you, you typically would receive a dynamic default route via BGP from your ISP as shown below in Figure 11.4. We will cover BGP in the ICND2 section.

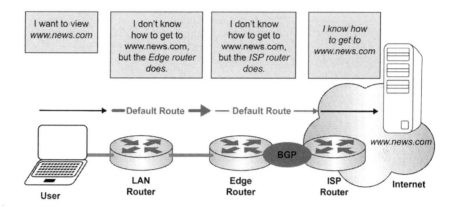

Figure 11.4—Static and Dynamic Default Routing

In Figure 11.4 above, the LAN router has a static default route pointing to the edge router, and the edge router has a dynamic default route that it learned via BGP from the ISP router that is pointing to the ISP router. Regardless of how a router learns the default route, the route works all the same.

In order to understand default routing, you must remember that routers will forward traffic to the most specific route. So, a router will forward a packet to 192.168.1.0/24 before it will send a packet to 192.168.0.0/16. Understanding this concept, the default route is a single route that matches all packets. This means that any valid route to a destination other than a default route will be preferred over the default route. The default route will only be used if there is no valid route to a destination. The default route is the "catch-all" route that says, "If I don't know where it goes, then I'm going to send it here as a last resort."

Default routing isn't limited to sending traffic to the Internet. Another popular way to leverage a default route is with enterprise networks. For example, if you have a core data center at your headquarters with two branch office sites, you could have all non-local branch office traffic forwarded to the core. If you host your e-mail, database, and intranet servers at your data center, you could leverage the default route on the branch office routers to forward all of that traffic instead of specifying individual routes for the e-mail, database, and intranet servers.

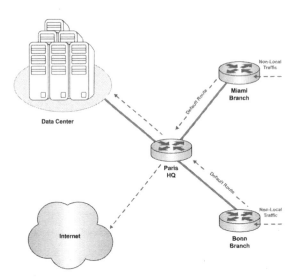

Figure 11.5—Static Default Routes in a Branch Office Design

In Figure 11.5 above, all non-local branch office traffic is sent to the Paris HQ hub router via a default route. The Paris HQ hub router has specific routes to either forward the traffic to the appropriate server in the data center or to forward the traffic out to the Internet.

This portion of the study guide will focus on static default routing, so going forward, all examples will reference static routing. Dynamic routing will be covered in other portions of this study guide.

Static Default Route Configuration

There are three commands you can use to statically assign a default route:

- `ip default-gateway`
- `ip default-network`
- `ip route 0.0.0.0 0.0.0.0`

ip default-gateway

The `ip default-gateway` command should only be used when IP routing is disabled on the Cisco router or switch. In the same way that a PC uses a default gateway to communicate on the network, the Cisco router can leverage the `ip default-gateway` command to communicate on the network. For example, you may want to use this command when you have a Cisco router in boot mode (when the routing doesn't have IP routing enabled) in order to TFTP a new Cisco IOS software image to the router.

The following example shows the router IP address 172.16.1.1 as the default route:

```
R1(config)#ip default-gateway 172.16.1.1
```

ip default-network

You can use the `ip default-network` command when IP routing is enabled on the Cisco router. When you configure the `ip default-network` command, the router considers routes to that network for installation as the gateway of last resort on the router. In the example below, 161.44.191.1 is a next hop router:

```
R1(config)#ip default-network 198.10.1.0
R1(config)#end
R1#show ip route
Codes: C - connected, S - static, I - IGRP, R - RIP, M - mobile,
       B—BGP, D - EIGRP, EX - EIGRP external, O - OSPF,
       IA - OSPF inter area, N1 - OSPF NSSA external type 1,
       N2 - OSPF NSSA external type 2, E1 - OSPF external type 1,
       E2 - OSPF external type 2, E—EGP, i - IS-IS,
       su - IS-IS summary, L1 - IS-IS level-1, L2 - IS-IS level-2,
       ia - IS-IS inter area, * - candidate default,
       U - per-user static route, o - ODR,
       P - periodic downloaded static route
```

Gateway of last resort is 161.44.191.1 to network 198.10.1.0.

```
     161.44.0.0/24 is subnetted, 1 subnets
C    161.44.192.0 is directly connected, Ethernet0
     131.108.0.0/24 is subnetted, 1 subnets
C    131.108.99.0 is directly connected, Serial0
S*   198.10.1.0/24 [1/0] via 161.44.191.1
```

The gateway of last resort is now set as 161.44.191.1 because 198.10.1.0 points to that as the next hop in the routing table.

ip route 0.0.0.0 0.0.0.0 (Destination IP)

In order for the `ip route 0.0.0.0 0.0.0.0` command to work, IP routing must be enabled on the router. Here is an example of configuring a gateway of last resort using the `ip route 0.0.0.0 0.0.0.0` command:

```
R1#configure terminal
Enter configuration commands, one per line. End with CTRL/Z.
R1(config)#ip route 0.0.0.0 0.0.0.0 170.170.3.4
R1(config)#^Z
R1#show ip route
  Codes: C - connected, S - static, I - IGRP, R - RIP, M - mobile,
         B—BGP, D - EIGRP, EX - EIGRP external, O - OSPF,
         IA - OSPF inter area, N1 - OSPF NSSA external type 1,
         N2 - OSPF NSSA external type 2, E1 - OSPF external type 1,
         E2 - OSPF external type 2, E—EGP, i - IS-IS,
         L1 - IS-IS level-1, L2 - IS-IS level-2,
         * - candidate default, U - per-user static route, o - ODR
```

Gateway of last resort is 170.170.3.4 to network 0.0.0.0.

```
170.170.0.0/24 is subnetted, 2 subnets
  C 170.170.2.0 is directly connected, Serial0
  C 170.170.3.0 is directly connected, Ethernet0
  S* 0.0.0.0/0 [1/0] via 170.170.3.4
```

Some important considerations for static default routing:

- If you use both the `ip default-network` and the `ip route 0.0.0.0 0.0.0.0` commands to configure candidate default networks, the network defined with the `ip default-network` command will take precedence.
- If you use multiple `ip route 0.0.0.0 0.0.0.0` commands to configure a default route, traffic will be load balanced over the multiple routes.
- EIGRP propagates a route to network 0.0.0.0 if the static route is redistributed into the routing protocol.
- In Cisco IOS Software Release 12.0T and later, RIP does not advertise the default route if the route is not learned via RIP. It may be necessary to redistribute the route into RIP.
- The default routes created using the `ip route 0.0.0.0 0.0.0.0` command are not propagated by OSPF.
- Use the `default-information originate` command to generate a default route into an OSPF routing domain.

Network Routing

Although the vast majority of your experience with routing to specific networks will be done using Interior Gateway (routing) Protocols, understanding the basics of how a static network route works will provide you with a solid foundation regardless of the environment you support. Static routing to networks is normally not the preferred method, but the reality is that static routes are still used and they certainly provide an excellent opportunity to understand how routing to networks is carried out.

A "network" as it applies to network routing is a remote subnet that you would like to reach. Some examples may be 10.1.0.0/24, 192.168.0.0/16, or 38.122.188.0/25. Basically, if it's anything below a /31 subnet, then you ultimately would need to rely on a network route to reach it.

Cisco IOS allows the definition of individual static routes using the `ip route` global configuration command. With this command, you will specify the subnet, the network mask, and the next hop address, that is, the next step in the path toward the destination. In lieu of a next hop address, you may also use the outgoing interface as shown below:

```
R1(config)#ip route 172.16.2.0 255.255.255.0 172.16.4.2
R1(config)#ip route 172.16.3.0 255.255.255.0 S0/0/1
```

In Figure 11.6 below, the end-user PC is trying to send traffic to 192.168.1.5, which resides on the 192.168.1.0/24 network. The gateway router (Router 1) for the end-user PC has a static route that tells the router to forward all traffic destined for 192.168.1.0/24 to the next hop of 192.168.10.1 (Router 2). The router then forwards that traffic, trusting that Router 2 knows how to handle the traffic flow from there.

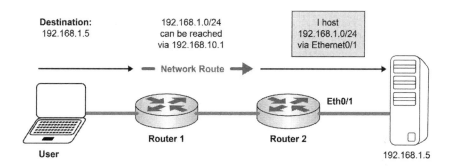

Figure 11.6—Network Routing

On Router 1, the route in the running configuration looks like this:

```
ip route 192.168.1.0 255.255.255.0 192.168.10.1
```

You can also implement this route using the router's outgoing interface instead of the next hop. So, for example, if Router 1 uses Ethernet 0/2 to connect to Router 2, it would look like this:

```
ip route 192.168.1.0 255.255.255.0 Ethernet0/2
```

Let's implement two different routes into the routing table using each method and see if you can discern the different behavior in the routing table.

```
R1(config)#ip route 192.168.2.0 255.255.255.0 172.16.4.2
R1(config)#ip route 192.168.4.0 255.255.255.0 Serial0/0/1
R1#show ip route static
Codes: L - local, C - connected, S - static, R - RIP, M - mobile,
       B -BGP
! lines omitted for brevity
Gateway of last resort is not set

   172.16.0.0/16 is variably subnetted, 6 subnets, 2 masks
S    192.168.2.0/24 [1/0] via 172.16.4.2
S    192.168.4.0/24 is directly connected, Serial0/0/1
```

Did you notice that the route that used the next hop IP address has a via keyword in the routing table entry? The route that references the outgoing Serial0/0/1 interface is listed as a connected route. Often, engineers will think that because a route is directly connected, the subnet must be hosted on the router itself, but as you can see, that's not always the case.

If Serial 0/0/1 went down due to a link failure, the static route would no longer show up in the routing table. If the link that connected to 172.16.4.2 went down, that route also would no longer show up in the routing table. That being said, using a different example, as shown in Figure 11.7 below, if the downstream router, Router 3, that is hosting 192.168.2.0/24 stopped working, R1 would continue to forward traffic to the next hop using static routes, because static routes are not aware of whether there are issues further downstream.

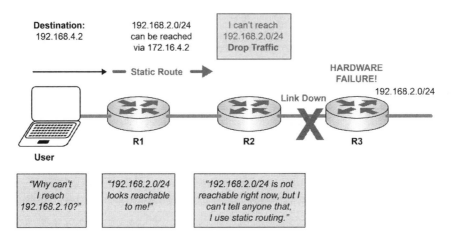

Figure 11.7—Static Routing Response to Downstream Failure

This is one reason why dynamic routing protocols are used. With dynamic routing protocols, the router experiencing the issue would notify the other routers on the network that there was a problem and that they should either stop passing traffic or forward it via a different path.

Static Host Routes

Now that you understand network routes from the previous section, it will be relatively easy to learn about host routes. A host route is a route for a single host address. It will always have a /32 subnet mask. As with network routes, the `ip route` command will create static routes for remote hosts by using a mask of 255.255.255.255. Here is an example:

```
ip route 192.168.1.10 255.255.255.255 10.0.0.1
```

As you can see above, the host IP address is 192.168.1.10 and the next hop in order to reach that host is 10.0.0.1.

So, why would you want to use host routes? There may be times when you have a redundant path to a host and you only want traffic to that host flowing over one path. In Figure 11.8 below, a branch office needs to communicate with a latency-sensitive application hosted on a server with the IP address 192.168.1.10. The WAN provider "Low Latency Networks" provides much better round-trip times than the WAN provider "Slow as You Go WAN

Solutions." Although you still want to load balance all traffic to the 192.168.1.0/24 network, when users communicate with the latency-sensitive server 192.168.1.10, you want that traffic to use the Low Latency Network circuit.

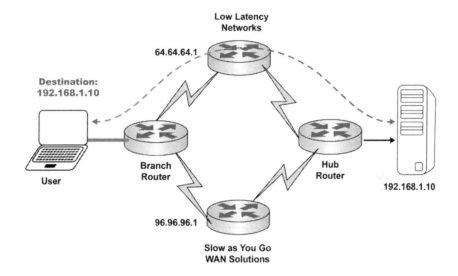

Figure 11.8—Host Routing

From a programming perspective, here is how it looks. First, make sure that you load balance 192.168.1.0/24 over both circuits.

```
BranchRouter(config)#ip route 192.168.1.0 255.255.255.0 64.64.64.1
BranchRouter(config)#ip route 192.168.1.0 255.255.255.0 96.96.96.1
```

Then, ensure that all traffic to 192.168.1.10 goes over the lower latency circuit destined for Low Latency Networks.

```
BranchRouter(config)#ip route 192.168.1.10 255.255.255.255 64.64.64.1
```

Since a router will always prefer a more specific route, any traffic destined for 192.168.1.10 will use the more specific host route and the router will not consider the /24 routes to forward this traffic. Now, any and all traffic coming from the Branch Router destined for 192.168.1.10 will traverse Low Latency Networks.

There are many other reasons why you may want to use a host route, but you get the idea. Just understand that the router will prefer the host route over any other options in the routing table.

Floating Static Routes

In order to understand how floating static routes work, you first need to learn (or be reminded of) the administrative distance (AD) attribute of the routes. Each type of route is assigned a numerical value that tells the router which route should be preferred. The lower the number, the stronger the candidate for insertion into the routing table.

In Table 11.1 below, you will see that Cisco routers prefer static routes over all of the routes learned via routing protocols (e.g., EIGRP, BGP, IGRP, OSPF, IS-IS, etc.). This is important to remember as we discuss floating static routes.

Table 11.1—Route sources and default distance values

Route Source	Default Distance Values
Connected interface	0
Static route	1
Enhanced Interior Gateway Routing Protocol (EIGRP) summary route	5
External Border Gateway Protocol (eBGP)	20
Internal EIGRP	90
IGRP	100
OSPF	110
Intermediate System-to-Intermediate System (IS-IS)	115
Routing Information Protocol (RIP)	120
Exterior Gateway Protocol (EGP)	140
On Demand Routing (ODR)	160
External EIGRP	170
Internal BGP	200
Unknown*	255

If you manually program a router with the `ip route` command, it will automatically take precedence over all other routes to the same destination (other than a directly connected route). Unless you plan wisely, this can cause routing issues on the network.

For example, let's say you are once again using the two network providers Low Latency and Slow as You Go. You have a GigabitEthernet link to Low Latency, which is the primary link, and only a T1 to Slow as You Go, which is the backup link. The decision was made to run a routing protocol (OSPF) over the Gigabit link but only use static routing over the T1 to lower the traffic overhead as shown below:

```
BranchRouter(config)#ip route 192.168.1.0 255.255.255.0 172.16.5.3
```

After this is implemented, you start getting calls from your end-users saying that their connectivity to the core site is very slow. What happened?

In the design, the network uses Open Shortest Path First version 2 (OSPFv2) over the primary link, learning the routes to the core dynamically. The Branch Router also defines static routes to the core over the backup link for the exact same subnets. Remember, static routes have an administrative distance of 1 and OSPF routes have an administrative distance of 110. Since the Cisco IOS considers static routes better than OSPF-learned routes, the Branch Router is sending all traffic to the core via the T1 line as indicated by the dotted traffic flow below:

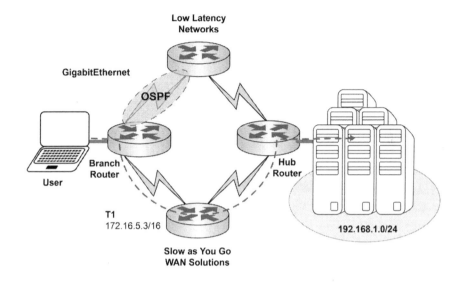

Figure 11.9—Static Route Preferred Over OSPF Route

You will need to fix this issue. You will still want to use OSPF over the primary link and static routing over the backup link. You also still want T1 to be used, but only as a backup if the primary link fails. You can accomplish this but you must adjust the static route and give it a higher administrative distance so that it is only chosen if the OSPF route is not available.

To make the router prefer the OSPF route, the configuration would need to change the administrative distance settings in order to create a floating static route. The floating static route "floats above" (from an AD perspective) the OSPF route and is only used if the OSPF route goes away. So, even though there is a static route in place, the router will not reference it unless it's a last resort, that is, unless all other options have disappeared.

To implement a floating static route, you need to override the default administrative distance on the static route and make sure that it's higher than the routing protocol you are running. Since OSPF has an AD of 110, change the AD of the static routes to 115 as follows:

```
BranchRouter(config)#ip route 192.168.1.0 255.255.255.0 172.16.5.3 115
```

Now take a look at the results of this change on the network:

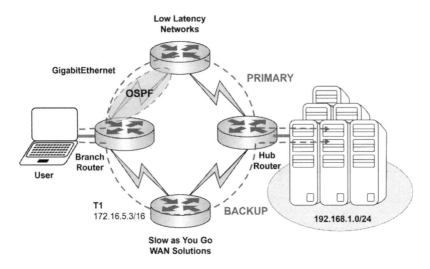

Figure 11.10—Floating AD Higher than the Routing AD

As you can see in Figure 11.10 above, the OSPF route is now preferred, but should OSPF indicate that the path is no longer valid through Low Latency Networks (possibly because of an interface or service provider failure), then the backup path using static routes over T1 will be used.

In real-world scenarios, you will typically see the route floating at or close to 250. The logic is that if you are going to make it an option for last resort, then go ahead and make the AD higher than any and all routing protocols. Here is a typical installation of a floating static route:

```
R1(config)#ip route 192.168.1.0 255.255.255.0 10.0.0.1 250
```

CONFIGURING STATIC IPV6 ROUTES

The configuration of static IPv6 routes follows similar logic to that of static IPv4 routes. In Cisco IOS software, the ipv6 route [ipv6-prefix/prefix-length] [next-hop-address | interface] [distance <1-254> | multicast | tag | unicast] global configuration command is used to configure static IPv6 routes.

While the other keywords are familiar, because they are also applicable to IPv4 static routes, the [multicast] keyword is exclusive to IPv6 and is used to configure an IPv6 static Multicast route. If this keyword is used, the route will not be entered into the Unicast routing table and will never be used to forward Unicast traffic. To ensure that the route is never installed into the Unicast RIB, Cisco IOS software sets the administrative distance value for the route to 255.

Inversely, the [unicast] keyword is used to configure an IPv6 static Unicast route. If this keyword is used, the route will not be entered into the Multicast routing table and will be used only to forward Unicast traffic. If neither the [multicast] keyword nor the [unicast] keyword is used, by default, the route will be used for both Unicast and Multicast packets.

The following configuration example illustrates how to configure three static IPv6 routes. The first route, to subnet 3FFF:1234:ABCD:0001::/64, will forward traffic out of the FastEthernet0/0 interface. This route will be used only for Unicast traffic. The second route, to subnet 3FFF:1234:ABCD:0002::/64, will forward packets to that subnet out of Serial0/0 using the Link-Local address of the next-hop router as the IPv6 next-hop address. This route will be used only for Multicast traffic. Finally, a default route pointing out of interface Serial0/1 is also configured. This default route will forward packets to unknown IPv6 destinations via Serial0/1 using the Link-Local address of the next-hop router as the IPv6 next-hop address. These routes are illustrated below:

```
R1(config)#ipv6 route 3FFF:1234:ABCD:0001::/64 Fa0/0 unicast
R1(config)#ipv6 route 3FFF:1234:ABCD:0002::/64 Se0/0 FE80::2222 multicast
R1(config)#ipv6 route ::/0 Serial0/1 FE80::3333
```

Following this configuration, the `show ipv6 route` command can be used to verify the static route configuration implemented on the local router, as illustrated below:

```
R1#show ipv6 route static
IPv6 Routing Table - 13 entries
Codes: C - Connected, L - Local, S - Static, R - RIP, B - BGP
       U - Per-user static route
       I1 - ISIS L1, I2 - ISIS L2, IA - ISIS inter area, IS - ISIS
summary
       O - OSPF intra, OI - OSPF inter, OE1 - OSPF ext 1, OE2 - OSPF ext
2
       ON1 - OSPF NSSA ext 1, ON2 - OSPF NSSA ext 2
S    ::/0 [1/0]
      via FE80::3333, Serial0/1
S    3FFF:1234:ABCD:1::/64 [1/0]
      via ::, FastEthernet0/0
S    3FFF:1234:ABCD:2::/64 [1/0]
      via FE80::2222, Serial0/0
```

In addition to using the `show ipv6 route` command, the `show ipv6 static [prefix] [detail]` command can also be used to view detailed information about all or just specified static routes. The following output illustrates how to use this command:

```
R1#show ipv6 static 3FFF:1234:ABCD:1::/64 detail
IPv6 static routes
Code: * - installed in RIB
* 3FFF:1234:ABCD:1::/64 via interface FastEthernet0/0, distance 1
```

TROUBLESHOOTING STATIC ROUTES

Troubleshooting will almost always involve a configuration issue (unless your interface is down). If traffic isn't arriving at the destination, you can test the route with the `traceroute` command or `tracert` command for a Windows PC.

Now please take today's exam at **https://www.in60days.com/free/ccnain60days/**

DAY 11 LABS

Static Routes

Topology

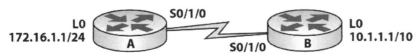

192.168.1.x/30

LO
172.16.1.1/24

S0/1/0

A

S0/1/0

B

LO
10.1.1.1/10

Purpose
Learn how to assign static routes to a router with a next-hop address and exit interface.

Walkthrough
1. Assign all the IP addresses according to the above topology. Router A can be 192.168.1.1/30 and Router B can be .2.

2. Ping across the Serial link to ensure that it is working.

3. Assign a static route on Router A, sending all traffic for the 10.1.1.0/10 network out of the Serial interface. Use your own serial number, of course; don't just copy mine if yours has a different number! I've not added the interface configs because you already know how.

```
RouterA(config)#ip route 10.0.0.0 255.192.0.0 Serial0/1/0
RouterA(config)#exit
RouterA#ping 10.1.1.1

Type escape sequence to abort.
Sending 5, 100-byte ICMP Echos to 10.1.1.1, timeout is 2 seconds:
!!!!!
Success rate is 100 percent (5/5), round-trip min/avg/max = 18/28/32
ms


RouterA#show ip route
Codes: C - Connected, S - Static, I - IGRP, R - RIP, M - Mobile, B
- BGP
        D - EIGRP, EX - EIGRP external, O - OSPF, IA - OSPF inter area
        N1 - OSPF NSSA external type 1, N2 - OSPF NSSA external type 2
        E1 - OSPF external type 1, E2 - OSPF external type 2, E - EGP
        i - IS-IS, L1 - IS-IS level-1, L2 - IS-IS level-2, ia - IS-IS
inter area
        * - Candidate default, U - Per-user static route, o - ODR
        P - Periodic downloaded static route

Gateway of last resort is not set

        10.0.0.0/10 is subnetted, 1 subnets
```

```
S        10.0.0.0 is directly connected, Serial0/1/0
       172.16.0.0/24 is subnetted, 1 subnets
C        172.16.1.0 is directly connected, Loopback0
       192.168.1.0/30 is subnetted, 1 subnets
C        192.168.1.0 is directly connected, Serial0/1/0
RouterA#

RouterA#show ip route 10.1.1.1
Routing entry for 10.0.0.0/10
Known via "static", distance 1, metric 0 (connected)
  Routing Descriptor Blocks:
  * directly connected, via Serial0/1/0
      Route metric is 0, traffic share count is 1
RouterA#
```

4. Configure a static route on Router B, sending all traffic for the 172.16.1.0/24 network to next-hop address 192.168.1.1.

```
RouterB(config)#ip route 172.16.1.0 255.255.255.0 192.168.1.1
RouterB(config)#exit

RouterB#ping 172.16.1.1
Type escape sequence to abort.
Sending 5, 100-byte ICMP Echos to 172.16.1.1, timeout is 2 seconds:
!!!!!

RouterB#show ip route 172.16.1.1
Routing entry for 172.16.1.0/24
Known via "static", distance 1, metric 0
  Routing Descriptor Blocks:
  * 192.168.1.1
      Route metric is 0, traffic share count is 1
RouterB#
```

IPv6 Static Routes

Topology

2001:aaaa:bbbb:cccc::/64

.1   .2

L0   L0

2001:aaaa:bbbb:dddd::1/64   2001:aaaa:bbbb:eeee::1/64

Purpose

Learn how to configure IPv6 static routes.

Walkthrough

1. Add IPv6 addresses to all the interfaces and then ping across the link. R1 is on the left.

```
R1(config)#ipv6 unicast-routing
R1(config)#int lo0
R1(config-if)#ipv6 add 2001:aaaa:bbbb:dddd::1/64
R1(config-if)#int f0/0
R1(config-if)#ipv6 add 2001:aaaa:bbbb:cccc::1/64
R1(config-if)#no shut

R2(config)#ipv6 unicast-routing
R2(config)#int f0/0
R2(config-if)#ipv6 address 2001:aaaa:bbbb:cccc::2/64
R2(config-if)#no shut
R2(config-if)#int lo0
R2(config-if)#ipv6 add 2001:aaaa:bbbb:eeee::1/64
R2(config-if)#end
R2#ping 2001:aaaa:bbbb:cccc::1

Type escape sequence to abort.
Sending 5, 100-byte ICMP Echos to 2001:AAAA:BBBB:CCCC::1, timeout is 2
seconds:
!!!!!
Success rate is 100 percent (5/5), round-trip min/avg/max = 12/22/36
ms
```

2. Issue some common show commands for IPv6.

```
R1#show ipv6 interface brief
R1#show ipv6 interface f0/0
R1#show ipv6 neighbors
```

3. Configure a static route on R2 so it can reach the network attached to Loopback 0 on R1. You will need to add a next-hop link local address because (in this example) we are using an exit interface (f0/0).

```
R2(config)#ipv6 route 2001:AAAA:BBBB:DDDD::0/64 f0/0
FE80::C003:8FF:FE2F:0
```

4. Now ping the remote network on R1 from R2.

```
R2#ping 2001:aaaa:bbbb:dddd::1

Type escape sequence to abort.
Sending 5, 100-byte ICMP Echos to 2001:AAAA:BBBB:DDDD::1, timeout is 2
seconds:
!!!!!
Success rate is 100 percent (5/5), round-trip min/avg/max = 8/16/24 ms
```

5. Now add a static default route on R1 to send any traffic for any network/host. You can try a next-hop address, I'll use an exit interface.

```
R1(config)#ipv6 route ::/0 f0/0 FE80::C004:8FF:FE2F:0
```

6. Now ping the IP address of L0 on R2.

```
R1#ping 2001:AAAA:BBBB:EEEE::1

Type escape sequence to abort.
Sending 5, 100-byte ICMP Echos to 2001:AAAA:BBBB:EEEE::1, timeout is 2
seconds:
!!!!!
Success rate is 100 percent (5/5), round-trip min/avg/max = 12/18/24
ms
R1#
```

7. Check the IPv6 static route table entries.

```
R1#show ipv6 route static
IPv6 Routing Table - 6 entries
Codes: C - Connected, L - Local, S - Static, R - RIP, B - BGP
       U - Per-user Static route, M - MIPv6
       I1 - ISIS L1, I2 - ISIS L2, IA - ISIS interarea, IS - ISIS
summary
       O - OSPF intra, OI - OSPF inter, OE1 - OSPF ext 1, OE2 - OSPF
ext 2
       ON1 - OSPF NSSA ext 1, ON2 - OSPF NSSA ext 2
       D - EIGRP, EX - EIGRP external
S    ::/0 [1/0]
     via FE80::C004:8FF:FE2F:0, FastEthernet0/0
```

Routing Information Protocol

DAY 12 TASKS

- Read today's theory notes
- Take today's exam
- Complete today's lab
- Read the ICND1 cram guide
- Spend 15 minutes on subnetting.org
- Review yesterday's theory notes and labs

RIP was taken out of the CCNA exam some years ago, much to my chagrin. Even though it's been around a long time (RIP was first specified in 1988 by RFC 1058), it works perfectly well in small networks. RIPv2 addressed many of the shortfalls in v1, meaning that it is still a viable option for you to consider. Even though RIP was removed from the CCNA syllabus, I still taught it in my classroom sessions and referred to it often in lessons because it provided a great foundation on which to build a strong understanding of routing protocols. It is now back in the syllabus (but only version 2).

RIP is now back in the syllabus but it only specifies version 2. I've outlined the original version so you can see the differences as well as understand how classful protocols operate.

Today you will learn about the following:

- RIP
- Troubleshooting RIP

This module maps to the following CCNA syllabus requirement:

- 3.7 Configure, verify, and troubleshoot RIPv2 for IPv4 (excluding authentication, filtering, manual summarization, redistribution)

ROUTING INFORMATION PROTOCOL

RIPv1 was created when networks were small so the hop (router) limit was set to 15. This was to prevent rogue RIP packets from endlessly traversing the network. You saw earlier with the `debug ip rip` output that RIP broadcasts updates and is classful so it has no concept of VLSM, meaning that if you had a 192.168.1.16/26 network, it would advertise it as 192.168.1.0/24. Also, it offers no authentication, making it an easy target for attackers wanting to inject false route updates into the network.

In Figure 12.1 below, you can see a packet capture from RIP demonstrating the fact that RIPv1 uses UDP for transport and port 520:

```
▷ Frame 17: 66 bytes on wire (528 bits), 66 bytes captured (528 bits)
▷ Ethernet II, Src: c2:01:06:da:00:00 (c2:01:06:da:00:00), Dst: Broadcast (ff:ff:ff:
▷ Internet Protocol Version 4, Src: 192.168.1.2 (192.168.1.2), Dst: 255.255.255.255
▽ User Datagram Protocol, Src Port: router (520), Dst Port: router (520)
     Source port: router (520)
     Destination port: router (520)
     Length: 32
   ▷ Checksum: 0x38e3 [validation disabled]
▽ Routing Information Protocol
     Command: Request (1)
     Version: RIPv1 (1)
   ▷ Address not specified, Metric: 16
```

Figure 12.1—RIPv1 Packet Capture

We covered the configuration for RIP earlier but as a refresher, Figure 12.2 below shows the topology used for the packet capture above, and the RIP part of the configuration is shown below for the router on the left:

192.168.1.0/24

Figure 12.2—Simple Network Topology for RIP

```
R1(config-if)#router rip
R1(config-router)#network 172.16.0.0
R1(config-router)#net 192.168.1.0
```

Note that you have to advertise the directly-connected network between the two routers. On R2, you would only advertise the 192 network as there are no other networks attached.

RIP uses various timers in order to mitigate routing issues such as hold down and invalid timers. You can also see the set timers for route updates, invalid, hold down, and flush, which were already discussed.

RIP will load balance over a maximum of 16 equal cost paths but the default is four (see below):

```
R1(config-router)#maximum-paths ?
  <1-16>  Number of paths
```

The go-to command for all routing information is `show ip protocols`. Take the time to read the outputs when you configure any routing labs.

```
R1#show ip protocols
Routing Protocol is "rip"
  Outgoing update filter list for all interfaces is not set
  Incoming update filter list for all interfaces is not set
  Sending updates every 30 seconds, next due in 10 seconds
  Invalid after 180 seconds, holddown 180, flushed after 240
  Redistributing: rip
  Default version control: send version 2, receive version 2
    Interface            Send  Recv  Triggered RIP  Key-chain
    FastEthernet0/0       2     2
  Automatic network summarization is not in effect
  Maximum path: 4
  Routing for Networks:
    172.16.0.0
    192.168.1.0
```

If you check the routing table, you will see the administrative distance for RIP and the output we covered earlier:

```
R2#show ip route
Codes: C - connected, S - static, R - RIP, M - mobile, B—BGP,
       D - EIGRP, EX - EIGRP external, O - OSPF, IA - OSPF inter area,
       N1 - OSPF NSSA external type 1, N2 - OSPF NSSA external type 2,
       E1 - OSPF external type 1, E2 - OSPF external type 2,
       i - IS-IS, su - IS-IS summary, L1 - IS-IS level-1,
       L2 - IS-IS level-2, ia - IS-IS inter area,
       * - candidate default, U - per-user static route,
       o - ODR, P - periodic downloaded static route

Gateway of last resort is not set

     172.16.0.0/24 is subnetted, 1 subnets
R      172.16.1.0 [120/1] via 192.168.1.1, 00:00:04, FastEthernet0/0
C    192.168.1.0/24 is directly connected, FastEthernet0/0
```

RIPv2

Many of the shortfalls with RIP were addressed in version 2. Support for VLSM and MD5 authentication was added and the updates via broadcasts were changed to multicasts on 224.0.0.9. I added the version 2 command to the topology above (on each router), and you can see the new packet capture in Figure 12.3 below:

```
R1(config)#router rip
R1(config-router)#version 2
```

```
▷ Ethernet II, Src: c2:00:06:da:00:00 (c2:00:06:da:00:00), Dst: IPv4mcast_00:00:09 (01:00:
▷ Internet Protocol Version 4, Src: 192.168.1.1 (192.168.1.1), Dst: 224.0.0.9 (224.0.0.9)
▽ User Datagram Protocol, Src Port: router (520), Dst Port: router (520)
     Source port: router (520)
     Destination port: router (520)
     Length: 32
   ▷ Checksum: 0xabd5 [validation disabled]
 ▽ Routing Information Protocol
     Command: Response (2)
     Version: RIPv2 (2)
   ▷ IP Address: 172.16.0.0, Metric: 1
```

Figure 12.3—RIPv2 Packet Capture

To test VLSM support, you can change the IP address on the Loopback interface on R1 to 172.16.1.1/24, but you also need to add the no auto-summary command because the default behavior for RIP is to summarize the network to its natural classful boundary when it crosses a major network boundary (a major network is a classful network that a particular network belongs to). You can see this with the show ip protocols command:

```
R1#show ip protocols
Routing Protocol is "rip"
  Outgoing update filter list for all interfaces is not set
  Incoming update filter list for all interfaces is not set
  Sending updates every 30 seconds, next due in 21 seconds
  Invalid after 180 seconds, holddown 180, flushed after 240
  Redistributing: rip
  Default version control: send version 2, receive version 2
    Interface         Send  Recv  Triggered RIP  Key-chain
    FastEthernet0/0    2     2
  Automatic network summarization is in effect
```

Turn it off with the no auto-summary command:

```
R1(config)#router rip
R1(config-router)#no auto-summary
R1(config-router)#int lo0
R1(config-if)#ip add 172.16.1.1 255.255.255.0
```

```
▽ Routing Information Protocol
    Command: Response (2)
    Version: RIPv2 (2)
  ▽ IP Address: 172.16.1.0, Metric: 1
      Address Family: IP (2)
      Route Tag: 0
      IP Address: 172.16.1.0 (172.16.1.0)
      Netmask: 255.255.255.0 (255.255.255.0)
      Next Hop: 0.0.0.0 (0.0.0.0)
      Metric: 1
```

Figure 12.4—RIPv2 Is Classless

Cisco has excluded the advanced features of RIP, such as authentication and redistribution, from the syllabus so we won't go into them here.

RIP Passive Interfaces

Most routing protocols offer the ability to turn off routing updates per interface. We covered the `passive-interface` command in detail throughout this guide. The actual behavior of this command will vary from protocol to protocol. For RIP, it will prevent route updates from being multicast from the interface it's applied to, but incoming updates will be received and processed for use in the routing table.

```
R1(config)#router rip
R1(config-router)#passive-interface loopback0
R1(config-router)#end
R1#show ip protocols
Routing Protocol is "rip"
  Outgoing update filter list for all interfaces is not set
  Incoming update filter list for all interfaces is not set
  Sending updates every 30 seconds, next due in 10 seconds
  Invalid after 180 seconds, holddown 180, flushed after 240
  Redistributing: rip
  Default version control: send version 2, receive version 2
    Interface          Send  Recv  Triggered RIP  Key-chain
    FastEthernet0/0     2     2
  Automatic network summarization is not in effect
  Maximum path: 4
  Routing for Networks:
    172.16.0.0
    192.168.1.0
  Passive Interface(s):
    Loopback0
  Routing Information Sources:
    Gateway          Distance      Last Update
  Distance: (default is 120)
```

In the exam, you could be presented with a troubleshooting lab or question asking why a neighbor router isn't receiving route updates. This may well be the cause!

Configuring, Verifying, and Troubleshooting RIP

We've already covered the commands you will need to use to configure RIP. Unlike other routing protocols, you don't need to add wildcard or subnet masks and there are limited options to fine-tune it. Once your IP addresses have been added to the interfaces (and they have been brought up with the `no shut` command), go into router configuration mode and add the networks that you want to advertise (including the attached networks). You can turn off auto summarization if you wish and add any other options, such as authentication and passive interfaces.

```
R1(config-if)#router rip
R1(config-router)#network 172.16.0.0
R1(config-router)#net 192.168.1.0
R1(config-router)#version 2
R1(config-router)#no auto-summary
R1(config-router)#passive-interface f0/1
```

We will discuss verification commands next.

TROUBLESHOOTING RIP

You will actually learn much more about troubleshooting RIP when you get to the configuration labs.

Most RIP issues are related to the administrator mistyping commands or misunderstanding VLSM. We will cover IP troubleshooting later on, but double-check that your router interfaces are up (physically and logically). Check that your IP address and subnet mask are correct as well.

If you can't ping across a directly-connected link, then you need to fix that issue before checking for routing issues. Next, check your routing configuration. You need to ensure that there are no unwanted passive interfaces and that you have configured the correct network.

If you have a discontiguous network such as the one below, you will need to ensure that you have no auto-summary configured on EVERY router. In Figure 12.5 below, the network designer has done a poor job, splitting the 172.16.x.x network on either side of another network class. If the auto summary feature is enabled, routing issues are guaranteed.

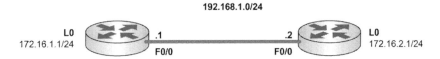

192.168.1.0/24

LO
172.16.1.1/24   .1   .2   LO
172.16.2.1/24
FO/0   FO/0

Figure 12.5—A Discontiguous Network

You can debug RIP on your network generally or drill down to three specific debugs, but bear in mind that this may generate a lot of output, causing either your router or the Telnet session to crash.

```
R1#debug ip rip ?
  database  RIP database events
  events    RIP protocol events
  trigger   RIP trigger extension
  <cr>
```

Other issues outside the CCNA syllabus include authentication mistakes and route filtering. You could be asked about split horizon (covered earlier), exceeding the maximum hop count, or a firewall blocking RIP traffic. Also, bear in mind that ACLs filter all traffic not specifically permitted. We cover permitting RIP via an ACL entry in the ACL section.

In order to verify and troubleshoot RIP, you would use the commands below (as well as the debugs above), which I recommend that you try out on any RIP lab that you configure.

```
show ip route
show ip route rip
show ip protocols
show ip rip database
```

Please take today's exam at https://www.in60days.com/free/ccnain60days/

DAY 12 LAB

RIPv2

Topology

192.168.1.4/30   172.16.0.0/16

R1   R2

Purpose
Learn how to configure and troubleshoot RIPv2.

Walkthrough

1. Add IP addresses to all the interfaces and then ping across the link. I've used Ethernet here but you can use a serial link if you wish as in the above topology.

```
R1(config)#int lo0
R1(config-if)#ip add 192.168.1.5 255.255.255.252
R1(config-if)#int f0/0
R1(config-if)#ip add 172.16.1.1 255.255.0.0
R1(config-if)#no shut
R2(config)#int f0/0
R2(config-if)#ip add 172.16.1.2 255.255.0.0
R2(config-if)#no shut
R2(config-if)#end
R2#ping 172.16.1.1
Type escape sequence to abort.
Sending 5, 100-byte ICMP Echos to 172.16.1.1, timeout is 2 seconds:
.!!!!
Success rate is 80 percent (4/5), round-trip min/avg/max = 24/31/44 ms
```

2. Advertise the networks using RIPv2.

```
R1(config)#router rip
R1(config-router)#version 2
R1(config-router)#network 192.168.1.0
R1(config-router)#network 172.16.0.0
R1(config-router)#end

R2(config)#router rip
R2(config-router)#ver 2
R2(config-router)#network 172.16.0.0
```

3. Issue the show ip route command on R2.

```
R2#show ip route
Codes: C - connected, S - static, R - RIP, M - mobile, B - BGP
       D - EIGRP, EX - EIGRP external, O - OSPF, IA - OSPF inter area
       N1 - OSPF NSSA external type 1, N2 - OSPF NSSA external type 2
       E1 - OSPF external type 1, E2 - OSPF external type 2
       i - IS-IS, su - IS-IS summary, L1 - IS-IS level-1, L2 - IS-IS
level-2
```

```
        ia - IS-IS inter area, * - candidate default, U - per-user
static route
        o - ODR, P - periodic downloaded static route
Gateway of last resort is not set
C    172.16.0.0/16 is directly connected, FastEthernet0/0
R    192.168.1.0/24 [120/1] via 172.16.1.1, 00:00:06, FastEthernet0/0
```

4. RIP is auto summarizing on the major network boundary. Fix R1 so this no longer happens. When you check on R2 you may see the old /24 route appear. This will eventually clear from the route table or you can issue the clear ip route * command.

```
R1(config)#router rip
R1(config-router)#no auto-summary
R2#show ip route
Codes: C - connected, S - static, R - RIP, M - mobile, B - BGP
       D - EIGRP, EX - EIGRP external, O - OSPF, IA - OSPF inter area
       N1 - OSPF NSSA external type 1, N2 - OSPF NSSA external type 2
       E1 - OSPF external type 1, E2 - OSPF external type 2
       i - IS-IS, su - IS-IS summary, L1 - IS-IS level-1, L2 - IS-IS
level-2
        ia - IS-IS inter area, * - candidate default, U - per-user
static route
        o - ODR, P - periodic downloaded static route
Gateway of last resort is not set
C    172.16.0.0/16 is directly connected, FastEthernet0/0
     192.168.1.0/24 is variably subnetted, 2 subnets, 2 masks
R       192.168.1.0/24 [120/1] via 172.16.1.1, 00:00:40, FE0/0
R       192.168.1.4/30 [120/1] via 172.16.1.1, 00:00:11, FE0/0
```

5. Now issue some show commands to check the RIP settings.

```
R2#show ip rip database
172.16.0.0/16     auto-summary
172.16.0.0/16     directly connected, FastEthernet0/0
192.168.1.0/24    auto-summary
192.168.1.4/30
    [1] via 172.16.1.1, 00:00:12, FastEthernet0/0
R1#show ip protocols
Routing Protocol is "rip"
  Outgoing update filter list for all interfaces is not set
  Incoming update filter list for all interfaces is not set
  Sending updates every 30 seconds, next due in 24 seconds
  Invalid after 180 seconds, hold down 180, flushed after 240
  Redistributing: rip
  Default version control: send version 2, receive version 2
    Interface          Send  Recv  Triggered RIP  Key-chain
    FastEthernet0/0     2     2
    Loopback0           2     2
  Automatic network summarization is not in effect
  Maximum path: 4
  Routing for Networks:
    172.16.0.0
    192.168.1.0
  Routing Information Sources:
    Gateway         Distance      Last Update
  Distance: (default is 120)
```

Review

DAY 13 TASKS

- Read today's notes (below)
- Review previous lessons and labs from day 9-12
- Read the ICND1 cram guide
- Take today's challenges
- Take today's exam at **https://www.in60days.com/free/ccnain60days/**
- Spend 15 minutes on subnetting.org

We have covered a lot of ground so far. Don't worry about how much is left to learn though. Review the main learning points from switch security, routing concepts, static routing and RIP.

Spend some time today repeating the labs from the last few days, do you best to configure them without looking at my walkthrough. Use the question mark rather than look at my answers. You need to start writing out the cram guide from memory also.

Challenge 1—Switch Security Lab

Topology

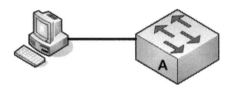

Instructions

Connect to the switch using a console connection.

1. Add an enable password to the switch of cisco.
2. Add a console password to the switch of cisco.
3. Set all passwords to be encrypted with level 7 encryption.
4. Issue a `show privilege` command and note the default level for users (covered later)

5. Issue the show line command and note how many vty lines you have. Then issue a username and password to be entered by users telnetting in.

6. Add a SVI to VLAN1 and then telnet to the switch using that IP address to test the username and password.

NOTE: You will need to set an IP address on the PC you are telnetting from on the same subnet as the switch e.g. 192.168.1.1 and 192.168.1.2

Challenge 2—Switchport Security Lab

Topology

Instructions

Connect to the switch using a console connection. Connect a PC to the switch or connect the switch to the fast ethernet port on a router.

1. Add port security to the switch.
2. Hard set the MAC address of the PC/Router interface as the permitted address.
3. Ensure the switch interface is up (and an IP address on the PC).
4. Set the port security violation action to restrict.
5. Change the MAC address of the PC or plug in another machine.
6. Issue a show port-security interface x on the switch.
7. Recover by adding the correct MAC address to the PC and resetting the interface with a shut and no shut command.

Challenge 3—Static Routes Lab

Topology

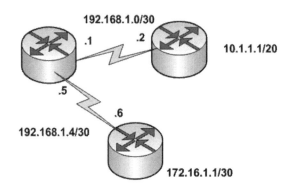

192.168.1.0/30

.1   .2

10.1.1.1/20

.5

.6

192.168.1.4/30

172.16.1.1/30

Instructions
Connect three routers together with serial or ethernet connections

1. Configure the connections between the routers and ping
2. Add loopback addresses to the two spoke routers as per the diagram
3. Add a static route exit interface on the hub router for 10.1.1.0/20 subnet
4. Add a next hop address for network 172.16.1.0/30
5. Ping both networks
6. Issue a `show ip route 172.16.1.1` and same for 10.1.1.1
7. Confirm you have exit interface and next hop listed
8. You won't be able to ping from edge router to edge router unless you add more static routes which you can if you wish

Challenge 4—RIPv2 Lab

Topology

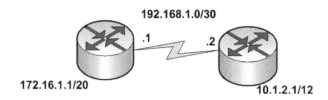

192.168.1.0/30

.1   .2

172.16.1.1/20

10.1.2.1/12

Instructions
Connect two routers together with serial or ethernet connections

1. Configure the connections between the routers and ping
2. Add loopback addresses to the two routers as per the diagram
3. Configure RIPv2 on both routers
4. Issue a `show ip route` and check all networks on both routers

5. Now configure 'no auto-summary' on both routers and check for /12 and /20 routes
6. Which command will show you the networks being advertised, the auto-summary and RIP timers?

Challenge 5—InterVLAN Routing (Subinterface) Lab

Topology

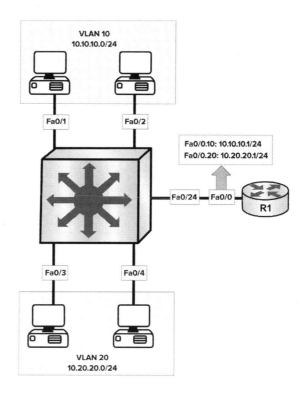

Instructions

Connect a switch to a router and at least two hosts, one per VLAN.

1. Add IP addresses for hosts inside the respective VLANs.
2. Add default gateways on the hosts to reach the router IPs.
3. Configure a trunk link between the switch and router using dot1q.
4. Configure Router 1 so it can route traffic between VLANs.
5. Test by pinging devices across the VLANs.
6. Check the mac address table on the switch.

DHCP, DNS and NTP

DAY 14 TASKS

- Read today's lesson notes (below)
- Complete today's lab
- Take today's exam
- Read the ICND1 cram guide
- Spend 15 minutes on the subnetting.org website

Dynamic Host Configuration Protocol (DHCP) is used by hosts to gather initial configuration information, which includes parameters such as IP address, subnet mask, and default gateway, upon boot up. Since each host needs an IP address to communicate in an IP network, DHCP eases the administrative burden of manually configuring each host with an IP address.

Domain Name System (DNS) maps host names to IP addresses, enabling you to type "www. in60days.com" into your web browser instead of the IP address of the server on which the site is hosted.

Network Time Protocol (NTP) synchronizes time across network devices.

Today you will learn about the following:

- DHCP functionality
- Configuring DHCP
- Troubleshooting DHCP issues
- DNS operations
- Troubleshooting DNS issues
- NTP

This lesson maps to the following CCNA syllabus requirement:

- 4.1 Describe DNS lookup operation
- 4.2 Troubleshoot client connectivity issues involving DNS
- 4.3 Configure and verify DHCP on a router (excluding static reservations)
- 4.3.a Server
- 4.3.b Relay

- 4.3.c Client
- 4.3.d TFTP, DNS, and gateway options
- 4.4 Troubleshoot client- and router-based DHCP connectivity issues
- 4.5 Configure and verify NTP operating in client/server mode

DHCP FUNCTIONALITY

DHCP Operations

DHCP simplifies network administrative tasks by automatically assigning IP information to hosts on a network. This information can include IP addresses, subnet masks, and default gateways, and is usually assigned when the host boots up but can also update periodically.

When the host first boots up, if it has been configured to use DHCP (which most hosts are), it will send a broadcast message asking for IP information to be allocated. The broadcast will be heard by the DHCP server and the information will be relayed.

 FARAI SAYS—"This is assuming that they are on the same subnet. If they are not, then see the `ip helper-address` command below."

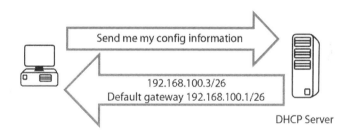

Send me my config information

192.168.100.3/26
Default gateway 192.168.100.1/26

DHCP Server

Figure 14.1—Host Requests IP Configuration Information

DHCP actually uses UDP ports 67 and 68 to communicate over the network, and, of course, actual servers are usually used as DHCP servers, although routers can also perform this role, if required. Routers can also be configured to obtain their IP address from a DHCP server, if required, although this is rarely done. The command to configure this is:

```
Router(config-if)#ip address dhcp
```

DHCP states for clients are as follows:

- Initialising
- Selecting
- Requesting
- Bound

- Renewing
- Rebinding

DHCP servers can be configured to give an IP address to a host for a specified period called the lease time. This can be for hours or days. You can and should reserve IP addresses which cannot be allocated to hosts on the network. These IP addresses will already be in use on router interfaces or for servers. If you fail to do this, you may see duplicate IP address warnings on your network because the DHCP server has allocated your address to a host.

The full DHCP request and assign process can be seen in Figure 14.2 below:

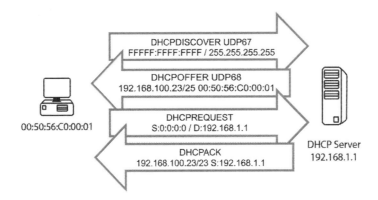

Figure 14.2—DHCP Request and Allocation Process

1. DHCP Discover packet: When a device boots up and it is configured to obtain an address via DHCP, it sends a broadcast sourced from UDP port 68 (bootpc) out to UDP port 67 (bootps). The packet will reach every device on the network, including any possible DHCP servers located there.
2. DHCP Offer packet: The DHCP servers on the local network see the broadcasted Discover message sent by the client and send back a response (DHCP Offer packet) using UDP source port bootps 67 and destination port bootpc 68, also in the form of a broadcast address, because the client still doesn't have an IP address so it cannot receive Unicast packets.
3. DHCP Request packet: Once the client workstation receives an offer made by the DHCP server, it will send a broadcast (to let all DHCP servers learn that it has accepted an offer from a server) DHCP Request message to a specific DHCP server, again using UDP source port bootpc 68 and destination port bootps 67. The client might have received offers from multiple DHCP servers, but it only needs a single IP address so it must choose a DHCP server (based on an identifier), and this is usually done on a "first-come, first-served" basis.
4. DHCP ACK packet: The DHCP server sends another broadcast message to confirm the IP address allocation to that specific client, again using UDP source port bootps 67 and destination port bootpc 68.

DHCP Reservations

A DHCP server can be configured to provide IP addresses in a number of different ways, including:

- Dynamic allocation
- Automatic allocation
- Static allocation

A very common approach to assigning addresses via the DHCP server is using a dynamic allocation process, in which the DHCP server is configured with a big pool of IP addresses and assigns one of them to clients based on their requests. When the device lease period expires or the device leaves the network, the particular IP address is handed back to the DHCP server, and then it can be assigned to another client.

Another method for assigning IP addresses using a DHCP server is called automatic allocation, which is a very similar process to dynamic allocation but using this approach, the DHCP server tries to keep a list of all the past assignments, and if an "old" client requests an IP address, it will be assigned the same one as before (i.e., the previous time it requested an IP address). Automatic allocation is a less efficient way of assigning IP addresses, but if you have a very large pool of IP addresses available, this is a very smart way to almost guarantee clients will get the same IP address every time they get active in a network.

Static allocation of IP addresses by a DHCP server implies defining the MAC addresses that you expect to see on the network and manually assigning a unique IP address for each of them, thus administratively building a MAC-to-IP association table. This is commonly used in a server environment because servers must use predictable IP addresses in order to be accessed.

DHCP Scopes

Network administrators who want to configure a DHCP server also need to configure DHCP scopes as part of this process. A scope is a grouping of IP addresses for a particular section of the network. Each subnet usually has its own scope.

A scope can also be a contiguous pool of addresses available for allocation by the DHCP server. Most servers also offer the functionality of excluding some addresses from the pool in order to avoid allocating them dynamically to clients. The excluded addresses are usually those IP addresses manually assigned to servers (and network devices) in the network.

Inside the defined DHCP scopes you can configure a number of parameters, such as:

- IP address range
- Subnet mask
- Lease duration
- Default gateway

- DNS server
- WINS server

Depending on the DHCP server used, you might be able to create different scopes with different parameters, usually associated with different subnets.

DHCP Leases

One of the major advantages offered by DHCP is the ability to lease an IP address, meaning assigning it on a temporary basis. Usually when a client leaves the network, that particular assigned IP address becomes free and can be allocated to another device by the DHCP server.

DHCP leases are related to every DHCP allocation and define for how long a user is allowed to use an allocated IP address. This parameter is usually administratively configured inside the DHCP scope. Whenever a client reboots it will have to ask the DHCP server again for an IP address. The DHCP server is usually configured to re-allocate the same address and extend the lease for the specific client.

Workstations can also manually release the IP address, for example, in these situations:

- The device is turned off indefinitely
- The device moves to another subnet (e.g, to a wireless network from a wired network)

The leasing process has a number of timers associated with it, so you can be sure that you are always going to have an IP address that is updated on every network device. The two important DHCP timers are as follows:

- Renewal (T1) timer (default 50% of the lease time): Whenever a workstation obtains an IP address, this timer starts up, and when 50% of the lease time has been reached, the DHCP client will try to renew its lease with the original DHCP server.
- Rebinding (T2) timer (default: 87.5% of the lease time): This second timer is used in situations in which the DHCP server does not answer or confirm the allocation extension after the renewal timer expires. This timer states that if 7/8ths of the lease time has passed, the client will try to find (send a DHCP Request) other DHCP servers which might be able to provide a DHCP address.

By having the lease process in place and correlated to the timers presented above, you can be assured that you will always have an IP address in a timely manner without any downtime associated with this and will automatically have a way to build redundancy into the DHCP process.

The T1 and T2 timers are presented in relation to the lease time in Figure 14.3 below:

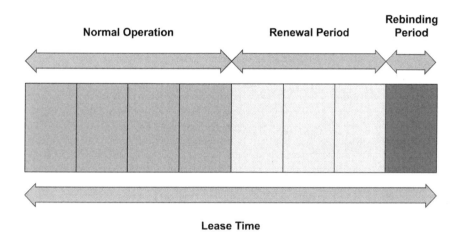

Figure 14.3—DHCP Lease Timers

DHCP Options

In DHCP, there is a special field available that helps extend the capabilities of this automatic configuration process. You can put many different configuration options inside this field, which are also present in the DHCP RFC.

NOTE: BOOTP options were called "vendor extensions."

DHCP offers 256 option values, from which only 254 are usable because 0 is the pad option and 255 is the end option. Many DHCP options are commonly known parameters used often, including:

- Subnet mask
- Domain name server
- Domain name

Over the years, additional DHCP options have been added, especially for VoIP use, such as the following:

- Option 129: call server IP address
- Option 135: HTTP proxy for phone-specific applications

All of these options are configured directly on the DHCP server, but not all DHCP servers offer the ability to set DHCP options. If network administrators would like to use these features, they should utilize an enterprise-level DHCP server. When using small routers as DHCP servers for home offices, there may be no benefit from such functionalities.

CONFIGURING DHCP

DHCP Servers on Cisco Routers

The first step is enabling the DHCP service on the router. This is done using the service dhcp command, as exemplified below:

```
Router#configure terminal
Enter configuration commands, one per line.  End with CNTL/Z.
Router(config)#service dhcp
```

The next step is to create a DHCP pool which defines the IP address pool that will be allocated to clients. In this example, pool name "SUBNET_A" will offer IP addresses from the 192.168.1.0/24 range:

```
Router(config)#ip dhcp pool SUBNET_A
Router(dhcp-config)#network 192.168.1.0 255.255.255.0
Router(dhcp-config)#default-router 192.168.1.1
Router(dhcp-config)#dns-server 8.8.8.8
Router(dhcp-config)#domain-name Network+
Router(dhcp-config)#lease 30
```

The DHCP Pool Configuration mode is also the place where you can configure other DHCP options. In the configuration output above, the following parameters were configured:

- Default gateway: 192.168.1.1 (the router interface assigned to the network it serves as a DHCP server)
- DNS server: 8.8.8.8
- Domain name: Network+
- Lease time: 30 days

If needed, you can also configure some excluded addresses from the 192.168.1.0/24 range. Let's say you want to exclude the router interface IP address (192.168.1.1) and the 192.168.1.250 to 192.168.1.255 address range, from which you would manually assign addresses to servers in your network. This is done using the configuration below:

```
Router(config)#ip dhcp excluded-address 192.168.1.1
Router(config)#ip dhcp excluded-address 192.168.1.250 192.168.1.255
```

You will notice that the above two commands are not executed in Router(dhcp-config)# mode. To verify the clients currently served by the router DHCP server, you can use the command below:

```
Router#show ip dhcp binding
Bindings from all pools not associated with VRF:
IP address   Client-ID/ Lease expiration  Type  Hardware address/
192.168.1.2  Mar 02 2014 12:07 AM     Automatic 0063.6973.636f.2d63
```

In the output above, a single client was served by the DHCP server and was assigned the first non-excluded IP address from the DHCP scope: 192.168.1.2. You can also see the lease expiration date and the device MAC address.

DHCP Clients on Cisco Routers

In addition to DHCP server functionality, Cisco IOS routers also permit configuring the interfaces as DHCP clients. This means that interfaces will require an address using the standard DHCP process, and any server present on the specific subnet can allocate the IP addresses.

The commands to configure a router interface as a DHCP client are as follows:

```
Router(config)#int FastEthernet0/0
Router(config-if)#ip address dhcp
```

Once a DHCP server allocates an IP address, the following notification (which includes the address and mask) will be visible on the router console:

```
*Mar  1 00:29:15.779: %DHCP-6-ADDRESS_ASSIGN: Interface FastEthernet0/0
assigned DHCP address 10.10.10.2, mask 255.255.255.0, hostname Router
```

The DHCP allocation method can be observed under the Method header with the show ip interface brief command:

```
Router#show ip interface brief
Interface       IP-Address    OK? Method  Status           Protocol
FastEthernet0/0 10.10.10.2    YES DHCP    up                 up
```

DHCP Packet Analysis

In order to practically understand the topics presented in this module, some traffic captures on the devices involved in the examples above will be generated. After the DHCP server is configured and the client workstation boots up, the four-step DHCP process occurs, as can be observed in Figure 14.4 below:

Time	Source	Destination	Protocol	Length	Info
191.391000	0.0.0.0	255.255.255.255	DHCP	618	DHCP Discover - Transaction ID 0x166f
191.421000	c2:00:27:bc:00:00	Broadcast	ARP	60	Who has 192.168.1.2? Tell 192.168.1.1
193.398000	192.168.1.1	255.255.255.255	DHCP	342	DHCP Offer - Transaction ID 0x166f
193.418000	0.0.0.0	255.255.255.255	DHCP	618	DHCP Request - Transaction ID 0x166f
193.438000	192.168.1.1	255.255.255.255	DHCP	342	DHCP ACK - Transaction ID 0x166f
193.448000	c2:02:27:bc:00:00	Broadcast	ARP	60	Gratuitous ARP for 192.168.1.2 (Reply)

Figure 14.4—DHCP Four-Step Process

The DHCP Discover packet components can be observed below:

```
⊞ Frame 48: 618 bytes on wire (4944 bits), 618 bytes captured (4944 bits) on interface 0
⊞ Ethernet II, Src: c2:02:27:bc:00:00 (c2:02:27:bc:00:00), Dst: Broadcast (ff:ff:ff:ff:ff:ff)
⊞ Internet Protocol Version 4, Src: 0.0.0.0 (0.0.0.0), Dst: 255.255.255.255 (255.255.255.255)
⊞ User Datagram Protocol, Src Port: bootpc (68), Dst Port: bootps (67)
⊟ Bootstrap Protocol
    Message type: Boot Request (1)
    Hardware type: Ethernet
    Hardware address length: 6
    Hops: 0
    Transaction ID: 0x0000166f
    Seconds elapsed: 0
  ⊞ Bootp flags: 0x8000 (Broadcast)
    Client IP address: 0.0.0.0 (0.0.0.0)
    Your (client) IP address: 0.0.0.0 (0.0.0.0)
    Next server IP address: 0.0.0.0 (0.0.0.0)
    Relay agent IP address: 0.0.0.0 (0.0.0.0)
    Client MAC address: c2:02:27:bc:00:00 (c2:02:27:bc:00:00)
    Client hardware address padding: 00000000000000000000
    Server host name not given
    Boot file name not given
    Magic cookie: DHCP
  ⊞ Option: (53) DHCP Message Type
  ⊞ Option: (57) Maximum DHCP Message Size
  ⊞ Option: (61) Client identifier
  ⊞ Option: (12) Host Name
  ⊞ Option: (55) Parameter Request List
  ⊞ Option: (255) End
    Padding
```

Figure 14.5—DHCP Discover Packet

As you can see in the Figure 14.5, the packet was sent by the client who broadcasted it on the network (Destination 255.255.255.255). You can also see the message type "Boot Request (1)."

The next packet is the DHCP Offer packet, presented below:

```
⊞ Frame 50: 342 bytes on wire (2736 bits), 342 bytes captured (2736 bits) on interface 0
⊞ Ethernet II, Src: c2:00:27:bc:00:00 (c2:00:27:bc:00:00), Dst: Broadcast (ff:ff:ff:ff:ff:ff)
⊞ Internet Protocol Version 4, Src: 192.168.1.1 (192.168.1.1), Dst: 255.255.255.255 (255.255.255.255)
⊞ User Datagram Protocol, Src Port: bootps (67), Dst Port: bootpc (68)
⊟ Bootstrap Protocol
    Message type: Boot Reply (2)
    Hardware type: Ethernet
    Hardware address length: 6
    Hops: 0
    Transaction ID: 0x0000166f
    Seconds elapsed: 0
  ⊞ Bootp flags: 0x8000 (Broadcast)
    Client IP address: 0.0.0.0 (0.0.0.0)
    Your (client) IP address: 192.168.1.2 (192.168.1.2)
    Next server IP address: 0.0.0.0 (0.0.0.0)
    Relay agent IP address: 0.0.0.0 (0.0.0.0)
    Client MAC address: c2:02:27:bc:00:00 (c2:02:27:bc:00:00)
    Client hardware address padding: 00000000000000000000
    Server host name not given
    Boot file name not given
    Magic cookie: DHCP
  ⊞ Option: (53) DHCP Message Type
  ⊞ Option: (54) DHCP Server Identifier
  ⊞ Option: (51) IP Address Lease Time
  ⊞ Option: (58) Renewal Time Value
  ⊞ Option: (59) Rebinding Time Value
  ⊞ Option: (1) Subnet Mask
  ⊞ Option: (3) Router
  ⊞ Option: (6) Domain Name Server
  ⊞ Option: (15) Domain Name
  ⊞ Option: (255) End
    Padding
```

Figure 14.6—DHCP Offer Packet

This packet was sent by the server (source IP: 192.168.1.1) to the broadcast address (destination: 255.255.255.255) and it contains the proposed IP address (192.168.1.2). You can also see the message type "Boot Reply (2)."

The third packet is the DHCP Request:

```
⊟ Frame 51: 618 bytes on wire (4944 bits), 618 bytes captured (4944 bits) on interface 0
⊞ Ethernet II, Src: c2:02:27:bc:00:00 (c2:02:27:bc:00:00), Dst: Broadcast (ff:ff:ff:ff:ff:ff)
⊞ Internet Protocol Version 4, Src: 0.0.0.0 (0.0.0.0), Dst: 255.255.255.255 (255.255.255.255)
⊞ User Datagram Protocol, Src Port: bootpc (68), Dst Port: bootps (67)
⊟ Bootstrap Protocol
      Message type: Boot Request (1)
      Hardware type: Ethernet
      Hardware address length: 6
      Hops: 0
      Transaction ID: 0x0000166f
      Seconds elapsed: 0
   ⊞ Bootp flags: 0x8000 (Broadcast)
      Client IP address: 0.0.0.0 (0.0.0.0)
      Your (client) IP address: 0.0.0.0 (0.0.0.0)
      Next server IP address: 0.0.0.0 (0.0.0.0)
      Relay agent IP address: 0.0.0.0 (0.0.0.0)
      Client MAC address: c2:02:27:bc:00:00 (c2:02:27:bc:00:00)
      Client hardware address padding: 00000000000000000000
      Server host name not given
      Boot file name not given
      Magic cookie: DHCP
   ⊞ Option: (53) DHCP Message Type
   ⊞ Option: (57) Maximum DHCP Message Size
   ⊞ Option: (61) Client identifier
   ⊞ Option: (54) DHCP Server Identifier
   ⊟ Option: (50) Requested IP Address
         Length: 4
         Requested IP Address: 192.168.1.2 (192.168.1.2)
   ⊞ Option: (51) IP Address Lease Time
   ⊞ Option: (12) Host Name
   ⊞ Option: (55) Parameter Request List
   ⊞ Option: (255) End
      Padding
```

Figure 14.7—DHCP Request Packet

The DHCP Request packet is sent by the client to the broadcast address. You can see the message type "Boot Request (1)." This packet is similar to the initial DHCP Discover packet but contains a very important field, which is Option 50: Requested IP Address (192.168.1.2). This is exactly the same IP address offered by the DHCP server in the DHCP Offer packet, and the client confirms it and accepts it.

The last packet in the DHCP allocation process is the DCHP ACK packet sent by the server:

```
⊟ Option: (53) DHCP Message Type
     Length: 1
     DHCP: ACK (5)
⊟ Option: (54) DHCP Server Identifier
     Length: 4
     DHCP Server Identifier: 192.168.1.1 (192.168.1.1)
⊟ Option: (51) IP Address Lease Time
     Length: 4
     IP Address Lease Time: (2592000s) 30 days
⊟ Option: (58) Renewal Time Value
     Length: 4
     Renewal Time Value: (1296000s) 15 days
⊟ Option: (59) Rebinding Time Value
     Length: 4
     Rebinding Time Value: (2268000s) 26 days, 6 hours
⊟ Option: (1) Subnet Mask
     Length: 4
     Subnet Mask: 255.255.255.0 (255.255.255.0)
⊟ Option: (3) Router
     Length: 4
     Router: 192.168.1.1 (192.168.1.1)
⊟ Option: (6) Domain Name Server
     Length: 4
     Domain Name Server: 8.8.8.8 (8.8.8.8)
⊟ Option: (15) Domain Name
     Length: 8
     Domain Name: Network+
⊟ Option: (255) End
     Option End: 255
   Padding
```

Figure 14.8—DHCP ACK Options Packet

This packet is sourced by the DHCP server and broadcasted on the network; it also contains some extra fields as seen in the Figure 14.8 above:

- DHCP Server Identifier: the DHCP server IP address (192.168.1.1)
- All of the options configured on the router:
  - Lease time: 30 days (and the derived renewal time and rebinding time values discussed earlier)
  - Subnet mask: 255.255.255.0
  - Default gateway (router): 192.168.1.1
  - DNS server: 8.8.8.8
  - Domain name: Network+

TROUBLESHOOTING DHCP ISSUES

As with NAT, DHCP issues are almost always due to an error in the configuration (jokingly referred to as a Layer 8 issue, meaning somebody messed up).

The `service dhcp` command is turned on by default, but sometimes it has been manually disabled by a network administrator for some reason. (I've seen network administrators call Cisco with urgent routing issues on their network after they entered the `no ip routing` command on their router—seriously!)

DHCP packets need to be permitted through your router if you are using a server on another subnet to administer DHCP configurations. DHCP uses broadcast messages as part of its process (which routers won't forward), so the IP address of the DHCP server needs to be added to the router to allow it to forward the broadcast message as a Unicast packet. The command ip helper-address [ip address] achieves this. This is another exam-favourite question! They refer to it as DHCP relay in the exam syllabus.

You can also use the following debug commands as part of your troubleshooting process:

```
debug ip dhcp server events
debug ip dhcp server packet
```

Please ensure that you type out ALL of these commands onto a router. There is no way on Earth that you will remember them by reading them on a page. Try out the configurations, make mistakes, post questions, break it on purpose (not on a live network), and fix it again.

DNS OPERATIONS

DNS maps hostnames to IP addresses (not the other way around). This allows you to browse a web address from your web browser instead of the server IP address.

DNS uses UDP port 53 when a host or a router wants to resolve a domain name to an IP address (or vice versa). TCP port 53 is used between two DNS servers when they want to sync or share their databases (zone transfers) or when the response size exceeds 512 bytes.

Configuring DNS

If you want to permit your router to find a DNS server on the web, then use the command ip name-server [ip address].

You can also set a hostname to the IP address table on your router to save time or to make it easier to remember which device to ping or connect to, as shown in the output below:

```
Router(config)#ip host R2 192.168.1.2
Router(config)#ip host R3 192.168.1.3
Router(config)#exit
Router#ping R2
Router#pinging 192.168.1.2
!!!!!
```

TROUBLESHOOTING DNS ISSUES

A default command on the router configuration will be ip domain-lookup. If this command has been disabled, then DNS won't work. Sometimes router administrators disable it because when you mistype a command you have to wait several seconds while the router performs a lookup. You can turn off DNS lookups with the following command:

```
Router(config)#no ip domain-lookup
```

Access control lists often block DNS, so this is another possible cause of problems. You can debug DNS on the router with the debug domain command.

NETWORK TIME PROTOCOL

NTP is a protocol that is designed to time-synchronize a network of machines. NTP is documented in RFC 1305 and runs over UDP.

An NTP network usually gets its time from an authoritative time source, such as a radio clock or an atomic clock attached to a time server. NTP then distributes this time across the network. NTP is extremely efficient; no more than one packet per minute is necessary to synchronize two machines to within a millisecond of one another.

NTP uses the concept of a stratum to describe how many NTP hops away a machine is from an authoritative time source. Keep in mind that this is not routing or switching hops, but NTP hops, which is a totally different concept. A stratum 1 time server typically has a radio or atomic clock directly attached, while a stratum 2 time server receives its time via NTP from a stratum 1 time server, and so on. When a device is configured with multiple NTP reference servers, it will automatically choose as its time source the machine with the lowest stratum number that it is configured to communicate with via NTP.

In Cisco IOS software, a device is configured with the IP addresses of one or more NTP servers using the ntp server [address] global configuration command. As previously stated, multiple NTP reference addresses can be specified by repeatedly using the same command. In addition, this command can also be used to configure security and other features between the server and the client. The following configuration example illustrates how to configure a device to synchronize its time with an NTP server with the IP address 10.0.0.1:

```
R2(config)#ntp server 10.0.0.1
```

Following this configuration, the show ntp associations command can be used to verify the communications between the NTP devices, as illustrated in the following output:

```
R2#show ntp associations

  address      ref clock    st  when  poll reach  delay  offset  disp
*~10.0.0.1  127.127.7.1   5    44    64   377    3.2    2.39    1.2
* master (synced), # master (unsynced), + selected, - candidate, ~
configured
```

The address field indicates the IP address of the NTP server as confirmed by the value 10.0.0.1 specified under this field. The ref clock field indicates the reference clock used by that NTP server. In this case, the IP address 127.127.7.1 indicates that the device is using an internal clock (127.0.0.0/8 subnet) as its reference time source. If this field contained another value, such as 192.168.1.254, for example, then that would be the IP address the server was using as its time reference.

Next, the st field indicates the stratum of the reference. From the output printed above, you can see that the 10.0.0.1 NTP device has a stratum of 5. The stratum on the local device will be incremented by 1 to a value of 6, as shown below, because it receives its time source from a server with a stratum value of 5. If another device was synchronized to the local router, it would reflect a stratum of 7 and so forth. The second command that is used to validate the NTP configuration is the show ntp status command, the output of which is illustrated below:

```
R2#show ntp status
Clock is synchronized, stratum 6, reference is 10.0.0.1
nominal freq is 249.5901 Hz, actual freq is 249.5900 Hz, precision is
2**18
reference time is C02C38D2.950DA968 (05:53:22.582 UTC Sun Mar 3 2002)
clock offset is 4.6267 msec, root delay is 3.16 msec
root dispersion is 4.88 msec, peer dispersion is 0.23 msec
```

The output of the show ntp status command indicates that the clock is synchronized to the configured NTP server (10.0.0.1). This server has a stratum of 5, hence the local device reflects a stratum of 6. An interesting observation when NTP is configured is that the local time still defaults to GMT, as can be seen in the bolded section above. To ensure that the device displays the correct time zone, you must issue the clock timezone command on the device.

If you wanted to set the router as the NTP server you would add the below command and (optionally) a stratum level.

```
R1(config)#ntp master ?
  <1-15>  Stratum number
```

Now please complete today's lab at https://www.in60days.com/free/ccnain60days/

DAY 14 LABS

DHCP on a Router

Topology

10.0.0.1/18

Purpose
Learn how routers can be used as DHCP servers.

Walkthrough

1. If you are using your home PC or laptop, set the network adapter to obtain the IP address automatically. You can also set this in Packet Tracer. Connect the PC to your router Ethernet port with a crossover cable.

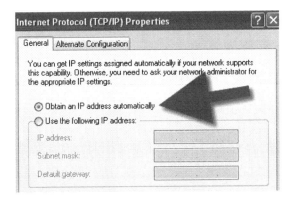

2. Add the IP address 172.16.1.1 255.255.0.0 to your router interface. Please see previous labs if you can't remember how to do this. Make sure you no shut it.

3. Configure your DHCP pool. Then, configure a lease of 3 days, 3 hours, and 5 minutes for your address. Lastly, exclude all the addresses from 1 to 10 from being assigned to hosts. Presume that these are already in use for other servers or interfaces.

```
Router#conf t
Router(config)#ip dhcp pool 60days
Router(dhcp-config)#network 172.16.0.0 255.255.0.0
Router1(dhcp-config)#lease 3 3 5 ← command won't work on Packet Tracer
Router1(dhcp-config)#exit
Router(config)#ip dhcp excluded-address 172.16.1.1 172.16.1.10
Router(config)#
```

4. Issue an `ipconfig /all` command to check whether an IP address has been assigned to your PC. You may need to issue an `ipconfig /renew` command if an old IP address is still in use.

```
PC>ipconfig /all

Physical Address...............: 0001.C7DD.CB19
IP Address.....................: 172.16.0.1
Subnet Mask....................: 255.255.0.0
Default Gateway................: 0.0.0.0
DNS Servers....................: 0.0.0.0
```

5. If you wish, you can go back into the DHCP pool and add a default gateway and a DNS server address, which will also be set on the host PC.

```
Router(config)#ip dhcp pool 60days
Router(dhcp-config)#default-router 172.16.1.2
Router(dhcp-config)#dns-server 172.16.1.3

PC>ipconfig /renew

IP Address.....................: 172.16.0.1
Subnet Mask....................: 255.255.0.0
Default Gateway................: 172.16.1.2
DNS Server.....................: 172.16.1.3
```

DNS on a Router Lab

Configure a name server on a router. Configure this as a name server (Google DNS server):

```
ip name-server 8.8.8.8
```

You won't be able to test this unless you have internet access on the router. Don't use live equipment if you have access to routers at work.

IPv4 Access Lists

DAY 15 TASKS

- Read today's lesson notes (below)
- Review yesterday's lesson notes and lab
- Complete today's labs
- Take today's exam
- Read the ICND1 cram guide
- Spend 15 minutes on the subnetting.org website

Along with subnetting and VLSM, access control lists (ACLs) are one of the bugbear subjects for new Cisco students. Among the problems are learning the IOS configuration commands, understanding ACL rules (including the implicit "deny all" rule), and learning the port numbers and protocol types.

Like any subject, you should take the learning process one step at a time, apply every command you see here to a router, and do lots and lots of labs.

Today you will learn about the following:

- ACL basics
- Port numbers
- ACL rules
- Wildcard masks
- ACL configuration
- ACL sequence numbers
- ACL logging
- Limit Telnet and SSH access
- Troubleshooting and verifying ACLs

This module maps to the following CCNA syllabus requirements:

- 4.6 Configure, verify, and troubleshoot IPv4 standard numbered and named access list for routed interfaces

ACL BASICS

The point of ACLs is to filter the traffic which passes through your router. I don't know of any network which should permit any traffic type to enter or leave it.

As well as filtering traffic, ACLs can be used to reference NAT pools, to filter your debugging commands, and with route maps (this is outside of the CCNA syllabus requirements). Depending upon the type of ACL you configure, you can filter traffic based on source network or IP addresses, destination network or IP addresses, protocols, or port numbers. You can apply ACLs to any router interface, including your Telnet (vty) ports.

The three main types of ACLs are as follows:

- Standard numbered
- Extended numbered
- Standard or extended named

Standard numbered ACLs are the most basic form of ACL you can apply to the router. While they are the easiest to configure, they have the most limited range of filters available. They can only filter based on the source IP address or network. The way to recognize a standard ACL is by the number which precedes the configuration lines; these numbers will be from 1 to 99.

Extended numbered ACLs allow far more granularity but can be trickier to configure and troubleshoot. They can filter a destination or source IP address or network, a protocol type, and a port number. The numbers you can use to configure extended ACLs are 100 to 199, inclusive.

Named ACLs allow you to associate a list of filters with a name rather than a number. This makes them easier to identify in router configurations. Named ACLs can actually be either extended or standard; you choose which at the initial configuration line of the ACL.

For success in the CCNA exam, and to make it as a new Cisco engineer, you need to understand the following:

- Port numbers
- ACL rules
- Command syntax for ACLs

PORT NUMBERS

You simply must know the common port numbers by heart if you want to pass the CCNA exam and to work on live networks. Looking up common port numbers isn't an option when you have customers watching what you are doing. Here are the most common port numbers you will encounter and need to know:

Table 15.1—Common CCNA Port Numbers

Port	Service	Port	Service
20	FTP Data	80	HTTP
21	FTP Control	110	POP3
22	SSH	119	NNTP
23	Telnet	123	NTP
25	SMTP	161/162	SNMP
53	DNS	443	HTTPS (HTTP with SSL)
69	TFTP		

ACCESS CONTROL LIST RULES

This is one of the hardest parts to understand. I've never seen a complete list of rules written down in one Cisco manual. Some refer to them generally or explain some of them, but then miss others completely. The difficulty is that the rules always apply but (until now) you found them only by trial and error. Here are the rules you need to know:

ACL Rule 1—Use only one ACL per interface per direction.

This makes good sense. You wouldn't want to have several ACLs doing different things on the same interface. Simply configure one ACL which does everything you need it to, rather than spreading out filters over two or more lists. I could have added "per protocol" to the above rule because you could have an IPX access control list, but IP is really the only protocol in use in modern networks.

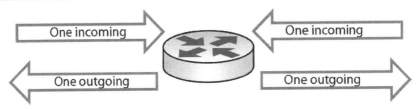

Figure 15.1—One ACL per Interface per Direction

ACL Rule 2—The lines are processed top-down.

Some engineers become confused when their ACL doesn't perform as expected. The router will look at the top line of the ACL, and if it sees a match, it will stop there and will not examine the other lines. For this reason, you need to put the most specific entries at the top of the ACL. For example, take the ACL blocking host 172.16.1.1:

Permit 10.0.0.0		No match
Permit 192.168.1.1		No match
Permit 172.16.0.0	✔	Match—Permit
Permit 172.16.1.0		Not processed
Deny 172.16.1.1		Not processed

In the example above, you should have put the Deny 172.16.1.1 line at the top, or at least above the Permit 172.16.0.0 statement.

ACL Rule 3—There is an implicit "deny all" at the bottom of every ACL.

This catches many engineers out. There is an invisible command at the bottom of every ACL. This command is set to deny all traffic which hasn't been matched yet. The only way to stop this command coming into effect is to configure a "permit all" at the bottom manually. For example, take an incoming packet from IP address 172.20.1.1:

Permit 10.0.0.0	No match
Permit 192.168.1.1	No match
Permit 172.16.0.0	No match
Permit 172.16.1.0	No match
[Deny all]	Match—DROP PACKET

You actually wanted the packet to be permitted by the router, but instead it denies it. The reason is the implicit "deny all," which is a security measure.

ACL Rule 4—The router can't filter self-generated traffic.

This can cause confusion when doing testing before implementing your ACL on a live network. A router won't filter traffic it generated itself. This is demonstrated in Figure 15.2 below:

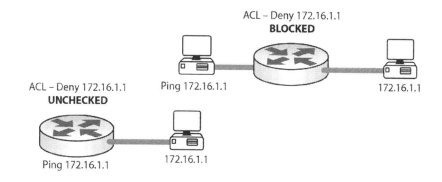

Figure 15.2—ACL Testing with Self-Generated Traffic

ACL Rule 5—You can't edit a live ACL.

In fact, until IOS 12.4 you could only edit a named ACL, not standard or extended ACLs. This was a limitation of ACL architecture. Before IOS 12.4, if you wanted to edit a standard or extended ACL, you had to follow these steps (I used list 99 as an example):

1. Stop ACL traffic on the interface with the `no ip access-group 99 in` command.
2. Copy and paste the ACL into Notepad and edit it there.
3. Go into ACL mode and paste in the new ACL.
4. Apply the ACL to the interface again.

Here are the steps on a live router:

ACL created and applied to interface:

```
Router>en
Router#conf t
Enter configuration commands, one per line.  End with CNTL/Z.
Router(config)#access-list 1 permit 172.16.1.1
Router(config)#access-list 1 permit 172.16.2.1
Router(config)#interface FastEthernet0/0
Router(config-if)#ip access-group 1 in
```

Take off the active interface:

```
Router(config)#int FastEthernet0/0
Router(config-if)#no ip access-group 1 in
Router(config-if)#^Z
```

Show the ACLs. Copy and paste into Notepad and make the changes:

```
Router#show run ← or show ip access lists
access-list 1 permit host 172.16.1.1
access-list 1 permit host 172.16.2.1
```

You actually need to add an exclamation mark in-between each line of configuration (if you are pasting it in) to tell the router to do a carriage return:

```
access-list 1 permit host 172.16.1.1
!
access-list 1 permit host 172.16.2.2
```

The lines being pasted into the router configuration are shown below. Delete the previous ACL and then paste in the new version:

```
Router#conf t
Enter configuration commands, one per line.  End with CNTL/Z.
Router(config)#no access-list 1
Router(config)#access-list 1 permit host 172.16.1.1
Router(config)#!
Router(config)#access-list 1 permit host 172.16.2.2
```

```
Router(config)#exit
Router#
%SYS-5-CONFIG_I: Configured from console by console
show ip access
Router#show ip access-lists
Standard IP access list 1
    permit host 172.16.1.1
    permit host 172.16.2.2
Router#
Router(config)#int FastEthernet0/0
Router(config-if)#ip access-group 1 in ← reapply to the interface
```

The commands above may not work if you are using Packet Tracer. Also, please do try these commands on a router because they are exam topics. Bear in mind that you should disable the ACL on the interface (so it's no longer live) before you edit it in order to avoid strange or unpredictable behavior. I'll show you how to edit live ACLs on IOS 12.4 and later shortly.

ACL Rule 6—Disable the ACL on the interface.

Many engineers, when they want to test or deactivate the ACL for a while, will actually delete it altogether. This isn't necessary. If you want to stop the ACL from working, simply remove it from the active interface it is applied to:

```
Router(config)#int FastEthernet0/0
Router(config-if)#no ip access-group 1 in
Router(config-if)#^Z
```

ACL Rule 7—You can reuse the same ACL.

I've seen this often on live networks. You will usually have the same ACL policy throughout your network. Rather than configuring several ACLs, simply refer to the same ACL and apply it to as many interfaces as you require. Figure 15.3 below illustrates this concept:

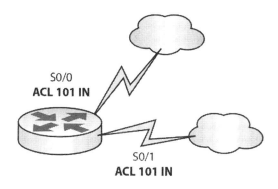

S0/0
ACL 101 IN

S0/1
ACL 101 IN

Figure 15.3—You Can Reuse an ACL

ACL Rule 8—Keep them short!

The basic rule with ACLs is to keep them short and focused. Many novice Cisco engineers stretch their ACL over many lines when, with some thought, it could be tightened to just a few lines of configuration. I've mentioned previously that you want your most specific lines of configuration on top. This is good practice and saves CPU cycles on the router.

Good ACL configuration skills come with knowledge and practice.

ACL Rule 9—Put your ACL as close to the source as possible.

Cisco documentation advises us to put an EXTENDED ACL as close to the SOURCE as possible and STANDARD ACL as close to the DESTINATION as possible, because that will prevent unnecessary overhead but will still allow any "legitimate" traffic.

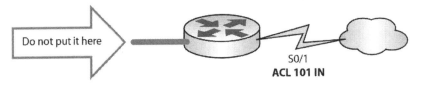

Figure 15.4—Put Your ACL Close to the Source

 FARAI SAYS—"The official Cisco advice is EXTENDED as close to the SOURCE as possible and STANDARD as close to the DESTINATION as possible."

WILDCARD MASKS

Wildcard masks are essential to learn because they are used as part of command line configuration in ACLs and some routing protocols. They exist because there has to be a way to tell the router which parts of an IP address or network address you want to match.

The matching is done at the binary level, but you can easily configure wildcard masks using the same notation you use for subnet masks. A binary 1 tells the router to ignore the digit and a 0 means match the digit.

The easy way to perform wildcard masking for the CCNA exam is simply to ensure that you add a number to the subnet mask to give you a total of 255. So, if your subnet mask in one octet was 192, you would add 63 to it to make 255. If it was 255, you would add 0. Take a look at the examples below:

Subnet	255	255	255	192
Wildcard	0	0	0	63
Equals	255	255	255	255

Subnet	255	255	224	0
Wildcard	0	0	31	255
Equals	255	255	255	255

Subnet	255	128	0	0
Wildcard	0	127	255	255
Equals	255	255	255	255

You need to enter a wildcard mask if you want your ACL to match a subnet or an entire network. For example, if you wanted to match 172.20.1.0 255.255.224.0, you would enter the following:

```
Router(config)#access-list 1 permit 172.20.1.0 0.0.31.255
```

Matching subnet 192.200.1.0 255.255.255.192 would require the following:

```
Router(config)#access-list 1 permit 192.200.1.0 0.0.0.63
```

Be careful when applying network statements with OSPF, which also requires a wildcard mask.

The same principle applies when you have a network with two host bits, as you will need to enter an ACL to match these. For example, matching subnet 192.168.1.0 255.255.255.252 or /30, you will need to enter the following:

```
Router(config)#access-list 1 permit 192.168.1.0 0.0.0.3
```

I have left off some configuration, as I just want to show the relevant part. This will match hosts 1 and 2 on the 192.168.1.0 network. If you wanted to match hosts 5 and 6 on the 192.168.1.4/30 network, you would enter the following:

```
Router(config)#access-list 1 permit 192.168.1.4 0.0.0.3
```

Read through the subnetting and VLSM notes to understand this concept further. It is important!

CONFIGURING ACCESS CONTROL LISTS

As with any skill, repetition makes mastery. As I've said before, you must type on a router every example I give, do as many labs as possible, and then make up your own examples. You need to be fast and you need to be accurate, both in the exam and in the real world.

The standard and extended ACLs presented in the next sections are numbered ACLs. These represent the classic way of configuring ACLs. Named ACLs are the other way of configuring ACLs and they are presented in a subsequent section.

Standard ACLs

Standard numbered ACLs are the easiest to configure, so this is the best place to start. Standard ACLs can only filter based on a source network or IP address.

Figure 15.5—Incoming Packet with Source and Destination

In Figure 15.5 above, the incoming packet has a source and destination address, but your standard ACL will only look at the source address. Your ACL would permit or deny this source address (see Figure 15.6):

```
Router(config)#access-list 1 permit host 172.16.1.1
```

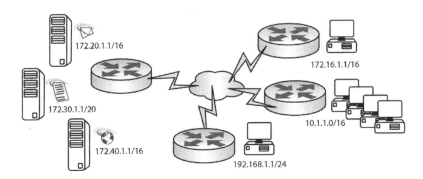

Figure 15.6—Network with Multiple Hosts/Networks

```
Router(config)#access-list 1 permit host 172.16.1.1
Router(config)#access-list 1 permit host 192.168.1.1
Router(config)#access-list 1 permit 10.1.0.0 0.0.255.255
```

This would be applied to the server side router. Remember that there will be an implicit "deny all" at the end of this list, so all other traffic will be blocked.

Extended ACLs

Far more granularity is built into extended numbered ACLs; however, this makes them trickier to configure. You can filter source or destination networks, ports, protocols, and services.

Generally, you can look at the configuration syntax for extended ACLs, as follows:

```
access list# permit/deny [service/protocol] [source network/IP]
[destination network/IP] [port#]
```

For example:

```
access-list 101 deny tcp 10.1.0.0 0.0.255.255 host 172.30.1.1 eq telnet
access-list 100 permit tcp 10.1.0.0 0.0.255.255 host 172.30.1.1 eq ftp
access-list 100 permit icmp any
```

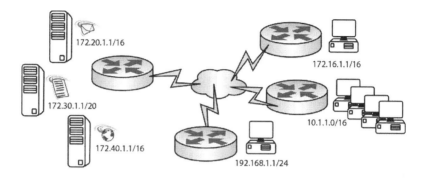

Figure 15.7—Blocking Server Access Example

An ACL you could configure for the network above, featuring e-mail, web, and file servers, would be as follows (applied on the server side):

```
access-list 100 permit tcp host 172.16.1.1 host 172.20.1.1 eq smtp
access-list 100 permit tcp 10.1.0.0 0.0.255.255 host 172.30.1.1 eq ftp
access-list 100 permit tcp host 192.168.1.1 host 172.40.1.1 eq www
```

Or, it could be the next ACL, if you had different requirements:

```
access-list 101 deny icmp any 172.20.0.0 0.0.255.255
access-list 101 deny tcp 10.1.0.0 0.0.255.255 host 172.30.1.1 eq telnet
```

Or, it could be as follows:

```
access-list 102 permit tcp any host 172.30.1.1 eq ftp established
```

The [established] keyword tells the router to permit the traffic only if it was originated by hosts on the inside. The three-way handshake flags (ACK or RST bit) will indicate this.

Named ACLs

Unlike numbered ACLs, named ACLs can be easily identified based on their descriptive name, and this is useful especially in large configurations. They were introduced to add flexibility and ease of management of ACLs. Named ACLs can be considered more of a configuration enhancement, as it does not modify the core ACL structure (it just modifies the way we refer to an ACL).

The syntax is similar to the numbered ACLs, with the major difference of using names instead of numbers to identify ACLs. Just like in the case of numbered ACLs, you can configure standard or extended named ACLs.

Another difference when configuring named ACLs is that you always have to use the `ip access-list` command, unlike with numbered ACLs, where you could also use the simple `access-list` command.

```
Router(config)#access-list ?
  <1-99>            IP standard access list
  <100-199>         IP extended access list
  <1100-1199>       Extended 48-bit MAC address access list
  <1300-1999>       IP standard access list (expanded range)
  <200-299>         Protocol type-code access list
  <2000-2699>       IP extended access list (expanded range)
  <700-799>         48-bit MAC address access list
  dynamic-extended  Extend the dynamic ACL absolute timer
  rate-limit        Simple rate-limit specific access list

Router(config)#ip access-list ?
  extended    Extended access list
  log-update  Control access list log updates
  logging     Control access list logging
  resequence  Resequence access list
  standard    Standard access list

R1(config)#ip access-list standard ?
  <1-99>        Standard IP access-list number
  <1300-1999>   Standard IP access-list number (expanded range)
  WORD          Access-list name

R1(config)#ip access-list extended ?
  <100-199>     Extended IP access-list number
  <2000-2699>   Extended IP access-list number (expanded range)
  WORD          Access-list name
```

Named ACLs have a slightly different syntax than the other types of ACLs do (standard numbered and extended numbered). You can also edit live named ACLs, which is a useful feature. You simply need to tell the router that you want to configure a named ACL, and whether you want it to be standard or extended. You can also edit numbered ACLs with later IOS releases, so please check the documentation for your platform.

When creating a named ACL using the `ip access-list` command, Cisco IOS will place you in the ACL configuration mode where you can enter or remove ACL entries (denied or permitted access conditions). Figure 15.8 below shows an example of a named ACL, followed by the corresponding output:

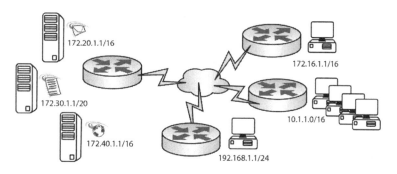

Figure 15.8—Named ACL

```
Router(config)#ip access-list extended BlockWEB
Router(config-ext-nacl)#?
Ext Access List configuration commands:
  <1-2147483647>  Sequence Number
  default         Set a command to its defaults
  deny            Specify packets to reject
  dynamic         Specify a DYNAMIC list of PERMITs or DENYs
  evaluate        Evaluate an access list
  exit            Exit from access-list configuration mode
  no              Negate a command or set its defaults
  permit          Specify packets to forward
  remark          Access list entry comment
Router(config-ext-nacl)#deny tcp any any eq 80
Router(config-ext-nacl)#permit ip any any
```

Named ACL verification can be done using the following commands:

- `show ip access-lists`—shows all ACLs created on the device.
- `show ip access-lists <acl_name>`—shows a particular named ACL

```
Router(config)#do show ip access-lists
Standard IP access list test
    30 permit 10.1.1.1
    20 permit 192.168.1.1
    15 permit 172.20.1.1
    10 permit 172.16.1.1
```

To learn how you can add or delete ACL entries in a named ACL, please refer to the "ACL Sequence Numbers" section below.

Applying ACLs

In order to come into effect, you must apply your ACL to an interface or router port. I say this because I've seen many novice Cisco engineers type the ACL and then wonder why it isn't working! Or they configure it but apply the wrong ACL number or name to the interface.

If you are applying an ACL to a line, you have to specify it with the `access-class` command, and to an interface, it is the `ip access-group` command. Why Cisco have you do this, I will never know!

Here are three examples of ACLs being applied to a port or interface.

Interface:

```
Router(config)#int FastEthernet0/0
Router(config-if)#ip access-group 101 in
```

Line:

```
Router(config)#line vty 0 15
Router(config-line)#access-class 101 in
```

Interface:

```
Router(config)#int FastEthernet0/0
Router(config-if)#ip access-group BlockWEB in
```

ACL SEQUENCE NUMBERS

With IOS 12.4 onwards, you can see that Cisco IOS adds sequence numbers to each ACL entry. So now I can create an access control list and then remove a line from it.

```
Router(config)#ip access-list standard test
Router(config-std-nacl)#permit 172.16.1.1
Router(config-std-nacl)#permit 192.168.1.1
Router(config-std-nacl)#permit 10.1.1.1
Router(config-std-nacl)#exit
Router(config)#exit
Router#show ip access-lists
Standard IP access list test
    30 permit 10.1.1.1
    20 permit 192.168.1.1
    10 permit 172.16.1.1
```

Note that the sequence numbers are not displayed in the router running configuration. In order to see them you have to issue a show [ip] access-list command.

Add an ACL Line

To add a new ACL line, you can simply enter the new sequence number and then the ACL statement. The example below shows how you can add line 15 to your existing ACL:

```
Router#conf t
Router(config)#ip access-list standard test
Router(config-std-nacl)#15 permit 172.20.1.1
Router(config-std-nacl)#do show ip access-lists
Standard IP access list test
    30 permit 10.1.1.1
    20 permit 192.168.1.1
    15 permit 172.20.1.1
    10 permit 172.16.1.1
```

Remove an ACL Line

To remove an ACL line, you can simply enter the `no <seq_number>` command, like in the example below where line 20 is deleted:

```
Router#conf t
Enter configuration commands, one per line.  End with CNTL/Z.
Router(config)#ip access
Router(config)#ip access-list standard test
Router(config-std-nacl)#no 20
Router(config-std-nacl)#do show ip access-lists
Standard IP access list test
    30 permit 10.1.1.1
    15 permit 172.20.1.1
    10 permit 172.16.1.1
```

Resequence an ACL

To resequence an ACL, you can use the `ip access-list resequence <acl_name> <starting_seq_number> <step_to_increment>` command. The behaviour of this command can be examined in the example below:

```
Router(config)#ip access-list resequence test 100 20
Router(config)#do show ip access-lists
Standard IP access list test
    100 permit 10.1.1.1
    120 permit 172.20.1.1
    140 permit 172.16.1.1
Router(config-std-nacl)#
```

The resequence command created new sequence numbers, starting from 100, and incremented them by 20 for each new ACL line.

ACL LOGGING

By default, ACL entries that are matched by packets traversing a router interface create incremental counters that can be analyzed using the `show ip access-lists` command, as can be seen in the example below:

```
Router#show ip access-lists
Extended IP access list test
    10 deny tcp any any eq 80 (10 matches)
    20 permit ip any any (56 matches)
```

If you need more detailed information about the traffic that is being matched by the ACL entries, you can configure the `log` or `log-input` parameters to the relevant ACL entries.

```
Router(config)#ip access-list extended test
Router(config)#no 10
Router(config)#10 deny tcp any any eq 80 log
```

```
Router#show ip access-lists
Extended IP access list test
    10 deny tcp any any eq 80 log
    20 permit ip any any (83 matches)
```

In the configuration sample above, ACL logging for test ACL entry 10 is configured. When a packet hits that ACL entry, the ACL counters will continue to increase but the router will also generate a log message that contains details about the specific ACL hit:

```
%SEC-6-IPACCESSLOGP: list test denied tcp 10.10.10.2(24667) ->
10.10.10.1(80), 1 packet
```

If you need more detail about the transaction, you can replace the log parameter with the log-input parameter, as you can see in the example below:

```
Router(config)#ip access-list extended test
Router(config)#no 10
Router(config)#10 deny tcp any any eq 80 log-input
Router#show ip access-lists
Extended IP access list test
    10 deny tcp any any eq 80 log-input
    20 permit ip any any (125 matches)
```

When the specific ACL entry is hit, a more detailed log message is generated by the router, which includes the incoming interface and the source MAC address:

```
%SEC-6-IPACCESSLOGP: list test denied tcp 10.10.10.2(14013)
(FastEthernet0/0 00aa.aabb.ccdd) -> 10.10.10.1(80), 1 packet
```

ACL logging can be very useful for troubleshooting to see what exactly is dropped/permitted, but one thing must be noted for real-world situations (this is beyond the scope of the CCNA exam): ACL entries that contain [log] or [log-input] keyword are process-switched by the router (as opposed to being CEF-switched, which is the default in modern routers). This requires more router CPU cycles, which can become a problem if there is a lot of traffic that is hitting the logged ACL entry.

USING ACLS TO LIMIT TELNET AND SSH ACCESS

Besides filtering the traffic on an interface level, ACLs can be associated with many other device features, including filtering traffic on VTY lines. In a previous module, you learned how you can configure Telnet or SSH access to a device (e.g., router or switch) using the line vty command.

Sometimes you may not want to accept all Telnet/SSH connections to or from the device. In order to manipulate this you must define an ACL that defines the type of traffic that will be allowed or denied on the VTY line. The ACL can be numbered or named. You associate the ACL to the VTY line using the access-class <acl> [in|out] command.

The following example defines an ACL permitting Telnet traffic from host 10.10.10.1, which will then be applied inbound to the VTY lines:

```
Router(config)#ip access-list extended VTY_ACCESS
Router(config-ext-nacl)#permit tcp host 10.10.10.1 any eq telnet
Router(config-ext-nacl)#deny tcp any any
Router(config-ext-nacl)#exit
Router(config)#line vty 0 4
Router(config-line)#access-class VTY_ACCESS in

You can verify the configuration using the following commands:
Router#show run | sect line vty
line vty 0 4
access-class VTY_ACCESS in
```

TROUBLESHOOTING AND VERIFYING ACLS

I think that with an understanding of the configuration commands and rules you should be fine with access control lists. If your ACL isn't working, first check that there is basic IP connectivity by pinging. Then check whether you have applied your ACL, that there are no typos, and whether you need to allow any IP traffic to pass (remember the implicit "deny all"). Some of the most important verification steps in the ACL troubleshooting process include:

- Verifying the ACL statistics
- Verifying the permitted networks
- Verifying the ACL interface and direction

Verifying the ACL Statistics

After you have successfully configured an ACL and applied it to an interface, it is very important to have a method by which you can verify the correct behavior of the ACL, especially how many times an ACL entry has been used (hit). Based on the number of hits, you can adjust your filtering policy or you can enhance your ACLs to improve the overall security. Based on your needs, you can verify the ACL statistics on a global level or per interface (starting with IOS 12.4).

Global ACL Statistics

Global ACL statistics can be verified using the show ip access-list or show access-list commands, which can refer to a numbered or a named ACL:

```
Router#show ip access-lists
Extended IP access list test
    10 deny tcp any any eq 80 (10 matches)
    20 permit ip any any (56 matches)
```

This method may not provide very specific information in situations in which you apply the same ACL on different interfaces, as it offers overall statistics.

Per Interface ACL Statistics

In situations where you want to examine per interface ACL hits, either inbound or outbound, you can use the `show ip access-list interface <interface_number> [in|out]` command, as illustrated below:

```
Router#show ip access-list interface FastEthernet0/1 in
Extended IP access list 100 in
    10 permit ip host 10.10.10.1 any (5 matches)
    30 permit ip host 10.10.10.2 any (31 matches)
```

If no direction is specified, any input or output ACL applied to the specific interface is displayed. This feature is also called "ACL Manageability" and is available starting with IOS 12.4.

Verifying the Permitted Networks

Sometimes, especially in large environments where you have to configure many ACLs, you can make typo errors when configuring the ACL entries and this can lead to wrong traffic flows being blocked on different interfaces. In order to verify the correct ACL entries (permit and deny statements) you can use either the `show run | section access-list` or the `show ip access-list` commands, as described in previous sections.

The implicit deny all will also block all routing protocol traffic so ensure you permit it if necessary.

To permit RIP, specify the following:

```
access-list 101 permit udp any any eq rip
```

To permit OSPF, specify the following:

```
access-list 101 permit ospf any any
```

To permit EIGRP, specify the following:

```
access-list 101 permit eigrp any any
```

Verifying the ACL Interface and Direction

One common error when applying an ACL to an interface is applying it in the wrong direction, meaning inbound instead of outbound and outbound instead of inbound. This can cause a lot of issues, both from a functionality and security perspective. One of the first steps you should take in an ACL troubleshooting process is verifying that the ACL is applied to the correct interface and in the correct direction.

Multiple commands exist to verify this, including the `show run` and the `show ip access-list interface <interface> [in|out]` commands.

Now please take today's exam at **https://www.in60days.com/free/ccnain60days/**

DAY 15 LABS

Standard ACL

Topology

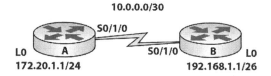

Purpose

Learn how to configure a standard ACL.

Walkthrough

1. Configure the network above. Add a static route on each router so any traffic for any network leaves the Serial interface. You are doing this because, though not a routing lab, you still need the traffic to route. Add .1 to the Router A Serial interface and .2 to the Router B Serial interface.

```
RouterA(config)#ip route 0.0.0.0 0.0.0.0 s0/1/0
RouterB(config)#ip route 0.0.0.0 0.0.0.0 s0/1/0
```

2. Configure a standard ACL on Router A permitting the 192.168.1.0/26 network. By default, all other networks will be blocked.

```
RouterA(config)#access-list 1 permit 192.168.1.0 0.0.0.63
RouterA(config)#int Serial0/1/0
RouterA(config-if)#ip access-group 1 in
RouterA(config-if)#exit
RouterA(config)#exit
RouterA#
```

3. Test the ACL by pinging from Router B, which by default will use the 10.0.0.1 address.

```
RouterB#ping 10.0.0.1
Type escape sequence to abort.
Sending 5, 100-byte ICMP Echos to 10.0.0.1, timeout is 2 seconds:
UUUUU
Success rate is 0 percent (0/5)
```

4. Test another ping, but source it from 192.168.1.1 and this should work.

```
RouterB#ping
Protocol [ip]:
Target IP address: 10.0.0.1
Repeat count [5]:
Datagram size [100]:
Timeout in seconds [2]:
Extended commands [n]: y
```

```
Source address or interface: 192.168.1.1
Type of service [0]:
Set DF bit in IP header? [no]:
Validate reply data? [no]:
Data pattern [0xABCD]:
Loose, Strict, Record, Timestamp, Verbose[none]:
Sweep range of sizes [n]:
Type escape sequence to abort.
Sending 5, 100-byte ICMP Echos to 10.0.0.1, timeout is 2 seconds:
Packet sent with a source address of 192.168.1.1
!!!!!
```

Success rate is 100 percent (5/5), round-trip min/avg/max = 31/31/32 ms

Extended ACL

Topology

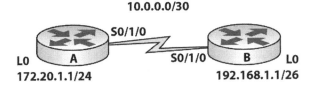

10.0.0.0/30

Purpose
Learn how to configure an extended ACL.

Walkthrough

1. Configure the network above. Add a static route on Router B so any traffic for any network leaves the Serial interface. You are doing this because, though not a routing lab, you still need the traffic to route.

   ```
   RouterB(config)#ip route 0.0.0.0 0.0.0.0 s0/1/0
   ```

2. Add an extended ACL to Router A. Permit Telnet traffic to your Loopback interface only. Remember to permit Telnet also.

   ```
   RouterA(config)#access-list 100 permit tcp any host 172.20.1.1 eq 23
   RouterA(config)#int s0/1/0
   RouterA(config-if)#ip access-group 100 in
   RouterA(config-if)#line vty 0 15
   RouterA(config-line)#password cisco
   RouterA(config-line)#login
   RouterA(config-line)#^Z
   RouterA#
   ```

   The ACL line above is number 100, which tells the router it is extended. The service you want to allow (telnet) uses TCP. It is allowing TCP from any network destined for host 172.20.1.1 on the Telnet port, which is 23. When you issue a show run command, the router actually replaces the port number with the name, as illustrated below:

```
access-list 100 permit tcp any host 172.20.1.1 eq telnet
```

3. Now test a Telnet from Router B. First, Telnet to the Serial interface on Router A, which should be blocked. Then test the Loopback interface.

```
RouterB#telnet 10.0.0.1
Trying 10.0.0.1 ...
% Connection timed out; remote host not responding

RouterB#telnet 172.20.1.1
Trying 172.20.1.1 ...Open

User Access Verification
Password: ←password won't show when you type it
RouterA> ←Hit Control+Shift+6 together and then let go and press the X key to quit.
```

NOTE: We will be covering ACLs in other labs, but you really need to know these cold. For this reason, try other TCP ports, such as 80, 25, etc. In addition, try UDP ports, such as 53. You won't be able to test them easily without a PC attached to Router B.

Going further, mix up the IP addresses, permitting Telnet (in this example) to the Serial interface but not the Loopback interface. Then put an ACL on Router B instead. I can't overemphasise how important this is. If you need to wipe the ACL, you can simply type the following:

```
RouterA(config)#no access-list 100
```

Named ACL

Topology

10.0.0.0/30

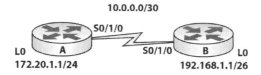

LO   A   S0/1/0   B   LO
172.20.1.1/24   192.168.1.1/26

Purpose

Learn how to configure a named ACL.

Walkthrough

1. Configure the network above. Add a static route on each router so any traffic for any network leaves the Serial interface. You are doing this because, though not a routing lab, you still need the traffic to route.

```
RouterA(config)#ip route 0.0.0.0 0.0.0.0 s0/1/0
RouterB(config)#ip route 0.0.0.0 0.0.0.0 s0/1/0
```

2. Add an extended named ACL on Router B. Permit pings from host 172.20.1.1 but no other hosts or networks.

```
RouterB(config)#ip access-list extended blockping
RouterB(config-ext-nacl)#permit icmp host 172.20.1.1 any
RouterB(config-ext-nacl)#exit
RouterB(config)#int s0/1/0
RouterB(config-if)#ip access-groupblockping in
RouterB(config-if)#
```

3. Now test the ACL with pings from the Serial interface on Router A and the Loopback interface (which should work).

```
RouterA#ping 192.168.1.1

Type escape sequence to abort.
Sending 5, 100-byte ICMP Echos to 192.168.1.1, timeout is 2 seconds:
UUUUU
Success rate is 0 percent (0/5)

RouterA#ping
Protocol [ip]:
Target IP address: 192.168.1.1
Repeat count [5]:
Datagram size [100]:
Timeout in seconds [2]:
Extended commands [n]: y
Source address or interface: 172.20.1.1
Type of service [0]:
Set DF bit in IP header? [no]:
Validate reply data? [no]:
Data pattern [0xABCD]:
Loose, Strict, Record, Timestamp, Verbose[none]:
Sweep range of sizes [n]:
Type escape sequence to abort.
Sending 5, 100-byte ICMP Echos to 192.168.1.1, timeout is 2 seconds:
Packet sent with a source address of 172.20.1.1
!!!!!
Success rate is 100 percent (5/5), round-trip min/avg/max = 31/34/47
ms
```

NOTE: You need to understand which service is which, as well as which port numbers various services use. Otherwise, you will really struggle to configure an ACL. This ACL is pretty straightforward and can be achieved with one line. If you had routing protocols running, then they would need to be permitted.

Network Address Translation

DAY 16 TASKS

- Read today's lesson notes (below)
- Review yesterday's lesson notes and lab
- Complete today's labs
- Take today's exam
- Read the ICND1 cram guide
- Spend 15 minutes on the subnetting.org website

Until we all transition to IPv6, NAT will be an essential tool enabling internet access from home users and small to large businesses. NAT can be somewhat tricky to configure and troubleshoot. I spent two years giving NAT support to customers when I worked at Cisco TAC.

Today you will learn about the following:

- NAT basics
- Configuring and verifying NAT
- NAT troubleshooting

This module maps to the following ICND1 syllabus requirements:

- 4.7 Configure, verify, and troubleshoot inside source NAT
- 4.7.a Static
- 4.7.b Pool
- 4.7.c PAT

NAT BASICS

Imagine for a moment that networks run on colors instead of using IP addresses. There is an unlimited supply of the colors blue and yellow but the other colors are in short supply. Your network is divided into many users using the colors blue and yellow because they are free to use. The blue users need to get out to the web fairly regularly, so you buy a few green tokens which your router can use to swap for the blue users' tokens when they need to reach hosts on the web. Your router would be doing this:

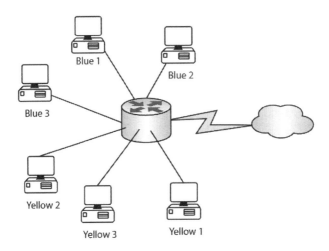

Figure 16.1—Inside Tokens Swapped for Outside Tokens

Inside Tokens	Outside Tokens
Blue 1	Green 1
Blue 2	Green 2
Blue 3	Green 3

When each of the blue devices has finished with the outside connection, the green token can be released for use by another blue device. The benefits to this are outside devices can't see your internal token IDs and you are helping conserve the limited amount of green tokens available for use on the Internet. NAT runs on this principle.

As you can see, NAT not only protects the identity of your network IP addresses but also is another method of address conservation. NAT is performed on routers or firewalls, so, instead of colors, you would see something like this:

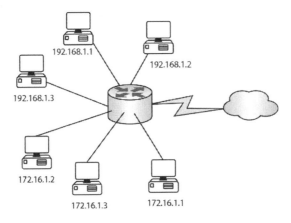

Figure 16.2—Inside Addresses Swapped for Outside Addresses

Inside Addresses	Outside Addresses
192.168.1.1	200.100.1.5
192.168.1.3	200.100.1.7

There are three ways to configure NAT on your router, depending upon your particular requirements. You will need to know all three for the CCNA exam.

In order to configure NAT, you need to tell the router which interfaces are on the inside and outside of your NAT network. This is because you could actually swap internal addresses for a pool of NAT addresses, or, at the very least, a single NAT address, and perform NAT between two Ethernet interfaces on your router.

Having said that, for the exam and in the real world, you will usually translate private Internet addresses into routable addresses on the Internet. You will see this on your home broadband router, which will usually give your laptop an IP in the 192.168.1 range but then have a routable address on the interface to the ISP.

NAT enables hosts on private networks to access resources on the Internet or other public networks. NAT is an IETF standard that enables a LAN to use one set of IP addresses for internal traffic, typically private address space as defined in RFC 1918, and another set of addresses for external traffic, typically publicly registered IP address space.

NAT converts the packet headers for incoming and outgoing traffic and keeps track of each session. The key to understanding NAT and, ultimately, troubleshooting NAT problems is having a solid understanding of NAT terminology. You should be familiar with the following NAT terms:

- The NAT inside interface
- Inside local address
- Inside global address
- The NAT outside interface
- Outside local address
- Outside global address

In NAT terminology, the inside interface is the border interface of the administrative domain controlled by the organization. This does not necessarily have to be the default gateway used by hosts that reside within the internal network.

The inside local address is the IP address of a host residing on the inside network. In most cases, the inside local address is an RFC 1918 address (i.e., non-routable, such as 192.168.x.x or 172.16.x.x). This address is translated to the outside global address, which is typically an IP address from a publicly assigned or registered pool. It is important to remember, however, that the inside local address could also be a public address.

The inside global address is the IP address of an internal host as it appears to the outside world. Once the inside IP address has been translated, it will appear as an inside global address to the Internet public or to any other external network or host.

The outside interface is the boundary for the administrative domain that is not controlled by the organization. In other words, the outside interface is connected to the external network, which may be the Internet or any other external network, such as a partner network, for example. Any hosts residing beyond the outside interface fall outside the local organization's administration.

The outside local address is the IP address of an outside, or external, host as it appears to inside hosts. Finally, the outside global address is an address that is legal and can be used on the Internet. Both outside local addresses and outside global addresses are typically allocated from a globally routable address or network space.

To clarify these concepts further, Figure 16.3 below shows the use of the addresses in a session between two hosts. NAT is enabled on the intermediate gateway:

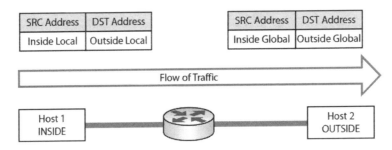

Figure 16.3—Understanding NAT Inside and Outside Addresses

NAT inside and outside addressing is a classic exam question, so come back to this concept a few times.

CONFIGURING AND VERIFYING NAT

The configuration and verification of Network Address Translation with Cisco IOS software is a straightforward task. When configuring NAT, perform the following:

- Designate one or more interfaces as the internal (inside) interface(s) using the ip nat inside interface configuration command.
- Designate an interface as the external (outside) interface using the ip nat outside interface configuration command.
- Configure an access control list (ACL) that will match all traffic for translation. This can be a standard or an extended named or numbered ACL.
- Optionally, configure a pool of global addresses using the ip nat pool <name> <start-ip> <end-ip> [netmask <mask> | prefix-length <length>] **global**

configuration command. This defines a pool of inside global addresses to which inside local addresses will be translated.

- Configure NAT globally using the `ip nat inside source list <ACL> [interface|pool] <name> [overload]` global configuration command.

The following output shows you one way to configure NAT (dynamic NAT) with Cisco IOS software. You can see that the configuration has used the `description` and `remark` features available to help administrators more easily manage and troubleshoot their networks:

```
R1(config)#interface FastEthernet0/0
R1(config-if)#description 'Connected To The Internal LAN'
R1(config-if)#ip address 10.5.5.1 255.255.255.248
R1(config-if)#ip nat inside
R1(config-if)#exit
R1(config)#interface Serial0/0
R1(config-if)#description 'Connected To The ISP'
R1(config-if)#ip address 150.1.1.1 255.255.255.248
R1(config-if)#ip nat outside
R1(config-if)#exit
R1(config)#access-list 100 remark 'Translate Internal Addresses Only'
R1(config)#access-list 100 permit ip 10.5.5.0 0.0.0.7 any
R1(config)#ip nat pool INSIDE-POOL 150.1.1.3 150.1.1.6 prefix-length 24
R1(config)#ip nat inside source list 100 pool INSIDE-POOL
R1(config)#exit
```

Following this configuration, the `show ip nat translations` command can be used to verify that translations are actually taking place on the router (once traffic starts traversing the router), as illustrated below:

```
R1#show ip nat translations
Pro  Inside global    Inside local    Outside local    Outside global
icmp 150.1.1.4:4      10.5.5.1:4      200.1.1.1:4      200.1.1.1:4
icmp 150.1.1.3:1      10.5.5.2:1      200.1.1.1:1      200.1.1.1:1
tcp  150.1.1.5:159    10.5.5.3:159    200.1.1.1:23     200.1.1.1:23
```

You actually have three choices when it comes to configuring NAT on your router:

- Swap one internal address for one external address (static NAT)
- Swap many internal addresses for two or more external addresses (dynamic NAT)
- Swap many internal addresses for many external ports (Port Address Translation or one-way NAT)

Static NAT

You would want to swap one specific address for another address when you have a web server (for example) on the inside of your network. If you keep using dynamic addressing, then there is no way to reach the destination address because it keeps changing.

FARAI SAYS—"You would use static NAT (see Figure 16.4 below) for any server that needs to be reachable via the Internet, such as e-mail or FTP."

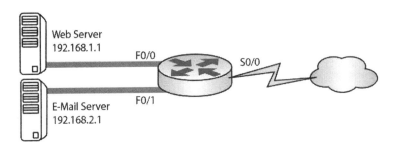

Figure 16.4—Static NAT in Use

Inside Addresses	Outside NAT Addresses
192.168.1.1	200.1.1.1
192.168.2.1	200.1.1.2

For the network above, your configuration would be as follows:

```
Router(config)#interface f0/0
Router(config-if)#ip address 192.168.1.1 255.255.255.0
Router(config-if)#ip nat inside
Router(config)#interface f0/1
Router(config-if)#ip address 192.168.2.1 255.255.255.0
Router(config-if)#ip nat inside
Router(config)#interface s0/0
Router(config-if)#ip nat outside
Router(config-if)#exit
Router(config)#ip nat inside source static 192.168.1.1 200.1.1.1
Router(config)#ip nat inside source static 192.168.2.1 200.1.1.2
```

The ip nat inside and ip nat outside commands tell the router which are the inside NAT interfaces and which are the outside NAT interfaces. The ip nat inside source command defines the static translations, of which you could have as many as you wish, so long as you paid for the public IP addresses. The vast majority of configuration mistakes I fixed whilst at Cisco were missing ip nat inside and ip nat outside statements! You might see questions in the exam where you have to spot configuration mistakes.

I strongly recommend that you type the commands above onto a router. You will do many NAT labs in this book, but the more you type whilst you read the theory section, the better the information will stick in your head.

Dynamic NAT or NAT Pool

You will often need to use a group, or pool, of routable addresses. One-to-one NAT mapping has its limitations, of course, expense and extensive lines of configuration on your router to name two. Dynamic NAT allows you to configure one or more groups of addresses to be used by your internal hosts.

Your router will keep a list of the internal addresses to external addresses, and eventually the translation in the table will time out. You can alter the timeout values but please do so on the advice of a Cisco TAC engineer.

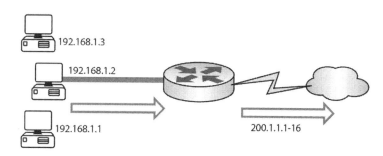

Figure 16.5—Internal Addresses to a NAT Pool of Routable Addresses

If you issued a `show ip nat translations` command on the router when the inside hosts have made outside connections, you would see a chart containing something like this:

Inside Addresses	Outside NAT Addresses
192.168.1.3	200.1.1.11
192.168.1.2	200.1.1.14

In Figure 16.5 above, you have internal addresses using a pool of addresses from 200.1.1.1 to 200.1.1.16. Here is the configuration file to achieve it. I have left off the router interface addresses for now:

```
Router(config)#interface f0/0
Router(config-if)#ip nat inside
Router(config)#interface s0/1
Router(config-if)#ip nat outside
Router(config)#ip nat pool poolname 200.1.1.1 200.1.1.16 netmask
255.255.255.0
Router(config)#ip nat inside source list 1 pool poolname
Router(config)#access-list 1 permit 192.168.1.0 0.0.0.255
```

The ACL is used to tell the router which addresses it can and cannot translate. The subnet mask is actually reversed and is called a wildcard mask, which was covered earlier. All NAT pools need a name, and in this example, it is simply called "poolname." The source list refers to the ACL.

NAT Overload/Port Address Translation/One-Way NAT

IP addresses are in short supply, and if you have hundreds or thousands of addresses which need to be routed, it could cost you a lot of money. In this instance, you can use NAT overload (see Figure 16.6), also referred to as Port Address Translation (PAT) or one-way NAT by Cisco. PAT cleverly allows a port number to be added to the IP address as a way of uniquely identifying it from another translation using the same IP address. There are over 65,000 ports available per IP address.

Although this is beyond the scope of the CCNA exam, it could be useful to know how PAT handles port numbers. Per Cisco documentation, it divides the available ports per global IP address into three ranges: 0–511, 512–1023, and 1024–65535. PAT assigns a unique source port to each UDP or TCP session. It will attempt to assign the same port value of the original request, but if the original source port has already been used, it will start scanning from the beginning of the particular port range to find the first available port and will assign it to the conversation.

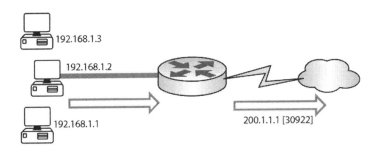

Figure 16.6—NAT Overload

The `show ip nat translations` table this time would show the IP addresses and port numbers:

Inside Addresses	Outside NAT Addresses (with Port Numbers)
192.168.1.1	200.1.1.1:30922
192.168.2.1	200.1.1.2:30975

To configure PAT, you would carry out the exact same configuration as for dynamic NAT, but you would add the keyword `overload` to the end of the pool:

```
Router(config)#interface f0/0
Router(config-if)#ip nat inside
Router(config)#interface s0/1
Router(config-if)#ip nat outside
Router(config)#ip nat pool poolname 200.1.1.1 200.1.1.1 netmask
255.255.255.0
Router(config)#ip nat inside source list 1 pool poolname overload
Router(config)#access-list 1 permit 192.168.1.0 0.0.0.255
```

This should be pretty easy to remember!

 FARAI SAYS—"Using PAT with more than one IP is a waste of address space because the router will use the first IP and increment port numbers for each subsequent connection. This is why PAT is typically configured to overload to the interface."

TROUBLESHOOTING NAT

Nine times out of ten, the router administrator has forgotten to add the `ip nat outside` or `ip nat inside` command to the router interfaces. In fact, this is almost always the problem! The next most frequent mistakes include the wrong ACL and a misspelled pool name (it is case sensitive).

You can debug NAT translations on the router by using the `debug ip nat [detailed]` command, and you can view the NAT pool with the `show ip nat translations` command.

Now please take today's exam at https://www.in60days.com/free/ccnain60days/

DAY 16 LABS

Static NAT

Topology

192.168.1.0 /24

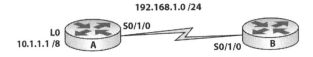

LO
10.1.1.1 /8   A

S0/1/0

S0/1/0   B

Purpose
Learn how to configure static NAT.

Walkthrough
1. Add IP address 192.168.1.1 255.255.255.0 to Router A and change the hostname to Router A. Add IP address 192.168.1.2 255.255.255.0 to Router B. Add a clock rate to the correct side and ping from A to B or from B to A. Check the previous labs if you need a reminder.

2. You need to add an IP address to Router A to simulate a host on the LAN. You can achieve this with a Loopback interface:

```
RouterA#conf t
Enter configuration commands, one per line.  End with CNTL/Z.
RouterA(config)#interface Loopback0
RouterA(config-if)#ip add 10.1.1.1 255.0.0.0
RouterA(config-if)#
```

3. For testing, you need to tell Router B to send any traffic to any network back out towards

    Router A. You will do this with a static route:

```
RouterB#conf t
Enter configuration commands, one per line.  End with CNTL/Z.
RouterB(config)#ip route 0.0.0.0 0.0.0.0 Serial0/1/0
RouterB(config)#
```

4. Test to see whether the static route is working by pinging from the Loopback interface on Router A to Router B:

```
RouterA#ping
Protocol [ip]:
Target IP address: 192.168.1.2
Repeat count [5]:
Datagram size [100]:
Timeout in seconds [2]:
Extended commands [n]: y
Source address or interface: 10.1.1.1
```

```
Type of service [0]:
Set DF bit in IP header? [no]:
Validate reply data? [no]:
Data pattern [0xABCD]:
Loose, Strict, Record, Timestamp, Verbose[none]:
Sweep range of sizes [n]:
Type escape sequence to abort.
Sending 5, 100-byte ICMP Echos to 192.168.1.2, timeout is 2 seconds:
Packet sent with a source address of 10.1.1.1
!!!!!
Success rate is 100 percent (5/5), round-trip min/avg/max = 31/31/32
ms

RouterA#
```

5. Configure a static NAT entry on Router A. Using NAT, translate the 10.1.1.1 address to 172.16.1.1 when it leaves the router. You also need to tell the router which is the inside and outside NAT interface:

```
RouterA#conf t
Enter configuration commands, one per line.  End with CNTL/Z.
RouterA(config)#int Loopback0
RouterA(config-if)#ip nat inside
RouterA(config-if)#int Serial0/1/0
RouterA(config-if)#ip nat outside
RouterA(config-if)#
RouterA(config-if)#ip nat inside source static 10.1.1.1 172.16.1.1
RouterA(config)#
```

6. Turn on NAT debugging so you can see the translations taking place. Then issue another extended ping (from L0) and check the NAT table. Your output may differ from mine due to changes in IOS.

```
RouterA#debug ip nat

IP NAT debugging is on
RouterA#
RouterA#ping
Protocol [ip]:
Target IP address: 192.168.1.2
Repeat count [5]:
Datagram size [100]:
Timeout in seconds [2]:
Extended commands [n]: y
Source address or interface: 10.1.1.1
Type of service [0]:
Set DF bit in IP header? [no]:
Validate reply data? [no]:
Data pattern [0xABCD]:
Loose, Strict, Record, Timestamp, Verbose[none]:
Sweep range of sizes [n]:
Type escape sequence to abort.
```

```
Sending 5, 100-byte ICMP Echos to 192.168.1.2, timeout is 2 seconds:
Packet sent with a source address of 10.1.1.1

NAT: s=10.1.1.1->172.16.1.1, d=192.168.1.2 [11]
!
NAT*: s=192.168.1.2, d=172.16.1.1->10.1.1.1 [11]

NAT: s=10.1.1.1->172.16.1.1, d=192.168.1.2 [12]
!
NAT*: s=192.168.1.2, d=172.16.1.1->10.1.1.1 [12]

NAT: s=10.1.1.1->172.16.1.1, d=192.168.1.2 [13]
!
NAT*: s=192.168.1.2, d=172.16.1.1->10.1.1.1 [13]

NAT: s=10.1.1.1->172.16.1.1, d=192.168.1.2 [14]
!
NAT*: s=192.168.1.2, d=172.16.1.1->10.1.1.1 [14]

NAT: s=10.1.1.1->172.16.1.1, d=192.168.1.2 [15]
!
Success rate is 100 percent (5/5), round-trip min/avg/max = 31/46/110
ms

RouterA#
NAT*: s=192.168.1.2, d=172.16.1.1->10.1.1.1 [15]

RouterA#show ip nat translations
Pro   Inside global  Inside local   Outside local    Outside global
icmp 172.16.1.1:10 10.1.1.1:10   192.168.1.2:10    192.168.1.2:10
icmp 172.16.1.1:6  10.1.1.1:6    192.168.1.2:6     192.168.1.2:6
icmp 172.16.1.1:7  10.1.1.1:7    192.168.1.2:7     192.168.1.2:7
icmp 172.16.1.1:8  10.1.1.1:8    192.168.1.2:8     192.168.1.2:8
icmp 172.16.1.1:9  10.1.1.1:9    192.168.1.2:9     192.168.1.2:9
---   172.16.1.1     10.1.1.1        ---               ---

RouterA#
```

7. Bear in mind that the router will clear the NAT translation soon afterward in order to clear the NAT address(es) for use by other IP addresses:

```
NAT: expiring 172.16.1.1 (10.1.1.1) icmp 6 (6)
NAT: expiring 172.16.1.1 (10.1.1.1) icmp 7 (7)
```

NAT Pool

Topology

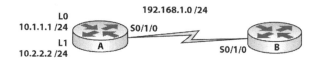

Purpose

Learn how to configure a NAT pool (dynamic NAT).

Walkthrough

1. Add IP address 192.168.1.1 255.255.255.0 to Router A and change the hostname to Router A. Add IP address 192.168.1.2 255.255.255.0 to Router B. Add a clock rate to the correct side and ping from A to B or from B to A. Check the previous lab if you need a reminder.

2. You need to add two IP addresses to Router A to simulate a host on the LAN. You can achieve this with two Loopback interfaces. They will be in different subnets but both start with a 10 address:

```
RouterA#conf t
Enter configuration commands, one per line.  End with CNTL/Z.
RouterA(config)#interface Loopback0
RouterA(config-if)#ip add 10.1.1.1 255.255.255.0
RouterA(config-if)#int l1    ← short for Loopback1
RouterA(config-if)#ip address 10.2.2.2 255.255.255.0
RouterA(config-if)#
```

3. For testing, you need to tell Router B to send any traffic to any network back out towards Router A. You will do this with a static route:

```
RouterB#conf t
Enter configuration commands, one per line.  End with CNTL/Z.
RouterB(config)#ip route 0.0.0.0 0.0.0.0 Serial0/1/0
RouterB(config)#
```

4. Test to see whether the static route is working by pinging from the Loopback interface on Router A to Router B:

```
RouterA#ping
Protocol [ip]:
Target IP address: 192.168.1.2
Repeat count [5]:
Datagram size [100]:
Timeout in seconds [2]:
Extended commands [n]: y
Source address or interface: 10.1.1.1
Type of service [0]:
```

```
Set DF bit in IP header? [no]:
Validate reply data? [no]:
Data pattern [0xABCD]:
Loose, Strict, Record, Timestamp, Verbose[none]:
Sweep range of sizes [n]:
Type escape sequence to abort.
Sending 5, 100-byte ICMP Echos to 192.168.1.2, timeout is 2 seconds:
Packet sent with a source address of 10.1.1.1
!!!!!
Success rate is 100 percent (5/5), round-trip min/avg/max = 31/31/32
ms

RouterA#
```

5. Configure a NAT pool on Router A. For this lab, use 172.16.1.1 to 172.16.1.10. Any address starting with 10 will be a NAT. Remember that you MUST specify the inside and outside NAT interfaces or NAT won't work:

```
RouterA#conf t
Enter configuration commands, one per line.  End with CNTL/Z.
RouterA(config)#int l0
RouterA(config-if)#ip nat inside
RouterA(config)#int l1
RouterA(config-if)#ip nat inside
RouterA(config-if)#int Serial0/1/0
RouterA(config-if)#ip nat outside
RouterA(config-if)#exit
RouterA(config)#ip nat pool 60days 172.16.1.1 172.16.1.10 netmask
255.255.255.0
RouterA(config)#ip nat inside source list 1 pool 60days
RouterA(config)#access-list 1 permit 10.1.1.0 0.0.0.255
RouterA(config)#access-list 1 permit 10.2.2.0 0.0.0.255
RouterA(config)#
```

The ip nat pool command creates the pool of addresses. You need to give the pool a name of your own choosing. The netmask command tells the router which network mask to apply to the pool.

The source list command tells the router which ACL to look at. The ACL tells the router which networks will match the NAT pool.

6. Turn on NAT debugging so you can see the translations taking place. Then issue extended pings (from L0 and L1) and check the NAT table. Your output may differ from mine due to changes in IOS. You should see two addresses from the NAT pool being used.

```
RouterA#debug ip nat

RouterA#ping
Protocol [ip]:
Target IP address: 192.168.1.2
```

```
Repeat count [5]:
Datagram size [100]:
Timeout in seconds [2]:
Extended commands [n]: y
Source address or interface: 10.1.1.1
Type of service [0]:
Set DF bit in IP header? [no]:
Validate reply data? [no]:
Data pattern [0xABCD]:
Loose, Strict, Record, Timestamp, Verbose[none]:
Sweep range of sizes [n]:
Type escape sequence to abort.
Sending 5, 100-byte ICMP Echos to 192.168.1.2, timeout is 2 seconds:
Packet sent with a source address of 10.1.1.1

NAT: s=10.1.1.1->172.16.1.1, d=192.168.1.2 [26]
!
NAT*: s=192.168.1.2, d=172.16.1.1->10.1.1.1 [16]

NAT: s=10.1.1.1->172.16.1.1, d=192.168.1.2 [27]
!
NAT*: s=192.168.1.2, d=172.16.1.1->10.1.1.1 [17]

NAT: s=10.1.1.1->172.16.1.1, d=192.168.1.2 [28]
!
NAT*: s=192.168.1.2, d=172.16.1.1->10.1.1.1 [18]

NAT: s=10.1.1.1->172.16.1.1, d=192.168.1.2 [29]
!
NAT*: s=192.168.1.2, d=172.16.1.1->10.1.1.1 [19]

NAT: s=10.1.1.1->172.16.1.1, d=192.168.1.2 [30]
!
Success rate is 100 percent (5/5), round-trip min/avg/max = 17/28/32
ms

RouterA#
NAT*: s=192.168.1.2, d=172.16.1.1->10.1.1.1 [20]

RouterA#ping
Protocol [ip]:
Target IP address: 192.168.1.2
Repeat count [5]:
Datagram size [100]:
Timeout in seconds [2]:
Extended commands [n]: y
Source address or interface: 10.2.2.2
Type of service [0]:
Set DF bit in IP header? [no]:
Validate reply data? [no]:
Data pattern [0xABCD]:
Loose, Strict, Record, Timestamp, Verbose[none]:
```

```
Sweep range of sizes [n]:
Type escape sequence to abort.
Sending 5, 100-byte ICMP Echos to 192.168.1.2, timeout is 2 seconds:
Packet sent with a source address of 10.2.2.2

NAT: s=10.2.2.2->172.16.1.2, d=192.168.1.2 [31]
!
NAT*: s=192.168.1.2, d=172.16.1.2->10.2.2.2 [21]

NAT: s=10.2.2.2->172.16.1.2, d=192.168.1.2 [32]
!
NAT*: s=192.168.1.2, d=172.16.1.2->10.2.2.2 [22]

NAT: s=10.2.2.2->172.16.1.2, d=192.168.1.2 [33]
!
NAT*: s=192.168.1.2, d=172.16.1.2->10.2.2.2 [23]

NAT: s=10.2.2.2->172.16.1.2, d=192.168.1.2 [34]
!
NAT*: s=192.168.1.2, d=172.16.1.2->10.2.2.2 [24]

NAT: s=10.2.2.2->172.16.1.2, d=192.168.1.2 [35]
!
Success rate is 100 percent (5/5), round-trip min/avg/max = 31/31/32
ms

RouterA#
NAT*: s=192.168.1.2, d=172.16.1.2->10.2.2.2 [25]

RouterA#show ip nat trans
Pro   Inside global  Inside local   Outside local     Outside global
icmp 172.16.1.1:16 10.1.1.1:16    192.168.1.2:16    192.168.1.2:16
icmp 172.16.1.1:17 10.1.1.1:17    192.168.1.2:17    192.168.1.2:17
icmp 172.16.1.1:18 10.1.1.1:18    192.168.1.2:18    192.168.1.2:18
icmp 172.16.1.1:19 10.1.1.1:19    192.168.1.2:19    192.168.1.2:19
icmp 172.16.1.1:20 10.1.1.1:20    192.168.1.2:20    192.168.1.2:20
icmp 172.16.1.2:21 10.2.2.2:21    192.168.1.2:21    192.168.1.2:21
icmp 172.16.1.2:22 10.2.2.2:22    192.168.1.2:22    192.168.1.2:22
icmp 172.16.1.2:23 10.2.2.2:23    192.168.1.2:23    192.168.1.2:23
icmp 172.16.1.2:24 10.2.2.2:24    192.168.1.2:24    192.168.1.2:24
icmp 172.16.1.2:25 10.2.2.2:25    192.168.1.2:25    192.168.1.2:25

RouterA#
```

NAT Overload

Repeat the previous lab. This time, when referring to the pool, add the `overload` command to the end of the configuration line. This instructs the router to use PAT. Leave off `Loopback1`. Please note that as Farai says, in the real world, your pool will usually have only one address or you will overload your outside interface.

```
RouterA(config)#ip nat inside source list 1 pool 60days overload
```

I've done some of the previous labs using Cisco Packet Tracer for convenience, so you will often see different output to mine. Here is a sample output from a PAT lab. You will see that the router is adding a port number to each translation. Unfortunately, you see a similar number at the end of the NAT pool labs, which is an annoyance of PAT.

```
RouterA#show ip nat tran
Inside global   Inside local        Outside local      Outside global
10.0.0.1:8759 172.16.1.129:8759 192.168.1.2:8759 192.168.1.2:8759
```

Spend time creating your own NAT labs if you really want to understand this difficult subject.

Review

DAY 17 TASKS

- Review days 14-16 and repeat the labs
- Take the challenge labs (if you wish)
- Read the ICND1 cram guide
- Take today's exam at https://www.in60days.com/free/ccnain60days/
- Spend 15 minutes on the subnetting.org website

We've covered some difficult subjects in the past three days. They are core TCP/IP topics which are sure to be featured in the exam and will also form part of your daily duties as a network engineer.

Challenge 1—DHCP Lab

Topology

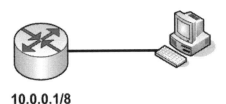

10.0.0.1/8

Instructions
Connect a PC to a router ethernet interface

1. Configure IP address 10.0.0.1 /8 onto the router.
2. Create a DHCP pool for the 10.0.0.0 /8 network.
3. Add an excluded address of the router interface.
4. Add a default router address of 192.168.1.1.
5. Configure the PC to obtain IP address via DHCP.
6. No shut the router interface.
7. Check the IP config of the PC for the IP address assignment.
8. Check the DHCP pool allocation on the router.

Challenge 2—NTP Lab

Topology

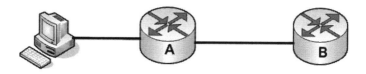

Instructions

Connect to a router with a console cable and Ethernet cable. Connect another router.

1. Configure an IP address on the two routers and ping across.
2. Configure Router A as an NTP server and Router B as an NTP client.
3. Issue a `show ntp associations` command on Router B.

Challenge 3—ACL Lab

Topology

Instructions

Connect to a router with a console cable and Ethernet cable.

1. Configure an IP address on the PC and the router in the same subnet.
2. Add a telnet username and password to the router and test by telnetting in.
3. Create an ACL to deny telnet to the router but permit all other IP traffic.
4. Test telnet again.

Challenge 4—Static NAT Lab

Topology

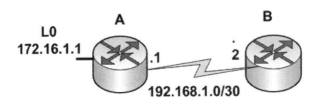

NAT 10.1.1.1

Instructions

Connect two routers together with a serial or crossover cable.

1. Add IP addresses to routers and loopback on Router A according to diagram
2. Designate NAT inside and outside interfaces
3. Add a static route on Router B to send all traffic back to Router A
4. Ping between Router A and B to test serial line (remember clock rates)
5. Create a static NAT for 172.16.1.1 to 10.1.1.1 and turn on NAT debug
6. Do an extended ping sourced from loopback 0
7. Check the NAT translation table

Challenge 4—NAT Pool Lab

Topology

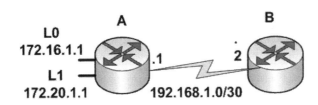

NAT 10.1.1.1-10/24

Instructions

Connect two routers together with a serial or crossover cable.

1. Add IP addresses to routers and loopback on Router A according to diagram
2. Designate NAT inside and outside interfaces
3. Add a static route on Router B to send all traffic back to Router A
4. Ping between Router A and B to test serial line (remember clock rates)
5. Create a NAT pool of 10.1.1.1-10 inclusive

6. Create two access list lines to permit the loopback networks (/16)
7. Turn on NAT debugging
8. Source two extended pings one each from L0 and L1
9. Check the NAT translation table

Challenge 5—PAT Lab

Topology

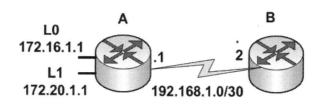

NAT 10.1.1.1

Instructions

Connect two routers together with a serial or crossover cable.

1. Add IP addresses to routers and loopback on Router A according to diagram
2. Designate NAT inside and outside interfaces
3. Add a static route on Router B to send all traffic back to Router A
4. Ping between Router A and B to test serial line (remember clock rates)
5. Create a NAT pool of 10.1.1.1 address only and overload this pool (address)
6. Create two access list lines to permit the loopback networks (/16)
7. Turn on NAT debugging
8. Source two extended pings one each from L0 and L1
9. Check the NAT translation table

Syslog and IOS

DAY 18 TASKS

- Read today's notes (below)
- Complete today's lab
- Take today's exam
- Spend 15 minutes on the subnetting.org website
- Watch the network design videos on www.in60days.com

Logging messages and events both locally and to a syslog server is a core maintenance task. Syslog is a protocol that allows a host to send event notification messages across IP networks to event message collectors—also known as syslog servers or syslog daemons. In other words, a host or a device can be configured in such a way that it generates a syslog message and forwards it to a specific syslog daemon.

Exam questions on Cisco Internetwork Operating System (IOS) includes architecture, which refers to the components which go into making the router and how they are used during the router booting process. This is all fundamental stuff to a Cisco CCNA engineer who needs to know what the various types of memory does and how to backup or manipulate them using IOS commands.

Today you will learn about the following:

- Router memory and files
- Managing the IOS
- Cisco password recovery
- File system management
- IOS licensing
- Syslog

This lesson maps to the following CCNA syllabus requirements:

- 5.1 Configure and verify device-monitoring using syslog
- 5.2 Configure and verify device management
- 5.2.a Backup and restore device configuration
- 5.2.c Licensing

- 5.2.d Logging
- 5.2.e Timezone
- 5.5 Perform device maintenance
- 5.5.a Cisco IOS upgrades and recovery (SCP, FTP, TFTP, and MD5 verify)
- 5.5.b Password recovery and configuration register
- 5.5.c File system management

ROUTER MEMORY AND FILES

Figure 18.1 below illustrates the main memory components inside the router. Each type of memory performs a different role and contains different files:

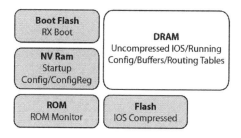

Figure 18.1—Router Memory Components

You can usually see memory banks inside the router when the cover is removed. You can often also see flash memory cards inserted into external router slots. Don't do this on routers at your office because it may invalidate the warranty if you have one. Figure 18.2 shows you the DRAM SIMMS on an old 2500 router I own.

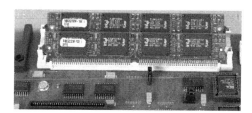

Figure 18.2—DRAM SIMMs on a Router Motherboard

Here is what each memory and file type does:

- Boot ROM—EEPROM for startup dialogue/Rommon and loads IOS. When the router boots, if no IOS file is present, it will boot into an emergency mode called Rommon, which allows some limited commands to be entered to recover the router and load another IOS. This is known as bootstrap mode and you can recognize it with either of the router prompts below:

```
>
Rommon>
```

- NVRAM—Stores router startup configuration and configuration register. The startup configuration is the file used to store the saved router configuration. It is not erased when the router reloads.
- Flash/PCMCIA—Contains IOS and some configuration files. Flash memory is also referred to as EEPROM, and Cisco IOS is usually stored here in a compressed form. You can in fact have more than one version of Cisco IOS on flash memory if there is room.
- DRAM—Also known as RAM, it stores the full IOS, running configuration, and routing tables. This is the working memory, which is erased upon the router being rebooted.
- ROM Monitor—System diagnostics and start-up. The ROM monitor has a very small code called bootstrap or boot helper in it to check for attached memory and interfaces.
- RxBoot—Mini-IOS, allows for an upload of the full IOS. It is also known as the boot loader and can be used to perform some router maintenance activities.
- Router Configuration—Although not strictly a router component, it is stored in NVRAM and pulled into DRAM on boot up. You put the configuration from DRAM into NVRAM with the copy run start command, while you put files from NVRAM into DRAM with the copy start run command.
- The Configuration Register—Sets instructions for booting. It is critical that you understand this because you will need to manipulate the configuration register on routers for use in labs (i.e., boot clean with no configuration) or to perform a password recovery. Some models differ but the two most common settings are as follows:

Boot and ignore startup configuration—0x2142

Boot normally—0x2102

```
Router(config)#config-register 0x2102
```

You can see the current configuration register setting with a show version command:

```
Router#show versionCisco Internetwork Operating System Software
IOS (tm) 2500 Software (C2500-JS-L), Version 12.1(17), RELEASE
SOFTWARE (fc1)
Copyright (c) 1986-2002 by Cisco Systems, Inc.
Compiled Wed 04-Sep-02 03:08 by kellythw Image text-base: 0x03073F40,
data-base: 0x00001000
ROM: System Bootstrap, Version 11.0(10c)XB2, PLATFORM SPECIFIC RELEASE
SOFTWARE (fc1)
BOOTLDR: 3000 Bootstrap Software (IGS-BOOT-R), Version 11.0(10c)XB2,
PLATFORM SPECIFIC RELEASE SOFTWARE (fc1)

Router uptime is 12 minutes
System returned to ROM by reload
System image file is "flash:c2500-js-l.121-17.bin"
```

```
Cisco 2500 (68030) processor (revision L) with 14336K/2048K bytes of
memory.
Processor board ID 01760497, with hardware revision 00000000 Bridging
software.
X.25 software, Version 3.0.0.
SuperLAT software (copyright 1990 by Meridian Technology Corp).
TN3270 Emulation software.
2 Ethernet/IEEE 802.3 interface(s)
2 Serial network interface(s)
32K bytes of non-volatile configuration memory.
16384K bytes of processor board System flash (Read ONLY)

Configuration register is 0x2102
```

The command also displays how long the router has been online and the reason for the last reload—handy if you need to troubleshoot a booting issue.

```
Router uptime is 12 minutes
System returned to ROM by reload
```

And the same command will display the various types of memory on the router:

```
Router#show version Cisco Internetwork Operating System Software IOS (tm)
2500 Software (C2500-IS-L), Version 12.2(4)T1, RELEASE SOFTWARE Copyright
(c) 1986-2001 by Cisco Systems, Inc.
ROM: System Bootstrap, Version 11.0(10c), SOFTWARE ← ROM code
BOOTLDR: 3000 Bootstrap Software (IGS-BOOT-R), Version 11.0(10c)
System image file is "flash:c2500-is-1_122-4_T1.bin" ← Flash image
Cisco 2522 (68030) processor CPU ← CPU
with 14336K/2048K bytes of memory. ← DRAM
Processor board ID 18086064, with hardware revision 00000003
32K bytes of non-volatile configuration memory. ← NVRAM
16384K bytes of processor System flash (Read ONLY) ← EEPROM/FLASH
```

Here is a graphical representation of the router booting process:

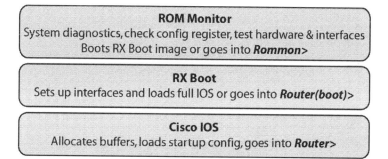

Figure 18.3—Router Booting Process

MANAGING THE IOS

Many network disasters could have been avoided with simple router and switch housekeeping. If your router configuration file is important to you and your business, then you should back it up.

If you are happy that the current running configuration of the router is going to be your working version, then you can copy this into NVRAM with the `copy run start` command.

In order to save the router configuration, you need to have a PC or server on your network running TFTP server software. You can download this free software from companies such as SolarWinds. The same process is used to upgrade the flash image.

Router configurations can be moved around the router or stored on a PC or server on the network. The running configuration on the router is stored in DRAM. Any changes to the configuration will remain in DRAM and will be lost if the router is reloaded for any reason.

You can copy the configuration onto a PC or server running TFTP server software:

```
Router#copy startup-config tftp:   ← You need to include the colon
```

You can also copy your IOS to a TFTP server. You must always do this if you are updating the router IOS to a newer version just in case of issues with the new version (often, network administrators try to fit a file onto the router which is too big for the installed memory).

```
Router#copy flash tftp:
```

The router will prompt you for the IP address of the TFTP server, which I recommend you have in the same subnet as your router. If you want to reverse the process, then you simply reverse the commands:

```
Router#copy tftp flash:
```

The issue with these commands is that most engineers use them only a couple of times a year or when there has been a network disaster. Usually, you will find that your Internet access has also gone down with your network, so you have to do this all from memory!

I strongly recommend that you do some backup and restoring of your configurations and IOS on your home network. In addition, check out my recovery lab on YouTube:

www.youtube.com/user/paulwbrowning

You can view the flash filename with the `show version` command or the `show flash` command, or you can drill down into the flash with the `dir flash:` command and this will show you all the files present in flash memory:

```
RouterA#show flash
System flash directory:
File      Length        Name/status
```

```
1         14692012      c2500-js-1.121-17.bin
[14692076 bytes used, 2085140 available, 16777216 total]
16384K bytes of processor board System flash (Read ONLY)
```

Booting Options

There are several options available when the router boots. Usually, there is one IOS image in flash memory so the router will boot using that. You may have more than one image, or the image may be too big for the flash memory to hold, so you might prefer the router to boot from a TFTP server on the network which holds the IOS.

The commands differ slightly, depending upon which boot options you want to configure. Try all of the options on a live router.

```
RouterA(config)#boot system ?
WORD          TFTP filename or URL
flash         Boot from flash memory
mop           Boot from a Decnet MOP server
ftp           Boot from server via ftp
rcp           Boot from server via rcp
tftp          Boot from tftp server
```

For flash:

```
RouterA(config)#boot system flash ? WORD System image filename <cr>
```

For TFTP:

```
Enter configuration commands, one per line. End with CNTL/Z.
RouterB(config)#boot system tftp: c2500-js-1.121-17.bin ? Hostname or
A.B.C.D Address from which to download the file <cr>
RouterA(config)#boot system tftp:
```

Booting Process and POST

A standard router boot sequence looks like this:

1. The device powers on and will first perform the POST (Power on Self Test). The POST tests the hardware in order to verify that all the components are present and healthy (interfaces, memory, CPU, ASICs, etc.). The POST is stored in and run from ROM (read only memory).
2. The bootstrap looks for and loads the Cisco IOS software. The bootstrap is a program in ROM that is used to execute programs and is responsible for finding where each IOS is located, and then loading the file. The bootstrap program locates the Cisco IOS software and loads it into RAM. Cisco IOS files can be located in one of three places: flash memory, a TFTP server, or another location indicated in the startup configuration file. By default, the IOS software is loaded from flash memory in all Cisco routers. The configuration settings must be changed to load from one of the other locations.

3. The IOS software looks for a valid configuration file in NVRAM (i.e., the startup-config file).

4. If a startup-config file is present in NVRAM, the router will load this file and the router will be operational. If a startup-config file is not present in NVRAM, the router will start the setup-mode configuration.

Any further modification on a running router will be stored on RAM, where you need to manually execute the command copy running-config startup-config to make your current configuration as a startup-config every time you boot your router.

Backing up and Restoring Device Configuration

It is wise to perform a regular backup of the startup and running configuration files (if they differ). As a reminder, the startup-config file is the saved configuration used each time the device boots, and the running-config file contains the current configuration stored inside RAM.

NOTE: Best practice is to always store configuration files on a remote server.

You can copy a configuration file to another location by using the aptly named copy command. Typically, the copy command leverages TFTP or FTP to store files but SCP can also be used. Another option is to copy the configuration file to a flash drive. As Cisco builds newer equipment, they have added USB slots so that you can insert or remove flash drives while the system is running. Here is an example of how you can do that:

```
R1#copy running-config usbflash1:running-config
Destination filename [running-config]?
3159 bytes copied in 0.544 secs (3346 bytes/sec)

R1#dir usbflash1:
Directory of usbflash1:/

! lines listing other files omitted for brevity.
   72  -rw-         2154  May 12 2017 20:10:00 +00:00   running-config

6683804228 bytes total (3685331808 bytes free)
```

You can see your available options if you append the ? to the end of the command:

```
Router#copy running-config ?
flash: Copy to flash file
ftp: Copy to current system configuration
startup-config: Copy to startup configuration
tftp: Copy to current system configuration
```

Recovering the configuration file is the reverse of saving it. You have to choose the correct name to restore the file. If you have saved your startup configuration with the date (standard practice), for example, startup-config-12June17, you need to restore it with the name startup-config, which is the file routers look for when booting.

```
Router#copy tftp: running-config
Address or name of remote host []? 10.0.0.1
Source filename []? running-config
Destination filename [running-config]?
```

Backing up and Restoring with the copy Command

The Cisco IOS `copy` command may not actually work in the way that you would expect when you execute it. Knowing this and other quirks actually makes the difference between a good network engineer and a great one. The IOS behavior quirk applies when you restore the configuration as opposed to when you back it up.

As opposed to replacing the entire running configuration file, the incoming file will compare the current configuration line by line, replacing or adding to them. For example, if you have an ACL present that has the same name, then any new lines will be added to it. This could leave you with problems if you had expected the one present on the router to be replaced. The `copy` command does not replace the running-config file when copying a configuration into RAM, but it will replace individual lines of code or add to them.

The IOS `copy tftp run` and `copy start run` commands will add lines, and the `copy run tftp` and `copy run start` commands will replace them. Please try this out for yourself if you have a router at home or Packet Tracer.

CISCO PASSWORD RECOVERY

We all forget passwords from time to time and this applies equally to routers. I've spent many hours on the phone with panicked engineers desperately trying to recover routers using the password recovery procedures. Unfortunately, it does involve power cycling the router. You will need to perform a password recovery if you have forgotten the password for enable mode and therefore can't configure the router, have bought a used router with a password left on it, or have taken over for another engineer who left the company without passing the passwords over.

The exact recovery procedure you perform will depend on the type of device you are trying to access. If you perform an Internet search for "Cisco Password Recovery for X Series," you should easily find the procedure for whatever "X" chassis you are trying to access. Switch password recovery can be much more complicated but we will not cover it here. The following is a typical example of the steps involved with password recovery on a Cisco router:

1. Power down the router.
2. If applicable, remove the compact flash that is at the back of the router.
3. Power on the router.
4. Once the `Rommon1>` prompt appears, change the configuration register to ignore NVRAM on bootup: `confreg 0x2142`.
5. Insert the compact flash, if applicable.

6. Type `reset`.
7. When you are prompted to *enter the initial configuration*, type No, and then press Enter.
8. At the `Router>` prompt, type `enable`.
9. At the `Router#` prompt, enter the `copy start run` command, and then press Enter in order to copy the startup configuration to the running configuration.

Remember, you have logged into the router with no configuration loaded, so now that you are in the router, you are loading the configuration that the router normally uses so that you can edit the password.

10. Use the `config t` command in order to enter global configuration mode.
11. Use this command to create a new username and password. In this example, the username is admin and the password is cisco: `Router(config)#username admin privilege 15 password cisco`.
12. Use this command to change the boot statement: `config-register 0x2102`.
13. Use this command in order to save the configuration: `copy run start`.
14. Reload the router, and then use the new username and password to log in to the router.

FILE SYSTEM MANAGEMENT

Cisco routers and switches have a single interface for you to manage the files stored on the system. This can include management of network files systems (e.g., FTP, TFTP, etc.), flash memory, or any endpoint that can read or write data used for the operation of the system.

Capabilities of IFS

With the Cisco IOS File System (IFS), all files can be viewed and classified from the command line interface. You can verify what type of file it is and view the file itself. For example, if you intend to load a configuration file from a remote system onto your router, you can view the contents of the configuration file first before you load it onto your router.

Regardless of the platform you are working on, the IFS commands have the same syntax. You can navigate to different directories and list the files in a directory. On newer platforms, you can create subdirectories in flash memory or on a disk.

IFS uses Uniform Resource Locators (URLs) to specify the location of a file. To specify a file on a network server, use one of the following commands:

- `ftp:[[//[username[:password]@]location]/directory]/filename`
- `rcp:[[//[username@]location]/directory]/filename`
- `tftp:[[//location]/directory]/filename`

The location can be an IP address or a hostname. For certain commands, you don't have to specify usernames and passwords if you have already set them using the following global commands:

- `ip rcmd remote-username`
- `ip ftp username`
- `ip ftp password`

That being said, when `username` is listed in a file transfer command, it will override the username specified by the `ip rcmd remote-username` or `ip ftp username` global configuration command, while `password` overrides the password specified by the `ip ftp password` global configuration command.

The following example specifies the file named c6500-j-mz.122 on the TFTP server named tftpserver.in60days.com. The file is located in the directory named /tftpboot/master.

```
tftp://tftpserver.in60days.com/master/c6500-j-mz.122
```

The following example specifies the file named dec-config on the server named ftp.in60days. com. The router uses the username admin and the password cisco to access this server via FTP.

```
ftp://admin:cisco@ftp.in60days.com/dec-config
```

Specifying Local Files

Use the `prefix:[directory/]filename` syntax to specify a file located on the router. You can use this form to specify a file in flash memory or NVRAM. For example:

- `nvram:startup-config` specifies the startup configuration in NVRAM
- `flash:configs/backup-config` specifies the file named backup-config in the configurations directory of flash memory
- `slot0:` can indicate the first PCMCIA flash memory card in slot 0

Using URL Prefixes

The list of available file systems differs by platform and operation. Use the `show file systems` EXEC command to determine which prefixes are available on your platform. Table 18.1 below shows all of the possible options:

Table 18.1—File System Prefixes

Prefix	File System
bootflash:	Boot flash memory
disk0:	Rotating media
flash:	Flash memory. This prefix is available on all platforms. For platforms that do not have a device named flash:, prefix flash: is aliased to slot0:. Therefore, you can use prefix flash: to refer to the main flash memory storage area on all platforms.
flh:	Flash load-helper log files
ftp:	FTP network server
null:	Null destination for copies. You can copy a remote file to null to determine its size.
nvram:	NVRAM
rcp:	Remote copy protocol network server
slavebootflash:	Internal flash memory on a slave route/switch processor (RSP) card of a router configured for high system availability (HSA)
slavenvram:	NVRAM on a slave RSP card of a router configured for HSA
slaveslot0:	First PCMCIA card on a slave RSP card of a router configured for HSA
slaveslot1:	Second PCMCIA card on a slave RSP card of a router configured for HSA
slot0:	First PCMCIA flash memory card
slot1:	Second PCMCIA flash memory card
system:	Contains the system memory, including the running configuration
tftp:	TFTP network server
xmodem:	Obtains the file from a network machine using the Xmodem protocol
ymodem:	Obtains the file from a network machine using the Ymodem protocol

Listing of the Files in a File System

You can obtain a listing of the files in a file system using the help feature. In the following example, the router lists all of the files in the NVRAM:

```
Router#show file info nvram:?
nvram:old-config nvram:startup-config nvram:archive-config
```

Displaying Information About Files

You can display a list of the contents of a file system before manipulating its contents. For example, before copying a new configuration file to flash memory, you may want to verify that the file system does not already contain a configuration file with the same name.

To display information about files in a file system, use the command in Table 4 in EXEC mode, as needed:

```
Router#dir [/all] [filesystem:][filename]
```

The following example compares the different commands used to display information about files for the PCMCIA card in the first slot. Note that deleted files will also appear if you use the dir /all command.

```
Router#dir slot0:
Directory of slot0:/
  1 -rw-   4720148  Aug 29 1997 17:49:36 cisco/nitro/c6500-j-mz
  2 -rw-   4767328  Oct 01 1997 18:42:53 c6500-js-mz
  5 -rw-       639  Oct 02 1997 12:09:32 view
  7 -rw-       639  Oct 02 1997 12:37:13 archive
20578304 bytes total (3104544 bytes free)
```

Displaying a File

It is often very helpful to be able to display the contents of any readable file, including a file on a remote file system. For example, if you wanted to view a new running configuration on a remote system prior to transferring it, you could run the more command to view the code and ensure that it's what you want to load on your system:

```
Router#more [/ascii | /binary | /ebcdic] [file-url]
```

The following example displays the contents of a configuration file on a TFTP server:

```
Router#more tftp://serverA/paris/savedconfig
!
! Saved configuration on server
!
version 11.3
service timestamps log datetime localtime
service linenumber
service udp-small-servers
service pt-vty-logging
!
End
```

Deleting Files

When you delete a file, the router marks the file as deleted, but it does not erase the file. This feature allows you to recover a deleted file. To delete a file from a specified flash memory device, use the delete command.

```
Router#delete [device:][filename]
```

The following example deletes the file named mybadconfig from a flash memory card inserted in slot 1:

```
delete slot1:mybadconfig
```

Recovering Deleted Files

To undelete a deleted file on a flash memory device, use the `dir` and `undelete` commands.

```
Router#dir /all [filesystem:]
Router#undelete index [filesystem:]
```

You must undelete a file by its index because you can have multiple deleted files with the same name.

The following example recovers the deleted file whose index number is 2 to the flash memory card inserted in slot 1:

```
undelete 2 slot1:
```

Permanently Deleting Files

To permanently delete files on a flash memory device, use the squeeze command.

```
Router#squeeze filesystem:
```

When you issue the `squeeze` command, the router copies all valid files to the beginning of flash memory and erases all files marked "deleted."

IOS LICENSING

Since the creation of the first Internetwork Operating System (IOS) for the first Cisco router, Cisco have followed the same method, each model of router having its own version and release built. Major versions were given the numbering system 12.0. Changes to these versions were then numbered 12.1, 12.2, etc. Within those versions were releases fixing bugs and adding support for modules and other features, such as 12.1(1a).

Unfortunately, as support was added and bugs fixed, the releases were split into trains so each model had its own IOS, which led to various versions and releases. If you wanted a security or voice image, then you would have to buy that specific image with the correct version for your router, with the correct feature support and bug fixes.

Cisco eventually released entire training tools and presentations so you could understand the naming conventions, release levels, and supported modules. As the software was tested and matured it was also given different names, such as ED for Early Deployment and GD for General Deployment! It all got very confusing for customers. Here is an image from some of Cisco's documentation explaining IOS releases:

Special Releases

Cisco.com

- Are similar to rebuilds but instead of quick fixes, special releases introduce new features or additional platform support to quickly meet market demands.
- A branch from a train code base.
- Does not conform to a strict naming convention. They use a double letter after the release number.
- The first letter could be a one-time release, the train identifier, or the technology identifier.
- The second letter could be a sequential revision or a one-time release.
- Special releases do not have an EoL, they are integrated back into the parent train.

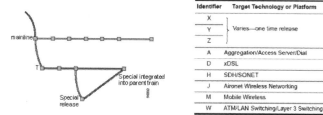

Identifier	Target Technology or Platform
X	
Y	Varies—one time release
Z	
A	Aggregation/Access Server/Dial
D	xDSL
H	SDH/SONET
J	Aironet Wireless Networking
M	Mobile Wireless
W	ATM/LAN Switching/Layer 3 Switching

Figure 18.4—IOS Special Releases (Image © Cisco Systems Inc.)

If you think it caused some confusion among customers you would be right. I can't tell you how many times while working at Cisco TAC I had to deal with confused and angry customers who had bought a router and IOS only to find it didn't support the features they required for their network infrastructure. Remember also that for large, enterprise networks, an IOS upgrade may have to be arranged months in advance during a tiny maintenance window.

A New Model

Cisco have now changed their IOS model and jumped from IOS release 12 to 15. Currently, there is one universal image built per model. This image features all the feature sets you require, but in order to gain access to the advanced features you need to buy the appropriate license and verify it on the actual device. This was done for convenience for both Cisco and their customers and to prevent theft or unauthorized sharing of Cisco software, which costs a considerable amount to develop, as you can imagine.

All new models bought from Cisco (resellers) come with a base image installed and the license enabled on the router. If the customer wants to enable advanced security or voice features, then these features need to be enabled. This is usually achieved using a free Cisco application called Cisco License Manager (CLM). You can easily search for this on Cisco.com:

Figure 18.5—Cisco License Manager Download Page

CLM can be installed on a server or host enabling the customer to interface between their devices and Cisco's license portal. CLM takes care of tracking current licenses and features per device using a GUI.

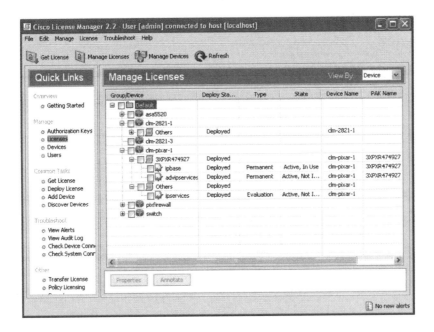

Figure 18.6—Cisco License Manager GUI (Image © Cisco Systems Inc.)

License Activation

Each model of Cisco router (that supports licensing) has been allocated a unique identifying number known as the unique device identifier (UDI). This is comprised of the serial number

(SN) and the product identification (PID). Issue the `show license udi` command to see this information.

```
Router#show license ?
  all     Show license all information
  detail  Show license detail information
  feature Show license feature information
  udi     Show license udi information

Router#show license udi
Device#   PID              SN            UDI
-------------------------------------------------------------------
*0        CISCO1941/K9     FTX15240000   CISCO1941/K9:FTX15240000
```

You would enter the UDI when registering the IOS with Cisco at www.cisco.com/go/license. You would also add the license you were issued by the reseller when you paid for the IOS (Product Authorization Key or PAK), which is checked against the UDI. If this is verified, you are emailed a license key by Cisco.

You can see below which features have been activated. The `ipbasek9` feature will always be enabled.

```
Router#show license all
License Store: Primary License Storage
StoreIndex: 0    Feature: ipbasek9              Version: 1.0
         License Type: Permanent
         License State: Active, In Use
         License Count: Non-Counted
         License Priority: Medium

License Store: Evaluation License Storage
StoreIndex: 0    Feature: securityk9            Version: 1.0
         License Type: Evaluation
         License State: Inactive
            Evaluation total period: 208 weeks 2 days
            Evaluation period left: 208 weeks 2 days
         License Count: Non-Counted
         License Priority: None
StoreIndex: 1    Feature: datak9                Version: 1.0
         License Type:
         License State: Inactive
            Evaluation total period: 208 weeks 2 days
            Evaluation period left: 208 weeks 2 days
         License Count: Non-Counted
         License Priority: None
```

The `show license feature` command will print a summary of features enabled:

```
Router#show license feature
Feature name    Enforcement   Evaluation   Subscription   Enabled
ipbasek9        no            no           no             yes
securityk9      yes           yes          no             no
datak9          yes           no           no             no
```

Once the license has been verified, the license key must be added to the router via the USB drive or network server and the `license install [url]` command issued from the command line. Notice the ".lic" filename.

```
Router#dir usbflash0:

Directory of usbflash0:/

    1  -rw-         3064  Apr 18 2013 03:31:18
+00:00   FHH1216P07R_20090528163510702.lic

255537152 bytes total (184524800 bytes free)
Router#
Router#license install  usbflash0:FHH1216P07R_2009052816351070.lic
Installing...Feature:datak9...Successful:Supported
1/1 licenses were successfully installed
0/1 licenses were existing licenses
0/1 licenses were failed to install
Router#
*Jun 25 11:18:20.234: %LICENSE-6-INSTALL: Feature datak9 1.0 was
installed in this device. UDI=CISCO2951:FHH1216P07R; StoreIndex=0:Primary
License Storage
*Jun 25 11:18:20.386: %IOS_LICENSE_IMAGE_APPLICATION-6-LICENSE_LEVEL:
Module name = c2951 Next reboot level = datak9 and License = datak9
```

The router will now have to be rebooted to activate the new feature set.

SYSLOG LOGGING

A syslog daemon or server is an entity that listens to the syslog messages that are sent to it. You cannot configure a syslog daemon to ask a specific device to send it syslog messages. In other words, if a specific device has no ability to generate syslog messages, then a syslog daemon cannot do anything about it. In the real world, corporations typically use SolarWinds (or similar) software for syslog capturing. Additionally, freeware such as the Kiwi Syslog daemon is also available for syslog capturing.

Syslog uses User Datagram Protocol (UDP) as the underlying transport mechanism, so the data packets are unsequenced and unacknowledged. While UDP does not have the overhead included in TCP, this means that on a heavily used network, some packets may be dropped and therefore logging information will be lost. However, Cisco IOS software allows administrators to configure multiple syslog servers for redundancy. A syslog solution is comprised of two main elements: a syslog server and a syslog client.

The syslog client sends syslog messages to the syslog server using UDP as the Transport Layer protocol, specifying a destination port of 514. These messages cannot exceed 1024 bytes in size; however, there is no minimum length. All syslog messages contain three distinct parts: the priority, the header, and the message.

The priority of a syslog message represents both the facility and the severity of the message. This number is an 8-bit number. The first 3 least significant bits represent the severity of the message (with 3 bits, you can represent 8 different severities) and the other 5 bits represent the facility. You can use these values to apply filters on the events in the syslog daemon.

NOTE: Keep in mind that these values are generated by the applications on which the event is generated, not by the syslog server itself.

The values set by Cisco IOS devices are listed and described below in Table 18.2 (please memorize the levels and level names):

Table 18.2—Cisco IOS Software Syslog Priority Levels and Definitions

Level	Level Name	Syslog Definition	Description
0	Emergencies	LOG_EMERG	This level is used for the most severe error conditions, which render the system unusable.
1	Alerts	LOG_ALERT	This level is used to indicate conditions that need immediate attention from administrators.
2	Critical	LOG_CRIT	This level is used to indicate critical conditions, which are less critical than Alerts but still require administrator intervention.
3	Errors	LOG_ERR	This level is used to indicate errors within the system; however, these errors do not render the system unusable.
4	Warnings	LOG_WARNING	This level is used to indicate warning conditions about system operations that did not complete successfully.
5	Notifications	LOG_NOTICE	This level is used to indicate state changes within the system (e.g., a routing protocol adjacency transitioning to a down state).
6	Informational	LOG_INFO	This level is used to indicate informational messages about the normal operation of the system.
7	Debugging	LOG_DEBUG	This level is used to indicate real-time (debugging) information that is typically used for troubleshooting purposes.

In syslog, the facility is used to represent the source that generated the message. This source can be a process on the local device, an application, or even an operating system. Facilities are represented by numbers (integers). In Cisco IOS software, there are eight local use facilities that can be used by processes and applications (as well as the device itself) for sending syslog messages. By default, Cisco IOS devices use facility local7 to send syslog messages. However, it should be noted that most Cisco devices provide options to change the default facility level. In Cisco IOS software, the `logging facility [facility]` global configuration command can be used to specify the syslog facility.

The options available with this command are as follows:

```
R1(config)#logging facility ?
  auth    Authorization system
  cron    Cron/at facility
  daemon  System daemons
  kern    Kernel
  local0  Local use
  local1  Local use
  local2  Local use
  local3  Local use
  local4  Local use
  local5  Local use
  local6  Local use
  local7  Local use
  lpr     Line printer system
  mail    Mail system
  news    USENET news
  sys10   System use
  sys11   System use
  sys12   System use
  sys13   System use
  sys14   System use
  sys9    System use
  syslog  Syslog itself
  user    User process
  uucp    Unix-to-Unix copy system
```

To send messages via syslog, you must perform the following sequence of steps on the device:

1. Globally enable logging on the router or switch using the `logging on` configuration command. By default, in Cisco IOS software, logging is enabled; however, it is only enabled to send messages to the console. The `logging on` command is a mandatory requirement when sending messages to any destination other than the console.
2. Specify the severity of messages to send to the syslog server using the `logging trap [severity]` global configuration command. You can specify the severity numerically or using the equivalent severity name.
3. Specify one or more syslog server destinations using the `logging [address]` or `logging host [address]` global configuration commands.
4. Optionally, specify the source IP address used in syslog messages using the `logging source-interface [name]`. This is a common practice on devices with multiple interfaces configured. If this command is not specified, then the syslog message will contain the IP address of the router or switch interface used to reach the server. If there are multiple interfaces for redundancy, this address may change when the primary path (interface) is down. Therefore, it is typically set to a Loopback interface.

The following configuration example illustrates how to send all informational (level 6) and below messages to a syslog server with the IP address 192.168.1.254:

```
R2(config)#logging on
R2(config)#logging trap informational
R2(config)#logging 192.168.1.254
```

This configuration can be validated using the show logging command, as illustrated below:

```
R2#show logging
Syslog logging: enabled (11 messages dropped, 1 messages rate-limited, 0
flushes, 0 overruns, xml disabled, filtering disabled)
    Console logging: disabled
    Monitor logging: level debugging, 0 messages logged, xml
disabled,filtering disabled
    Buffer logging: disabled, xml disabled, filtering disabled
    Logging Exception size (4096 bytes)
    Count and timestamp logging messages: disabled

No active filter modules.

    Trap logging: level informational, 33 message lines logged
        Logging to 192.168.1.254(global) (udp port 514, audit disabled,
link up), 2 message lines logged, xml disabled,filtering disabled
```

When configuring logging in general, it is important to ensure that the router or switch clocks reflect the actual current time, which allows you to correlate the fault data. Inaccurate or incorrect time stamps on log messages make the fault and problem isolation using a filtration and correlation process very difficult and very time-consuming. In Cisco IOS devices, the system clock can be configured manually or the device can be configured to synchronize its clock with a Network Time Protocol (NTP) server. These clock option is discussed in the following section.

Manual clock or time configuration is fine if you have only a few internetwork devices in your network. In Cisco IOS software, the system time is configured using the clock set hh:mm:ss [day & month | month & day] [year] privileged EXEC command. It is not configured or specified in Global Configuration mode. The following configuration example illustrates how to set the system clock to October 20 12:15 AM:

```
R2#clock set 12:15:00 20 october 2010
```

Alternatively, the same configuration could be implemented on the router as follows:

```
R2#clock set 12:15:00 october 20 2010
```

Following this configuration, the show clock command can be used to view the system time:

```
R2#show clock
12:15:19.419 UTC Wed Oct 20 2010
```

One interesting observation of note is that when the system time is configured manually or set using the clock set command, it defaults to the GMT (UTC) time zone, as can be seen above. In order to ensure that the system clock reflects the correct time zone, for those who are not in the GMT time zone, you must use the `clock timezone [time zone name] [GMT offset]` global configuration command. For example, the United States has six different time zones, each with a different GMT offset. These time zones are Eastern Time, Central Time, Mountain Time, Pacific Time, Hawaii Time, and Alaska Time.

In addition, some of the time zones use Standard Time and Daylight Saving Time. Given this, it is important to ensure that the system time is set correctly (Standard or Daylight Saving) on all devices when manually configuring the system clock. The following configuration example illustrates how to set the system clock to 12:40 AM on October 20 for the Central Standard Time (CST) time zone, which is six hours behind GMT:

```
R2#config t
Enter configuration commands, one per line.  End with CNTL/Z.
R2(config)#clock timezone CST -6
R2(config)#end
R2#clock set 12:40:00 october 20 2010
```

Following this configuration, the system clock on the local router now shows the following:

```
R2#show clock
12:40:17.921 CST Wed Oct 20 2010
```

NOTE: If you use the `clock set` command before the `clock timezone` command, then the time that you specified using the `clock set` command will be offset by using the `clock timezone` command. For example, assume that the configuration commands that are used in the example above were entered on the router as follows:

```
R2#clock set 12:40:00 october 20 2010
R2#config t
Enter configuration commands, one per line.  End with CNTL/Z.
R2(config)#clock timezone CST -6
R2(config)#end
```

Because the `clock set` command is used first, the output of the `show clock` command on the router would show the system clock offset by 6 hours, as specified using the `clock timezone` command. This behavior is illustrated in the following output on the same router:

```
R2#show clock
06:40:52.181 CST Wed Oct 20 2010
```

NOTE: Cisco IOS routers and switches can be configured to switch automatically to summertime (Daylight Saving Time) using the `clock summer-time zone recurring [week day month hh:mm week day month hh:mm [offset]]` global configuration command. This negates the need to have to adjust the system clock manually on all manually configured devices during Standard Time and Daylight Saving Time periods.

The second method of setting or synchronizing the system clock is to use a Network Time Protocol (NTP) server as a reference time source. This is the preferred method in larger networks with more than just a few internetwork devices. We covered NTP earlier.

After the system clock has been set, either manually or via NTP, it is important to ensure that the logs sent to the server contain the correct timestamps. This is performed using the service timestamps log [datetime | uptime] global configuration command. The [datetime] keyword supports the following self-explanatory additional sub keywords:

```
R2(config)#service timestamps log datetime ?
  localtime      Use local time zone for timestamps
  msec           Include milliseconds in timestamp
  show-timezone  Add time zone information to timestamp
  year           Include year in timestamp
  <cr>
```

The [uptime] keyword has no additional sub keywords and configures the local router to include only the system uptime as the timestamp for sent messages. The following configuration example illustrates how to configure the local router to include the local time, millisecond information, and the time zone for all messages:

```
R2#configure terminal
Enter configuration commands, one per line.  End with CNTL/Z.
R2(config)#logging on
R2(config)#logging console informational
R2(config)#logging host 150.1.1.254
R2(config)#logging trap informational
R2(config)#service timestamps log datetime localtime msec show-timezone
```

Following this configuration, the local router console would print the following message:

```
Oct 20 02:14:10.519 CST: %SYS-5-CONFIG_I: Configured from console by
console
Oct 20 02:14:11.521 CST: %SYS-6-LOGGINGHOST_STARTSTOP: Logging to host
150.1.1.254 started - CLI initiated
```

In addition, the syslog daemon on server 150.1.1.254 would also reflect the same, as illustrated in the Kiwi Syslog Manager screenshot in Figure 18.7 below:

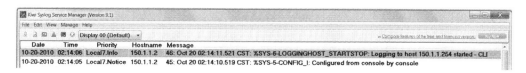

Figure 18.7—Configuring Log Timestamps

Please take today's exam at https://www.in60days.com/free/ccnain60days/

DAY 18 LABS

Logging

Configure logging on a Cisco router:

- Choose the logging facility local3: logging facility local2
- Issue the global `logging on` command
- Choose logging severity informational
- Configure a free syslog server on a PC and connect it to the router
- Issue the `logging [address]` command to specify the syslog server
- Specify the `logging source-interface` command
- Verify the `show logging` command
- Configure the `service timestamps log datetime localtime msec show-timezone` command
- Verify the syslog messages on the PC

Copy IOS and Startup Configuration

Topology

Gig0/0   Fa0

1941   Server - PT

Purpose

Learn how to update the Cisco IOS version and save the startup configuration. Packet Tracer offers an easy solution by allowing you to connect a router to a server using a crossover cable and enabling TFTP on the server. Packet Tracer TFTP server offers a limited number of IOS versions so check your router model matches what is available.

Walkthrough

1. Add IP addresses in the same subnet to the router and server interfaces.

```
Router(config)#int g0/0
Router(config-if)#ip add 192.168.1.1 255.255.255.0
Router(config-if)#no shut
```

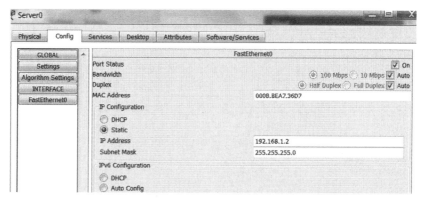

```
Router#ping 192.168.1.2
Type escape sequence to abort.
Sending 5, 100-byte ICMP Echos to 192.168.1.2, timeout is 2 seconds:
.!!!!
Success rate is 80 percent (4/5), round-trip min/avg/max = 0/0/1 ms
```

2. Check the IOS flash file on the router.

```
Router#dir flash:
Directory of flash0:/
    3  -rw-   33591768 <no date>  c1900-universalk9-mz.SPA.151-4.M4.bin
    2  -rw-      28282       <no date>  sigdef-category.xml
    1  -rw-     227537       <no date>  sigdef-default.xml

255744000 bytes total (221896413 bytes free)
Router#
```

3. Check that TFTP server software is enabled on the server (and note that there are no IOS images for the 1900 router).

4. Copy the IOS from the router to the TFTP server.

```
Router#copy flash: tftp:
```

```
Source filename []? c1900-universalk9-mz.SPA.151-4.M4.bin
Address or name of remote host []? 192.168.1.2
Destination filename [c1900-universalk9-mz.SPA.151-4.M4.bin]?

Writing c1900-universalk9-mz.SPA.151-4.M4.bin...!!!!!!!!!!!!!!!!!!!!!!!!!
!!!!!!!!!!!!!!!!!!!!!!!!!!!!!!!!!!!!!!!!!!!!!!!!!!!!!!!!!!!!!!!!!!!!!!!!!!!!
!!!!!!!!!!!!!!!!!!!!!!!!
[OK - 33591768 bytes]

33591768 bytes copied in 0.57 secs (6187713 bytes/sec)
Router#
```

5.   Note that the IOS file is now present on the TFTP server. You may need to come out
     of the page and return in order to refresh the contents.

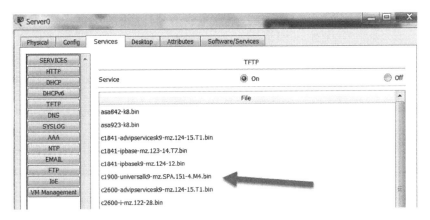

6.   Now copy the startup configuration file to the TFTP server. You may need to issue a
     copy run start first if it's never been saved. You can change the name of the file so
     it's more memorable so long as you copy it back with the original name.

```
Router#copy startup-config tftp
%% Non-volatile configuration memory invalid or not present
Router#copy run start
Destination filename [startup-config]?
Building configuration...
[OK]
Router#copy startup-config tftp:
Address or name of remote host []? 192.168.1.2
Destination filename [Router-confg]? config16may

Writing startup-config...!!
[OK - 620 bytes]

620 bytes copied in 0 secs
Router#
```

7.   Check the TFTP files again.

Router Security

DAY 19 TASKS

- Read today's notes (below)
- Complete today's lab
- Review yesterdays notes and lab
- Take today's exam
- Spend 15 minutes on the subnetting.org website

Many of the steps you need to follow to secure your router also apply to switches running IOS so please review Day 9 (switch security) in conjunction with today's tasks. You can disregard securing VLANs, Trunks and switch ports of course.

My first job at Cisco was on the core team. Our role involved helping customers with access control lists, IOS upgrades, disaster recovery, and related tasks. One of the first things which struck me was how many engineers didn't lock down their routers with a password. Many of those who did used the password "password" or "cisco"—probably two of the most easily guessed, I would imagine!

In this section of the guide, we will look at the basic steps you should take on every network to protect your routers.

Today you will learn about the following:

- Securing the router

This module maps to the following CCNA syllabus requirements:

- 5.4 Configure, verify, and troubleshoot basic device hardening
- 5.4.a Local authentication
- 5.4.b Secure password
- 5.4.c Access to device
- 5.4.c. (i) Source address
- 5.4.c. (ii) Telnet/SSH
- 5.4.d Login banner

SECURING THE ROUTER

Protecting Physical Access

Strange that when you consider the disastrous consequences of losing network access for a business, you often find their router sitting underneath somebody's desk!

Network equipment should be stored in a secure room with keypad access, or at least lock and key access. Cisco routers can be very valuable pieces of equipment, and they are attractive targets to thieves. The larger the network, the more valuable the equipment, and the higher the need to protect the data and router configuration files.

Console Access

The console port is designed to give physical access to the router to permit initial configurations and disaster recovery. Anybody having console access can completely wipe or reconfigure the files, so, for this reason, the console port should be protected with a password by adding either a password or a local username and password, as illustrated below:

- Add a password:

```
Router(config)#line console 0
Router(config-line)#password cisco
Router(config-line)#login
```

- Or add a local username and password:

```
Router(config)#username paul password cisco
Router(config)#line console 0
Router(config-line)#login local
```

You can also create a timeout on the console (and VTY) lines so that it disconnects after a certain period of time. The default is 5 minutes.

```
Router(config)#line console 0

Router(config-line)#exec-timeout ?
  <0-35791>  Timeout in minutes

Router(config-line)#exec-timeout 2 ?
  <0-2147483>  Timeout in seconds
  <cr>

Router(config-line)#exec-timeout 2 30
```

Telnet Access

You can't actually Telnet into a router unless somebody adds a password to the Telnet (vty) lines. As above, you can add a password to the VTY lines or tell the router to look for a local username and password (in the configuration file or username and password stored on a RADIUS/TACACS server), as shown below:

```
Router(config-line)#line vty 0 15
Router(config-line)#password cisco
Router(config-line)#login ← or login local
```

The output below is a Telnet session from one router to another. You can see the hostname change when you get Telnet access. The password will not show as you type it:

```
Router1#telnet 192.168.1.2
Trying 192.168.1.2 ...Open
User Access Verification
Username: paul
Password:
Router2>
```

If you have a security IOS image, you can configure the router to permit only SSH access rather than Telnet. The benefit of this is that all data is encrypted. If you try to Telnet after SSH has been enabled, the connection will be terminated:

```
Router1(config)#line vty 0 15
Router1(config-line)#transport input ssh
Router2#telnet 192.168.1.2
Trying 192.168.1.2 ...Open
[Connection to 192.168.1.2 closed by foreign host]
```

Protecting Enable Mode

Enable mode gives configuration access to the router, so you will want to protect this also. You can configure an enable secret or an enable password. In fact, you could have both at the same time, but this is a bad idea.

An enable password is unencrypted, so it can be seen in the router configuration. An enable secret is given level 5 (MD5) encryption, which is hard to break. Newer IOS releases (starting with 15.0(1)S) can also use level 4 (SHA256) encryption, which is superior to MD5 encryption (this level 5 encryption will be deprecated eventually). You can add the command service password encryption to your enable password, but this can be cracked easily because it is level 7 encryption (i.e., low security; Cisco calls it "over the shoulder security," as it only requires someone looking over your shoulder to memorise a slightly harder phrase and then crack it using password 7 decryption tools on the Internet). You can see level 7 and level 5 encryption in the output below:

```
Router(config)#enable password cisco
Router(config)#exit
Router#show run
enable password cisco

Router(config)#enable password cisco
```

```
Router(config)#service password-encryption
Router#show run
enable password 7 0822455D0A16

Router(config)#enable secret cisco
Router(config)#exit
Router#show run
enable secret 5 $1$mERr$hx5rVt7rPNoS4wqbXKX7mO
```

Bear in mind that if you forget the enable password, you will have to perform a password recovery on the router or switch. Google the term for the particular model you are using because the process differs. For routers, it involves reloading the device, pressing the designated break key on your keyboard, setting the configuration register to skip the startup configuration file (usually to 0x2142), and then issuing a copy start run command so you can create a new password.

For switches, it is a bit more complicated (again, Google the term for the particular model you are using), but it can also be done using a little trick—hold down the MODE button for eight seconds while powering on the switch. The switch will boot up with a blank configuration, and the last startup configuration will be saved to the flash in the file named config.text. renamed so it can be copied back to running configuration and modified with another password.

Protecting User Access

Cisco IOS offers the ability to give users individual passwords and usernames, as well as access to a restricted list of commands. This would be useful if you have tiers of network support. An example of this is shown in the following output:

```
RouterA#config term
Enter configuration commands, one per line. End with CNTL/Z.
RouterA(config)#username paul password cisco
RouterA(config)#username stuart password hello
RouterA(config)#username davie password football
RouterA(config)#line vty 0 4
RouterA(config-line)#login local
RouterA(config-line)#exit
RouterA(config)#exit
```

You can specify access levels for user accounts on the router. You may want, for example, junior network team members to be able to use only some basic troubleshooting commands. It is also worth remembering that Cisco routers have two modes of password security, User mode (Exec) and Privileged mode (Enable).

Cisco routers have 16 different privilege levels (0 to 15) available to configure, where 15 is full access, as illustrated below:

```
RouterA#conf t
Enter configuration commands, one per line. End with CNTL/Z.
RouterA(config)#username support privilege 4 password soccer
```

```
    LINE Initial keywords of the command to modify
RouterA(config)#privilege exec level 4 ping
RouterA(config)#privilege exec level 4 traceroute
RouterA(config)#privilege exec level 4 show ip interface brief
RouterA(config)#line console 0
RouterA(config-line)#password basketball
RouterA(config-line)#login local  ← password is needed
RouterA(config-line)#^z
```

The support person logs in to the router and tries to go into configuration mode, but this command and any other command not available are not valid and cannot be seen:

```
RouterA con0 is now available
Press RETURN to get started.
User Access Verification
Username: support
Password:
RouterA#config t  ← not allowed to use this command
          ^
% Invalid input detected at '^' marker.
```

You can see the default privilege levels at the router prompts:

```
Router>show privilege
Current privilege level is 1
Router>en
Router#show privilege
Current privilege level is 15
```

Updating the IOS

Admittedly, updating the IOS can sometimes introduce new bugs or problems into your network, so it is best practice to do this on the advice of Cisco if you have a TAC support contract. In general, though, keeping your IOS up to date is highly recommended.

Updating your IOS:

- Fixes known bugs
- Closes security vulnerabilities
- Offers enhanced features and IOS capabilities

Router Logging

Routers offer the ability to log events. They can send the log messages to your screen or a server if you wish. You should log router messages, and there are eight levels of logging severity available (you need to know them for the exam), as shown in bold in the output below:

```
logging buffered ?
<0-7>Logging severity level
alerts—Immediate action needed (severity=1)
```

```
critical—Critical conditions (severity=2)
debugging—Debugging messages (severity=7)
emergencies—System is unusable (severity=0)
errors—Error conditions (severity=3)
informational—Informational messages (severity=6)
notifications—Normal but significant conditions (severity=5)
warnings—Warning conditions (severity=4)
```

You can send the logging messages to several places:

```
Router(config)#logging ?
  A.B.C.D    IP address of the logging host
  buffered   Set buffered logging parameters
  console    Set console logging parameters
  host       Set syslog server IP address and parameters
  on         Enable logging to all enabled destinations
  trap       Set syslog server logging level
  userinfo   Enable logging of user info on privileged mode enabling
```

Logging messages will usually be displayed on the screen when you are consoled into the router. This can prove somewhat annoying if you are typing configuration commands. Here, I'm typing a command (underlined) when it's interrupted by a console logging message:

```
Router(config)#int f0/1
Router(config-if)#no shut
Router(config-if)#end
Router#
*Jun 27 02:06:59.951: %SYS-5-CONFIG_I: Configured from console by console
show ver
*Jun 27 02:07:01.151: %LINK-3-UPDOWN: Interface FastEthernet0/1, changed
state to up
```

You can either turn off logging messages with the `no logging console` command or you can set them to not interrupt as you type with the `logging synchronous` command, which re-enters the line you were typing before being interrupted by the logging message (also available on VTY lines).

```
Router(config)#line con 0
Router(config-line)#logging synchronous
Router(config-line)#exit
Router(config)#int f0/1
Router(config-if)#shut
Router(config-if)#exit
Router(config)#
*Jun 27 02:12:46.143: %LINK-5-CHANGED: Interface FastEthernet0/1, changed
state to administratively down
Router(config)#exit
```

It's worth mentioning here that you won't see console output when you are Telnetted (or using SSH) into the router. If you want to see logging messages when Telnetted in, then issue the `terminal monitor` command.

Simple Network Management Protocol (SNMP)

SNMP is a service you can use to manage your network remotely. It consists of a central station maintained by an administrator running the SNMP management software and smaller files (agents) on each of your network devices, including routers, switches, and servers.

Several vendors have designed SNMP software, including HP, Cisco, IBM, and SolarWinds. There are also open source versions available. This software allows you to monitor bandwidth and activity on devices, such as logins and port status.

You can remotely configure or shut down ports and devices using SNMP. You can also configure it to send alerts when certain conditions are met, such as high bandwidth or ports going down. We will cover SNMP in more detail on Day 52 because it is part of the ICND2 syllabus.

External Authentication Methods

Rather than store usernames and passwords locally, you can use a server which typically runs either AAA or TACACS+. The advantage to this method is not having to manually enter usernames and passwords on each individual router and switch. Instead, they are stored on the server database.

TACACS+ stands for Terminal Access Controller Access Control System Plus. It is a Cisco proprietary protocol that uses TCP port 49. TACACS+ provides access control for network devices, including routers, and network access servers via one or more centralized servers.

RADIUS stands for Remote Authentication Dial-In User Service. It is a system of distributed network security that secures remote access to the network and a client/server protocol that uses UDP. RADIUS is open standard.

If you have TACACS+ or RADIUS, you may wish to enable Authentication, Authorization, and Accounting (AAA). AAA is installed on a server and monitors a database of user accounts for the network. Users' access, protocols, connections, and disconnect reasons, as well as many other features, can be monitored.

Routers and switches can be configured to query the server when a user attempts to log in. The server then validates the user. We cover this in more detail in the ICND2 section.

Router Clock and NTP

The time on a switch is often overlooked; however, it is very important. When you encounter security violations, SNMP traps, or logging of events, it uses a timestamp. If the time on your switch is incorrect, it will be difficult figuring out when the event happened. We've already covered this in detail.

Now take today's exam at https://www.in60days.com/free/ccnain60days/

DAY 19 LAB

Basic Router Security

Topology

Purpose

Learn some basic steps to take to lock down your router.

Walkthrough

1. Log in using Protect Enable mode with an enable secret password. Test this by logging out of Privileged mode and then logging back in.

```
Router#conf t
Enter configuration commands, one per line.  End with CNTL/Z.
Router(config)#enable secret cisco
Router(config)#exit
Router#
%SYS-5-CONFIG_I: Configured from console by console
Router#exi
Router con0 is now available

Press RETURN to get started.
Router>en
Password:
Router#
```

2. Set an enable password and then add service password encryption. This is rarely done on live routers because it is not secure.

```
Router(config)#no enable secret
Router(config)#enable password cisco
Router(config)#service password-encryption
Router(config)#exit
Router#
%SYS-5-CONFIG_I: Configured from console by console

Router#show run
Building configuration...

Current configuration: 480 bytes
!
version 12.4
no service timestamps log datetime msec
no service timestamps debug datetime msec
service password-encryption
```

```
!
hostname Router
!
enable password 7 0822455D0A16
```

3. Protect the Telnet lines. Set a local username and password and have users enter this when connecting to the router.

```
Router(config)#line vty 0 ?
  <1-15>  Last Line number
  <cr>
Router(config)#line vty 0 15
Router(config-line)#login local
Router(config-line)#exit
Router(config)#username in60days password cisco
Router(config)#
```

You have tested Telnet before, but feel free to add a PC and Telnet into the router so you are prompted for a username and password.

4. Protect the console port with a password. Set one directly on the console port.

```
Router(config)#line console 0
Router(config-line)#password cisco
```

You can test this by unplugging and plugging your console lead back into the router. You can also protect the auxiliary port (used for modem access) on your router if you have one:

```
Router(config)#line aux 0
Router(config-line)#password cisco
```

5. Protect the Telnet lines by permitting only SSH traffic in. You can also permit only SSH traffic outbound. You will need a security image for this command to work.

```
Router(config)#line vty 0 15
Router(config-line)#transport input ssh
Router(config-line)#transport output ssh
```

6. Add a banner message of the day (MOTD). Set the character which tells the router you have finished your message as "X" (the delimiting character).

```
Router(config)#banner motd X
Enter TEXT message.  End with the character 'X'.
Do not use this router without authorization. X

Router(config)#
Router(config)#exit
Router#
%SYS-5-CONFIG_I: Configured from console by console
Exit
```

```
Router con0 is now available
Press RETURN to get started.

Do not use this router without authorization.
Router>
```

7. Turn off CDP on the entire router. You could disable it on an interface only with the
    `no cdp enable` interface command.

    ```
    Router(config)#no cdp run
    ```

    You can test whether this is working by connecting a switch or router to your router
    before you turn off CDP and issuing the `show cdp neighbor (detail)` command.

8. Set the router to send logging messages to a host on the network.

    ```
    Router#conf t
    Enter configuration commands, one per line.  End with CNTL/Z.
    Router(config)#logging ?
      A.B.C.D   IP address of the logging host
      buffered  Set buffered logging parameters
      console   Set console logging parameters
      host      Set syslog server IP address and parameters
      on        Enable logging to all enabled destinations
      trap      Set syslog server logging level
      userinfo  Enable logging of user info on privileged mode enabling
    Router(config)#logging 10.1.1.1
    ```

Review

DAY 20 TASKS

- Review the lessons and labs from the previous two days
- Repeat the labs from the previous two days
- Review any other lessons or labs you feel necessary
- Read the ICND1 cram guide
- Spend 15 minutes on the subnetting.org website
- Take today's exam at https://www.in60days.com/free/ccnain60days/

Troubleshooting Layers 1 and 2

DAY 21 TASKS

- Read today's notes (below)
- Complete today's lab
- Spend 15 minutes on the subnetting.org website
- Take today's exam

We have covered much of the ICND1 troubleshooting requirements in previous lessons, particularly ACLs and IP addressing. Layers 1 and 2 cover a lot of possible issues and their causes, which will be the focus of today's lesson.

LAN switching is a form of packet switching that is used in Local Area Networks (LANs). LAN switching is performed in hardware at the Data Link Layer. Because LAN switching is hardware-based, it uses hardware addresses that are referred to as Media Access Control (MAC) addresses. The MAC addresses are then used by LAN switches to forward frames.

Today you will learn about the following:

- Troubleshooting at the Physical Layer
- Using the command line to troubleshoot links
- Troubleshooting switch port configuration
- Troubleshooting VLANs and trunking
- Extended ping and traceroute
- Terminal monitor
- Logging events

This module maps to the following CCNA syllabus requirements:

- 1.7 Apply troubleshooting methodologies to resolve problems
- 1.7.a Perform fault isolation and document
- 1.7.b Resolve or escalate
- 1.7.c Verify and monitor resolution
- 2.5 Configure, verify, and troubleshoot inter-switch connectivity

- 5.6 Use Cisco IOS tools to troubleshoot and resolve problems
- 5.6.a Ping and traceroute with extended option
- 5.6.b Terminal monitor
- 5.6.c Log events

TROUBLESHOOTING AT THE PHYSICAL LAYER

Cisco IOS switches support several commands that can be used to troubleshoot Layer 1, or at least suspected Layer 1, issues. However, in addition to being familiar with the software command suite, it is also important to have a solid understanding of physical indicators (i.e., LEDs) that can be used to troubleshoot link status or that indicate an error condition.

Troubleshooting Link Status Using Light Emitting Diodes (LEDs)

If you have physical access to the switch or switches, LEDs can be a useful troubleshooting tool. Different Cisco Catalyst switches provide different LED capabilities. Understanding the meaning of the LEDs is an integral part of Catalyst switch link status and system troubleshooting. Cisco Catalyst switches have front-panel LEDs that can be used to determine link status, as well as other variables such as system status.

Check Cisco documentation for the Catalyst 2960 switch model by Googling "Catalyst 2960 Switch Hardware Installation Guide." The installation and configuration guides consist of many hundreds of pages of notes, advice, and technical information. It's worth browsing through it but you shouldn't be expected to know the contents of it for the CCNA exam beyond what is in the syllabus (which is covered in this guide).

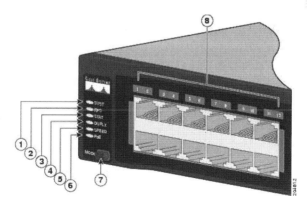

1	System LED	5	Speed LED
2	RPS LED	6	PoE LED
3	Status LED	7	Mode button
4	Duplex LED	8	Port LEDs

Figure 21.1—Cisco 2960 Switch LEDs. Image © Cisco Systems

The PoE LED is found only on the Catalyst 2960 switch model.

System LED

The system LED indicates that the system is receiving power (or is not) and is functioning properly. Table 21.1 below lists the LED colors and the status that they indicate:

Table 21.1—System LEDs

System LED Color	System Status
Off	System is not powered on.
Green	System is operating normally.
Amber	System is powered on but is not functioning correctly.

RPS LED

The RPS LED is only present on switches featuring a redundant power supply. Table 21.2 below lists the LED colors and their meanings:

Table 21.2—RPS LEDs

System LED Color	System Status
Green	RPS is connected and ready to provide backup power, if required.
Blinking Green	RPS is connected but is unavailable because it is providing power to another device (redundancy has been allocated to a neighboring device).
Amber	The RPS is in standby mode or in a fault condition. Press the Standby/ Active button on the RPS, and the LED should turn green. If it does not, the RPS fan could have failed. Contact Cisco Systems.
Blinking Amber	The internal power supply in a switch has failed, and the RPS is providing power to the switch (redundancy has been allocated to this device).

Port LEDs and Modes

Port LEDs give information about a group of ports or individual ports, as shown in Table 21.3 below:

Table 21.3—Modes for Port LEDs

Selected Mode LED	Port Mode	Description
1—System		
2—RPS		Status of the RPS
3—Status	Port status	The port status (default mode)
4—Duplex		Duplex mode: full duplex or half duplex
5—Speed	Port speed	Port operating speed: 10, 100, or 1000Mbps
6—PoE	PoE port power	PoE status
7—Mode		Cycles through Status, Duplex, and Speed LEDs
8—Port		Meaning differs according to mode

You can cycle through modes by pressing the Mode button until you reach the mode setting you require. This will change the meaning of the port LED colors, as shown in Table 21.4 below:

Table 21.4—Mode Settings

Port Mode	LED Color	System Status
Status	Off	No link or port was administratively shut down.
	Green	Link is present.
	Blinking Green	Activity: Port is sending or receiving data.
	Alternating Green-Amber	Link fault: Error frames can affect connectivity, and errors such as excessive collisions, cyclic redundancy check (CRC), and alignment and jabber are monitored for a link-fault indication.
	Amber	Port is blocked by Spanning Tree Protocol (STP) and is not forwarding data. **NOTE:** After a port is reconfigured, the port LED can remain amber for up to 30 seconds as STP checks the network topology for possible loops.
	Blinking Amber	Port is blocked by STP and is not sending or receiving packets.
Duplex	Off	Port is operating in half duplex.
	Green	Port is operating in full duplex.
Speed	10/100 and 10/100/1000 Ports	
	Off	Port is operating at 10Mbps.
	Green	Port is operating at 100Mbps.
	Blinking Green	Port is operating at 1000Mbps.
	SFP Ports	
	Off	Port is operating at 10Mbps.
	Green	Port is operating at 100Mbps.
	Blinking Green	Port is operating at 1000Mbps. **NOTE:** When installed in Catalyst 2960 switches, 1000BASE-T SFP modules can operate at 10, 100, or 1000Mbps in full-duplex mode or at 10 or 100Mbps in half-duplex mode.
PoE	Off	PoE is off. If the powered device is receiving power from an AC power source, the PoE port LED is off even if the powered device is connected to the switch port.
	Green	PoE is on. The port LED is green only when the switch port is providing power.
	Alternating Green-Amber	PoE is denied because providing power to the powered device will exceed the switch power capacity. The Catalyst 2960-24PC-L, 2960 48PST-L, 2960-48PST-S, and 2960-24PC-S switches provide up to 370 W of power. The Catalyst 2960-24LT-L and 2960-24LC-S switches provide up to 124 W of power.
	Blinking Amber	PoE is off due to a fault. **Caution:** PoE faults are caused when noncompliant cabling or powered devices are connected to a PoE port. Only standard-compliant cabling can be used to connect Cisco pre-standard IP phones, wireless access points, or IEEE 802.3af-compliant devices to PoE ports. You must remove the cable or device that caused the PoE fault from the network.
	Amber	PoE for the port has been disabled. By default, PoE is enabled.

In addition to understanding what the different LED colors mean, it is also important to have an understanding of what action to take to remedy the issue. For example, assume that you are troubleshooting a Catalyst 6500 Series switch and you notice that the status LEDs on the supervisor engine (or any switching modules) is red or off. In such cases, it is possible that the module might have shifted out of its slot, or, in the event of a new module, was not correctly inserted into the chassis. In this case, the recommended action is to reseat the module. In some cases, it also may be necessary to reboot the entire system.

While a link or port LED color other than green typically indicates some kind of failure or other issue, it is important to remember that a green link light does not always mean that the cable is fully functional. For example, a single broken wire or one shut down port can cause the problem of one side showing a green link light while the other side does not. This could be because the cable encountered physical stress that caused it to be functional at a marginal level. In such cases, the CLI can be used to perform additional troubleshooting.

Troubleshooting Cable Issues

When troubleshooting cabling issues (Layer 1 troubleshooting), it can sometimes be very easy to find the problem because you can directly see and inspect the cable. However, sometimes cabling problems can be invisible, so you will have to engage in a systematic troubleshooting process to make sure the problem is really localized at Layer 1. A general recommendation is to properly test all cabling before engaging in a complex infrastructure implementation. Some common cabling problems include the following:

- Plugging in a cable but getting no connection
- Plugging in a cable and getting a connection but with very low throughput on that connection
- Everything is working normally but suddenly the connection goes away, and then comes back, and then goes away again (i.e., flapping)
- Intermittent connectivity, where it seems to work fine but the signal gets lost from time to time
- Some of the recommended tests for these problems include:
- Verifying that the switch link light is on
- Verifying that the link light is not turning on and off intermittently
- Verifying that the cable is punched correctly
- Verifying that the cable is not physically damaged
- Verifying that the cable is not too long (this may cause signal degradation)
- Verifying that the cable connectors are not faulty (you might need to use other connectors)
- Verifying that the wires are pinned in the correct order (in the case of copper cables)

If you want to be sure that you are not dealing with a cabling issue, one of the simplest things to do is to replace the cable and run the same tests again. This is very easy to do and might help in immediately fixing the issue without investing much time and resources into the troubleshooting process.

NOTE: Sometimes even brand new cables can come with a defect, so do not assume that a new cable should function as expected.

Troubleshooting Module Issues

Most routers and switches used in an enterprise network offer copper port connectivity, but also dedicated ports that can be populated with different kind of transceivers. These transceivers are usually used for fiber connectivity, but there are also copper-compatible transceivers.

Fiber connections may run over very long distances, and generally those particular ports are modular and require a compatible SFP (small form-factor pluggable transceiver), like the one presented in Figure 21.2 below:

Figure 21.2—SFP Module

Although they look similar, depending upon the type of connectivity used, the appropriate SFP module should be used based on several parameters, including:

- Type of media: optical fiber or copper
- Fiber type: single-mode or multimode fiber
- Bandwidth
- Wavelength
- Core size
- Modal bandwidth
- Operating distance

NOTE: When purchasing transceivers for your network, you should always check the compatibility between the device ports, type of module, and type of fiber used.

Transceivers can be plugged into and unplugged from the network device (e.g., switch, router, firewall, etc.) at any time without restarting the device. When there is no connection you will see no activity on the SFP modules, and this is one of the easiest issues to troubleshoot if you have access to the device.

On the other hand, you might plug in a fiber cable that will activate that port but the connectivity suffers from different issues (e.g., performance degradation or intermittent connectivity) or simply does not exist. In this case, there are several approaches you could take:

- Verify that the correct cable types have been used (multi-mode vs. single-mode) depending upon the type of transceiver
- Verify that the cable is not broken, using dedicated fiber optic testing tools
- Verify that the correct type of transceiver has been used
- Verify that the transceiver does not have hardware issues (swap it and test the connection with another SFP)
- Verify that the device port is configured with the correct parameters based on the type of transceiver and cable used

To minimize connection downtime, you should monitor the ports populated with SFP modules in order to see possible errors that appear in the statistics. This can be done with standard monitoring tools, most often using SNMP.

USING THE COMMAND LINE INTERFACE TO TROUBLESHOOT LINK ISSUES

Several Command Line Interface (CLI) commands can be used to troubleshoot Layer 1 issues on Cisco IOS Catalyst switches. Commonly used commands include the show interfaces, the show controllers, and the show interface [name] counters errors commands. In addition to knowing these commands, you also are required to be able to interpret accurately the output or information that these commands provide.

The show interfaces command is a powerful troubleshooting tool that provides a plethora of information, which includes the following:

- The administrative status of a switching port
- The port operational state
- The media type (for select switches and ports)
- Port input and output packets
- Port buffer failures and port errors
- Port input and output errors
- Port input and output queue drops

The output of the show interfaces command for a GigabitEthernet switch port is illustrated below:

```
Switch#show interfaces GigabitEthernet3/0/1
GigabitEthernet0/1 is up, line protocol is down (notconnect)
 Hardware is GigabitEthernet, address is 000f.2303.2db1 (bia
000f.2303.2db1)
 MTU 1500 bytes, BW 10000 Kbit, DLY 1000 usec,
    reliability 255/255, txload 1/255, rxload 1/255
```

```
Encapsulation ARPA, Loopback not set
Keepalive not set
Auto-duplex, Auto-speed, link type is auto, media type is unknown
input flow-control is off, output flow-control is desired
ARP type: ARPA, ARP Timeout 04:00:00
Last input never, output never, output hang never
Last clearing of "show interface" counters never
Input queue: 0/75/0/0 (size/max/drops/flushes); Total output drops: 0
Queueing strategy: fifo
Output queue: 0/40 (size/max)
5 minute input rate 0 bits/sec, 0 packets/sec
5 minute output rate 0 bits/sec, 0 packets/sec
   0 packets input, 0 bytes, 0 no buffer
   Received 0 broadcasts (0 multicasts)
   0 runts, 0 giants, 0 throttles
   0 input errors, 0 CRC, 0 frame, 0 overrun, 0 ignored
   0 watchdog, 0 multicast, 0 pause input
   0 input packets with dribble condition detected
   0 packets output, 0 bytes, 0 underruns
   0 output errors, 0 collisions, 1 interface resets
   0 babbles, 0 late collision, 0 deferred
   0 lost carrier, 0 no carrier, 0 PAUSE output
   0 output buffer failures, 0 output buffers swapped out
```

Most Cisco Catalyst switch ports default to the notconnect state, as illustrated in the first line of the output printed by this command. However, a port can also transition to this state if a cable is removed from the port or is not correctly connected. This status is also reflected when the connected cable is faulty or when the other end of the cable is not connected to an active port or device (e.g., if a workstation connected to the switch port is powered off).

> **NOTE:** When troubleshooting GigabitEthernet ports, this port status may also be a result of incorrect Gigabit Interface Converters (GBICs) being used between the two ends.

The first part of the output in the first line printed by this command (i.e., [interface] is up) refers to the Physical Layer status of the particular interface. The second part of the output (i.e., line protocol is down) indicates the Data Link Layer status of the interface. If this indicates an "up," then it means that the interface can send and receive keepalives. Keep in mind that it is possible for the switch port to indicate that the Physical Layer is up while the Data Link Layer is down, for example, such as when the port is a SPAN destination port (for sniffer traffic) or if the local port is connected to a CatOS (older switch operating system) switch with its port disabled.

The Input queue indicates the actual number of frames dropped because the maximum queue size was exceeded. The flushes column counts Selective Packet Discard (SPD) drops on the Catalyst 6000 Series switches. SPD drops low-priority packets when the CPU is overloaded in order to save some processing capacity for high-priority packets. The flushes counter in the show interfaces command output increments as part of SPD, which implements a selective packet drop policy on the IP process queue of the router. Therefore, it applies only to process-switched traffic.

The total output drops indicates the number of packets dropped because the output queue is full. This is often seen when traffic from multiple inbound high-bandwidth links (e.g., GigabitEthernet links) is being switched to a single outbound lower-bandwidth link (e.g., a FastEthernet link). The output drops increment because the interface is overwhelmed by the excess traffic due to the speed mismatch between the inbound and outbound bandwidths.

Some of the other interface-specific terms that can be analyzed from the show interfaces output and can be very useful during Layers 1 and 2 troubleshooting are:

- **Frame number:** This field describes the number of packets received incorrectly having a CRC error and a non-integer number of octets. This is usually the result of collisions due to a malfunctioning Ethernet device (hardware fault).
- **CRC:** This field indicates that the CRC (cyclic redundancy checksum) generated by the sending device does not match the checksum calculated at the receiving device. This usually indicates transmission problems on a LAN, collisions, or a system transmitting bad data.
- **Runts:** This field indicates the number of packets that are discarded due to being smaller than the minimum packet size. On Ethernet segments, packets smaller than 64 bytes are considered runts.
- **Giants:** This field indicates the number of packets that are discarded due to being larger than the maximum packet size. On Ethernet segments, packets larger than 1518 bytes are considered giants.
- **Late collisions:** Late collisions usually occur when Ethernet cables are too long or when there are too many repeaters in the network. The number of collisions represents the number of messages retransmitted due to an Ethernet collision. This is usually caused by an overextended LAN.
- **Input errors:** This field provides the total sum of runts, giants, CRC, overruns, and ignored packets.
- **Output errors:** This field provides the total sum of all errors that prevented the final transmission of datagrams out of the interface.

In addition to the show interfaces command, the show interfaces [name] counters errors command can also be used to view interface errors and facilitate Layer 1 troubleshooting. The output that is printed by the show interfaces [name] counters errors command is as follows:

```
Switch#show interfaces GigabitEthernet3/0/1 counters errors
Port        Align-Err    FCS-Err   Xmit-Err    Rcv-Err UnderSize
Gi3/0/1         0            0         0           0         0
Port      Single-Col Multi-Col  Late-Col Excess-Col Carri-Sen    Runts
Gi3/0/1        0         0         0          0         0         0
Port        Giants
Gi3/0/1        0
```

The following section describes some of the error fields included in the output of the show interfaces [name] counters errors command, and which issues or problems are indicated by non-zero values under these fields.

The `Align-Err` field reflects a count of the number of frames received that do not end with an even number of octets and that have a bad CRC. These errors are usually the result of a duplex mismatch or a physical problem, such as cabling, a bad port, or a bad network interface controller (NIC). When the cable is first connected to the port, some of these errors can occur. In addition, if there is a hub connected to the port, collisions between other devices on the hub can cause these errors.

The `FCS-Err` field reflects the number of valid-sized frames with Frame Check Sequence (FCS) errors but no framing errors. This is typically a physical issue, such as cabling, a bad port, or a bad NIC. Additionally, a non-zero value under this field could indicate a duplex mismatch.

A non-zero value in the `Xmit-Err` field is an indication that the internal send (Tx) buffer is full. This is commonly seen when traffic from multiple inbound high-bandwidth links (e.g., GigabitEthernet links) is being switched to a single outbound lower-bandwidth link (i.e., a FastEthernet link), for example.

The `Rcv-Err` field indicates the sum of all received errors. This counter is incremented when the interface receives an error such as a runt, a giant, or an FCS, for example.

The `UnderSize` field is incremented when the switch receives frames that are smaller than 64 bytes in length. This is commonly caused by a faulty sending device.

The various `collision` fields indicate collisions on the interface. This is common for half-duplex Ethernet, which is almost non-existent in modern networks. However, these counters should not increment for full-duplex links. In the event that non-zero values are present under these counters, this typically indicates a duplex mismatch issue. When a duplex mismatch is detected, the switch prints a message similar to the following on the console or in the log:

```
%CDP-4-DUPLEX_MISMATCH: duplex mismatch discovered on FastEthernet0/1
(not full duplex), with R2 FastEthernet0/0 (full duplex)
```

As will be described in the section pertaining to Spanning Tree Protocol (STP), duplex mismatches can cause STP loops in the switched network if a port is connected to another switch. These mismatches can be resolved by manually configuring the speed and the duplex of the switch ports.

The `Carri-Sen` (carrier sense) counter increments every time an Ethernet controller wants to send data on a half-duplex connection. The controller senses the wire and ensures that it is not busy before transmitting. A non-zero value under this field indicates that the interface is operating in half-duplex mode. This is normal for half-duplex.

Non-zero values can also be seen under the `Runts` field due to a duplex mismatch or because of other Physical Layer problems, such as a bad cable, port, or NIC on the attached device. Runts are received frames with a bad CRC that are smaller than the minimum IEEE 802.3 frame size, which is 64 bytes for Ethernet.

Finally, the Giants counter is incremented when frames are received that exceed the IEEE 802.3 maximum frame size, which is 1518 bytes for non-jumbo Ethernet, and that have a bad FCS. For ports or interfaces connected to a workstation, a non-zero value under this field is typically caused by a bad NIC on the connected device. However, for ports or interfaces that are connected to another switch (e.g., via a trunk link), this field will contain a non-zero value if 802.1Q encapsulation is used. With 802.1Q, the tagging mechanism implies a modification of the frame because the trunking device inserts a 4-byte tag and then re-computes the FCS.

Inserting a 4-byte tag into a frame that already has the maximum Ethernet size creates a 1522-byte frame that can be considered a baby giant frame by the receiving equipment. Therefore, while the switch will still process such frames, this counter will increment and contain a non-zero value. To resolve this issue, the 802.3 committee created a subgroup called 802.3ac to extend the maximum Ethernet size to 1522 bytes; however, it is not uncommon to see a non-zero value under this field when using 802.1Q trunking.

The show controllers ethernet-controller <interface> command can also be used to display traffic counter and error counter information similar to that printed by the show interfaces and show interfaces <name> counters errors commands. The output of the show controllers ethernet-controller <interface> command is shown below:

```
Switch#show controllers ethernet-controller GigabitEthernet3/0/1
  Transmit GigabitEthernet3/0/1          Receive
4069327795 Bytes                     3301740741 Bytes
 559424024 Unicast frames             376047608 Unicast frames
  27784795 Multicast frames            1141946 Multicast frames
   7281524 Broadcast frames            1281591 Broadcast frames
         0 Too old frames            429934641 Unicast bytes
         0 Deferred frames           226764843 Multicast bytes
         0 MTU exceeded frames       137921433 Broadcast bytes
         0 1 collision frames                0 Alignment errors
         0 2 collision frames                0 FCS errors
         0 3 collision frames                0 Oversize frames
         0 4 collision frames                0 Undersize frames
         0 5 collision frames                0 Collision fragments
         0 6 collision frames
         0 7 collision frames           257477 Minimum size frames
         0 8 collision frames        259422986 65 to 127 byte frames
         0 9 collision frames         51377167 128 to 255 byte frames
         0 10 collision frames        41117556 256 to 511 byte frames
         0 11 collision frames         2342527 512 to 1023 byte frames
         0 12 collision frames         5843545 1024 to 1518 byte frames
         0 13 collision frames                0 Overrun frames
         0 14 collision frames                0 Pause frames
         0 15 collision frames
         0 Excessive collisions              0 Symbol error frames
         0 Late collisions                   0 Invalid frames, too large
         0 VLAN discard frames        18109887 Valid frames, too large
         0 Excess defer frames               0 Invalid frames, too small
    264522 64 byte frames                    0 Valid frames, too small
  99898057 127 byte frames
```

```
 76457337 255 byte frames           0 Too old frames
  4927192 511 byte frames           0 Valid oversize frames
 21176897 1023 byte frames          0 System FCS error frames
127643707 1518 byte frames          0 RxPortFifoFull drop frames
264122631 Too large frames
        0 Good (1 coll) frames
        0 Good (>1 coll) frames
```

> **NOTE:** The output above will vary slightly depending upon the switch platform on which this command is executed. For example, Catalyst 3550 series switches also include a Discarded frames field, which shows the total number of frames whose transmission attempt is abandoned due to insufficient resources. A large number in this field typically indicates a network congestion issue. In the output above, you would look at the RxPortFifoFull drop frame field, which indicates the total number of frames received on an interface that are dropped because the ingress queue is full.

TROUBLESHOOTING PORT CONFIGURATION

Each networking device can be configured in different ways. Most types of misconfigurations generate problems within the network, including:

- Poor throughput
- Lack of connectivity

A device can be connected to the network, have a signal, and be able to communicate to the Internet and to other devices but the performance might be low, in a consistent and easily reproducible way. This can manifest during normal operations, including file transfer or other types of communications with the rest of the network.

With major configuration issues, the issue might manifest as complete lack of connectivity, including no link lights on the specific device ports. Sometimes the link lights are on but you still lack any kind of connectivity. This shows that the signal is passing through the cable, which means that you don't have a cabling issue but rather a port configuration issue on one port or the other. This requires problem investigation in the device's configuration.

There are a number of different settings when configuring a port, including:

- Speed
- Duplex
- Encapsulation/VLAN.

Most of these parameters have to be synchronized on both sides of the link, either by manually configuring them or by enabling port autoconfiguration. If detected, this method will send negotiation packets on the link to each device to detect the capabilities on the other end device and commonly agree on the best possible parameters supported by both of them to ensure an optimal transmission. The problem is that sometimes autoconfiguration does not select the best parameters for your needs, so you should also verify this and manually configure the ports according to each specific case.

If you are performing manual configuration on each port, one of the first parameters you have to take care of is the interface speed. This has to be identical on both sides of a link. If you configure it incorrectly on one side, the link might not be operational. Another related setting is port duplex, which can be configured to be either half duplex or full duplex. You can configure a link with half duplex on one side and full duplex on the other side, and even though the link will come up, the throughput will be highly affected because each side is expecting to handle communication in a different way. This will result in collisions which will affect the transmission on that particular link. Make sure that both sides use the same duplex settings in order for the traffic to be sent as efficiently as possible.

If you are operating in an enterprise-level environment, you might need to use different VLANs to segment the traffic. Each switch must be properly configured in this regard so each switch port is assigned to the correct VLAN. If you are directly connecting ports configured to use different VLAN IDs, the communication will be broken at Layer 2, even though the Physical Layer shows no issues.

By examining all the port configuration options presented above and making sure that you have everything synchronized at both ends of a link, you can be assured that the connectivity and throughput of the configured devices will be optimized.

TROUBLESHOOTING VLANS AND TRUNKING

On days 5 and 6 we covered this topic but it's worth discussing again but we won't repeat what was already said, instead covering some other troubleshooting aspects.

Earlier, we discussed the use of three CLI commands that can be used for troubleshooting Physical Layer issues. This section describes some common approaches to identifying and troubleshooting intra-VLAN connectivity issues. Some of the more common causes of intra-VLAN connectivity issues include the following:

- Duplex mismatches
- Bad NIC or cable
- Congestion
- Hardware issues
- Software issues
- Resource oversubscription
- Configuration issues

Duplex mismatches can result in very slow network performance and connectivity. While some improvements in auto-negotiation have been made, and the use of auto-negotiation is considered a valid practice, it is still possible for duplex mismatches to occur. As an example, when the NIC is set to 100/Full and the switch port is auto-negotiating, the NIC will retain its 100/Full setting, but the switch port will be set to 100/Half. Another example would be the inverse; that is, the NIC is set to auto-negotiate, while the switch port is set to 100/Full. In that case, the NIC would auto-negotiate to 100/Half, while the switch retained its static 100/Full configuration, resulting in a duplex mismatch.

It is therefore good practice to specify manually the speed and duplex settings for 10/100 Ethernet connections, where feasible, to avoid duplex mismatches with auto-negotiation. Duplex mismatches can affect not only users directly connected to the switch but also network traffic that traverses inter-switch links that have mismatched duplex settings. The port interface speed and duplex settings can be viewed using the show interfaces command.

> **NOTE:** Because Catalyst switches support only full-duplex for 1Gbps links, this is not commonly an issue for GigabitEthernet connections.

Multiple counters in Cisco IOS software can be used to identify a potentially bad NIC or cabling issue. NIC or cabling issues can be identified by checking the values of certain counters in different show commands. For example, if the switch port counters show an incrementing number of frames with a bad CRC or with FCS errors, this can most likely be attributed either to a bad NIC on the workstation or machine or to a bad network cable.

Network congestion can also cause intermittent connectivity issues in the switched network. The first sign that your VLAN is overloaded is if the Rx or Tx buffers on a port are oversubscribed. Additionally, excessive frame drops on a port can also be an indication of network congestion. A common cause of network congestion is due to underestimating aggregate bandwidth requirements for backbone connections. In such cases, congestion issues can be resolved by configuring EtherChannels or by adding additional ports to existing EtherChannels. While network congestion is a common cause of connectivity issues, it is also important to know that the switch itself can experience congestion issues, which can have a similar impact on network performance.

Limited switch bandwidth can result in congestion issues, which can severely impact network performance. In LAN switching, bandwidth refers to the capacity of the switch fabric. Therefore, if the switch fabric is on 5Gbps and you attempt to push 7Gbps worth of traffic through the switch, the end result is packet loss and poor network performance. This is a common issue in oversubscribed platforms, where the aggregate capacity of all ports can exceed the total backplane capacity.

Hardware problems can also cause connectivity issues in the switched LAN. Examples of such issues include bad ports or bad switch modules. While you could troubleshoot such issues by looking at physical indicators such as LEDs, if possible, such issues are sometimes difficult to troubleshoot and diagnose. In most cases, you should seek the assistance of the Technical Assistance Centre (TAC) when you suspect potentially faulty hardware issues.

Software bugs are even more difficult to identify because they cause deviation, which is hard to troubleshoot. In the event that you suspect a software bug may be causing connectivity issues, you should contact the TAC with your findings. Additionally, if error messages are printed on the console or are in the logs, you can also use some of the online tools available from Cisco to implement a workaround or get a recommendation for a version of software in which the issue has been resolved and verified.

As with any other hardware device, switches have limited resources, such as physical memory. When these resources are oversubscribed, this can lead to severe performance issues. Issues such as high CPU utilization can have a drastic impact on both switch and network performance.

Finally, as with any other technology, incorrect configurations may also cause connectivity issues, either directly or indirectly. For example, the poor placement of the Root Bridge may result in slow connectivity for users. Directly integrating or adding an incorrectly configured switch into the production network could result in an outright outage for some or all users. The following sections describe some common VLAN-related issues, their probable causes, and the actions that can be taken to remedy them.

Troubleshooting Dynamic VLAN Advertisements

Cisco Catalyst switches use VLAN Trunk Protocol (VTP) to propagate VLAN information dynamically throughout the switched domain. VTP is a Cisco proprietary Layer 2 messaging protocol that manages the addition, deletion, and renaming of VLANs for switches in the same VTP domain.

There are several reasons why a switch might not be able to receive any VLAN information dynamically when added to the VTP domain. Some common causes include the following:

- Layer 2 trunking misconfigurations
- Incorrect VTP configuration
- Configuration revision number
- Physical Layer issues
- Software or hardware issues or bugs
- Switch performance issues

In order for switches to exchange VLAN information using VTP, a trunk must be established between the switches. Cisco IOS switches support both ISL and 802.1Q trunking mechanisms. While some switches default to ISL, which is a Cisco proprietary trunking mechanism, the current Cisco IOS Catalyst switches default to 802.1Q. When provisioning trunking between switches, it is considered good practice to specify manually the trunking encapsulation protocol. This is accomplished using the switchport trunk encapsulation [isl|dot1q] interface configuration command when configuring the link as a trunk port.

There are several commands that you can use to troubleshoot trunk connectivity issues. You can use the show interfaces command to verify basic port operational and administrative status. Additionally, you can append the [trunk] or [errors] keyword to perform additional troubleshooting and verification. The `show interfaces [name] counters trunk` command can be used to view the number of frames transmitted and received on trunk ports.

The output of this command also includes encapsulation errors, which can be used to verify 802.1Q and ISL, and trunking encapsulation mismatches, as illustrated in the following output:

```
Switch#show interfaces FastEthernet0/12 counters trunk
Port          TrunkFramesTx   TrunkFramesRx   WrongEncap
Fa0/12              1696           32257            0
```

Referencing the output above, you can repeat the same command to ensure that both the Tx and Rx columns are incrementing and perform additional troubleshooting from there. For example, if the switch is not sending any frames, then the interface might not be configured as a trunk, or it might be down or disabled. If the Rx column is not incrementing, then it may be that the remote switch is not configured correctly.

Another command that can be used to troubleshoot possible Layer 2 trunk misconfigurations is the `show interfaces [name] trunk` command. The output of this command includes the trunking encapsulation protocol and mode, the native VLAN for 802.1Q, the VLANs that are allowed to traverse the trunk, the VLANs that are active in the VTP domain, and the VLANs that are pruned. A common issue with VLAN propagation is that the upstream switch has been configured to filter certain VLANs on the trunk link using the `switchport trunk allowed vlan` interface configuration command. The output of the `show interfaces [name] trunk` command is shown below:

```
Switch#show interfaces trunk

Port        Mode            Encapsulation  Status      Native vlan
Fa0/12      desirable       n-802.1q       trunking    1
Fa0/13      desirable       n-802.1q       trunking    1
Fa0/14      desirable       n-isl          trunking    1
Fa0/15      desirable       n-isl          trunking    1

Port        Vlans allowed on trunk
Fa0/12      1-4094
Fa0/13      1-4094
Fa0/14      1-4094
Fa0/15      1-4094

Port        Vlans allowed and active in management domain
Fa0/12      1-4
Fa0/13      1-4
Fa0/14      1-4
Fa0/15      1-4

Port        Vlans in spanning tree forwarding state and not pruned
Fa0/12      1-4
Fa0/13      none
Fa0/14      none
Fa0/15      none
```

Another common trunking misconfiguration issue is native VLAN mismatches. When you are configuring 802.1Q trunks, the native VLAN must match on both sides of the trunk link; otherwise, the link will not work. If there is a native VLAN mismatch, then STP places the port in a port VLAN ID (PVID) inconsistent state and will not forward on the link. In such cases, an error message similar to the following will be printed on the console or in the log:

```
*Mar  1 03:16:43.935: %SPANTREE-2-RECV_PVID_ERR: Received BPDU with
inconsistent peer vlan id 1 on FastEthernet0/11 VLAN2.
*Mar  1 03:16:43.935: %SPANTREE-2-BLOCK_PVID_PEER: Blocking
FastEthernet0/11 on VLAN0001. Inconsistent peer vlan.
*Mar  1 03:16:43.935: %SPANTREE-2-BLOCK_PVID_LOCAL: Blocking
FastEthernet0/11 on VLAN0002. Inconsistent local vlan.
```

While STP troubleshooting will be described later in this guide, this inconsistent state could be validated using the show spanning-tree command, as illustrated below:

```
Switch#show spanning-tree interface FastEthernet0/11

Vlan                    Role Sts  Cost      Prio.Nbr Type
------------------- ---- ---  --------- -------- ----------------
VLAN0001                Desg BKN* 19        128.11   P2p *PVID_Inc
VLAN0002                Desg BKN* 19        128.11   P2p *PVID_Inc
```

If you have checked and validated that the trunk is indeed correctly configured and operational between the two switches, then the next step would be to validate VTP configuration parameters. These parameters include the VTP domain name, the correct VTP mode, and the VTP password, if one has been configured for the domain, using the show vtp status and show vtp password commands, respectively. The output of the show vtp status command is shown below:

```
Switch#show vtp status
VTP Version                       : running VTP2
Configuration Revision            : 0
Maximum VLANs supported locally   : 1005
Number of existing VLANs          : 8
VTP Operating Mode                : Server
VTP Domain Name                   : TSHOOT
VTP Pruning Mode                  : Enabled
VTP V2 Mode                       : Enabled
VTP Traps Generation              : Disabled
MD5 digest                        : 0x26 0x99 0xB7 0x93 0xBE 0xDA 0x76 0x9C
[Truncated Output]
```

When using the show vtp status command, ensure that the switches are running the same version of VTP. By default, Catalyst switches run VTP version 1. A switch running VTP version 1 cannot participate in a VTP version 2 domain. If the switch is incapable of running VTP version 2, then all VTP version 2 switches should be configured to run version 1 instead using the vtp version global configuration command.

NOTE: If you change the VTP version on the server, then the change will be propagated automatically to client switches in the VTP domain.

VTP propagation is enabled for VTP client/server or server/server devices. If VTP is disabled on a switch (i.e., transparent mode), then the switch will not receive VLAN information dynamically via VTP. However, be mindful of the fact that with version 2, transparent mode switches will forward received VTP advertisements out of their trunk ports and act as VTP relays. This happens even if the VTP version is not the same. The VTP domain name should also be consistent on the switches.

The output of the show vtp status command also includes the MD5 hash used for authentication purposes. This hash, which is derived from the VTP domain name and password, should be consistent on all switches in the domain. If the VTP passwords or domain names are different on the switches, then the calculated MD5 will also be different. If the domain name or password is different, then the show vtp status command will indicate an MD5 digest checksum mismatch, as illustrated in the following output:

```
Switch#show vtp status
VTP Version                       : running VTP2
Configuration Revision            : 0
Maximum VLANs supported locally   : 1005
Number of existing VLANs          : 8
VTP Operating Mode                : Server
VTP Domain Name                   : TSHOOT
VTP Pruning Mode                  : Enabled
VTP V2 Mode                       : Enabled
VTP Traps Generation              : Disabled
MD5 Digest                        : 0x26 0x99 0xB7 0x93 0xBE 0xDA 0x76 0x9C
*** MD5 digest checksum mismatch on trunk: Fa0/11 ***
*** MD5 digest checksum mismatch on trunk: Fa0/12 ***
[Truncated Output]
```

Finally, the configuration revision number can wreak havoc when using VTP. Switches use the configuration revision number to keep track of the most recent information in the VTP domain. Every switch in the domain stores the configuration revision number that it last heard from a VTP advertisement, and this number is incremented every time new information is received. When any switch in the VTP domain receives an advertisement message with a higher configuration revision number than its own, it will overwrite any stored VLAN information and synchronize its own stored VLAN information with the information received in the advertisement message.

Therefore, if you are wondering why the switch that you integrated into the VTP domain is not receiving any VLAN information, it may be that the same switch had a higher configuration revision number and caused all other switches to overwrite their local VLAN information and replace it with the information received in the advertisement message from the new switch. To avoid such situations, always ensure that the configuration revision number is set to 0 prior to integrating a new switch into the domain. This can be done by changing the VTP mode or changing the VTP domain name on the switch. The configuration revision number is included in the output of the `show vtp status` command.

Troubleshooting Loss of End-to-End Intra-VLAN Connectivity

There are several possible reasons for a loss of end-to-end connectivity within a VLAN. Some of the most common causes include the following:

- Physical Layer issues
- VTP pruning
- VLAN trunk filtering
- New switches
- Switch performance issues
- Network congestion
- Software or hardware issues or bugs

> **NOTE:** For brevity, only trunking, VTP pruning, trunk filtering, and the integration of new switches into the domain will be described in this section. Software or hardware issues or bugs and switch performance issues are described throughout this guide. Physical Layer troubleshooting was described earlier in this module.

VTP pruning removes VLANs from the VLAN database of the local switch when no local ports are a part of that VLAN. VTP pruning increases the efficiency of trunks by eliminating unnecessary Broadcast, Multicast, and unknown traffic from being flooded across the network.

While VTP pruning is a desirable feature to implement, incorrect configuration or implementation can result in a loss of end-to-end VLAN connectivity. VTP pruning should be enabled only in client/server environments. Implementing pruning in a network that includes transparent mode switches may result in a loss of connectivity. If one or more switches in the network are in VTP transparent mode, you should either globally disable pruning for the entire domain or ensure that all VLANs on the trunk link(s) to the upstream transparent mode switch(es) are pruning ineligible (i.e., they are not pruned), using the `switchport trunk pruning vlan` interface configuration command under the applicable interfaces.

Verify Allowed VLANs and Trunk Status

In addition to VTP pruning, incorrectly filtering VLANs on switch trunk links can result in a loss of end-to-end VLAN connectivity. By default, all VLANs are allowed to traverse all trunk links; however, Cisco IOS software allows administrators to remove (or add) VLANs selectively to specific trunk links using the `switchport trunk allowed vlan` interface configuration command. You can use the `show interfaces [name] trunk` and the `show interfaces [name] switchport` commands to view pruned and restricted VLANs on trunk links. The output of the `show interfaces [name] trunk` command, which is the easiest way to verify the allowed VLANs on a trunk, is shown below:

```
Switch#show interfaces trunk

Port        Mode         Encapsulation  Status       Native vlan
Fa0/1       on           802.1q         trunking     1
Fa0/2       on           802.1q         trunking     1

Port        Vlans allowed on trunk
Fa0/1       1,10,20,30,40,50
Fa0/2       1-99,201-4094

Port        Vlans allowed and active in management domain
Fa0/1       1,10,20,30,40,50
Fa0/2       1,10,20,30,40,50,60,70,80,90,254

Port        Vlans in spanning tree forwarding state and not pruned
Fa0/1       1,10,20,30,40,50
Fa0/2       1,40,50,60,70,80,90,254
```

You should also check that the correct VLANs are advertised on your trunk links. Improper VLANs allowed on the link can lead to a lack of functionality or security issues. Also, you want to make sure that the same VLANs are allowed on both ends of a trunk.

> **NOTE:** You should be very careful not to forget the [add] keyword when adding another VLAN(s) that should be allowed over a trunk link. For example, if you already have switchport trunk allowed vlan 10, 20 configured and you want to allow VLAN 30 as well, you need to enter the command switchport trunk allowed vlan add 30. If you simply configured switchport trunk allowed vlan 30, previously permitted VLANs 10 and 20 would be removed from the trunk, which would cause a break of communication for VLANs 10 and 20.

Another important piece of information that is offered by the show interface trunk command is the trunk status. This confirms whether the trunk is formed or not and has to be checked at both ends of the link. If the interface is not in "trunking" mode, one of the most important things that have to be verified is the mode of operation (on, auto, etc.) to see whether it allows forming a trunking state with the other end of the link.

Verify Encapsulation Type

Another important step in resolving trunking problems is verifying that the correct encapsulation is configured at both ends of a trunk link. Most Cisco switches allow both ISL and dot1Q encapsulation types. Although most modern network designs use dot1Q, there might be situations in which ISL is the preferred method. The encapsulation type is configured using the switchport trunk encapsulation <type> command. Some of the commands that can be used to verify the encapsulation types are:

- show interface trunk
- show interface <number> switchport

The output of the `show interfaces [name] switchport` command on a port that has been configured statically as an 802.1Q trunk link is shown below:

```
Switch2#show interfaces FastEthernet0/7 switchport
Name: Fa0/7
Switchport: Enabled
Administrative Mode: trunk
Operational Mode: trunk
Administrative Trunking Encapsulation: dot1q
Operational Trunking Encapsulation: dot1q
Negotiation of Trunking: On
Access Mode VLAN: 1 (default)
Trunking Native Mode VLAN: 1 (default)
Administrative Native VLAN tagging: enabled
Voice VLAN: none
Administrative private-vlan host-association: none
Administrative private-vlan mapping: none
Administrative private-vlan trunk native VLAN: none
Administrative private-vlan trunk native VLAN tagging: enabled
Administrative private-vlan trunk encapsulation: dot1q
Administrative private-vlan trunk normal VLANs: none
Administrative private-vlan trunk associations: none
Administrative private-vlan trunk mappings: none
Operational private-vlan: none
Trunking VLANs Enabled: 3,5,7
Pruning VLANs Enabled: 2-8
Capture Mode Disabled
Capture VLANs Allowed: ALL

Protected: false
Unknown unicast blocked: disabled
Unknown multicast blocked: disabled
Appliance trust: none
```

As was described in the previous section, the integration of a new switch into the network can result in a loss of VLAN information in the management domain. This loss of VLAN information can result in a loss of connectivity between devices within the same VLAN. Ensure that the configuration revision number is reset prior to integrating a new switch into the LAN.

Using the "show vlan" Command

In addition to the commands that were described in the previous sections, there are additional Cisco IOS software commands that are useful for both verifying and troubleshooting VLAN configurations. One of the most commonly used VLAN verification and troubleshooting commands is the `show vlan` command. This command displays parameters for all VLANs within the administrative domain, as illustrated in the following output:

```
Switch#show vlan

VLAN Name                             Status    Ports
---- -------------------------------- --------- --------------------
1    default                          active    Fa0/11, Fa0/12,
```

```
                                                      Fa0/13, Fa0/14,
                                                      Fa0/20, Fa0/21,
                                                      Fa0/22, Fa0/23,
                                                      Fa0/24
 150  VLAN_150                            active      Fa0/2, Fa0/3, Fa0/4,
                                                      Fa0/5, Fa0/6, Fa0/7,
                                                      Fa0/8, Fa0/9, Fa0/10
 160  VLAN_160                            active      Fa0/15, Fa0/16,
                                                      Fa0/17, Fa0/18,
                                                      Fa0/19
 170  VLAN_170                            active      Gi0/1, Gi0/2
1002  fddi-default                        active
1003  token-ring-default                  active
1004  fddinet-default                     active
1005  trnet-default                       active

VLAN Type  SAID       MTU   Parent RingNo BridgeNo Stp  BrdgMode
---- ----- ---------- ----- ------ ------ -------- ---- --------
1    enet  100001     1500  -      -      -        -    -
150  enet  100150     1500  -      -      -        -    -
160  enet  100160     1500  -      -      -        -    -
170  enet  100170     1500  -      -      -        -    -
1002 fddi  101002     1500  -      -      -        -    -
1003 tr    101003     1500  -      -      -        -    -
1004 fdnet 101004     1500  -      -      -        ieee -
1005 trnet 101005     1500  -      -      -        ibm  -

Trans1 Trans2
------ ------
0      0
0      0
0      0
0      0
0      0
0      0
0      0
0      0

Remote SPAN VLANs
------------------------------------------------------------------

Primary Secondary Type              Ports
------- --------- ----------------- ------------------------------
```

This command prints all available VLANs, along with the ports that are assigned to each of the individual VLANs. Only access ports, regardless of whether they are up or down, will be included in the output of this command. Trunk links will not be included, as these belong to all VLANs. The show vlan command also provides information on RSPAN VLANs, as well as Private VLAN (PVLAN) configuration on the switch (this is a CCNP subject). The show vlan command can be used with additional keywords to provide information that is more specific. The following output displays the supported additional keywords that can be used with this command:

```
Switch#show vlan ?
  brief        VTP all VLAN status in brief
  id           VTP VLAN status by VLAN id
  ifindex      SNMP ifIndex
  name         VTP VLAN status by VLAN name
  private-vlan Private VLAN information
  remote-span  Remote SPAN VLANs
  summary      VLAN summary information
  |            Output modifiers
  <cr>
```

The brief field prints a brief status of all active VLANs. The output that is printed by this command is the same as the output above, with the only difference being that the last two sections will be omitted. The id field provides the same information as the show vlan command, but only for the specified VLAN, as shown in the following output:

```
Switch-1#show vlan id 150

VLAN Name                             Status    Ports
---- -------------------------------- --------- --------------------
150  VLAN_150                         active    Fa0/1, Fa0/2, Fa0/3,
                                                Fa0/4, Fa0/5, Fa0/6,
                                                Fa0/7, Fa0/8, Fa0/9,
                                                Fa0/10

VLAN Type  SAID       MTU   Parent RingNo BridgeNo Stp  BrdgMode
---- ----- ---------- ----- ------ ------ -------- ---- --------
150  enet  100150     1500  -      -      -        -    -

Trans1 Trans2
------ ------
0      0
0      0

Remote SPAN VLAN
----------------
Disabled

Primary Secondary Type               Ports
------- --------- ------------------ --------------------------------
```

Again, the VLAN name is included in the output, as are all of the access ports that belong to the VLAN. Trunk ports are not included in this output because they belong to all VLANs. Additional information also includes the VLAN MTU, RSPAN configuration (if applicable), and PVLAN configuration parameters (if applicable).

The name field allows the VLAN name to be specified instead of the ID. This command prints the same information as the show vlan id <number> command. The ifindex field displays the SNMP IfIndex for the VLAN (if applicable), while the private-vlan and remote-span fields print PVLAN and RSPAN configuration information, respectively. Finally, the summary field prints a summary of the number of VLANs that are active in the management domain. This includes standard and extended VLANs.

The show vlan command, with or without parameters, is the most useful command in the following aspects of the troubleshooting process:

- Identifying that VLANs are configured on the device
- Verifying port membership

Another useful VLAN troubleshooting command is the show vtp counters command. This command prints information on VTP packet statistics. The output of the show vtp counters command on a switch configured as a VTP server (default) is shown below:

```
Switch#show vtp counters
VTP statistics:
Summary advertisements received    : 15
Subset advertisements received     : 10
Request advertisements received    : 2
Summary advertisements transmitted : 19
Subset advertisements transmitted  : 12
Request advertisements transmitted : 0
Number of config revision errors   : 0
Number of config digest errors     : 0
Number of V1 summary errors        : 0

VTP pruning statistics:

Trunk    Join Transmitted   Join Received   Summary advts received
                                            from non-pruning-
                                            capable device
-----    ----------------   -------------   ------------------------
Fa0/11                  0               1                          0
Fa0/12                  0               1                          0
```

The first six lines of the output printed by the show vtp counters command provide the statistics for the three types of VTP packets: advertisement requests, summary advertisements, and subset advertisements. These different messages will be described in the following section.

VTP advertisement requests are requests for configuration information. These messages are sent by VTP clients to VTP servers to request VLAN and VTP information they may be missing. A VTP advertisement request is sent out when the switch resets, the VTP domain name changes, or in the event that the switch has received a VTP summary advertisement frame with a higher configuration revision number than its own. VTP servers should show only the received counters incrementing, while any VTP clients should show only the transmitted counters incrementing.

VTP summary advertisements are sent out by servers every five minutes, by default. These types of messages are used to inform an adjacent switch of the current VTP domain name the configuration revision number and the status of the VLAN configuration, as well as other VTP information, which includes the time stamp, the MD5 hash, and the number of subset advertisements to follow. If these counters are incrementing on the server, then there is more than one switch acting or configured as a server in the domain.

VTP subset advertisements are sent out by VTP servers when a VLAN configuration changes, such as when a VLAN is added, suspended, changed, deleted, or other VLAN-specific parameters (e.g., VLAN MTU) have changed. One or more subset advertisements will be sent following the VTP summary advertisement. A subset advertisement contains a list of VLAN information. If there are several VLANs, more than one subset advertisement may be required in order to advertise all the VLANs.

The Number of config revision errors field shows the number of advertisements that the switch cannot accept because it received packets with the same configuration revision number but with a different MD5 hash value. This is common when changes are made to two or more server switches in the same domain at the same time and an intermediate switch receives these advertisements at the same time. This concept is illustrated in Figure 21.3 below, which illustrates a basic switched network:

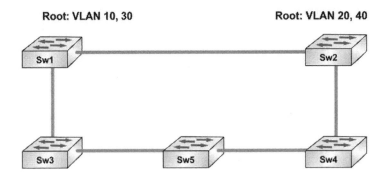

Figure 21.3—Troubleshooting Configuration Revision Number Errors

Figure 21.3 illustrates a basic network that incorporates redundancy and load sharing. It should be assumed that Sw1 and Sw2 are configured as servers, while Sw3 is configured as a client. Sw1 is the root for VLANs 10 and 30, while Sw2 is the root for VLANs 20 and 40. Assume that a simultaneous change is implemented on Sw1 and Sw2, adding VLAN 50 to Sw1 and VLAN 60 to Sw2. Both switches send out an advertisement following the change to the database.

The change is propagated throughout the domain, overwriting the previous databases of the other switches that receive this information. Assume that Sw5 receives the same information from neighbors at the same time and both advertisements contain the same configuration revision number. In such situations, the switch will not be able to accept either advertisement because they have the same configuration revision number but different MD5 hash values.

When this occurs, the switch increments the Number of config revision errors counter field and does not update its database. This situation can result in a loss of connectivity within one or more VLANs because VLAN information is not updated on the switch. To resolve this issue and ensure that the local database on the switch is updated, configure a dummy VLAN on one of the server switches, which results in another update with an incremented configuration revision number. This will overwrite the local database of all switches, allowing Sw5 to update its database as well. Keep in mind that this is not a common occurrence; however, it is possible, hence, the reason for this counter.

The `Number of config digest errors counter` field increments whenever the switch receives an advertisement with a different MD5 hash value than it calculated. This is the result of different VTP passwords configured on the switches. You can use the `show vtp password` command to verify that the configured VTP password is correct. It is also important to remember that the passwords may be the same, but hardware or software issues or bugs could be causing data corruption of VTP packets, resulting in these errors.

Finally, the `VTP pruning statistics` field will only ever contain non-zero values when pruning is enabled for the VTP domain. Pruning is enabled on servers and this configuration is propagated throughout the VTP domain. Servers will receive joins from clients when pruning has been enabled for the VTP domain.

PING, TRACEROUTE, AND THEIR EXTENDED OPTIONS

Few tools in the IOS are used more frequently than the `ping` and `traceroute` commands. Every network administrator and engineer has used these commands but, surprisingly, very few know about all of the capabilities that are available with them. This section will go into a deep dive of the `ping` and `traceroute` commands, not only so you do well on your exam but, more importantly, so you can use this information to support the network you are entrusted with.

The Ping Command

The `ping` (Packet InterNet Groper) command is typically used to troubleshoot accessibility between two devices. Ping leverages the ICMP to determine whether a remote device is accessible or not. If it is accessible, ICMP will measure the amount of time it takes to receive the echo reply from the destination.

A ping is successful only if an ECHO_REQUEST gets to the destination and the destination is able to get an ECHO_REPLY back to the source of the ping within a predefined time (maximum) interval. This is illustrated in Figure 21.4 below:

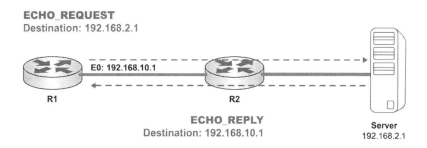

Figure 21.4—Ping Command in Action

In the output below, you can see that the max interval is set to 36 milliseconds.

```
R1#ping 192.168.1.2

Type escape sequence to abort.
Sending 5, 100-byte ICMP Echos to 192.168.1.2, timeout is 2 seconds:
.!!!!
Success rate is 80 percent (4/5), round-trip min/avg/max = 20/26/36 ms
```

The Extended Ping Command

When a `ping` command is sent from a router, the default source address of the `ping` is the IP address of the interface that the packet uses to exit the router. This may not be ideal, as you will see in the following example, if you have a firewall in between that would deny a source ping from the default interface 192.168.10.1. You would need to change the source address to something that is allowed, for example, to 192.168.20.1, using the inside interface E1. With the `extended ping` command, you can change the source address to any IP address hosted by the router.

Figure 21.5 below illustrates a blocked ping packet and one permitted when sourced from a different interface:

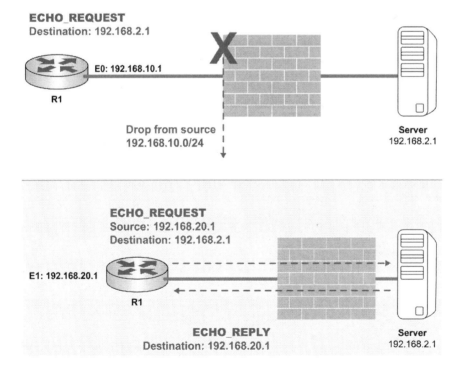

Figure 21.5—Extended ping using the source interface

Ping Command Field Descriptions

Before we do a deep dive into the extended ping options, let's first login to a router and take a look at the options from a high level:

```
Router1#ping
Protocol [ip]:
Target IP address: 192.168.2.1
Repeat count [5]: 50
Datagram size [100]: 1400
Timeout in seconds [2]:
Extended commands [n]: y
Source address or interface: 172.16.1.1
Type of service [0]:
Set DF bit in IP header? [no]:
Validate reply data? [no]:
Data pattern [0xABCD]:
Loose, Strict, Record, Timestamp, Verbose[none]:
Sweep range of sizes [n]:
Type escape sequence to abort.
Sending 50, 1400-byte ICMP Echos to 192.168.2.1, timeout is 2 seconds:
Packet sent with a source address of 172.16.1.1
```

Now that you have seen all the options that are offered, let's dive into each one.

Table 21.5—Ping options

Field	Description
Protocol [ip]:	Prompts for a supported protocol. Enter appletalk, clns, ip, novell, apollo, vines, decnet, or xns. The default is ip.
Target IP address:	Prompts for the address or hostname of the destination node you plan to ping
Repeat count [5]:	Number of ping packets that are sent to the destination address; the default is 5
Datagram size [100]:	Size of the ping packet (in bytes); the default is 100 bytes
Timeout in seconds [2]:	Timeout interval. The default is 2 (seconds). The ping is declared successful only if the ECHO_REPLY packet is received before this time interval.
Extended commands [n]:	Specifies whether or not a series of additional commands will appear. The default is "no" and if selected, the ping operation will begin without further prompting. If "yes" is selected, you will be prompted with the following:
Source address or interface:	The interface or IP address of the router to use as a source address for the probes. The router normally picks the IP address of the outbound interface to use.
Type of service [0]:	Specifies the Type of Service (ToS). The requested ToS is placed in each probe. The default is 0.

Set DF bit in IP header? [no]:	Specifies whether or not the Don't Fragment (DF) bit is to be set on the ping packet. If yes is specified, the Don't Fragment option will not allow this packet to be fragmented.
Validate reply data? [no]:	Specifies whether or not to validate the reply data; the default is "no"
Data pattern [0xABCD]	Specifies the data pattern to troubleshoot framing errors and clocking problems on Serial lines; the default is [0xABCD]
Verbose[none]:, Record, Loose, Strict, Timestamp,	IP header options. This prompt offers more than one option to be selected: • Verbose is automatically selected along with any other option. • Record displays the address(es) of the hops. • Loose specifies the address(es) of the hop(s) you want the packet to go through. • Strict specifies the hop(s) that you want the packet to go through, but no other hop(s) are allowed to be visited. • Timestamp is used to measure roundtrip time to hosts.
Sweep range of sizes [n]:	Allows you to vary the sizes of the echo packets that are sent; the default is "no"

When you send a ping, you will receive immediate notification of success or failure. A "!" indicates a successful response and a "." indicates no response. Here is an example output of a successful ping attempt:

```
!!!!!!!!!!!!!!!!!!!!!!!!!!!!!!!!!!!!!!!!!!!!!!!!!!!!!!!!!!!!!!!!!!!!!!!!!!!!
Success rate is 100 percent, round-trip min/avg/max = 1/2/4 ms
```

As you can see, there were no lost packets and there was even information on round-trip time. The fastest round-trip time (RTT) was 1 ms, the average RTT was 2 ms, and the longest RTT was 4 ms. Round-trip time is how long the ping signal/pulse/packet takes to get there and back.

Just because you lose a packet doesn't necessarily mean that something is wrong. For example, when performing tests, you will often see this:

```
.!!!!
Success rate is 80 percent, round-trip min/avg/max = 1/2/4 ms
```

In the output above, the first packet failed because there was no ARP entry, but once a MAC address was mapped to an IP address, the remaining packets reached their destination and responded. All other tests to this endpoint were successful.

You may also see something like this:

```
.!!!....!!!..!!.!.....!!!
```

This would indicate an intermittent connectivity issue that could be anything from a Spanning Tree issue to MAC flapping or a Physical Layer issue, all of which would have to be investigated further. We will use the extended ping option in several of our labs for testing purposes.

The Traceroute Command

Although ping is used to verify connectivity between two devices, it doesn't provide information on the path between them. For example, if you cannot ping a data center server from your branch office, you will want to understand where the ping is failing. Is it failing at the firewall, the edge router, the core router, or at the data center switch? You won't know the answer unless you use the traceroute command.

For example, if you want to fly to New York, you can call a travel agent and say, "Please book me a ticket to New York." Most people want to know how many layovers they will have to get to New York and when they ask this, they may be told that there will be a layover in Atlanta first and then arrival at New York. That's the difference between a ping and a traceroute command. The ping command simply tells you the status of the destination, but the traceroute command tells you the path you will take to get there. The purpose behind the traceroute command is to "trace" the path the packet took to reach the destination.

Let's go ahead and run the traceroute command and check the path to 4.2.2.1:

```
Router1#traceroute 4.2.2.1
Type escape sequence to abort.
Tracing the route to a.resolvers.level3.net (4.2.2.1)
 1 te0-1-0-6.rcr21.ord07.atlas.ispco.com (38.122.188.17) 0 msec 12 msec 4
msec
 2 be2110.router42.ord01.atlas.ispco.com (114.14.1.37) 0 msec 4 msec
 3 be2761.router41.ord03.atlas.ispco.com (114.14.41.18) 4 msec
 4 proispinc.ord03.atlas.ispco.com (114.14.12.82) 2132 msec 432 msec
 5 a.resolvers.level3.net (4.2.2.1) 0 msec 4 msec 0 msec
Router1#
```

As you can see, there are a total of five "hops" between the network device and 4.2.2.1. Each hop is a router forwarding the packet to the next router. You can also see the amount of time it took for the packet to traverse between each hop. For example, you can see that once you hit hop 4, you may have a network issue to look into with the owner of "proispinc.ord03" at ispco.com.

So, how did we obtain all of this information?

1. Three datagrams are sent, each with a TTL field value set to 1, which causes the datagram to "timeout" as soon as it hits the first router in the path. This router then responds with an ICMP "time exceeded" message.
2. Three more UDP messages are sent, each with the TTL value set to 2. This causes the second router in the path to the destination to return ICMP "time exceeded" messages.
3. This process continues until the packets reach the destination and until the system that originated the traceroute receives ICMP "time exceeded" messages from every router in the path to the destination.

The Extended Traceroute Command

The extended traceroute command offers additional troubleshooting tools:

```
Router#traceroute
Protocol [ip]:
Target IP address: 4.2.2.1
Source address: 31.111.118.29
Numeric display [n]:
Timeout in seconds [3]:
Probe count [3]:
Minimum Time to Live [1]:
Maximum Time to Live [30]:
Port Number [33434]:
Loose, Strict, Record, Timestamp, Verbose[none]:
Type escape sequence to abort.
Tracing the route to a.resolvers.level3.net (4.2.2.1)
```

Table 21.6 below lists the traceroute command field descriptions:

Table 21.6—Traceroute options

Field	Description
Protocol [ip]:	Prompts for a supported protocol; the default is ip
Target IP address	You must enter a hostname or an IP address. There is no default.
Source address:	The interface or IP address of the router to use as a source address for the probes
Numeric display [n]:	The default is to have both a symbolic and numeric display; however, you can suppress the symbolic display.
Timeout in seconds [3]:	The number of seconds to wait for a response to a probe packet; the default is 3 seconds
Probe count [3]:	The number of probes to be sent at each TTL level; the default count is 3
Minimum Time to Live [1]:	The TTL value for the first probes; the default is 1
Maximum Time to Live [30]:	The largest TTL value that can be used. The default is 30. The traceroute command terminates when the destination is reached or when this value is reached.
Port Number [33434]:	The destination port used by the UDP probe messages; the default is 33434
Loose, Strict, Record, Timestamp, Verbose[none]:	IP header options. You can specify any combination. The traceroute command issues prompts for the required fields.

If the timer goes off before a response comes in, traceroute prints an asterisk (*) as you can see below:

```
Router1#traceroute 9.1.2.3
Type escape sequence to abort.
Tracing the route to 9.1.2.3
  1 * * *
  2 * * *
  3 * * *
  4 * *
Router1#
```

TERMINAL MONITOR

There will be times when you will want to display the results of debug commands or system error messages in your terminal session (i.e., when you have a remote connection as opposed to a console connection). By default, this information will not show up on your screen, which can lead novice engineers to believe that the debug isn't running or that no errors are being printed. So, if you enable a debug session, you won't see the results of that process even though it is running.

This is by design, as debug or system information normally will overwhelm the screen you are on, and it's likely that any attempt to view other data through show commands will be futile. Also, trying to program a Cisco device while the debug information is filling your screen is quite a challenge. Cisco provides commands to turn on and off the display of debug and system information during your terminal session.

To display debug command output and system error messages for the current terminal and session, use the `terminal monitor` command in EXEC mode. This setting is set locally and will not remain in effect if you close your terminal session.

In the following example, the system is configured to display debug command output and error messages during the current terminal session:

```
Router#terminal monitor
```

Now, let's look at what happens when we enable a debug session for AAA and then enable the `terminal monitor` command:

```
Router1#debug aaa authorization
AAA Authorization debugging is on
Router1#terminal monitor
Router1#
26w3d: AAA/ACCT/3844(003D3E51): Pick method list "default"
26w3d: AAA/ACCT/SETMLIST(003D3E51): Handle 0, mlist 4A4B97C0, Name
default
26w3d: Getting session id for CMD(003D3E51) : db=53F3A34C
26w3d: AAA/ACCT/CMD(003D3E51): add, count 3
26w3d: AAA/ACCT/EVENT/(003D3E51): COMMAND
```

This data will continue to quickly fill up the screen. If you want to shut it off, you would enter the following:

```
Router1#terminal no monitor
```

LOGGING EVENTS

There are many different ways you can monitor the status of your network device, but one of the more useful ways is to leverage the logging function within the IOS. Specifically, you can use the `logging` command to track important updates on areas of concern. Events related to the selection you make will be entered into the log of the Cisco router for you to view immediately or at a later date. Here are the many options for you to select from:

```
Router1(config)#logging ?
  Hostname or A.B.C.D  IP address of the logging host
  alarm                Configure syslog for alarms
  buffered             Set buffered logging parameters
  buginf               Enable buginf logging for debugging
  cns-events           Set CNS Event logging level
  console              Set console logging parameters
  count                every log message and timestamp last
                       occurrence
  delimiter            Append delimiter to syslog messages
  discriminator        Create or modify a message discriminator
  esm                  Set ESM filter restrictions
  event                Global interface events
  exception            Limit size of exception flush output
  facility             Facility parameter for syslog messages
  filter               Specify logging filter
  history              Configure syslog history table
  host                 Set syslog server IP address and parameters
  ip                   IP configuration
  listen               MWAM remote console and logging listen enabler
  message-counter      Configure log message to include certain
                       counter value
  monitor              Set terminal line (monitor) logging parameters
  on                   Enable logging to all enabled destinations
  origin-id            Add origin ID to syslog messages
  persistent           Set persistent logging parameters
  queue-limit          Set logger message queue size
  rate-limit           Set messages per second limit
  reload               Set reload logging level
  source-interface     Specify interface for source address in logging
                       transactions
  system               enable/disable System Event Log
  trap                 Set syslog server logging level
  userinfo             Enable logging of user info on privileged mode
                       enabling
```

Let's say you want to log the status of a trunk you've been having issues with lately. To enable trunk status messaging, use the `logging event trunk-status` command in interface configuration mode. To disable trunk status messaging, use the no form of this command.

```
Router(config)#logging event trunk-status
Router(config)#end
Router#show logging event trunk-status
```

NOTE: Use the ? to reveal many of the commands. How can you ensure the pool only contains the addresses you want to lease? Check step 3 for the answer.

The following will show up in the log via the`show log` command (or a terminal session if you have the `terminal monitor` command enabled):

```
*Aug 4 17:27:01.404 UTC: %DTP-SPSTBY-5-NONTRUNKPORTON: Port Gi3/3 has
become non-trunk
*Aug 4 17:27:00.773 UTC: %DTP-SP-5-NONTRUNKPORTON: Port Gi3/3 has become
non-trunk
```

You can dig deeper and perform a `logging event link-status` command to track the status of problem interfaces. Here is an example of how to implement this type of tracking:

```
Router1#config t
Enter configuration commands, one per line. End with CTRL/Z.
Router1(config)#logging event ?
  link-status  Globally enable/disable link UPDOWN message

Router1(config)#logging event link-status ?
  boot     Suppress/Allow link UPDOWN messages during boot
  default  Link UPDOWN messages for all interfaces

Router1(config)#logging event link-status default
```

Please take today's exam at https://www.in60days.com/free/ccnain60days/

DAY 21 LABS

Layer 1 Troubleshooting

Test the relevant Layer 1 troubleshooting commands presented in this module on real devices:

- Examine switch system and port LED status for different scenarios, as described in the module
- Issue a `show interface` command and examine all the related information as per the description in this module
- Issue the same for `show controllers` and `show interface counters errors` commands

Layer 2 Troubleshooting

Test the relevant Layer 2 troubleshooting commands presented in this module on real devices:

- Configure VTP between the switches and advertise some VLANs from the VTP server to the VTP client (see the VTP lab in Day 3)
- Configure a trunk between two switches and generate some traffic (ping)
- Test the `show vlan` command
- Test the `show interface counters trunk` command
- Test the `show interface switchport` command
- Test the `show interface trunk` command
- Test the `show VTP status` command
- Test the `show VTP counter` command

Review

DAY 22 TASKS

- Review yesterdays troubleshooting lesson and labs
- Read over days 1-3 and redo any labs if necessary
- Complete challenges below
- Read the ICND1 cram guide
- Take today's exam at **https://www.in60days.com/free/ccnain60days/**
- Spend 15 minutes on the subnetting.org website

We will now embark upon review days taking you up to the ICND1 exam for day 30. If you are taking the CCNA exam (one exam route) then you will still do these review days and then take the CCNA exam on day 60. In this case you will need to come back and review the ICND1 notes periodically.

I've set tasks and labs for you to follow over the next few days. Feel free to adjust my plan if you need to work on other areas.

Challenge 1—VLSM Exercise

Reality Press Ltd

Network: 200.10.200.x /24
Subnet Mask: ???

50 hosts

60 hosts

55 hosts

You are the network administrator for the network 200.10.200.0/24. You are asked to redesign the network to cater for a change in the company. Now they require the network to be broken into three smaller networks. One requires 55 hosts, one requires 50, and another 60. There will also be two WAN connections required.

Challenge 2—VLANs Lab

Topology

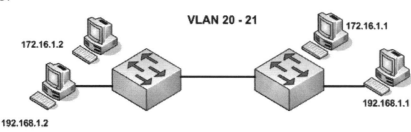

Instructions

Connect to the switch using a console connection. Connect two PCs to each switch or connect the switch to the fast ethernet port on two routers.

1. Add IP addresses to the PCs or router Ethernet interfaces
2. Create VLAN 20 and 21 on the switch
3. Set the ports the PCs connect to as access ports (default but do it anyway)
4. Put the two switch ports into VLAN 20 and two into VLAN 21 you can choose which subnets go into which vlans 172 or 192
5. Ping from 172.16.1.1 to 172.16.1.2 and then 192.168.1.1 to 192.168.1.2—you won't be able to ping between subnets as there is no router involved
6. Add switchport security to both switches. Allow only 2 MAC addresses to be learned and make them sticky. Do this for both host ports on either switch. Set the default action to 'restrict.'

Challenge 3—NAT and Static Routes

Topology

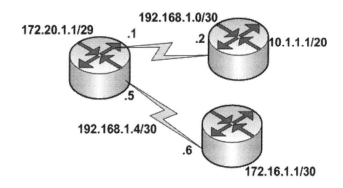

172.20.1.1/29

192.168.1.0/30

.1

.2

10.1.1.1/20

.5

192.168.1.4/30

.6

172.16.1.1/30

Instructions

Connect three routers together with serial or ethernet connections

1. Configure the connections between the routers and ping
2. Add loopback addresses to the three routers as per the diagram
3. Add a static routes so all networks can ping one another. Mix up exit interface and next hop.
4. Ping all networks from all routers
5. Configure a NAT pool on the hub (middle) router for network 172.20.1.0/29 to be NATted to pool 192.168.20.0/24
6. Source a ping from 172.20.1.1 to the loopback addresses on the spoke routers. Turn on a NAT debug first and check the NAT translation table afterward

Challenge 4—Named ACL

Topology

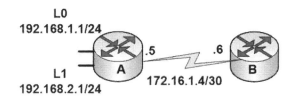

L0
192.168.1.1/24

.5

.6

A

B

L1
192.168.2.1/24

172.16.1.4/30

Instructions

Connect two routers together with a serial or crossover cable.

1. Add IP addresses to routers and loopback on Router A according to diagram.
2. Add a static route on Router B to send all traffic back to Router A.
1. Ping between Router A and B to test the serial line (remember clock rates).
2. Create a local username and password for the routers.

3. Permit connections to the telnet (vty) lines on the Router B and login local.
4. Permit only SSH traffic into the vty lines on Router A.
5. Create a named ACL on Router A it should block all ping traffic unless it is destined for 192.168.1.1 and of course apply the ACL to the serial interface on RouterA.
6. Test by pinging the serial and other loopback addresses.
3. Issue a show `ip access-lists.`

Answers to VLSM Challenge

One proposal could be like this:

55 hosts: 200.10.200.0/26

50 hosts: 200.10.200.128/26

60 hosts: 200.10.200.64/26

Spare network: 200.10.200.192/26. This can be further subnetted for the WAN links:

Point-to-Point network 1: 200.10.200.192/30

Point-to-Point network 2: 200.10.200.196/30

Please take today's exam at **https://www.in60days.com/free/ccnain60days/**

Review

DAY 23 TASKS

- Review theory and labs from days 5-7
- Review any other theory (if required)
- Complete challenges
- Read the ICND1 cram guide
- Spend 15 minutes on the subnetting.org website

Take the exam at **https://www.in60days.com/free/ccnain60days/**

Challenge 1—NAT and RIP

Topology

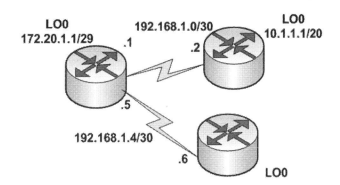

Instructions
Connect three routers together with serial or ethernet connections

1. Configure the connections between the routers and ping
2. Add loopback addresses to the three routers as per the diagram
3. Put the 172.16.1.0/30 and 10.1.1.0/20 and both 192 networks into RIPv2
4. Add a static route on the two spoke routers for network 192.168.20.0/24 to go to the hub

5. Configure a NAT pool on the hub router for network 172.20.1.0/29 to be NATted to pool 192.168.20.0/24
6. Check all RIP routes are in the routing table with correct networks
7. Source a ping from 172.20.1.1 to the loopback addresses on the spoke routers. Turn on a NAT debug first and check the NAT translation table afterward

Challenge 2—VLANs and Port Security

Topology

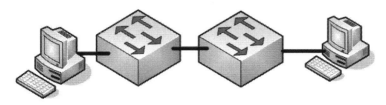

Instructions

Connect to the switch using a console connection. Connect a PC to the switch or connect the switch to the fast ethernet port on a router.

1. Add port security to the switches allowing only the MACs of the attached PCs
2. Create VLAN10 on the switches
3. Set the ports to the PCs as Access and Switch to Switch as trunk
4. Put switch interfaces into VLAN10
5. Add IP addresses for both PCs in the same subnet and ping across (after approx 30 secs)
6. Issue a `show port-security interface` x on the switch

Challenge 3—Trunking and DTP

Topology

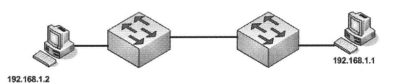

VLAN 4

192.168.1.1

192.168.1.2

Instructions

Connect to the switch using a console connection. Connect a PC to each switch or connect the switch to the fast ethernet port on a router.

1. Add IP addresses to the PCs or router Ethernet interfaces.
2. Create VLAN 4 on the switches.
3. Set the ports the PCs connect to as access ports (default but do it anyway).
4. Put the two switch ports into VLAN 4.
5. Configure the link between the switches as trunk ports and no shut them.
6. Disable DTP on both switches.
7. Configure the trunk link to permit only VLAN4.
8. Set the native VLAN as VLAN4.
9. Wait about 30 seconds at most and then ping from PC to PC.

Review

DAY 24 TASKS

- Review theory and labs from days 9-12
- Complete the challenges below
- Read the ICND1 cram guide
- Take the exam at https://www.in60days.com/free/ccnain60days/
- Spend 15 minutes on the subnetting.org website

Challenge 1—CDP

Topology

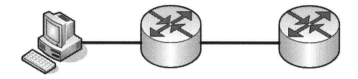

Instructions

Connect to a router with a console cable and Ethernet cable. Connect another router.

1. Configure an IP address on the two routers and ping across.
2. Using CDP commands see what information you can gather about the other router.
3. On the left router turn CDP off the interface.
4. On the right router, turn CDP off the entire device..

Challenge 2—DHCP

Topology

172.16.0.1/24

Instructions
Connect a PC to a router Ethernet interface

1. Configure IP address 172.16.0.1 /24 onto the router.
2. Create a DHCP pool for the 172.16.0.100-200 /24 network.
3. Add an excluded address of the router interface.
4. Add a default router address of 192.168.1.1.
5. Add a DNS server name of in60days.com
6. Add a lease duration of 4 hours
7. Configure the PC to obtain IP address via DHCP.
8. No shut the router interface.
9. Check the IP config of the PC for the IP address assignment.
10. Check the DHCP pool allocation on the router.

Challenge 3—InterVLAN Routing Subinterfaces

Topology

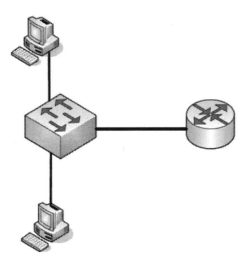

Instructions

Connect to the switch using a console connection. Connect two PCs to the switch and the switch to a router Ethernet interface. Set VLAN2 as 172.16.0.0/16 and VLAN3 as 192.168.1.0/24.

1. Configure two VLANs on the switch and put each PC in one of the VLANs. Set default gateways as necessary.
2. Configure a trunk between the switch and the router.
3. Set sub-interfaces on the router to enable routing between the two VLANs.
4. Put the two switch ports into VLAN 20 and two into VLAN 21 you can choose which subnets go into which vlans 172 or 192.
5. Ping from one PC to another. Check the switch MAC address table.

Review

DAY 25 TASKS

- Take the exam at https://www.in60days.com/free/ccnain60days/
- Review lessons and labs from days 14-16
- Complete the challenges below
- Complete any earlier lab (without looking at the solution)
- Read the ICND1 cram guide
- Spend 15 minutes on the subnetting.org website

Challenge 1—VLANs

Topology

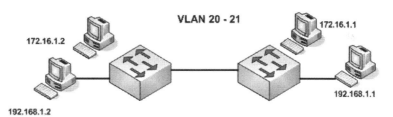

Instructions

Connect to the switch using a console connection. Connect two PCs to each switch or connect the switch to the fast ethernet port on two routers.

1. Add IP addresses to the PCs or router Ethernet interfaces
2. Create VLAN 20 and 21 on the switch
3. Set the ports the PCs connect to as access ports (default but do it anyway)
4. Put the two switch ports into VLAN 20 and two into VLAN 21 you can choose which subnets go into which vlans 172 or 192
5. Ping from 172.16.1.1 to 172.16.1.2 and then 192.168.1.1 to 192.168.1.2—you won't be able to ping between subnets as there is no router involved

Challenge 2—DHCP

Topology

10.0.0.1/24

Instructions
Connect a PC to a router Ethernet interface

1. Configure IP address 10.0.0.1 /24 onto the router.
2. Create a DHCP pool for the 10.0.0.100-200/24 network.
3. Add an excluded address of the router interface.
4. Add a default router address of 10.1.1.201
5. Add a DNS server name of in60days.com
6. Add a lease duration of 4 hours
7. Configure the PC to obtain IP address via DHCP.
8. No shut the router interface.
9. Check the IP config of the PC for the IP address assignment.
10. Check the DHCP pool allocation on the router.

NOTE: Use the ? to reveal many of the commands. How can you ensure the pool only contains the addresses you want to lease? Check step 3 for the answer.

Review

DAY 26 TASKS

- Take the exam at https://www.in60days.com/free/ccnain60days/
- Review days 18-19 theory and labs
- Complete any lab you wish or challenge labs below
- Write the ICND1 cram guide from memory
- Spend 15 minutes on the subnetting.org website

Is there anything else you need to cover from the ICND1 syllabus? You should have nailed all of your weak areas by now.

You should be able to do the following:

- Recite the entire cram guide
- Configure ACLs, NAT, and IP addressing
- Configure basic switch security and VLANs
- Configure port security on switches
- Enable and disable CDP and LLDP
- Configure and troubleshoot trunks
- Configure DHCP, DNS and NTP
- Answer VLSM and subnetting questions very quickly
- Understand TCP, OSI, cables, and specifications
- Understand the routing process including static IPv4/IPv6
- Understand IPv6 addressing and IPv4.
- Configure RIP with passive interfaces
- And of course troubleshoot the above!

Challenge 1—IPv6 Static Routes

Topology

2001:aaaa:bbbb:cccc::/64

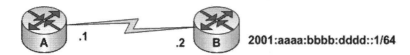

.1 .2 **2001:aaaa:bbbb:dddd::1/64**

Instructions
Connect two routers together with a serial or crossover cable.

1. Add IPv6 addresses to routers and loopback on Router B according to diagram.
2. Set enable secret password cisco on Router A and enable password on Router B.
3. Ping between Router A and B to test serial line (remember clock rates).
4. Configure a static route on Router A to reach the network on the loopback of Router B.
5. Ping the IPv6 host on Router B from Router A.

Add a telnet password on Router B and telnet to it from Router A.

Challenge 2—LLDP

Topology

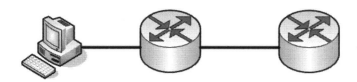

Instructions
Connect to a router with a console cable and Ethernet cable. Connect another router.

1. Configure an IP address on the two routers and ping across.
2. Enable LLDP on both routers.
3. Using LLDP commands see what information you can gather about the other router.
4. On the left router turn LLDP off the interface.
5. On the right router, turn LLDP off the entire device.

Challenge 3—RIP Lab

Topology

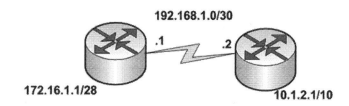

192.168.1.0/30

.1   .2

172.16.1.1/28

10.1.2.1/10

Instructions

Connect two routers together with serial or ethernet connections

1. Configure the connections between the routers and ping
2. Add loopback addresses to the two routers as per the diagram
3. Configure RIPv2 on both routers
4. Issue a show ip route and check all networks on both routers
5. Now configure no auto-summary on both routers and check for /10 and /28 routes
6. Make the loopback on R2 (on the right) passive.

DAY 27

Review

DAY 27 TASKS

- Take the exam at https://www.in60days.com/free/ccnain60days/
- Review troubleshooting any theory (if required), especially the IPv6-related sections
- Complete any lab you wish or make your own up
- Write the ICND1 cram guide from memory
- Spend 15 minutes on the subnetting.org website

Review

DAY 28 TASKS

- Take the exam at **https://www.in60days.com/free/ccnain60days/**
- Review any theory (if required)
- Complete any labs you wish
- Write the ICND1 cram guide from memory
- Spend 15 minutes on the subnetting.org website

Can you do the following?

- Secure a switch with Telnet passwords/SSH and switch ports
- Secure a router with Banner messages and passwords
- Put switch ports into VLANs
- Troubleshoot simple switch and VLAN issues
- Configure static routes
- Configure static NAT, dynamic NAT, and PAT
- Configure named and numbered IPv4 ACLs
- Carve a network down using VLSM
- Find the correct subnet for a host
- Configure a DHCP pool
- Configure IPv6 basic addressing

Review

DAY 29 TASKS

- Take the exam at https://www.in60days.com/free/ccnain60days/
- Review any theory (if required)
- Complete any lab you wish
- Spend 10 minutes on the subnetting.org website

Review

DAY 30 TASKS

- Take the exam at **https://www.in60days.com/free/ccnain60days/**
- Review any theory (if required), especially the IPv6-related sections
- Complete any lab you wish
- Write the ICND1 cram guide from memory
- Spend 15 minutes on the subnetting.org website

Exam Day

Today you should be taking the ICND1 exam. If you are doing the full CCNA route, then take a day off. You have earned it. We have a lot of hard work to come.

You will need to dip back into ICND1 topics if you are taking the one exam route. I'm going to leave this to you because by now you will know what to do and how to do it. You literally only need to spend 10-15 minutes per day reviewing a lab or theory.

Spanning Tree Protocol

DAY 31 TASKS

- Read today's lesson notes (below)
- Complete today's lab
- Take today's exam at **https://www.in60days.com/free/ccnain60days/**
- Read the ICND2 cram guide
- Spend 15 minutes on the subnetting.org website

The role of Spanning Tree Protocol (STP) is to prevent loops from occurring on your network by creating a loop-free logical topology, while allowing physical links in redundant switched network topologies. With the huge growth in the use of switches on networks, and the main goal of propagating VLAN information, the problem of frames looping endlessly around the network began to occur.

The previous CCNA exam required only a basic understanding of STP. The current version, however, expects you to have a very good grasp of the subject.

The IEEE 802.1D standard was designed at a time when the recovery of connectivity after an outage was within a minute or so, which was considered adequate performance. With the IEEE 802.1D STP, recovery takes around 50 seconds, which includes 20 seconds for the Max Age timer to expire and then an additional 30 seconds for the port to transition from the Blocking state to the Forwarding state.

As computer technology evolved, and networks became more critical, it became apparent that more rapid network convergence was required. Cisco addressed this requirement by developing some proprietary enhancements to STP that include Backbone Fast and Uplink Fast.

Today you will learn about the following:

- The need for STP
- BPDUs
- STP Bridge ID
- STP Root Bridge election
- STP cost and priority

- STP Root and Designated Ports
- STP enhancements
- Troubleshooting STP
- The need for RSTP
- RSTP configuration
- Extended VLANs

This lesson maps to the following ICND2 syllabus requirement:

- 1.1 Configure, verify, and troubleshoot VLANs (normal/extended range) spanning multiple switches
- 1.3 Configure, verify, and troubleshoot STP protocols
- 1.3.a STP mode (PVST+ and RPVST+)
- 1.3.b STP root bridge selection
- 1.4 Configure, verify, and troubleshoot STP-related optional features
- 1.4.a PortFast
- 1.4.b BPDU guard

THE NEED FOR STP

STP is defined in the IEEE 802.1D standard. Its sole purpose is to prevent loops on your LAN by shutting down ports which could cause them. In order to maintain a loop-free logical topology, every two seconds, switches pass Bridge Protocol Data Units (BPDUs). BPDUs are data messages used within a spanning tree topology to pass information about ports, addresses, priorities, and costs. The BPDUs are tagged with the VLAN ID.

Figure 31.1 below shows how loops can be created in a network. Because each switch learns about VLAN 20, it also advertises to other switches that it can reach VLAN 20. Soon enough, each switch thinks it is the source for VLAN 20 traffic and a loop is caused, so any frame destined for VLAN 20 is passed from switch to switch.

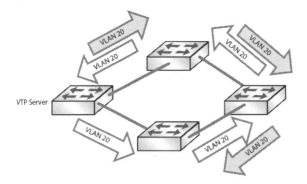

Figure 31.1—How Loops Are Created

STP runs an algorithm to decide which switch ports stay open (active), as far as a particular VLAN is concerned, and which ones need to be shut for that particular VLAN. This means that a port could be actively forwarding traffic for one VLAN but closed for another.

All switches that reside in the Spanning Tree domain communicate and exchange messages using BPDUs. STP uses the exchange of BPDUs to determine the network topology, which is determined by the following three variables:

- The unique MAC address (switch identifier) that is associated with each switch
- The path cost to the Root Bridge associated with each switch port
- The port identifier (MAC address of the port) associated with each switch port

BPDUs are sent every two seconds, which allows for rapid network loop detection and topology information exchanges. The two types of BPDUs are Configuration BPDUs and Topology Change Notification BPDUs; only Configuration BPDUs will be covered here.

IEEE 802.1D CONFIGURATION BPDUS

Configuration BPDUs are sent by LAN switches and are used to communicate and compute the Spanning Tree topology. After the switch port initializes, the port is placed into the Blocking state and a BPDU is sent to each port in the switch. By default, all switches initially assume that they are the Root of the Spanning Tree, until they exchange Configuration BPDUs with other switches. As long as a port continues to see its Configuration BPDU as the most attractive, it will continue sending Configuration BPDUs. Switches determine the best Configuration BPDU based on the following four factors (in the order listed):

1. Lowest Root Bridge ID
2. Lowest Root path cost to Root Bridge
3. Lowest sender Bridge ID
4. Lowest sender Port ID

The completion of the Configuration BPDU exchange results in the following actions:

- A Root Switch is elected for the entire Spanning Tree domain
- A Root Port is elected on every Non-Root Switch in the Spanning Tree domain
- A Designated Switch is elected for every LAN segment
- A Designated Port is elected on the Designated Switch for every segment (all active ports on the Root Switch are also designated)
- Loops in the network are eliminated by blocking redundant paths

NOTE: These characteristics will be described in detail as you progress through this module.

Once the Spanning Tree network has converged, which happens when all switch ports are in a Forwarding or Blocking state, Configuration BPDUs are sent by the Root Bridge every

Hello time interval, which defaults to two seconds. This is referred to as the origination of Configuration BPDUs. The Configuration BPDUs are forwarded to downstream neighboring switches via the Designated Port on the Root Bridge.

When a Non-Root Bridge receives a Configuration BPDU on its Root Port, which is the port that provides the best path to the Root Bridge, it sends an updated version of the BPDU via its Designated Port(s). This is referred to as the propagation of BPDUs.

The Designated Port is a port on the Designated Switch that has the lowest path cost when forwarding packets from that LAN segment to the Root Bridge.

Once the Spanning Tree network has converged, a Configuration BPDU is always transmitted away from the Root Bridge to the rest of the switches within the STP domain. The simplest way to remember the flow of Configuration BPDUs after the Spanning Tree network has converged is to memorize the following four rules:

1. A Configuration BPDU originates on the Root Bridge and is sent via the Designated Port.
2. A Configuration BPDU is received by a Non-Root Bridge on a Root Port.
3. A Configuration BPDU is transmitted by a Non-Root Bridge on a Designated Port.
4. There is only one Designated Port (on a Designated Switch) on any single LAN segment.

Figure 31.2 below illustrates the flow of the Configuration BPDU in the STP domain, demonstrating the four simple rules listed above:

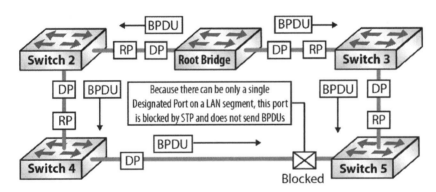

Figure 31.2—A Configuration BPDU Flows throughout the STP Domain

1. Referencing Figure 31.2, the Configuration BPDU is originated by the Root Bridge and sent out via the Designated Ports on the Root Bridge towards the Non-Root Bridge switches, Switch 2 and Switch 3.
2. Non-Root Bridge Switch 2 and Switch 3 receive the Configuration BPDU on their Root Ports, which provide the best path to the Root Bridge.

3. Switch 2 and Switch 3 modify (update) the received Configuration BPDU and forward it out of their Designated Ports. Switch 2 is the Designated Switch on the LAN segment for itself and Switch 4, while Switch 3 is the Designated Switch on the LAN segment for itself and Switch 5. The Designated Port resides on the Designated Switch and is the port that has the lowest path cost when forwarding packets from that LAN segment to the Root Bridge.

4. On the LAN Segment between Switch 4 and Switch 5, Switch 4 is elected Designated Switch and the Designated Port resides on that switch. Because there can be only a single Designated Switch on a segment, the port on Switch 5 for that LAN segment is blocked. This port will not forward any BPDUs.

SPANNING TREE PORT STATES

The Spanning Tree Algorithm (STA) defines a number of states that a port under STP control will progress through before being in an active Forwarding state. 802.1D port states are as follows:

- Blocking—BPDUs received only (20 seconds)
- Listening—BPDUs sent and received (15 seconds)
- Learning—Bridging table is built (15 seconds)
- Forwarding—Sending/receiving data
- Disabled—Administratively down

A port moves through these states in the following manner:

1. From Initialization to Blocking
2. From Blocking to either Listening or Disabled
3. From Listening to either Learning or Disabled
4. From Learning to either Forwarding or Disabled
5. From Forwarding to Disabled

STP timers are used in the process to control convergence:

- Hello—2 seconds (time between each Configuration BPDU)
- Forward Delay—15 seconds (controls durations of Listening/Learning states)
- Max Age—20 seconds (controls the duration of the Blocking state)

Default convergence time is 30 to 50 seconds.

Spanning Tree Blocking State

A switch port that is in the Blocking state performs the following actions:

- Discards frames received on the port from the attached segment
- Discards frames switched from another port

- Does not incorporate station location into its address database
- Receives BPDUs and directs them to the system module
- Does not transmit BPDUs received from the system module
- Receives and responds to network management messages

Spanning Tree Listening State

The Listening state is the first transitional state that the port enters following the Blocking state. The port enters this state when STP determines that the port should participate in frame forwarding. A switch port that is in the Listening state performs the following actions:

- Discards frames received on the port from the attached segment
- Discards frames switched from another port
- Does not incorporate station location into its address database
- Receives BPDUs and directs them to the system module
- Receives, processes, and transmits BPDUs received from the system module
- Receives and responds to network management messages

Spanning Tree Learning State

The Learning state is the second transitional state the port enters. This state comes after the Listening state and before the port enters the Forwarding state. In this state, the port learns and installs MAC addresses into its forwarding table. A switch port that is in the Learning state performs the following actions:

- Discards frames received from the attached segment
- Discards frames switched from another port
- Incorporates (installs) station location into its address database
- Receives BPDUs and directs them to the system module
- Receives, processes, and transmits BPDUs received from the system module
- Receives and responds to network management messages

Spanning Tree Forwarding State

The Forwarding state is the final transitional state the port enters after the Learning state. A port in the Forwarding state forwards frames. A switch port that is in the Forwarding state performs the following actions:

- Forwards frames received from the attached segment
- Forwards frames switched from another port
- Incorporates (installs) station location information into its address database
- Receives BPDUs and directs them to the system module
- Processes BPDUs received from the system module
- Receives and responds to network management messages

Spanning Tree Disabled State

The Disabled state is not part of the normal STP progression for a port. Instead, a port that is administratively shut down by the network administrator, or by the system because of a fault condition, is considered to be in the Disabled state. A disabled port performs the following actions:

- Discards frames received from the attached segment
- Discards frames switched from another port
- Does not incorporate station location into its address database
- Receives BPDUs but does not direct them to the system module
- Does not receive BPDUs from the system module
- Receives and responds to network management messages

SPANNING TREE BRIDGE ID

Switches in a Spanning Tree domain have a Bridge ID (BID), which is used to identify uniquely the switch within the STP domain. The BID is also used to assist in the election of an STP Root Bridge, which will be described later. The BID is an 8-byte field that is composed from a 6-byte MAC address and a 2-byte Bridge Priority. The BID is illustrated in Figure 31.3 below:

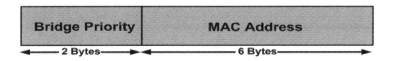

Bridge Priority	MAC Address
◄— 2 Bytes —►	◄———— 6 Bytes ————►

Figure 31.3—Bridge ID Format

The Bridge Priority is the priority of the switch in relation to all other switches. The Bridge Priority values range from 0 to 65535. The default value for Cisco Catalyst switches is 32768.

```
Switch2#show spanning-tree vlan 2

VLAN0002
  Spanning tree enabled protocol ieee
  Root ID    Priority    32768
             Address     0009.7c87.9081
             Cost        19
             Port        1 (FastEthernet0/1)
             Hello Time 2 sec Max Age 20 sec Forward Delay 15 sec
  Bridge ID Priority    32770 (priority 32768 sys-id-ext 2)
             Address     0008.21a9.4f80
             Hello Time 2 sec Max Age 20 sec Forward Delay 15 sec
             Aging Time 300

Interface   Port ID                Designated              Port ID
Name        Prio.Nbr  Cost  Sts Cost        Bridge ID        Prio.Nbr
----------  --------  ----  --- ------------ --------------  --------
```

```
Fa0/1       128.1     19    FWD 0 32768      0009.7c87.9081 128.13
Fa0/2       128.2     19    FWD 19 32770     0008.21a9.4f80 128.2
```

The MAC address in the output above is the hardware address derived from the switch backplane or supervisor engine. In the 802.1D standard, each VLAN requires a unique BID.

Most Cisco Catalyst switches have a pool of 1024 MAC addresses that can be used as BIDs for VLANs. These MAC addresses are allocated sequentially, with the first MAC address in the range assigned to VLAN 1, the second to VLAN 2, the third to VLAN 3, and so forth. This provides the capability to support the standard range of VLANs, but more MAC addresses would be needed to support the extended range of VLANs. This issue was resolved in the 802.1t (Technical and Editorial corrections for 802.1D) standard.

SPANNING TREE ROOT BRIDGE ELECTION

By default, following initialization, all switches initially assume that they are the Root of the Spanning Tree, until they exchange BPDUs with other switches. When switches exchange BPDUs, an election is held and the switch with the lowest Bridge ID in the network is elected the STP Root Bridge. If two or more switches have the same priority, the switch with the lowest order MAC address is chosen. This concept is illustrated in Figure 31.4 below:

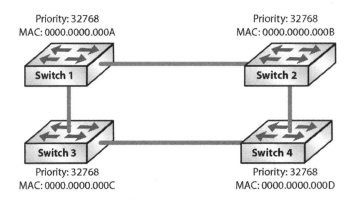

Figure 31.4—Electing the STP Root Bridge

In Figure 31.4, four switches—Switch 1, Switch 2, Switch 3, and Switch 4—are all part of the same STP domain. By default, all of the switches have a Bridge Priority of 32768. In order to determine which switch will become the Root Bridge, and thus break the tie, STP will select the switch based on the lowest-order MAC address. Based on this criterion, and referencing the information shown in Figure 31.4, Switch 1 will be elected the Root Bridge.

Once elected, the Root Bridge becomes the logical center of the Spanning Tree network. This is not to say that the Root Bridge is physically at the center of the network. Ensure that you do not make that false assumption.

NOTE: It is important to remember that during STP Root Bridge election, no traffic is forwarded over any switch in the same STP domain.

Cisco IOS software allows administrators to influence the election of the Root Bridge. In addition, administrators can also configure a backup Root Bridge. The backup Root Bridge is a switch that administrators would prefer to become the Root Bridge in the event that the current Root Bridge failed or was removed from the network.

It is always good practice to configure a backup Root Bridge for the Spanning Tree domain. This allows the network to be deterministic in the event that the Root Bridge fails. The most common practice is to configure the highest priority (i.e., the lowest numerical value) on the Root Bridge and then the second-highest priority on the switch that should assume Root Bridge functionality in the event that the current Root Bridge fails. This is illustrated in Figure 31.5 below:

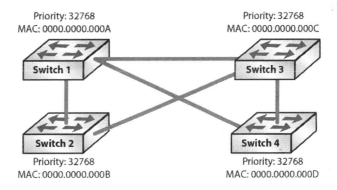

Figure 31.5—Electing the STP Root Bridge (Continued)

Based on the configuration in Figure 31.5, the most likely switch to be elected as the Root Bridge in this network is Switch 1. This is because, although all priority values are the same, this switch has the lowest-order MAC address. In the event that Switch 1 failed, STP would elect Switch 2 as the Root Bridge, because it has the second-lowest MAC address. However, this would result in a suboptimal network topology.

To address this, administrators can manually configure the priority on Switch 1 to the lowest possible value (0) and that of Switch 2 to the second-lowest possible value (4096). This will ensure that in the event that the Root Bridge (Switch 1) fails, Switch 2 will be elected the Root Bridge. Because administrators are aware of the topology and know which switch would assume Root Bridge functionality, they created a deterministic network that is easier to troubleshoot. The Root ID is carried in BPDUs and includes the Bridge Priority and MAC address of the Root Bridge.

EXAM TIP: If you want to force a switch to become the Root Bridge, you can perform the following (see also Figure 31.6 below):

- You can manually set the priority

```
Switch(config)#spanning-tree vlan 2 priority ?
  <0-61440>  bridge priority in increments of 4096
```

- Or set it as the Root Bridge using macro the commands primary or secondary

```
Switch(config)#spanning-tree vlan 2 root ?
  primary    Configure this switch as primary root for this spanning
tree
  secondary  Configure switch as secondary root
```

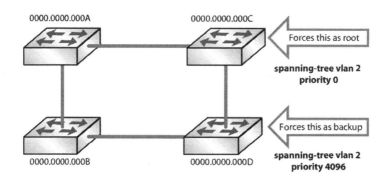

Figure 31.6—Forcing a Switch to Become the Root Bridge

```
SwitchC#show spanning-tree vlan 5
VLAN0005
Spanning tree enabled protocol ieee
Root ID        Priority       0
Address0000.0000.000c
This bridge is the root
Bridge ID      Priority       0 (priority 0 sys-id-ext 5)
SwitchD#show spanning-tree vlan 5
VLAN0005
Spanning tree enabled protocol ieee
Root ID        Priority       4096
Address0000.0000.000d
Bridge ID      Priority       4096 (priority 8192 sys-id-ext 5)

SwitchD#show spanning-tree vlan 5
VLAN0005
Spanning tree enabled protocol ieee
Root ID        Priority       4096
Address0000.0000.000d
Bridge ID      Priority       4096 (priority 8192 sys-id-ext 5)
```

Note that the VLAN number is often added to the priority number, as shown in the output below:

```
SwitchA#show spanning-tree vlan 5
Bridge ID Priority 32773 (priority 32768 sys-id-ext 5)
```

```
Address 0013.c3e8.2500
Hello Time 2 sec Max Age 20 sec Forward Delay 15 sec
Aging Time 300

Interface   Role   Sts   Cost   Prio.Nbr     Type
---------   ----   ---   ----   --------     ----
Fa0/15      Desg   FWD   19     128.15 P2p
Fa0/18      Desg   FWD   19     128.18 P2
```

SPANNING TREE COST AND PRIORITY

STP uses cost and priority values to determine the best path to the Root Bridge. These values are then used in the election of the Root Port, which will be described in the following section. It is important to understand the calculation of the cost and priority values in order to understand how Spanning Tree selects one port over another, for example.

One of the key functions of the STA is to attempt to provide the shortest path to each switch in the network from the Root Bridge. Once selected, this path is then used to forward data, whilst redundant links are placed into a Blocking state. STA uses two values to determine which port will be placed into a Forwarding state (i.e., is the best path to the Root Bridge) and which port(s) will be placed into a Blocking state. These values are the port cost and the port priority. Both are described in the sections that follow.

Spanning Tree Port Cost

The 802.1D specification assigns 16-bit (short) default port cost values to each port that is based on the port's bandwidth. Because administrators also have the capability to assign port cost values manually (between 1 and 65535), the 16-bit values are used only for ports that have not been specifically configured for port cost. Table 31.1 below lists the default values for each type of port when using the short method to calculate the port cost:

Table 31.1—Default STP Port Cost Values

Bandwidth	Default Port Cost
4Mbps	250
10Mbps	100
16Mbps	62
100Mbps	19
1Gbps	4
10Gbps	2

In Cisco IOS Catalyst switches, default port cost values can be verified by issuing the show spanning-tree interface [name] command, as illustrated in the following output, which shows the default short port cost for a FastEthernet interface:

```
Switch#show spanning-tree interface FastEthernet0/2
Vlan            Role  Sts   Cost      Prio.Nbr Type
--------        ----  ---   ----      -------------
VLAN0050        Desg  FWD   19        128.2    P2p
The following output shows the same for long port cost assignment:
Switch#show spanning-tree interface FastEthernet0/2
Vlan            Role Sts Cost      Prio.Nbr Type
--------        ---- --- ------    -------- ----
VLAN0050        Desg FWD 200000    128.2    P2p
```

It is important to remember that ports with lower (numerical) costs are more preferred; the lower the port cost, the higher the probability of that particular port being elected the Root Port. The port cost value is globally significant and affects the entire Spanning Tree network. This value is configured on all Non-Root Switches in the Spanning Tree domain.

SPANNING TREE ROOT AND DESIGNATED PORTS

STP elects two types of ports that are used to forward BPDUs: the Root Port, which points towards the Root Bridge, and the Designated Port, which points away from the Root Bridge. It is important to understand the functionality of these two port types and how they are elected by STP.

Spanning Tree Root Port Election

STA defines three types of ports: the Root Port, the Designated Port, and the Non-Designated Port. These port types are elected by the STA and placed into the appropriate state (e.g., Forwarding or Blocking). During the Spanning Tree election process, in the event of a tie, the following values will be used (in the order listed) as tiebreakers:

1. Lowest Root Bridge ID
2. Lowest Root path cost to Root Bridge
3. Lowest sender Bridge ID
4. Lowest sender Port ID

NOTE: It is important to remember these tiebreaking criteria in order to understand how Spanning Tree elects and designates different port types in any given situation. Not only is this something that you will most likely be tested on, but also it is very important to have a solid understanding of this in order to design, implement, and support internetworks in the real world.

The Spanning Tree Root Port is the port that provides the best path, or lowest cost, when the device forwards packets to the Root Bridge. In other words, the Root Port is the port that receives the best BPDU for the switch, which indicates that it is the shortest path to the Root Bridge in terms of path cost. The Root Port is elected based on the Root Bridge path cost.

The Root Bridge path cost is calculated based on the cumulative cost (path cost) of all the links leading up to the Root Bridge. The path cost is the value that each port contributes to the Root Bridge path cost. Because this concept is often quite confusing, it is illustrated in Figure 31.7 below:

NOTE: All but one of the links illustrated in Figure 31.7 are GigabitEthernet links. It should be assumed that the traditional 802.1D method is used for port cost calculation. Therefore, the default port cost of GigabitEthernet is 4, whilst that of FastEthernet is 19.

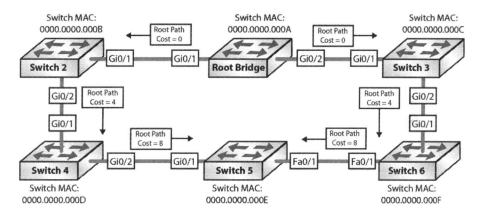

Figure 31.7—Spanning Tree Root Port Election

NOTE: The following explanation illustrates the flow of BPDUs between the switches in the network. Along with other information, these BPDUs contain the Root Bridge path cost information, which is incremented by the ingress port on the receiving switch.

1. The Root Bridge sends out a BPDU with a Root Bridge path cost value of 0 because its ports reside directly on the Root Bridge. This BPDU is sent to Switch 2 and Switch 3.
2. When Switch 2 and Switch 3 receive the BPDU from the Root Bridge, they add their own path cost based on the ingress interface. Because Switch 2 and Switch 3 are both connected to the Root Bridge via GigabitEthernet connections, they add the path cost value received from the Root Bridge (0) to their GigabitEthernet path cost values (4). The Root Bridge path cost from Switch 2 and Switch 3 via GigabitEthernet0/1 to the Root Bridge is 0 + 4 = 4.
3. Switch 2 and Switch 3 send out new BPDUs to their respective neighbors, which are Switch 4 and Switch 6, respectively. These BPDUs contain the new cumulative value (4) as the Root Bridge path cost.
4. When Switch 4 and Switch 6 receive the BPDUs from Switch 2 and Switch 3, they increment the received Root Bridge path cost value based on the ingress interface. Since GigabitEthernet connections are being used, the value received from Switch 2 and Switch 3 is incremented by 4. The Root Bridge path cost to the Root Bridge on

Switch 4 and Switch 6 via their respective GigabitEthernet0/1 interfaces is therefore $0 + 4 + 4 = 8$.

5.   Switch 5 receives two BPDUs: one from Switch 4 and the other from Switch 6. The BPDU received from Switch 4 has a Root Bridge path cost of $0 + 4 + 4 + 4 = 12$. The BPDU received from Switch 6 has a Root Bridge path cost of $0 + 4 + 4 + 19 = 27$. Because the Root Bridge path cost value contained in the BPDU received from Switch 4 is better than that received from Switch 6, Switch 5 elects GigabitEthernet0/1 as the Root Port.

NOTE: Switches 2, 3, 4, and 6 will all elect their GigabitEthernet0/1 ports as Root Ports.

FURTHER EXPLANATION:

To explain further and to help you understand the election of the Root Port, let's assume that all ports in the diagram in Figure 31.7 above are GigabitEthernet ports. This would mean that in Step 5 above, Switch 5 would receive two BPDUs with the same Root Bridge ID, both with a Root path cost value of $0 + 4 + 4 + 4 = 12$. In order for the Root Port to be elected, STP will progress to the next option in the tiebreaker criteria listed below (the first two options, which have already been used, have been removed):

•   Lowest sender Bridge ID
•   Lowest sender Port ID

Based on the third selection criteria, Switch 5 will prefer the BPDU received from Switch 4 because its BID (0000.0000.000D) is lower than that of Switch 6 (0000.0000.000F). Switch 5 elects port GigabitEthernet0/1 as the Root Port.

Spanning Tree Designated Port Election

Unlike the Root Port, the Designated Port is a port that points away from the STP Root. This port is the one in which the designated device is attached to the LAN. It is also the port that has the lowest path cost when forwarding packets from that LAN to the Root Bridge.

NOTE: Some people refer to the Designated Port as the Designated Switch. The terms are interchangeable and refer to the same thing; that is, this is the switch, or port, that is used to forward frames from a particular LAN segment to the Root Bridge

The primary purpose of the Designated Port is to prevent loops. When more than one switch is connected to the same LAN segment, all switches will attempt to forward a frame received on that segment. This default behavior can result in multiple copies of the same frame being forwarded by multiple switches—resulting in a network loop. To avoid this default behavior, a Designated Port is elected on all LAN segments. By default, all ports on the Root Bridge are Designated Ports. This is because the Root Bridge path cost will always be 0. The STA election of the Designated Port is illustrated in Figure 31.8 below:

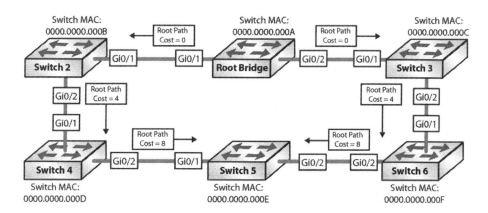

Figure 31.8—Spanning Tree Designated Port Election

- On the segment between the Root Bridge and Switch 2, the Root Bridge GigabitEthernet0/1 is elected as the Designated Port because it has the lower Root Bridge path cost, which is 0.
- On the segment between the Root Bridge and Switch 3, the Root Bridge GigabitEthernet0/2 is elected as the Designated Port because it has the lower Root Bridge path cost, which is 0.
- On the segment between Switch 2 and Switch 4, the GigabitEthernet0/2 port on Switch 2 is elected as the Designated Port because Switch 2 has the lowest Root Bridge path cost, which is 4.
- On the segment between Switch 3 and Switch 6, the GigabitEthernet0/2 port on Switch 3 is elected as the Designated Port because Switch 3 has the lowest Root Bridge path cost, which is 4.
- On the segment between Switch 4 and Switch 5, the GigabitEthernet0/2 port on Switch 4 is elected as the Designated Port because Switch 4 has the lowest Root Bridge path cost, which is 8.
- On the segment between Switch 5 and Switch 6, the GigabitEthernet0/2 port on Switch 6 is elected as the Designated Port because Switch 6 has the lowest Root Bridge path cost, which is 8.

The Non-Designated Port is not really a Spanning Tree Port type. Instead, it is a term that simply means a port that is not the Designated Port on a LAN segment. This port will always be placed into a Blocking state by STP. Based on the calculation of Root and Designated Ports, the resultant Spanning Tree topology for the switched network that was used in the Root Port and Designated Port election examples is shown in Figure 31.9 below:

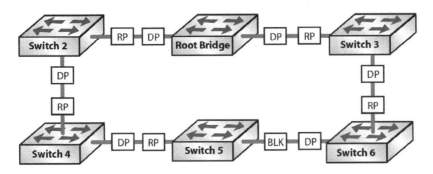

Figure 31.9—Converged Spanning Tree Network

CISCO SPANNING TREE ENHANCEMENTS

As stated earlier, STP makes two assumptions about the environment in which it has been enabled, as follows:

- All links are bidirectional and can both send and receive Bridge Protocol Data Units
- All switches can regularly receive, process, and send Bridge Protocol Data Units

In real-world networks, these two assumptions are not always correct. In situations where that is the case, STP may not be able to prevent loops from being formed within the network. Because of this possibility, and to improve the performance of the basic IEEE 802.1D STA, Cisco has introduced a number of enhancements to the IEEE 802.1D standard, which are described below.

Port Fast

Port Fast is a feature that is typically enabled only for a port or interface that connects to a host. When the link comes up on this port, the switch skips the first stages of the STA and directly transitions to the Forwarding state. Contrary to popular belief, the Port Fast feature does not disable Spanning Tree on the selected port. This is because even with the Port Fast feature, the port can still send and receive BPDUs.

This is not a problem when the port is connected to a network device that does not send or respond to BPDUs, such as the NIC on a workstation, for example. However, this may result in a switching loop if the port is connected to a device that does send BPDUs, such as another switch. This is because the port skips the Listening and Learning states and proceeds immediately to the Forwarding state. Port Fast simply allows the port to begin forwarding frames much sooner than a port going through all normal STA steps.

BPDU Guard

The BPDU Guard feature is used to protect the Spanning Tree domain from external influence. BPDU Guard is disabled by default but is recommended for all ports on which the

Port Fast feature has been enabled. When a port that is configured with the BPDU Guard feature receives a BPDU, it immediately transitions to the errdisable state.

This prevents false information from being injected into the Spanning Tree domain on ports that have Spanning Tree disabled. The operation of BPDU Guard, in conjunction with Port Fast, is illustrated in Figures 31.10, 31.11, and 31.12, below and following:

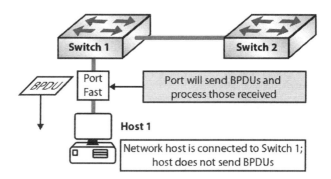

Figure 31.10—Understanding BPDU Guard

In Figure 31.10, Port Fast is enabled on Switch 1 on its connection to Host 1. Following initialization, the port transitions to a Forwarding state, which eliminates 30 seconds of delay that would have been encountered if STA was not bypassed and the port went through the Listening and Learning states. Because the network host is a workstation, it sends no BPDUs on that port.

Either by accident or due to some other malicious intent, Host 1 is disconnected from Switch 1. Using the same port, Switch 3 is connected to Switch 1. Switch 3 is also connected to Switch 2. Because Port Fast is enabled on the port connecting Switch 1 to Switch 3, this port moves from initialization to the Forwarding state, bypassing normal STP initialisation. This port will also receive and process any BPDUs that are sent by Switch 3, as illustrated in Figure 31.11 below:

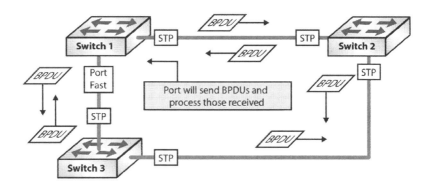

Figure 31.11—Understanding BPDU Guard (Continued)

Based on the port states illustrated above, you can quickly see how a loop would be created in this network. To prevent this from occurring, BPDU Guard should be enabled on all ports with Port Fast enabled. This is illustrated in Figure 31.12 below:

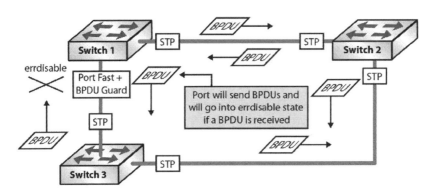

Figure 31.12—Understanding BPDU Guard (Continued)

With BPDU Guard enabled on the Port Fast port, when Switch 1 receives a BPDU from Switch 3, it immediately transitions the port into the errdisable state. The result is that the STP calculation is not affected by this redundant link and the network will not have any loops.

BPDU Filter

The BPDU Guard and the BPDU Filter features are often confused or even thought to be the same. They are, however, different, and it is important to understand the differences between them. When Port Fast is enabled on a port, the port will send out BPDUs and will accept and process received BPDUs. The BPDU Guard feature prevents the port from receiving any BPDUs but does not prevent it from sending them. If any BPDUs are received, the port will be errdisabled.

The BPDU Filter feature has dual functionality. When configured at interface level it effectively disables STP on the selected ports by preventing them from sending or receiving any BPDUs. When configured globally and used in conjunction with global Port Fast, it will revert out of Port Fast any port that receives BPDUs. This is illustrated in Figure 31.13 below:

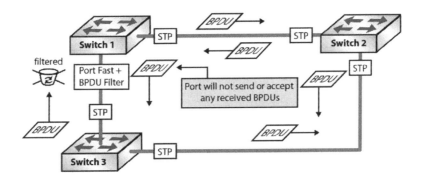

Figure 31.13—Understanding BPDU Filter

Loop Guard

The Loop Guard feature is used to prevent the formation of loops within the Spanning Tree network. Loop Guard detects Root Ports and blocked ports and ensures that they continue to receive BPDUs. When switches receive BPDUs on blocked ports, the information is ignored because the best BPDU is still being received from the Root Bridge via the Root Port.

If the switch link is up and no BPDUs are received (due to a unidirectional link), the switch assumes that it is safe to bring this link up, and the port transitions to the Forwarding state and begins relaying received BPUDs. If a switch is connected to the other end of the link, this effectively creates a Spanning Tree loop. This concept is illustrated in Figure 31.14 below:

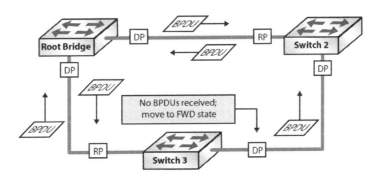

Figure 31.14—Understanding Loop Guard

In Figure 31.14, the Spanning Tree network has converged and all ports are in a Blocking or Forwarding state. However, the Blocking port on Switch 3 stops receiving BPDUs from the Designated Port on Switch 2 due to a unidirectional link. Switch 3 assumes that the port can be transitioned into a Forwarding state and so begins this move. The switch then relays received BPDUs out of that port, resulting in a network loop.

When Loop Guard is enabled, the switch keeps track of all Non-Designated Ports. As long as the port continues to receive BPDUs, it is fine; however, if the port stops receiving BPDUs, it is moved into a loop-inconsistent state. In other words, when Loop Guard is enabled, the STP port state machine is modified to prevent the port from transitioning from the Non-Designated Port role to the Designated Port role in the absence of BPDUs. When implementing Loop Guard, you should be aware of the following implementation guidelines:

- Loop Guard cannot be enabled on a switch that also has Root Guard enabled
- Loop Guard does not affect Uplink Fast or Backbone Fast operation
- Loop Guard must be enabled on Point-to-Point links only
- Loop Guard operation is not affected by the Spanning Tree timers
- Loop Guard cannot actually detect a unidirectional link
- Loop Guard cannot be enabled on Port Fast or Dynamic VLAN ports

Root Guard

The Root Guard feature prevents a Designated Port from becoming a Root Port. If a port on which the Root Guard feature is enabled receives a superior BPDU, it moves the port into a root-inconsistent state, thus maintaining the current Root Bridge status quo. This concept is illustrated in Figure 31.15 below:

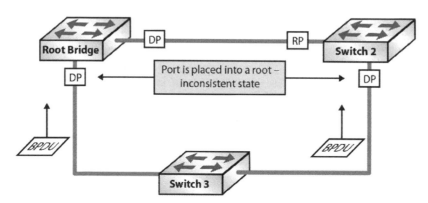

Figure 31.15—Understanding Root Guard

In Figure 31.15, Switch 3 is added to the current STP network and sends out BPDUs that are superior to those of the current Root Bridge. Under ordinary circumstances, STP would recalculate the entire topology and Switch 3 would be elected the Root Bridge. However, because the Root Guard feature is enabled on the Designated Ports on the current Root Bridge, as well as on Switch 2, both switches will place these ports into a root-inconsistent state when they receive the superior BPDUs from Switch 3. This preserves the Spanning Tree topology.

The Root Guard feature prevents a port from becoming a Root Port, thus ensuring that the port is always a Designated Port. Unlike other STP enhancements, which can also be enabled on a global basis, Root Guard must be manually enabled on all ports where the Root Bridge should not appear. Because of this, it is important to ensure a deterministic topology when designing and implementing STP in the LAN. Root Guard enables an administrator to enforce the Root Bridge placement in the network, ensuring that no customer device inadvertently or otherwise becomes the Root of the Spanning Tree, so it is usually used on the network edge of the ISP towards the customer's equipment.

Uplink Fast

The Uplink Fast feature provides faster failover to a redundant link when the primary link fails (i.e., direct failure of the Root Port). The primary purpose of this feature is to improve the convergence time of STP in the event of a failure of an uplink. This feature is of most use on Access Layer switches with redundant uplinks to the Distribution Layer; hence, the name.

When Access Layer switches are dual-homed to the Distribution Layer, one of the links is placed into a Blocking state by STP to prevent loops. When the primary link to the Distribution Layer fails, the port in the Blocking state must transition through the Listening and Learning states before it begins forwarding traffic. This results in a 30-second delay before the switch is able to forward frames destined to other network segments. Uplink Fast operation is illustrated in Figure 31.16 below:

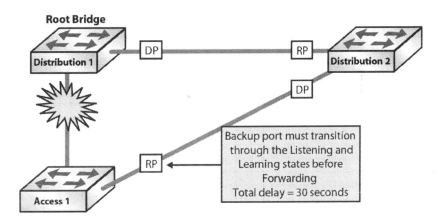

Figure 31.16—Understanding Uplink Fast

In Figure 31.16, a failure on the link between Access 1 and Distribution 1, which is also the STP Root Bridge, would mean that STP would move the link between Access 1 and Distribution 1 into a Forwarding state (i.e., Blocking > Listening > Learning > Forwarding). The Listening and Learning states take 15 seconds each, so the port would begin to forward frames only after a total of 30 seconds had elapsed. When the Uplink Fast feature is enabled, the backup port to the Distribution Layer is immediately placed into a Forwarding state, resulting in no network downtime. This concept is illustrated in Figure 31.17 below:

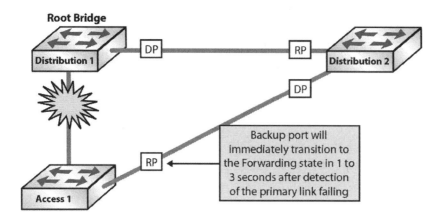

Figure 31.17—Understanding Uplink Fast (Continued)

Backbone Fast

The Backbone Fast feature provides fast failover when an indirect link failure occurs in the STP domain. Failover occurs when the switch receives an inferior BPDU from its designated bridge (on it's Root Port). An inferior BPDU indicates that the designated bridge has lost its connection to the Root Bridge, so the switch knows there was an upstream failure and without waiting for timers to expire changes the Root Port. This is illustrated in Figure 31.18 below:

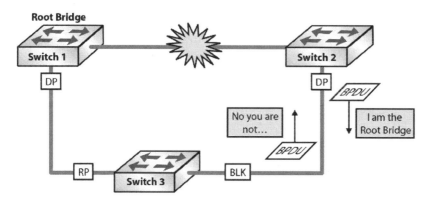

Figure 31.18—Understanding Backbone Fast

In Figure 31.18, the link between Switch 1 and Switch 2 fails. Switch 2 detects this and sends out BPDUs indicating that it is the Root Bridge. The inferior BPDUs are received on Switch 3, which still has the BPDU information received from Switch 1 saved.

Switch 3 will ignore the inferior BPDUs until the Max Age value expires. During this time, Switch 2 continues to send BPDUs to Switch 3. When the Max Age expires, Switch 3 will age out the stored BPDU information from the Root Bridge and transition into a Listening state, and will then send out the received BPDU from the Root Bridge out to Switch 2.

Because this BPDU is better than its own, Switch 2 stops sending BPDUs, and the port between Switch 2 and Switch 3 transitions through the Listening and Learning states, and, finally, into the Forwarding state. This default method of operation by the STP process will mean that Switch 2 will be unable to forward frames for at least 50 seconds.

The Backbone Fast feature includes a mechanism that allows an immediate check to see whether the BPDU information stored on a port is still valid if an inferior BPDU is received. This is implemented with a new PDU and the Root Link Query (RLQ), which is referred to as the RLQ PDU.

Upon receipt of an inferior BPDU, the switch will send out an RLQ PDU on all Non-Designated Ports, except for the port on which the inferior BPDU was received. If the switch is the Root Bridge or it has lost its connection to the Root Bridge, it will respond to the RLQ. Otherwise, the RLQ will be propagated upstream. If the switch receives an RLQ response on its Root Port, connectivity to the Root Bridge is still intact. If the response is received on a Non-Root Port, it means that connectivity to the Root Bridge is lost, and the local switch Spanning Tree must be recalculated on the switch and the Max Age timer expired so that a new Root Port can be found. This concept is illustrated in Figure 31.19 below:

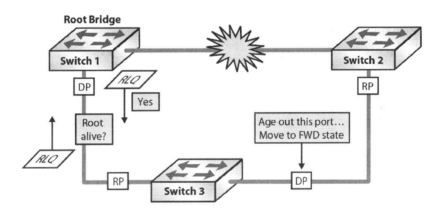

Figure 31.19—Understanding Backbone Fast (Continued)

Referencing Figure 31.19, upon receipt of the inferior BPDU, Switch 3 sends out an RLQ request on all Non-Designated Ports, except for the port on which the BPDU was received. The Root Bridge responds via an RLQ response sent out of its Designated Port. Because the response is received on the Root Port of Switch 3, it is considered a positive response. However, if the response was received on a Non-Root Port, the response would be considered negative and the switch would need to go through the whole Spanning Tree calculation again.

Based on the positive response received on Switch 3, it can age out the port connected to Switch 2 without waiting for the Max Age timer to expire. The port, however, must still go through the Listening and Learning states. By immediately aging out the Max Age timer, Backbone Fast reduces the convergence time from 50 seconds (20 seconds Max Age + 30 seconds Listening and Learning) to 30 seconds (the time for the Listening and Learning states).

There are two types of RLQs: RLQ requests and RLQ responses. RLQ requests are typically sent out on the Root Port to check for connectivity to the Root Bridge. All RLQ responses are sent out on Designated Ports. Because the RLQ request contains the BID of the Root Bridge that sent it, if another switch in the path to the Root Bridge can still reach the Root Bridge specified in the RLQ response, it will respond back to the sending switch. If this is not the case, the switch simply forwards the query towards the Root Bridge through its Root Port.

> **NOTE:** The RLQ PDU has the same packet format as a normal BPDU, with the only difference being that the RLQ PDU contains two Cisco SNAP addresses that are used for requests and replies.

TROUBLESHOOTING STP

Most Layer 2 issues are related to some kind of loop within the domain and this has multiple problems associated with it, including network downtime. When you are working with switch configuration and are plugging/unplugging a device, you should make sure that you aren't creating a loop in the process. To mitigate against such problems, you should usually configure Spanning Tree Protocol on switches in order to avoid situations that might occur if you happen to accidentally create a loop somewhere in the network.

Every switch in a network is communicating using MAC addresses. As packets come in, the MAC address is analyzed and the switch determines where that packet goes based on the destination MAC address in the Layer 2 header. Every device in the network has its own MAC address, so all the packets are very specific as to where they are going. Unfortunately, things like broadcasts and Multicasts go to every port on the switch. If a broadcast frame arrives at a switch port, it copies that broadcast to every other device that might be connected to that switch. This process can often be a problem when you have loops in the network.

You should also keep in mind that the MAC address packets have no mechanism inside them to time out. In the case of TCP/IP, the IP protocol has within its header a function called TTL (Time to Live), which refers to the number of hops through a router, not actually to a specific unit of time. So if IP packets happen to be in a loop and are going through multiple routers, they will eventually time out and be removed from the network. On the other hand, switches do not offer that kind of mechanism. Layer 2 frames can theoretically loop forever, as there is no mechanism to time them out, meaning that if you create a loop, it is going to be there until you manually remove it from the network.

If you are plugging in one workstation to the network and a broadcast reaches it, it will terminate at that point and will not be a problem for the network. On the other hand, if you misconfigure a port configuration on the switch side or you plug both ends into a switch without enabling STP, this might lead to a broadcast storm within the Layer 2 domain. This happens because broadcast packets are forwarded to all other ports, so the broadcast packet keeps exiting and entering the switch on the same cable, causing a Layer 2 loop. This can lead to high resource usage and even network downtime.

If you enable STP on such a misconfigured network, the switch will recognize that a loop has occurred and it would block certain ports to avoid broadcast storms. Every other port in the switch continues to operate normally, so the network is not affected. If STP is not configured, the only option would be to unplug the network cable that is causing the problem or administratively disable it if you can still operate the switch at that moment.

STP issues usually fall within the following three categories:

- Incorrect Root Bridge
- Incorrect Root Port
- Incorrect Designated Port

Incorrect Root Bridge

Priority and base MAC addresses decide whether the Root Bridge is incorrect. You can issue the `show spanning-tree vlan <vlan#>` command to see the MAC address and switch priority. You can fix this problem with the `spanning-tree vlan <vlan#> priority <priority>` command.

Incorrect Root Port

The Root Port provides the fastest path from the switch to the Root Bridge, and the cost is cumulative across the entire path. If you suspect an incorrect Root Port, you can issue the `show spanning-tree vlan <vlan#>` command. If the Root Port is incorrect, you can issue the `spanning-tree cost <cost>` command to fix it.

Incorrect Designated Port

The Designated Port is the lowest cost port connecting a network segment to the rest of the network. If you suspect a problem with the Designated Port, you can issue the `show spanning-tree vlan <vlan#>` and `spanning-tree cost <cost>` commands.

A useful STP troubleshooting command that can debug related events is `Switch#debug spanning-tree events`.

THE NEED FOR RSTP

With the continued evolution of technology, and the amalgamation of routing and switching capabilities on the same physical platform, it soon became apparent that switched network convergence lagged behind that of routing protocols such as OSPF and EIGRP, which are able to provide an alternate path in less time. The 802.1W standard was designed to address this.

The IEEE 802.1W standard, or Rapid Spanning Tree Protocol (RSTP), significantly reduces the time taken for STP to converge when a link failure occurs. With RSTP, network failover to an alternate path or link can occur in a sub-second timeframe. RSTP is an extension of 802.1D that performs functions similar to Uplink Fast and Backbone Fast. RSTP performs better than traditional STP, with no additional configuration. Additionally, RSTP is backward compatible with the original IEEE 802.1D STP standard. It does this by using a modified BPDU, as shown in the screenshot below:

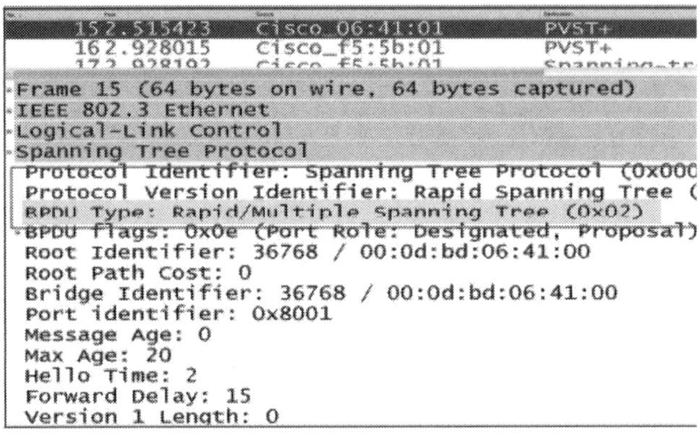

Figure 31.20—Modified BPDU

RSTP port states can be mapped against STP port states as follows:

- Disabled—Discarding
- Blocking—Discarding
- Listening—Discarding
- Learning—Learning
- Forwarding—Forwarding

RSTP port roles include the following:

- Root (Forwarding state)
- Designated (Forwarding state)
- Alternate (Blocking state)
- Backup (Blocking state)

For the exam it's very important that you understand the bullet points above, especially which port states forward traffic (once the network is converged). Figures 31.21 and 31.22 illustrate an RSTP Alternate Port and an RSTP Backup Port, respectively:

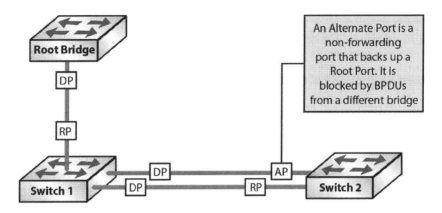

Figure 31.21—RSTP Alternate Port

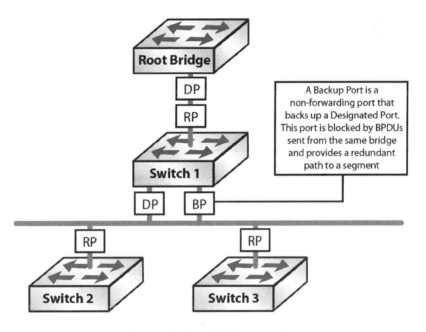

Figure 31.22—RSTP Backup Port

RSTP with PVST+

Per VLAN Spanning Tree Plus (PVST+) allows for an individual STP instance per VLAN. Traditional or Normal PVST+ mode relies on the use of the older 802.1D STP for switched network convergence in the event of a link failure.

RPVST+

Rapid Per VLAN Spanning Tree Plus (R-PVST+) allows for the use of 802.1W with PVST+. This allows for an individual RSTP instance per VLAN, whilst providing much faster convergence than would be attained with the traditional 802.1D STP. By default, when RSTP is enabled on a Cisco switch, R-PVST+ is enabled on the switch.

Here is a little memory trick you can use to remember the letter designation of the various IEEE STP specification:

- 802.1D ("Classic" Spanning Tree)—It's dog-gone slow
- 802.1W (Rapid Spanning Tree)—Imagine Elmer Fudd saying "rapid" as "wapid"

802.1S (Multiple Spanning Tree)—You add the letter "s" to nouns to make them plural (multiple) but this is a CCNP SWITCH subject

CONFIGURING RSTP

This can be achieved with one command!

```
Switch#spanning-tree mode rapid-pvst
Switch#show spanning-tree summary
Switch is in rapid-pvst mode
Root bridge for: VLAN0050, VLAN0060, VLAN0070
```

EXTENDED VLANS

We discussed extended VLANs in the ICND1 section when we covered VTP transparent mode so this section will be brief. Extended VLANs are numbered from 1006 to 4094, inclusive. You won't actually see them listed when you issue the show vlan brief command as illustrated below:

```
ALS1#show vlan brief

VLAN Name                     Status     Ports
---- ---------------------- ---------- ---------------------------
1    default                  active     Fa0/1, Fa0/2, Fa0/3, Fa0/4
                                         Fa0/5, Fa0/6, Fa0/13, Fa0/14
                                         Fa0/15, Fa0/16, Fa0/17, Fa0/18
                                         Fa0/19, Fa0/20, Fa0/21, Fa0/22
                                         Fa0/23, Fa0/24, Gi0/1, Gi0/2

2    VLAN0002                 active
1002 fddi-default             act/unsup
1003 token-ring-default       act/unsup
1004 fddinet-default          act/unsup
1005 trnet-default            act/unsup
```

Extended VLANs are not stored in the vlan.dat file (i.e., the VLAN database) and are not advertised via VTP. If you want to configure them, you must put the switch into VTP transparent mode (or disable VTP completely). At the time of writing this, you can't configure extended VLANs in Packet Tracer so you will need to get access to remote live racks or your own switch if you want to do so.

You can see in the output below that when we tried to create an extended VLAN (1006), the command was accepted but it failed to take until we changed the switch from VTP server mode to VTP transparent mode:

```
ALS1#show vtp status
VTP Version                       : running VTP1 (VTP2 capable)
Configuration Revision            : 1
Maximum VLANs supported locally   : 1005
Number of existing VLANs          : 6
VTP Operating Mode                : Server
VTP Domain Name                   :
VTP Pruning Mode                  : Disabled
VTP V2 Mode                       : Disabled
VTP Traps Generation              : Disabled
MD5 digest                        : 0xAD 0x80 0xCE 0x6D 0x7F 0x3A 0xA9 0x21
Configuration last modified by 0.0.0.0 at 3-1-93 21:42:31
Local updater ID is 0.0.0.0 (no valid interface found)

ALS1#conf t
Enter configuration commands, one per line.  End with CTRL/Z.
ALS1(config)#vlan 1006
ALS1(config-vlan)#end
% Failed to create VLANs 1006
Extended VLAN(s) not allowed in current VTP mode.
%Failed to commit extended VLAN(s) changes.

ALS1#conf t
ALS1(config)#vtp mode transparent
Setting device to VTP TRANSPARENT mode.
ALS1(config)#end
ALS1#show vtp status
VTP Version                       : running VTP1 (VTP2 capable)
Configuration Revision            : 0
Maximum VLANs supported locally   : 1005
Number of existing VLANs          : 6
VTP Operating Mode                : Transparent
VTP Domain Name                   :
VTP Pruning Mode                  : Disabled
VTP V2 Mode                       : Disabled
VTP Traps Generation              : Disabled
MD5 digest                        : 0xAD 0x80 0xCE 0x6D 0x7F 0x3A 0xA9 0x21
Configuration last modified by 0.0.0.0 at 3-1-93 21:42:31
ALS1#conf t
ALS1(config)#vlan 1006
ALS1(config-vlan)#end
ALS1#show vlan brief

VLAN Name                 Status    Ports
---- -------------------- --------- -------------------------------
1    default              active    Fa0/1, Fa0/2, Fa0/3, Fa0/4
                                    Fa0/5, Fa0/6, Fa0/13, Fa0/14
                                    Fa0/15, Fa0/16, Fa0/17, Fa0/18
                                    Fa0/19, Fa0/20, Fa0/21, Fa0/22
```

```
                                       Fa0/23, Fa0/24, Gi0/1, Gi0/2
2    VLAN0002              active
1002 fddi-default          act/unsup
1003 token-ring-default    act/unsup
1004 fddinet-default       act/unsup
1005 trnet-default         act/unsup
1006 VLAN1006              active
```

Troubleshooting extended VLANs involves the same process as standard VLANs. Bear in mind that your switches will need to be in transparent mode in order to configure them.

Take the exam at **https://www.in60days.com/free/ccnain60days/**

DAY 31 LAB

Spanning Tree Root Selection

Topology

Purpose

Learn how to influence which switch becomes the Spanning Tree Root Bridge.

Walkthrough

1. Set the hostname of each switch and connect them with a crossover cable. You can then check whether the interface between them is set to "trunk."

```
SwitchA#show interface trunk
```

2. You may not see the trunk link become active until you set one side as a trunk link.

```
SwitchB#conf t
Enter configuration commands, one per line.  End with CNTL/Z.
SwitchB(config)#int FastEthernet0/1
SwitchB(config-if)#switchport mode trunk
SwitchB(config-if)#^Z
SwitchB#sh int trunk

Port         Mode          Encapsulation  Status        Native vlan
Fa0/1        on            802.1q         trunking      1

Port         Vlans allowed on trunk
Fa0/1        1-1005

Port         Vlans allowed and active in management domain
Fa0/1        1
```

3. You will see that the other switch is left on auto mode.

```
SwitchA#show int trunk
Port         Mode          Encapsulation  Status        Native vlan
Fa0/1        auto          n-802.1q       trunking      1

Port         Vlans allowed on trunk
Fa0/1        1-1005

Port         Vlans allowed and active in management domain
Fa0/1        1
```

4. Create two VLANs on each switch.

```
SwitchA#conf t
```

```
Enter configuration commands, one per line.  End with CNTL/Z.
SwitchA(config)#vlan 2
SwitchA(config-vlan)#vlan 3
SwitchA(config-vlan)#^Z
SwitchA#
%SYS-5-CONFIG_I: Configured from console by console

SwitchA#show vlan brief

VLAN Name                           Status    Ports
---- --------------------          -------   --------------------
1    default                        active    Fa0/2, Fa0/3, Fa0/4,
                                              Fa0/5, Fa0/6, Fa0/7,
                                              Fa0/8, Fa0/9, Fa0/10,
                                              Fa0/11, Fa0/12, Fa0/13,
                                              Fa0/14, Fa0/15, Fa0/16,
                                              Fa0/17, Fa0/18, Fa0/19,
                                              Fa0/20, Fa0/21, Fa0/22,
                                              Fa0/23, Fa0/24
2    VLAN0002                       active
3    VLAN0003                       active
1002 fddi-default                   active
1003 token-ring-default             active
```

Create the VLANs on Switch B as well (copy the commands above).

5. Determine which switch is the Root Bridge for VLANs 2 and 3.

```
SwitchB#show spanning-tree vlan 2
VLAN0002
  Spanning tree enabled protocol ieee
  Root ID    Priority    32770
             Address     0001.972A.7A23
             This bridge is the root
             Hello Time  2 sec  Max Age 20 sec  Forward Delay 15 sec

  Bridge ID  Priority    32770  (priority 32768 sys-id-ext 2)
             Address     0001.972A.7A23
             Hello Time  2 sec  Max Age 20 sec  Forward Delay 15 sec
             Aging Time  20

Interface        Role Sts Cost      Prio.Nbr Type
---------        ---- --- ----      -------- ----
Fa0/1            Desg FWD  19       128.1    P2p
```

You can see that Switch B is the Root. Do the same command on Switch A and check for VLAN 3. The priority is 32768 plus the VLAN number, which is 2 in this case. The lowest MAC address will then determine the Root Bridge.

```
SwitchB#show spanning-tree vlan 3
VLAN0003
  Spanning tree enabled protocol ieee
  Root ID    Priority    32771
```

```
        Address        0001.972A.7A23
        This bridge is the root
        Hello Time   2 sec   Max Age 20 sec   Forward Delay 15 sec

Bridge ID  Priority     32771 (priority 32768 sys-id-ext 3)
           Address      0001.972A.7A23
           Hello Time   2 sec   Max Age 20 sec   Forward Delay 15 sec
           Aging Time   20

Interface         Role  Sts  Cost      Prio.Nbr Type
----------        ----  ---  ----      -------- ----
Fa0/1             Desg  FWD  19        128.1    P2p
```

The MAC address I have for Switch A is higher, which is why it didn't become the Root Bridge:

```
0010.1123.D245
```

6. Set the other switch to be the Root Bridge for VLANs 2 and 3. Use the `spanning-tree vlan 2 priority 4096` command for VLAN 2 and the `spanning-tree`

Vlan 3 root primary for VLAN 3.

```
SwitchA(config)#spanning-tree vlan 2 priority 4096
SwitchA(config)#spanning-tree vlan 3 root primary

SwitchA#show spanning-tree vlan 2
VLAN0002
  Spanning tree enabled protocol ieee
  Root ID    Priority     4098
             Address      0010.1123.D245
             This bridge is the root
             Hello Time   2 sec   Max Age 20 sec   Forward Delay 15 sec

  Bridge ID  Priority     4098 (priority 4096 sys-id-ext 2)
             Address      0010.1123.D245
             Hello Time   2 sec   Max Age 20 sec   Forward Delay 15 sec
             Aging Time   20

Interface         Role  Sts  Cost      Prio.Nbr Type
---------         ----  ---  ----      -------- ----
Fa0/1             Desg  FWD  19        128.1    P2p

SwitchA#show spanning-tree vlan 3
VLAN0003
  Spanning tree enabled protocol ieee
  Root ID    Priority     24579
             Address      0010.1123.D245
             This bridge is the root
             Hello Time   2 sec   Max Age 20 sec   Forward Delay 15 sec

  Bridge ID  Priority     24579 (priority 24576 sys-id-ext 3)
             Address      0010.1123.D245
             Hello Time   2 sec   Max Age 20 sec   Forward Delay 15 sec
```

```
         Aging Time  20

Interface        Role  Sts  Cost      Prio.Nbr Type
---------        ----  ---  ----      -------- ----
Fa0/1            Desg  FWD  19        128.1    P2p

SwitchA#
```

> **NOTE:** Despite Switch B having the lower Bridge ID, Switch A was forced to be the Root Bridge.

RSTP

Topology

Purpose

Learn the configuration command for RSTP.

Walkthrough

1. Check the Spanning Tree mode on your switch.

   ```
   SwitchA#show spanning-tree summary
   Switch is in pvst mode
   Root bridge for: VLAN0002 VLAN0003
   ```

2. Change the mode to RSTP and check again.

   ```
   SwitchA(config)#spanning-tree mode rapid-pvst
   SwitchA#show spanning-tree summary
   Switch is in rapid-pvst mode
   Root bridge for: VLAN0002 VLAN0003
   ```

3. Repeat Day 31 (STP) lab using RSTP mode instead.

4. Can you predict which ports will be Root/Designated/Blocking beforehand?

EtherChannels and Link Aggregation Protocols

DAY 32 TASKS

- Read today's lesson notes (below)
- Review yesterday's lesson notes and labs
- Take today's exam
- Read the ICND2 cram guide
- Spend 15 minutes on the subnetting.org website

Cisco IOS software allows administrators to combine multiple physical links in the chassis into a single logical link. This provides an ideal solution for load sharing, as well as link redundancy, and can be used by both Layer 2 and Layer 3 subsystems. EtherChannels is actually a CCNP topic but is now in the CCNA exam syllabus also.

Today you will learn about the following:

- Understanding EtherChannels
- Port Aggregation Protocol (PAgP) overview
- Link Aggregation Control Protocol (LACP) overview
- EtherChannel load-distribution methods
- EtherChannel configuration guidelines

This lesson maps to the following ICND2 syllabus requirement:

- 1.5 Configure, verify, and troubleshoot (Layer 2/Layer 3) EtherChannel
- 1.5.a Static
- 1.5.b PAGP
- 1.5.c LACP

UNDERSTANDING ETHERCHANNELS

An EtherChannel is comprised of physical, individual FastEthernet, GigabitEthernet, or Ten-GigabitEthernet (10Gbps) links that are bundled together into a single logical link, as illustrated in Figure 32.1 below. An EtherChannel comprised of FastEthernet links is referred to as a FastEtherChannel (FEC); an EtherChannel comprised of GigabitEthernet links is referred to as a GigabitEtherChannel (GEC); and, finally, an EtherChannel comprised of Ten-GigabitEthernet links is referred to as a Ten-GigabitEtherChannel (10GEC):

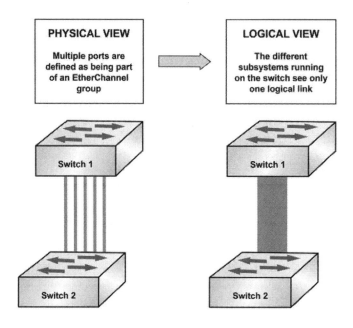

Figure 32.1—EtherChannel Physical and Logical Views

Each EtherChannel can consist of up to eight ports. Physical links in an EtherChannel must share similar characteristics, such as be defined in the same VLAN or have the same speed and duplex settings, for example. When configuring EtherChannels on Cisco Catalyst switches, it is important to remember that the number of supported EtherChannels will vary between the different Catalyst switch models.

For example, on the Catalyst 3750 series switches, the range is 1 to 48; on the Catalyst 4500 series switches, the range is 1 to 64; and on the flagship Catalyst 6500 series switches, the number of valid values for EtherChannel configuration depends on the software release. For releases prior to Release 12.1(3a)E3, valid values are from 1 to 256; for Releases 12.1(3a)E3, 12.1(3a)E4, and 12.1(4)E1, valid values are from 1 to 64. Release 12.1(5c)EX and later support a maximum of 64 values, ranging from 1 to 256.

NOTE: You are not expected to known the values supported in each different IOS version.

There are two link aggregation protocol options that can be used to automate the creation of an EtherChannel group: Port Aggregation Protocol (PAgP) and Link Aggregation Control Protocol (LACP). PAgP is a Cisco proprietary protocol, while LACP is part of the IEEE

802.3ad specification for creating a logical link from multiple physical links. These two protocols will be described in detail throughout this module.

PORT AGGREGATION PROTOCOL OVERVIEW

Port Aggregation Protocol (PAgP) is a Cisco proprietary link aggregation protocol that enables the automatic creation of EtherChannels. By default, PAgP packets are sent between EtherChannel-capable ports in order to negotiate the forming of an EtherChannel. These packets are sent to the destination Multicast MAC address 01-00-0C-CC-CC-CC, which is also the same Multicast address that is used by CDP, UDLD, VTP, and DTP. Figure 33.2 below shows the fields contained within a PAgP frame as seen on the wire:

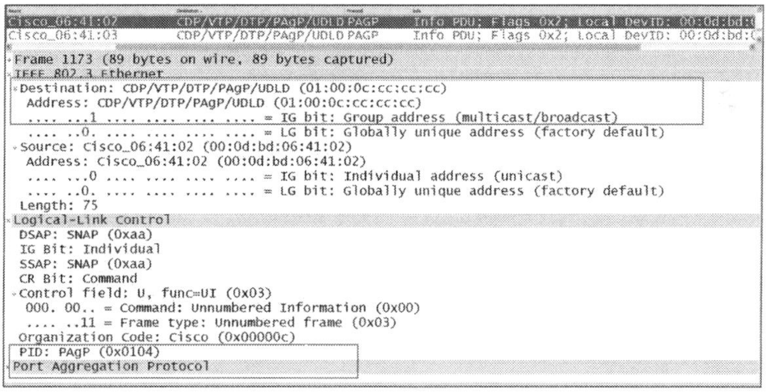

Figure 32.2—PAgP Ethernet Header

Although going into detail on the PAgP packet format is beyond the scope of the CCNA exam requirements, Figure 32.3 below shows the fields contained in a typical PAgP packet. Some of the fields contained within the PAgP packet are of relevance to the CCNA exam and will be described in detail as we progress through this module:

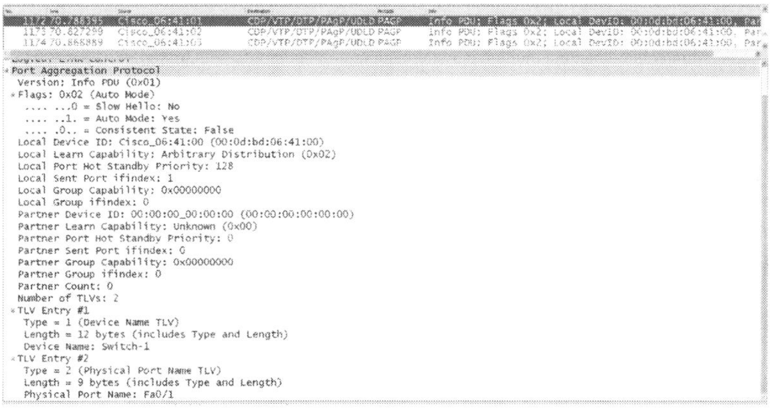

Figure 32.3—The Port Aggregation Protocol Frame

PAgP Port Modes

PAgP supports different port modes that determine whether an EtherChannel will be formed between two PAgP-capable switches. Before we delve into the two PAgP port modes, one particular mode deserves special attention. This mode (the "on" mode) is sometimes incorrectly referenced as a PAgP mode. The truth, however, is that it is not a PAgP port mode.

The on mode forces a port to be placed into a channel unconditionally. The channel will only be created if another switch port is connected and is configured in the on mode. When this mode is enabled, there is no negotiation of the channel performed by the local EtherChannel protocol. In other words, this effectively disables EtherChannel negotiation and forces the port to the channel. The operation of this mode is similar to the operation of the `switchport nonegotiate` command on trunk links. It is important to remember that switch interfaces that are configured in the on mode do not exchange PAgP packets.

Switch EtherChannels using PAgP may be configured to operate in one of two modes: auto or desirable. These two PAgP modes of operation are described in the following sections.

Auto Mode

Auto mode is a PAgP mode that will negotiate with another PAgP port only if the port receives a PAgP packet. When this mode is enabled, the port(s) will never initiate PAgP communications but will instead listen passively for any received PAgP packets before creating an EtherChannel with the neighboring switch.

Desirable Mode

Desirable mode is a PAgP mode that causes the port to initiate PAgP negotiation for a channel with another PAgP port. In other words, in this mode, the port actively attempts to establish an EtherChannel with another switch running PAgP.

In summation, it is important to remember that switch interfaces configured in the on mode do not exchange PAgP packets, but they do exchange PAgP packets with partner interfaces configured in the auto or desirable modes. Table 32.1 shows the different PAgP combinations and the result of their use in establishing an EtherChannel:

Table 32.1—EtherChannel Formation Using Different PAgP Modes

Switch 1 PAgP Mode	Switch 2 PAgP Mode	EtherChannel Result
Auto	Auto	No EtherChannel Formed
Auto	Desirable	EtherChannel Formed
Desirable	Auto	EtherChannel Formed
Desirable	Desirable	EtherChannel Formed

PAgP EtherChannel Protocol Packet Forwarding

While PAgP allows for all links within the EtherChannel to be used to forward and receive user traffic, there are some restrictions that you should be familiar with regarding the forwarding of traffic from other protocols. DTP and CDP send and receive packets over all the physical interfaces in the EtherChannel. PAgP sends and receives PAgP Protocol Data Units only from interfaces that are up and have PAgP enabled for auto or desirable modes.

When an EtherChannel bundle is configured as a trunk port, the trunk sends and receives PAgP frames on the lowest numbered VLAN. Spanning Tree Protocol (STP) always chooses the first operational port in an EtherChannel bundle. The show pagp [channel number] neighbor command, which can also be used to validate the port that will be used by STP to send and receive packets, determines the port STP will use in an EtherChannel bundle, as shown in the following output:

```
Switch-1#show pagp neighbor
Flags:  S - Device is sending Slow hello. C - Device is in Consistent
state.
        A - Device is in Auto mode.      P - Device learns on physical
port.

Channel group 1 neighbors
            Partner      Partner                    Partner Group
Port        Name         Device ID      Port     Age Flags   Cap.
Fa0/1       Switch-2     0014.a9e5.d640 Fa0/1    2s  SC      10001
Fa0/2       Switch-2     0014.a9e5.d640 Fa0/2    1s  SC      10001
Fa0/3       Switch-2     0014.a9e5.d640 Fa0/3    15s SC      10001
```

Referencing the above output, STP will send packets only out of port FastEthernet0/1 because it is the first operational interface. If that port fails, STP will send packets out of FastEthernet0/2. The default port used by PAgP can be viewed with the show EtherChannel summary command, as illustrated in the following output:

```
Switch-1#show EtherChannel summary
Flags:  D - down
        I - stand-alone
        H - Hot-standby (LACP only)
        R - Layer3
        u - unsuitable for bundling
        U - in use
        d - default port
        P - in port-channel
        s - suspended
        S - Layer2
        f - failed to allocate aggregator

Number of channel-groups in use: 1
Number of aggregators:           1

Group  Port-channel  Protocol    Ports
```

```
- - - - - - +- - - - - - - - - - - - +- - - - - - - - - - - +- - - - - - - - - - - - - - - - - - - - - - - - - - - - - -
  1      Po1(SU)        PAgP        Fa0/1(Pd)    Fa0/2(P)      Fa0/3(P)
```

When configuring additional STP features such as Loop Guard on an EtherChannel, it is very important to remember that if Loop Guard blocks the first port, no BPDUs will be sent over the channel, even if other ports in the channel bundle are operational. This is because PAgP will enforce uniform Loop Guard configuration on all of the ports that are part of the EtherChannel group.

REAL-WORLD IMPLEMENTATION:

In production networks, you may run across the Cisco Virtual Switching System (VSS), which is comprised of two physical Catalyst 6500 series switches acting as a single logical switch. In the VSS, one switch is selected as the active switch, while the other is selected as the standby switch. The two switches are connected together via an EtherChannel, which allows for the sending and receiving of control packets between them.

Access switches are connected to the VSS using Multichassis EtherChannel (MEC). An MEC is simply an EtherChannel that spans the two physical Catalyst 6500 switches but terminates to the single logical VSS. Enhanced PAgP (PAgP+) can be used to allow the Catalyst 6500 switches to communicate via the MEC in the event that the EtherChannel between them fails, which would result in both switches assuming the active role (dual active), effectively affecting forwarding of traffic within the switched network. This is illustrated in the diagram below:

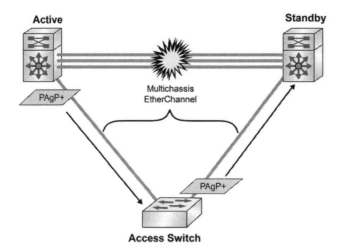

CISCO VIRTUAL SWITCHING SYSTEM:
Two chassis acting as a single switch

While VSS is beyond the scope of the CCNA exam requirements, it is beneficial to know that only PAgP can be used to relay VSS control packets. Therefore, if implementing EtherChannels in a VSS environment, or an environment in which VSS may eventually be implemented, you may want to consider running PAgP instead of LACP, which is an open standard that does not support the proprietary VSS frames. VSS will not be described any further in this guide.

LINK AGGREGATION CONTROL PROTOCOL OVERVIEW

Link Aggregation Control Protocol (LACP) is part of the IEEE 802.3ad specification for creating a logical link from multiple physical links. Because LACP and PAgP are incompatible, both ends of the link need to run LACP in order to automate the formation of EtherChannel groups.

As is the case with PAgP, when configuring LACP EtherChannels, all LAN ports must be the same speed and must all be configured as either Layer 2 or Layer 3 LAN ports. If a link within a port channel fails, traffic previously carried over the failed link is switched over to the remaining links within the port channel. Additionally, when you change the number of active bundled ports in a port channel, traffic patterns will reflect the rebalanced state of the port channel.

LACP supports the automatic creation of port channels by exchanging LACP packets between ports. It learns the capabilities of port groups dynamically and informs the other ports. Once LACP identifies correctly matched Ethernet links, it facilitates grouping the links into a GigabitEthernet port channel. Unlike PAgP, where ports are required to have the same speed and duplex settings, LACP mandates that ports be only full-duplex, as half-duplex is not supported. Half-duplex ports in an LACP EtherChannel are placed into the suspended state.

By default, all inbound Broadcast and Multicast packets on one link in a port channel are blocked from returning on any other link of the port channel. LACP packets are sent to the IEEE 802.3 Slow Protocols Multicast group address 01-80-C2-00-00-02. LACP frames are encoded with the EtherType value 0x8809. Figure 32.4 below illustrates these fields in an Ethernet frame:

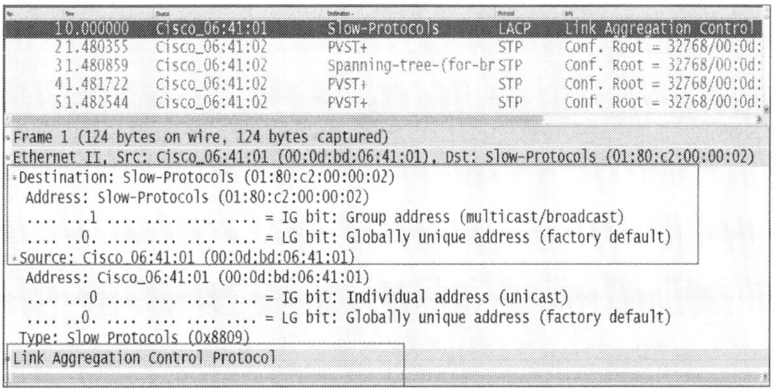

Figure 32.4—IEEE 802.3 LACP Frame

LACP Port Modes

LACP supports the automatic creation of port channels by exchanging LACP packets between ports. LACP does this by learning the capabilities of port groups dynamically and informing the other ports. Once LACP identifies correctly matched Ethernet links, it facilitates grouping the links into a port channel. Once an LACP mode has been configured, it can only be changed if a single interface has been assigned to the specified channel group. LACP supports two modes: active and passive. These two modes of operation are described in the following sections.

LACP Active Mode

LACP active mode places a switch port into an active negotiating state in which the switch port initiates negotiations with remote ports by sending LACP packets. Active mode is the LACP equivalent of PAgP desirable mode. In other words, in this mode, the switch port actively attempts to establish an EtherChannel with another switch that is also running LACP.

LACP Passive Mode

When a switch port is configured in passive mode, it will negotiate with an LACP channel only if it receives another LACP packet. In passive mode, the port responds to LACP packets that the interface receives but does not start LACP packet negotiation. This setting minimizes the transmission of LACP packets. In this mode, the port channel group attaches the interface to the EtherChannel bundle. This mode is similar to the auto mode that is used with PAgP.

It is important to remember that the active and passive modes are valid on non-PAgP interfaces only. However, if you have a PAgP EtherChannel and want to convert it to LACP, then Cisco IOS software allows you to change the protocol at any time. The only caveat is that this change causes all existing EtherChannels to reset to the default channel mode for the new protocol. Table 32.2 below shows the different LACP combinations and the result of their use in establishing an EtherChannel between two switches:

Table 32.2—EtherChannel Formation Using Different LACP Modes

Switch 1 LACP Mode	Switch 2 LACP Mode	EtherChannel Result
Passive	Passive	No EtherChannel Formed
Passive	Active	EtherChannel Formed
Active	Active	EtherChannel Formed
Active	Passive	EtherChannel Formed

ETHERCHANNEL LOAD-DISTRIBUTION METHODS

For both PAgP and LACP EtherChannels, Catalyst switches use a polymorphic algorithm that utilizes key fields from the header of the packet to generate a hash, which is then matched to a physical link in the EtherChannel group. In other words, the switch distributes the traffic load across the links in an EtherChannel by reducing part of the binary pattern formed from the addresses in the frame to a numerical value that selects one of the links in the EtherChannel.

This operation can be performed on MAC addresses or IP addresses and can be based solely on source or destination addresses, or even both source and destination addresses. While delving into detail on the actual computation of the hash used in EtherChannel load distribution is beyond the scope of the CCNA exam requirements, it is important to know that the administrator can define which fields in the header can be used as input to the algorithm used to determine the physical link transport to the packet.

The load-distribution method is configured via the `port-channel load-balance [method]` global configuration command. Only a single method can be used at any given time. Table 32.3 below lists and describes the different methods available in Cisco IOS Catalyst switches when configuring EtherChannel load distribution:

Table 32.3—EtherChannel Load-Distribution (Load-Balancing) Options

Method	Description
dst-ip	Performs load distribution based on the destination IP address
dst-mac	Performs load distribution based on the destination MAC address
dst-port	Performs load distribution based on the destination Layer 4 port
src-dst-ip	Performs load distribution based on the source and destination IP address
src-dst-mac	Performs load distribution based on the source and destination MAC address
src-dst-port	Performs load distribution based on the source and destination Layer 4 port
src-ip	Performs load distribution based on the source IP address
src-mac	Performs load distribution based on the source MAC address
src-port	Performs load distribution based on the source Layer 4 port

ETHERCHANNEL CONFIGURATION GUIDELINES

The following section lists and describes the steps that are required to configure Layer 2 PAgP EtherChannels. However, before we delve into these configuration steps, it is important that you are familiar with the following caveats when configuring Layer 2 EtherChannels:

- Each EtherChannel can have up to eight compatibly configured Ethernet interfaces. LACP allows you to have more than eight ports in an EtherChannel group. These additional ports are hot-standby ports.
- All interfaces in the EtherChannel must operate at the same speed and duplex modes. Keep in mind, however, that unlike PAgP, LACP does not support half-duplex ports.
- Ensure that all interfaces in the EtherChannel are enabled. In some cases, if the interfaces are not enabled, the logical port channel interface will not be created automatically.

- When first configuring an EtherChannel group, it is important to remember that ports follow the parameters set for the first group port added.
- If Switch Port Analyzer (SPAN) is configured for a member port in an EtherChannel, then the port will be removed from the EtherChannel group.
- It is important to assign all interfaces in the EtherChannel to the same VLAN or configure them as trunk links. If these parameters are different, the channel will not form.
- Keep in mind that similar interfaces with different STP path costs (manipulated by an administrator) can still be used to form an EtherChannel.

It is recommended to shut down all member interfaces prior to beginning channeling configuration.

Configuring and Verifying Layer 2 EtherChannels

This section describes the configuration of Layer 2 EtherChannels by unconditionally forcing the selected interfaces to establish an EtherChannel.

1. The first configuration step is to enter Interface Configuration mode for the desired EtherChannel interface(s) via the `interface [name]` or `interface range [range]` global configuration command.
2. The second configuration step is to configure the interfaces as Layer 2 switch ports via the `switchport` interface configuration command.
3. The third configuration step is to configure the switch ports as either trunk or access links via the `switchport mode [access|trunk]` interface configuration command.
4. Optionally, if the interface or interfaces have been configured as access ports, assign them to the same VLAN using the `switchport access vlan [number]` command. If the interface or interfaces have been configured as a trunk port, select the VLANs allowed to traverse the trunk by issuing the `switchport trunk allowed vlan [range]` interface configuration command; if VLAN 1 will not be used as the native VLAN (for 802.1Q), enter the native VLAN by issuing the `switchport trunk native vlan [number]` interface configuration command. This configuration must be the same on all of the port channel member interfaces.
5. The next configuration step is to configure the interfaces to unconditionally trunk via the `channel-group [number] mode on` interface configuration command.

The configuration of unconditional EtherChannels using the steps described above will be based on the network topology illustrated in Figure 32.5 below:

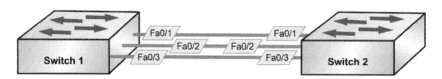

Figure 32.5—Network Topology for EtherChannel Configuration Output Examples

The following output illustrates how to configure unconditional channeling on Switch 1 and Switch 2 based on the network topology depicted in Figure 32.5. The EtherChannel will be configured as a Layer 2 802.1Q trunk using default parameters:

```
Switch-1#conf t
Enter configuration commands, one per line.  End with CNTL/Z.
Switch-1(config)#interface range fa0/1—3
Switch-1(config-if-range)#no shutdown
Switch-1(config-if-range)#switchport
Switch-1(config-if-range)#switchport trunk encapsulation dot1q
Switch-1(config-if-range)#switchport mode trunk
Switch-1(config-if-range)#channel-group 1 mode on
Creating a port-channel interface Port-channel 1
Switch-1(config-if-range)#exit
Switch-1(config)#exit
```

NOTE: Notice that the switch automatically creates interface port-channel 1 by default (refer to the output below). No explicit user configuration is required to configure this interface.

```
Switch-2#conf t
Enter configuration commands, one per line.  End with CNTL/Z.
Switch-2(config)#interface range fa0/1 - 3
Switch-2(config-if-range)#switchport
Switch-2(config-if-range)#switchport trunk encapsulation dot1q
Switch-2(config-if-range)#switchport mode trunk
Switch-2(config-if-range)#channel-group 1 mode on
Creating a port-channel interface Port-channel 1
Switch-2(config-if-range)#exit
Switch-2(config)#exit
```

The show EtherChannel [options] command can then be used to verify the configuration of the EtherChannel. The available options (which may vary depending upon platform) are printed in the following output:

```
Switch-2#show EtherChannel ?
  <1-6>          Channel group number
  detail         Detail information
  load-balance   Load-balance/frame-distribution scheme among ports in
port-channel
  port           Port information
  port-channel   Port-channel information
  protocol       protocol enabled
  summary        One-line summary per channel-group
  |              Output modifiers
  <cr>
```

The following output illustrates the show EtherChannel summary command:

```
Switch-2#show EtherChannel summary
Flags:  D - down
```

```
              I - stand-alone
              H - Hot-standby (LACP only)
              R - Layer3
              u - unsuitable for bundling
              U - in use
              d - default port
              P - in port-channel
              s - suspended
              S - Layer2
              f - failed to allocate aggregator

Number of channel-groups in use: 1
Number of aggregators:           1

Group  Port-channel  Protocol    Ports
------+-------------+-----------+------------------------------
1      Po1(SU)           -       Fa0/1(Pd)   Fa0/2(P)   Fa0/3(P)
```

In the output above, you can see that there are three links in Channel Group 1. Interface FastEthernet0/1 is the default port; this port will be used to send STP packets, for example. If this port fails, FastEthernet0/2 will be designated as the default port, and so forth. You can also see that this is an active Layer 2 EtherChannel by looking at the SU flag next to Po1. The following output shows the information printed by the show EtherChannel detail command:

```
Switch-2#show EtherChannel detail
                    Channel-group listing:
                    ----------------------

Group: 1
----------
Group state = L2
Ports: 3   Maxports = 8
Port-channels: 1 Max Port-channels = 1
Protocol:    -
                    Ports in the group:
                    -------------------
Port: Fa0/1
------------

Port state     = Up Mstr In-Bndl
Channel group = 1           Mode = On/FEC            Gcchange = -
Port-channel  = Po1         GC   = -     Pseudo port-channel = Po1
Port index    = 0           Load = 0x00            Protocol = -

Age of the port in the current state: 0d:00h:20m:20s

Port: Fa0/2
------------

Port state     = Up Mstr In-Bndl
Channel group = 1           Mode = On/FEC            Gcchange = -
```

```
Port-channel  = Po1        GC   = -    Pseudo port-channel = Po1
Port index    = 0          Load = 0x00              Protocol = -

Age of the port in the current state: 0d:00h:21m:20s

Port: Fa0/3
- - - - - - - - - - -

Port state     = Up Mstr In-Bndl
Channel group = 1          Mode = On/FEC           Gcchange = -
Port-channel  = Po1        GC   = -    Pseudo port-channel = Po1
Port index    = 0          Load = 0x00              Protocol = -

Age of the port in the current state: 0d:00h:21m:20s

                    Port-channels in the group:
                    - - - - - - - - - - - - - - - - - - - - - - - - -

Port-channel: Po1
- - - - - - - - - - -

Age of the Port-channel   = 0d:00h:26m:23s
Logical slot/port   = 1/0            Number of ports = 3
GC                  = 0x00000000     HotStandBy port = null
Port state          = Port-channel Ag-Inuse
Protocol            = -

Ports in the Port-channel:

Index  Load   Port    EC state            No of bits
- - - - - -+- - - - - -+- - - - - -+- - - - - - - - - - - - - - - - - -+- - - - - - - - - - -
0       00     Fa0/1   On/FEC              0
0       00     Fa0/2   On/FEC              0
0       00     Fa0/3   On/FEC              0

Time since last port bundled:     0d:00h:21m:20s     Fa0/3
```

In the output above, you can see that this is a Layer 2 EtherChannel with three out of a maximum of eight possible ports in the channel group. You can also see that the EtherChannel mode is on, based on the protocol being denoted by a dash (-). In addition, you can also see that this is a FastEtherChannel (FEC).

Finally, you can also verify the Layer 2 operational status of the logical port-channel interface by issuing the show interfaces port-channel [number] switchport command. This is illustrated in the following output:

```
Switch-2#show interfaces port-channel 1 switchport
Name: Po1
Switchport: Enabled
Administrative Mode: trunk
Operational Mode: trunk
Administrative Trunking Encapsulation: dot1q
```

```
Operational Trunking Encapsulation: dot1q
Negotiation of Trunking: On
Access Mode VLAN: 1 (default)
Trunking Native Mode VLAN: 1 (default)
Voice VLAN: none
Administrative private-vlan host-association: none
Administrative private-vlan mapping: none
Administrative private-vlan trunk native VLAN: none
Administrative private-vlan trunk encapsulation: dot1q
Administrative private-vlan trunk normal VLANs: none
Administrative private-vlan trunk private VLANs: none
Operational private-vlan: none
Trunking VLANs Enabled: ALL
Pruning VLANs Enabled: 2-1001
Protected: false
Appliance trust: none
```

Configuring and Verifying PAgP EtherChannels

This section describes the configuration of PAgP Layer 2 EtherChannels. The following steps need to be executed in order to configure and establish a PAgP EtherChannel.

1. The first configuration step is to enter Interface Configuration mode for the desired EtherChannel interface(s) via the interface [name] or interface range [range] global configuration command.
2. The second configuration step is to configure the interfaces as Layer 2 switch ports via the switchport interface configuration command.
3. The third configuration step is to configure the switch ports as either trunk or access links via the switchport mode [access|trunk] interface configuration command.
4. Optionally, if the interface or interfaces have been configured as access ports, assign them to the same VLAN using the switchport access vlan [number] command. If the interface or interfaces have been configured as a trunk port, select the VLANs allowed to traverse the trunk by issuing the switchport trunk allowed vlan [range] interface configuration command; if VLAN 1 will not be used as the native VLAN (for 802.1Q), enter the native VLAN by issuing the switchport trunk native vlan [number] interface configuration command. This configuration must be the same on all of the port channel member interfaces.
5. Optionally, configure PAgP as the EtherChannel protocol by issuing the channel-protocol pagp interface configuration command. Because EtherChannels default to PAgP, this command is considered optional and is not required. It is considered good practice to issue this command just to be absolutely sure of your configuration.
6. The next configuration step is to configure the interfaces to unconditionally trunk via the channel-group [number] mode interface configuration command.

The following output illustrates how to configure PAgP channeling on Switch 1 and Switch 2 based on the network topology depicted in Figure 32.5 above. The EtherChannel will be configured as a Layer 2 802.1Q trunk using default parameters:

```
Switch-1#conf t
Enter configuration commands, one per line.  End with CNTL/Z.
Switch-1(config)#interface range fa0/1 - 3
Switch-1(config-if-range)#switchport
Switch-1(config-if-range)#switchport trunk encap dot1q
Switch-1(config-if-range)#switchport mode trunk
Switch-1(config-if-range)#channel-group 1 mode desirable
Creating a port-channel interface Port-channel 1
Switch-1(config-if-range)#exit
```

NOTE: In the output above, the port channel desirable mode has been selected. An additional keyword, [non-silent], may also be appended to the end of this command. This is because, by default, PAgP auto and desirable modes default to a silent mode. The silent mode is used when the switch is connected to a device that is not PAgP-capable and that seldom, if ever, transmits packets. An example of a silent partner is a file server or a packet analyzer that is not generating traffic. It is also used if a device will not be sending PAgP packets (such as in auto mode).

In this case, running PAgP on a physical port connected to a silent partner prevents that switch port from ever becoming operational; however, the silent setting allows PAgP to operate, to attach the interface to a channel group, and to use the interface for transmission. In this example, because Switch 2 will be configured for auto mode (passive mode), it is preferred that the port uses the default silent mode operation. This is illustrated in the PAgP EtherChannel configuration output below:

```
Switch-1#conf t
Enter configuration commands, one per line.  End with CNTL/Z.
Switch-1(config)#interface range fa0/1 - 3
Switch-1(config-if-range)#switchport
Switch-1(config-if-range)#switchport trunk encap dot1q
Switch-1(config-if-range)#switchport mode trunk
Switch-1(config-if-range)#channel-group 1 mode desirable ?
  non-silent  Start negotiation only after data packets received
  <cr>
Switch-1(config-if-range)#channel-group 1 mode desirable non-silent
Creating a port-channel interface Port-channel 1
Switch-1(config-if-range)#exit
```

Proceeding with PAgP EtherChannel configuration, Switch 2 is configured as follows:

```
Switch-2#conf t
Enter configuration commands, one per line.  End with CNTL/Z.
Switch-2(config)#int range fa0/1 - 3
Switch-2(config-if-range)#switchport
Switch-2(config-if-range)#switchport trunk encapsulation dot1q
Switch-2(config-if-range)#switchport mode trunk
Switch-2(config-if-range)#channel-group 1 mode auto
Creating a port-channel interface Port-channel 1
Switch-2(config-if-range)#exit
```

The following output illustrates how to verify the PAgP EtherChannel configuration by using the `show EtherChannel summary` command on Switch 1 and Switch 2:

```
Switch-1#show EtherChannel summary
Flags:  D - down
        I - stand-alone
        H - Hot-standby (LACP only)
        R - Layer3
        u - unsuitable for bundling
        U - in use
        d - default port
        P - in port-channel
        s - suspended
        S - Layer2
        f - failed to allocate aggregator

Number of channel-groups in use: 1
Number of aggregators:            1

Group  Port-channel  Protocol   Ports
------+-------------+----------+-----------------------------
1      Po1(SU)        PAgP      Fa0/1(Pd)   Fa0/2(P)   Fa0/3(P)
```

PAgP EtherChannel configuration and statistics may also be viewed by issuing the `show pagp [options]` command. The options available with this command are illustrated in the following output:

```
Switch-1#show pagp ?
  <1-6>     Channel group number
  counters  Traffic information
  internal  Internal information
  neighbor  Neighbor information
```

NOTE: Entering the desired port channel number provides the same options as the last three options printed above. This is illustrated in the following output:

```
Switch-1#show pagp 1 ?
  counters  Traffic information
  internal  Internal information
  neighbor  Neighbor information
```

The `[counters]` keyword provides information on PAgP sent and received packets. The `[internal]` keyword provides information such as the port state, Hello interval, PAgP port priority, and the port learning method, for example. Using the `show pagp internal` command, this is illustrated in the following output:

```
Switch-1#show pagp 1 internal
Flags:  S - Device is sending Slow hello.  C - Device is in Consistent
state.
        A - Device is in Auto mode.        d - PAgP is down.
Timers: H - Hello timer is running.        Q - Quit timer is running.
```

```
        S - Switching timer is running.    I - Interface timer is
running.

Channel group 1
                                 Hello    Partner PAgP      Learning Group
   Port  Flags State Timers Interval Count Priority Method  Ifindex
   Fa0/1 SC    U6/S7 H      30s      1     128      Any     29
   Fa0/2 SC    U6/S7 H      30s      1     128      Any     29
   Fa0/3 SC    U6/S7 H      30s      1     128      Any     29
```

The [neighbor] keyword prints out the neighbor name, ID of the PAgP neighbor, the neighbor device ID (MAC), and the neighbor port. The flags also indicate the mode the neighbor is operating in, as well as if it is a physical learner, for example. Using the show pagp neighbor command, this is illustrated in the following output:

```
Switch-1#show pagp 1 neighbor
Flags:  S - Device is sending Slow hello. C - Device is in Consistent
state.
        A - Device is in Auto mode.      P - Device learns on physical
port.

Channel group 1 neighbors
          Partner    Partner            Partner         Partner Group
   Port   Name       Device ID          Port     Age    Flags   Cap.
   Fa0/1  Switch-2   0014.a9e5.d640     Fa0/1    19s    SAC     10001
   Fa0/2  Switch-2   0014.a9e5.d640     Fa0/2    24s    SAC     10001
   Fa0/3  Switch-2   0014.a9e5.d640     Fa0/3    18s    SAC     10001
```

Configuring and Verifying LACP EtherChannels

This section describes the configuration of LACP Layer 2 EtherChannels. The following steps need to be executed in order to configure and establish an LACP EtherChannel.

1. The first configuration step is to enter Interface Configuration mode for the desired EtherChannel interface(s) via the interface [name] or interface range [range] global configuration command.
2. The second configuration step is to configure the interfaces as Layer 2 switch ports via the switchport interface configuration command.
3. The third configuration step is to configure the switch ports as either trunk or access links via the switchport mode [access|trunk] interface configuration command.
4. Optionally, if the interface or interfaces have been configured as access ports, assign them to the same VLAN using the switchport access vlan [number] command. If the interface or interfaces have been configured as a trunk port, select the VLANs allowed to traverse the trunk by issuing the switchport trunk allowed vlan [range] interface configuration command; if VLAN 1 will not be used as the native VLAN (for 802.1Q), enter the native VLAN by issuing the switchport trunk native vlan [number] interface configuration command. This configuration must be the same on all of the port channel member interfaces.

5. Configure LACP as the EtherChannel protocol by issuing the `channel-protocol lacp` interface configuration command. Because EtherChannels default to PAgP, this command is considered mandatory for LACP and is required.
6. The next configuration step is to configure the interfaces to unconditionally trunk via the `channel-group [number] mode` interface configuration command.

In the above output illustrating how to configure LACP channeling on Switch 1 and Switch 2 based on the network topology depicted in Figure 32.5, the EtherChannel will be configured as a Layer 2 802.1Q trunk using default parameters, as shown in the following outputs:

```
Switch-1#conf t
Enter configuration commands, one per line.  End with CNTL/Z.
Switch-1(config)#int range FastEthernet0/1 - 3
Switch-1(config-if-range)#switchport
Switch-1(config-if-range)#switchport trunk encapsulation dot1q
Switch-1(config-if-range)#switchport mode trunk
Switch-1(config-if-range)#channel-protocol lacp
Switch-1(config-if-range)#channel-group 1 mode active
Creating a port-channel interface Port-channel 1
Switch-1(config-if-range)#exit

Switch-2#conf t
Enter configuration commands, one per line.  End with CNTL/Z.
Switch-2(config)#interface range FastEthernet0/1 - 3
Switch-2(config-if-range)#switchport
Switch-2(config-if-range)#switchport trunk encapsulation dot1q
Switch-2(config-if-range)#switchport mode trunk
Switch-2(config-if-range)#channel-protocol lacp
Switch-2(config-if-range)#channel-group 1 mode passive
Creating a port-channel interface Port-channel 1
Switch-2(config-if-range)#exit
```

The following output illustrates how to verify the LACP EtherChannel configuration by using the `show EtherChannel summary` command on Switch 1 and Switch 2:

```
Switch-1#show EtherChannel summary
Flags:  D - down
        I - stand-alone
        H - Hot-standby (LACP only)
        R - Layer3
        u - unsuitable for bundling
        U - in use
        d - default port
        P - in port-channel
        s - suspended
        S - Layer2
        f - failed to allocate aggregator

Number of channel-groups in use: 1
Number of aggregators:           1
```

```
Group  Port-channel  Protocol    Ports
------+-------------+-----------+-----------------------------------
1      Po1(SU)       LACP        Fa0/1(Pd)   Fa0/2(P)    Fa0/3(P)
```

By default, LACP allows up to 16 ports to be entered into a port channel group. The first eight operational interfaces will be used by LACP, while the remaining eight interfaces will be placed into the hot-standby state. The show EtherChannel detail command shows the maximum number of supported links in an LACP EtherChannel, as illustrated in the following output:

```
Switch-1#show EtherChannel 1 detail
Group state = L2
Ports: 3   Maxports = 16
Port-channels: 1 Max Port-channels = 16
Protocol:   LACP
                Ports in the group:
                -------------------
Port: Fa0/1
------------

Port state      = Up Mstr In-Bndl
Channel group = 1           Mode = Active       Gcchange = -
Port-channel  = Po1         GC   = -        Pseudo port-channel = Po1
Port index    = 0           Load = 0x00         Protocol = LACP

Flags:  S - Device is sending Slow LACPDUs.  F - Device is sending fast
                                                 LACPDUs.
            A - Device is in active mode.       P - Device is in passive
mode.

Local information:


                      LACP port    Admin     Oper     Port      Port
Port    Flags  State  Priority     Key       Key      Number    State
Fa0/1   SA     bndl   32768        0x1       0x1      0x0       0x3D

Partner's information:

          Partner              Partner                    Partner
Port      System ID            Port Number      Age       Flags
Fa0/1     00001,0014.a9e5.d640 0x1              4s        SP

          LACP Partner         Partner          Partner
          Port Priority        Oper Key         Port State
          32768                0x1              0x3C

Age of the port in the current state: 00d:00h:00m:35s

Port: Fa0/2
------------
```

```
Port state    = Up Mstr In-Bndl
Channel group = 1              Mode = Active      Gcchange = -
Port-channel  = Po1            GC   = -       Pseudo port-channel = Po1
Port index    = 0              Load = 0x00        Protocol = LACP

Flags:  S - Device is sending Slow LACPDUs.  F - Device is sending fast
                                                 LACPDUs.
        A - Device is in active mode.         P - Device is in passive
mode.

Local information:

                        LACP port   Admin    Oper    Port     Port
Port    Flags  State  Priority     Key      Key     Number   State
Fa0/2   SA     bndl   32768        0x1      0x1     0x1      0x3D

Partner's information:

          Partner               Partner                    Partner
Port      System ID             Port Number    Age         Flags
Fa0/2     00001.0014.a9e5.d640  0x2            28s         SP

          LACP Partner          Partner        Partner
          Port Priority         Oper Key       Port State
          32768                 0x1            0x3C

Age of the port in the current state: 00d:00h:00m:33s

Port: Fa0/3
------------

Port state    = Up Mstr In-Bndl
Channel group = 1              Mode = Active      Gcchange = -
Port-channel  = Po1            GC   = -       Pseudo port-channel = Po1
Port index    = 0              Load = 0x00        Protocol = LACP

Flags:  S - Device is sending Slow LACPDUs.  F - Device is sending fast
                                                 LACPDUs.
        A - Device is in active mode.         P - Device is in passive
mode.

Local information:

                        LACP port   Admin    Oper    Port     Port
Port    Flags  State  Priority     Key      Key     Number   State
Fa0/3   SA     bndl   32768        0x1      0x1     0x2      0x3D

Partner's information:

          Partner               Partner                    Partner
Port      System ID             Port Number    Age         Flags
Fa0/3     00001.0014.a9e5.d640  0x3            5s          SP
```

```
            LACP Partner          Partner           Partner
            Port Priority         Oper Key          Port State
            32768                 0x1               0x3C

Age of the port in the current state: 00d:00h:00m:29s

                    Port-channels in the group:
                    - - - - - - - - - - - - - - - - - - - - -

Port-channel: Po1     (Primary Aggregator)


- - - - - - - - - - - -

Age of the Port-channel = 00d:00h:13m:50s
Logical slot/port    = 1/0             Number of ports = 3
HotStandBy port = null
Port state           = Port-channel Ag-Inuse
Protocol             = LACP

Ports in the Port-channel:

Index   Load    Port    EC state
------+------+------+------------
0       00      Fa0/1   Active
0       00      Fa0/2   Active
0       00      Fa0/3   Active

Time since last port bundled:    00d:00h:00m:32s    Fa0/3
Time since last port Un-bundled: 00d:00h:00m:49s    Fa0/1
```

LACP configuration and statistics may also be viewed by issuing the show lacp [options] command. The options available with this command are illustrated in the following output:

```
Switch-1#show lacp ?
  <1-6>     Channel group number
  counters  Traffic information
  internal  Internal information
  neighbor  Neighbor information
  sys-id    LACP System ID
```

The [counters] keyword provides information on LACP sent and received packets. The output printed by this command is illustrated below:

```
Switch-1#show lacp counters
                LACPDUs         Marker      Marker Response    LACPDUs
Port        Sent   Recv     Sent   Recv     Sent   Recv       Pkts Err
------------------------------------------------------------------------
Channel group: 1
Fa0/1       14     12       0      0        0      0          0
Fa0/2       21     18       0      0        0      0          0
Fa0/3       21     18       0      0        0      0          0
```

The [internal] keyword provides information such as the port state, administrative key, LACP port priority, and the port number, for example. This is illustrated in the following output:

```
Switch-1#show lacp internal
Flags:  S - Device is sending Slow LACPDUs.  F - Device is sending Fast
                                                 LACPDUs.
        A - Device is in Active mode.       P - Device is in Passive
mode.

Channel group 1
                          LACP port    Admin    Oper    Port    Port
Port       Flags   State  Priority     Key      Key     Number  State
Fa0/1      SA      bndl   32768        0x1      0x1     0x0     0x3D
Fa0/2      SA      bndl   32768        0x1      0x1     0x1     0x3D
Fa0/3      SA      bndl   32768        0x1      0x1     0x2     0x3D
```

The [neighbor] keyword prints out the neighbor name, ID of the LACP neighbor, the neighbor device ID (MAC), and the neighbor port. The flags also indicate the mode the neighbor is operating in, as well as whether it is a physical learner, for example. This is illustrated in the following output:

```
Switch-1#show lacp neighbor
Flags:  S - Device is sending Slow LACPDUs.  F - Device is sending Fast
                                                 LACPDUs.
        A - Device is in Active mode.       P - Device is in Passive
mode.

Channel group 1 neighbors

Partner's information:

           Partner                Partner                     Partner
Port       System ID              Port Number    Age          Flags
Fa0/1      00001,0014.a9e5.d640   0x1            11s          SP

           LACP Partner           Partner        Partner
           Port Priority          Oper Key       Port State
           32768                  0x1            0x3C

Partner's information:

           Partner                Partner                     Partner
Port       System ID              Port Number    Age          Flags
Fa0/2      00001,0014.a9e5.d640   0x2            19s          SP

           LACP Partner           Partner        Partner
           Port Priority          Oper Key       Port State
           32768                  0x1            0x3C

Partner's information:
```

```
             Partner               Partner                        Partner
Port         System ID             Port Number      Age           Flags
Fa0/3        00001,0014.a9e5.d640  0x3              24s           SP

             LACP Partner          Partner          Partner
             Port Priority         Oper Key         Port State
             32768                 0x1              0x3C
```

Finally, the [sys-id] keyword provides the system ID of the local switch. This is a combination of the switch MAC and LACP priority, as illustrated in the following output:

```
Switch-1#show lacp sys-id
1      ,000d.bd06.4100
```

Please take today's exam at **https://www.in60days.com/free/ccnain60days**

DAY 32 LAB

EtherChannels

Test the configuration commands presented in this module on a simple topology that includes two directly connected switches (at least two links between them). Connect them via Fa1/1 and Fa2/2 (Fa1/1 to Fa1/1 and Fa2/2 to Fa2/2) or Fa0/1 etc. Whatever is available on your device :

- Configure PagP on the two links in mode auto-desirable
- Configure the EtherChannel link as a trunk and allow a couple of VLANs through it
- Issue a `show etherchannel summary` command and verify that the port channel is up
- Issue a `show mac-address-table` command and see the learned MAC addresses on each switch
- Issue a `show papg neighbor` command and verify the results
- Repeat the steps above using LACP mode passive-active
- Verify the configuration using the `show EtherChannel detail` and `show lacp neighbor` commands
- Verify the configuration using the `show interface port-channel [number] switchport` command
- Issue some traffic (ping) across the port channel and verify the counters using the `show lacp counters` command
- Configure a different `lacp system-priority` output and verify it with the `show lacp sys-id` command
- Configure a different `lacp port-priority` output and verify it with the `show lacp internal` command

Configure LACP load balancing using the `port-channel load-balance` command and verify this with the `show etherchannel load-balance` command

Switch Stacking and Layer 2 Mitigation Techniques

DAY 33 TASKS

- Read today's lesson notes (below)
- Review yesterday's lesson notes and lab
- Read the ICND2 cram guide
- Take today's exam
- Spend 15 minutes on the subnetting.org website

Switch stacking was Cisco's solution to a problem faced by network support and installation engineers who had the cumbersome task of configuring a number of switches with management IP addresses, default gateways, and SSH or Telnet access. In addition, if troubleshooting was needed, each switch had to be interrogated for the MAC address table, STP, VTP, and CDP entries.

Gaining access to network ports is fairly easy for any visitor to your company or even an employee with malicious intent, as they only need to find a free LAN port or unplug an existing device. This is why it's so important to secure your network from the edge. A company may not be able to always control who physically connects a device to the network, but it can control which computers can actually access network resources.

Today you will learn about the following:

- Switch Stacking
- Common access layer threat mitigation techniques

This lesson maps to the following ICND2 syllabus requirements:

- 1.6 Describe the benefits of switch stacking and chassis aggregation
- 1.7 Describe common access layer threat mitigation techniques
- 1.7.a 802.1x
- 1.7.b DHCP snooping

SWITCH STACKING AND CHASSIS AGGREGATION

Switch stacking enables you to physically connect a number of Cisco switches with special cables so that they logically appear on the network as one switch. This group of switches has a single IP address for management, a single MAC address table, and one instance of STP.

Stackable switches feature special ports at the rear of the chassis that allow two or more to be daisy-chained. Figure 33.1 below demonstrates a typical stack connection:

Figure 33.1—Stacked Switches (Image © http://wannabelab.blogspot.com.au)

There are several benefits to using stacking technology:

- Simplified administration
- Scalability with no overhead
- Ease of deployment (adding or removing switches)

One of the switches is elected as the master switch and acts as the primary source for incoming telnet or ping responses, routing information exchange, QoS, etc., while relevant information is passed down to subordinate switches. In order for stacking to work, each switch must be running the same IOS release and feature set.

Cisco offers stacking in two varieties, Cisco FlexStack and FlexStack-Plus. Which one you adopt depends on the model of switch you have purchased. FlexStack was introduced with the 2960-S model series, and then enhanced with FlexStack-Plus for the 2960-X and XR series switches. According to Cisco, "[a] single FlexStack connection between two 2960 stack members is a full-duplex 10Gbps connection. A single FlexStack-Plus connection between two 2960-X members is full-duplex 20Gbps."

You can stack up to four switches with FlexStack and eight with FlexStack-Plus.

COMMON ACCESS LAYER THREAT MITIGATION TECHNIQUES

Home users are all too aware of some of the types of attacks hackers can use such as viruses and hoax e-mails. As network administrators, we need to understand and mitigate against many other types of attacks. Cisco has updated the CCNA syllabus to reflect some of the most common network attacks, which adds to the previous device-hardening steps that have been present for a few years now.

In this section, we will cover the tools that have been specifically created for access layer deployment. There are several types of attacks and mitigation steps available; however, we will focus on 802.1X and DHCP snooping, which are exam syllabus topics.

Securing Access with IEEE 802.1x

Using 802.1X, users cannot simply receive network access just because they have plugged their PC into a network port. All users must be authenticated in order for the LAN switch to which they are connected to allow them to pass traffic. The combination of 802.1X and a AAA server will protect the network from unwanted parties.

802.1X provides Port-based Network Access Control (PNAC) and authenticates users or devices before they have access to the LAN or Wireless LAN. It provides port-level policy enforcement and then places users into a predetermined VLAN granting certain network rights.

802.1X employs the concepts of supplicant, authenticator, and authentication server. Once implemented, the LAN switch acts as the authenticator, as shown in Figure 33.2 below. In order for a client (supplicant) to gain access to the network, he or she must be authenticated by the connected switch (authenticator), which in turn contacts the authentication server for authorization. For this to work, the end-user device must be using 802.1X client software, which is included with most major operating systems such as Windows and Ubuntu.

The client software must support both 802.1X and Extensible Authentication Protocol (EAP) protocols, which is how the client sends the authentication request. The authenticator switch acts as a proxy by relaying messages between the client and the authentication server. This process is outlined in Figure 33.2 below. I've added the EAP message types; however, this is just for information because they are outside the scope of the exam syllabus.

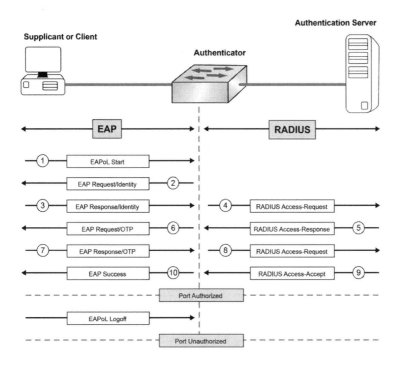

Figure 33.2—Supplicant, Authenticator, and Authentication Server

In summary, the switch, acting as the 802.1X authenticator, queries the AAA server if the supplied username and password are correct, and the AAA server provides the appropriate response. If there is a match, the switch will then enable the port for use. If there is no match, the port will not forward traffic to or from the device connected to it.

If authenticated, the port will transition to "authorized" and the supplicant will be able to forward packets to the network. Although the configuration is beyond the scope of the exam, it is worth noting that the switchport must be set to static access or the configuration commands won't be applied.

```
Switch(config)#int f0/1
Switch(config-if)#dot1x port-control auto
% Error: 802.1X cannot be configured on a dynamic port
```

DHCP Snooping

DHCP was devised to protect the network from rogue DHCP servers, which is another way to create a Layer 2 network attack. DHCP spoofing and starvation attacks are methods used by attackers to exhaust DHCP address pools, resulting in resource starvation (i.e., no IP addresses available for network hosts).

The next step for the attacker is to introduce a rogue DHCP server into the network to respond to host requests for IP information. Rogue default gateway and DNS server information is then provided to the hosts, allowing other forms of attacks to take place. This type of attack can be mitigated with port security, which will be covered in the following DHCP snooping section.

DHCP Snooping Basics

DHCP snooping provides network protection from rogue DHCP servers by creating a logical firewall between untrusted hosts and DHCP servers. When DHCP snooping is enabled, the switch builds and maintains a DHCP snooping table (which is also referred to as the DHCP binding table), and it is used to prevent and filter untrusted messages from the network.

DHCP snooping uses the concept of trusted and untrusted interfaces. This means that incoming packets received on untrusted ports are dropped if the source MAC address of those packets does not match the MAC address in the binding table. Figure 33.3 below illustrates the operation of the DHCP snooping feature:

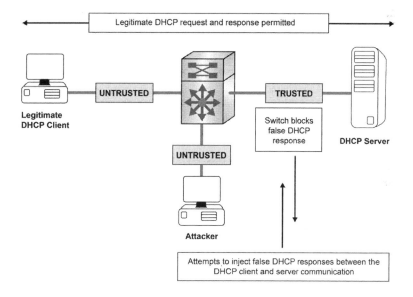

Figure 33.3—DHCP Snooping in Operation

You can see in Figure 33.3 above that the attacker has attempted to inject rogue DHCP messages into the legitimate exchange between the DHCP server and the client. DHCP snooping means that these packets are dropped because they originated from an untrusted interface and the source MAC isn't present in the MAC binding table. The exchange between the legitimate client who is on an untrusted interface and the DHCP server is permitted because the source address does match the MAC address in the binding table entry.

Figure 33.4 below illustrates the use of the DHCP snooping table, which is used to filter untrusted DHCP messages from the network:

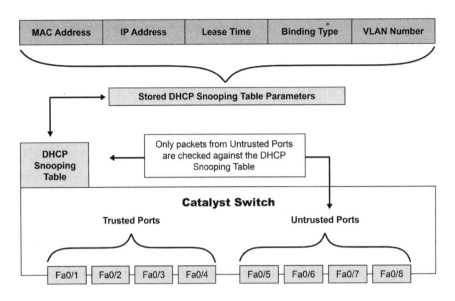

Figure 33.4—The DHCP Snooping (Binding) Table

In Figure 33.4 above, packets sourced from trusted ports are not subject to DHCP snooping checks. Trusted interfaces for DHCP snooping would be configured for ports directly connected to DHCP servers. However, all packets from untrusted interfaces are checked against the entries in the DHCP snooping table.

This means that if an attacker attempts to use randomly-generated MAC addresses to initiate a DHCP snooping and starvation attack, all packets will be checked against the DHCP snooping table, and because there will be no matches for those specific MAC addresses, all packets will be discarded by the switch, effectively preventing this type of attack from occurring.

DHCP snooping assumes that end-user devices are untrusted. Therefore, any port that is not specifically marked as a trusted port will be monitored. DHCP snooping must be enabled either globally on a switch or by VLAN. When enabled, all ports are considered untrusted. In order for a switchport to be trusted, you would enable it on the port(s) connected to the DHCP servers.

Configuring DHCP snooping is beyond the scope of the exam syllabus; however, the following output shows how to configure DHCP snooping for VLAN100. Once DHCP snooping has been enabled, administrators can use the show ip dhcp snooping command to validate their configuration. DHCP snooping is disabled by default.

```
Switch(config)#ip dhcp snooping
Switch(config)#ip dhcp snooping vlan100
Switch(config)#int gi2/24
Switch(config-if)#description "Connected to Legitimate DHCP Server"
Switch(config-if)#ip dhcp snooping trust
```

```
Switch#show ip dhcp snooping
Switch DHCP snooping is enabled.
DHCP Snooping is configured on the following VLANs:
100
Insertion of option 82 information is enabled.
Interface           Trusted         Rate limit (pps)
---------           -------         ----------------
GigabitEthernet2/24 yes             none
```

Please take today's exam at **https://www.in60days.com/free/ccnain60days/**

Review

DAY 34 TASKS

- Review the last three days lesson notes and labs
- Take today's exam at **https://www.in60days.com/free/ccnain60days/**
- Read the ICND2 cram guide
- Do the below challenge labs if you wish

Challenge 1—STP

Topology

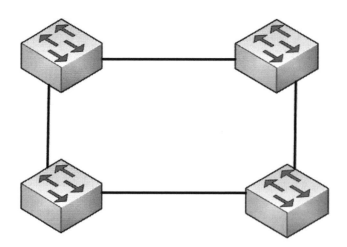

Instructions

Connect two or four switches together.

1. Configure VLANs 20 and 30 on all switches
2. Configure trunking between all switches
3. Disable DTP on all switches
4. Establish which switch will be the root just by looking at each MAC address
5. Establish which interface will be blocking
6. Check your working out with show commands. Were you correct?

Challenge 2—VLANs and STP

Topology

VLAN 4

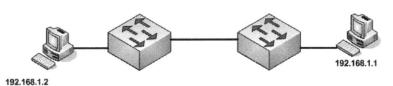

192.168.1.1

192.168.1.2

Instructions

Connect to the switch using a console connection. Connect a PC to each switch or connect the switch to the fast ethernet port on a router.

1. Add IP addresses to the PCs or router Ethernet interfaces
2. Create VLAN 4 on the switches
3. Set the ports the PCs connect to as access ports (default but do it anyway)
4. Put the two switch ports into VLAN 4
5. Configure the link between the switches as trunk ports and no shut them
6. Wait about 30 seconds at most and then ping from PC to PC.
7. Check which switch is the root with `show spanning-tree vlan 4`
8. Set the other switch as the root with the `spanning-tree vlan 4 priority 0` command
9. Now check the switch has become the root
10. Remove the command to reset the original switch as root (put 'no' in front of command)
11. Now set the other switch as root with the `spanning-tree vlan 4 root primary` command

Challenge 3—Etherchannels

Topology

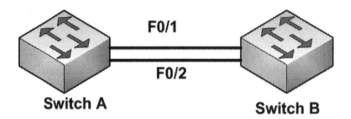

Switch A   **Switch B**

Instructions

Connect two switches together with crossover cables (or use Packet Tracer)

1. Put all ports into VLAN 10 and set as access ports
2. Create an etherchannel using LCAP. Switch A should actively try to create an etherchannel but B should only do so when it receives a request to do so
3. Issue 'show etherchannel summary' to check the channel came up
4. Reload the switches and do the same but this time use PAgP

InterVLAN Routing—Switched Virtual Interfaces

DAY 35 TASKS

- Read today's lesson notes (below)
- Complete today's lab
- Take today's exam
- Read the ICND2 cram guide

The most common way to configure inter-VLAN routing is by using SVIs. Cisco cover the other two methods in the ICND1 syllabus. In order to configure inter-VLAN routing with SVIs you will need access to a layer 3 switch (such as a 3560) or Packet Tracer.

Today you will learn about the following:

- InterVLAN routing using Switched Virtual Interfaces

This lesson maps to the following CCNA syllabus requirements:

- 2.1.b SVI

INTER-VLAN ROUTING USING SWITCHED VIRTUAL INTERFACES

Multilayer switches support the configuration of IP addressing on physical interfaces. These interfaces, however, must be configured with the `no switchport` interface configuration command to allow administrators to configure IP addressing on them. In addition to using physical interfaces, Multilayer switches also support Switched Virtual Interfaces (SVIs).

SVIs are logical interfaces that represent a VLAN. Although the SVI represents a VLAN, it is not automatically configured when a Layer 2 VLAN is configured on the switch; it must be manually configured by the administrator using the `interface vlan [number]` global configuration command. The Layer 3 configuration parameters, such as IP addressing, are then configured on the SVI in the same manner as they would be on a physical interface.

The following output illustrates the configuration of SVIs to allow inter-VLAN routing on a single switch. This output references the VLANs used in the previous configuration outputs in this section:

```
Switch(config)#vlan 10
Switch(config-vlan)#name Example-VLAN-10
Switch(config-vlan)#exit
Switch(config)#vlan 20
Switch(config-vlan)#name Example-VLAN-20
Switch(config-vlan)#exit
Switch(config)#interface range FastEthernet0/1-2
Switch(config-if-range)#switchport
Switch(config-if-range)#switchport mode access
Switch(config-if-range)#switchport access vlan 10
Switch(config-if-range)#exit
Switch(config)#interface range FastEthernet0/3-4
Switch(config-if-range)#switchport
Switch(config-if-range)#switchport mode access
Switch(config-if-range)#switchport access vlan 20
Switch(config-if-range)#exit
Switch(config)#interface vlan 10
Switch(config-if)#description "SVI for VLAN 10"
Switch(config-if)#ip address 10.10.10.1 255.255.255.0
Switch(config-if)#no shutdown
Switch(config-if)#exit
Switch(config)#interface vlan 20
Switch(config-if)#description 'SVI for VLAN 20'
Switch(config-if)#ip address 10.20.20.1 255.255.255.0
Switch(config-if)#no shutdown
Switch(config-if)#exit
```

When using Multilayer switches, SVIs are the recommended method for configuring and implementing an inter-VLAN routing solution.

You can verify that the SVI is properly configured (IP addressing, etc.) by using the show interface vlan x command. The output is identical to a show interface x command:

```
Switch#show interfaces vlan 100
Vlan100 is up, line protocol is down
  Hardware is EtherSVI, address is c200.06c8.0000 (bia c200.06c8.0000)
  Internet address is 10.10.10.1/24
  MTU 1500 bytes, BW 100000 Kbit/sec, DLY 100 usec,
     reliability 255/255, txload 1/255, rxload 1/255
  Encapsulation ARPA, loopback not set
  ARP type: ARPA, ARP Timeout 04:00:00
```

If you wish to use a 2960 switch to route IP packets, it will require a configuration change and reload. The reason for this is the 2960 and newer model switches are tuned to allocate resources in a certain way. The resource management is called the Switch Database Management (SDM) template. Your choices include the following:

- Default—balances all functions
- Dual IPv4/IPv6—for use in dual-stack environments
- Lanbase-routing—supports Unicast routes
- QoS—gives support for QoS features

Here are the options on my 3750 switch. They don't match the 2960 options exactly, but you get the idea. Also, bear in mind that your switch model and IOS will affect the configuration options, so check the configuration guide for your model:

```
Switch(config)#sdm prefer ?
  access               Access bias
  default              Default bias
  dual-ipv4-and-ipv6   Support both IPv4 and IPv6
  ipe                  IPe bias
  lanbase-routing      Unicast bias
  vlan                 VLAN bias
```

Lanbase-routing will need to be enabled if you wish to configure inter-VLAN routing on your 2960 switch. You will also need to reload the switch before the change will take effect. Here is the output of the show sdm prefer command, which tells you the current SDM configuration and resource allocation:

```
Switch#show sdm prefer
 The current template is "desktop default" template.
 The selected template optimizes the resources in
 the switch to support this level of features for
 8 routed interfaces and 1024 VLANs.

    number of unicast mac addresses:                  6K
    number of IPv4 IGMP groups + multicast routes:    1K
    number of IPv4 unicast routes:                    8K
      number of directly-connected IPv4 hosts:        6K
      number of indirect IPv4 routes:                 2K
    number of IPv4 policy based routing aces:         0
    number of IPv4/MAC qos aces:                      0.5K
    number of IPv4/MAC security aces:                 1K
```

Take today's exam at **https://www.in60days.com/free/ccnain60days/**

DAY 35 LAB

Inter-VLAN SVIs

Topology

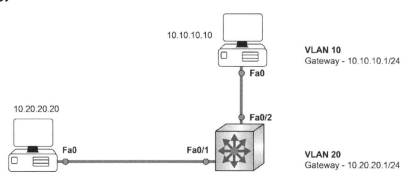

Purpose

Learn how to configure inter-VLAN routing using SVIs.

I've used Packet Tracer for this lab and the built in Layer 3 switch but you can use your own home lab if you have access to all the available equipment. Set the displayed IP address on each PC and put the default gateway as marked in the diagram.

Walkthrough

1. Create VLAN 10 and 20 on the switch and set the correct ports for the correct VLANs.

    ```
    Switch#conf t
    Enter configuration commands, one per line.  End with CNTL/Z.
    Switch(config)#vlan 10
    Switch(config-vlan)#vlan 20
    Switch(config-vlan)#int f0/2
    Switch(config-if)#switchport
    Switch(config-if)#switchport mode access
    Switch(config-if)#switchport access vlan 10
    Switch(config-if)#no shut
    Switch(config-if)#int f0/1
    Switch(config-if)#switchport
    Switch(config-if)#switchport mode access
    Switch(config-if)#switchport access vlan 20
    ```

2. Because I'm using a Layer 3 switch we have to set the interface to Layer 2 with the `switchport` command which you saw above. We next need to add an IP address for the VLAN because we aren't connected to a router.

    ```
    Switch(config)#interface vlan 10
    %LINK-5-CHANGED: Interface Vlan10, changed state to up
    ```

```
%LINEPROTO-5-UPDOWN: Line protocol on Interface Vlan10, changed state
to up
ip add 10.10.10.1 255.255.255.0
Switch(config-if)#no shut
Switch(config-if)#int vlan 20
%LINK-5-CHANGED: Interface Vlan20, changed state to up
%LINEPROTO-5-UPDOWN: Line protocol on Interface Vlan20, changed state
to up
ip add 10.20.20.1 255.255.255.0
Switch(config-if)#no shut
Switch(config-if)#exit
Switch#show vlan brief

VLAN Name Status                        Ports
---- -------------- ---------- --------------------------------
1 default active                        Fa0/3, Fa0/4, Fa0/5, Fa0/6
                                        Fa0/7, Fa0/8, Fa0/9, Fa0/10
                                        Fa0/11, Fa0/12, Fa0/13, Fa0/14
                                        Fa0/15, Fa0/16, Fa0/17, Fa0/18
                                        Fa0/19, Fa0/20, Fa0/21, Fa0/22
                                        Fa0/23, Fa0/24, Gig0/1, Gig0/2
                                        Gig0/1, Gig0/2
10   VLAN0010                           active    Fa0/2
20   VLAN0020                           active    Fa0/1
1002 fddi-default                       active
1003 token-ring-default                 active
1004 fddinet-default                    active
1005 trnet-default                      active
```

3. Because we're not using a router, we need to enable IP routing on the switch so it can route between the two subnets.

```
Switch(config)#ip routing
```

4. Check that the VLAN interfaces are up.

```
Switch#show ip interface brief
GigabitEthernet0/1 unassigned  YES unset  down                      down
GigabitEthernet0/2 unassigned  YES unset  down                      down
Vlan1              unassigned  YES unset  administratively down down
Vlan10             10.10.10.1  YES manual up                        up
Vlan20             10.20.20.1  YES manual up                        up
[Output Truncated]
```

5. Ping the default gateway and then the PC on the other VLAN to check inter-VLAN routing is working.

```
C:\>ping 10.10.10.1

Pinging 10.10.10.1 with 32 bytes of data:

Reply from 10.10.10.1: bytes=32 time<1ms TTL=255
Reply from 10.10.10.1: bytes=32 time<1ms TTL=255
```

```
Reply from 10.10.10.1: bytes=32 time<1ms TTL=255
Reply from 10.10.10.1: bytes=32 time<1ms TTL=255

Ping statistics for 10.10.10.1:
    Packets: Sent = 4, Received = 4, Lost = 0 (0% loss),
Approximate round trip times in milli-seconds:
    Minimum = 0ms, Maximum = 0ms, Average = 0ms

C:\>ping 10.20.20.20

Pinging 10.20.20.20 with 32 bytes of data:

Request timed out.
Reply from 10.20.20.20: bytes=32 time<1ms TTL=127
Reply from 10.20.20.20: bytes=32 time<1ms TTL=127
Reply from 10.20.20.20: bytes=32 time<1ms TTL=127

Ping statistics for 10.20.20.20:
    Packets: Sent = 4, Received = 3, Lost = 1 (25% loss),
Approximate round trip times in milli-seconds:
    Minimum = 0ms, Maximum = 0ms, Average = 0ms

C:\>
```

EIGRP

DAY 36 TASKS

- Read today's lesson notes (below)
- Review yesterday's lesson notes
- Take today's exam
- Complete today's lab
- Read the ICND2 cram guide

Note—Today is a tough day so feel free to spread it over two days because the next chapter is really short (and very similar). I've had to keep it pretty detailed because Cisco Press do the same in their books. You may well want to stop at the EIGRP Troubleshooting section and then continue tomorrow.

Enhanced Interior Gateway Routing Protocol (EIGRP) is a proprietary Interior Gateway Protocol (IGP) that was developed by Cisco. EIGRP includes traditional Distance Vector characteristics, such as split horizon, as well as characteristics that are similar to those used by Link State routing protocols, such as incremental updates.

Although EIGRP has Link State routing protocol characteristics, EIGRP falls under the Distance Vector routing protocol classification and is referred to as an advanced Distance Vector routing protocol instead. EIGRP runs directly over IP using protocol number 88.

While it is not possible to delve into all potential EIGRP problem scenarios, this module will discuss some of the most common problem scenarios when EIGRP is implemented as the Interior Gateway Protocol (IGP) of choice.

This lesson maps to the following CCNA syllabus requirement:

- 2.6 Configure, verify, and troubleshoot EIGRP for IPv4 (excluding authentication, filtering, manual summarization, redistribution, stub)

Today you will learn about the following:

- Cisco EIGRP overview and fundamentals
- EIGRP configuration fundamentals

- EIGRP messages
- EIGRP neighbor discovery and maintenance
- Metrics, DUAL, and the topology table
- Equal cost and unequal cost load sharing
- Default routing using EIGRP
- Split horizon in EIGRP networks
- EIGRP route summarization
- Understanding passive interfaces
- Understanding the use of the EIGRP router ID
- Troubleshooting EIGRP

CISCO EIGRP OVERVIEW AND FUNDAMENTALS

Cisco developed Enhanced IGRP to overcome some of the limitations of its proprietary Distance Vector routing protocol, Interior Gateway Routing Protocol (IGRP) which was dropped as a CCNA exam topic a few years ago. IGRP offered improvements over Routing Information Protocol (RIP), such as support for an increased number of hops; however, IGRP still succumbed to the traditional Distance Vector routing protocol limitations, which included the following:

- Sending full periodic routing updates
- A hop limitation
- The lack of VLSM support
- Slow convergence
- The lack of loop prevention mechanisms

Unlike the traditional Distance Vector routing protocols, which send their neighbors periodic routing updates that contain all routing information, EIGRP sends non-periodic incremental routing updates to distribute routing information throughout the routing domain. The EIGRP incremental updates are sent when there is a change in the network topology.

By default, RIP (a former CCNA-level topic) has a hop-count limitation of up to 15 hops, which makes RIP suitable only for smaller networks. EIGRP has a default hop-count limitation of 100; however, this value can be manually adjusted by the administrator using the `metric maximum-hops <1-255>` router configuration command when configuring EIGRP. This allows EIGRP to support networks that contain hundreds of routers, making it more scalable and better suited for larger networks.

Enhanced IGRP uses two unique Type/Length/Value (TLV) triplets to carry route entries. These TLVs are the Internal EIGRP Route TLV and the External EIGRP Route TLV, which are used for internal and external EIGRP routes, respectively. Both TLVs include an 8-bit Prefix Length field that specifies the number of bits used for the subnet mask of the destination network. The information that is contained in this field allows EIGRP to support variably subnetted networks.

Enhanced IGRP converges much faster than the traditional Distance Vector routing protocols. Instead of relying solely on timers, EIGRP uses information contained in its topology table to locate alternate paths. EIGRP can also query neighboring routers for information if an alternate path is not located in the local router's topology table. The EIGRP topology table will be described in detail later in this module.

In order to ensure that there are loop-free paths through the network, EIGRP uses the Diffusing Update Algorithm (DUAL), which is used to track all routes advertised by neighbors and then select the best loop-free path to the destination network. DUAL is a core EIGRP concept that will be described in detail later in this module.

EIGRP CONFIGURATION FUNDAMENTALS

Enhanced IGRP is enabled in Cisco IOS software using the router eigrp [ASN] global configuration command. The [ASN] keyword designates the EIGRP autonomous system number (ASN). This is a 32-bit integer between 1 and 65535. In addition to other factors, which will be described later in this lesson, routers running EIGRP must reside within the same autonomous system to form a neighbor relationship successfully. Following the configuration of the router eigrp [ASN] global configuration command, the router transitions to EIGRP Router Configuration mode wherein you can configure parameters pertaining to EIGRP. The configured ASN can be verified in the output of the show ip protocols command, as follows:

```
R1#show ip protocols
Routing Protocol is "eigrp 150"
  Outgoing update filter list for all interfaces is not set
  Incoming update filter list for all interfaces is not set
  Default networks flagged in outgoing updates
  Default networks accepted from incoming updates
  EIGRP metric weight K1=1, K2=0, K3=1, K4=0, K5=0
  EIGRP maximum hopcount 100
  EIGRP maximum metric variance 1
[Truncated Output]
```

In addition to the show ip protocols command, the show ip eigrp neighbors command prints information on all known EIGRP neighbors and their respective autonomous systems. This command, and its available options, will be described in detail later in this module. On routers running multiple instances of EIGRP, the show ip eigrp [ASN] command can be used to view information pertaining only to the autonomous system that is specified in this command. The use of this command is illustrated in the following output:

```
R1#show ip eigrp 150 ?
  interfaces  IP-EIGRP interfaces
  neighbors   IP-EIGRP neighbors
  topology    IP-EIGRP topology table
  traffic     IP-EIGRP traffic statistics
```

In the output above, 150 is the ASN. The default in Cisco IOS software is to print information on all EIGRP instances if an autonomous system is not specified with any `show ip eigrp` commands.

Once in Router Configuration mode, the `network` command is used to specify the network(s) (interfaces) for which EIGRP routing will be enabled. When the `network` command is used and a major classful network is specified, the following actions are performed on the EIGRP-enabled router:

- EIGRP is enabled for networks that fall within the specified classful network range.
- The topology table is populated with these directly connected subnets.
- EIGRP Hello packets are sent out of the interfaces associated with these subnets.
- EIGRP advertises the network(s) to EIGRP neighbors in Update messages.
- Based on the exchange of messages, EIGRP routes are then added to the IP routing table.

For example, assume that the router has the following Loopback interfaces configured:

- Loopback0—IP Address 10.0.0.1/24
- Loopback1—IP Address 10.1.1.1/24
- Loopback2—IP Address 10.2.2.1/24
- Loopback3—IP Address 10.3.3.1/24

If EIGRP is enabled for use and the major classful 10.0.0.0/8 network is used in conjunction with the `network` router configuration command, all four Loopback interfaces are enabled for EIGRP routing. This is illustrated in the following output:

```
R1#show ip eigrp interfaces
IP-EIGRP interfaces for process 150

                     Xmit Queue   Mean   Pacing Time   Multicast    Pending
Interface Peers Un/Reliable  SRTT   Un/Reliable  Flow Timer   Routes
Lo0         0        0/0       0       0/10          0            0
Lo1         0        0/0       0       0/10          0            0
Lo2         0        0/0       0       ·0/10          0            0
Lo3         0        0/0       0       0/10          0            0
```

You can use the `show ip protocols` command to verify that EIGRP is enabled for the major classful 10.0.0.0/8 network. The output of this command is illustrated below:

```
R1#show ip protocols
Routing Protocol is "eigrp 150"
  Outgoing update filter list for all interfaces is not set
  Incoming update filter list for all interfaces is not set
  Default networks flagged in outgoing updates
  Default networks accepted from incoming updates
  EIGRP metric weight K1=1, K2=0, K3=1, K4=0, K5=0
  EIGRP maximum hopcount 100
  EIGRP maximum metric variance 1
```

```
Redistributing: eigrp 150
EIGRP NSF-aware route hold timer is 240s
Automatic network summarization is in effect
Maximum path: 4
Routing for Networks:
  10.0.0.0
Routing Information Sources:
  Gateway          Distance        Last Update

Distance: internal 90 external 170
```

The EIGRP topology table can be viewed using the show ip eigrp topology command. The output of this command is illustrated below:

```
R1#show ip eigrp topology
IP-EIGRP Topology Table for AS(150)/ID(10.3.3.1)

Codes: P - Passive, A - Active, U - Update, Q - Query, R - Reply,
       r - reply Status, s - sia Status

P 10.3.3.0/24, 1 successors, FD is 128256
        via Connected, Loopback3
P 10.2.2.0/24, 1 successors, FD is 128256
        via Connected, Loopback2
P 10.1.1.0/24, 1 successors, FD is 128256
        via Connected, Loopback1
P 10.0.0.0/24, 1 successors, FD is 128256
        via Connected, Loopback0
```

NOTE: The topology table, EIGRP Hello packets, and Update messages are described in detail later in this module. The focus of this section is restricted to EIGRP configuration implementation.

Using the network command to specify a major classful network allows multiple subnets that fall within the classful network range to be advertised at the same time with minimal configuration. However, there may be situations where administrators may not want all of the subnets within a classful network to be enabled for EIGRP routing. For example, referencing the Loopback interfaces configured on R1 in the previous example, assume that you want EIGRP routing enabled only for the 10.1.1.0/24 and 10.3.3.0/24 subnets, and not for the 10.0.0.0/24 and 10.2.2.0/24 subnets. While it appears that this would be possible if you specified the networks (i.e., 10.1.1.0 and 10.3.3.0) when using the network command, Cisco IOS software still converts these statements to the major classful 10.0.0.0/8 network, as illustrated below:

```
R1(config)#router eigrp 150
R1(config-router)#network 10.1.1.0
R1(config-router)#network 10.3.3.0
R1(config-router)#exit
```

Despite the configuration above, the show ip protocols command reveals the following:

```
R1#show ip protocols
Routing Protocol is "eigrp 150"
  Outgoing update filter list for all interfaces is not set
  Incoming update filter list for all interfaces is not set
  Default networks flagged in outgoing updates
  Default networks accepted from incoming updates
  EIGRP metric weight K1=1, K2=0, K3=1, K4=0, K5=0
  EIGRP maximum hopcount 100
  EIGRP maximum metric variance 1
  Redistributing: eigrp 150
  EIGRP NSF-aware route hold timer is 240s
  Automatic network summarization is in effect
  Maximum path: 4
```
Routing for Networks:
```
    10.0.0.0
  Routing Information Sources:
    Gateway         Distance     Last Update

Distance: internal 90 external 170
```

NOTE: A common misconception is that disabling the EIGRP automatic summarization feature addresses this issue; however, this has nothing to do with the auto-summary command. For example, assume that you issued the no auto-summary command to the configuration used in the previous example, as follows:

```
R1(config)#router eigrp 150
R1(config-router)#network 10.1.1.0
R1(config-router)#network 10.3.3.0
R1(config-router)#no auto-summary
R1(config-router)#exit
```

The show ip protocols command still shows that EIGRP is enabled for network 10.0.0.0/8, as illustrated below:

```
R1#show ip protocols
Routing Protocol is "eigrp 150"
  Outgoing update filter list for all interfaces is not set
  Incoming update filter list for all interfaces is not set
  Default networks flagged in outgoing updates
  Default networks accepted from incoming updates
  EIGRP metric weight K1=1, K2=0, K3=1, K4=0, K5=0
  EIGRP maximum hopcount 100
  EIGRP maximum metric variance 1
  Redistributing: eigrp 150
  EIGRP NSF-aware route hold timer is 240s
```
Automatic network summarization is not in effect
```
  Maximum path: 4
```
Routing for Networks:
```
    10.0.0.0
  Routing Information Sources:
    Gateway         Distance     Last Update

Distance: internal 90 external 170
```

In order to provide more granular control of the networks that are enabled for EIGRP routing, Cisco IOS software supports the use of wildcard masks in conjunction with the `network` statement when configuring EIGRP. The wildcard mask operates in a manner similar to the wildcard mask used in ACLs and is independent of the subnet mask for the network.

As an example, the command `network 10.1.1.0 0.0.0.255` would match the 10.1.1.0/24 network, the 10.1.1.0/26 network, and the 10.1.1.0/30 network. Referencing the Loopback interfaces configured in the previous output, R1 would be configured as follows to enable EIGRP routing for the 10.1.1.0/24 and 10.3.3.0/24 subnets, and not for the 10.0.0.0/24 subnet or the 10.2.2.0/24 subnet:

```
R1(config)#router eigrp 150
R1(config-router)#network 10.1.1.0 0.0.0.255
R1(config-router)#network 10.3.3.0 0.0.0.255
R1(config-router)#exit
```

This configuration can be validated using the `show ip protocols` command, as follows:

```
R1#show ip protocols
Routing Protocol is "eigrp 150"
  Outgoing update filter list for all interfaces is not set
  Incoming update filter list for all interfaces is not set
  Default networks flagged in outgoing updates
  Default networks accepted from incoming updates
  EIGRP metric weight K1=1, K2=0, K3=1, K4=0, K5=0
  EIGRP maximum hopcount 100
  EIGRP maximum metric variance 1
  Redistributing: eigrp 150
  EIGRP NSF-aware route hold timer is 240s
  Automatic network summarization is in effect
  Maximum path: 4
  Routing for Networks:
    10.1.1.0/24
    10.3.3.0/24
  Routing Information Sources:
    Gateway         Distance      Last Update

  Distance: internal 90 external 170
```

Additionally, the `show ip eigrp interfaces` command can be used to validate that EIGRP routing has been enabled only for Loopback1 and Loopback3:

```
R1#show ip eigrp interfaces
IP-EIGRP interfaces for process 150

                 Xmit Queue   Mean   Pacing Time   Multicast    Pending
Interface Peers Un/Reliable  SRTT   Un/Reliable   Flow Timer   Routes
Lo1       0        0/0         0        0/10           0            0
Lo3       0        0/0         0        0/10           0            0
```

As illustrated in the output above, EIGRP routing is enabled only for Loopback1 and Loopback3 because of the wildcard mask configuration.

It is important to remember that the network command can be configured using the subnet mask, rather than the wildcard mask. When this is the case, Cisco IOS software inverts the subnet mask and the command is saved using the wildcard mask. For example, referencing the same Loopback interfaces on the router, R1 could also be configured as follows:

```
R1(config-router)#router eigrp 150
R1(config-router)#network 10.1.1.0 255.255.255.0
R1(config-router)#network 10.3.3.0 255.255.255.0
R1(config-router)#exit
```

Based on this configuration, the following is entered in the running configuration (I've used a pipe to drill down to the part of config I'm interested in):

```
R1#show running-config | begin router eigrp
router eigrp 150
 network 10.1.1.0 0.0.0.255
 network 10.3.3.0 0.0.0.255
 auto-summary
```

You can see by the above configuration that you can use pipes with show commands in order to get more granularity. This will be a familiar concept to anyone with previous programming knowledge.

If a specific address on the network is used, in conjunction with the wildcard mask, Cisco IOS software performs a logical AND operation to determine the network that will be enabled for EIGRP. For example, if the network 10.1.1.15 0.0.0.255 command is issued, Cisco IOS software performs the following actions:

- Inverts the wildcard mask to the subnet mask value of 255.255.255.0
- Performs a logical AND operation
- Adds the network 10.1.1.0 0.0.0.255 command to the configuration

The network configuration used in this example is illustrated in the following output:

```
R1(config)#router eigrp 150
R1(config-router)#network 10.1.1.15 0.0.0.255
R1(config-router)#exit
```

Based on this, the running configuration on the router displays the following:

```
R1#show running-config | begin router eigrp
router eigrp 150
 network 10.1.1.0 0.0.0.255
 auto-summary
```

If a specific address on the network is used in conjunction with the subnet mask, the router performs the same logical AND operation and adds the network command to the running configuration using the wildcard mask format. This is illustrated in the configuration below:

```
R1(config)#router eigrp 150
R1(config-router)#network 10.1.1.15 255.255.255.0
R1(config-router)#exit
```

Based on this configuration, the following is added to the current configuration on the router:

```
R1#show running-config | begin router eigrp
router eigrp 150
 network 10.1.1.0 0.0.0.255
 auto-summary
```

As illustrated in the configuration above, the use of either the wildcard mask or the subnet mask results in the same operation and network statement configuration in Cisco IOS software.

REAL-WORLD IMPLEMENTATION:

When configuring EIGRP in production networks, it is common practice to use a wildcard mask of all zeros or a subnet mask of all 1s. For example, the network 10.1.1.1 0.0.0.0 and network 10.1.1.1 255.255.255.255 commands perform the same actions. Using all zeros in the wildcard mask or all ones in the subnet mask configures Cisco IOS software to match an exact interface address, regardless of the subnet mask configured on the interface itself. Either one of these commands would match interfaces configured with the 10.1.1.1/8, 10.1.1.1/16, 10.1.1.1/24, and 10.1.1.1/30 address, for example. The use of these commands is illustrated in the following output:

```
R1(config)#router eigrp 150
R1(config-router)#network 10.0.0.1 0.0.0.0
R1(config-router)#network 10.1.1.1 255.255.255.255
R1(config-router)#exit
```

The show ip protocols command verifies that the configuration of both network statements is treated in a similar manner on the router, as illustrated below:

```
R1#show ip protocols
Routing Protocol is "eigrp 150"
  Outgoing update filter list for all interfaces is not set
  Incoming update filter list for all interfaces is not set
  Default networks flagged in outgoing updates
  Default networks accepted from incoming updates
  EIGRP metric weight K1=1, K2=0, K3=1, K4=0, K5=0
  EIGRP maximum hopcount 100
  EIGRP maximum metric variance 1
  Redistributing: eigrp 150
  EIGRP NSF-aware route hold timer is 240s
  Automatic network summarization is in effect
  Maximum path: 4
```

```
Routing for Networks:
   10.0.0.1/32
   10.1.1.1/32
Routing Information Sources:
   Gateway          Distance       Last Update
Distance: internal 90 external 170
```

When a subnet mask with all ones or a wildcard mask with all zeros is used, EIGRP is enabled for the specified (matched) interface and the network the interface resides on is advertised. In other words, EIGRP will not advertise the /32 address in the output above but, instead, the actual network based on the subnet mask configured on the matched interface. The use of this configuration is independent of the subnet mask configured on the actual interface matched.

EIGRP MESSAGES

This section describes the different types of messages used by EIGRP. However, before delving into the specifics of the different message types, it is important to have a solid understanding of the EIGRP packet header, wherein these messages are contained.

EIGRP Packet Header

Although going into specifics on the EIGRP packet formats is beyond the scope of the CCNA exam requirements, a fundamental understanding of the EIGRP packet header is important in order to understand completely the overall operation of the EIGRP routing protocol. Figure 36.1 below illustrates the format of the EIGRP packet header:

Version	OPCode	Checksum
Flags		
Sequence		
Acknowledgement		
Autonomous System Number		
TLVs		

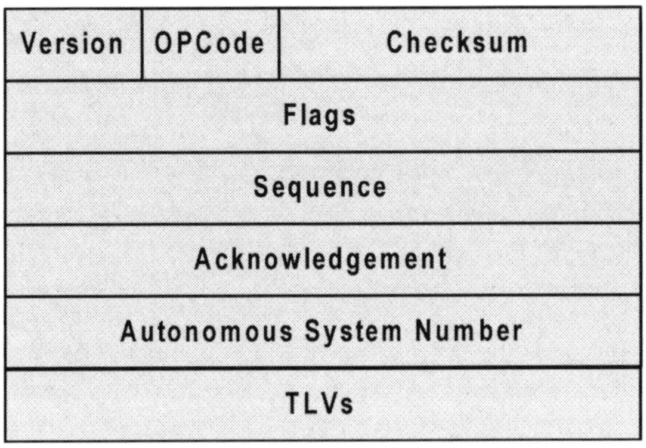

Figure 36.1—EIGRP Packet Header Fields

Within the EIGRP packet header, the 4-bit Version field is used to indicate the protocol version. Current Cisco IOS images support EIGRP version 1.x. The 4-bit OPCode field specifies the EIGRP packet or message type. The different EIGRP packet types are each assigned a unique OPCode value, which allows them to be differentiated from other packet types. These messages will be described in detail later in this module.

The 24-bit Checksum field is used to run a sanity check on the EIGRP packet. This field is based on the entire EIGRP packet, excluding the IP header. The 32-bit Flags field is used to indicate an INIT either for a new EIGRP neighbor or for the Conditional Receive (CR) for EIGRP Reliable Transport Protocol (RTP). RTP and CR will be described in detail later in this module.

The 32-bit Sequence field specifies the sequence number used by EIGRP RTP to ensure orderly delivery of reliable packets. The 32-bit Acknowledgment field is used to acknowledge the receipt of an EIGRP reliable packet.

The 32-bit Autonomous System Number field specifies the ASN of the EIGRP domain. Finally, the 32-bit Type/Length/Value (TLV) triplet field is used to carry route entries and provides EIGRP DUAL information. EIGRP supports several different types of TLVs, with the most common being the following:

- The Parameters TLV, which has the parameters to establish neighbor relationships
- The Sequence TLV, which is used by RTP
- The Next Multicast Sequence TLV, which is used by RTP
- The EIGRP Internal Route TLV, which is used for internal EIGRP routes
- The EIGRP External Route TLV, which is used for external EIGRP routes

NOTE: You are not required to go into detail on the different EIGRP TLVs.

Figure 36.2 below illustrates the different fields as they appear in a wire capture of an EIGRP packet:

```
Cisco EIGRP
 Version    = 2
 Opcode = 5 (Hello)
 Checksum   = 0xee36
 Flags      = 0x00000000
 Sequence   = 0
 Acknowledge = 0
 Autonomous System  : 150
·EIGRP Parameters
·Software Version: IOS=12.4, EIGRP=1.2
```

Figure 36.2—EIGRP Packet Header Wire Capture

Within the EIGRP packet header, the 4-bit OPCode field is used to specify the EIGRP packet type or message. EIGRP uses different message or packet types, which are Hello packets, Acknowledgement packets, Update packets, Query packets, Reply packets, and Request packets. These packet types are described in detail in the following sections.

Hello Packets

Enhanced IGRP sends Hello packets once it has been enabled on a router for a particular network. These messages are used to identify neighbors and, once identified, serve or function as a keepalive mechanism between neighbors. EIGRP neighbor discovery and maintenance is described in detail later in this module.

Enhanced IGRP Hello packets are sent to the Link Local Multicast group address 224.0.0.10. Hello packets sent by EIGRP do not require an Acknowledgment to be sent confirming that they were received. Because they require no explicit acknowledgment, Hello packets are classified as unreliable EIGRP packets. EIGRP Hello packets have an OPCode of 5.

Acknowledgement Packets

An EIGRP Acknowledgment (ACK) packet is simply an EIGRP Hello packet that contains no data. Acknowledgment packets are used by EIGRP to confirm reliable delivery of EIGRP packets. The ACK packets are always sent to a Unicast address, which is the source address of the sender of the reliable packet, and not to the EIGRP Multicast group address. In addition, ACK packets will always contain a non-zero acknowledgment number. The ACK packet uses the same OPCode as the Hello packet because it is essentially a Hello packet that contains no information. The OPCode is 5.

Update Packets

Enhanced IGRP Update packets are used to convey reachability of destinations. In other words, Update packets contain EIGRP routing updates. When a new neighbor is discovered, Update packets are sent via Unicast so that the neighbor can build up its EIGRP topology table. In other cases, such as a link cost change, updates are sent via Multicast. It is important to know that Update packets are always transmitted reliably and always require explicit acknowledgment. Update packets are assigned an OPCode of 1. An EIGRP Update packet is illustrated in Figure 36.3 below:

```
Cisco EIGRP
  Version      = 2
  Opcode = 1 (Update)
  Checksum     = 0x1629
  Flags        = 0x00000008
  Sequence     = 7
  Acknowledge  = 10
  Autonomous System   : 150
  IP internal route  =    1.0.0.0/8
    Type = 0x0102 (IP internal route)
    Size = 26 bytes
    Next Hop    = 0.0.0.0
    Delay       = 128000
    Bandwidth   = 256
    MTU         = 1514
    Hop Count   = 0
    Reliability = 255
    Load        = 1
    Reserved
    Prefix Length = 8
    Destination = 1.0.0.0
```

Figure 36.3—EIGRP Update Packet

NOTE: You are not required to go into detail on the information contained in EIGRP packets.

Query Packets

Enhanced IGRP Query packets are Multicast and are used to request reliable routing information. EIGRP Query packets are sent to neighbors when a route is not available and the router needs to ask about the status of the route for fast convergence. If the router that sends out a Query does not receive a response from any of its neighbors, it resends the Query as a Unicast packet to the non-responsive neighbor(s). If no response is received in 16 attempts, the EIGRP neighbor relationship is reset. This concept will be described in further detail later in this module. EIGRP Query packets are assigned an OPCode of 3.

Reply Packets

Enhanced IGRP Reply packets are sent in response to Query packets. The Reply packets are used to respond reliably to a Query packet. Reply packets are Unicast to the originator of the Query. The EIGRP Reply packets are assigned an OPCode of 4.

Request Packets

Enhanced IGRP Request packets are used to get specific information from one or more neighbors and are used in route server applications. These packet types can be sent via either Multicast or Unicast but are always transmitted unreliably. In other words, they do not require an explicit acknowledgment.

NOTE: While EIGRP Hello and ACK packets have been described as two individual packet types, it is important to remember that in some texts, EIGRP Hello and ACK packets are considered the same type of packet. This is because, as was stated earlier in this section, an ACK packet is simply an EIGRP Hello packet that contains no data.

The debug eigrp packets command may be used to print real-time debugging information on the different EIGRP packets described in this section. Keep in mind that this command also includes additional packets that are not described, as they are beyond the scope of the current CCNA exam requirements. The following output illustrates the use of this command:

```
R1#debug eigrp packets ?
  SIAquery   EIGRP SIA-Query packets
  SIAreply   EIGRP SIA-Reply packets
  ack        EIGRP ack packets
  hello      EIGRP hello packets
  ipxsap     EIGRP ipxsap packets
  probe      EIGRP probe packets
  query      EIGRP query packets
  reply      EIGRP reply packets
  request    EIGRP request packets
  retry      EIGRP retransmissions
```

```
stub      EIGRP stub packets
terse     Display all EIGRP packets except Hellos
update    EIGRP update packets
verbose   Display all EIGRP packets
<cr>
```

The show ip eigrp traffic command is used to view the number of EIGRP packets sent and received by the local router. This command is also a powerful troubleshooting tool. For example, if the routing is sending out Hello packets but is not receiving any back, this could indicate that the intended neighbor is not configured, or even that an ACK may be blocking EIGRP packets. The following output illustrates this command:

```
R2#show ip eigrp traffic
IP-EIGRP Traffic Statistics for AS 150
  Hellos sent/received: 21918/21922
  Updates sent/received: 10/6
  Queries sent/received: 1/0
  Replies sent/received: 0/1
  Acks sent/received: 6/10
  SIA-Queries sent/received: 0/0
  SIA-Replies sent/received: 0/0
  Hello Process ID: 178
  PDM Process ID: 154
  IP Socket queue:   0/2000/2/0 (current/max/highest/drops)
  Eigrp input queue: 0/2000/2/0 (current/max/highest/drops)
```

Table 36.1 summarizes the EIGRP packets described in this section and whether they are sent unreliably or reliably:

Table 36.1—EIGRP Packet Summary

Message Type	Description	Sent
Hello	Used for neighbor discovery, maintenance, and keepalives	Unreliably
Acknowledgement	Used to acknowledge receipt of information	Unreliably
Update	Used to convey routing information	Reliably
Query	Used to request specific routing information	Reliably
Reply	Used to respond to a Query	Reliably
Request	Used to request information in route server applications	Unreliably

EIGRP NEIGHBOR DISCOVERY AND MAINTENANCE

Enhanced IGRP may be configured to discover neighboring routers dynamically (default) or via manual administrator configuration. Both methods, as well as other EIGRP neighbor-related topics, will be described in the following sections.

Dynamic Neighbor Discovery

Dynamic neighbor discovery is performed by sending EIGRP Hello packets to the destination Multicast group address 224.0.0.10. This is performed as soon as the `network` command is issued when configuring EIGRP on the router. In addition, as stated earlier, EIGRP packets are sent directly over IP using protocol number 88. Figure 36.4 below illustrates the basic EIGRP neighbor discovery and route exchange process:

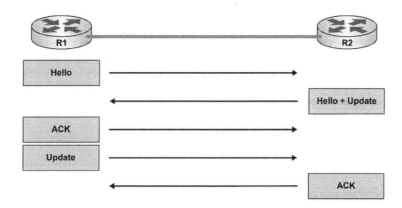

Figure 36.4—EIGRP Neighbor Discovery and Route Exchange

Referencing Figure 36.4, upon initialization, the EIGRP neighbors send Hello packets to discover other neighbors. The neighbors then exchange their full routing tables via full Updates. These Updates contain information about all known routes. Because Update packets are sent reliably, they must be explicitly acknowledged by the recipient.

After the neighbors have exchanged their routing information, they continue to exchange Hello packets to maintain the neighbor relationship. Additionally, the EIGRP neighbor routers will only send incremental updates to advise neighbors of status or routing changes. They will no longer send full Updates to neighbor routers.

It is important to understand that simply enabling EIGRP between two or more routers does not guarantee that a neighbor relationship will be established. Instead, some parameters must match in order for the routers to become neighbors. The EIGRP neighbor relationship may not establish due to any of the following circumstances:

- Mismatched EIGRP authentication parameters (if configured)
- Mismatched EIGRP K values
- Mismatched EIGRP autonomous system number
- Using secondary addresses for EIGRP neighbor relationships
- The neighbors are not on a common subnet

While the `show ip eigrp neighbors` command does not differentiate between dynamically and statically configured neighbors, the `show ip eigrp interfaces detail <name>`

command can be used to verify that the router interface is sending out Multicast packets to discover and maintain neighbor relationships. The output of this command on a router enabled for dynamic neighbor discovery is illustrated below:

```
R2#show ip eigrp interfaces detail FastEthernet0/0
IP-EIGRP interfaces for process 150
               Xmit Queue  Mean    Pacing Time   Multicast    Pending
Interface Peers Un/Reliable SRTT  Un/Reliable  Flow Timer   Routes
Fa0/0          1        0/0        1        0/1          50
0
   Hello interval is 5 sec
   Next xmit serial <none>
   Un/reliable mcasts: 0/2  Un/reliable ucasts: 2/2
   Mcast exceptions: 0  CR packets: 0  ACKs suppressed: 0
   Retransmissions sent: 1  Out-of-sequence rcvd: 0
   Authentication mode is not set
   Use multicast
```

NOTE: The `show ip eigrp neighbors` command will be described in detail later. When looking at the output of the `show ip eigrp interfaces detail <name>` command, keep in mind that because EIGRP uses both Multicast and Unicast packets, the command counters will include values for both types of packets, as shown in the output above

Static Neighbor Discovery

Unlike the dynamic EIGRP neighbor discovery process, static EIGRP neighbor relationships require manual neighbor configuration on the router. When static EIGRP neighbors are configured, the local router uses the Unicast neighbor address to send packets to these routers.

Static neighbor relationships are seldom used in EIGRP networks. The primary reason for this is the manual configuration of neighbors does not scale well in large networks. However, it is important to understand why this option is available in Cisco IOS software and the situations in which this feature can be utilized. A prime example of when static neighbor configuration could be used would be in a situation where EIGRP is being deployed across media that does not natively support Broadcast or Multicast packets, such as Frame Relay.

A second example would be to prevent sending unnecessary EIGRP packets on Multi-Access networks, such as Ethernet, when only a few EIGRP-enabled routers exist. In addition to basic EIGRP configuration, the `neighbor` command must be configured on the local router for all static EIGRP neighbors. EIGRP-enabled routers will not establish an adjacency if one router is configured to use Unicast (static) while another uses Multicast (dynamic).

In Cisco IOS software, static EIGRP neighbors are configured using the `neighbor <address> <interface>` router configuration command. Keep in mind that this is simply in addition to the basic EIGRP configuration. The simple network topology that is illustrated in Figure

36.5 below will be used both to demonstrate and to verify the configuration of static EIGRP neighbors:

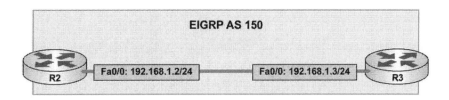

Figure 36.5—Configuring Static EIGRP Neighbors

Referencing the topology illustrated in Figure 36.5, router R2 is configured as follows:

```
R2(config)#router eigrp 150
R2(config-router)#network 192.168.1.0 0.0.0.255
R2(config-router)#neighbor 192.168.1.3 FastEthernet0/0
R2(config-router)#no auto-summary
R2(config-router)#exit
```

The configuration implemented on router R3 is as follows:

```
R3(config)#router eigrp 150
R3(config-router)#network 192.168.1.0 0.0.0.255
R3(config-router)#neighbor 192.168.1.2 FastEthernet0/0
R3(config-router)#no auto-summary
R3(config-router)#exit
```

The show ip eigrp interfaces detail <name> command can be used to determine whether the router interface is sending Multicast (dynamic) or Unicast (static) packets for neighbor discovery and maintenance. This is illustrated in the following output:

```
R2#show ip eigrp interfaces detail FastEthernet0/0
IP-EIGRP interfaces for process 150
                  Xmit Queue   Mean   Pacing Time   Multicast    Pending
Interface Peers Un/Reliable  SRTT   Un/Reliable   Flow Timer   Routes
Fa0/0      1        0/0        2        0/1           50           0
  Hello interval is 5 sec
  Next xmit serial <none>
  Un/reliable mcasts: 0/1  Un/reliable ucasts: 3/8
  Mcast exceptions: 1  CR packets: 1  ACKs suppressed: 2
  Retransmissions sent: 1  Out-of-sequence rcvd: 0
  Authentication mode is not set
  Use unicast
```

Additionally, the show ip eigrp neighbors [detail] command can be used to determine the type of EIGRP neighbor. This command will be described in detail later in this module.

EIGRP Hello and Hold Timers

Enhanced IGRP uses different Hello and Hold timers for different types of media. Hello timers are used to determine the interval rate EIGRP Hello packets are sent. The Hold timer is used to determine the time that will elapse before a router considers an EIGRP neighbor as down. By default, the Hold time is three times the Hello interval.

Enhanced IGRP sends Hello packets every 5 seconds on Broadcast, Point-to-Point Serial, Point-to-Point sub interfaces, and Multipoint circuits greater than T1 speed. The default Hold time is 15 seconds. EIGRP sends Hello packets every 60 seconds on other link types. These include low-bandwidth WAN links less than T1 speed. The default Hold time for neighbor relationships across these links is also three times the Hello interval and therefore defaults to 180 seconds.

Enhanced IGRP timer values do not have to be the same on neighboring routers in order for a neighbor relationship to be established. In addition, there is no mandatory requirement that the Hold time be three times the Hello interval. This is only a recommended guideline, which can be manually adjusted in Cisco IOS software. The EIGRP Hello time can be adjusted using the `ip hello-interval eigrp <ASN> <secs>` interface configuration command, while the EIGRP Hold time can be adjusted using the `ip hold-time eigrp <ASN> <secs>` interface configuration command.

It is important to understand the use of both Hello timers and Hold timers as they pertain to EIGRP. The Hold time value is advertised in the EIGRP Hello packet, while the Hello time value tells the local router how often to send its neighbor(s) Hello packets. The Hold time, on the other hand, tells the neighbor router(s) of the local router how long to wait before declaring the local router "dead." The EIGRP Hello packet and the Hold Time field is illustrated in Figure 36.6 below:

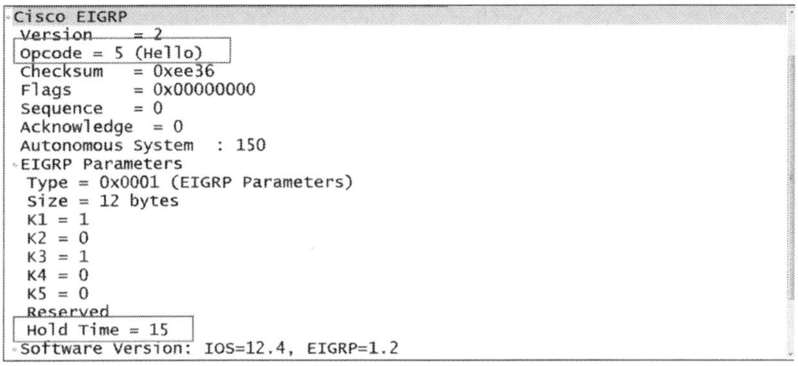

```
Cisco EIGRP
  Version      = 2
  Opcode = 5 (Hello)
  Checksum    = 0xee36
  Flags       = 0x00000000
  Sequence    = 0
  Acknowledge  = 0
  Autonomous System  : 150
 EIGRP Parameters
  Type = 0x0001 (EIGRP Parameters)
  Size = 12 bytes
  K1 = 1
  K2 = 0
  K3 = 1
  K4 = 0
  K5 = 0
  Reserved
  Hold Time = 15
 Software Version: IOS=12.4, EIGRP=1.2
```

Figure 36.6—EIGRP Hold Time in the EIGRP Hello Packet

Referencing Figure 36.6, the EIGRP Hello packet (OPCode 5) contains, among other things, the configured Hold time value. The value of 15 illustrated in Figure 36.6 is a non-default configured value implemented using the `ip hold-time eigrp <ASN> <secs>` interface configuration command. It is important to remember that the actual Hello time interval is not included. However, the configured Hello time can be viewed using the `show ip eigrp interfaces detail <name>` command. The information printed by this command is illustrated below:

```
R2#show ip eigrp interfaces detail FastEthernet0/0
IP-EIGRP interfaces for process 150
                Xmit Queue   Mean   Pacing Time   Multicast    Pending
Interface Peers Un/Reliable  SRTT   Un/Reliable   Flow Timer   Routes
Fa0/0       1      0/0         7        0/1           50           0
   Hello interval is 5 sec
   Next xmit serial <none>
   Un/reliable mcasts: 0/1  Un/reliable ucasts: 2/5
   Mcast exceptions: 1  CR packets: 1  ACKs suppressed: 0
   Retransmissions sent: 1  Out-of-sequence rcvd: 0
   Authentication mode is not set
   Use multicast
```

The most common reason for adjusting the default EIGRP timer values is to speed up routing protocol convergence. For example, on a low-speed WAN link, a Hold time of 180 seconds might be a long time to wait before EIGRP declares a neighbor router down. Inversely, in some situations, it may be necessary to increase the EIGRP timer values on high-speed links in order to ensure a stable routing topology. This is common when implementing a solution for Stuck-In-Active (SIA) routes. SIA will be described in detail later in this module.

EIGRP Neighbor Table

The EIGRP neighbor table is used by routers running EIGRP to maintain state information about EIGRP neighbors. When newly discovered neighbors are learned, the address and interface of the neighbor is recorded. This is applicable to both dynamically discovered neighbors and statically defined neighbors. There is a single EIGRP neighbor table for each Protocol-Dependent Module (PDM).

When an EIGRP neighbor sends a Hello packet, it advertises a Hold time, which is the amount of time a router treats a neighbor as reachable and operational. After a router receives a Hello packet, the Hold time value begins to decrement and count down to zero. When another Hello packet is received, the Hold time value restarts from the beginning and the process is continually repeated. If a Hello packet is not received within the Hold time, then the Hold time expires (goes to 0). When the Hold time expires, DUAL is informed of the topology change and the neighbor is declared down by EIGRP. A message similar to the following is then printed and logged by the router:

```
%DUAL-5-NBRCHANGE: IP-EIGRP(0) 1: Neighbor 10.1.1.2 (Serial0/0) is down:
holding time expired
```

The EIGRP neighbor table entry also includes information required by the Reliable Transport Protocol (RTP). RTP is used by EIGRP to ensure that Update, Query, and Reply packets are sent reliably. In addition, sequence numbers are also used to match acknowledgments with data packets. The last sequence number received from the neighbor is recorded in order to detect out-of-order packets. This ensures reliable packet delivery.

NOTE: RTP is described in detail later in this module.

The neighbor table includes a transmission list that is used to queue packets for possible retransmission on a per-neighbor basis. Additionally, round-trip timers are kept in the neighbor data structure to estimate an optimal retransmission interval. All of this information is printed in the output of the show ip eigrp neighbors command, as illustrated below:

```
R2#show ip eigrp neighbors
IP-EIGRP neighbors for process 150
H   Address       Interface  Hold   Uptime    SRTT   RTO   Q    Seq
                              (sec)            (ms)         Cnt  Num
0   192.168.1.3  Fa0/0      14     00:43:08  2      200   0    12
```

It is important to understand the information printed by this command, both as a basis for demonstrating competency on a core EIGRP component and for troubleshooting EIGRP issues. Table 36.2 below lists and describes the fields contained in the output of this command:

Table 36.2—EIGRP Neighbor Table Fields

Field	Description
H	The list of neighbors in the order they are learned, starting at 0
Address	The IP address of the neighbor
Interface	The interface via which the neighbor is learned
Hold	The Hold timer for the neighbor; if it gets to 0, the neighbor is down
Uptime	Timer for how long the neighbor relationship has been up
SRTT	Smooth Round-Trip Time, which is the time it takes to send and receive a reliable EIGRP packet
RTO	Retransmission Timeout, which is the amount of time the router will wait to retransmit the EIGRP reliable packet if an ACK is not received
Q Cnt	The number of EIGRP packets (Update, Query, and Reply) that the software is waiting to send
Sequence Number	The sequence number of the last EIGRP reliable packets being received from the neighbor to ensure that packets received from the neighbor are in order

While the show ip eigrp neighbors command prints out information on known EIGRP neighbors, it does not differentiate between dynamically discovered and manually configured neighbors. For example, the output of the show ip eigrp neighbors command on R2 indicates that the router has two EIGRP neighbor relationships. Based on this configuration, one is a statically configured neighbor, while the other is dynamically discovered. As you can see, it is not possible to determine which is which based on the following output:

```
R2#show ip eigrp neighbors
IP-EIGRP neighbors for process 150
H   Address          Interface    Hold  Uptime     SRTT   RTO    Q    Seq
                                  (sec)            (ms)          Cnt  Num
1   150.2.2.2        Se0/0        13    00:00:48   153    918    0    4
0   192.168.1.3      Fa0/0        10    08:33:23   1      200    0    20
```

In environments where the router has both dynamically discovered and manually configured neighbor relationships, the show ip eigrp neighbors detail command can be used to determine which neighbor is statically configured and which is dynamically discovered, as illustrated below:

```
R2#show ip eigrp neighbors detail
IP-EIGRP neighbors for process 150
H   Address          Interface    Hold  Uptime     SRTT   RTO    Q    Seq
                                  (sec)            (ms)          Cnt  Num
1   150.2.2.2        Se0/0        11    00:04:22   153    918    0    4
    Version 12.3/1.2, Retrans: 0, Retries: 0, Prefixes: 1
0   192.168.1.3      Fa0/0        10    08:36:58   1      200    0    20
    Static neighbor
    Version 12.4/1.2, Retrans: 0, Retries: 0, Prefixes: 1
```

Referencing the output above, neighbor 192.168.1.3 is a manually configured neighbor and neighbor 150.2.2.2 is a dynamically discovered neighbor. The static neighbors can also be viewed using the show ip eigrp neighbors static <interface> command, as illustrated below:

```
R2#show ip eigrp neighbors static FastEthernet0/0
IP-EIGRP neighbors for process 150
Static Address            Interface
192.168.1.3               FastEthernet0/0
```

Reliable Transport Protocol

Enhanced IGRP needs its own transport protocol to ensure the reliable delivery of packets. RTP is used by EIGRP to ensure that Update, Query, and Reply packets are sent reliably. The use of sequence numbers also ensures that the EIGRP packets are received in the correct order.

When reliable EIGRP packets are sent to a neighbor, the sending router expects an ACK from the receiving routers stating that the packet has been received. Using RTP, EIGRP maintains a transport window of one unacknowledged packet, which means that every single reliable packet that is sent out must be acknowledged before the next reliable packet can be sent. The sending router will retransmit the unacknowledged reliable packet until it receives an ACK.

It is important to note, however, that the unacknowledged packet will be retransmitted only up to 16 times. If there is still no acknowledgment after 16 retransmissions, EIGRP will reset the neighbor relationship. RTP uses both Multicast and Unicast packets. On Broadcast Multi-Access networks such as Ethernet, EIGRP uses Multicast packets instead of sending an individual packet (Unicast) to each router on the segment. However, packets may also be sent using Unicast if a response is not received from one or more of the neighbors on the Multi-Access segment. This is described referencing the diagram in Figure 36.7 below:

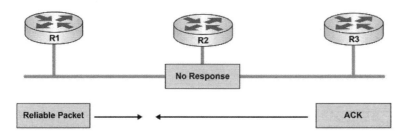

Figure 36.7—EIGRP RTP Operation

In Figure 36.7, routers R1, R2, and R3 reside on a common subnet on the Multi-Access segment. Given the media, EIGRP will use Multicast to send reliable packets between the routers. Assume, for example, that R1 sends out a packet that requires acknowledgment to routers R2 and R3. R1 then waits for acknowledgment from R2 and R3 confirming receipt of this packet.

Assume that R3 responds but R2 is unable to respond to this packet. Given that EIGRP maintains a transport window of one unacknowledged packet, which means that every individual reliable packet that is sent out must be acknowledged explicitly by the neighbor router(s) before the next reliable packet can be sent, this presents a possible issue on the Multi-Access segment because R1 will not be able to send out packets until it has received the acknowledgment from R2. R3 is therefore indirectly affected by the issues on R2.

To avoid this potential pitfall, R1 will wait for the Multicast Flow Timer (MFT) on the Ethernet interface connected to the Multi-Access segment to expire. The MFT, or simply the Flow Timer, is the maximum amount of time that the sending router will wait for an ACK packet from a group member. When the timer expires, R1 will Multicast a special EIGRP packet called a Sequence TLV. This packet lists R2 (the offender) and indicates an out-of-sequence Multicast packet. Because R3 is not listed in this packet, it enters Conditional Receive (CR) mode and continues listening to Multicast packets. R1 uses Unicast to retransmit the packet to R2. The Retransmission Timeout (RTO) indicates the time that the router waits for an acknowledgment of that Unicast packet. If after 16 total attempts there is still no response from R2, then EIGRP will reset the neighbor.

NOTE: You are not required to go into any detail on MFT or RTO in the current CCNA exam.

METRICS, DUAL, AND THE TOPOLOGY TABLE

When implementing EIGRP, it is important to understand the various aspects used within and by the protocol before routes are actually placed into the IP routing table. In this section, you will learn about the EIGRP composite metric and how it is calculated. You will also learn about the different ways to influence metric calculation, as well as to adjust the calculated metric.

Following that, you will learn about the Diffusing Update Algorithm (DUAL) and the EIGRP topology table. This section concludes with a discussion on how all this information meshes when it comes to populating the IP routing table on a router running EIGRP.

EIGRP Composite Metric Calculation

Enhanced IGRP uses a composite metric, which includes different variables referred to as the K values. The K values are constants that are used to distribute weight to different path aspects, which may be included in the composite EIGRP metric. The default values for the K values are K1 = K3 = 1 and K2 = K4 = K5 = 0. In other words, K1 and K3 are set to a default value of 1, while K2, K4, and K5 are set to a default value of 0.

Assuming the default K value settings, the complete EIGRP metric can be calculated using the following mathematical formula:

[K1 * bandwidth + (K2 * bandwidth) / (256 - load) + K3 * delay] * [K5 / (reliability + K4)]

However, given that only K1 and K3 have any positive values by default, the default EIGRP metric calculation is performed using the following mathematical formula:

$[(10^7/\text{least bandwidth on path}) + (\text{sum of all delays})] \times 256$

This essentially means that, by default, EIGRP uses the minimum bandwidth on the path to a destination network and the total cumulative delay to compute routing metrics. However, Cisco IOS software allows administrators to set other K values to non-zero values to incorporate other variables into the composite metric. This may be performed using the `metric weights [tos] k1 k2 k3 k4 k5` router configuration command.

When using the `metric weights` command, `[tos]` stands for Type of Service. Although Cisco IOS software shows that any value between 0 and 8 may be used, as of the time this guide was written, this field can currently be set only to zero. The K values can be set to any value between 0 and 255. The default EIGRP K values can be viewed by issuing the `show ip protocols` command. This is illustrated in the following output:

```
R2#show ip protocols
Routing Protocol is "eigrp 150"
  Outgoing update filter list for all interfaces is not set
  Incoming update filter list for all interfaces is not set
  Default networks flagged in outgoing updates
```

```
Default networks accepted from incoming updates
EIGRP metric weight K1=1, K2=0, K3=1, K4=0, K5=0
EIGRP maximum hopcount 100
EIGRP maximum metric variance 1
Redistributing: eigrp 150
EIGRP NSF-aware route hold timer is 240s
Automatic network summarization is not in effect
Maximum path: 4
Routing for Networks:
  192.168.1.0
Routing Information Sources:
  Gateway         Distance      Last Update
  192.168.1.3           90      00:00:15
Distance: internal 90 external 170
```

When adjusting the EIGRP K values, it is important to remember that the same values must be configured on all routers within the EIGRP domain. If the K values are mismatched, EIGRP neighbor relationships will not be established.

NOTE: Adjusting the default K value settings is not recommended. It should be done only with the assistance of seasoned senior-level engineers who have a solid understanding of the implications of such actions within the network or based upon the recommendation of the Cisco Technical Assistance Centre (TAC).

Using Interface Bandwidth to Influence EIGRP Metric Calculation

Enhanced IGRP metric calculation can be directly influenced by adjusting the default bandwidth values assigned to individual interfaces using the bandwidth command. The bandwidth values specified by this command are in Kilobits. The bandwidth used in EIGRP metric calculation is also in Kilobits. Figure 36.8 below illustrates a network comprised of two routers connected via two Serial (T1) links that have a bandwidth value of 1544Kbps:

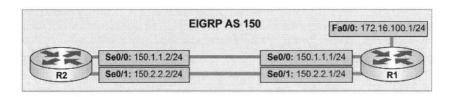

Figure 36.8—EIGRP Metric Bandwidth Manipulation

Referencing the diagram in Figure 36.8, because of the equal bandwidth (and delay) values of the links between R1 and R2, the same EIGRP metric will be derived for both paths from R2 to the 172.16.100.0/24 subnet. EIGRP will load-share traffic between the two Serial links, as illustrated in the following output on R2:

```
R2#show ip route 172.16.100.0 255.255.255.0
Routing entry for 172.16.100.0/24
```

```
Known via "eigrp 150", distance 90, metric 2172416, type internal
Redistributing via eigrp 150
Last update from 150.2.2.1 on Serial0/1, 00:48:09 ago
Routing Descriptor Blocks:
   150.2.2.1, from 150.2.2.1, 00:48:09 ago, via Serial0/1
      Route metric is 2172416, traffic share count is 1
      Total delay is 20100 microseconds, minimum bandwidth is 1544 Kbit
      Reliability 255/255, minimum MTU 1500 bytes
      Loading 1/255, Hops 1
 * 150.1.1.1, from 150.1.1.1, 00:48:09 ago, via Serial0/0
      Route metric is 2172416, traffic share count is 1
      Total delay is 20100 microseconds, minimum bandwidth is 1544 Kbit
      Reliability 255/255, minimum MTU 1500 bytes
      Loading 1/255, Hops 1
```

Adjusting the default bandwidth value on either interface will directly influence the EIGRP metric calculation for the path to the destination network. Such actions can be used for path control within larger networks (i.e., controlling the path that traffic takes based on administrator-defined values and configurations). For example, if it was preferred that EIGRP use Serial0/0 as the primary path to the destination network and Serial0/1 as the backup path to the destination, one of two actions could be taken.

The first is that the bandwidth value on Serial0/0 could be incremented, resulting in a better (lower) metric for this path. The second is that the bandwidth value on Serial0/1 could be decremented, resulting in a worse (higher) metric for this path. Either option is acceptable and will achieve the desired result. The following output illustrates how to decrement the default bandwidth value on Serial0/1, effectively ensuring that Serial0/0 is used as the primary path between R2 and the 172.16.100.0/24 network:

```
R2(config)#interface Serial0/1
R2(config-if)#bandwidth 1024
R2(config-if)#exit
```

NOTE: This configuration does not mean that Serial0/1 is now capable of only 1024Kbps of throughput through this interface.

The result of this configuration is that Serial0/0 is the primary path used by R2 to get to the 172.16.100.0/24 destination network. This is illustrated in the following output:

```
R2#show ip route 172.16.100.0 255.255.255.0
Routing entry for 172.16.100.0/24
   Known via "eigrp 150", distance 90, metric 2172416, type internal
   Redistributing via eigrp 150
   Last update from 150.1.1.1 on Serial0/0, 00:01:55 ago
   Routing Descriptor Blocks:
 * 150.1.1.1, from 150.1.1.1, 00:01:55 ago, via Serial0/0
      Route metric is 2172416, traffic share count is 1
      Total delay is 20100 microseconds, minimum bandwidth is 1544 Kbit
      Reliability 255/255, minimum MTU 1500 bytes
      Loading 1/255, Hops 1
```

NOTE: The asterisk (*) points to the interface over which the next packet is sent. In the event that there are multiple equal-cost routes in the routing table, the position of the * rotates among the equal-cost paths.

Although the path via the Serial0/1 interface is not installed into the routing table, when using EIGRP as the routing protocol, it is important to remember that this path is not completely ignored. Instead, this path is stored in the EIGRP topology table, which contains the primary and alternate (backup) paths to remote destination networks. The EIGRP topology table will be described in detail later in this module.

NOTE: By default, when EIGRP is enabled, it can use up to 50% of the interface bandwidth to send EIGRP packets (EIGRP is a very chatty protocol, so it limits itself in possible bandwidth usage). EIGRP determines the bandwidth amount based on the bandwidth interface configuration command. Therefore, when adjusting interface bandwidth values, it is important to keep this fact in mind. This default setting can be adjusted by using the ip bandwidth-percent eigrp [ASN] [percentage] interface configuration command.

In summation, when using the bandwidth command to influence EIGRP metric calculation, it is important to remember that EIGRP uses the minimum bandwidth on the path to a destination network, along with the cumulative delay, to compute routing metrics. It is important to have a solid understanding of the network topology to best determine where to use the bandwidth command to influence EIGRP metric calculation. In the real world, however, delay is the preferred method of influencing EIGRP metrics.

Using Interface Delay to Influence EIGRP Metric Calculation

The interface delay value is presented in microseconds. The delay value used in EIGRP metric calculation is in tens of microseconds. Therefore, the delay value on the interface must be divided by 10 in order to compute the EIGRP metric. Table 36.3 below shows the default interface bandwidth and delay values used in Cisco IOS software:

Table 36.3—Default Interface Bandwidth and Delay Values

Interface	Bandwidth (Kilobits)	Delay (Microseconds)
Ethernet	10000	1000
FastEthernet	100000	100
GigabitEthernet	1000000	10
Ten-GigabitEthernet	10000000	10
Serial (T1)	1544	20000
Serial (E1)	2048	20000
Serial (T3)	44736	200
Serial (E3)	34010	200

When working with the interface bandwidth and delay values, it is very important to remember that adjusting the interface bandwidth value does not automatically adjust the interface delay value, and vice-versa. The two values are independent of each other. As an example, the output that follows shows the default bandwidth and delay values for a FastEthernet interface:

```
R2#show interfaces FastEthernet0/0
FastEthernet0/0 is up, line protocol is up
  Hardware is AmdFE, address is 0013.1986.0a20 (bia 0013.1986.0a20)
  Internet address is 192.168.1.2/24
  MTU 1500 bytes, BW 100000 Kbit/sec, DLY 100 usec,
      reliability 255/255, txload 1/255, rxload 1/255

[Truncated Output]
```

To reinforce this concept, the bandwidth value on the FastEthernet interface is adjusted to 1544Kbps using the bandwidth interface configuration command, as follows:

```
R2(config)#interface FastEthernet0/0
R2(config-if)#bandwidth 1544
R2(config-if)#exit
```

While the bandwidth value now displayed in the output of the show interfaces command reflects the implemented configuration, the default interface delay value remains the same, as illustrated below:

```
R2#show interfaces FastEthernet0/0
FastEthernet0/0 is up, line protocol is up
  Hardware is AmdFE, address is 0013.1986.0a20 (bia 0013.1986.0a20)
  Internet address is 192.168.1.2/24
  MTU 1500 bytes, BW 1544 Kbit/sec, DLY 100 usec,
      reliability 255/255, txload 1/255, rxload 1/255
```

The cumulative delay used by EIGRP is the sum of all interface delays between the source and the destination network. Changing any of the delay values in the path influences EIGRP metric calculation. The interface delay value is adjusted using the delay interface configuration command. This value is then divided by 10 when used in EIGRP metric calculation. Figure 36.9 below illustrates a network comprised of two routers connected via two Serial (T1) links that have a bandwidth value of 1544Kbps and a default delay of 20000 microseconds. In addition, the 172.16.100.0/24 network is directly connected to a FastEthernet interface, which has a default bandwidth of 100000Kbps and a default delay value of 100 microseconds:

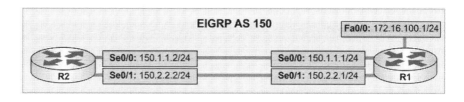

Figure 36.9—EIGRP Metric Delay Manipulation

The EIGRP metric from R2 to the 172.16.100.0/24 network is calculated as follows:

Metric = $[(10^7/\text{least bandwidth on path}) + (\text{sum of all delays})] \times 256$
Metric = $[(10000000/1544) + (2000 + 10)] \times 256$

NOTE: Remember to divide the interface delay values by 10 for EIGRP metric calculation.

Metric = $[(10000000/1544) + (2000 + 10)] \times 256$

NOTE: The calculated value should always be rounded down to the nearest integer.

Metric = $[6476 + 2010] \times 256$
Metric = 8486×256
Metric = 2172416

This calculation can be verified by the show ip route command, as follows:

```
R2#show ip route 172.16.100.0 255.255.255.0
Routing entry for 172.16.100.0/24
  Known via "eigrp 150", distance 90, metric 2172416, type internal
  Redistributing via eigrp 150
  Last update from 150.2.2.1 on Serial0/1, 00:03:28 ago
  Routing Descriptor Blocks:
    150.2.2.1, from 150.2.2.1, 00:03:28 ago, via Serial0/1
      Route metric is 2172416, traffic share count is 1
      Total delay is 20100 microseconds, minimum bandwidth is 1544 Kbit
      Reliability 255/255, minimum MTU 1500 bytes
      Loading 1/255, Hops 1
  * 150.1.1.1, from 150.1.1.1, 00:03:28 ago, via Serial0/0
      Route metric is 2172416, traffic share count is 1
      Total delay is 20100 microseconds, minimum bandwidth is 1544 Kbit
      Reliability 255/255, minimum MTU 1500 bytes
      Loading 1/255, Hops 1
```

As with the bandwidth command, you can either increment or decrement the interface delay value using the delay command to influence EIGRP metric calculation. For example, to configure R2 to use the Serial0/0 link to get to the 172.16.100.0/24 network, with Serial0/1 being used as a backup link only, the delay value on Serial0/0 could be decremented as follows:

```
R2(config)#int s0/0
R2(config-if)#delay 100
R2(config-if)#exit
```

This configuration adjusts the EIGRP metric for the path via Serial0/0, as illustrated below:

```
R2#show ip route 172.16.100.0 255.255.255.0
Routing entry for 172.16.100.0/24
  Known via "eigrp 150", distance 90, metric 1686016, type internal
  Redistributing via eigrp 150
  Last update from 150.1.1.1 on Serial0/0, 00:01:09 ago
```

```
Routing Descriptor Blocks:
* 150.1.1.1, from 150.1.1.1, 00:01:09 ago, via Serial0/0
    Route metric is 1686016, traffic share count is 1
    Total delay is 1100 microseconds, minimum bandwidth is 1544 Kbit
    Reliability 255/255, minimum MTU 1500 bytes
    Loading 1/255, Hops 1
```

The path via Serial0/1 is retained in the topology table as an alternate path to the network.

The Diffusing Update Algorithm (DUAL)

The Diffusing Update Algorithm is at the crux of the EIGRP routing protocol. DUAL looks at all routes received from neighbor routers, compares them, and then selects the lowest metric (best) loop-free path to the destination network, which is the Feasible Distance (FD), resulting in the Successor route. The FD includes both the metric of a network as advertised by the connected neighbor plus the cost of reaching that particular neighbor.

The metric that is advertised by the neighbor router is referred to as the Reported Distance (RD) or as the Advertised Distance (AD) to the destination network. Therefore, the FD includes the RD plus the cost of reaching that particular neighbor. The next-hop router for the Successor route is referred to as the Successor. The Successor route is placed into the IP routing table and the EIGRP topology table and points to the Successor.

Any other routes to the same destination network that have a lower RD than the FD of the Successor path are guaranteed to be loop-free and are referred to as Feasible Successor (FS) routes. These routes are not placed into the IP routing table; however, they are still placed into the EIGRP topology table, along with the Successor routes.

In order for a route to become an FS route, it must meet the Feasibility Condition (FC), which occurs only when the RD to the destination network is less than the FD. In the event that the RD is more than the FD, the route is not selected as an FS. This is used by EIGRP to prevent the possibility of loops. The network topology illustrated in Figure 36.10 below will be used to clarify the terminology referred to in this section:

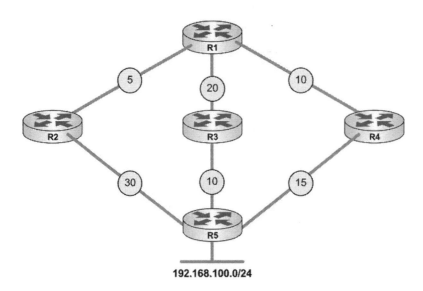

192.168.100.0/24

Figure 36.10—Understanding the Diffusing Update Algorithm

Referencing Figure 36.10, Table 36.4 below shows the Feasible Distance and the Reported Distance values as seen on R1 for the 192.168.100.0/24 network:

Table 36.4—R1 Paths and Distances

Network Path	R1 Neighbor	Neighbor Metric (RD)	R1 Feasible Distance
R1—R2—R5	R2	30	35
R1—R3—R5	R3	10	30
R1—R4—R5	R4	15	25

Based on the information in Table 36.4, R1 will select the path through R4 as the Successor route based on the FD for the route, which is 25. This route will be placed into the IP routing table as well as the EIGRP topology table. R1 then looks at alternate paths to the 192.168.100.0/24 network. The metric for neighbor R3 to the 192.168.100.0/24 network, also referred to as the RD or AD, is 10. This is less than the FD and so this route meets the FC and is placed into the EIGRP topology table. The metric for neighbor R2 to the 192.168.100.0/24 network is 30. This value is higher than the FD of 25. This route does not meet the FC and is not considered an FS. The route, however, is still placed into the EIGRP topology table. This is illustrated in the section on the EIGRP topology table that follows.

When a neighbor changes a metric, or when a topology change occurs, and the Successor route is removed or changes, DUAL checks for FSs for the route and if one is found, then DUAL uses it to avoid re-computing the route unnecessarily. This is referred to as local computation. Performing a local computation saves CPU power because the FS has been chosen and already exists before the Successor or primary route fails.

When no FS for the destination network exists, the local router will send a Query to neighboring routers asking if they have information on the destination network. If the information is available and another neighbor does have a route to the destination network, then the router performs a diffusing computation to determine a new Successor.

The EIGRP Topology Table

The EIGRP topology table is populated by EIGRP PDMs acted upon by the DUAL Finite State Machine. All known destination networks and subnets that are advertised by neighboring EIGRP routers are stored in the EIGRP topology table. This includes Successor routes, FS routes, and even routes that have not met the FC.

The topology table allows all EIGRP routers to have a consistent view of the entire network. It also allows for rapid convergence in EIGRP networks. Each individual entry in the topology table contains the destination network and the neighbor(s) that have advertised the destination network. Both the FD and the RD are stored in the topology table. The EIGRP topology table contains the information needed to build a set of distances and vectors to each reachable network, including the following:

- The lowest bandwidth on the path to the destination network
- The total or cumulative delay to the destination network
- The reliability of the path to the destination network
- The loading of the path to the destination network
- The minimum Maximum Transmission Unit (MTU) to the destination network
- The Feasible Distance to the destination network
- The Reported Distance by the neighbor router to the destination network
- The route source (only external routes) of the destination network

NOTE: While the MTU is included in the topology table, EIGRP does not use this value in actual metric computation. Instead, the MTU is simply tracked to determine the minimum value to the destination network. The interface MTU specifies the largest size of datagram that can be transferred across a certain link without the need for fragmentation, or breaking the datagram or packet into smaller pieces.

The contents of the EIGRP topology table are viewed using the show ip eigrp topology command. The options that are available with this command are illustrated below:

```
R2#show ip eigrp topology ?
  <1-65535>      AS Number
  A.B.C.D        IP prefix <network>/<length>, e.g., 192.168.0.0/16
  A.B.C.D        Network to display information about
  active         Show only active entries
  all-links      Show all links in topology table
  detail-links   Show all links in topology table
  pending        Show only entries pending transmission
  summary        Show a summary of the topology table
```

```
zero-successors Show only zero successor entries
|                Output modifiers
<cr>
```

The show ip eigrp topology command with no options prints only the Successor and Feasible Successor information for routes in the topology table and for all of the EIGRP instances enabled on the router. The output printed by this command is illustrated below:

```
R2#show ip eigrp topology
IP-EIGRP Topology Table for AS(150)/ID(2.2.2.2)
Codes: P - Passive, A - Active, U - Update, Q - Query, R - Reply,
       r - reply Status, s - sia Status

P 150.2.2.0/24, 1 successors, FD is 20512000
        via Connected, Serial0/1
        via 150.1.1.1 (2195456/2169856), Serial0/0
P 150.1.1.0/24, 1 successors, FD is 1683456
        via Connected, Serial0/0
P 172.16.100.0/24, 1 successors, FD is 1686016
        via 150.1.1.1 (1686016/28160), Serial0/0
```

The show ip eigrp topology [network]/[prefix] and show ip eigrp topology [network] [mask] commands print Successor routes, FS routes, and routes that have not met the FC for the route specified in either command. The following illustrates the use of the show ip eigrp topology [network]/[prefix] command:

```
R2#show ip eigrp topology 172.16.100.0/24
IP-EIGRP (AS 150): Topology entry for 172.16.100.0/24
  State is Passive, Query origin flag is 1, 1 Successor(s), FD is 1686016
  Routing Descriptor Blocks:
  150.1.1.1 (Serial0/0), from 150.1.1.1, Send flag is 0x0
      Composite metric is (1686016/28160), Route is Internal
      Vector metric:
        Minimum bandwidth is 1544 Kbit
        Total delay is 1100 microseconds
        Reliability is 255/255
        Load is 1/255
        Minimum MTU is 1500
        Hop count is 1
  150.2.2.1 (Serial0/1), from 150.2.2.1, Send flag is 0x0
      Composite metric is (2167998207/2147511807), Route is Internal
      Vector metric:
        Minimum bandwidth is 128 Kbit
        Total delay is 83906179 microseconds
        Reliability is 255/255
        Load is 1/255
        Minimum MTU is 1500
        Hop count is 1
```

In the output above, you can see that the path via Serial0/1 does not meet the FC because the RD exceeds the FD. This is why the path is not printed in the output of the show ip eigrp topology command. Instead of viewing each prefix on an individual basis to determine

Successor routes, FS routes, and routes that did not meet the FC, you can use the show ip eigrp topology all-links command to view all possible routes for all of the prefixes in the EIGRP topology table. The output of this command is illustrated below:

```
R2#show ip eigrp topology all-links
IP-EIGRP Topology Table for AS(150)/ID(2.2.2.2)
Codes: P - Passive, A - Active, U - Update, Q - Query, R - Reply,
       r - reply Status, s - sia Status

P 150.2.2.0/24, 1 successors, FD is 20512000, serno 42
        via Connected, Serial0/1
        via 150.1.1.1 (2195456/2169856), Serial0/0
P 150.1.1.0/24, 1 successors, FD is 1683456, serno 32
        via Connected, Serial0/0
        via 150.2.2.1 (21024000/2169856), Serial0/1
P 172.16.100.0/24, 1 successors, FD is 1686016, serno 47
        via 150.1.1.1 (1686016/28160), Serial0/0
        via 150.2.2.1 (2167998207/2147511807), Serial0/1
```

Within the EIGRP topology table, entries may be marked either as Passive (P) or as Active (A). A route in the Passive state indicates that EIGRP has completed actively computing the metric for the route and traffic can be forwarded to the destination network using the Successor route. This is the preferred state for all routes in the topology table.

Enhanced IGRP routes are in an Active state when the Successor route has been lost and the router sends out a Query packet to determine an FS. Usually, an FS is present and EIGRP promotes that to the Successor route. This way, the router converges without involving other routers in the network. This process is referred to as a local computation.

However, if the Successor route has been lost or removed, and there is no FS, then the router will begin diffused computation. In diffused computation, EIGRP will send a Query out to all neighbors and out of all interfaces, except for the interface to the Successor route. When an EIGRP neighbor receives a Query for a route, and if that neighbor's EIGRP topology table does not contain an entry for the route, then the neighbor immediately replies to the Query with an unreachable message, stating that there is no path for this route through this neighbor.

If the EIGRP topology table on the neighbor lists the router sending the Query as the Successor for that route, and an FS exists, then the FS is installed and the router replies to the neighbor Query that it has a route to the lost destination network.

However, if the EIGRP topology table lists the router sending the Query as the Successor for this route and there is no FS, then the router queries all of its EIGRP neighbors, except those that were sent out of the same interface as its former Successor. The router will not reply to the Query until it has received a Reply to all Queries that it originated for this route.

Finally, if the Query was received from a neighbor that is not the Successor for this destination, then the router replies with its own Successor information. If the neighboring routers do not have the lost route information, then Queries are sent from those neighboring routers to their neighboring routers until the Query boundary is reached. The Query boundary is either the end of the network, the distribute list boundary, or the summarization boundary.

Once the Query has been sent, the EIGRP router must wait for all replies to be received before it calculates the Successor route. If any neighbor has not replied within three minutes, the route is said to be Stuck-in-Active (SIA). When a route is SIA, the neighbor relationship of the router(s) that did not respond to the Query will be reset. In such cases, you will see a message logged by the router similar to the following:

```
%DUAL-5-NBRCHANGE: IP-EIGRP 150:
    Neighbor 150.1.1.1(Serial0/0) is down: stuck in active
%DUAL-3-SIA:
    Route 172.16.100.0/24 stuck-in-active state in IP-EIGRP 150.
Cleaning up
```

There are several reasons why the EIGRP neighbor router(s) may not respond to the Query, which include the following:

- The neighbor router's CPU is overloaded and it cannot respond in time
- The neighbor router itself has no information about the lost route
- Quality issues on the circuit are causing packets to be lost

```
Low-bandwidth links are congested and packets are being delayed
```

To prevent SIA issues due to delayed responses from other EIGRP neighbors, the local router can be configured to wait for longer than the default of three minutes to receive responses back to its Query packets using the timers active-time command in Router Configuration mode.

> **NOTE:** It is important to note that if you change this default parameter on one EIGRP router in your network, you must change it on all the other routers within your EIGRP routing domain.

EQUAL COST AND UNEQUAL COST LOAD SHARING

Cisco IOS software supports equal cost load sharing for a default of up to four paths for all routing protocols. This is illustrated below in the output of the show ip protocols command:

```
R2#show ip protocols
Routing Protocol is "eigrp 150"
  Outgoing update filter list for all interfaces is not set
  Incoming update filter list for all interfaces is not set
  Default networks flagged in outgoing updates
  Default networks accepted from incoming updates
  EIGRP metric weight K1=1, K2=0, K3=1, K4=0, K5=0
  EIGRP maximum hopcount 100
  EIGRP maximum metric variance 1
  Redistributing: eigrp 150
```

```
EIGRP NSF-aware route hold timer is 240s
Automatic network summarization is not in effect
Maximum path: 4
Routing for Networks:
   150.1.1.2/32
   150.2.2.2/32
Routing Information Sources:
   Gateway          Distance        Last Update
   Gateway          Distance        Last Update
   150.2.2.1              90         00:00:52
   150.1.1.1              90         00:00:52
Distance: internal 90 external 170
```

The maximum-paths <1-6> router configuration command can be used to change the default value of four maximum paths up to a maximum of six equal cost paths. When performing equal cost load balancing, the router distributes the load evenly among all paths. The traffic share count identifies the number of outgoing packets on each path. When performing equal cost load balancing, one packet is sent on each individual path, as illustrated in the following output:

```
R2#show ip route 172.16.100.0 255.255.255.0
Routing entry for 172.16.100.0/24
   Known via "eigrp 150", distance 90, metric 2172416, type internal
   Redistributing via eigrp 150
   Last update from 150.2.2.1 on Serial0/1, 00:04:00 ago
   Routing Descriptor Blocks:
     150.2.2.1, from 150.2.2.1, 00:04:00 ago, via Serial0/1
       Route metric is 2172416, traffic share count is 1
       Total delay is 20100 microseconds, minimum bandwidth is 1544 Kbit
       Reliability 255/255, minimum MTU 1500 bytes
       Loading 1/255, Hops 1
   * 150.1.1.1, from 150.1.1.1, 00:04:00 ago, via Serial0/0
       Route metric is 2172416, traffic share count is 1
       Total delay is 20100 microseconds, minimum bandwidth is 1544 Kbit
       Reliability 255/255, minimum MTU 1500 bytes
       Loading 1/255, Hops 1
```

In addition to equal cost load balancing capabilities, EIGRP is also able to perform unequal cost load sharing. This unique ability allows EIGRP to use unequal cost paths to send outgoing packets to the destination network based on weighted traffic share values. Unequal cost load sharing is enabled using the variance <multiplier> router configuration command.

The <multiplier> keyword is an integer between 1 and 128. A multiplier of 1, which is the default, implies that no unequal cost load sharing is being performed. This default setting is illustrated below in the output of the show ip protocols command:

```
R2#show ip protocols
Routing Protocol is "eigrp 150"
   Outgoing update filter list for all interfaces is not set
   Incoming update filter list for all interfaces is not set
   Default networks flagged in outgoing updates
```

```
Default networks accepted from incoming updates
EIGRP metric weight K1=1, K2=0, K3=1, K4=0, K5=0
EIGRP maximum hopcount 100
EIGRP maximum metric variance 1
Redistributing: eigrp 150
EIGRP NSF-aware route hold timer is 240s
Automatic network summarization is not in effect
Maximum path: 4
Routing for Networks:
    150.1.1.2/32
    150.2.2.2/32
Routing Information Sources:
    Gateway         Distance        Last Update
    150.2.2.1            90          00:00:52
    150.1.1.1           90          00:00:52
Distance: internal 90 external 170
```

The multiplier is a variable integer that tells the router to load share across routes that have a metric that is less than the minimum metric multiplied by the multiplier. For example, specifying a variance of 5 instructs the router to load share across routes whose metric is less than 5 times the minimum metric. The default variance of 1 tells the router to perform equal cost load balancing. When the variance command is used and a value other than 1 is specified as the multiplier, the router will distribute traffic among the routes proportionately, with respect to the metric of each individual route. In other words, the router will send more traffic using those paths with lower metric values than those with higher metric values.

Figure 36.11 below illustrates a basic network running EIGRP. R1 and R2 are connected via back-to-back Serial links. The 150.1.1.0/24 link between the two routers has a bandwidth of 1024Kbps. The 150.2.2.0/24 link between the routers has a bandwidth of 768Kbps. R1 is advertising the 172.16.100.0/24 prefix via EIGRP to R2:

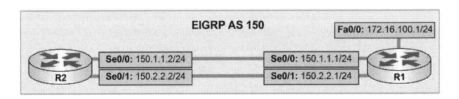

Figure 36.11—Understanding EIGRP Variance

Based on the topology illustrated in Figure 36.11, the routing table on R2 for the 172.16.100.0/24 prefix is shown in the following output:

```
R2#show ip route 172.16.100.0 255.255.255.0
Routing entry for 172.16.100.0/24
  Known via "eigrp 150", distance 90, metric 3014400, type internal
  Redistributing via eigrp 150
  Last update from 150.1.1.1 on Serial0/0, 00:00:11 ago
  Routing Descriptor Blocks:
```

```
*  150.1.1.1, from 150.1.1.1, 00:00:11 ago, via Serial0/0
      Route metric is 3014400, traffic share count is 1
      Total delay is 20100 microseconds, minimum bandwidth is 1024 Kbit
      Reliability 255/255, minimum MTU 1500 bytes
      Loading 1/255, Hops 1
```

The following EIGRP topology table shows both the Successor and the Feasible Successor routes:

```
R2#show ip eigrp topology 172.16.100.0 255.255.255.0
IP-EIGRP (AS 150): Topology entry for 172.16.100.0/24
   State is Passive, Query origin flag is 1, 1 Successor(s), FD is 3014400
   Routing Descriptor Blocks:
   150.1.1.1 (Serial0/0), from 150.1.1.1, Send flag is 0x0
      Composite metric is (3014400/28160), Route is Internal
      Vector metric:
        Minimum bandwidth is 1024 Kbit
        Total delay is 20100 microseconds
        Reliability is 255/255
        Load is 1/255
        Minimum MTU is 1500
        Hop count is 1
   150.2.2.1 (Serial0/1), from 150.2.2.1, Send flag is 0x0
      Composite metric is (3847680/28160), Route is Internal
      Vector metric:
        Minimum bandwidth is 768 Kbit
        Total delay is 20100 microseconds
        Reliability is 255/255
        Load is 1/255
        Minimum MTU is 1500
        Hop count is 1
```

To determine the variance value to configure on the router, you can use the following formula:

Variance = Highest metric for the paths being considered / Metric for the best route

Using this formula, you can calculate the variance value to configure on R2 as follows:

Variance = Highest metric for the paths being considered / Metric for the best route
Variance = 3847680 / 3014400
Variance = 1.28

This value must then be rounded up to the nearest whole integer, which in this case is 2. Given this, R2 can be configured to perform unequal cost load sharing by implementing the following configuration in Router Configuration mode:

```
R2(config)#router eigrp 150
R2(config-router)#variance 2
R2(config-router)#exit
```

Following this configuration, the routing table entry for 172.16.100.0/24 is illustrated below:

```
R2#show ip route 172.16.100.0 255.255.255.0
Routing entry for 172.16.100.0/24
  Known via "eigrp 150", distance 90, metric 3014400, type internal
  Redistributing via eigrp 150
  Last update from 150.2.2.1 on Serial0/1, 00:00:36 ago
  Routing Descriptor Blocks:
    150.2.2.1, from 150.2.2.1, 00:00:36 ago, via Serial0/1
      Route metric is 3847680, traffic share count is 47
      Total delay is 20100 microseconds, minimum bandwidth is 768 Kbit
      Reliability 255/255, minimum MTU 1500 bytes
      Loading 1/255, Hops 1
  * 150.1.1.1, from 150.1.1.1, 00:00:36 ago, via Serial0/0
      Route metric is 3014400, traffic share count is 60
      Total delay is 20100 microseconds, minimum bandwidth is 1024 Kbit
      Reliability 255/255, minimum MTU 1500 bytes
      Loading 1/255, Hops 1
```

The traffic share count indicates that for every 60 packets forwarded via Serial0/0, the router will forward 47 packets via Serial0/1. This is performed proportionally in respect to the route metric of either path. This is the default behavior when the `variance` command is implemented. This intelligent traffic sharing functionality is enabled via the `traffic-share balanced` router configuration command, which requires no explicit configuration.

NOTE: The `traffic-share balanced` command is enabled by default and does not appear in the running configuration, even if manually configured. This is illustrated below:

```
R2(config)#router eigrp 150
R2(config-router)#vari 2
R2(config-router)#traffic-share balanced
R2(config-router)#exit
R2(config)#do show run | begin router
router eigrp 150
 variance 2
 network 150.1.1.2 0.0.0.0
 network 150.2.2.2 0.0.0.0
 no auto-summary
```

As stated previously in this section, when the `variance` command is used, all paths that both meet the Feasibility Condition and have a metric that is less than the minimum metric multiplied by the multiplier will be installed into the routing table. The router will then use all paths and load share traffic proportionally based on the route metric.

In some cases, you may want to allow alternate routes, such as the Feasible Successor route, to be placed into the routing table but not be used unless the Successor route is removed. Such actions are typically performed to reduce convergence times in EIGRP-enabled networks. To understand this concept, recall that, by default, the router only places the Successor route into the IP routing table. In the event that the Successor route is no longer available, the

Feasible Successor route is promoted to the Successor route. This route is then installed into the routing table as the primary path to the destination network.

The `traffic-share min across-interfaces` router configuration command can be used in conjunction with the `variance` command to install all routes that have a metric less than the minimum metric multiplied by the multiplier into the routing table, but use only the route with the minimum (best) metric to forward packets until that route becomes unavailable. The primary objective of this configuration is that in the event that the primary route is lost, the alternative route is already in the routing table and can be used immediately.

The following configuration example uses the topology shown in Figure 36.11 above to illustrate how to configure the router to place routes with a metric less than two times the minimum metric into the routing table, but use only the route with the lowest metric to actually forward packets:

```
R2(config)#router eigrp 150
R2(config-router)#vari 2
R2(config-router)#traffic-share min across-interfaces
R2(config-router)#exit
```

This configuration results in the following output for 172.16.100.0/24 in the routing table:

```
R2#show ip route 172.16.100.0 255.255.255.0
Routing entry for 172.16.100.0/24
  Known via "eigrp 150", distance 90, metric 3014400, type internal
  Redistributing via eigrp 150
  Last update from 150.2.2.1 on Serial0/1, 00:09:01 ago
  Routing Descriptor Blocks:
    150.2.2.1, from 150.2.2.1, 00:09:01 ago, via Serial0/1
      Route metric is 3847680, traffic share count is 0
      Total delay is 20100 microseconds, minimum bandwidth is 768 Kbit
      Reliability 255/255, minimum MTU 1500 bytes
      Loading 1/255, Hops 1
  * 150.1.1.1, from 150.1.1.1, 00:09:01 ago, via Serial0/0
      Route metric is 3014400, traffic share count is 1
      Total delay is 20100 microseconds, minimum bandwidth is 1024 Kbit
      Reliability 255/255, minimum MTU 1500 bytes
      Loading 1/255, Hops 1
```

As is illustrated in the output above, the two different metric routes have been installed into the routing table based on the variance configuration. However, notice the traffic share count for the route via Serial0/1 is 0 while the traffic share count for the route via Serial0/0 is 1. This means that the router will not send any packets to 172.16.100.0/24 via Serial0/1, even though the route entry is installed into the routing table, until the path via Serial0/0 is no longer available.

DEFAULT ROUTING USING EIGRP

Enhanced IGRP supports numerous ways to advertise dynamically the gateway or network of last resort to other routers within the routing domain. A gateway of last resort, or default route, is a method for the router to direct traffic when the destination network is not specifically listed in the routing table. These methods are as follows:

- Using the `ip default-network` command
- Using the `network` command to advertise network 0.0.0.0/0
- Redistributing the default static route
- Using the `ip summary-address eigrp [asn] [network] [mask]` command

The use of the `ip default-network` command is considered a legacy method of advertising the default route dynamically using EIGRP. However, because it is still supported in current IOS software versions, it is worth mentioning.

The `ip default-network` configuration command flags a network as the default network by inserting an asterisk (*) next to the network in the routing table. Traffic for destinations to which there is no specific routing table entry is then forwarded by the router to this network. The implementation of this feature is illustrated referencing the EIGRP topology in Figure 36.12 below:

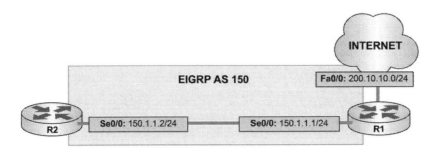

Figure 36.12—EIGRP Default Routing

Referencing Figure 36.12, assume that the 200.10.10.0/24 subnet is connected to the Internet. This subnet resides off the FastEthernet0/0 interface of R1. R1 and R2 are in turn connected via a back-to-back Serial connection. Both routers reside in EIGRP AS 150. To flag the 200.10.10.0/24 network as the network of last resort, the following configuration is implemented on R1:

```
R1(config)#router eigrp 150
R1(config-router)#network 200.10.10.0 0.0.0.255
R1(config-router)#exit
R1(config)#ip default-network 200.10.10.0
R1(config)#exit
```

Based on this configuration, R2 receives 200.10.10.0/24 as the network of last resort, as follows:

```
R2#show ip route
Codes: C - connected, S - static, R - RIP, M - mobile, B - BGP
       D - EIGRP, EX - EIGRP external, O - OSPF, IA - OSPF inter area
       N1 - OSPF NSSA external type 1, N2 - OSPF NSSA external type 2
       E1 - OSPF external type 1, E2 - OSPF external type 2
       i - IS-IS, su - IS-IS summary, L1 - IS-IS level-1, L2 - IS-IS
level-2
       ia - IS-IS inter area, * - candidate default, U - per-user static
route
       o - ODR, P - periodic downloaded static route

Gateway of last resort is 150.2.2.1 to network 200.10.10.0

D*     200.10.10.0/24 [90/2172416] via 150.2.2.1, 00:01:03, Serial0/0
       150.1.0.0/24 is subnetted, 1 subnets
C         150.1.1.0 is directly connected, Serial0/0
```

The network command can be used to advertise an existing static default route point to either a physical or a logical interface, typically the Null0 interface.

> **NOTE:** The Null0 interface is a virtual interface on the router that discards all traffic that is routed to it. If you have a static route pointing to Null0, all traffic destined for the network specified in the static route is simply discarded. Think of the Null0 interface as a black hole: packets enter, but none ever leaves. It is essentially a bit-bucket on the router.

Referencing the diagram in Figure 36.12 above, the use of the network command in conjunction with an existing default static route is illustrated in the following configuration on R1:

```
R1(config)#ip route 0.0.0.0 0.0.0.0 FastEthernet0/0
R1(config)#router eigrp 150
R1(config-router)#network 0.0.0.0
R1(config-router)#exit
```

Based on this configuration, the IP routing table on R2 is illustrated in the following output:

```
R2#show ip route
Codes: C - connected, S - static, R - RIP, M - mobile, B - BGP
       D - EIGRP, EX - EIGRP external, O - OSPF, IA - OSPF inter area
       N1 - OSPF NSSA external type 1, N2 - OSPF NSSA external type 2
       E1 - OSPF external type 1, E2 - OSPF external type 2
       i - IS-IS, su - IS-IS summary, L1 - IS-IS level-1, L2 - IS-IS
level-2
       ia - IS-IS inter area, * - candidate default, U - per-user static
route
       o - ODR, P - periodic downloaded static route
```

```
Gateway of last resort is 150.1.1.1 to network 0.0.0.0

D    200.10.10.0/24 [90/2172416] via 150.1.1.1, 00:01:11, Serial0/0
     150.1.0.0/24 is subnetted, 1 subnets
C        150.1.1.0 is directly connected, Serial0/0
D*   0.0.0.0/0 [90/2172416] via 150.1.1.1, 00:00:43, Serial0/0
```

Although route redistribution isn't part of the CCNA exam, it will be outlined here. This is the third method of advertising a default route via EIGRP. To redistribute the existing static default route into EIGRP, use the `redistribute static metric [bandwidth] [delay] [reliability] [load] [MTU]` router configuration command. The same network topology used for the previous outputs in this section will be used to illustrate the implementation of this method, as illustrated in Figure 36.13 below:

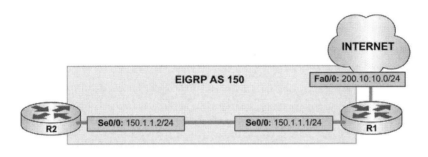

Figure 36.13—EIGRP Default Routing (Continued)

Referencing Figure 36.13, which is the same as Figure 36.12, the following is performed on R1:

```
R1(config)#ip route 0.0.0.0 0.0.0.0 FastEthernet0/0
R1(config)#router eigrp 150
R1(config-router)#redistribute static metric 100000 100 255 1 1500
R1(config-router)#exit
```

NOTE: The values used in the metric can be derived from the interface, or you can specify any values that you want when using this command.

Based on this configuration, the routing table on R2 is illustrated below:

```
R2#show ip route
Codes: C - connected, S - static, R - RIP, M - mobile, B - BGP
       D - EIGRP, EX - EIGRP external, O - OSPF, IA - OSPF inter area
       N1 - OSPF NSSA external type 1, N2 - OSPF NSSA external type 2
       E1 - OSPF external type 1, E2 - OSPF external type 2
       i - IS-IS, su - IS-IS summary, L1 - IS-IS level-1, L2 - IS-IS
level-2
       ia - IS-IS inter area, * - candidate default, U - per-user static
route
       o - ODR, P - periodic downloaded static route
```

```
Gateway of last resort is 150.1.1.1 to network 0.0.0.0

     150.1.0.0/24 is subnetted, 1 subnets
C       150.1.1.0 is directly connected, Serial0/0
D*EX 0.0.0.0/0 [170/2195456] via 150.1.1.1, 00:01:16, Serial0/0
```

Because the route was redistributed into EIGRP on R1, it is an external EIGRP route, as reflected in the output above. For external routes, the EIGRP topology table includes information such as the router that originated the route, the protocol the route was received for, and the metric of the external route, for example. This is illustrated in the following output:

```
R2#show ip eigrp topology 0.0.0.0/0
IP-EIGRP (AS 150): Topology entry for 0.0.0.0/0
  State is Passive, Query origin flag is 1, 1 Successor(s), FD is 2195456
  Routing Descriptor Blocks:
  150.1.1.1 (Serial0/0), from 150.1.1.1, Send flag is 0x0
      Composite metric is (2195456/51200), Route is External
      Vector metric:
        Minimum bandwidth is 1544 Kbit
        Total delay is 21000 microseconds
        Reliability is 255/255
        Load is 1/255
        Minimum MTU is 1500
        Hop count is 1
      External data:
        Originating router is 1.1.1.1
        AS number of route is 0
        External protocol is Static, external metric is 0
        Administrator tag is 0 (0x00000000)
        Exterior flag is set
```

From the information in bold, you can see that the default route is a static route that was redistributed into EIGRP on R1. This route has a metric of 0. In addition, you can also see that the EIGRP router ID (RID) of R1 is 1.1.1.1.

The final method of advertising the default route is by using the ip summary-address eigrp [asn] [network] [mask] interface configuration command. EIGRP route summarization will be described in detail later in this module. For the moment, concentrate on the use of this command to advertise the default route when using EIGRP.

Referencing the network topology diagram illustrated in Figure 36.13 above, R1 is configured with the ip summary-address eigrp [asn] [network] [mask] interface configuration command to advertise the default route to R2, as follows:

```
R1(config)#interface Serial0/0
R1(config-if)#description 'Back-to-Back Serial Connection To R2
Serial0/0'
R1(config-if)#ip summary-address eigrp 150 0.0.0.0 0.0.0.0
R1(config-if)#exit
```

The primary advantage to using this command is that a default route or network does not need to exist in the routing table in order for EIGRP to advertise network 0.0.0.0/0 to its neighbor routers. When this command is issued, the local router generates a summary route to the Null0 interface and flags the entry as the candidate default route. This is illustrated below:

```
R1#show ip route
Codes: C - connected, S - static, R - RIP, M - mobile, B - BGP
       D - EIGRP, EX - EIGRP external, O - OSPF, IA - OSPF inter area
       N1 - OSPF NSSA external type 1, N2 - OSPF NSSA external type 2
       E1 - OSPF external type 1, E2 - OSPF external type 2
       i - IS-IS, su - IS-IS summary, L1 - IS-IS level-1, L2 - IS-IS
level-2
       ia - IS-IS inter area, * - candidate default, U - per-user static
route
       o - ODR, P - periodic downloaded static route

Gateway of last resort is 0.0.0.0 to network 0.0.0.0

     150.1.0.0/24 is subnetted, 1 subnets
C       150.1.1.0 is directly connected, Serial0/0
D*    0.0.0.0/0 is a summary, 00:02:26, Null0
```

The summary route is received as an internal EIGRP route on R2, as illustrated below:

```
R2#show ip route
Codes: C - connected, S - static, R - RIP, M - mobile, B - BGP
       D - EIGRP, EX - EIGRP external, O - OSPF, IA - OSPF inter area
       N1 - OSPF NSSA external type 1, N2 - OSPF NSSA external type 2
       E1 - OSPF external type 1, E2 - OSPF external type 2
       i - IS-IS, su - IS-IS summary, L1 - IS-IS level-1, L2 - IS-IS
level-2
       ia - IS-IS inter area, * - candidate default, U - per-user static
route
       o - ODR, P - periodic downloaded static route

Gateway of last resort is 150.1.1.1 to network 0.0.0.0

     150.1.0.0/24 is subnetted, 1 subnets
C       150.1.1.0 is directly connected, Serial0/0
D*    0.0.0.0/0 [90/2297856] via 150.1.1.1, 00:03:07, Serial0/0
```

SPLIT HORIZON IN EIGRP NETWORKS

Previously, you learned that split horizon is a Distance Vector protocol feature mandating that routing information cannot be sent back out of the same interface through which it was received. This prevents the re-advertising of information back to the source from which it was learned. While this characteristic is a great loop prevention mechanism, it is also a significant drawback, especially in hub-and-spoke networks. To better understand the drawbacks of this feature, refer to the EIGRP hub-and-spoke network in Figure 36.14 below:

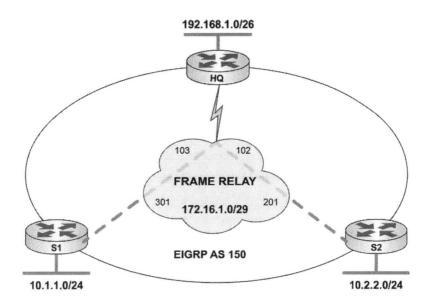

Figure 36.14—EIGRP Split Horizon

The topology in Figure 36.14 illustrates a classic hub-and-spoke network, with router HQ as the hub router and routers S1 and S2 as the two spoke routers. On the Frame Relay WAN, each spoke router has a single DLCI provisioned between itself and the HQ router in a partial-mesh topology. The Frame Relay configuration on the routers is verified as follows:

```
HQ#show frame-relay map
Serial0/0 (up): ip 172.16.1.2 dlci 102(0x66,0x1860), static,
              broadcast,
              CISCO, status defined, active
Serial0/0 (up): ip 172.16.1.1 dlci 103(0x67,0x1870), static,
              broadcast,
              CISCO, status defined, active

S1#show frame-relay map
Serial0/0 (up): ip 172.16.1.2 dlci 301(0x12D,0x48D0), static,
              broadcast,
              CISCO, status defined, active
Serial0/0 (up): ip 172.16.1.3 dlci 301(0x12D,0x48D0), static,
              broadcast,
              CISCO, status defined, active

S2#show frame-relay map
Serial0/0 (up): ip 172.16.1.1 dlci 201(0xC9,0x3090), static,
              broadcast,
              CISCO, status defined, active
Serial0/0 (up): ip 172.16.1.3 dlci 201(0xC9,0x3090), static,
              broadcast,
              CISCO, status defined, active
```

Frame Relay has been dropped from the CCNA syllabus, unfortunately split horizon issues which they cause has no so we'll cover the issue but not the theory behind the technology.

Enhanced IGRP has been enabled on all three routers, using AS 150. The following output illustrates the EIGRP neighbor relationships between the HQ router and the spoke routers:

```
HQ#show ip eigrp neighbors
IP-EIGRP neighbors for process 150
H   Address         Interface     Hold   Uptime    SRTT  RTO  Q   Seq
                                  (sec)            (ms)       Cnt Num
1   172.16.1.1      Se0/0         165    00:01:07  24    200  0   2
0   172.16.1.2      Se0/0         153    00:01:25  124   744  0   2
```

The following output illustrates the EIGRP neighbor relationship between the first spoke router, S1, and the HQ router:

```
S1#show ip eigrp neighbors
IP-EIGRP neighbors for process 150
H   Address         Interface     Hold   Uptime    SRTT RTO   Q   Seq
                                  (sec)            (ms)       Cnt Num
0   172.16.1.3      Se0/0         128    00:00:53  911  5000  0   4
```

The following output illustrates the EIGRP neighbor relationship between the second spoke router, S2, and the HQ router:

```
S2#show ip eigrp neighbors
IP-EIGRP neighbors for process 150
H   Address         Interface     Hold   Uptime    SRTT  RTO  Q   Seq
                                  (sec)            (ms)       Cnt Num
0   172.16.1.3      Se0/0         156    00:02:20  8     200  0   4
```

By default, EIGRP split horizon is enabled, which is undesirable in partial-mesh NBMA networks. This means that the HQ router will not advertise routing information learned on Serial0/0 out of the same interface. The effect of this default behavior is that the HQ router will not advertise the 10.1.1.0/24 prefix received from S1 to S2 because the route is received via the Serial0/0 interface, and the split horizon feature prevents the router from advertising information learned on that interface back out onto the same interface. The same is also applicable for the 10.2.2.0/24 prefix the HQ router receives from S2.

This default behavior means that while the HQ router is aware of both prefixes, the spoke routers have only partial routing tables. The routing table on the HQ router is as follows:

```
HQ#show ip route eigrp
     10.0.0.0/8 is variably subnetted, 2 subnets, 2 masks
D       10.1.1.0/24 [90/2195456] via 172.16.1.1, 00:12:04, Serial0/0
D       10.2.2.0/24 [90/2195456] via 172.16.1.2, 00:12:06, Serial0/0
```

The routing table on spoke S1 is as follows:

```
S1#show ip route eigrp
      192.168.1.0/26 is subnetted, 1 subnets
D        192.168.1.0 [90/2195456] via 172.16.1.3, 00:10:53, Serial0/0
```

The routing table on spoke S2 is as follows:

```
S2#show ip route eigrp
      192.168.1.0/26 is subnetted, 1 subnets
D        192.168.1.0 [90/2195456] via 172.16.1.3, 00:10:55, Serial0/0
```

The result of this default behavior is that while the HQ router will be able to reach both of the spoke router networks, neither spoke router will be able to reach the network of the other. There are several ways such a situation can be addressed and they are as follows:

- Disabling split horizon on the HQ (hub) router
- Advertising a default route from the HQ router to the spoke routers
- Manually configuring EIGRP neighbors on the routers

Disabling split horizon is performed at the interface level using the `no ip split-horizon eigrp [AS]` interface configuration command on the hub router. The command `show ip split-horizon interface_name` does not show the state of EIGRP split horizon as it does for RIP. To see if it is disabled, you have to examine the interface configuration section (i.e, `show run interface_name`). Referencing the network topology illustrated in Figure 36.14 above, this interface configuration command would be applied to the Serial0/0 interface on the HQ router. This is performed as follows:

```
HQ(config)#interface Serial0/0
HQ(config-if)#no ip split-horizon eigrp 150
```

After split horizon is disabled, the HQ router can advertise information back out onto the same interface on which it was received. For example, the routing table on spoke S2 now shows a routing entry for the 10.1.1.0/24 prefix advertised by spoke S1 to the HQ router:

```
S2#show ip route eigrp
      10.0.0.0/8 is variably subnetted, 2 subnets, 2 masks
D        10.1.1.0/24 [90/2707456] via 172.16.1.3, 00:00:47, Serial0/0
      192.168.1.0/26 is subnetted, 1 subnets
D        192.168.1.0 [90/2195456] via 172.16.1.3, 00:00:47, Serial0/0
```

A simple ping test from spoke router S2 to the 10.1.1.0/24 subnet can be used to verify connectivity, as illustrated below:

```
S2#ping 10.1.1.2
Type escape sequence to abort.
Sending 5, 100-byte ICMP Echos to 10.1.1.2, timeout is 2 seconds:
!!!!!
Success rate is 100 percent (5/5), round-trip min/avg/max = 24/27/32 ms
```

The second method of disabling split horizon is simply to advertise a default route from the HQ router to the spoke routers. In this situation, the `ip summary-address eigrp 150 0.0.0.0 0.0.0.0` interface configuration command could be applied to the Serial0/0 interface of the HQ router. This would allow the spoke routers to reach each other through the HQ router, which contains the full routing table, negating the need to disable split horizon.

The final alternative method of disabling split horizon is to configure manually EIGRP neighbor statements on all routers using the `neighbor` router configuration command. Because updates between neighbors are Unicast when this configuration is used, the split horizon limitation is removed. This option works well in small networks; however, as the network grows and the number of spoke routers increases, so does the configuration overhead.

Given that the configuration of both EIGRP default routing and static neighbors was described in detail in earlier sections in this module, the configuration of these features is omitted for brevity.

EIGRP ROUTE SUMMARIZATION

Route summarization reduces the amount of information that routers must process, which allows for faster convergence within the network. Summarization also restricts the size of the area that is affected by network changes by hiding detailed topology information from certain areas within the network. Finally, as was stated earlier in this module, summarization is used to define a Query boundary for EIGRP, which supports two types of route summarization, as follows:

- Automatic route summarization
- Manual route summarization

By default, automatic route summarization is in effect when EIGRP is enabled on the router. This is implemented using the `auto-summary` command. This command allows EIGRP to perform automatic route summarization at classful boundaries. The operation of this default feature is illustrated referencing the network topology in Figure 36.15 below:

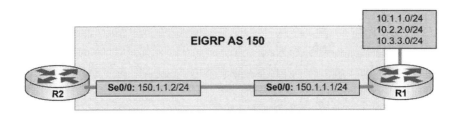

Figure 36.15—EIGRP Automatic Route Summarization

Referencing the EIGRP network illustrated in Figure 36.15, R1 and R2 are running EIGRP and are using autonomous system 150. The 10.1.1.0/24, 10.2.2.0/24, and 10.3.3.0/24 subnets are directly connected to R1. R1 is advertising these routes to R2. R1 and R2 are connected using a back-to-back Serial connection on the 150.1.1.0/24 subnet (which is a different major network than the 10.1.1.0/24, 10.2.2.0/24, and 10.3.3.0/24 subnets). Based on the networks connected to these routers, by default, EIGRP will perform automatic summarization, as follows:

- The 10.1.1.0/24, 10.2.2.0/24, and 10.3.3.0/24 subnets will be summarised to 10.0.0.0/8
- The 150.1.1.0/24 subnet will be summarized to 150.1.0.0/16

This default behavior can be validated by viewing the output of the show ip protocols command. The output of this command on R1 is illustrated below:

```
R1#show ip protocols
Routing Protocol is "eigrp 150"
  Outgoing update filter list for all interfaces is not set
  Incoming update filter list for all interfaces is not set
  Default networks flagged in outgoing updates
  Default networks accepted from incoming updates
  EIGRP metric weight K1=1, K2=0, K3=1, K4=0, K5=0
  EIGRP maximum hopcount 100
  EIGRP maximum metric variance 1
  Redistributing: eigrp 150
  EIGRP NSF-aware route hold timer is 240s
  Automatic network summarization is in effect
  Automatic address summarization:
    150.1.0.0/16 for Loopback1, Loopback2, Loopback3
      Summarizing with metric 2169856
    10.0.0.0/8 for Serial0/0
      Summarizing with metric 128256
  Maximum path: 4
  Routing for Networks:
    10.1.1.0/24
    10.2.2.0/24
    10.3.3.0/24
    150.1.1.0/24
  Routing Information Sources:
    Gateway         Distance      Last Update
    (this router)         90      00:03:12
    150.1.1.2             90      00:03:12
  Distance: internal 90 external 170
```

In the output above, the 10.1.1.0/24, 10.2.2.0/24, and 10.3.3.0/24 subnets have been automatically summarized to 10.0.0.0/8. This summary address is advertised out of Serial0/0. The 150.1.1.0/24 subnet has been summarized to 150.1.0.0/16. This summary address is advertised out of Loopback1, Loopback2, and Loopback3. Remember, by default, EIGRP will send out updates on all interfaces for which EIGRP routing is enabled.

Referencing the output printed above, you can see that sending updates on a Loopback interface is a waste of resources because a device cannot be connected physically to a router

Loopback interface listening for such updates. This default behavior can be disabled by using the passive-interface router configuration command, as follows:

```
R1(config)#router eigrp 150
R1(config-router)#passive-interface Loopback1
R1(config-router)#passive-interface Loopback2
R1(config-router)#passive-interface Loopback3
R1(config-router)#exit
```

The result of this configuration is that EIGRP packets are no longer sent out of the Loopback interfaces. Therefore, as illustrated below, the summary address is not advertised out of these interfaces:

```
R1#show ip protocols
Routing Protocol is "eigrp 150"
  Outgoing update filter list for all interfaces is not set
  Incoming update filter list for all interfaces is not set
  Default networks flagged in outgoing updates
  Default networks accepted from incoming updates
  EIGRP metric weight K1=1, K2=0, K3=1, K4=0, K5=0
  EIGRP maximum hopcount 100
  EIGRP maximum metric variance 1
  Redistributing: eigrp 150
  EIGRP NSF-aware route hold timer is 240s
  Automatic network summarization is in effect
  Automatic address summarization:
    10.0.0.0/8 for Serial0/0
      Summarizing with metric 128256
  Maximum path: 4
  Routing for Networks:
    10.0.0.0
    150.1.0.0
  Passive Interface(s):
    Loopback0
    Loopback1
    Loopback2
    Loopback3
  Routing Information Sources:
    Gateway         Distance      Last Update
    (this router)         90      00:03:07
    150.1.1.2             90      00:01:12
  Distance: internal 90 external 170
```

NOTE: The passive-interface command is described in detail later in this module.

Continuing with automatic summarization, following automatic summarization at the classful boundary, EIGRP installs a route to the summary address into the EIGRP topology table and the IP routing table. The route is highlighted below in the EIGRP topology table, along with the more specific entries and their respective directly connected interfaces:

```
R1#show ip eigrp topology
IP-EIGRP Topology Table for AS(150)/ID(10.3.3.1)
```

```
Codes: P - Passive, A - Active, U - Update, Q - Query, R - Reply,
       r - reply Status, s - sia Status

P 10.0.0.0/8, 1 successors, FD is 128256
        via Summary (128256/0), Null0
P 10.3.3.0/24, 1 successors, FD is 128256
        via Connected, Loopback3
P 10.2.2.0/24, 1 successors, FD is 128256
        via Connected, Loopback2
P 10.1.1.0/24, 1 successors, FD is 128256
        via Connected, Loopback1

[Truncated Output]
```

In the routing table, the summary route is connected directly to the Null0 interface. The route has a default administrative distance value of 5. This is illustrated in the following output:

```
R1#show ip route 10.0.0.0 255.0.0.0
Routing entry for 10.0.0.0/8
  Known via "eigrp 150", distance 5, metric 128256, type internal
  Redistributing via eigrp 150
  Routing Descriptor Blocks:
  * directly connected, via Null0
      Route metric is 128256, traffic share count is 1
      Total delay is 5000 microseconds, minimum bandwidth is 10000000
Kbit
      Reliability 255/255, minimum MTU 1514 bytes
      Loading 1/255, Hops 0
```

When EIGRP performs automatic summarization, the router advertises the summary route and suppresses the more specific routes. In other words, while the summary route is advertised, the more specific prefixes are suppressed in updates to EIGRP neighbors. This can be validated by looking at the routing table on R2, as illustrated below:

```
R2#show ip route eigrp
D    10.0.0.0/8 [90/2298856] via 150.1.1.1, 00:29:05, Serial0/0
```

This default behavior works well in basic networks, such as the one illustrated in Figure 36.15 above. However, it can have an adverse impact in a discontiguous network, which comprises a major network that separates another major network, as illustrated in Figure 36.16 below:

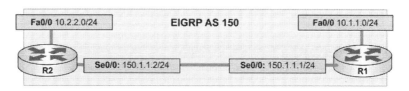

Figure 36.16—Discontiguous Network

Referencing the diagram illustrated in Figure 36.16, the major 150.1.0.0/16 network separates the two major 10.0.0.0/8 networks. When automatic summarization is enabled, both R1 and R2 will summarize the 10.1.1.0/24 and 10.2.2.0/24 subnets, respectively, to the 10.0.0.0/8 address. This summary route will be installed with a next-hop interface of Null0. The Null0 interface is a "bit-bucket." Any packets sent to this interface are effectively discarded.

Because both routers advertise to each other only the summary addresses, neither router will be able to reach the 10.x.x.x/24 subnet of the other router. To understand the ramifications of automatic summarization in the network illustrated in Figure 36.16, let's go through the steps one at a time, beginning with the configuration on R1 and R2, which is as follows:

```
R1(config)#router eigrp 150
R1(config-router)#network 10.1.1.0 0.0.0.255
R1(config-router)#network 150.1.1.0 0.0.0.255
R1(config-router)#exit

R2(config)#router eigrp 150
R2(config-router)#network 10.2.2.0 0.0.0.255
R2(config-router)#network 150.1.1.0 0.0.0.255
R2(config-router)#exit
```

Because automatic summarization at the classful boundary is enabled by default on both of the routers, they will both generate two summary addresses: one for 10.0.0.0/8 and another for 150.1.0.0/16. These summary addresses will both point to the Null0 interface, and the routing table on R1 will display the following entries:

```
R1#show ip route eigrp
     10.0.0.0/8 is variably subnetted, 2 subnets, 2 masks
D       10.0.0.0/8 is a summary, 00:04:51, Null0
     150.1.0.0/16 is variably subnetted, 2 subnets, 2 masks
D       150.1.0.0/16 is a summary, 00:06:22, Null0
```

Similarly, the routing table on R2 also reflects the same, as follows:

```
R2#show ip route eigrp
     10.0.0.0/8 is variably subnetted, 2 subnets, 2 masks
D       10.0.0.0/8 is a summary, 00:01:58, Null0
     150.1.0.0/16 is variably subnetted, 2 subnets, 2 masks
D       150.1.0.0/16 is a summary, 00:01:58, Null0
```

Even though a summary address of 150.1.0.0/16 has been installed into the IP routing table, R1 and R2 are still able to ping each other because the more route-specific entry (150.1.1.0/24) resides on a directly connected interface. The more specific entries in a summary route can be viewed by issuing the show ip route [address][mask] longer-prefixes command. The output of this command is illustrated below for the 150.1.0.0/16 summary:

```
R1#show ip route 150.1.0.0 255.255.0.0 longer-prefixes
Codes: C - connected, S - static, R - RIP, M - mobile, B - BGP
       D - EIGRP, EX - EIGRP external, O - OSPF, IA - OSPF inter area
       N1 - OSPF NSSA external type 1, N2 - OSPF NSSA external type 2
```

```
        E1 - OSPF external type 1, E2 - OSPF external type 2
        i - IS-IS, su - IS-IS summary, L1 - IS-IS level-1, L2 - IS-IS
level-2
        ia - IS-IS inter area, * - candidate default, U - per-user static
route
        o - ODR, P - periodic downloaded static route

Gateway of last resort is not set

     150.1.0.0/16 is variably subnetted, 2 subnets, 2 masks
C       150.1.1.0/24 is directly connected, Serial0/0
D       150.1.0.0/16 is a summary, 00:10:29, Null0
```

Because the more specific 150.1.1.0/24 route entry exists, packets sent to the 150.1.1.2 address will be forwarded via the Serial0/0 interface. This allows connectivity between R1 and R2, as illustrated below:

```
R1#ping 150.1.1.2

Type escape sequence to abort.
Sending 5, 100-byte ICMP Echos to 150.1.1.2, timeout is 2 seconds:
!!!!!
Success rate is 100 percent (5/5), round-trip min/avg/max = 1/3/4 ms
```

However, packets to any other subnets of the major 150.1.0.0/16 network will be sent to the Null0 interface because no specific route entries exist.

So far, everything appears to be in order. You can see that due to the more specific route entry of the major 150.1.0.0/16 network, R1 and R2 are able to ping each other. The problem, however, is connectivity between the major 10.0.0.0/8 subnets on R1 and R2. Router R1 displays the following specific route entries for its generated 10.0.0.0/8 summary address:

```
R1#show ip route 10.0.0.0 255.0.0.0 longer-prefixes
Codes: C - connected, S - static, R - RIP, M - mobile, B - BGP
       D - EIGRP, EX - EIGRP external, O - OSPF, IA - OSPF inter area
       N1 - OSPF NSSA external type 1, N2 - OSPF NSSA external type 2
       E1 - OSPF external type 1, E2 - OSPF external type 2
       i - IS-IS, su - IS-IS summary, L1 - IS-IS level-1, L2 - IS-IS
level-2
       ia - IS-IS inter area, * - candidate default, U - per-user static
route
       o - ODR, P - periodic downloaded static route

Gateway of last resort is not set

     10.0.0.0/8 is variably subnetted, 2 subnets, 2 masks
C       10.1.1.0/24 is directly connected, FastEthernet0/0
D       10.0.0.0/8 is a summary, 00:14:23, Null0
```

Similarly, router R2 displays the following specific entries for its generated 10.0.0.0/8 summary:

```
R2#show ip route 10.0.0.0 255.0.0.0 longer-prefixes
Codes: C - connected, S - static, R - RIP, M - mobile, B - BGP
       D - EIGRP, EX - EIGRP external, O - OSPF, IA - OSPF inter area
       N1 - OSPF NSSA external type 1, N2 - OSPF NSSA external type 2
       E1 - OSPF external type 1, E2 - OSPF external type 2
       i - IS-IS, su - IS-IS summary, L1 - IS-IS level-1, L2 - IS-IS
level-2
       ia - IS-IS inter area, * - candidate default, U - per-user static
route
       o - ODR, P - periodic downloaded static route

Gateway of last resort is not set

     10.0.0.0/8 is variably subnetted, 2 subnets, 2 masks
C       10.2.2.0/24 is directly connected, FastEthernet0/0
D       10.0.0.0/8 is a summary, 00:15:11, Null0
```

Neither router has a route to the other router's 10.*x.x.x*/24 subnet. If, for example, R1 attempts to send packets to 10.2.2.0/24, the summary address will be used and the packets will be forwarded to the Null0 interface. This is illustrated in the following output:

```
R1#show ip route 10.2.2.0
Routing entry for 10.0.0.0/8
  Known via "eigrp 150", distance 5, metric 28160, type internal
  Redistributing via eigrp 150
  Routing Descriptor Blocks:
  * directly connected, via Null0
      Route metric is 28160, traffic share count is 1
      Total delay is 100 microseconds, minimum bandwidth is 100000 Kbit
      Reliability 255/255, minimum MTU 1500 bytes
      Loading 1/255, Hops 0
```

R1 will be unable to ping the 10.*x.x.x*/24 subnet on R2 and vice-versa, as illustrated below:

```
R1#ping 10.2.2.2
Type escape sequence to abort.
Sending 5, 100-byte ICMP Echos to 10.2.2.2, timeout is 2 seconds:
.....
Success rate is 0 percent (0/5)
```

Two solutions to this issue are as follows:

- Manually configure static routes for the 10.*x.x.x*/24 subnets on both routers
- Disable EIGRP automatic classful network summarization

The first option is very basic. However, static route configuration is not scalable and requires a great deal of configuration overhead in large networks. The second option, which is also the recommended option, is both scalable and requires less configuration overhead than the first. Automatic summarization is disabled by issuing the no auto-summary command (disabled by default in newer IOS releases), as illustrated below:

```
R1(config)#router eigrp 150
R1(config-router)#no auto-summary
R1(config-router)#exit

R2(config)#router eigrp 150
R2(config-router)#no auto-summary
R2(config-router)#exit
```

The result of this configuration is that the specific subnets of the major network are advertised by both routers. A summary route is not generated, as illustrated below:

```
R2#show ip route eigrp
      10.0.0.0/24 is subnetted, 2 subnets
D        10.1.1.0 [90/2172416] via 150.1.1.1, 00:01:17, Serial0/0
```

IP connectivity between the 10.*x.x.x*/24 subnets can be validated using a simple ping, as illustrated below:

```
R2#ping 10.1.1.1 source 10.2.2.2 repeat 10

Type escape sequence to abort.
Sending 10, 100-byte ICMP Echos to 10.1.1.1, timeout is 2 seconds:
Packet sent with a source address of 10.2.2.2
!!!!!!!!!!
Success rate is 100 percent (10/10), round-trip min/avg/max = 1/3/4 ms
```

Before we mention manual route summarization (not in the syllabus), it is important to know that EIGRP will not automatically summarize external networks unless there is an internal network that will be included in the summary. To better understand this concept, refer to Figure 36.17 below, which illustrates a basic EIGRP network:

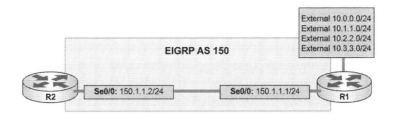

Figure 36.17—Summarising External Networks

Referencing Figure 36.17, R1 is redistributing (which makes them external) and then advertising the 10.0.0.0/24, 10.1.1.0/24, 10.2.2.0/24, and 10.3.3.0/24 external networks via EIGRP. Automatic route summarization is enabled on R1. The initial configuration on R1 is as follows:

```
R1(config)#router eigrp 150
R1(config-router)#redistribute connected metric 8000000 5000 255 1 1514
R1(config-router)#network 150.1.1.1 0.0.0.0
R1(config-router)#exit
```

The `show ip protocols` command shows that EIGRP is enabled for Serial0/0 and is redistributing connected networks. Automatic summarization is also enabled, as illustrated below:

```
R1#show ip protocols
Routing Protocol is "eigrp 150"
  Outgoing update filter list for all interfaces is not set
  Incoming update filter list for all interfaces is not set
  Default networks flagged in outgoing updates
  Default networks accepted from incoming updates
  EIGRP metric weight K1=1, K2=0, K3=1, K4=0, K5=0
  EIGRP maximum hopcount 100
  EIGRP maximum metric variance 1
  Redistributing: connected, eigrp 150
  EIGRP NSF-aware route hold timer is 240s
  Automatic network summarization is in effect
  Maximum path: 4
  Routing for Networks:
    150.1.1.1/32
  Routing Information Sources:
    Gateway         Distance      Last Update
    150.1.1.2             90       00:00:07
  Distance: internal 90 external 170
```

Because the 10.x.x.x/24 prefixes are all external routes, EIGRP will not automatically summarize these prefixes, as illustrated in the previous example. Therefore, EIGRP will not add a summary route to either the topology table or the IP routing table for these entries. This is illustrated in the following output:

```
R1#show ip eigrp topology
IP-EIGRP Topology Table for AS(150)/ID(10.3.3.1)

Codes: P - Passive, A - Active, U - Update, Q - Query, R - Reply,
       r - reply Status, s - sia Status

P 10.0.0.0/24, 1 successors, FD is 1280256
        via Rconnected (1280256/0)
P 10.1.1.0/24, 1 successors, FD is 1280256
        via Rconnected (1280256/0)
P 10.2.2.0/24, 1 successors, FD is 1280256
        via Rconnected (1280256/0)
P 10.3.3.0/24, 1 successors, FD is 1280256
        via Rconnected (1280256/0)

[Truncated Output]
```

The specific route entries are advertised to R2 as external EIGRP routes, as illustrated below:

```
R2#show ip route eigrp
      10.0.0.0/24 is subnetted, 4 subnets
D EX    10.3.3.0 [170/3449856] via 150.1.1.1, 00:07:02, Serial0/0
D EX    10.2.2.0 [170/3449856] via 150.1.1.1, 00:07:02, Serial0/0
```

```
D EX    10.1.1.0 [170/3449856] via 150.1.1.1, 00:07:02, Serial0/0
D EX    10.0.0.0 [170/3449856] via 150.1.1.1, 00:07:02, Serial0/0
```

Now, assume that the 10.0.0.0/24 subnet is an internal network, while the 10.1.1.0/24, 10.2.2.0/24, and 10.3.3.0/24 subnets are external routes. Because one of the routes that will comprise the classful summary address 10.0.0.0/8 is an internal route, EIGRP will create a summary address and include that in the EIGRP topology table and the IP routing table. The show ip protocols command shows that the 10.0.0.0/24 network is now an internal EIGRP network, as illustrated below:

```
R1#show ip protocols
Routing Protocol is "eigrp 150"
  Outgoing update filter list for all interfaces is not set
  Incoming update filter list for all interfaces is not set
  Default networks flagged in outgoing updates
  Default networks accepted from incoming updates
  EIGRP metric weight K1=1, K2=0, K3=1, K4=0, K5=0
  EIGRP maximum hopcount 100
  EIGRP maximum metric variance 1
  Redistributing: connected, eigrp 150
  EIGRP NSF-aware route hold timer is 240s
  Automatic network summarization is in effect
  Automatic address summarization:
    150.1.0.0/16 for Loopback0
      Summarizing with metric 2169856
    10.0.0.0/8 for Serial0/0
      Summarizing with metric 128256
  Maximum path: 4
  Routing for Networks:
    10.0.0.1/32
    150.1.1.1/32
  Routing Information Sources:
    Gateway         Distance      Last Update
    (this router)         90      00:00:05
    150.1.1.2             90      00:00:02
  Distance: internal 90 external 170
```

In the output above, EIGRP automatic summarization has generated a summary address for 10.0.0.0/8 because the 10.0.0.0/24 internal subnet is a part of the aggregate address. The EIGRP topology table displays the external and internal entries, as well as the summary address, as illustrated below:

```
R1#show ip eigrp topology
IP-EIGRP Topology Table for AS(150)/ID(10.3.3.1)

Codes: P - Passive, A - Active, U - Update, Q - Query, R - Reply,
       r - reply Status, s - sia Status

P 10.0.0.0/8, 1 successors, FD is 128256
       via Summary (128256/0), Null0
P 10.0.0.0/24, 1 successors, FD is 128256
```

```
        via Connected, Loopback0
P 10.1.1.0/24, 1 successors, FD is 1280256
        via Rconnected (1280256/0)
P 10.2.2.0/24, 1 successors, FD is 1280256
        via Rconnected (1280256/0)
P 10.3.3.0/24, 1 successors, FD is 1280256
        via Rconnected (1280256/0)

[Truncated Output]
```

This time, only a single route is advertised to R2, as illustrated in the following output:

```
R2#show ip route eigrp
D    10.0.0.0/8 [90/2297856] via 150.1.1.1, 00:04:05, Serial0/0
```

From the perspective of R2, this is simply an internal EIGRP route. In other words, the router does not have any knowledge that the summary address is also comprised of external routes, as illustrated below:

```
R2#show ip route 10.0.0.0 255.0.0.0
Routing entry for 10.0.0.0/8
  Known via "eigrp 150", distance 90, metric 2297856, type internal
  Redistributing via eigrp 150
  Last update from 150.1.1.1 on Serial0/0, 00:05:34 ago
  Routing Descriptor Blocks:
  * 150.1.1.1, from 150.1.1.1, 00:05:34 ago, via Serial0/0
      Route metric is 2297856, traffic share count is 1
      Total delay is 25000 microseconds, minimum bandwidth is 1544 Kbit
      Reliability 255/255, minimum MTU 1500 bytes
      Loading 1/255, Hops 1
```

R2 is able to reach both the internal 10.0.0.0/24 network and the other external 10.*x.x.x*/24 networks via the received summary route, as illustrated below:

```
R2#ping 10.0.0.1

Type escape sequence to abort.
Sending 5, 100-byte ICMP Echos to 10.0.0.1, timeout is 2 seconds:
!!!!!
Success rate is 100 percent (5/5), round-trip min/avg/max = 1/2/4 ms

R2#ping 10.3.3.1

Type escape sequence to abort.
Sending 5, 100-byte ICMP Echos to 10.3.3.1, timeout is 2 seconds:
!!!!!
Success rate is 100 percent (5/5), round-trip min/avg/max = 1/3/4 ms
```

Unlike EIGRP automatic summarization, EIGRP manual route summarization is configured and implemented at the interface level using the `ip summary-address eigrp [ASN] [network] [mask] [distance] [leak-map <name>]` interface configuration command.

By default, an EIGRP summary address is assigned a default administrative distance value of 5. This default assignment can be changed by specifying the desired administrative distance value as specified by the [distance] keyword.

We will not go into further details because manual summarization is outside the CCNA syllabus.

UNDERSTANDING PASSIVE INTERFACES

As stated earlier in this module, when EIGRP is enabled for a network, the router begins to send out Hello packets on all interfaces that fall within the specified network range. This allows EIGRP to discover neighbors dynamically and establish network relationships. This is desired on interfaces that are actually connected to physical media, such as Ethernet and Serial interfaces. However, this default behavior also results in an unnecessary waste of router resources on logical interfaces, such as Loopback interfaces, that will never have any other device connected to them with which the router could ever establish an EIGRP neighbor relationship.

Cisco IOS software allows administrators to use the passive-interface [name|default] router configuration command to specify the named interface as passive, or all interfaces as passive. EIGRP packets are not sent out on passive interfaces; therefore, no neighbor relationship will ever be established between passive interfaces. The following output illustrates how to configure two EIGRP-enabled interfaces as passive on a router:

```
R1(config)#interface Loopback0
R1(config-if)#ip address 10.0.0.1 255.255.255.0
R1(config-if)#exit
R1(config)#interface Loopback1
R1(config-if)#ip address 10.1.1.1 255.255.255.0
R1(config-if)#exit
R1(config)#interface Serial0/0
R1(config-if)#ip address 150.1.1.1 255.255.255.0
R1(config-if)#exit
R1(config)#router eigrp 150
R1(config-router)#no auto-summary
R1(config-router)#network 150.1.1.0 0.0.0.255
R1(config-router)#network 10.0.0.0 0.0.0.255
R1(config-router)#network 10.1.1.0 0.0.0.255
R1(config-router)#passive-interface Loopback0
R1(config-router)#passive-interface Loopback1
R1(config-router)#exit
```

Based on this configuration, Loopback0 and Loopback1 are enabled for EIGRP routing and the directly connected networks will be advertised to EIGRP neighbors. However, no EIGRP packets will be sent by R1 out of these interfaces. Serial0/0, on the other hand, is also configured for EIGRP routing, but EIGRP is allowed to send packets on this interface because it is not a passive interface. All three network entries are installed in the EIGRP topology table, as illustrated below:

```
R1#show ip eigrp topology
IP-EIGRP Topology Table for AS(150)/ID(10.3.3.1)

Codes: P - Passive, A - Active, U - Update, Q - Query, R - Reply,
       r - reply Status, s - sia Status

P 10.1.1.0/24, 1 successors, FD is 128256
        via Connected, Loopback1
P 10.0.0.0/24, 1 successors, FD is 128256
        via Connected, Loopback0
P 150.1.1.0/24, 1 successors, FD is 2169856
        via Connected, Serial0/0
```

However, the output of the show ip eigrp interfaces command shows that EIGRP routing is enabled only for the Serial0/0 interface, as illustrated below:

```
R1#show ip eigrp interfaces
IP-EIGRP interfaces for process 150

                        Xmit Queue    Mean   Pacing Time   Multicast
Pending
Interface     Peers   Un/Reliable   SRTT   Un/Reliable   Flow Timer
Routes
Se0/0           1         0/0         0        0/15           0          0
```

You can also view the interfaces configured as passive in the output of the show ip protocols command, as illustrated below:

```
R1#show ip protocols
Routing Protocol is "eigrp 150"
  Outgoing update filter list for all interfaces is not set
  Incoming update filter list for all interfaces is not set
  Default networks flagged in outgoing updates
  Default networks accepted from incoming updates
  EIGRP metric weight K1=1, K2=0, K3=1, K4=0, K5=0
  EIGRP maximum hopcount 100
  EIGRP maximum metric variance 1
  Redistributing: eigrp 150
  EIGRP NSF-aware route hold timer is 240s
  Automatic network summarization is not in effect
  Maximum path: 4
  Routing for Networks:
    10.0.0.0/24
    10.1.1.0/24
    150.1.1.0/24
  Passive Interface(s):
    Loopback0
    Loopback1
  Routing Information Sources:
    Gateway        Distance      Last Update

  Distance: internal 90 external 170
```

The [default] keyword makes all interfaces passive. Assume that a router is configured with 50 Loopback interfaces configured. If you wanted to make each Loopback interface passive, you would need to add 50 lines of code. The passive-interface default command can be used to make all interfaces passive. Those interfaces that you do want to send EIGRP packets to can then be configured with the no passive-interface [name] command. The following illustrates the use of the passive-interface default command:

```
R1(config)#interface Loopback0
R1(config-if)#ip address 10.0.0.1 255.255.255.0
R1(config-if)#exit
R1(config)#interface Loopback1
R1(config-if)#ip address 10.1.1.1 255.255.255.0
R1(config-if)#exit
R1(config)#interface Loopback3
R1(config-if)#ip address 10.3.3.1 255.255.255.0
R1(config-if)#exit
R1(config)#interface Loopback2
R1(config-if)#ip address 10.2.2.1 255.255.255.0
R1(config-if)#exit
R1(config)#interface Serial0/0
R1(config-if)#ip address 150.1.1.1 255.255.255.0
R1(config-if)#exit
R1(config)#router eigrp 150
R1(config-router)#network 10.0.0.1 255.255.255.0
R1(config-router)#network 10.1.1.1 255.255.255.0
R1(config-router)#network 10.3.3.1 255.255.255.0
R1(config-router)#network 10.2.2.1 255.255.255.0
R1(config-router)#network 150.1.1.1 255.255.255.0
R1(config-router)#passive-interface default
R1(config-router)#no passive-interface Serial0/0
R1(config-router)#exit
```

The show ip protocols can be used to view which interfaces are passive under EIGRP, as illustrated below:

```
R1#show ip protocols
Routing Protocol is "eigrp 150"
  Outgoing update filter list for all interfaces is not set
  Incoming update filter list for all interfaces is not set
  Default networks flagged in outgoing updates
  Default networks accepted from incoming updates
  EIGRP metric weight K1=1, K2=0, K3=1, K4=0, K5=0
  EIGRP maximum hopcount 100
  EIGRP maximum metric variance 1
  Redistributing: eigrp 150
  EIGRP NSF-aware route hold timer is 240s
  Automatic network summarization is not in effect
  Maximum path: 4
  Routing for Networks:
    10.0.0.0/24
    10.1.1.0/24
```

```
       10.2.2.0/24
       10.3.3.0/24
       150.1.1.0/24
     Passive Interface(s):
       Loopback1
       Loopback2
       Loopback3
       Loopback4
     Routing Information Sources:
       Gateway         Distance      Last Update
       (this router)         90      00:02:52
     Distance: internal 90 external 170
```

By using the `passive-interface default` command, the configuration of multiple passive interfaces is simplified and reduced. Used in conjunction with the `no passive-interface Serial0/0` command, EIGRP packets are still sent out on Serial0/0, allowing EIGRP neighbor relationships to be established across that interface, as illustrated below:

```
R1#show ip eigrp neighbors
IP-EIGRP neighbors for process 150
H   Address       Interface  Hold Uptime   SRTT  RTO   Q    Seq
                             (sec)         (ms)        Cnt  Num
0   150.1.1.2     Se0/0      12   00:02:47  1     3000  0    69
```

UNDERSTANDING THE USE OF THE EIGRP ROUTER ID

Unlike OSPF, which uses the router ID (RID) to identify the OSPF neighbor, the primary use of the EIGRP RID is to prevent routing loops. The RID is used to identify the originating router for external routes. If an external route is received with the same RID as the local router, the route is discarded. This feature is designed to reduce the possibility of routing loops in networks where route redistribution is being performed on more than one ASBR.

When determining the RID, EIGRP will select the highest IP address that is configured on the router. If Loopback interfaces are also configured on the router, those interfaces are preferred, since a Loopback interface is the most stable interface that can exist on a router. The RID will never change unless the EIGRP process is removed (i.e., if the RID is manually configured). The RID will always be listed in the EIGRP topology table, as illustrated below:

```
R1#show ip eigrp topology
IP-EIGRP Topology Table for AS(150)/ID(10.3.3.1)

Codes: P - Passive, A - Active, U - Update, Q - Query, R - Reply,
       r - reply Status, s - sia Status

P 10.2.2.0/24, 1 successors, FD is 128256
        via Connected, Loopback2
P 10.3.3.0/24, 1 successors, FD is 128256
        via Connected, Loopback3
P 10.1.1.0/24, 1 successors, FD is 128256
        via Connected, Loopback1
```

```
P 10.0.0.0/24, 1 successors, FD is 128256
       via Connected, Loopback0
P 150.1.1.0/24, 1 successors, FD is 2169856
       via Connected, Serial0/0
```

> **NOTE:** It is important to understand that the RID and the neighbor ID will typically be different, although this may not be the case in routers with a single interface, for example.

The EIGRP RID is configured using the `eigrp router-id [address]` router configuration command. When this command is entered, the RID is automatically updated with the new address in the EIGRP topology table. To demonstrate this point, let's begin by looking at the current RID on the router, as stated in the topology table below:

```
R1#show ip eigrp topology
IP-EIGRP Topology Table for AS(150)/ID(10.3.3.1)

Codes: P - Passive, A - Active, U - Update, Q - Query, R - Reply,
       r - reply Status, s - sia Status

[Truncated Output]
```

A RID of 1.1.1.1 is now configured on the router, as follows:

```
R1(config)#router eigrp 150
R1(config-router)#eigrp router-id 1.1.1.1
R1(config-router)#
*Mar  1 05:50:13.642: %DUAL-5-NBRCHANGE: IP-EIGRP(0) 150: Neighbor
150.1.1.2 (Serial0/0) is down: route configuration changed
*Mar  1 05:50:16.014: %DUAL-5-NBRCHANGE: IP-EIGRP(0) 150: Neighbor
150.1.1.2 (Serial0/0) is up: new adjacency
```

Following the change, the EIGRP neighbor relationship is reset and the new RID is reflected immediately in the EIGRP topology table, as illustrated below:

```
R1#show ip eigrp topology
IP-EIGRP Topology Table for AS(150)/ID(1.1.1.1)

Codes: P - Passive, A - Active, U - Update, Q - Query, R - Reply,
       r - reply Status, s - sia Status

[Truncated Output]
```

When configuring the EIGRP RID, the following should be remembered:

- You cannot configure the RID as 0.0.0.0
- You cannot configure the RID as 255.255.255.255

All external routes that are originated by the router now contain the EIGRP RID. This can be verified in the following output of neighbor router R2:

```
R2#show ip eigrp topology 192.168.254.0/24
IP-EIGRP (AS 150): Topology entry for 192.168.254.0/24
  State is Passive, Query origin flag is 1, 1 Successor(s), FD is 7289856
  Routing Descriptor Blocks:
  150.1.1.1 (Serial0/0), from 150.1.1.1, Send flag is 0x0
      Composite metric is (7289856/6777856), Route is External
      Vector metric:
        Minimum bandwidth is 1544 Kbit
        Total delay is 220000 microseconds
        Reliability is 255/255
        Load is 1/255
        Minimum MTU is 1500
        Hop count is 1
      External data:
        Originating router is 1.1.1.1
        AS number of route is 0
        External protocol is Connected, external metric is 0
        Administrator tag is 0 (0x00000000)
```

The RID is not included for internal EIGRP routes, as illustrated in the following output:

```
R2#show ip eigrp topology 10.3.3.0/24
IP-EIGRP (AS 150): Topology entry for 10.3.3.0/24
  State is Passive, Query origin flag is 1, 1 Successor(s), FD is 2297856
  Routing Descriptor Blocks:
  150.1.1.1 (Serial0/0), from 150.1.1.1, Send flag is 0x0
      Composite metric is (2297856/128256), Route is Internal
      Vector metric:
        Minimum bandwidth is 1544 Kbit
        Total delay is 25000 microseconds
        Reliability is 255/255
        Load is 1/255
        Minimum MTU is 1500
        Hop count is 1
```

TROUBLESHOOTING EIGRP

Neighbor Relationships

It is important to understand that simply enabling EIGRP between two or more routers does not guarantee that a neighbor relationship will be established. In addition to certain parameters-matching, additional factors can also result in a failure of EIGRP neighbor relationship establishment. The EIGRP neighbor relationship may not establish due to any of the following:

- The neighbor routers are not on a common subnet
- Mismatched primary and secondary subnets
- Mismatched K values
- Mismatched ASN
- Access control lists are filtering EIGRP packets

- Physical Layer issues
- Data Link Layer issues
- Mismatched authentication parameters

Uncommon subnet issues are one of the most common problems experienced when attempting to establish EIGRP neighbor relationships. When EIGRP cannot establish a neighbor relationship because of an uncommon subnet, the following error message will be printed on the console, or will be logged by the router or switch:

```
*Mar  2 22:12:46.589 CST: IP-EIGRP(Default-IP-Routing-Table:1): Neighbor
150.1.1.2 not on common subnet for FastEthernet0/0
```

The most common reason for the neighbor routers being on an uncommon subnet is a misconfiguration issue. It may be that the router interfaces have been accidentally configured on two different subnets. However, if the neighbors are connected via a VLAN, it is possible that Multicast packets could be leaking between VLANs, resulting in this error. The first troubleshooting step, however, simply would be to verify the interface configuration on the devices. Following this, additional troubleshooting steps, such as VLAN troubleshooting (if applicable) could be undertaken to isolate and resolve the issue.

Another common reason for this error message is using secondary addresses when attempting to establish EIGRP neighbor relationships. Again, the simplest way to troubleshoot such issues is to verify the router or switch configurations. For example, assume the error message above was being printed on the console of the local router. The first troubleshooting step would be to validate the IP addresses configured on the interface, as follows:

```
R1#show running-config interface FastEthernet0/0
Building configuration...

Current configuration : 140 bytes
!
interface FastEthernet0/0
 ip address 150.2.2.1 255.255.255.0
 duplex auto
 speed auto
end
```

Next, validate that the configuration is the same on the device with the IP address 150.1.1.2, as follows:

```
R2#show running-config interface FastEthernet0/0
Building configuration...

Current configuration : 140 bytes
!
interface FastEthernet0/0
 ip address 150.2.2.2 255.255.255.0 secondary
 ip address 150.1.1.2 255.255.255.0
 duplex auto
```

```
speed auto
end
```

From the output above, you can see that the primary subnet on R1 is the secondary subnet on the local router. EIGRP will not establish neighbor relationships using a secondary address. The resolution for this issue simply would be to correct the IP addressing configuration under the FastEthernet0/0 interface of R2, as follows:

```
R2#config terminal
Enter configuration commands, one per line.  End with CNTL/Z.
R2(config)#interface FastEthernet0/0
R2(config-if)#ip address 150.2.2.2 255.255.255.0
R2(config-if)#ip address 150.1.1.2 255.255.255.0 secondary
R2(config-if)#end
*Oct 20 03:10:27.185 CST: %DUAL-5-NBRCHANGE: IP-EIGRP(0) 1: Neighbor
150.2.2.1 (FastEthernet0/0) is up: new adjacency
```

EIGRP K values are constants that are used to distribute weight to different path aspects, which may be included in the composite EIGRP metric. Once again, the default values for the K values are K1 = K3 = 1 and K2 = K4 = K5 = 0. If changed on one router or switch, then these values must be adjusted for all other routers or switches within the autonomous system. The default EIGRP K values can be viewed using the show ip protocols command, as illustrated below:

```
R1#show ip protocols
Routing Protocol is "eigrp 150"
  Outgoing update filter list for all interfaces is not set
  Incoming update filter list for all interfaces is 1
  Default networks flagged in outgoing updates
  Default networks accepted from incoming updates
  EIGRP metric weight K1=1, K2=0, K3=1, K4=0, K5=0
  EIGRP maximum hopcount 100
  EIGRP maximum metric variance 1
  Redistributing: eigrp 150, ospf 1
  EIGRP NSF-aware route hold timer is 240s
  Automatic network summarization is not in effect
  Maximum path: 4
  Routing for Networks:
    10.1.0.0/24
    172.16.1.0/30
  Routing Information Sources:
    Gateway         Distance      Last Update
    (this router)         90      15:59:19
    172.16.0.2            90      12:51:56
    172.16.1.2            90      00:27:17
  Distance: internal 90 external 170
```

When K values are reset on a router, all neighbor relationships for the local router will be reset. If the values are not consistent on all routers following the reset, the following error message will be printed on the console, and the EIGRP neighbor relationship(s) will not be established:

```
*Oct 20 03:19:14.140 CST: %DUAL-5-NBRCHANGE: IP-EIGRP(0) 1: Neighbor
150.2.2.1 (FastEthernet0/0) is down: Interface Goodbye received

*Oct 20 03:19:18.732 CST: %DUAL-5-NBRCHANGE: IP-EIGRP(0) 1: Neighbor
150.2.2.1 (FastEthernet0/0) is down: K-value mismatch
```

NOTE: While EIGRP K values can be adjusted using the `metric-weights` command, this is not recommended without assistance from seasoned network engineers or the Technical Assistance Centre (TAC).

Unlike OSPF, which uses a locally significant process ID, EIGRP requires the same ASN (among other variables) when establishing neighbor relationships with other routers. Troubleshoot such issues by comparing configurations of devices and ensuring that the ASN (among other variables) is consistent between routers that should establish neighbor relationships. A good indicator that neighbors are in a different AS would be a lack of bidirectional Hellos, even in the presence of basic IP connectivity between the routers. This can be validated using the `show ip eigrp traffic` command, the output of which is illustrated in the section that follows.

ACLs and other filters are also common causes for routers failing to establish EIGRP neighbor relationships. Check router configurations and those of intermediate devices to ensure that EIGRP or Multicast packets are not filtered. A very useful troubleshooting command to use is the `show ip eigrp traffic` command. This command provides statistics on all EIGRP packets. Assume, for example, that you have verified basic connectivity and configurations between two devices, but the EIGRP neighbor relationship is still not up. In that case, you could use this command to check to see whether the routers are exchanging Hello packets, before enabling debugging on the local device, as illustrated below:

```
R2#show ip eigrp traffic
IP-EIGRP Traffic Statistics for AS 2
  Hellos sent/received: 144/0
  Updates sent/received: 0/0
  Queries sent/received: 0/0
  Replies sent/received: 0/0
  Acks sent/received: 0/0
  SIA-Queries sent/received: 0/0
  SIA-Replies sent/received: 0/0
  Hello Process ID: 149
  PDM Process ID: 120
  IP Socket queue:   0/2000/0/0 (current/max/highest/drops)
  Eigrp input queue: 0/2000/0/0 (current/max/highest/drops)
```

In the output above, notice that the local router has not received any Hello packets, although it has sent out 144 Hellos. Assuming that you have verified IP connectivity between the two devices, as well as the configuration, you could also check ACL configurations on the local routers, as well as intermediate devices (if applicable), to ensure that EIGRP or Multicast traffic is not being filtered. For example, you might find an ACL that is configured to deny Class D and Class E traffic, while allowing all other traffic, such as the following ACL:

```
R2#show ip access-lists
Extended IP access list 100
    10 deny ip 224.0.0.0 15.255.255.255 any
    20 deny ip any 224.0.0.0 15.255.255.255 (47 matches)
    30 permit ip any any (27 matches)
```

Physical and Data Link Layer issues, and ways in which these can affect routing protocols and other traffic, have been described in detail in previous modules. You can troubleshoot these issues using the show interfaces, show interfaces counters, show vlan, and show spanning-tree commands, among other commands described in those modules. To avoid being redundant, we will not restate the Physical and Data Link Layer troubleshooting steps.

Finally, common authentication configuration mistakes include using different key IDs when configuring key chains and specifying different or mismatched passwords. When authentication is enabled under an interface, the EIGRP neighbor relationships are reset and reinitialized. If previously established neighbor relationships do not come up following authentication implementation, verify the authentication configuration parameters by looking at the running configuration or using the show key chain and show ip eigrp interfaces detail [name] commands on the router. Following is a sample output of the information that is printed by the show key chain command:

```
R2#show key chain
Key-chain EIGRP-1:
    key 1 -- text "eigrp-1"
        accept lifetime (always valid) - (always valid) [valid now]
        send lifetime (always valid) - (always valid) [valid now]
Key-chain EIGRP-2:
    key 1 -- text "eigrp-2"
        accept lifetime (00:00:01 UTC Nov 1 2010) - (infinite)
        send lifetime (00:00:01 UTC Nov 1 2010) - (infinite)
Key-chain EIGRP-3:
    key 1 -- text "eigrp-3"
        accept lifetime (00:00:01 UTC Dec 1 2010) - (00:00:01 UTC Dec 31 2010)
        send lifetime (00:00:01 UTC Dec 1 2010) - (00:00:01 UTC Dec 31 2010)
```

The following is a sample output of the information that is printed by the show ip eigrp interfaces detail [name] command:

```
R2#show ip eigrp interfaces detail Serial0/0
IP-EIGRP interfaces for process 1
                  Xmit Queue   Mean   Pacing Time   Multicast    Pending
Interface Peers Un/Reliable  SRTT  Un/Reliable  Flow Timer   Routes
Se0/0      0        0/0        0        0/1          0            0
    Hello interval is 5 sec
    Next xmit serial <none>
    Un/reliable mcasts: 0/0  Un/reliable ucasts: 0/0
    Mcast exceptions: 0  CR packets: 0  ACKs suppressed: 0
    Retransmissions sent: 0  Out-of-sequence rcvd: 0
```

```
Authentication mode is md5, key-chain is "EIGRP-1"
Use unicast
```

When troubleshooting in general, it is recommended that you use show commands in Cisco IOS software instead of enabling debug commands. While debugging provides real-time information, it is very processor intensive, and it could result in high CPU utilization of the device and, in some cases, even crashing the device. In addition to show commands, you should also pay attention to the various error messages that are printed by the software, as these provide useful information that can be used to troubleshoot and isolate the root cause of the problem.

Troubleshooting Route Installation

There are instances where you might notice that EIGRP is not installing certain routes into the routing table. For the most part, this is typically due to some misconfigurations versus a protocol failure. Some common reasons for route installation failure include the following:

- The same route is received via another protocol with a lower administrative distance
- EIGRP summarization
- Duplicate router IDs are present within the EIGRP domain
- The routes do not meet the Feasibility Condition

The administrative distance (AD) concept is used to determine how reliable the route source is. The lower the AD, the more reliable the route source is. If the same route is received from three different protocols, the route with the lowest AD will be installed into the routing table. When using EIGRP, keep in mind that EIGRP uses different AD values for summary, internal, and external routes. If you are running multiple routing protocols, it is important to ensure that you understand AD values and how they impact routing table population. This is especially of concern when you are redistributing routes between multiple routing protocols.

By default, EIGRP automatically summarizes at classful boundaries and creates a summary route pointing to the Null0 interface. Because the summary is installed with a default AD value of 5, any other similar dynamically received routes will not be installed into the routing table. Consider the topology illustrated in Figure 36.18 below, for example:

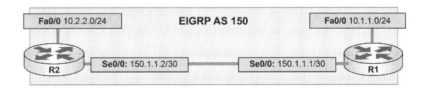

Figure 36.18—EIGRP Automatic Summarization

Referencing the diagram illustrated in Figure 36.18, the 150.1.1.0./30 subnet separates 10.1.1.0/24 and 10.2.2.0/24. When automatic summarization is enabled, both R1 and R2 will summarize the 10.1.1.0/24 and 10.2.2.0/24 subnets, respectively, to 10.0.0.0/8. This summary route will be installed into the routing table with an AD of 5 and a next-hop interface of Null0. This lower administrative distance value will prevent either router from accepting or installing the 10.0.0.0/8 summary from the other router, as illustrated in the following output:

```
R2#debug eigrp fsm
EIGRP FSM Events/Actions debugging is on
R2#
R2#
*Mar 13 03:24:31.983: %DUAL-5-NBRCHANGE: IP-EIGRP(0) 1: Neighbor
150.1.1.1 (FastEthernet0/0) is up: new adjacency
*Mar 13 03:24:33.995: DUAL: dest(10.0.0.0/8) not active
*Mar 13 03:24:33.995: DUAL: rcvupdate: 10.0.0.0/8 via 150.1.1.1 metric
156160/128256
*Mar 13 03:24:33.995: DUAL: Find FS for dest 10.0.0.0/8. FD is 128256, RD
is 128256
*Mar 13 03:24:33.995: DUAL:    0.0.0.0 metric 128256/0
*Mar 13 03:24:33.995: DUAL:    150.1.1.1 metric 156160/128256 found Dmin
is 128256
*Mar 13 03:24:33.999: DUAL: RT installed 10.0.0.0/8 via 0.0.0.0
```

In the debug output above, the local router receives the 10.0.0.0/8 route from neighbor 150.1.1.1 with a route metric of 156160/128256. However, DUAL also has the same route locally, due to summarization, and this route has a route metric of 128256/0. The local route is therefore installed into the routing table instead because it has the better metric. The same would also be applicable on R1, which would install its local 10.0.0.0/8 route into the RIB instead. The result is that neither router would be able to ping the 10.x.x.x subnet of the other router. To resolve this issue, automatic summarization should be disabled using the `no auto-summary` command on both of the routers, allowing the specific route entries to be advertised instead.

The primary use of the EIGRP router ID (RID) is to prevent routing loops. The RID is used to identify the originating router for external routes. If an external route is received with the same RID as the local router, the route will be discarded. However, duplicate RIDs do not affect any internal EIGRP routes. This feature is designed to reduce the possibility of routing loops in networks where route redistribution is being performed on more than one ASBR. The originating RID can be viewed in the output of the `show ip eigrp topology` command, as illustrated below:

```
R1#show ip eigrp topology 2.2.2.2 255.255.255.255
IP-EIGRP (AS 1): Topology entry for 2.2.2.2/32
  State is Passive, Query origin flag is 1, 1 Successor(s), FD is 156160
  Routing Descriptor Blocks:
  150.1.1.2 (FastEthernet0/0), from 150.1.1.2, Send flag is 0x0
      Composite metric is (156160/128256), Route is External
      Vector metric:
        Minimum bandwidth is 100000 Kbit
        Total delay is 5100 microseconds
        Reliability is 255/255
        Load is 1/255
        Minimum MTU is 1500
        Hop count is 1
```

```
External data:
  Originating router is 2.2.2.2
  AS number of route is 0
  External protocol is Connected, external metric is 0
  Administrator tag is 0 (0x00000000)
```

If you suspect a potential duplicate RID issue, you can check the events in the EIGRP event log to see if any routes have been rejected because of a duplicate RID. The following illustrates a sample output of the EIGRP event log, showing routes that have been rejected because they were received from a router with the same RID as the local router:

```
R2#show ip eigrp events
Event information for AS 1:

21    03:05:39.747 Ignored route, neighbor info: 10.0.0.1 Serial0/0
22    03:05:39.747 Ignored route, dup router: 150.1.1.254
23    03:05:06.659 Ignored route, metric: 192.168.2.0 284160
24    03:05:06.659 Ignored route, neighbor info: 10.0.0.1 Serial0/0
25    03:05:06.659 Ignored route, dup router: 150.1.1.254
26    03:04:33.311 Ignored route, metric: 192.168.1.0 284160
27    03:04:33.311 Ignored route, neighbor info: 10.0.0.1 Serial0/0
28    03:04:33.311 Ignored route, dup router: 150.1.1.254
[Truncated Output]
```

The resolution for the solution above would be to change the RID on neighbor router 10.0.0.1 or on the local router, depending upon which one of the two has been incorrectly configured.

Finally, it is important to remember that EIGRP will not install routes into the routing table if they do not meet the Feasibility Condition. This is true even if the variance command has been configured on the local router. It is a common misconception that issuing the variance command will allow EIGRP to load share over any paths whose route metric is x times that of the successor metric. Consider the topology illustrated in Figure 36.19 below, for example:

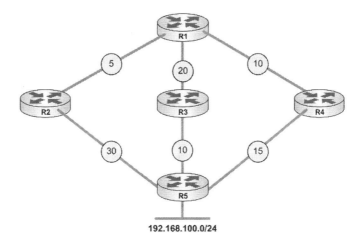

Figure 36.19—Understanding the Feasibility Condition

Figure 36.19 shows a basic network that includes metrics from R1 to the 192.168.100.0/24 subnet. Referencing Figure 36.19, Table 36.5 below displays the Reported Distance and Feasible Distance values as seen on R1 for the 192.168.100.0/24 network:

Table 36.5—R1 Paths and Distances

Network Path	R1 Neighbor	Neighbor Metric (RD)	R1 Feasible Distance
R1—R2—R5	R2	30	35
R1—R3—R5	R3	10	30
R1—R4—R5	R4	15	25

R1 has been configured to load share across all paths and the `variance 2` command is added to the router configuration. This allows EIGRP to load share across paths with up to twice the metric of the Successor route, which would include all three paths based on the default metric calculation. However, despite this configuration, only two paths will be installed and used.

First, R1 will select the path through R4 as the Successor route based on the FD for the route, which is 25. This route will be placed into the IP routing table as well as the EIGRP topology table. The metric for neighbor R3 to the 192.168.100.0/24 network, also referred to as the Reported Distance or Advertised Distance, is 10. This is less than the FD, and so this route meets the FC and is placed into the EIGRP topology table.

The metric for neighbor R2 to the 192.168.100.0/24 network is 30. This value is higher than the FD of 25. This route does not meet the FC and is not considered a Feasible Successor. The route, however, is still placed into the EIGRP topology table. However, the path will not be used for load sharing, even though the metric falls within the range specified by the configuration of the `variance 2` EIGRP router configuration command. In such situations, consider using EIGRP offset lists to ensure that all routes are considered.

Troubleshooting Route Advertisement

There are times when it may seem that EIGRP is either not advertising the networks that it has been configured to advertise or is advertising networks that it has not been configured to advertise. For the most part, such issues are typically due to router and switch misconfigurations. There are several reasons why EIGRP might not advertise a network that it has been configured to advertise. Some of these reasons include the following:

- Distribute lists (outside CCNA syllabus)
- Split horizon
- Summarization

Incorrectly configured distribute lists are one reason why EIGRP might not advertise a network that it has been configured to advertise. When configuring distribute lists, ensure that all networks that should be advertised are permitted by the referenced IP ACL or IP Prefix List.

Another common issue pertaining to network advertisement when using EIGRP is the default behavior of split horizon. Split horizon is a Distance Vector protocol feature that mandates that routing information cannot be sent back out of the same interface through which it was received. This prevents the re-advertising of information back to the source from which it was learned, effectively preventing routing loops. This concept is illustrated in Figure 36.20 below:

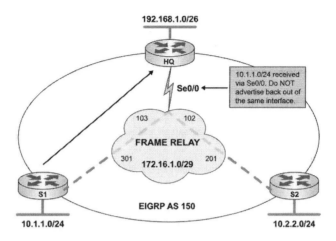

Figure 36.20—EIGRP Split Horizon

The topology in Figure 36.20 illustrates a classic hub-and-spoke network, with router HQ as the hub router and routers S1 and S2 as the two spoke routers. On the Frame Relay WAN, each spoke router has a single DLCI provisioned between itself and the HQ router in a partial-mesh topology. By default, EIGRP split horizon is enabled for WAN interfaces connected to packet-switched networks, such as Frame Relay. This means that the HQ router will not advertise routing information learned on Serial0/0 out of the same interface.

The effect of this default behavior is that the HQ router will not advertise the 10.1.1.0/24 prefix received from S1 to S2 because the route is received via the Serial0/0 interface, and the split horizon feature prevents the router from advertising information learned on that interface back out of the same interface. The same is also applicable for the 10.2.2.0/24 prefix the HQ router receives from S2. The recommended solution for this problem would be to disable the split horizon feature on the WAN interface using the `no ip split-horizon eigrp [asn]` interface configuration command on the HQ router.

By default, automatic summarization at the classful boundary is enabled for EIGRP. This can be validated using the `show ip protocols` command. In addition to automatic summarization, EIGRP also supports manual summarization at the interface level. Regardless of the method implemented, summarization prevents the more specific route entries that are encompassed by the summary from being advertised to neighbor routers. If route summarization is configured incorrectly, it may appear that EIGRP is not advertising certain networks. For example, consider the basic network topology that is illustrated in Figure 36.21 below:

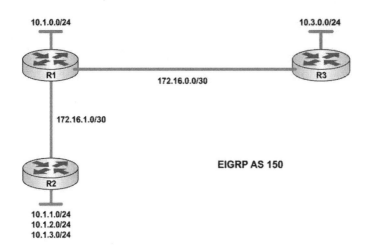

Figure 36.21—EIGRP Summarization

Referencing Figure 36.21, all routers reside in EIGRP Autonomous System 150. R2 is advertising the 10.1.1.0/24, 10.1.2.0/24, and 10.1.3.0/24 subnets to R1 via EIGRP. R1, which also has an interface assigned to the 10.1.0.0/24 subnet, should in turn advertise these subnets to R3. The EIGRP configuration on router R2 has been implemented as follows:

```
R2(config)#router eigrp 150
R2(config-router)#network 10.1.1.0 0.0.0.255
R2(config-router)#network 10.1.2.0 0.0.0.255
R2(config-router)#network 10.1.3.0 0.0.0.255
R2(config-router)#network 172.16.1.0 0.0.0.3
R2(config-router)#no auto-summary
R2(config-router)#exit
```

The EIGRP configuration on R1 has been implemented as follows:

```
R1(config)#router eigrp 150
R1(config-router)#network 10.1.0.0 0.0.0.255
R1(config-router)#network 172.16.0.0 0.0.0.3
R1(config-router)#network 172.16.1.0 0.0.0.3
R1(config-router)#exit
```

Finally, the EIGRP configuration on R3 has been implemented as follows:

```
R3(config)#router eigrp 150
R3(config-router)#network 172.16.0.0 0.0.0.3
R3(config-router)#no auto-summary
R3(config-router)#exit
```

After this configuration, the routing table on R2 displays the following entries:

```
R2#show ip route eigrp
     172.16.0.0/30 is subnetted, 2 subnets
D       172.16.0.0 [90/2172416] via 172.16.1.1, 00:02:38, FastEthernet0/0
```

```
         10.0.0.0/8 is variably subnetted, 4 subnets, 2 masks
D            10.0.0.0/8 [90/156160] via 172.16.1.1, 00:00:36, FastEthernet0/0
```

The routing table on R1 displays the following entries:

```
R1#show ip route eigrp
         172.16.0.0/16 is variably subnetted, 3 subnets, 2 masks
D            172.16.0.0/16 is a summary, 00:01:01, Null0
         10.0.0.0/8 is variably subnetted, 6 subnets, 2 masks
D            10.1.3.0/24 [90/156160] via 172.16.1.2, 00:21:01, FastEthernet0/0
D            10.3.0.0/24 [90/2297856] via 172.16.0.2, 00:00:39, Serial0/0
D            10.1.2.0/24 [90/156160] via 172.16.1.2, 00:21:01, FastEthernet0/0
D            10.1.1.0/24 [90/156160] via 172.16.1.2, 00:21:01, FastEthernet0/0
D            10.0.0.0/8 is a summary, 00:01:01, Null0
```

Finally, the routing table on R3 displays the following entries:

```
R3#show ip route eigrp
         172.16.0.0/30 is subnetted, 2 subnets
D            172.16.1.0 [90/2172416] via 172.16.0.1, 00:21:21, Serial0/0
         10.0.0.0/8 is variably subnetted, 2 subnets, 2 masks
D            10.0.0.0/8 [90/2297856] via 172.16.0.1, 00:01:15, Serial0/0
```

Because summarization is enabled on R1, it appears that the EIGRP is no longer advertising the specific subnets encompassed by the 10.0.0.0/8 summary. To allow the specific subnets to be advertised via EIGRP, automatic summarization should be disabled on R1, as illustrated below:

```
R1(config)#router eigrp 150
R1(config-router)#no auto-summary
R1(config-router)#exit
```

After this, the routing table on R3 would display the following route entries:

```
R3#show ip route eigrp
         172.16.0.0/30 is subnetted, 2 subnets
D            172.16.1.0 [90/2172416] via 172.16.0.1, 00:00:09, Serial0/0
         10.0.0.0/24 is subnetted, 5 subnets
D            10.1.3.0 [90/2300416] via 172.16.0.1, 00:00:09, Serial0/0
D            10.1.2.0 [90/2300416] via 172.16.0.1, 00:00:09, Serial0/0
D            10.1.1.0 [90/2300416] via 172.16.0.1, 00:00:09, Serial0/0
D            10.1.0.0 [90/2297856] via 172.16.0.1, 00:00:09, Serial0/0
```

The same would also be applicable to R2, which would now display the specific entries for the 10.1.0.0/24 and 10.3.0.0/24 subnets, as follows:

```
R2#show ip route eigrp
         172.16.0.0/30 is subnetted, 2 subnets
D            172.16.0.0 [90/2172416] via 172.16.1.1, 00:00:10, FastEthernet0/0
         10.0.0.0/24 is subnetted, 5 subnets
D            10.3.0.0 [90/2300416] via 172.16.1.1, 00:00:10, FastEthernet0/0
D            10.1.0.0 [90/156160] via 172.16.1.1, 00:00:10, FastEthernet0/0
```

Debugging EIGRP Routing Issues

While primary emphasis has been placed on the use of show commands in the previous sections, this final section describes some of the debugging commands that can also be used to troubleshoot EIGRP. Keep in mind, however, that debugging is very processor intensive and should be used only as a last resort (i.e., after all show commands and other troubleshooting methods and tools have been applied or attempted).

The debug ip routing [acl|static] command is a powerful troubleshooting tool and command. It should be noted, however, that while this command is not EIGRP-specific, it provides useful and detailed information on routing table events. Following is a sample of the information that is printed by this command:

```
R1#debug ip routing
IP routing debugging is on
R1#
*Mar  3 23:03:35.673: %LINEPROTO-5-UPDOWN: Line protocol on Interface
FastEthernet0/0, changed state to down

*Mar  3 23:03:35.673: RT: is_up: FastEthernet0/0 0 state: 4 sub state: 1
line: 0 has_route: True
*Mar  3 23:03:35.677: RT: interface FastEthernet0/0 removed from routing
table
*Mar  3 23:03:35.677: RT: del 172.16.1.0/30 via 0.0.0.0, connected metric
[0/0]
*Mar  3 23:03:35.677: RT: delete subnet route to 172.16.1.0/30
*Mar  3 23:03:35.677: RT: NET-RED 172.16.1.0/30
*Mar  3 23:03:35.677: RT: Pruning routes for FastEthernet0/0 (3)
*Mar  3 23:03:35.689: RT: delete route to 10.1.3.0 via 172.16.1.2,
FastEthernet0/0
*Mar  3 23:03:35.689: RT: no routes to 10.1.3.0, flushing
*Mar  3 23:03:35.689: RT: NET-RED 10.1.3.0/24
*Mar  3 23:03:35.689: RT: delete route to 10.1.2.0 via 172.16.1.2,
FastEthernet0/0
*Mar  3 23:03:35.689: RT: no routes to 10.1.2.0, flushing
*Mar  3 23:03:35.689: RT: NET-RED 10.1.2.0/24
*Mar  3 23:03:35.689: RT: delete route to 10.1.1.0 via 172.16.1.2,
FastEthernet0/0
*Mar  3 23:03:35.689: RT: no routes to 10.1.1.0, flushing
*Mar  3 23:03:35.693: RT: NET-RED 10.1.1.0/24

*Mar  3 23:03:35.693: %DUAL-5-NBRCHANGE: IP-EIGRP(0) 150: Neighbor
172.16.1.2 (FastEthernet0/0) is down: interface down

*Mar  3 23:03:39.599: %DUAL-5-NBRCHANGE: IP-EIGRP(0) 150: Neighbor
172.16.1.2 (FastEthernet0/0) is up: new adjacency
*Mar  3 23:03:40.601: %LINEPROTO-5-UPDOWN: Line protocol on Interface
FastEthernet0/0, changed state to up

*Mar  3 23:03:40.601: RT: is_up: FastEthernet0/0 1 state: 4 sub state: 1
line: 1 has_route: False
*Mar  3 23:03:40.605: RT: SET_LAST_RDB for 172.16.1.0/30
  NEW rdb: is directly connected
```

```
*Mar  3 23:03:40.605: RT: add 172.16.1.0/30 via 0.0.0.0, connected metric
[0/0]
*Mar  3 23:03:40.605: RT: NET-RED 172.16.1.0/30
*Mar  3 23:03:40.605: RT: interface FastEthernet0/0 added to routing
table
*Mar  3 23:03:49.119: RT: SET_LAST_RDB for 10.1.1.0/24
  NEW rdb: via 172.16.1.2
*Mar  3 23:03:49.119: RT: add 10.1.1.0/24 via 172.16.1.2, eigrp metric
[90/156160]
```

You can use this command in conjunction with an ACL to view information about the route or routes referenced in the ACL. Additionally, the same command can also be used for troubleshooting static route events on the local device. As a side note, instead of using this command, if you are running EIGRP, consider using the show ip eigrp events command instead, as it provides a history of EIGRP internal events and can be used to troubleshoot SIA issues, as well as route flaps and other events. Following is a sample of the information that is printed by this command:

```
R1#show ip eigrp events
Event information for AS 150:
1    23:03:49.135 Ignored route, metric: 192.168.3.0 28160
2    23:03:49.135 Ignored route, metric: 192.168.2.0 28160
3    23:03:49.135 Ignored route, metric: 192.168.1.0 28160
4    23:03:49.131 Rcv EOT update src/seq: 172.16.1.2 85
5    23:03:49.127 Change queue emptied, entries: 3
6    23:03:49.127 Ignored route, metric: 192.168.3.0 28160
7    23:03:49.127 Ignored route, metric: 192.168.2.0 28160
8    23:03:49.127 Ignored route, metric: 192.168.1.0 28160
9    23:03:49.127 Metric set: 10.1.3.0/24 156160
10   23:03:49.127 Update reason, delay: new if 4294967295
11   23:03:49.127 Update sent, RD: 10.1.3.0/24 4294967295
12   23:03:49.127 Update reason, delay: metric chg 4294967295
13   23:03:49.127 Update sent, RD: 10.1.3.0/24 4294967295
14   23:03:49.123 Route install: 10.1.3.0/24 172.16.1.2
15   23:03:49.123 Find FS: 10.1.3.0/24 4294967295
16   23:03:49.123 Rcv update met/succmet: 156160 128256
17   23:03:49.123 Rcv update dest/nh: 10.1.3.0/24 172.16.1.2
18   23:03:49.123 Metric set: 10.1.3.0/24 4294967295
19   23:03:49.123 Metric set: 10.1.2.0/24 156160
20   23:03:49.123 Update reason, delay: new if 4294967295
21   23:03:49.123 Update sent, RD: 10.1.2.0/24 4294967295
22   23:03:49.123 Update reason, delay: metric chg 4294967295

[Truncated Output]
```

In addition to the debug ip routing command, two additional EIGRP-specific debugging commands are also available in Cisco IOS software. The debug eigrp command can be used to provide real-time information on the DUAL Finite State Machine, EIGRP neighbor relationships, Non-Stop Forwarding events, packets, and transmission events. The options that are available with this command are illustrated below:

```
R1#debug eigrp ?
  fsm        EIGRP Dual Finite State Machine events/actions
  neighbors  EIGRP neighbors
  nsf        EIGRP Non-Stop Forwarding events/actions
  packets    EIGRP packets
  transmit   EIGRP transmission events
```

In addition to the debug eigrp command, the debug ip eigrp command prints detailed information on EIGRP route events, such as how EIGRP processes incoming updates. The additional keywords that can be used in conjunction with this command are illustrated below:

```
R1#debug ip eigrp ?
  <1-65535>      Autonomous System
  neighbor       IP-EIGRP neighbor debugging
  notifications  IP-EIGRP event notifications
  summary        IP-EIGRP summary route processing
  vrf            Select a VPN Routing/Forwarding instance
  <cr>
```

In conclusion, the following is a sample output of the debug ip eigrp command:

```
R1#debug ip eigrp
IP-EIGRP Route Events debugging is on
R1#
*Mar  3 23:49:47.028: %DUAL-5-NBRCHANGE: IP-EIGRP(0) 150: Neighbor
172.16.1.2 (FastEthernet0/0) is up: new adjacency
*Mar  3 23:49:47.044: IP-EIGRP(Default-IP-Routing-Table:150): 10.1.0.0/24
- do advertise out FastEthernet0/0
*Mar  3 23:49:47.044: IP-EIGRP(Default-IP-Routing-Table:150): Int
10.1.0.0/24 metric 128256 - 256 128000
*Mar  3 23:49:48.030: %LINEPROTO-5-UPDOWN: Line protocol on Interface
FastEthernet0/0, changed state to up
*Mar  3 23:49:56.179: IP-EIGRP(Default-IP-Routing-Table:150): Processing
incoming UPDATE packet
*Mar  3 23:49:56.544: IP-EIGRP(Default-IP-Routing-Table:150): Processing
incoming UPDATE packet
*Mar  3 23:49:56.544: IP-EIGRP(Default-IP-Routing-Table:150): Int
10.1.1.0/24 M 156160 - 25600 130560 SM 128256 - 256 128000
*Mar  3 23:49:56.544: IP-EIGRP(Default-IP-Routing-Table:150): route
installed for 10.1.1.0  ()
*Mar  3 23:49:56.544: IP-EIGRP(Default-IP-Routing-Table:150): Int
10.1.2.0/24 M 156160 - 25600 130560 SM 128256 - 256 128000
*Mar  3 23:49:56.548: IP-EIGRP(Default-IP-Routing-Table:150): route
installed for 10.1.2.0  ()
*Mar  3 23:49:56.548: IP-EIGRP(Default-IP-Routing-Table:150): Int
10.1.3.0/24 M 156160 - 25600 130560 SM 128256 - 256 128000

[Truncated Output]
```

Take today's exam at **https://www.in60days.com/free/ccnain60days/**

DAY 36 LAB

EIGRP Lab

Topology

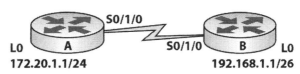

10.0.0.0/30

L0   **A**   S0/1/0   S0/1/0   **B**   L0

172.20.1.1/24   **192.168.1.1/26**

Purpose
Learn how to configure basic EIGRP.

Walkthrough
1. Configure all IP addresses based on the topology above. Make sure you can ping across the Serial link.

2. Configure EIGRP with AS 30 on each router.

```
RouterA(config)#router eigrp 30
RouterA(config-router)#net 172.20.0.0
RouterA(config-router)#net 10.0.0.0
RouterA(config-router)#^Z
RouterA#

RouterB#conf t
Enter configuration commands, one per line.  End with CNTL/Z.
RouterB(config)#router eigrp 30
RouterB(config-router)#net 10.0.0.0
%DUAL-5-NBRCHANGE: IP-EIGRP 30: Neighbor 10.0.0.1 (Serial0/1/0) is up:
new adjacency
RouterB(config-router)#net 192.168.1.0
```

3. Check the routing table on each router.

```
RouterA#sh ip route
Codes: C - connected, S - static, I - IGRP, R - RIP, M - mobile, B
- BGP
       D - EIGRP, EX - EIGRP external, O - OSPF, IA - OSPF inter area
       N1 - OSPF NSSA external type 1, N2 - OSPF NSSA external type 2
       E1 - OSPF external type 1, E2 - OSPF external type 2, E - EGP
       i - IS-IS, L1 - IS-IS level-1, L2 - IS-IS level-2, ia - IS-IS
inter area
       * - candidate default, U - per-user static route, o - ODR
       P - periodic downloaded static route

Gateway of last resort is not set
```

```
      10.0.0.0/8 is variably subnetted, 2 subnets, 2 masks
D        10.0.0.0/8 is a summary, 00:01:43, Null0
C        10.0.0.0/30 is directly connected, Serial0/1/0
      172.20.0.0/16 is variably subnetted, 2 subnets, 2 masks
D        172.20.0.0/16 is a summary, 00:01:43, Null0
C        172.20.1.0/24 is directly connected, Loopback0
D     192.168.1.0/24 [90/20640000] via 10.0.0.2, 00:00:49, Serial0/1/0
RouterA

RouterB#show ip route
[Truncated Output]

      10.0.0.0/8 is variably subnetted, 2 subnets, 2 masks
D        10.0.0.0/8 is a summary, 00:01:21, Null0
C        10.0.0.0/30 is directly connected, Serial0/1/0
D     172.20.0.0/16 [90/20640000] via 10.0.0.1, 00:01:27, Serial0/1/0
      192.168.1.0/24 is variably subnetted, 2 subnets, 2 masks
D        192.168.1.0/24 is a summary, 00:01:21, Null0
C        192.168.1.0/26 is directly connected, Loopback0
RouterB#
```

4. Check to ensure that each router is auto-summarizing each network. Then turn off auto-summary on Router B.

```
RouterB#show ip protocols

Routing Protocol is "eigrp  30"
  Outgoing update filter list for all interfaces is not set
  Incoming update filter list for all interfaces is not set
  Default networks flagged in outgoing updates
  Default networks accepted from incoming updates
  EIGRP metric weight K1=1, K2=0, K3=1, K4=0, K5=0
  EIGRP maximum hopcount 100
  EIGRP maximum metric variance 1
Redistributing: eigrp 30
  Automatic network summarization is in effect
  Automatic address summarization:
    192.168.1.0/24 for Serial0/1/0
      Summarizing with metric 128256
    10.0.0.0/8 for Loopback0
      Summarizing with metric 20512000
  Maximum path: 4
  Routing for Networks:
    10.0.0.0
    192.168.1.0
  Routing Information Sources:
    Gateway         Distance      Last Update
    10.0.0.1          90            496078
  Distance: internal 90 external 170

RouterB(config)#router eigrp 30
RouterB(config-router)#no auto-summary
```

5. Check the routing table on Router A.

```
RouterA#show ip route
[Truncated Output]

Gateway of last resort is not set

      10.0.0.0/8 is variably subnetted, 2 subnets, 2 masks
D        10.0.0.0/8 is a summary, 00:00:04, Null0
C        10.0.0.0/30 is directly connected, Serial0/1/0
      172.20.0.0/16 is variably subnetted, 2 subnets, 2 masks
D        172.20.0.0/16 is a summary, 00:00:04, Null0
C        172.20.1.0/24 is directly connected, Loopback0
      192.168.1.0/26 is subnetted, 1 subnets
D        192.168.1.0 [90/20640000] via 10.0.0.2, 00:00:04, Serial0/1/0
RouterA#
```

Troubleshooting EIGRP

Repeat the EIGRP lab above again. In addition, test the EIGRP troubleshooting commands presented in this lesson:

- See the EIGRP parameters using the show ip protocol command
- Modify K values on both routers and issue the command again
- Notice that different configured K values lead to EIGRP neighbor relationships being lost
- Verify the Hello packets being transmitted by issuing the show ip eigrp traffic command
- Test the debug eigrp fsm command
- Test the show ip eigrp topology command for the advertised route and notice the originating RID; change the RID on the remote router and issue the command again
- Verify the show ip eigrp events command
- Start the debug ip routing before advertising the network into EIGRP; notice the generated debug updates

EIGRP For IPv6

DAY 37 TASKS

- Read today's lesson notes (below)
- Complete today's lab
- Take today's exam
- Review yesterdays lesson notes

Yesterday was a tough day so I'm guessing you will spend some of today finishing off reading EIGRP. Don't sweat too much because the actual exam will only test you on a fraction of the information we covered and I'll try to cover that in labs and practice tests.

In addition to open standard protocols, the Cisco-proprietary EIGRP has also been modified to support IPv6. This modified version of EIGRP is sometimes referred to as EIGRPv6 because of its support for IPv6, not because it is revision 6 of the EIGRP routing protocol. Similarly, EIGRP for IPv4 is also sometimes referred to as EIGRPv4 to differentiate between the routing protocol versions supported by either version.

Today you will learn about the following:

- Cisco EIGRP for IPv6 vs EIGRP
- Configuring and verifying EIGRPv6

This lesson maps to the following CCNA syllabus requirement:

- 2.7 Configure, verify, and troubleshoot EIGRP for IPv6 (excluding authentication, filtering, manual summarization, redistribution, stub)

For the most part, EIGRPv6 retains the same basic core functions as EIGRPv4. For example, both versions still use DUAL to ensure loop-free paths, and both protocols use Multicast packets to send updates—although EIGRPv6 uses IPv6 Multicast address FF02::A instead of the 224.0.0.10 group address used by EIGRPv4. While the same core fundamentals are retained, there are some differences between these versions. Table 37.1 below lists the differences between EIGRPv4 and EIGRPv6, or simply and more commonly between EIGRP for IPv4 and EIGRP for IPv6:

Table 37.1—EIGRPv4 and EIGRPv6 Differences

Protocol Characteristic	EIGRP for IPv4	EIGRP for IPv6
Automatic Summarization	Yes	Not Applicable
Authentication or Security	MD5	Built into IPv6
Common Subnet for Peers	Yes	No
Advertisement Contents	Subnet/Mask	Prefix/Length
Packet Encapsulation	IPv4	IPv6

NOTE: Because EIGRPv6 uses the Link-Local address of the neighbor as the next-hop address, the global IPv6 Unicast subnets do not need to be the same for a neighbor relationship to be established between two routers that reside within the same autonomous system and are on a common network segment. This is one of the most significant differences between EIGRPv4, which requires neighbors to be on a common subnet, and EIGRPv6, which negates this need by using the Link-Local addresses for neighbor relationships instead.

CISCO IOS SOFTWARE EIGRPV4 AND EIGRPV6 CONFIGURATION DIFFERENCES

There are some notable differences in the configuration of EIGRPv4 and EIGRPv6 in Cisco IOS software. The first notable difference is the way in which the routing protocol is enabled. For EIGRPv4, the `router eigrp [ASN]` global configuration command is required to enable EIGRPv4 routing and to specify the EIGRPv4 autonomous system number (ASN). When configuring EIGRPv6, the `ipv6 router eigrp [ASN]` global configuration command is used instead to enable EIGRPv6 and to specify the local router ASN.

While enabling EIGRPv4 and EIGRPv6 is somewhat similar, there is a very notable and significant difference in the protocol states once the routing process has been enabled. By default, when EIGRPv4 is enabled, the protocol automatically starts and, assuming correct configuration, begins sending Hello packets on all specified operational interfaces. When enabling EIGRPv6 in Cisco IOS software, by default, after the protocol has been enabled, it remains in the shutdown state. This means that even if enabled under specified interfaces, the EIGRP process will not be operational until the `no shutdown` router configuration command is issued.

Yet another configuration difference between EIGRPv4 and EIGRPv6 is that with EIGRPv6, the router ID is mandatory and must be specified in IPv4 dotted-decimal notation. When assigning the RID, keep in mind that the address does not have to be a routable or reachable address.

NOTE: If there are any interfaces with IPv4 addresses configured on the local router, then the router will select the router ID from these interfaces—preferring Loopback interfaces, and then using physical interfaces if no Loopback interfaces are configured or operational on the router. The highest IP address of the Loopback interface(s), if up, will be selected. If not, the RID will be selected from the highest IP address of the physical interfaces, if up. If neither is configured on the router, the `eigrp router-id [IPv4 Address]` command must be used.

CONFIGURING AND VERIFYING EIGRPV6 IN CISCO IOS SOFTWARE

Continuing from the previous section, which highlighted the configuration differences between EIGRPv4 and EIGRPv6, this section goes through the sequence of steps required to enable and verify EIGRPv6 functionality and routing in Cisco IOS software, as follows:

1. Globally enable IPv6 routing using the `ipv6 unicast-routing` global configuration command. By default, IPv6 routing is disabled in Cisco IOS software.
2. Configure one or more EIGRPv6 processes using the `ipv6 router eigrp [ASN]` global configuration command.
3. If there are no operational interfaces with an IPv4 address configured on the router, then configure the EIGRPv6 RID manually using the `eigrp router-id [IPv4 Address]` router configuration command.
4. Enable the EIGRPv6 process(es) using the `no shutdown` router configuration command.
5. Enable IPv6 on the desired interfaces using the `ipv6 address` and `ipv6 enable` interface configuration commands.
6. Enable one or more EIGRPv6 processes under the interface using the `ipv6 eigrp [ASN]` interface configuration command.

Because automatic summarization is not applicable to EIGRPv6, there is no need to disable this behavior. To solidify the configuration of EIGRPv6, consider the topology illustrated in Figure 37.1 using AS 1. Router R3 will be advertising two additional prefixes via EIGRPv6:

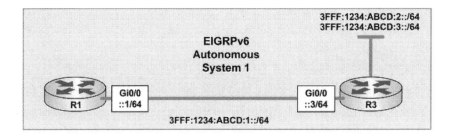

Figure 37.1—Configuring EIGRPv6 in Cisco IOS Software

Following the sequence of configuration steps described above, EIGRPv6 will be configured on router R1 as follows:

```
R1(config)#ipv6 unicast-routing
R1(config)#ipv6 router eigrp 1
R1(config-rtr)#eigrp router-id 1.1.1.1
R1(config-rtr)#no shutdown
R1(config-rtr)#exit
R1(config)#interface GigabitEthernet0/0
R1(config-if)#ipv6 address 3fff:1234:abcd:1::1/64
R1(config-if)#ipv6 enable
R1(config-if)#ipv6 eigrp 1
R1(config-if)#exit
```

Following the same sequence of steps, EIGRPv6 routing is configured on router R3 as follows:

```
R3(config)#ipv6 unicast-routing
R3(config)#ipv6 router eigrp 1
R3(config-rtr)#eigrp router-id 3.3.3.3
R3(config-rtr)#no shutdown
R3(config-rtr)#exit
R3(config)#interface GigabitEthernet0/0
R3(config-if)#ipv6 address 3fff:1234:abcd:1::3/64
R3(config-if)#ipv6 enable
R3(config-if)#ipv6 eigrp 1
R3(config-if)#exit
R3(config)#interface GigabitEthernet0/1
R3(config-if)#ipv6 address 3fff:1234:abcd:2::3/64
R3(config-if)#ipv6 address 3fff:1234:abcd:3::3/64
R3(config-if)#ipv6 enable
R3(config-if)#ipv6 eigrp 1
R3(config-if)#exit
```

The verification process for EIGRPv6 follows the same as that for EIGRPv4. First, verify that the EIGRP neighbor relationships have been established successfully. For EIGRPv6, this is performed using the show ipv6 eigrp neighbors command, as illustrated below:

```
R1#show ipv6 eigrp neighbors
EIGRP-IPv6 Neighbors for AS(1)
H    Address                  Interface Hold Uptime    SRTT   RTO Q   Seq
                                        (sec)          (ms)       Cnt Num
0    Link-local address:  Gi0/0     13  00:01:37  1200      0   3
     FE80::1AEF:63FF:FE63:1B00
```

As was stated earlier, notice that the next-hop address (i.e., EIGRP neighbor address) is specified as the Link-Local address, rather than the global Unicast address. All of the other information printed by this command is the same as that printed for the show ip eigrp neighbors command. To view detailed neighbor information, you can simply append the [detail] keyword to the end of the show ipv6 eigrp neighbors command. Using this option prints information on the EIGRP version, as well as the number of prefixes received from that particular EIGRP neighbor, as illustrated below:

```
R1#show ipv6 eigrp neighbors detail
EIGRP-IPv6 Neighbors for AS(1)
H   Address                Interface Hold Uptime   SRTT   RTO Q   Seq
                                     (sec)         (ms)       Cnt Num
0   Link-local address:    Gi0/0      12  00:01:52 1200       0   3
    FE80::1AEF:63FF:FE63:1B00
    Version 5.0/3.0, Retrans: 1, Retries: 0, Prefixes: 3
    Topology-ids from peer - 0
```

Following the verification of the EIGRPv6 neighbor relationships, you can then verify routing information. For example, to view the IPv6 prefixes received from EIGRPv6 neighbors, you would use the show ipv6 route command, as illustrated in the following output:

```
R1#show ipv6 route eigrp
IPv6 Routing Table - default - 6 entries
Codes: C - Connected, L - Local, S - Static, U - Per-user Static route
       B - BGP, HA - Home Agent, MR - Mobile Router, R - RIP
       I1 - ISIS L1, I2 - ISIS L2, IA - ISIS inter area, IS - ISIS
summary
       D - EIGRP, EX - EIGRP external, ND - Neighbor Discovery
D   3FFF:1234:ABCD:2::/64 [90/3072]
     via FE80::1AEF:63FF:FE63:1B00, GigabitEthernet0/0
D   3FFF:1234:ABCD:3::/64 [90/3072]
     via FE80::1AEF:63FF:FE63:1B00, GigabitEthernet0/0
```

Again, notice that the received prefixes all contain the Link-Local address of the neighbor as the next-hop IPv6 address for all received prefixes. To view the EIGRPv6 topology table, the show ipv6 eigrp topology command should be used. This command supports the same options as those available with the show ip eigrp topology command used to view the EIGRPv4 topology table. Based on the implemented configuration, the topology table on R1 displays the following IPv6 prefix information:

```
R1#show ipv6 eigrp topology
EIGRP-IPv6 Topology Table for AS(1)/ID(1.1.1.1)
Codes: P - Passive, A - Active, U - Update, Q - Query, R - Reply,
       r - reply Status, s - sia Status

P 3FFF:1234:ABCD:2::/64, 1 successors, FD is 3072
        via FE80::1AEF:63FF:FE63:1B00 (3072/2816), GigabitEthernet0/0
P 3FFF:1234:ABCD:1::/64, 1 successors, FD is 2816
        via Connected, GigabitEthernet0/0
P 3FFF:1234:ABCD:3::/64, 1 successors, FD is 3072
        via FE80::1AEF:63FF:FE63:1B00 (3072/2816), GigabitEthernet0/0
```

As is the case with EIGRPv4, you can append a prefix to the end of this command in order to view the detailed information on that prefix or subnet. For example, to view detailed information on the 3FFF:1234:ABCD:2::/64 subnet, you would simply enter the show ipv6 eigrp topology 3FFF:1234:ABCD:2::/64 command, as illustrated below:

```
R1#show ipv6 eigrp topology 3FFF:1234:ABCD:2::/64
EIGRP-IPv6 Topology Entry for AS(1)/ID(1.1.1.1) for 3FFF:1234:ABCD:2::/64
```

```
    State is Passive, Query origin flag is 1, 1 Successor(s), FD is 3072
    Descriptor Blocks:
    FE80::1AEF:63FF:FE63:1B00 (GigabitEthernet0/0), from
FE80::1AEF:63FF:FE63:1B00, Send flag is 0x0
        Composite metric is (3072/2816), route is Internal
        Vector metric:
          Minimum bandwidth is 1000000 Kbit
          Total delay is 20 microseconds
          Reliability is 255/255
          Load is 1/255
          Minimum MTU is 1500
          Hop count is 1
          Originating router is 3.3.3.3
```

Finally, a simple ping can and should be used to verify connectivity between subnets. The following is a ping from R1 to the 3FFF:1234:ABCD:2::3 address on R3:

```
R1#ping 3FFF:1234:ABCD:2::3 repeat 10

Type escape sequence to abort.
Sending 10, 100-byte ICMP Echos to 3FFF:1234:ABCD:2::3, timeout is 2
seconds:
!!!!!!!!!!
Success rate is 100 percent (10/10), round-trip min/avg/max = 0/0/4 ms
```

As is the case with EIGRPv4, the default protocol values for EIGRPv6 can be validated using the show ipv6 protocols command, the output of which is printed below. This command includes the interfaces enabled for the EIGRP instance, the route redistribution information (if applicable), and the manually specified or configured dotted-decimal EIGRPv6 router ID.

```
R1#show ipv6 protocols
IPv6 Routing Protocol is "eigrp 1"
EIGRP-IPv6 Protocol for AS(1)
  Metric weight K1=1, K2=0, K3=1, K4=0, K5=0
  NSF-aware route hold timer is 240
  Router-ID: 1.1.1.1
  Topology : 0 (base)
    Active Timer: 3 min
    Distance: internal 90 external 170
    Maximum path: 16
    Maximum hopcount 100
    Maximum metric variance 1

  Interfaces:
    GigabitEthernet0/0
  Redistribution:
```

Now take today's exam at **https://www.in60days.com/free/ccnain60days/**

DAY 37 LAB

Repeat the EIGRP lab from Day 36, this time using IPv6 addresses and activating EIGRP for IPv6:

- Enable IPv6 Unicast routing on both routers
- Configure IPv6 addresses on the interfaces
- Configure the EIGRP process using the `ipv6 router eigrp 100` command
- Configure a RID using the `eigrp router-id 10.10.10.10` command
- Activate the process using the `no shutdown` command
- Enable EIGRP on the IPv6 interfaces using the `ipv6 eigrp 100` command
- Verify the neighbor relationships using the `show ipv6 eigrp neighbors [detail]` command
- Verify the advertised route(s) using the `show ipv6 route eigrp` command
- Verify the EIGRP topology using the `show ipv6 eigrp topology` command

Review

DAY 38 TASKS

- Review lesson notes from days 35-37
- Complete the labs from the above chapters
- Complete the challenge labs if you wish
- Take today's exam at https://www.in60days.com/free/ccnain60days/
- Read the ICND2 cram guide
- Spend 15 minutes on the subnetting.org website

We've covered some tough subjects over the last few days. Don't get bogged down in the details. Just review and make notes, repeat the labs and start to get familiar with important commands. We will be reviewing it all again.

Challenge 1—InterVLAN SVI Lab

Topology

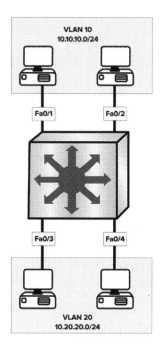

Instructions

Connect host to a switch as above. You will need a layer 3 switch such as a 3550/3560/3570 or packet tracer.

1. Add IP addresses for hosts inside the respective VLANs.
2. Put the ports into the correct VLANs.
3. Configure an SVI for VLAN 10 - 10.10.10.1 255.255.255.0
4. Configure an SVI for VLAN 20 - 10.20.20.1 255.255.255.0
5. Set the default gateway on the hosts for the respective SVI addresses.
6. Test by pinging devices across the VLANs.
7. Check the mac address table on the switch.

Challenge 2—EIGRP Lab

Topology

EIGRP 40

10.10.30.0/24   172.16.1.0/24   10.10.10.0/24

10.10.40.0/24   **R1**   **R2**   10.10.20.0/24

Instructions

Connect two routers together with a serial or crossover cable.

1. Add IP addresses to routers and loopback on Routers according to diagram
2. Ping between Router A and B to test serial line (remember clock rates)
3. Now set the serial lines to use PPP with CHAP (set usernames and passwords also)
4. Configure EIGRP 40 on all routers and add all networks
5. Fix the issue that prevents R2 pinging hosts on 10.10.30.0 and 10.10.40.0 and R1 from pinging the 10 addresses on R2.
6. Now change the routing so only 10.10.10.0 on R2 and 10.10.30.0 on R1 are advertised. Put the loopbacks using the other 10 networks into passive mode for EIGRP

Challenge 3—EIGRPv6 Lab

Topology

EIGRP 40

2001:abcd:1234:aaaa::/64

2001:abcd:1234:cccc::/64   **R1**   **R2**   2001:abcd:1234:cccc::/64

Instructions

Connect two routers together with a serial or crossover cable.

1. Add IP addresses to routers and loopback on Routers according to diagram
2. Ping between Router A and B to test serial line (remember clock rates)
3. Configure EIGRP 40 on all routers and add all networks
4. Check the IPv6 routing table and EIGRPv6 neighbors
5. Make the loopback on R2 passive (and confirm with a show command)

OSPF

DAY 39 TASKS

- Read today's lesson notes (below)
- Complete today's lab
- Take today's exam
- Read the ICND2 cram guide
- Spend 15 minutes on the subnetting.org website

Previous versions of the CCNA exam required only a basic understanding of OSPF. The current version now requires a deeper understanding of OSPF and multi-area OSPF as well as troubleshooting.

Today you will learn about the following:

- OSPF overview and fundamentals
- Configuring OSPF
- Designated and backup designated routers
- Additional router types
- OSPF packet types
- Establishing adjacencies
- OSPF LSAs
- OSPF areas
- Route metrics
- OSPF default routing
- Configuring OSPF
- Troubleshooting OSPF

This module maps to the following CCNA syllabus requirement:

- 2.4 Configure, verify, and troubleshoot single area and multi area OSPFv2 for IPv4 (excluding authentication, filtering, manual summarization, redistribution, stub, virtual-link, and LSAs)

As with EIGRP, we could discuss OSPF over several days, but we need to stick to what you need to know for your exam. Even CCNA-level OSPF knowledge wouldn't be sufficient to design and deploy it on most networks.

Open Shortest Path First (OSPF) is an open-standard Link State routing protocol. Link State routing protocols advertise the state of their links. When a Link State router begins operating on a network link, information associated with that logical network is added to its local Link State Database (LSDB). The local router then sends Hello messages on its operational links to determine whether other Link State routers are operating on the interfaces as well. OSPF runs directly over Internet Protocol using IP protocol number 89.

OSPF OVERVIEW AND FUNDAMENTALS

Several Requests for Comments (RFCs) have been written for OSPF. In this section, we will learn about the history of OSPF based on some of the most common RFCs that pertain to OSPF. The OSPF working group was formed in 1987 and it has since released numerous RFCs. Some of the most common RFCs on OSPF are listed below:

- RFC 1131 — OSPF Specification
- RFC 1584 — Multicast Extensions to OSPF
- RFC 1587 — The OSPF NSSA Option
- RFC 1850 — OSPF Version 2 Management Information Base
- RFC 2328 — OSPF Version 2
- RFC 2740 — OSPF Version 3

RFC 1131 describes the first iteration of OSPF, and it was used in initial tests to determine whether the protocol worked.

RFC 1584 provides extensions to OSPF for the support of IP Multicast traffic. This is commonly referred to as Multicast OSPF (MOSPF). However, this standard is seldom used and, most importantly, it is not supported by Cisco.

RFC 1587 describes the operation of an OSPF Not-So-Stubby Area (NSSA). An NSSA allows for the injection of external routing knowledge by an Autonomous System Boundary Router (ASBR) using an NSSA External LSA. NSSAs will be described in detail later in this module.

RFC 1850 allows network management of OSPF using the Simple Network Management Protocol (SNMP). SNMP is used in network management systems to monitor network-attached devices for conditions that warrant administrative attention. The implementation of this standard is beyond the scope of the CCNA exam requirements and is not described in this guide.

RFC 2328 details the latest update to OSPF version 2 (OSPFv2), which is the default version of OSPF in use today. OSPFv2 was initially described in RFC 1247, which addressed a number of issues discovered during the initial rollout of OSPF version 1 (OSPFv1) and modified the protocol to allow future modifications without generating backward-compatibility issues. Because of this, OSPFv2 is not compatible with OSPFv1.

Finally, RFC 2740 describes the modifications to OSPF to support IPv6. It should be assumed that all references to OSPF in this module are for OSPFv2.

Link State Fundamentals

When a Link State routing protocol is enabled for a particular link, information associated with that network is added to the local Link State Database (LSDB). The local router then sends Hello messages on its operational links to determine whether other Link State routers are operating on the interfaces as well. The Hello messages are used for neighbor discovery and to maintain adjacencies between neighbor routers. These messages will be described in detail later in this module.

When a neighbor router is located, the local router attempts to establish an adjacency, assuming both routers share the same common subnet, are in the same area, and that other parameters, such as authentication and timers, are identical. This adjacency enables the two routers to advertise summary LSDB information to each other. This exchange is not the actual detailed database information but is instead a summary of the data.

Each individual router evaluates the summary information against its local LSDB to ensure that it has the most up-to-date information. If one side of the adjacency realizes that it requires an update, the router requests the new information from the adjacent router. The update from the neighbor includes the actual data contained in the LSDB. This exchange process continues until both routers have identical LSDBs. OSPF uses different types of messages to exchange the database information and to ensure that all routers have a consistent view of the network. These different packet types will be described in detail later in this module.

Following the database exchange, the SPF algorithm runs and creates a shortest-path tree to all hosts in an area or in the network backbone, with the router that is performing the calculation at the root of that tree. The SPF algorithm was described briefly in Day 10.

OSPF Fundamentals

Unlike EIGRP, which can support multiple Network Layer protocols, OSPF can only support the Internet Protocol (IP), specifically IPv4 and IPv6. Like EIGRP, OSPF supports VLSM and authentication and utilizes IP Multicast when sending and receiving updates on Multi-Access networks, such as Ethernet.

OSPF is a hierarchical routing protocol that logically divides the network into subdomains referred to as areas. This logical segmentation is used to limit the scope of Link State Advertisements (LSAs) flooding throughout the OSPF domain. LSAs are special types of packets sent by routers running OSPF. Different types of LSAs are used within an area and between areas. By restricting the propagation of certain types of LSAs between areas, the

OSPF hierarchical implementation effectively reduces the amount of routing protocol traffic within the OSPF network.

In a multi-area OSPF network, one area must be designated as the backbone area, or Area 0. The OSPF backbone is the logical center of the OSPF network. All other non-backbone areas must be connected physically to the backbone. However, because it is not always possible or feasible to have a physical connection between a non-backbone area and the backbone, the OSPF standard allows the use of virtual connections to the backbone. These virtual connections are known as virtual links, but this concept is not included in the current CCNA syllabus.

Routers within each area store detailed topology information for the area in which they reside. Within each area, one or more routers, referred to as Area Border Routers (ABRs), facilitate inter-area routing by advertising summarized routing information between the different areas. This functionality allows for the following within the OSPF network:

- Reduces the scope of LSAs flooding throughout the OSPF domain
- Hides detailed topology information between areas
- Allows for end-to-end connectivity within the OSPF domain
- Creates logical boundaries within the OSPF domain

The OSPF backbone area receives summarized routing information from the ABRs. The routing information is disseminated to all other non-backbone areas within the OSPF network. When a change to the network topology occurs, this information is disseminated throughout the entire OSPF domain, allowing all routers in all areas to have a consistent view of the network. The network topology illustrated in Figure 39.1 below is an example of a multi-area OSPF implementation:

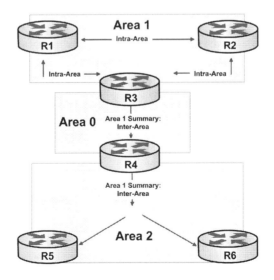

Figure 39.1—A Multi-Area OSPF Network

Figure 39.1 illustrates a basic multi-area OSPF network. Areas 1 and 2 are connected to Area 0, the OSPF backbone. Within Area 1, routers R1, R2, and R3 exchange intra-area routing information and maintain detailed topology for that area. R3, the ABR, generates an inter-area summary route and advertises this to the OSPF backbone.

R4, the ABR for Area 2, receives the summary information from Area 0 and floods it into its adjacent area. This allows routers R5 and R6 to know of the routes that reside outside of their local area but within the OSPF domain. The same concept would also be applicable to the routing information within Area 2.

In summation, the ABRs maintain LSDB information for all the areas in which they are connected. All routers within each area have detailed topology information pertaining to that specific area. These routers exchange intra-area routing information. The ABRs advertise summary information from each of their connected areas to other OSPF areas, allowing for inter-area routing within the domain.

NOTE: OSPF ABRs and other OSPF router types will be described in detail later in this guide.

Network Types

OSPF uses different default network types for different media, which are as follows:

- Non-Broadcast (default on Multipoint NBMA (FR and ATM))
- Point-to-Point (default on HDLC, PPP, P2P sub interface on FR and ATM, and ISDN)
- Broadcast (default on Ethernet and Token Ring)
- Point-to-Multipoint
- Point-to-Multipoint Non-Broadcast
- Loopback (default on Loopback interfaces)

Non-Broadcast networks are network types that do not support natively broadcast or Multicast traffic. The most common example of a Non-Broadcast network type is Frame Relay. Non-Broadcast network types require additional configuration to allow for both Broadcast and Multicast support. On such networks, OSPF elects a Designated Router (DR) and/or a Backup Designated Router (BDR). These two routers are described later in this guide.

In Cisco IOS software, OSPF-enabled routers send Hello packets every 30 seconds by default on Non-Broadcast network types. If a Hello packet is not received in four times the Hello interval, or 120 seconds, the neighbor router is considered "dead." The following output illustrates the show ip ospf interface command on a Frame Relay Serial interface:

```
R2#show ip ospf interface Serial0/0
Serial0/0 is up, line protocol is up
  Internet Address 150.1.1.2/24, Area 0
  Process ID 2, Router ID 2.2.2.2, Network Type NON_BROADCAST, Cost: 64
  Transmit Delay is 1 sec, State DR, Priority 1
```

```
Designated Router (ID) 2.2.2.2, Interface address 150.1.1.2
Backup Designated Router (ID) 1.1.1.1, Interface address 150.1.1.1
Timer intervals configured, Hello 30, Dead 120, Wait 120, Retransmit 5
  oob-resync timeout 120
  Hello due in 00:00:00
Supports Link-local Signaling (LLS)
Index 2/2, flood queue length 0
Next 0x0(0)/0x0(0)
Last flood scan length is 2, maximum is 2
Last flood scan time is 0 msec, maximum is 0 msec
Neighbor Count is 1, Adjacent neighbor count is 1
  Adjacent with neighbor 1.1.1.1  (Backup Designated Router)
Suppress Hello for 0 neighbor(s)
```

A Point-to-Point (P2P) connection is simply a connection between two endpoints only. Examples of P2P connections include physical WAN interfaces using HDLC and PPP encapsulation, and Frame Relay (FR) and Asynchronous Transfer Mode (ATM) Point-to-Point sub interfaces. No DR or BDR is elected on OSPF Point-to-Point network types. By default, OSPF sends Hello packets out every 10 seconds on P2P network types. The "dead" interval on these network types is four times the Hello interval, which is 40 seconds. The following output illustrates the show ip ospf interface command on a P2P link:

```
R2#show ip ospf interface Serial0/0
Serial0/0 is up, line protocol is up
  Internet Address 150.1.1.2/24, Area 0
  Process ID 2, Router ID 2.2.2.2, Network Type POINT_TO_POINT, Cost: 64
  Transmit Delay is 1 sec, State POINT_TO_POINT
  Timer intervals configured, Hello 10, Dead 40, Wait 40, Retransmit 5
    oob-resync timeout 40
    Hello due in 00:00:03
  Supports Link-local Signaling (LLS)
  Index 2/2, flood queue length 0
  Next 0x0(0)/0x0(0)
  Last flood scan length is 1, maximum is 1
  Last flood scan time is 0 msec, maximum is 0 msec
  Neighbor Count is 1, Adjacent neighbor count is 1
    Adjacent with neighbor 1.1.1.1
  Suppress Hello for 0 neighbor(s)
```

Broadcast network types are those that natively support Broadcast and Multicast traffic, the most common example being Ethernet. As is the case with Non-Broadcast networks, OSPF also elects a DR and/or a BDR on Broadcast networks. By default, OSPF sends Hello packets every 10 seconds on these network types and a neighbor is declared "dead" if no Hello packets are received within four times the Hello interval, which is 40 seconds. The following output illustrates the show ip ospf interface command on a FastEthernet interface:

```
R2#show ip ospf interface FastEthernet0/0
FastEthernet0/0 is up, line protocol is up
  Internet Address 192.168.1.2/24, Area 0
  Process ID 2, Router ID 2.2.2.2, Network Type BROADCAST, Cost: 64
```

```
Transmit Delay is 1 sec, State BDR, Priority 1
Designated Router (ID) 192.168.1.3, Interface address 192.168.1.3
Backup Designated Router (ID) 2.2.2.2, Interface address 192.168.1.2
Timer intervals configured, Hello 10, Dead 40, Wait 40, Retransmit 5
  oob-resync timeout 40
  Hello due in 00:00:04
Supports Link-local Signaling (LLS)
Index 1/1, flood queue length 0
Next 0x0(0)/0x0(0)
Last flood scan length is 1, maximum is 1
Last flood scan time is 0 msec, maximum is 0 msec
Neighbor Count is 1, Adjacent neighbor count is 1
  Adjacent with neighbor 192.168.1.3  (Designated Router)
Suppress Hello for 0 neighbor(s)
```

Point-to-Multipoint is a non-default OSPF network type. In other words, this network type must be configured manually using the `ip ospf network point-to-multipoint [non-broadcast]` interface configuration command. By default, this command defaults to a Broadcast Point-to-Multipoint network type. This default network type allows OSPF to use Multicast packets to discover dynamically its neighbor routers. In addition, there is no DR/BDR election held on Broadcast Point-to-Multipoint network types.

The `[non-broadcast]` keyword configures the Point-to-Multipoint network type as a Non-Broadcast Point-to-Multipoint network. This requires static OSPF neighbor configuration, as OSPF will not use Multicast to discover dynamically its neighbor routers. Additionally, this network type does not require the election of a DR and/or a BDR router for the designated segment. The primary use of this network type is to allow neighbor costs to be assigned to neighbors instead of using the interface-assigned cost for routes received from all neighbors.

The Point-to-Multipoint network type is typically used in partial-mesh hub-and-spoke Non-Broadcast Multi-Access (NBMA) networks. However, this network type can also be specified for other network types, such as Broadcast Multi-Access networks (e.g., Ethernet). By default, OSPF sends Hello packets every 30 seconds on Point-to-Multipoint networks. The default dead interval is four times the Hello interval, which is 120 seconds.

The following output illustrates the `show ip ospf interface` command on a Frame Relay Serial interface that has been configured manually as a Point-to-Multipoint network:

```
R2#show ip ospf interface Serial0/0
Serial0/0 is up, line protocol is up
  Internet Address 150.1.1.2/24, Area 0
  Process ID 2, Router ID 2.2.2.2, Network Type POINT_TO_MULTIPOINT, Cost:
64
  Transmit Delay is 1 sec, State POINT_TO_MULTIPOINT
  Timer intervals configured, Hello 30, Dead 120, Wait 120, Retransmit 5
    oob-resync timeout 120
    Hello due in 00:00:04
  Supports Link-local Signaling (LLS)
```

```
Index 2/2, flood queue length 0
Next 0x0(0)/0x0(0)
Last flood scan length is 1, maximum is 2
Last flood scan time is 0 msec, maximum is 0 msec
Neighbor Count is 1, Adjacent neighbor count is 1
  Adjacent with neighbor 1.1.1.1
Suppress Hello for 0 neighbor(s)
```

The primary reason for the OSPF requirement that the network type be the same on both routers (by the same this means that they either hold or don't hold elections) is because of the timer values. As illustrated in the outputs above, different network types use different Hello and Dead timer intervals. In order for an OSPF adjacency to be established successfully, these values must match on both routers.

Cisco IOS software allows the default OSPF Hello and Dead timers to be changed using the `ip ospf hello-interval <1-65535>` and the `ip ospf dead-interval [<1-65535>|minimal]` interface configuration commands. The `ip ospf hello-interval <1-65535>` command is used to specify the Hello interval in seconds. When issued, the software automatically configures the Dead interval to a value four times the configured Hello interval. For example, assume that a router was configured as follows:

```
R2(config)#interface Serial0/0
R2(config-if)#ip ospf hello-interval 1
R2(config-if)#exit
```

By setting the Hello interval to 1 on R2 above, Cisco IOS software automatically adjusts the default Dead timer to four times the Hello interval, which is 4 seconds. This is illustrated in the following output:

```
R2#show ip ospf interface Serial0/0
Serial0/0 is up, line protocol is up
  Internet Address 10.0.2.4/24, Area 2
  Process ID 4, Router ID 4.4.4.4, Network Type POINT_TO_POINT, Cost: 64
  Transmit Delay is 1 sec, State POINT_TO_POINT
  Timer intervals configured, Hello 1, Dead 4, Wait 4, Retransmit 5
    oob-resync timeout 40
    Hello due in 00:00:00

[Truncated Output]
```

OSPF CONFIGURATION

This section describes OSPF configuration fundamentals.

Enabling OSPF in Cisco IOS Software

OSPF is enabled in Cisco IOS software by issuing the `router ospf [process id]` global configuration command. The `[process id]` keyword is locally significant and does not need to be the same on all routers in the network in order to establish an adjacency. The use of the locally significant process ID allows you to configure multiple instances of OSPF on the same router.

The OSPF process ID is an integer between 1 and 65535. Each OSPF process maintains its own separate Link State Database; however, all routes are entered into the same IP routing table. In other words, there is no unique IP routing table for each individual OSPF process configured on the router.

In earlier versions of Cisco IOS software, OSPF would not be enabled if the router did not have at least one interface configured with a valid IP address in the up/up state. This restriction has been removed in current versions of Cisco IOS software. In the event that the router has no interfaces configured with a valid IP address and in the up/up state, Cisco IOS will create a Proximity Database (PDB) and allow the process to be created. However, it is important to remember that the process will be inactive until a router ID is selected, which can be performed in the following two ways:

- Configuring a valid IP address on an interface and bringing the interface up
- Configuring the router ID manually using the `router-id` command (see below)

As an example, consider the following router, which has all interfaces disabled:

```
R3#show ip interface brief
Interface       IP-Address   OK? Method Status                Protocol
FastEthernet0/0 unassigned   YES manual administratively down down
Serial0/0       unassigned   YES NVRAM  administratively down down
Serial0/1       unassigned   YES unset  administratively down down
```

Next, OSPF is enabled on the router using the `router ospf [process id]` global configuration command, as illustrated in the following output:

```
R3(config)#router ospf 1
R3(config-router)#exit
```

Based on this configuration, Cisco IOS software assigns the process a default router ID of 0.0.0.0, as illustrated in the following output of the `show ip protocols` command:

```
R3#show ip protocols
Routing Protocol is "ospf 1"
  Outgoing update filter list for all interfaces is not set
  Incoming update filter list for all interfaces is not set
  Router ID 0.0.0.0
  Number of areas in this router is 0. 0 normal 0 stub 0 nssa
  Maximum path: 4
  Routing for Networks:
 Reference bandwidth unit is 100 mbps
  Routing Information Sources:
    Gateway          Distance      Last Update

  Distance: (default is 110)
```

However, the `show ip ospf [process id]` command reveals that the process is not actually active and indicates that a router ID needs to be configured, as illustrated below:

```
R3#show ip ospf 1
%OSPF: Router process 1 is not running, please configure a router-id
```

Enabling OSPF Routing for Interfaces or Networks

After OSPF has been enabled, two actions can be performed to enable OSPF routing for one or more networks or interfaces on the router, as follows:

- Using the `[network] [wildcard] area [area id]` router configuration command
- Using the `ip ospf [process id] area [area id]` interface configuration command

Unlike EIGRP, the wildcard mask is mandatory in OSPF and must be configured; however, as is the case with EIGRP, it serves the same function in that it matches interfaces within the range specified. As an example, the statement `network 10.0.0.0 0.255.255.255 area 0` would enable OSPF routing for interfaces with the IP address and subnet mask combination of 10.0.0.1/30, 10.5.5.1/24, and even 10.10.10.1/25. The interfaces would all be assigned to OSPF Area 0 based on the OSPF network configuration.

> **NOTE:** The wildcard mask for OSPF can also be entered in the same format as a traditional subnet mask, for example, `network 10.0.0.0 255.0.0.0 area 0`. In this case, Cisco IOS software will invert the subnet mask and the wildcard mask will be entered into the running configuration. In addition, it is important to remember that OSPF also supports the use of the all ones or all zeros wildcard mask to enable OSPF routing for a specific interface. This configuration enables OSPF on a particular interface but the router advertises the actual subnet mask configured on the interface itself.

After the `network [network] [wildcard] area [area id]` command has been issued, the router sends out Hello packets on interfaces matching the specified network and wildcard mask combination and attempts to discover neighbors. The connected subnet is then advertised to one or more neighbor routers during the OSPF database exchange, and, finally, this information is then added to the OSPF Link State Database of the OSPF routers.

When the `network [network] [wildcard] area [area id]` command is issued, the router matches the most specific entry in order to determine the area the interface will be assigned to. Consider the following OSPF network statement configurations, as an example:

- First configuration statement: `network 10.0.0.0 0.255.255.255 Area 0`
- Second configuration statement: `network 10.1.0.0 0.0.255.255 Area 1`
- Third configuration statement: `network 10.1.1.0 0.0.0.255 Area 2`
- Fourth configuration statement: `network 10.1.1.1 0.0.0.0 Area 3`
- Fifth configuration statement: `network 0.0.0.0 255.255.255.255 Area 4`

Following this configuration on the router, the Loopback interfaces shown in Table 39.1 below are then configured on the same router:

Table 39.1—Assigning Interfaces to OSPF Areas

Interface	IP Address/Mask
Loopback 0	10.0.0.1/32
Loopback 1	10.0.1.1/32
Loopback 2	10.1.0.1/32
Loopback 3	10.1.1.1/32
Loopback 4	10.2.0.1/32

As was previously stated, when the `network [network] [wildcard] area [area id]` command is issued, the router matches the most specific entry in order to determine the area in which the interface will be assigned. For the network statement configuration and the Loopback interfaces configured on the router, the `show ip ospf interface brief` command would show that the interfaces were assigned to the following OSPF areas:

```
R1#show ip ospf interface brief
Interface    PID   Area    IP Address/Mask     Cost  State Nbrs F/C
Lo4          1     0       10.2.0.1/32         1     LOOP  0/0
Lo1          1     0       10.0.1.1/32         1     LOOP  0/0
Lo0          1     0       10.0.0.1/32         1     LOOP  0/0
Lo2          1     1       10.1.0.1/32         1     LOOP  0/0
Lo3          1     3       10.1.1.1/32         1     LOOP  0/0
```

NOTE: Regardless of the order in which the network statements are entered, within the running configuration, the most specific entries are listed first in the output of the `show running-config` command on the router.

The `ip ospf [process id] area [area id]` interface configuration command negates the need to use the `network [network] [wildcard] area [area id]` router configuration command. This command enables OSPF routing for the specified interface and assigns the interface to the specified OSPF area. These two commands perform the same basic function and may be used interchangeably.

Additionally, if, for example, two routers are connected back to back, with one router configured using the `ip ospf [process id] area [area id]` interface configuration command and the neighbor router configured using the `network [network] [wildcard] area [area id]` router configuration command, then, assuming the area IDs are the same, the routers will successfully establish an OSPF adjacency.

OSPF Areas

The OSPF area ID may be configured either as an integer between 0 and 4294967295 or using dotted-decimal notation (i.e., using the IP address format). Unlike the OSPF process ID, the

OSPF area ID must match in order for adjacency to be established. The most common type of OSPF area configuration is using an integer to specify the OSPF area. However, ensure that you are familiar with both supported methods of area configuration.

OSPF Router ID

In order for OSPF to operate on a network, each router must have a unique identifying number, and in the context of OSPF the router ID number is used.

When determining the OSPF router ID, Cisco IOS selects the highest IP address of configured Loopback interfaces. If no Loopback interfaces are configured, the software uses the highest IP address of all configured physical interfaces as the OSPF router ID. Cisco IOS software also allows administrators to specify the router ID manually using the router-id [address] router configuration command.

Loopback interfaces are very useful, especially during testing because they require no hardware and are logical, so they can never be down.

On the router below, I have configured IP address 1.1.1.1/32 for Loopback0 and 2.2.2.2/24 for F0/0. I then configured OSPF for all interfaces on the router:

```
Router(config-if)#router ospf 1
Router(config-router)#net 0.0.0.0 255.255.255.255 area 0
Router(config-router)#end
Router#
%SYS-5-CONFIG_I: Configured from console by console

Router#show ip protocols

Routing Protocol is "ospf 1"
  Outgoing update filter list for all interfaces is not set
  Incoming update filter list for all interfaces is not set
  Router ID 1.1.1.1
  Number of areas in this router is 1. 1 normal 0 stub 0 nssa
  Maximum path: 4
  Routing for Networks:
    0.0.0.0 255.255.255.255 area 0
  Routing Information Sources:
    Gateway         Distance      Last Update
    1.1.1.1              110      00:00:14
  Distance: (default is 110)
```

I want to hard code the router ID to 10.10.10.1. I could have done this by configuring another Loopback interface with this IP address, or I can simply add this at the OSPF router ID. I will have to either reload the router or clear the IP OSPF process on the router in order for this to take effect.

```
Router#conf t
Enter configuration commands, one per line.  End with CNTL/Z.
Router(config)#router ospf 1
```

```
Router(config-router)#router-id 10.10.10.1
Reload or use "clear ip ospf process" command, for this to take effect

Router(config-router)#end
Router#
%SYS-5-CONFIG_I: Configured from console by console

Router#clear ip ospf process
Reset ALL OSPF processes? [no]: yes

Router#show ip prot

Routing Protocol is "ospf 1"
  Outgoing update filter list for all interfaces is not set
  Incoming update filter list for all interfaces is not set
  Router ID 10.10.10.1
  Number of areas in this router is 1. 1 normal 0 stub 0 nssa
  Maximum path: 4
  Routing for Networks:
    0.0.0.0 255.255.255.255 area 0
  Routing Information Sources:
    Gateway          Distance      Last Update
    1.1.1.1               110      00:03:15
  Distance: (default is 110)
```

The router ID is of particular importance when it comes to electing the DR and BDR as you will see in Day 39.

OSPF Passive Interfaces

Passive interfaces can be described as interfaces over which no routing updates are sent. In Cisco IOS software, an interface is configured as passive by using the `passive-interface` `[name]` router configuration command. If there are multiple interfaces on the router that need to be configured as passive, the `passive-interface` `default` router configuration command should be used. This command configures all interfaces that fall within the configured network range on the router to be passive. Interfaces on which adjacencies or neighbor relationships should be allowed can then be configured using the `no passive-interface` `[name]` router configuration command.

Passive interface configuration works the same for both OSPF and EIGRP in that if an interface is marked as passive, all neighbor relationships via that interface will be torn down and Hello packets will not send or receive packets via that interface. However, the interface will continue to be advertised based on the configured network statement configuration on the router:

```
Router(config)#router ospf 10
Router(config-router)#passive-interface f0/0

Router#show ip ospf int f0/0
FastEthernet0/0 is up, line protocol is up
```

```
Internet address is 192.168.1.1/24, Area 0
Process ID 10,Router ID 172.16.1.1,Network Type BROADCAST, Cost: 1
Transmit Delay is 1 sec, State WAITING, Priority 1
No designated router on this network
No backup designated router on this network
Timer intervals configured,Hello 10, Dead 40, Wait 40,Retransmit 5
  No Hellos (Passive interface)
```

DESIGNATED AND BACKUP DESIGNATED ROUTERS

As stated earlier, OSPF elects a Designated Router (DR) and/or a Backup Designated Router (BDR) on Broadcast and Non-Broadcast network types. It is important to understand that the BDR is not a mandatory component on these network types. In fact, OSPF will work just as well when only a DR is elected and there is no BDR; however, there will be no redundancy if the DR fails and the OSPF routers need to go through the election process again to elect a new DR.

On the segment (on Broadcast and Non-Broadcast network types), each individual non-DR/BDR router establishes an adjacency with the DR and, if one has also been elected, the BDR, but not with any other non-DR/BDR routers on the segment. The DR and BDR routers are fully adjacent with each other and all other routers on the segment. The non-DR/BDR routers send messages and updates to the AllDRRouters Multicast group address 224.0.0.6. Only the DR/BDR routers listen to Multicast messages sent to this group address. The DR then advertises messages to the AllSPFRouters Multicast group address 224.0.0.5. This allows all other OSPF routers on the segment to receive the updates.

It is important to understand the sequence of message exchanges when a DR and/or a BDR router have been elected. As an example, imagine a Broadcast network with four routers, which are R1, R2, R3, and R4. Assume that R4 has been elected DR, and R3 has been elected BDR. R2 and R1 are neither DR nor BDR and are therefore referred to as DROther routers in Cisco OSPF terminology. A configuration change is made on R1, and R1 then sends an update to the AllDRRouters Multicast group address 224.0.0.6. R4, the DR, receives this update and sends an acknowledgment back to the AllSPFRouters Multicast group address 224.0.0.5. R4 then sends this update to all other non-DR/BDR routers using the AllSPFRouters Multicast group address. This update is received by the other DROther router, R2, and R2 sends an acknowledgment to the AllDRRouters Multicast group 224.0.0.6. This is illustrated in Figure 39.2 below:

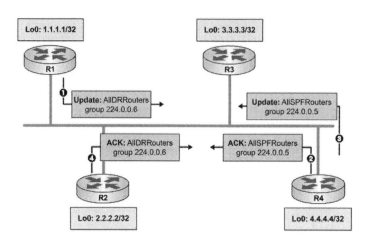

Figure 39.2—OSPF DR and BDR Advertisements

NOTE: The BDR simply listens to the packets sent to both Multicast groups.

In order for a router to be the DR or the BDR for the segment, the router must be elected. This election is based on the following:

- The highest router priority value
- The highest router ID

By default, all routers have a default priority value of 1. This value can be adjusted using the `ip ospf priority <0-255>` interface configuration command. The higher the priority, the greater the likelihood the router will be elected DR for the segment. The router with the second-highest priority will then be elected BDR. If a priority value of 0 is configured, the router will not participate in the DR/BDR election process. The highest router priority and router ID are important only if OSPF processes loads at the same time on all routers participating in the DR/BDR election process. Otherwise the router that finishes loading the OSPF process first will become the DR on the segment.

When determining the OSPF router ID, Cisco IOS selects the highest IP address of configured Loopback interfaces. If no Loopback interfaces are configured, the software uses the highest IP address of all configured physical interfaces as the OSPF router ID. Cisco IOS software also allows administrators to specify the router ID manually using the `router-id [address]` router configuration command.

It is important to remember that with OSPF, once the DR and the BDR have been elected, they will remain as DR/BDR routers until a new election is held. For example, if a DR and a BDR exist on a Multi-Access network and a router with a higher priority or IP address is added to the same segment, the existing DR and BDR routers will not change. If the DR fails, the BDR will assume the role of the DR, not the new router with the higher priority or IP address. Instead, a new election will be held and that router will most likely be elected BDR.

In order for that router to become the DR, the BDR must be removed or the OSPF process must be reset using the `clear ip ospf` command, forcing a new DR/BDR election. Once elected, OSPF uses the DR and the BDR routers as follows:

- To reduce the number of adjacencies required on the segment
- To advertise the routers on the Multi-Access segment
- To ensure that updates are sent to all routers on the segment

To better understand these fundamental concepts, reference the basic OSPF network topology illustrated in Figure 39.3 below:

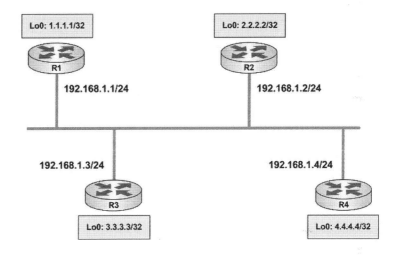

Figure 39.3—OSPF DR and BDR Fundamentals

Referencing Figure 39.3, each router on the segment establishes an adjacency with the DR and the BDR but not with each other. In other words, non-DR/BDR routers do not establish an adjacency with each other. This prevents the routers on the segment from forming N(N-1) adjacencies with each other, which reduces excessive OSPF packet flooding on the segment.

For example, without the concept of a DR/BDR on the segment, each individual router would need to establish an adjacency with every other router on the segment. This would result in 4(4-1) or 12 adjacencies on the segment. However, with the DR/BDR, each individual router needs to establish an adjacency with only these two routers and no other non-DR and BDR routers. The DR and the BDR also establish an adjacency between themselves. This reduces the number of adjacencies required on the segment and on each individual OSPF router, which in turn reduces resources consumption (e.g., memory and processor utilization) on the routers.

Regarding the second point, OSPF views a link as a connection between two routers or nodes. In Multi-Access networks, such as Ethernet, multiple routers can reside on the same segment, as illustrated in Figure 39.3. On such networks, OSPF uses the Network Link State

Advertisement (Type 2 LSA) to advertise the routers on the Multi-Access segment. This LSA is generated by the DR and is flooded only within the area. Because the other non-DR/BDR routers do not establish adjacencies with each other, this LSA allows those routers to know about the other routers on the Multi-Access segment.

To further clarify this point, referencing Figure 39.3, assuming that all routers on the segment have the default OSPF priority value of 1 (and load the OSPF process at the same time), R4 is elected as the DR for the segment because it has the highest router ID. R3 is elected as the BDR for the segment because it has the second-highest router ID. Because R2 and R1 are neither the DR nor the BDR, they are referred to as DROther routers in Cisco terminology. This can be validated using the show ip ospf neighbor command on all routers, as follows:

```
R1#show ip ospf neighbor

Neighbor ID  Pri  State          Dead Time   Address        Interface
2.2.2.2       1   2WAY/DROTHER  00:00:38    192.168.1.2    FastEth0/0
3.3.3.3       1   FULL/BDR      00:00:39    192.168.1.3    FastEth0/0
4.4.4.4       1   FULL/DR       00:00:38    192.168.1.4    FastEth0/0

R2#show ip ospf neighbor

Neighbor ID Pri  State          Dead Time   Address        Interface
1.1.1.1      1   2WAY/DROTHER  00:00:32    192.168.1.1    FastEth0/0
3.3.3.3      1   FULL/BDR      00:00:33    192.168.1.3    FastEth0/0
4.4.4.4      1   FULL/DR       00:00:32    192.168.1.4    FastEth0/0

R3#show ip ospf neighbor

Neighbor ID Pri  State          Dead Time   Address        Interface
1.1.1.1      1   FULL/DROTHER  00:00:36    192.168.1.1    FastEth0/0
2.2.2.2      1   FULL/DROTHER  00:00:36    192.168.1.2    FastEth0/0
4.4.4.4      1   FULL/DR       00:00:35    192.168.1.4    FastEth0/0

R4#show ip ospf neighbor

Neighbor ID Pri  State          Dead Time   Address        Interface
1.1.1.1      1   FULL/DROTHER  00:00:39    192.168.1.1    FastEth0/0
2.2.2.2      1   FULL/DROTHER  00:00:39    192.168.1.2    FastEth0/0
3.3.3.3      1   FULL/BDR      00:00:30    192.168.1.3    FastEth0/0
```

NOTE: The DROther routers remain in the 2WAY/DROTHER state because they exchange their databases only with the DR and BDR routers. Therefore, because there is no full database exchange between the DROther routers, they will never reach the OSPF FULL adjacency state.

Because R4 has been elected DR, it generates the Network LSA, which advertises the other routers on the Multi-Access segment. This can be verified using the show ip ospf database network [link state ID] command on any router on the segment or the show ip ospf database network self-originate command on the DR only. The following illustrates the output of the show ip ospf database network self-originate command on the DR (R4):

```
R4#show ip ospf database network self-originate

              OSPF Router with ID (4.4.4.4) (Process ID 4)

                Net Link States (Area 0)

    Routing Bit Set on this LSA
    LS age: 429
    Options: (No TOS-capability, DC)
    LS Type: Network Links
    Link State ID: 192.168.1.4 (address of Designated Router)
    Advertising Router: 4.4.4.4
    LS Seq Number: 80000006
    Checksum: 0x7E08
    Length: 40
    Network Mask: /24
          Attached Router: 4.4.4.4
          Attached Router: 1.1.1.1
          Attached Router: 2.2.2.2
          Attached Router: 3.3.3.3
```

Referencing the output above, the DR (R4) originates the Type 2 (Network) LSA representing the 192.168.1.0/24 subnet. Because multiple routers exist on this subnet, this 192.168.1.0/24 subnet is referred to as a transit link in OSPF terminology. The Advertising Router field shows the router that originated this LSA. The Network Mask field shows the subnet mask of the transit network, which is 24-bit or 255.255.255.0.

The Attached Router field lists the router IDs of all routers that are on the network segment. This allows all of the routers on the segment to know what other routers also reside on the segment. The output of the show ip ospf database network [link state ID] command on R1, R2, and R3 reflects the same information, as illustrated in the following outputs:

```
R2#show ip ospf database network

              OSPF Router with ID (2.2.2.2) (Process ID 2)

                Net Link States (Area 0)

    Routing Bit Set on this LSA
    LS age: 923
    Options: (No TOS-capability, DC)
    LS Type: Network Links
    Link State ID: 192.168.1.4 (address of Designated Router)
    Advertising Router: 4.4.4.4
    LS Seq Number: 80000006
    Checksum: 0x7E08
    Length: 40
    Network Mask: /24
```

```
        Attached Router: 4.4.4.4
        Attached Router: 1.1.1.1
        Attached Router: 2.2.2.2
        Attached Router: 3.3.3.3

R1#show ip ospf database network

            OSPF Router with ID (1.1.1.1) (Process ID 1)

                Net Link States (Area 0)

  Routing Bit Set on this LSA
  LS age: 951
  Options: (No TOS-capability, DC)
  LS Type: Network Links
  Link State ID: 192.168.1.4 (address of Designated Router)
  Advertising Router: 4.4.4.4
  LS Seq Number: 80000006
  Checksum: 0x7E08
  Length: 40
  Network Mask: /24
        Attached Router: 4.4.4.4
        Attached Router: 1.1.1.1
        Attached Router: 2.2.2.2
        Attached Router: 3.3.3.3


            OSPF Router with ID (4.4.4.4) (Process ID 4)

R3#show ip ospf database network

            OSPF Router with ID (3.3.3.3) (Process ID 3)

                Net Link States (Area 0)

  Routing Bit Set on this LSA
  LS age: 988
  Options: (No TOS-capability, DC)
  LS Type: Network Links
  Link State ID: 192.168.1.4 (address of Designated Router)
  Advertising Router: 4.4.4.4
  LS Seq Number: 80000006
. Checksum: 0x7E08
  Length: 40
  Network Mask: /24
        Attached Router: 4.4.4.4
        Attached Router: 1.1.1.1
        Attached Router: 2.2.2.2
        Attached Router: 3.3.3.3
```

The functionality of the Network LSA and how it is correlated to another LSA, specifically the Router LSA (Type 1), will be described in detail later in this module. For this section, primary emphasis should be placed on understanding that the DR generates and advertises the Network LSA on the Multi-Access segment to advertise other routers that reside on the same segment. This is because routers on the segment establish an adjacency only with the DR and BDR routers and not with each other. Without an adjacency with each other, the routers will never know about other non-DR/BDR routers on the Multi-Access segment.

Finally, regarding the third point made on DR/BDR routers, the DR/BDR routers ensure that all routers on the segment have complete databases. Non-DR/BDR routers send updates to the Multicast group address 224.0.0.6 (AllDRRouters). The DR then advertises these updates to other non-DR/BDR routers by sending the update to the Multicast group address 224.0.0.5 (AllSPFRouters). Figure 39.4 below illustrates an update from R1 (a DROther) to the DR group address referencing the routers illustrated in Figure 39.3:

```
Internet Protocol, Src: 192.168.1.1 (192.168.1.1), Dst: 224.0.0.6 (224.0.0.6)
Open Shortest Path First
OSPF Header
LS Update Packet
  Number of LSAs: 1
  LS Type: Router-LSA
    LS Age: 1 seconds
    Do Not Age: False
    Options: 0x22 (DC, E)
    Link-State Advertisement Type: Router-LSA (1)
    Link State ID: 1.1.1.1
    Advertising Router: 1.1.1.1 (1.1.1.1)
    LS Sequence Number: 0x80000006
    LS Checksum: 0x5f95
    Length: 60
    Flags: 0x00 ()
    Number of Links: 3
    Type: Stub     ID: 10.10.10.10    Data: 255.255.255.255 Metric: 1
    Type: Stub     ID: 1.1.1.1        Data: 255.255.255.255 Metric: 1
    Type: Transit  ID: 192.168.1.4    Data: 192.168.1.1     Metric: 10
```

Figure 39.4—DROther Update to DR/BDR Group Address

R4 (DR) receives this update and in turn sends the same to Multicast group address 224.0.0.5. This group address is used by all OSPF routers, ensuring that all other routers on the segment receive this update. This update from the DR (R4) is illustrated in Figure 39.5 below:

```
Internet Protocol, Src: 192.168.1.4 (192.168.1.4), Dst: 224.0.0.5 (224.0.0.5)
Open Shortest Path First
OSPF Header
LS Update Packet
  Number of LSAs: 1
  LS Type: Router-LSA
    LS Age: 2 seconds
    Do Not Age: False
    Options: 0x22 (DC, E)
    Link-State Advertisement Type: Router-LSA (1)
    Link State ID: 1.1.1.1
    Advertising Router: 1.1.1.1 (1.1.1.1)
    LS Sequence Number: 0x80000006
    LS Checksum: 0x5f95
    Length: 60
    Flags: 0x00 ()
    Number of Links: 3
    Type: Stub     ID: 10.10.10.10    Data: 255.255.255.255 Metric: 1
    Type: Stub     ID: 1.1.1.1        Data: 255.255.255.255 Metric: 1
    Type: Transit  ID: 192.168.1.4    Data: 192.168.1.1     Metric: 10
```

Figure 39.5—DR Update to OSPF Group Address

NOTE: You can see that this is the Update from R1 because the Advertising Router field in both Figures 39.4 and 39.5 contains the router ID (RID) of R1, which is 1.1.1.1.

NOTE: The other LSAs used by OSPF will be described in detail later in this module.

ADDITIONAL ROUTER TYPES

In addition to the Designated Router and the Backup Designated Router on Multi-Access segments, OSPF routers are also described based on their location and function within the OSPF network. The additional router types that are commonly found within the OSPF network include the following:

- Area Border Routers
- Autonomous System Boundary Routers
- Internal routers
- Backbone routers

Figure 39.6 below illustrates a basic OSPF network comprised of two areas, the OSPF backbone area (Area 0) and an additional normal OSPF area (Area 2). R2 has an external BGP neighbor relationship with R1. This diagram will be used to describe the different OSPF router types within this network.

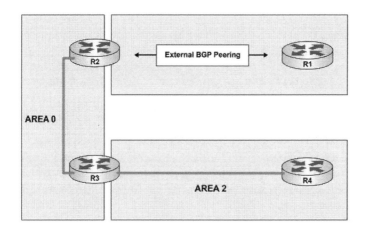

Figure 39.6 Additional OSPF Router Types

An Area Border Router (ABR) is an OSPF router that connects one or more OSPF areas to the OSPF backbone. This means that it must have at least one interface in Area 0 and another interface, or interfaces, within a different OSPF area. ABRs are members of all areas to which they belong, and they keep a separate Link State Database for every area to which they belong. Referencing Figure 39.6, R3 would be considered an ABR, as it connects Area 2 to the OSPF backbone, or Area 0.

An Autonomous System Boundary Router (ASBR), in the traditional sense, resides at the edge of the routing domain and defines the boundary between the internal and the external networks. Referencing Figure 39.6, R2 would be considered an ASBR. In addition to injecting routing information from other protocols (e.g., BGP), a router can also be classified as an ASBR if it injects static routes or connected subnets into the OSPF domain.

Internal routers maintain all operational interfaces within a single OSPF area. Based on the network topology illustrated in Figure 39.6, R4 would be considered an internal router because its only interface resides within a single OSPF area.

Backbone routers are routers that have an interface in the OSPF backbone. Backbone routers can include routers that have interfaces only in the OSPF backbone area, or routers that have an interface in the OSPF backbone area as well as interfaces in other areas (ABRs). Based on the topology illustrated in Figure 39.6, both R2 and R3 would be considered backbone routers.

> **NOTE:** OSPF routers can have multiple roles. For example, R2 is both an ASBR and a backbone router, while R3 is both a backbone router and an ABR. Throughout this module, we will take a detailed look at these types of routers and their roles and functions within the OSPF domain.

OSPF PACKET TYPES

The different types of packets sent by OSPF routers are contained in the common 24-byte OSPF header. While delving into the specifics of the OSPF header is beyond the scope of the CCNA exam requirements, it is still important to have a basic understanding of the fields contained within this header and what they are used for. Figure 39.7 below illustrates the common 24-octet OSPF header:

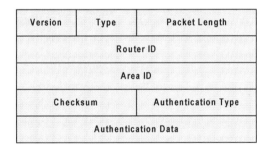

Figure 39.7—The OSPF Packet Header

The 8-bit Version field specifies the OSPF version. The default value for this field is 2. However, when OSPFv3 is enabled, this field is also set to 3.

The 8-bit Type field is used to specify the OSPF packet type. The five main OSPF packet types, which are described in detail later in this module, are as follows:

- Type 1 = Hello packet
- Type 2 = Database Description packet

- Type 3 = Link State Request packet
- Type 4 = Link State Update packet
- Type 5 = Link State Acknowledgement packet

The 16-bit Packet Length field is used to specify the length of the protocol packet. This length includes the standard OSPF header.

The 32-bit Router ID field is used to specify the IP address of the router from which the packet originated. On Cisco IOS devices, this field will contain the highest IP address of all physical interfaces configured on the device running OSPF. If Loopback interfaces are configured on the device, the field will contain the highest IP address of all configured Loopback interfaces. Alternatively, this field can also contain a manually configured router ID if one has been explicitly configured or specified by the administrator.

> **NOTE:** When the router ID has been selected, it will never change unless the router is reloaded, the interface that the IP address was derived from is shut down or removed, or the OSPF process is reset using the clear ip ospf process privileged EXEC command on the router.

The 32-bit Area ID field is used to identify the OSPF area of the packet. A packet can belong only to a single OSPF area. If the packet is received via a virtual link, then the Area ID will be the OSPF backbone, or Area 0. Virtual links are described in detail later in this module.

The Checksum field is 16-bits long and indicates the standard IP checksum of the entire contents of the packet, starting with the OSPF packet header but excluding the 64-bit Authentication Data field. If the packet's length is not an integral number of 16-bit words, the packet is padded with a byte of zero before being checksummed.

The 16-bit Authentication (Auth) Type field identifies the type of authentication used. This field is valid only for OSPFv2 and may contain one of the following three codes:

- Code 0—This means that there is null (no) authentication; this is the default
- Code 1—This means that the authentication type is plain text
- Code 2—This means that the authentication type is Message Digest 5 (MD5)

Finally, the 64-bit Authentication Data field is for the actual authentication information or data, if authentication has been enabled. It is important to remember that this field is valid only for OSPFv2. If plain text authentication is being used, this field contains the authentication key. However, if MD5 authentication is being used, this field is redefined into several other fields, which are beyond the scope of the CCNA exam requirements. Figure 39.8 below shows the different fields as they appear in a wire capture of an OSPF packet:

```
Frame 20 (94 bytes on wire, 94 bytes captured)
Ethernet II, Src: Cisco_a7:f3:a0 (00:0c:ce:a7:f3:a0), Dst: IP
Internet Protocol, Src: 192.168.1.3 (192.168.1.3), Dst: 224.0
Open Shortest Path First
OSPF Header
 OSPF Version: 2
 Message Type: Hello Packet (1)
 Packet Length: 48
 Source OSPF Router: 3.3.3.3 (3.3.3.3)
 Area ID: 0.0.0.0 (Backbone)
 Packet Checksum: 0x4d3a [correct]
 Auth Type: Null
 Auth Data (none)
OSPF Hello Packet
OSPF LLS Data Block
```

Figure 39.8—OSPF Packet Header Wire Capture

Within the OSPF packet header, the 8-bit Type field is used to specify the OSPF packet type. Again, the five OSPF packet types are as follows:

- Type 1 = Hello packet
- Type 2 = Database Description packet
- Type 3 = Link State Request packet
- Type 4 = Link State Update packet
- Type 5 = Link State Acknowledgement packet

OSPF Hello Packets

Hello packets are used to discover other directly connected OSPF routers and to establish OSPF adjacencies between OSPF routers. OSPF uses Multicast to send Hello packets for Broadcast and Point-to-Point network types. These packets are addressed to the AllSPFRouters Multicast group address 224.0.0.5. For Non-Broadcast links (e.g., Frame Relay), OSPF uses Unicast to send Hello packets directly to statically configured neighbors.

> **NOTE:** By default, all OSPF packets (i.e., Multicast and Unicast) are sent with an IP TTL of 1. This limits these packets to the local link. In other words, you cannot establish an OSPF adjacency with another router that is more than one hop away. This is also applicable to EIGRP.

OSPF Hello packets are also used on Broadcast links to elect a DR and a BDR. The DR listens specifically to the Multicast address 224.0.0.6 (AllDRRouters). The DR and the BDR were described in detail previously in this module. Figure 39.9 below illustrates the fields contained within the OSPF Hello packet:

```
Open Shortest Path First
 OSPF Header
 OSPF Hello Packet
   Network Mask: 255.255.255.0
   Hello Interval: 10 seconds
   Options: 0x12 (L, E)
     0... .... = DN: DN-bit is NOT set
     .0.. .... = 0: O-bit is NOT set
     ..0. .... = DC: Demand circuits are NOT supported
     ...1 .... = L: The packet contains LLS data block
     .... 0... = NP: Nssa is NOT supported
     .... .0.. = MC: NOT multicast capable
     .... ..1. = E: ExternalRoutingCapability
   Router Priority: 1
   Router Dead Interval: 40 seconds
   Designated Router: 192.168.1.3
   Backup Designated Router: 192.168.1.2
   Active Neighbor: 20.2.2.2
 OSPF LLS Data Block
```

Figure 39.9—OSPF Hello Packet

The 4-byte Network Mask field contains the subnet mask of the advertising OSPF interface. The network mask is checked only on Broadcast media. Unnumbered Point-to-Point interfaces and virtual links, both of which will be described later in this module, set this value to 0.0.0.0.

The 2-byte Hello field displays the value of the Hello interval, which is the number of seconds between two Hello packets, requested by the advertising router. Possible values range from 1 to 255. By default, the Hello interval is 10 seconds on Broadcast and Point-to-Point media and 30 seconds on all other media.

The 1-byte Options field is used by the local router to advertise optional capabilities. Each bit in the Options field represents a different function. Going into them is outside the scope of the CCNA exam requirements.

The 1-byte Router Priority field contains the priority of the local router. By default, this field has a value of 1. The value is used in the election of the DR and the BDR. Possible values range from 0 to 255. The higher the priority, the higher the chances the local router will become the DR. A priority value of 0 means that the local router will not participate in the DR or the BDR election.

The 4-byte Router Dead Interval field shows the value of the dead interval. The dead interval is the time (seconds) before a neighbor router is declared dead. This value is requested by the advertising router. The default value for the dead interval is four times the value of the Hello interval, which would be a default of 40 seconds on Broadcast and Point-to-Point interfaces and 120 seconds on all other types of media.

The 4-byte Designated Router field lists the IP address of the DR. A value of 0.0.0.0 is used when no DR has been elected, for example, on a Point-to-Point link or when a router has been explicitly configured not to participate in this election.

The 4-byte Backup Designated Router field identifies the BDR and lists the interface address of the current BDR. A value of 0.0.0.0 is used when no BDR has been elected.

Finally, the (Active) Neighbor field is a variable length field that displays the router ID of all OSPF routers for which a Hello packet has been received on the network segment.

Database Description Packets

Database Description packets are used during the database exchange when each OSPF router advertises its local database information. These packets are commonly referred to as DBD packets or as DD packets. The first DBD packet is used for the Master and Slave election for database exchange. The DBD packet also contains the initial sequence number selected by the Master. The router with the highest router ID becomes the Master and initiates database synchronization. This is the only router that can increment the sequence number. The Master router begins the database exchange and polls the Slave for information. The Master and Slave election is held on a per-neighbor basis.

It is important to understand that the Master and Slave election process is not the same as the DR and BDR election process. This is commonly incorrectly assumed. The Master and Slave election process is based solely on the router with the highest IP address; however, the DR/BDR election process may be determined using either the IP address or the priority value.

Assume, for example, two routers named R1 and R2 are beginning the adjacency establishment process. R1 has a RID of 1.1.1.1, while R2 has a RID of 2.2.2.2. The network administrator has configured R1 with an OSPF priority value of 255 to ensure that this router will be elected the DR. During the Master and Slave determination process, R2 will be elected master by virtue of the higher RID. However, the priority value configured on R1 results in R1 being elected the DR. In essence, the DR (R1) can be the Slave during the Master and Slave election process.

After the Master and Slave have been elected, DBD packets are used to summarize the local database by sending LSA headers to the remote router. The remote router analyses these headers to determine whether it lacks any information within its own copy of the LSDB. The OSPF Database Description packet is illustrated in Figure 39.10 below:

```
Open Shortest Path First
 OSPF Header
 OSPF DB Description
   Interface MTU: 1500
  Options: 0x52 (O, L, E)
     0... .... = DN: DN-bit is NOT set
     .1.. .... = O: O-bit is SET
     ..0. .... = DC: Demand circuits are NOT supported
     ...1 .... = L: The packet contains LLS data block
     .... 0... = NP: Nssa is NOT supported
     .... .0.. = MC: NOT multicast capable
     .... ..1. = E: ExternalRoutingCapability
  DB Description: 0x02 (M)
     .... 0... = R: OOBResync bit is NOT set
     .... .0.. = I: Init bit is NOT set
     .... ..1. = M: More bit is SET
     .... ...0 = MS: Master/Slave bit is NOT set
   DD Sequence: 5409
 LSA Header
 LSA Header
 OSPF LLS Data Block
```

Figure 39.10—OSPF Database Description Packet

Within the DBD packet, the 2-byte Interface MTU field contains the MTU value, in octets, of the outgoing interface. In other words, this field contains the largest data size that can be sent through the associated interface (in bytes). When the interface is used on a virtual link, the field is set to a value of 0x0000. In order for an OSPF neighbor adjacency to be established successfully, the MTU must be the same on all routers. If you change this value on one router, you must configure the same value on all other routers on the same subnet (or use the `ip ospf mtu-ignore` command).

> **NOTE:** The interface MTU values for EIGRP do not have to be the same in order for an EIGRP neighbor relationship to be established successfully.

The 1-byte Options field contains the same options contained within the OSPF Hello packet. For brevity, these options will not be described again.

The Database Description or Flags field is a 1-byte field that provides an OSPF router with the capability to exchange multiple DBD packets with a neighbor during an adjacency formation.

The 4-byte DBD Sequence Number field is used to guarantee that all DBD packets are received and processed during the synchronization process through the use of a sequence number. The Master router initializes this field to a unique value in the first DBD packet, with each subsequent packet being incremented by 1. The sequence number is incremented only by the Master.

Finally, the variable length LSA Header field carries the LSA headers describing the local router's database information. Each header is 20 octets in length and uniquely identifies each LSA in the database. Each DBD packet may contain multiple LSA headers.

Link State Request Packets

Link State Request (LSR) packets are sent by OSPF routers to request missing or out-of-date database information. These packets contain identifiers that uniquely describe the requested Link State Advertisement. An individual LSR packet may contain a single set of identifiers or multiple sets of identifiers to request multiple LSAs. LSR packets are also used after database exchange to request LSAs that were seen during the database exchange that the local router does not have. Figure 39.11 below illustrates the format of the OSPF LSR packet:

```
Open Shortest Path First
OSPF Header
Link State Request
  Link-State Advertisement Type: Router-LSA (1)
  Link State ID: 3.3.3.3
  Advertising Router: 3.3.3.3 (3.3.3.3)
Link State Request
  Link-State Advertisement Type: Network-LSA (2)
  Link State ID: 192.168.1.3
  Advertising Router: 3.3.3.3 (3.3.3.3)
```

Fig. 39.11—OSPF Link State Request Packet

The 4-byte Link State Advertisement Type field contains the type of LSA being requested. It may contain one of the following fields:

- Type 1 = Router Link State Advertisement
- Type 2 = Network Link State Advertisement
- Type 3 = Network Summary Link State Advertisement
- Type 4 = ASBR Summary Link State Advertisement
- Type 5 = AS External Link State Advertisement
- Type 6 = Multicast Link State Advertisement
- Type 7 = NSSA External Link State Advertisement
- Type 8 = External Attributes Link State Advertisement
- Type 9 = Opaque Link State Advertisement—Link Local
- Type 10 = Opaque Link State Advertisement—Area
- Type 11 = Opaque Link State Advertisement—Autonomous System

NOTE: Some of the LSAs listed above are described in detail in the following sections.

The 4-byte Link State ID field encodes information specific to the LSA. The information that is contained in this field depends upon the type of LSA. Finally, the 4-byte Advertising Router field contains the RID of the router that first originated the LSA.

Link State Update Packets

Link State Update (LSU) packets are used by the router to advertise LSAs. LSU packets may be Unicast to an OSPF neighbor in response to a received LSR from that neighbor. Most commonly, however, they are reliably flooded throughout the network to the AllSPFRouters Multicast group address 224.0.0.5 until each router has a copy. The flooded updates are then acknowledged in the LSA Acknowledgement packet. If the LSA is not acknowledged, it will be retransmitted every five seconds, by default. Figure 39.12 below shows an LSU sent to a neighbor in response to an LSR:

```
Internet Protocol, Src: 192.168.1.3 (192.168.1.3), Dst: 192.168.1.2 (192.168.1.2)
Open Shortest Path First
 OSPF Header
 LS Update Packet
  Number of LSAs: 1
 LS Type: Summary-LSA (IP network)
  LS Age: 3600 seconds
  Do Not Age: False
 Options: 0x22 (DC, E)
  Link-State Advertisement Type: Summary-LSA (IP network) (3)
  Link State ID: 150.1.1.0
  Advertising Router: 20.2.2.2 (20.2.2.2)
  LS Sequence Number: 0x80000001
  LS Checksum: 0x70d9
  Length: 28
  Netmask: 255.255.255.0
  Metric: 64
```

Figure 39.12—Unicast LSU Packet

Figure 39.13 below illustrates an LSU that is reliably flooded to the Multicast group address 224.0.0.5:

```
 Internet Protocol, Src: 192.168.1.2 (192.168.1.2), Dst: 224.0.0.5 (224.0.0.5)
 Open Shortest Path First
 OSPF Header
 LS Update Packet
  Number of LSAs: 1
  LS Type: Summary-LSA (IP network)
  LS Age: 1 seconds
  Do Not Age: False
  Options: 0x22 (DC, E)
  Link-State Advertisement Type: Summary-LSA (IP network) (3)
  Link State ID: 150.1.1.0
  Advertising Router: 20.2.2.2 (20.2.2.2)
  LS Sequence Number: 0x80000002
  LS Checksum: 0x6eda
  Length: 28
  Netmask: 255.255.255.0
  Metric: 64
```

Figure 39.13—Multicast LSU Packet

The LSU is comprised of two parts. The first part is the 4-byte Number of LSAs field. This field displays the number of LSAs carried within the LSU packet. The second part is one or more Link State Advertisements. This variable-length field contains the complete LSA. Each type of LSA has a common header format along with specific data fields to describe its information. An LSU packet may contain a single LSA or multiple LSAs.

Link State Acknowledgement Packets

The Link State Acknowledgement (LSAck) packet is used to acknowledge each LSA and is sent in response to LSU packets. By explicitly acknowledging packets with LSAcks, the flooding mechanism used by OSPF is considered reliable.

The LSAck contains the common OSPF header followed by a list of LSA headers. This variable-length field allows the local router to acknowledge multiple LSAs using a single packet. LSAcks are sent using Multicast. On Multi-Access networks, if the router sending the LSAck is a DR or a BDR, then LSAcks are sent to the Multicast group address 224.0.0.5 (AllSPFRouters). However, if the router sending the LSAcks is not a DR or a BDR device, then LSAck packets are sent to the Multicast group address 224.0.0.6 (AllDRRouters). Figure 39.14 below illustrates the format of the LSAck:

```
 Open Shortest Path First
 OSPF Header
  OSPF Version: 2
  Message Type: LS Acknowledge (5)
  Packet Length: 84
  Source OSPF Router: 20.2.2.2 (20.2.2.2)
  Area ID: 0.0.0.0 (Backbone)
  Packet Checksum: 0xca63 [correct]
  Auth Type: Null
  Auth Data (none)
 LSA Header
 LSA Header
 LSA Header
```

Figure 39.14—Link State Acknowledgement Packet

In conclusion, it is important to remember the different OSPF packet types and what information they contain. This not only will benefit you in the exam but also will aid you in understanding the overall operation of OSPF as a protocol.

In Cisco IOS software, you can use the `show ip ospf traffic` command to view OSPF packet statistics. This command shows the total count for the sent and received OSPF packets, and then segments this further to the individual OSPF process and, finally, to the interfaces enabled for OSPF routing under that process. This command can also be used to troubleshoot OSPF adjacency establishment and is not as processor intensive as debugging. The information printed by this command is illustrated in the following output:

```
R4#show ip ospf traffic

OSPF statistics:
  Rcvd: 702 total, 0 checksum errors
        682 hello, 3 database desc, 0 link state req
        12 link state updates, 5 link state acks

  Sent: 1378 total
        1364 hello, 2 database desc, 1 link state req
        5 link state updates, 6 link state acks


            OSPF Router with ID (4.4.4.4) (Process ID 4)

OSPF queue statistics for process ID 4:

                    InputQ      UpdateQ      OutputQ
    Limit           0           200          0
    Drops           0           0            0
    Max delay [msec] 4          0            0
    Max size        2           2            2
      Invalid       0           0            0
      Hello         0           0            1
      DB des        2           2            1
      LS req        0           0            0
      LS upd        0           0            0
      LS ack        0           0            0
    Current size    0           0            0
      Invalid       0           0            0
      Hello         0           0            0
      DB des        0           0            0
      LS req        0           0            0
      LS upd        0           0            0
      LS ack        0           0            0

  Interface statistics:

    Interface Serial0/0

OSPF packets received/sent
```

```
         Invalid  Hellos  DB-des  LS-req  LS-upd  LS-ack  Total
Rx: 0             683     3       0       12      5       703
Tx: 0             684     2       1       5       6       698

OSPF header errors
   Length 0, Auth Type 0, Checksum 0, Version 0,
   Bad Source 0, No Virtual Link 0, Area Mismatch 0,
   No Sham Link 0, Self Originated 0, Duplicate ID 0,
   Hello 0, MTU Mismatch 0, Nbr Ignored 0,
   LLS 0, Unknown Neighbor 0, Authentication 0,
   TTL Check Fail 0,

OSPF LSA errors
   Type 0, Length 0, Data 0, Checksum 0,

      Interface FastEthernet0/0

OSPF packets received/sent
         Invalid  Hellos  DB-des  LS-req  LS-upd  LS-ack  Total
Rx: 0             0       0       0       0       0       0
Tx: 0             682     0       0       0       0       682

OSPF header errors
   Length 0, Auth Type 0, Checksum 0, Version 0,
   Bad Source 0, No Virtual Link 0, Area Mismatch 0,
   No Sham Link 0, Self Originated 0, Duplicate ID 0,
   Hello 0, MTU Mismatch 0, Nbr Ignored 0,
   LLS 0, Unknown Neighbor 0, Authentication 0,
   TTL Check Fail 0,

OSPF LSA errors
   Type 0, Length 0, Data 0, Checksum 0,

Summary traffic statistics for process ID 4:

   Rcvd: 703 total, 0 errors
         683 hello, 3 database desc, 0 link state req
         12 link state upds, 5 link state acks, 0 invalid
   Sent: 1380 total
         1366 hello, 2 database desc, 1 link state req
         5 link state upds, 6 link state acks, 0 invalid
```

ESTABLISHING ADJACENCIES

Routers running OSPF transition through several states before establishing an adjacency. The routers exchange different types of packets during these states. This exchange of messages allows all routers that establish an adjacency to have a consistent view of the network. Additional changes to the current network are simply sent out as incremental updates. The different states are the Down, Attempt, Init, 2-Way, Exstart, Exchange, Loading, and Full states, as described below:

- The Down state is the starting state for all OSPF routers. However, the local router may also show a neighbor in this state when no Hello packets have been received within the specified router dead interval for that interface.
- The Attempt state is valid only for OSPF neighbors on NBMA networks. In this state, a Hello has been sent but no information has been received from the statically configured neighbor within the dead interval; however, some effort is being made to establish an adjacency with this neighbor.
- The Init state is reached when an OSPF router receives a Hello packet from a neighbor but the local RID is not listed in the received Neighbor field. If OSPF Hello parameters, such as timer values, do not match, then OSPF routers will never progress beyond this state.
- The 2-Way state indicates bi-directional communication (each router has seen the other's Hello packet) with the OSPF neighbor(s). In this state, the local router has received a Hello packet with its own RID in the Neighbor field and Hello packet parameters are identical on the two routers. At this state, a router decides whether to become adjacent with this neighbor. On Multi-Access networks, the DR and the BDR are elected during this phase.
- The Exstart state is used for the initialization of the database synchronization process. It is at this stage that the local router and its neighbor establish which router is in charge of the database synchronization process. The Master and Slave are elected in this state, and the first sequence number for DBD exchange is decided by the Master in this stage.
- The Exchange state is where routers describe the contents of their databases using DBD packets. Each DBD sequence is explicitly acknowledged, and only one outstanding DBD is allowed at a time. During this phase, LSR packets are also sent to request a new instance of the LSA. The M (More) bit is used to request missing information during this stage. When both routers have exchanged their complete databases, they will both set the M bit to 0.
- In the Loading state, OSPF routers build an LSR and Link State Retransmission list. LSR packets are sent to request the more recent instance of an LSA that has not been received during the Exchange process. Updates that are sent during this phase are placed on the Link State Retransmission list until the local router receives an acknowledgment. If the local router also receives an LSR during this phase, it will respond with a Link State Update that contains the requested information.
- The Full state indicates that the OSPF neighbors have exchanged their entire databases and both agree (i.e., have the same view of the network). Both neighboring routers in this state add the adjacency to their local database and advertise the relationship in a Link State Update packet. At this point, the routing tables are calculated, or recalculated if the adjacency was reset. Full is the normal state for an OSPF router. If a router is stuck in another state, it's an indication that there are problems in forming adjacencies. The only exception to this is the 2-Way state, which is normal in Broadcast and Non-Broadcast Multi-Access networks where routers achieve the Full state with their DR and BDR only. Other neighbors always see each other as 2-Way.

In order for an OSPF adjacency to be established successfully, certain parameters on both routers must match. These parameters include the following:

- The interface MTU values (can be configured to be ignored)
- The Hello and Dead timers
- The Area ID
- The Authentication type and password
- The Stub Area flag
- Compatible network types

These parameters will be described as we progress through this module. If these parameters do not match, the OSPF adjacency will never fully establish.

NOTE: In addition to mismatched parameters, it is also important to remember that on a Multi-Access network, if both routers are configured with a priority value of 0, then the adjacency will not be established. The DR must be present on such network types.

OSPF LSAS AND THE LINK STATE DATABASE (LSDB)

As stated in the previous section, OSPF uses several types of Link State Advertisements. Each LSA begins with a standard 20-byte LSA header. This header contains the following fields:

- Link State Age
- Options
- Link State Type
- Link State ID
- Advertising Router
- Link State Sequence Number
- Link State Checksum
- Length

The 2-byte Link State Age field states the time (in seconds) since the LSA was originated. The maximum age of the LSA is 3600 seconds, which means that if the age reaches 3600 seconds, the LSA is removed from the database. To avoid this, the LSA is refreshed every 1800 seconds.

The 1-byte Options field contains the same options as those in the OSPF Hello packet.

The 1-byte Link State Type field represents the types of LSAs. These different LSA packet types are described in detail in the following sections.

The 4-byte Link State ID field identifies the portion of the network that is being described by the LSA. The contents of this field depend upon the advertisement's LS type.

The 4-byte Advertising Router field represents the router ID of the router originating the LSA.

The 1-byte Link State Sequence Number field detects old or duplicate Link State Advertisements. Successive instances of an LSA are given successive Link State Sequence Numbers. The first sequence number 0x80000000 is reserved; therefore, the actual first sequence number is always 0x80000001. This value is incremented as packets are sent. The maximum sequence number is 0x7FFFFFFF.

The 2-byte Link State Checksum field performs the Fletcher checksum of the complete contents of the LSA, including the LSA header. The Link State Age field is not included in the checksum. The checksum is performed because Link State Advertisements can be corrupted while being stored in memory due to router software or hardware issues or during flooding due to Physical Layer errors, for example.

> **NOTE:** The checksum is performed at the time the LSA is generated or is received. In addition, the checksum is performed at every CheckAge interval, which is 10 minutes. If this field has a value of 0, then it means that the checksum has not been performed.

The 2-byte Length field is the final field and includes the length (in bytes) of the LSA. This includes the 20-byte LSA header. Figure 39.15 below illustrates the LSA header:

```
Open Shortest Path First
 OSPF Header
 LSA Header
  LS Age: 3600 seconds
  Do Not Age: False
  Options: 0x22 (DC, E)
  Link-State Advertisement Type: Router-LSA (1)
  Link State ID: 20.2.2.2
  Advertising Router: 20.2.2.2 (20.2.2.2)
  LS Sequence Number: 0x80000005
  LS Checksum: 0xcb54
  Length: 36
 LSA Header
 LSA Header
```

Figure 39.15—Link State Advertisement Header

While OSPF supports 11 different types of Link State Advertisements, only LSA Types 1, 2, and 3, which are used to calculate internal routes, and LSA Types 4, 5, and 7, which are used to calculate external routes, are within the scope of the CCNA exam requirements. Because there is really no need to go into great detail on the other LSAs for the CCNA exam, these LSAs will not be described further in this guide.

In Cisco IOS software, the `show ip ospf database` command is used to view the contents of the Link State Database. This command, when used without any keywords, prints out a summary of LSAs in all areas to which the router is connected. The command supports several keywords that provide greater granularity in allowing network administrators to restrict output only to specific types of LSAs, LSAs advertised by the local router, or even LSAs advertised by other routers within the OSPF domain.

While illustrating the output of the usage of each keyword is unrealistic, the following section describes the different LSAs and the common keywords used in conjunction with the show ip ospf database command to view detailed information on these LSAs. The keywords supported by this command are illustrated in the following output:

```
R3#show ip ospf database ?
  adv-router          Advertising Router link states
  asbr-summary        ASBR Summary link states
  database-summary    Summary of database
  external            External link states
  network             Network link states
  nssa-external       NSSA External link states
  opaque-area         Opaque Area link states
  opaque-as           Opaque AS link states
  opaque-link         Opaque Link-Local link states
  router              Router link states
  self-originate      Self-originated link states
  summary             Network Summary link states
  |                   Output modifiers
  <cr>
```

Router Link State Advertisements (Type 1)

Type 1 LSAs are generated by each router for each area to which it belongs. The Router LSA lists the originating router's router ID (RID). Each individual router will generate a Type 1 LSA for the area in which it resides. The Router LSAs are the first LSA types printed in the output of the show ip ospf database command.

Network Link State Advertisements (Type 2)

OSPF uses the Network Link State Advertisement (Type 2 LSA) to advertise the routers on the Multi-Access segment. This LSA is generated by the DR and is flooded only within the area. Because the other non-DR/BDRs do not establish adjacencies with each other, the Network LSA allows those routers to know about the other routers on the Multi-Access segment.

Network Summary Link State Advertisements (Type 3)

The Network (Type 3) LSA is a summary of destinations outside of the local area but within the OSPF domain. In other words, this LSA advertises both inter-area and intra-area routing information. The Network Summary LSA does not carry any topological information. Instead, the only information contained in the LSA is an IP prefix. Type 3 LSAs are generated by ABRs and are flooded to all adjacent areas. By default, each Type 3 LSA matches a single Router or Network LSA on a one-for-one basis. In other words, a Type 3 LSA exists for each individual Type 1 and Type 2 LSA. Special attention must be paid to how these LSAs are propagated in relation to the OSPF backbone. This propagation or flooding is performed as follows:

- Network Summary (Type 3) LSAs are advertised from a non-backbone area to the OSPF backbone for intra-area routes (i.e., for Type 1 and Type 2 LSAs).

- Network Summary (Type 3) LSAs are advertised from the OSPF backbone to other non- backbone areas for both intra-area (i.e., Area 0 Type 1 and Type 2 LSAs) and inter-area routes (i.e., for the Type 3 LSAs flooded into the backbone by other ABRs).

The next three Link State Advertisements, Type 4, Type 5, and Type 7, are used in external route calculation. Type 4 and Type 5 LSAs will be described in the following sections. Type 7 LSAs will be described later in this module when we discuss the different types of OSPF areas.

ASBR Summary Link State Advertisements (Type 4)

The Type 4 LSA describes information regarding the Autonomous System Boundary Router (ASBR). This LSA contains the same packet format as the Type 3 LSA and performs the same basic functionality, with some notable differences. Like the Type 3 LSA, the Type 4 LSA is generated by the ABR. For both LSAs, the Advertising Router field contains the RID of the ABR that generated the Summary LSA. However, the Type 4 LSA is created by the ABR for each ASBR reachable by a Router LSA. The ABR then injects the Type 4 LSA into the appropriate area. This LSA provides reachability information on the ASBR itself. The key differences between the Type 3 and Type 4 LSAs that you should be familiar with are listed below in Table 39.2:

Table 39.2—Type 3 and Type 4 Summary LSAs

Type 3 Summary LSA	Type 4 Summary LSA
Provides information about the network link.	Provides information about the ASBR.
The Network Mask field contains the subnet mask value of the network.	The Network Mask field will always contain a value of 0.0.0.0, or simply just 0.
The Link State ID field contains the actual network number.	The Link State ID field contains the router ID of the ASBR.

AS External Link State Advertisements (Type 5)

The External Link State Advertisement is used to describe destinations that are external to the autonomous system. In other words, Type 5 LSAs provide the network information necessary to reach the external networks. In addition to external routes, the default route for an OSPF routing domain can also be injected as a Type 5 Link State Advertisement.

OSPF AREAS

In addition to the backbone (Area 0) and other non-backbone areas described and used in the examples in previous sections of this module, the OSPF specification also defines several "special" types of areas. The configuration of these areas is used primarily to reduce the size of the Link State Database on routers residing within those areas by preventing the injection of different types of LSAs (primarily Type 5 LSAs) into certain areas, which include the following:

- Not-so-stubby Areas
- Totally Not-so-stubby Areas
- Stub Areas
- Totally Stubby Areas

Not-so-stubby Areas (NSSAs)

Not-so-stubby Areas (NSSAs) are a type of OSPF Stub Area that allows the injection of external routing information by an ASBR using an NSSA External LSA (Type 7). As stated in the previous section, Type 4, Type 5, and Type 7 LSAs are used for external route calculation. We will not examine Type 7 LSAs in detail or how they are used in NSSAs.

Totally Not-so-stubby Areas (TNSSAs)

Totally Not-so-stubby Areas (TNSSAs) are an extension of NSSAs. Like NSSAs, Type 5 LSAs are not allowed into a TNSSA; unlike NSSAs, Summary LSAs are also not allowed into a TNSSA. In addition, when a TNSSA is configured, the default route is injected into the area as a Type 7 LSA. TNSSAs have the following characteristics:

- Type 7 LSAs are converted into Type 5 LSAs at the NSSA ABR
- They do not allow Network Summary LSAs
- They do not allow External LSAs
- The default route is injected as a Summary LSA

Stub Areas

Stub areas are somewhat similar to NSSAs, with the major exception being that external routes (Type 5 or Type 7) are not allowed into Stub Areas. It is important to understand that Stub functionality in OSPF and EIGRP is not at all similar. In OSPF, the configuration of an area as a Stub Area reduces the size of the routing table and the OSPF database for the routers within the Stub Area by preventing external LSAs from being advertised into such areas without any further configuration. Stub Areas have the following characteristics:

- The default route is injected into the Stub Area by the ABR as a Type 3 LSA
- Type 3 LSAs from other areas are permitted into these areas
- External route LSAs (i.e., Type 4 and Type 5 LSAs) are not allowed

Totally Stubby Areas

Totally Stubby Areas (TSAs) are an extension of Stub Areas. However, unlike Stub Areas, TSAs further reduce the size of the LSDB on routers in the TSA by restricting Type 3 LSAs, in addition to the external LSAs. TSAs are typically configured on routers that have a single ingress and egress point into the network, for example in a traditional hub-and-spoke network. The area routers forward all external traffic to the ABR. The ABR is also the exit point for all backbone and inter-area traffic to the TSA, which has the following characteristics:

- The default route is injected into Stub Areas as a Type 3 Network Summary LSA
- Type 3, Type 4, and Type 5 LSAs from other areas are not permitted into these areas

ROUTE METRICS AND BEST ROUTE SELECTION

In the following sections, you will learn about the OSPF metric and how it is calculated.

Calculating the OSPF Metric

The OSPF metric is commonly referred to as the cost. The cost is derived from the bandwidth of a link using the formula 10^8 / bandwidth (in bps). This means that different links are assigned different cost values, depending on their bandwidth. Using this formula, the OSPF cost of a 10Mbps Ethernet interface would be calculated as follows:

- Cost = 10^8 / bandwidth (bps)
- Cost = 100 000 000 / 10 000 000
- Cost = 10

Using the same formula, the OSPF cost of a T1 link would be calculated as follows:

- Cost = 10^8 / bandwidth (bps)
- Cost = 100 000 000 / 1 544 000
- Cost = 64.77

NOTE: When calculating the OSPF metric, point math is not used. Therefore, any such values are always rounded down to the nearest integer. Regarding the previous example, the actual cost for a T1 link would be rounded down to 64.

The OSPF cost of an interface can be viewed using the show ip ospf interface [name] command, as was illustrated previously. The default reference bandwidth used in metric calculation can be viewed in the output of the show ip protocols command, as is illustrated in the following output:

```
R4#show ip protocols
Routing Protocol is "ospf 4"
  Outgoing update filter list for all interfaces is not set
  Incoming update filter list for all interfaces is not set
  Router ID 4.4.4.4
  Number of areas in this router is 1. 1 normal 0 stub 0 nssa
  Maximum path: 4
  Routing for Networks:
    0.0.0.0 255.255.255.255 Area 2
  Reference bandwidth unit is 100 mbps
  Routing Information Sources:
    Gateway         Distance      Last Update
    3.3.3.3              110       00:00:03
  Distance: (default is 110)
```

The default reference bandwidth used in OSPF cost calculation can be adjusted using the `auto-cost reference-bandwidth <1-4294967>` router configuration command and specifying the reference bandwidth value in Mbps. This is particularly important in networks that have links that have a bandwidth value over 100Mbps, for example, GigabitEthernet links. In such networks, the default value assigned to the GigabitEthernet link would be the same as that of a FastEthernet link. In most cases, this is certainly not desirable, especially if OSPF attempts to load balance across both links.

To prevent this skewed calculation of cost value, the `auto-cost reference-bandwidth 1000` router configuration command should be issued on the router. This results in a recalculation of cost values on the router using the new reference bandwidth value. For example, following this configuration, the cost of a T1 link would be recalculated as follows:

- Cost = 10^9 / bandwidth (bps)
- Cost = 1 000 000 000 / 1 544 000
- Cost = 647.66

NOTE: Again, because the OSPF metric does not support point values, this would be rounded down to a metric value of simply 647, as illustrated in the following output:

```
R4#show ip ospf interface Serial0/0
Serial0/0 is up, line protocol is up
  Internet Address 10.0.2.4/24, Area 2
  Process ID 4, Router ID 4.4.4.4, Network Type POINT_TO_POINT, Cost: 647
  Transmit Delay is 1 sec, State POINT_TO_POINT
  Timer intervals configured, Hello 10, Dead 60, Wait 60, Retransmit 5
    oob-resync timeout 60
    Hello due in 00:00:01
  Supports Link-local Signaling (LLS)
  Index 2/2, flood queue length 0
  Next 0x0(0)/0x0(0)
  Last flood scan length is 1, maximum is 1
  Last flood scan time is 0 msec, maximum is 0 msec
  Neighbor Count is 0, Adjacent neighbor count is 0
  Suppress Hello for 0 neighbor(s)
```

When the `auto-cost reference-bandwidth 1000` router configuration command is issued, Cisco IOS software prints the following message indicating that this same value should be applied to all routers within the OSPF domain. This is illustrated in the following output:

```
R4(config)#router ospf 4
R4(config-router)#auto-cost reference-bandwidth 1000
% OSPF: Reference bandwidth is changed.
        Please ensure reference bandwidth is consistent across all
routers.
```

While this may seem like an important warning, keep in mind that the use of this command simply affects the local router. It is not mandatory to configure it on all routers; however, for exam purposes, ensure that a consistent configuration is implemented on all routers.

Influencing OSPF Metric Calculation

The calculation of the OSPF metric can be directly influenced by performing the following:

- Adjusting the interface bandwidth using the `bandwidth` command
- Manually specifying a cost using the `ip ospf cost` command

The use of the `bandwidth` command was described in a previous module when we discussed EIGRP metric calculation. As stated earlier, the default OSPF cost is calculated by dividing the link bandwidth by a reference bandwidth of 10^8, or 100 Mbps. Either incrementing or decrementing the link bandwidth directly affects the OSPF cost for the particular link. This is typically a path control mechanism used to ensure that one path is preferred over another.

However, as was described in the previous module, the `bandwidth` command affects more than just the routing protocol. It is for this reason that the second method, manually specifying a cost value, is the recommended method for influencing OSPF metric calculation.

The `ip ospf cost <1-65535>` interface configuration command is used to manually specify the cost of a link. The lower the value, the greater the probability that the link will be preferred over other links to the same destination network but with higher cost values. The following example illustrates how to configure an OSPF cost of 5 for a Serial (T1) link:

```
R1(config)#interface Serial0/0
R1(config-if)#ip ospf cost 5
R1(config-if)#exit
```

This configuration can be validated using the `show ip ospf interface [name]` command, as illustrated in the following output:

```
R1#show ip ospf interface Serial0/0
Serial0/0 is up, line protocol is up
  Internet Address 10.0.0.1/24, Area 0
  Process ID 1, Router ID 1.1.1.1, Network Type POINT_TO_POINT, Cost: 5
  Transmit Delay is 1 sec, State POINT_TO_POINT,
  Timer intervals configured, Hello 10, Dead 40, Wait 40, Retransmit 5
    oob-resync timeout 40
    Hello due in 00:00:04
  Index 2/2, flood queue length 0
  Next 0x0(0)/0x0(0)
  Last flood scan length is 1, maximum is 4
  Last flood scan time is 0 msec, maximum is 0 msec
  Neighbor Count is 1, Adjacent neighbor count is 1
    Adjacent with neighbor 2.2.2.2
  Suppress Hello for 0 neighbor(s)
```

OSPF DEFAULT ROUTING

Unlike EIGRP, which supports several different ways of generating and advertising the default route, OSPF uses only the `default-information originate [always] [metric <value>] [metric-type <1|2>] [route-map <name>]` router configuration command to advertise dynamically the default route.

The `default-information originate` command used by itself will configure the router to advertise a default route only if a default route is already present in the routing table. However, the `[always]` keyword can be appended to this command to force the router to generate a default route, even when one does not exist in the routing table. This keyword should be used with caution, as it may result in the blackholing of traffic within the OSPF domain or the forwarding of packets for all unknown destinations to the configured router.

The `[metric <value>]` keyword is used to specify the route metric for the generated default route. The `[metric-type <1|2>]` keyword can be used to change the metric type for the default route. Finally, the `[route-map <name>]` keyword configures the router to generate a default route only if the conditions specified in the named route map are met.

The following configuration example illustrates how to configure an OSPF-enabled router to generate and advertise a default route if one already exists in the routing table. The existing default route can be a static route or even a default route from another routing protocol if multiple routing protocols have been configured on the router. The output below illustrates this configuration based on a configured static default route:

```
R4(config)#ip route 0.0.0.0 0.0.0.0 FastEthernet0/0 172.16.4.254
R4(config)#router ospf 4
R4(config-router)#network 172.16.4.0 0.0.0.255 Area 2
R4(config-router)#default-information originate
R4(config-router)#exit
```

By default, the default route is advertised as a Type 5 LSA.

CONFIGURING OSPF

Basic OSPF can be enabled on the router with one line of configuration, and then by adding the network statement that specifies on which interfaces you want to run OSPF, not necessarily networks you wish to advertise:

- `Router ospf 9` ← locally significant number
- `network 10.0.0.0 0.255.255.255 area 0`

OSPF won't become active until at least one interface is up/up, and remember that at least one area must be Area 0. A Sample OSPF network is illustrated in Figure 39.16 below:

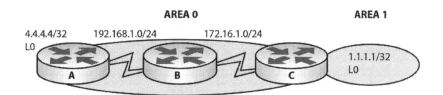

Figure 39.16—A Sample OSPF Network

Router A configuration:

```
router ospf 20
network 4.4.4.4 0.0.0.0 area 0
network 192.168.1.0 0.0.0.255 area 0
router-id 4.4.4.4
```

Router B configuration:

```
router ospf 22
network 172.16.1.0 0.0.0.255 area 0
network 192.168.1.0 0.0.0.255 area 0
router-id 192.168.1.2
```

Router C configuration:

```
router ospf 44
network 1.1.1.1 0.0.0.0 area 1
network 172.16.1.0 0.0.0.255 area 0
router-id 1.1.1.1

RouterC#show ip route
Gateway of last resort is not set
     1.0.0.0/32 is subnetted, 1 subnets
C        1.1.1.1 is directly connected, Loopback0
     4.0.0.0/32 is subnetted, 1 subnets
O        4.4.4.4 [110/129] via 172.16.1.1, 00:10:39, Serial0/0/0
     172.16.0.0/24 is subnetted, 1 subnets
C        172.16.1.0 is directly connected, Serial0/0/0
O    192.168.1.0/24 [110/128] via 172.16.1.1, 00:10:39, Serial0/0/0
```

TROUBLESHOOTING OSPF

Once again, Open Shortest Path First is an open-standard Link State routing protocol that advertises the state of its links. When a Link State router begins operating on a network link, information associated with that logical network is added to its local Link State Database (LSDB). The local router then sends Hello messages on its operational links to determine whether other Link State routers are operating on the interfaces as well. OSPF runs directly over Internet Protocol using IP number 89.

While it is not possible to delve into all potential OSPF problem scenarios, the sections to follow discuss some of the most common problem scenarios when OSPF is implemented as the IGP of choice.

Troubleshooting Neighbor Relationships

Routers running OSPF transition through several states before establishing an adjacency. These different states are the Down, Attempt, Init, 2-Way, Exstart, Exchange, Loading, and Full states. The preferred state for an OSPF adjacency is the Full state. This state indicates that the neighbors have exchanged their entire databases and both have the same view of the network. While the Full state is the preferred adjacency state, it is possible that during the adjacency establishment process, the neighbors get "stuck" in one of the other states. For this reason, it is important to understand what to look for in order to troubleshoot the issue.

The Neighbor Table Is Empty

There are several reasons why the OSPF neighbor table may be empty (i.e., why the output of the show ip ospf neighbor command might not yield any results). Common reasons are as follows:

- Basic OSPF misconfigurations
- Layer 1 and Layer 2 issues
- ACL filtering
- Interface misconfigurations

Basic OSPF misconfigurations span a broad number of things. These could include mismatched timers, area IDs, authentication parameters, and stub configuration, for example. A plethora of tools is available in Cisco IOS software to troubleshoot basic OSPF misconfigurations. For example, you could use the show ip protocols command to determine information (e.g., about OSPF-enabled networks); the show ip ospf command to determine area configuration and the interfaces per area; and the show ip ospf interface brief command to determine which interfaces reside in which area, and for which OSPF process IDs those interfaces have been enabled, assuming that OSPF has been enabled for the interface.

Another common misconfiguration is specifying the interface as passive. If this is so, then the interface will not send out Hello packets, and a neighbor relationship will not be established using that interface. You can verify which interfaces have been configured or specified as passive using either the show ip protocols or the show ip ospf interface commands. The following is a sample output of the latter command on a passive interface:

```
R1#show ip ospf interface Serial0/0
Serial0/0 is up, line protocol is up
  Internet Address 172.16.0.1/30, Area 0
  Process ID 1, Router ID 10.1.0.1, Network Type POINT_TO_POINT, Cost: 64
  Transmit Delay is 1 sec, State POINT_TO_POINT
  Timer intervals configured, Hello 10, Dead 40, Wait 40, Retransmit 5
    oob-resync timeout 40
```

```
    No Hellos (Passive interface)
  Supports Link-Local Signaling (LLS)
  Index 1/1, flood queue length 0
  Next 0x0(0)/0x0(0)
  Last flood scan length is 0, maximum is 0
  Last flood scan time is 0 msec, maximum is 0 msec
  Neighbor Count is 0, Adjacent neighbor count is 0
  Suppress hello for 0 neighbor(s)
```

Finally, when enabling OSPF over NBMA technologies such as Frame Relay, remember that the neighbors must be defined statically, as OSPF does not use Multicast transmission for neighbor discovery for the default Non-Broadcast network type. This is a common reason for empty neighbor tables when implementing OSPF. We discuss NBMA in the WAN section.

Layer 1 and Layer 2 issues can also result in no formation of OSPF neighbor relationships. Layer 1 and Layer 2 troubleshooting was described in detail in previous modules. Use commands such as the show interfaces command to check for interface status (i.e., line protocol), as well as any received errors on the interface. If the OSPF-enabled routers reside in a VLAN that spans multiple switches, verify that there is end-to-end connectivity within the VLAN and that all ports or interfaces are in the correct Spanning Tree states, for example.

ACL filtering is another common cause for adjacencies failing to establish. It is important to be familiar with the topology in order to troubleshoot such issues. For example, if the routers failing to establish an adjacency are connected via different physical switches, it may be that the ACL filtering is being implemented in the form of a VACL that has been configured on the switches for security purposes. A useful troubleshooting tool that may indicate that OSPF packets are being either blocked or discarded is the show ip ospf traffic command, which prints information on transmitted and sent OSPF packets as illustrated in the output below:

```
R1#show ip ospf traffic Serial0/0

    Interface Serial0/0

OSPF packets received/sent
    Invalid  Hellos   DB-des   LS-req   LS-upd   LS-ack   Total
Rx: 0        0        0        0        0        0        0
Tx: 0        6        0        0        0        0        6

OSPF header errors
  Length 0, Auth Type 0, Checksum 0, Version 0,
  Bad Source 0, No Virtual Link 0, Area Mismatch 0,
  No Sham Link 0, Self Originated 0, Duplicate ID 0,
  Hello 0, MTU Mismatch 0, Nbr Ignored 0,
  LLS 0, Unknown Neighbor 0, Authentication 0,
  TTL Check Fail 0,

OSPF LSA errors
  Type 0, Length 0, Data 0, Checksum 0,
```

In the output above, notice that the local router is sending OSPF Hello packets but is not receiving any. If the configuration on the routers is correct, check ACLs on the routers or intermediate devices to ensure that OSPF packets are not being filtered or discarded.

Another common reason for an empty neighbor table is interface misconfigurations. Similar to EIGRP, OSPF will not establish a neighbor relationship using secondary interface addresses. However, unlike EIGRP, OSPF will also not establish a neighbor relationship if interface subnet masks are not consistent.

EIGRP-enabled routers will establish neighbor relationships even if the interface subnet masks are different. For example, if two routers, one with an interface using the address 10.1.1.1/24 and another with an interface using the address 10.1.1.2/30 are configured in back-to-back EIGRP implementation, they will successfully establish a neighbor relationship. However, it should be noted that such implementations could cause routing loops between the routers. In addition to mismatched subnet masks, EIGRP-enabled routers also ignore Maximum Transmission Unit (MTU) configurations and establish neighbor relationships even if the interface MTU values are different. Use the show ip interfaces and show interfaces commands to verify IP address and mask configuration.

Troubleshooting Route Advertisement

As is the case with EIGRP, there may be times when you notice that OSPF is not advertising certain routes. For the most part, this is typically due to some misconfigurations versus a protocol failure. Some common reasons for this include the following:

- OSPF is not enabled on the interface(s)
- The interface(s) is/are down
- Interface addresses are in a different area
- OSPF misconfigurations

A common reason why OSPF does not advertise routes is that the network is not advertised via OSPF. In current Cisco IOS versions, networks can be advertised using the network router configuration command or the ip ospf interface configuration command. Regardless of the method used, the show ip protocols command can be used to view which networks OSPF is configured to advertise, as can be seen in the following output:

```
R2#show ip protocols
Routing Protocol is "ospf 1"
  Outgoing update filter list for all interfaces is not set
  Incoming update filter list for all interfaces is not set
  Router ID 2.2.2.2
  Number of areas in this router is 1. 1 normal 0 stub 0 nssa
  Maximum path: 4
  Routing for Networks:
    10.2.2.0 0.0.0.128 Area 1
    20.2.2.0 0.0.0.255 Area 1
  Routing on Interfaces Configured Explicitly (Area 1):
```

```
    Loopback0
  Reference bandwidth unit is 100 mbps
    Routing Information Sources:
      Gateway         Distance      Last Update
      1.1.1.1            110        00:00:17
  Distance: (default is 110)
```

Additionally, keep in mind that you can also use the show ip ospf interfaces command to find out for which interfaces OSPF has been enabled, among other things. In addition to network configuration, if the interface is down, OSPF will not advertise the route. You can use the show ip ospf interface command to determine the interface state, as follows:

```
R1#show ip ospf interface brief
Interface    PID   Area      IP Address/Mask   Cost  State  Nbrs F/C
Lo100        1     0         100.1.1.1/24      1     DOWN   0/0
Fa0/0        1     0         10.0.0.1/24       1     BDR    1/1
```

Referencing the output above, you can see that Loopback100 is in a DOWN state. Taking a closer look, you can see that the issue is because the interface has been administratively shut, as illustrated in the following output:

```
R1#show ip ospf interface Loopback100
Loopback100 is administratively down, line protocol is down
  Internet Address 100.1.1.1/24, Area 0
  Process ID 1, Router ID 1.1.1.1, Network Type LOOPBACK, Cost: 1
  Enabled by interface config, including secondary ip addresses
  Loopback interface is treated as a stub Host
```

If you debugged IP routing events using the debug ip routing command and then issued the no shutdown command under the Loopback100 interface, then you would see the following:

```
R1#debug ip routing
IP routing debugging is on
R1#conf t
Enter configuration commands, one per line.  End with CNTL/Z.
R1(config)#interface Loopback100
R1(config-if)#no shutdown
R1(config-if)#end
R1#
*Mar 18 20:03:34.687: RT: is_up: Loopback100 1 state: 4 sub state: 1
line: 0 has_route: False
*Mar 18 20:03:34.687: RT: SET_LAST_RDB for 100.1.1.0/24
  NEW rdb: is directly connected

*Mar 18 20:03:34.687: RT: add 100.1.1.0/24 via 0.0.0.0, connected metric
[0/0]
*Mar 18 20:03:34.687: RT: NET-RED 100.1.1.0/24
*Mar 18 20:03:34.687: RT: interface Loopback100 added to routing table

[Truncated Output]
```

When multiple addresses are configured under an interface, all secondary addresses must be in the same area as the primary address; otherwise, OSPF will not advertise these networks. As an example, consider the network topology illustrated in Figure 39.17 below:

Figure 39.17—OSPF Secondary Subnet Advertisement

Referencing Figure 39.17, routers R1 and R2 are connected via a back-to-back connection. These two routers share the 10.0.0.0/24 subnet. However, in addition, R1 has been configured with some additional (secondary) subnets under its FastEthernet0/0 interface so that the interface configuration on R1 is printed as follows:

```
R1#show running-config interface FastEthernet0/0
Building configuration...

Current configuration : 183 bytes
!
interface FastEthernet0/0
 ip address 10.0.1.1 255.255.255.0 secondary
 ip address 10.0.2.1 255.255.255.0 secondary
 ip address 10.0.0.1 255.255.255.0
 duplex auto
 speed auto
end
```

OSPF is enabled on both R1 and R2. The configuration implemented on R1 is as follows:

```
R1#show running-config | section ospf
router ospf 1
 router-id 1.1.1.1
 log-adjacency-changes
 network 10.0.0.1 0.0.0.0 Area 0
 network 10.0.1.1 0.0.0.0 Area 1
 network 10.0.2.1 0.0.0.0 Area 1
```

The configuration implemented on R2 is as follows:

```
R2#show running-config | section ospf
router ospf 2
 router-id 2.2.2.2
 log-adjacency-changes
 network 10.0.0.2 0.0.0.0 Area 0
```

By default, because the secondary subnets have been placed into a different OSPF area on R1, they will not be advertised by the router. This can be seen on R2, which displays the following when the show ip route command is issued:

```
R2#show ip route
Codes: C - connected, S - static, R - RIP, M - mobile, B - BGP
       D - EIGRP, EX - EIGRP external, O - OSPF, IA - OSPF inter area
       N1 - OSPF NSSA external type 1, N2 - OSPF NSSA external type 2
       E1 - OSPF external type 1, E2 - OSPF external type 2
       i - IS-IS, su - IS-IS summary, L1 - IS-IS level-1, L2 - IS-IS
level-2
       ia - IS-IS inter area, * - candidate default, U - per-user static
route
       o - ODR, P - periodic downloaded static route

Gateway of last resort is not set

     10.0.0.0/24 is subnetted, 1 subnets
C       10.0.0.0 is directly connected, FastEthernet0/0
```

To resolve this issue, the secondary subnets must also be assigned to Area 0, as follows:

```
R1(config)#router ospf 1
R1(config-router)#network 10.0.1.1 0.0.0.0 Area 0
*Mar 18 20:20:37.491: %OSPF-6-AREACHG: 10.0.1.1/32 changed from Area 1 to
Area 0
R1(config-router)#network 10.0.2.1 0.0.0.0 Area 0
*Mar 18 20:20:42.211: %OSPF-6-AREACHG: 10.0.2.1/32 changed from Area 1 to
Area 0
R1(config-router)#end
```

After this configuration change, the networks are now advertised to router R2, as follows:

```
R2#show ip route
Codes: C - connected, S - static, R - RIP, M - mobile, B - BGP
       D - EIGRP, EX - EIGRP external, O - OSPF, IA - OSPF inter area
       N1 - OSPF NSSA external type 1, N2 - OSPF NSSA external type 2
       E1 - OSPF external type 1, E2 - OSPF external type 2
       i - IS-IS, su - IS-IS summary, L1 - IS-IS level-1, L2 - IS-IS
level-2
       ia - IS-IS inter area, * - candidate default, U - per-user static
route
       o - ODR, P - periodic downloaded static route

Gateway of last resort is not set

     10.0.0.0/24 is subnetted, 3 subnets
O       10.0.2.0 [110/2] via 10.0.0.1, 00:01:08, FastEthernet0/0
C       10.0.0.0 is directly connected, FastEthernet0/0
O       10.0.1.0 [110/2] via 10.0.0.1, 00:01:08, FastEthernet0/0
```

In addition to the three common causes described above, poor design, implementation, and misconfigurations are another reason OSPF may not advertise networks as expected. Common design issues that cause such issues include a discontiguous or partitioned backbone and area type misconfigurations, such as configuring areas as Totally Stubby, for example. For this reason, it is important to have a solid understanding of how the protocol works and how it has been implemented in your environment. This understanding will greatly simplify the troubleshooting process, as half the battle is already won before you even start troubleshooting the problem or issue.

Debugging OSPF Routing Issues

In the final section of this module, we will look at some of the more commonly used OSPF debugging commands. OSPF debugging is enabled using the debug ip ospf command. This command can be used in conjunction with the following additional keywords:

```
R1#debug ip ospf ?
  adj                OSPF adjacency events
  database-timer     OSPF database timer
  events             OSPF events
  flood              OSPF flooding
  hello              OSPF hello events
  lsa-generation     OSPF lsa generation
  mpls               OSPF MPLS
  nsf                OSPF non-stop forwarding events
  packet             OSPF packets
  retransmission     OSPF retransmission events
  spf                OSPF spf
  tree               OSPF database tree
```

The debug ip ospf adj command prints real-time information on adjacency events. This is a useful troubleshooting tool when troubleshooting OSPF neighbor adjacency problems. Following is a sample of the information that is printed by this command. The example below illustrates how this command can be used to determine that an MTU mismatch is preventing the neighbor adjacency from reaching the Full state:

```
R1#debug ip ospf adj
OSPF adjacency events debugging is on
R1#
*Mar 18 23:13:21.279: OSPF: DR/BDR election on FastEthernet0/0
*Mar 18 23:13:21.279: OSPF: Elect BDR 2.2.2.2
*Mar 18 23:13:21.279: OSPF: Elect DR 1.1.1.1
*Mar 18 23:13:21.279:        DR: 1.1.1.1 (Id)   BDR: 2.2.2.2 (Id)
*Mar 18 23:13:21.283: OSPF: Neighbor change Event on interface
FastEthernet0/0
*Mar 18 23:13:21.283: OSPF: DR/BDR election on FastEthernet0/0
*Mar 18 23:13:21.283: OSPF: Elect BDR 2.2.2.2
*Mar 18 23:13:21.283: OSPF: Elect DR 1.1.1.1
*Mar 18 23:13:21.283:        DR: 1.1.1.1 (Id)   BDR: 2.2.2.2 (Id)
```

```
*Mar 18 23:13:21.283: OSPF: Rcv DBD from 2.2.2.2 on FastEthernet0/0 seq
0xA65 opt 0x52 flag 0x7 len 32  mtu 1480 state EXSTART
*Mar 18 23:13:21.283: OSPF: Nbr 2.2.2.2 has smaller interface MTU
*Mar 18 23:13:21.283: OSPF: NBR Negotiation Done. We are the SLAVE
*Mar 18 23:13:21.287: OSPF: Send DBD to 2.2.2.2 on FastEthernet0/0 seq
0xA65 opt 0x52 flag 0x2 len 192
*Mar 18 23:13:26.275: OSPF: Rcv DBD from 2.2.2.2 on FastEthernet0/0 seq
0xA65 opt 0x52 flag 0x7 len 32  mtu 1480 state EXCHANGE
*Mar 18 23:13:26.279: OSPF: Nbr 2.2.2.2 has smaller interface MTU
*Mar 18 23:13:26.279: OSPF: Send DBD to 2.2.2.2 on FastEthernet0/0 seq
0xA65 opt 0x52 flag 0x2 len 192

[Truncated Output]
```

From the output above, you can conclude that the MTU on the local router is larger than 1480 bytes because the debug output shows that the neighbor has the smaller MTU value. The recommended solution would be to adjust the smaller MTU value so that both neighbors have the same interface MTU values. This will allow the adjacency to reach the Full state.

The debug ip ospf lsa-generation command prints information on OSPF LSAs. This command can be used to troubleshoot route advertisement when using OSPF. Following is a sample output of the information that is printed by this command:

```
R1#debug ip ospf lsa-generation
OSPF summary lsa generation debugging is on
*Mar 18 23:25:59.447: %OSPF-5-ADJCHG: Process 1, Nbr 2.2.2.2 on
FastEthernet0/0 from FULL to DOWN, Neighbor Down: Interface down or
detached
*Mar 18 23:25:59.511: %OSPF-5-ADJCHG: Process 1, Nbr 2.2.2.2 on
FastEthernet0/0 from LOADING to FULL, Loading Done
*Mar 18 23:26:00.491: OSPF: Start redist-scanning
*Mar 18 23:26:00.491: OSPF: Scan the RIB for both redistribution and
translation
*Mar 18 23:26:00.499: OSPF: max-aged external LSA for summary 150.0.0.0
255.255.0.0, scope: Translation
*Mar 18 23:26:00.499: OSPF: End scanning, Elapsed time 8ms
*Mar 18 23:26:00.499: OSPF: Generate external LSA 192.168.4.0, mask
255.255.255.0, type 5, age 0, metric 20, tag 0, metric-type 2, seq
0x80000001
*Mar 18 23:26:00.503: OSPF: Generate external LSA 192.168.5.0, mask
255.255.255.0, type 5, age 0, metric 20, tag 0, metric-type 2, seq
0x80000001
*Mar 18 23:26:00.503: OSPF: Generate external LSA 192.168.1.0, mask
255.255.255.0, type 5, age 0, metric 20, tag 0, metric-type 2, seq
0x80000001
*Mar 18 23:26:00.503: OSPF: Generate external LSA 192.168.2.0, mask
255.255.255.0, type 5, age 0, metric 20, tag 0, metric-type 2, seq
0x80000001
*Mar 18 23:26:00.507: OSPF: Generate external LSA 192.168.3.0, mask
255.255.255.0, type 5, age 0, metric 20, tag 0, metric-type 2, seq
0x80000001
```

```
*Mar 18 23:26:05.507: OSPF: Generate external LSA 192.168.4.0, mask
255.255.255.0, type 5, age 0, metric 20, tag 0, metric-type 2, seq
0x80000006
*Mar 18 23:26:05.535: OSPF: Generate external LSA 192.168.5.0, mask
255.255.255.0, type 5, age 0, metric 20, tag 0, metric-type 2, seq
0x80000006
```

The debug ip ospf spf command provides real-time information about Shortest Path First algorithm events. This command can be used in conjunction with the following keywords:

```
R1#debug ip ospf spf ?
  external   OSPF spf external-route
  inter      OSPF spf inter-route
  intra      OSPF spf intra-route
  statistic  OSPF spf statistics
  <cr>
```

As is the case with all debug commands, consideration should be given to factors such as the size of the network and the resource utilization on the router before debugging SPF events. The following is a sample of the output from the debug ip ospf spf statistic command:

```
R1#debug ip ospf spf statistic
OSPF spf statistic debugging is on
R1#clear ip ospf process
Reset ALL OSPF processes? [no]: y
R1#
*Mar 18 23:37:27.795: %OSPF-5-ADJCHG: Process 1, Nbr 2.2.2.2 on
FastEthernet0/0 from FULL to DOWN, Neighbor Down: Interface down or
detached
*Mar 18 23:37:27.859: %OSPF-5-ADJCHG: Process 1, Nbr 2.2.2.2 on
FastEthernet0/0 from LOADING to FULL, Loading Done

*Mar 18 23:37:32.859: OSPF: Begin SPF at 28081.328ms, process time 608ms
*Mar 18 23:37:32.859:       spf_time 07:47:56.328, wait_interval 5000ms
*Mar 18 23:37:32.859: OSPF: End SPF at 28081.328ms, Total elapsed time
0ms
*Mar 18 23:37:32.859:       Schedule time 07:48:01.328, Next wait_
interval 10000ms
*Mar 18 23:37:32.859:       Intra: 0ms, Inter: 0ms, External: 0ms
*Mar 18 23:37:32.859:       R: 2, N: 1, Stubs: 2
*Mar 18 23:37:32.859:       SN: 0, SA: 0, X5: 0, X7: 0
*Mar 18 23:37:32.863:       SPF suspends: 0 intra, 0 total
```

NOTE: Prior to enabling SPF debug commands, consider using show commands first, such as the show ip ospf statistics and show ip ospf commands, when beginning the troubleshooting process.

Now please take today's exam at **https://www.in60days.com/free/ccnain60days/**

DAY 39 LABS

OSPF

Topology

10.0.0.0/30

S0/1/0

LO **A** **S0/1/0** **B** **LO**

172.20.1.1/24 **192.168.1.1/26**

Purpose

Learn how to configure basic OSPF.

Walkthrough

1. Configure all IP addresses based on the topology above. Make sure you can ping across the Serial link.

2. Add OSPF to Router A. Put the network on Loopback0 into Area 1 and the 10 network into Area 0.

```
RouterA(config)#router ospf 4
RouterA(config-router)#network 172.20.1.0 0.0.0.255 area 1
RouterA(config-router)#network 10.0.0.0 0.0.0.3 area 0
RouterA(config-router)#^Z
RouterA#
%SYS-5-CONFIG_I: Configured from console by console

RouterA#show ip protocols

Routing Protocol is "ospf 4"
  Outgoing update filter list for all interfaces is not set
  Incoming update filter list for all interfaces is not set
  Router ID 172.20.1.1
  Number of areas in this router is 2. 2 normal 0 stub 0 nssa
  Maximum path: 4
  Routing for Networks:
    172.20.1.0 0.0.0.255 area 1
    10.0.0.0 0.0.0.3 area 0
  Routing Information Sources:
    Gateway         Distance      Last Update
    172.20.1.1          110       00:00:09
  Distance: (default is 110)
```

3. Add OSPF on Router B. Put the Loopback network into OSPF Area 40.

```
RouterB(config)#router ospf 2
RouterB(config-router)#net 10.0.0.0 0.0.0.3 area 0
RouterB(config-router)#
```

```
00:22:35: %OSPF-5-ADJCHG: Process 2, Nbr 172.20.1.1 on Serial0/1/0
from LOADING to FULL, Loading Done

RouterB(config-router)#net 192.168.1.0 0.0.0.63 area 40
RouterB(config-router)# ^Z

RouterB#show ip protocols

Routing Protocol is "ospf 2"
  Outgoing update filter list for all interfaces is not set
  Incoming update filter list for all interfaces is not set
  Router ID 192.168.1.1
  Number of areas in this router is 2. 2 normal 0 stub 0 nssa
  Maximum path: 4
  Routing for Networks:
    10.0.0.0 0.0.0.3 area 0
    192.168.1.0 0.0.0.63 area 40
  Routing Information Sources:
    Gateway         Distance      Last Update
    172.20.1.1           110      00:01:18
    192.168.1.1          110      00:00:44
  Distance: (default is 110)
```

4. Check the routing table on your routers. Look for the OSPF advertised network. You will see an IA, which means IA—OSPF inter-area. You will also see the AD for OSPF, which is 110.

```
RouterA#sh ip route

[Truncated Output]

     10.0.0.0/30 is subnetted, 1 subnets
C       10.0.0.0 is directly connected, Serial0/1/0
     172.20.0.0/24 is subnetted, 1 subnets
C       172.20.1.0 is directly connected, Loopback0
     192.168.1.0/32 is subnetted, 1 subnets
O IA    192.168.1.1 [110/65] via 10.0.0.2, 00:01:36, Serial0/1/0
RouterA#
```

5. Issue some of the available OSPF commands on either router.

```
RouterA#sh ip ospf ?
  <1-65535>       Process ID number
  border-routers  Border and Boundary Router Information
  database        Database summary
  interface       Interface information
  neighbor        Neighbor list
```

Basic OSPF

Repeat the previous lab, again but using different IP addressing. Use OSPF Area 0 again:

- Assign an IPv4 address to the directly connected interfaces (10.10.10.1/24 and 10.10.10.2/24)
- Test direct connectivity using ping
- Configure a Loopback interface on each router and assign addresses from two different ranges (11.11.11.1/32 and 12.12.12.2/32)
- Configure standard OSPF process 1 and advertise all the local networks in Area 0. Also, configure a router ID for each device:

R1:

```
router ospf 1
router-id 1.1.1.1
network 10.10.10.0 0.0.0.255 area 0
network 11.11.11.0 0.0.0.0 area 0
```

R2:

```
router ospf 1
router-id 2.2.2.2
network 10.10.10.0 0.0.0.255 area 0
network 12.12.12.0 0.0.0.0 area 0
```

- Ping R2 Loopback from R1 to test connectivity
- Issue a `show ip route` command to verify that routes are being received via OSPF
- Issue a `show ip protocols` command to verify that OSPF is configured and active on the devices
- Verify the interface OSPF-specific parameters: `show ip ospf interface` and `show ip ospf interface brief`
- Change the OSPF Hello and Dead timers on both routers (directly connected interfaces): `ip ospf hello` and `ip ospf dead`
- Issue a `show ip ospf 1` command to see the routing process parameters
- Repeat the lab but this time advertise the networks in OSPF using the `ip ospf 1 area 0 interface specific` command instead of the `network` command under router OSPF

OSPFv3

DAY 40 TASKS

- Read today's lesson notes (below)
- Review yesterday's lesson notes and labs
- Complete today's lab
- Take today's exam
- Read the ICND2 cram guide
- Spend 15 minutes on the subnetting.org website

Today we will look at OSPFv3, where you will learn about the following:

- OSPFv3
- Configuration differences between OSPF and OSPFv3
- Configuring and verifying OSPFv3

This module maps to the following CCNA syllabus requirements:

- 2.5 Configure, verify, and troubleshoot single area and multi area OSPFv3 for IPv6 (excluding authentication, filtering, manual summarization, redistribution, stub, virtual-link, and LSAs)

OSPF VERSION 3

OSPFv3 is defined in RFC 2740 and is the counterpart of OSPFv2, but it is designed explicitly for the IPv6 routed protocol. The version is derived from the Version field in the OSPF packet, which has been updated to a value of 3. The OSPFv3 specification is based mainly on OSPFv2 but contains additional enhancements because of the added support for IPv6.

Both OSPFv2 and OSPFv3 can run on the same router. In other words, the same physical router can route for both IPv4 and IPv6 because each address family has a different SPF process. This does not mean that the SPF algorithm itself is different for OSPFv2 and OSPFv3; the statement simply means that a separate instance of the same SPF algorithm is run for OSPFv2 and OSPFv3. The similarities shared by OSPFv2 and OSPFv3 are as follows:

- OSPFv3 continues to use the same packets that are also used by OSPFv2. These packets include Database Description (DBD), Link State Requests (LSRs), Link State Updates (LSUs), and Link State Advertisements (LSAs).
- The mechanisms for dynamic neighbor discovery and the adjacency formation process (i.e., the different neighbor states that OSPF transitions through from the Init or Attempt state through to the Full state) remain the same in OSPFv3 as in OSPFv2.
- OSPFv3 still remains RFC-compliant on different technologies. For example, if OSPFv3 is enabled over a PPP link, the network type is still specified as Point-to-Point. In a similar manner, if OSPFv3 is enabled over Frame Relay, the default network type is still specified as Non-Broadcast. In addition, the default network type can still be changed manually using the different interface-specific commands in Cisco IOS software.
- Both OSPFv2 and OSPFv3 use the same LSA flooding and aging mechanisms.
- Like OSPFv2, the OSPFv3 router ID (RID) still requires the use of a 32-bit IPv4 address. When OSPFv3 is enabled on a router running dual-stack (i.e., both IPv4 and IPv6), the same RID selection process used by Cisco IOS routers for OSPFv2 is used to determine the router ID to be used. However, when OSPFv3 is enabled on a router that has no operational IPv4 interfaces, then it is mandatory that the OSPFv3 router ID be configured manually using the `router-id` router configuration command.
- The OSPFv3 link ID indicates that the links are not IPv6-specific and are still based on a 32-bit IPv4 address, as is the case in OSPFv2.

While there are similarities between OSPFv2 and OSPFv3, it is important to understand that some significant differences exist with which you must be familiar. These include the following:

- In a manner similar to EIGRP, OSPFv3 runs over a link. This negates the need to have a network statement for OSPFv3. Instead, the link is configured as part of an OSPF process by using the `ipv6 router ospf [process ID] area [area ID]` interface configuration command. However, like OSPFv2, the OSPF process ID is still specified in Global Configuration mode using the `ipv6 router ospf [process ID]` global configuration command.
- OSPFv3 uses Link-Local addresses to identify the OSPFv3 adjacencies. Like EIGRPv6, the next-hop IPv6 address for OSPFv3 routes will reflect the Link-Local address of the adjacent or neighboring router(s).
- OSPFv3 introduces two new OSPF LSA types. These are the Link LSA, defined as LSA Type 0x0008 (or LSA Type 8), and the Intra-Area-Prefix LSA, defined as LSA Type 0x2009 (or LSA Type 9). The Link LSA provides the router's Link-Local address and provides all the IPv6 prefixes attached to the link. There is one Link LSA per link. There can be multiple Intra-Area-Prefix LSAs with different Link-State IDs. The Area flooding scope can therefore be an associated prefix with the transit network referencing a Network LSA or it can be an associated prefix with a router or Stub referencing a Router LSA.
- The transport used by OSPFv2 and OSPFv3 is different in that OSPFv3 messages are sent over (encapsulated in) IPv6 packets.
- OSPFv3 uses two standard IPv6 Multicast addresses. The Multicast address FF02::5 is the equivalent of the AllSPFRouters Multicast address 224.0.0.5 used in OSPFv2,

while the Multicast address FF02::6 address is the AllDRRouters Multicast address and is the equivalent of the 224.0.0.6 group address used in OSPFv2. (This will be covered in the ICND2 section.)

- OSPFv3 leverages the built-in capabilities of IPSec and uses the AH and ESP extension headers as an authentication mechanism instead of the numerous authentication mechanisms configurable in OSPFv2. Therefore, the Authentication and AuType fields have been removed from the OSPF packet header in OSPFv3.

- Finally, the last significant difference is that the OSPFv3 Hello packet now contains no address information at all but includes an interface ID, which the originating router has assigned to uniquely identify its interface to the link. This interface ID becomes the Network LSA's Link State ID, should the router become the Designated Router on the link.

OSPFV2 AND OSPFV3 CONFIGURATION DIFFERENCES

There are some configuration differences in Cisco IOS software when configuring OSPFv2 versus OSPFv3. However, it should be noted that these differences are not as significant as those between other versions of IPv4 routing protocols and their IPv6 counterparts.

In Cisco IOS software, OSPFv3 routing is enabled using the `ipv6 router ospf [process ID]` global configuration command. As is the case with OSPFv2, the OSPF process ID is locally significant to the router and does not need to be the same on adjacent routers in order for an adjacency to be established.

As is required for EIGRPv6, the router ID for OSPFv3 must be either specified manually or configured as an operational interface with an IPv4 address (e.g., a Loopback interface). Similar to EIGRPv6, there are no network commands used when enabling OSPFv3. Instead, OSPFv3 is enabled on a per-interface basis and multiple instances may be enabled on the same interface.

Finally, when configuring OSPFv3 over NBMA networks, such as Frame Relay and ATM, the neighbor statements are specified under the specific interface using the `ipv6 ospf neighbor [link local address]` interface configuration command. In OSPFv2, these would be configured in Router Configuration mode.

> **NOTE:** When configuring OSPFv3 over NBMA technologies, you should create static Frame Relay map statements using Link-Local addresses. This is because the Link-Local address is used to establish adjacencies, not the global Unicast address. For example, to create a static Frame Relay map statement and specify an OSPF neighbor for a Frame Relay implementation, the following configuration would be implemented on the router.

```
R1(config)#ipv6 unicast-routing
R1(config)#ipv6 router ospf 1
R1(config-rtr)#router-id 1.1.1.1
R1(config-rtr)#exit
R1(config)#interface Serial0/0
R1(config-if)#frame-relay map ipv6 FE80::205:5EFF:FE6E:5C80 111 broadcast
```

```
R1(config-if)#ipv6 ospf neighbor FE80::205:5EFF:FE6E:5C80
R1(config-if)#exit
```

CONFIGURING AND VERIFYING OSPFV3 IN CISCO IOS SOFTWARE

Continuing from the previous section, which highlighted the configuration differences between OSPFv2 and OSPFv3, this section goes through the steps required to enable and verify OSPFv3 functionality and routing in Cisco IOS software. The following sequence of steps should be taken to enable OSPFv3 routing in Cisco IOS software:

1. Globally enable IPv6 routing using the `ipv6 unicast-routing` global configuration command. By default, IPv6 routing is disabled in Cisco IOS software.
2. Configure one or more OSPFv3 processes using the `ipv6 router ospf [process ID]` global configuration command.
3. If there are no operational interfaces with an IPv4 address configured on the router, then configure the OSPFv3 RID manually using the `router-id [ipv4 address]` router configuration command.
4. Enable IPv6 on the desired interfaces using the `ipv6 address` and `ipv6 enable` interface configuration commands.
5. Enable one or more OSPFv3 processes under the interface using the `ipv6 ospf [process ID] area [area ID]` interface configuration command.

The first basic multi-area OSPFv3 configuration example is based on the topology that is illustrated in Figure 40.1 below:

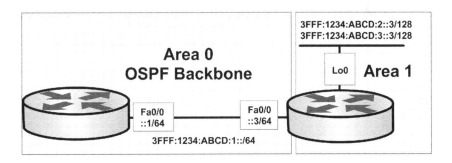

Figure 40.1—Configuring Basic Multi-Area OSPFv3 in Cisco IOS Software

Following the sequence of configuration steps described in the previous section, OSPFv3 will be configured on router R1 as follows:

```
R1(config)#ipv6 unicast-routing
R1(config)#ipv6 router ospf 1
R1(config-rtr)#router-id 1.1.1.1
R1(config-rtr)#exit
R1(config)#interface FastEthernet0/0
```

```
R1(config-if)#ipv6 address 3fff:1234:abcd:1::1/64
R1(config-if)#ipv6 enable
R1(config-if)#ipv6 ospf 1 Area 0
R1(config-if)#exit
```

Following the same sequence of steps, OSPFv3 routing is configured on router R3 as follows:

```
R3(config)#ipv6 unicast-routing
R3(config)#ipv6 router ospf 3
R3(config-rtr)#router-id 3.3.3.3
R3(config-rtr)#exit
R3(config)#interface FastEthernet0/0
R3(config-if)#ipv6 address 3fff:1234:abcd:1::3/64
R3(config-if)#ipv6 enable
R3(config-if)#ipv6 ospf 3 Area 0
R3(config-if)#exit
R3(config)#interface Loopback0
R3(config-if)#ipv6 address 3fff:1234:abcd:2::3/128
R3(config-if)#ipv6 address 3fff:1234:abcd:3::3/128
R3(config-if)#ipv6 enable
R3(config-if)#ipv6 ospf 3 Area 1
R3(config-if)#exit
```

Following the configuration of OSPFv3 on both routers, you can use the show ipv6 ospf neighbors command to verify the state of the OSPFv3 adjacency, as illustrated below on R1:

```
R1#show ipv6 ospf neighbor
Neighbor    ID Pri   State      Dead Time   Interface ID    Interface
3.3.3.3          1   FULL/BDR   00:00:36    4
FastEthernet0/0
```

You can also view detailed neighbor information by appending the [detail] keyword to the end of this command:

```
R1#show ipv6 ospf neighbor detail
 Neighbor 3.3.3.3
    In the area 0 via interface FastEthernet0/0
    Neighbor: interface-id 4, link-local address FE80::213:19FF:FE86:A20
    Neighbor priority is 1, State is FULL, 6 state changes
    DR is 1.1.1.1 BDR is 3.3.3.3
    Options is 0x000013 in Hello (V6-Bit E-Bit R-bit )
    Options is 0x000013 in DBD (V6-Bit E-Bit R-bit )
    Dead timer due in 00:00:39
    Neighbor is up for 00:06:40
    Index 1/1/1, retransmission queue length 0, number of retransmission
0
    First 0x0(0)/0x0(0)/0x0(0) Next 0x0(0)/0x0(0)/0x0(0)
    Last retransmission scan length is 0, maximum is 0
    Last retransmission scan time is 0 msec, maximum is 0 msec
```

In the output above, notice that the actual neighbor interface address is the Link-Local address, not the configured global IPv6 Unicast address.

https://www.in60days.com/free/ccnain60days/

DAY 40 LABS

Basic OSPFv3

Repeat the scenario from Day 39 (two routers directly connected, Loopback interface on each of them) but instead of configuring OSPF for IPv4, configure IPv6 addresses and advertise them using OSPFv3 between the devices:

- Assign an IPv6 address to the directly connected interfaces (2001:100::1/64 and 2001:100::2/64)
- Test direct connectivity using ping
- Configure a Loopback interface on each router and assign addresses from two different ranges (2002::1/128 and 2002::2/128)
- Configure standard OSPFv3 process 1 and advertise all the local networks in Area 0. Also, configure a router ID for each device

R1:

```
ipv6 router ospf 1
router-id 1.1.1.1
int fa0/0 (or the specific interface number)
ipv6 ospf 1 area 0
int lo0 (or the specific interface number)
ipv6 ospf 1 area 0
```

R2:

```
ipv6 router ospf 1
router-id 2.2.2.2
int fa0/0 (or the specific interface number)
ipv6 ospf 1 area 0
int lo0 (or the specific interface number)
ipv6 ospf 1 area 0
```

- Ping R2 IPv6 Loopback from R1 to test connectivity
- Issue a `show ipv6 route` command to verify that routes are being received via OSPFv3
- Issue a `show ipv6 protocols` command to verify that OSPFv3 is configured and active on the devices
- Verify the interface OSPF-specific parameters: `show ipv6 ospf interface` and `show ipv6 ospf interface brief`
- Change the OSPF Hello and Dead timers on both routers (directly connected interfaces): `ipv6 ospf hello` and `ipv6 ospf dead`
- Issue a `show ipv6 ospf 1` command to see the routing process parameters

Multi-area OSPFv3 Lab

Topology

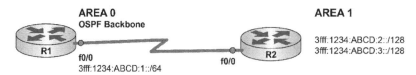

AREA 0
OSPF Backbone

R1
f0/0
3fff:1234:ABCD:1::/64

f0/0
R2

AREA 1

3fff:1234:ABCD:2::/128
3fff:1234:ABCD:3::/128

Purpose

Learn how to configure multi-area OSPFv3 using two routers.

Walkthrough

1. Enable the indicated IPv6 addresses on R2. Repeat on R1 but we only need the Ethernet interface.

```
R2(config)#ipv6 uni
R2(config)#int lo0
R2(config-if)#ipv6 add 3fff:1234:abcd:2::1/128
R2(config-if)#int lo1
R2(config-if)#ipv6 add 3fff:1234:abcd:3::1/128
R2(config-if)#int f0/0
R2(config-if)#ipv6 add 3fff:1234:abcd:1::2/64
R2(config-if)#no shut
```

2. After the R1 IPv6 interface is addressed test the link with a ping.

```
R2#ping 3fff:1234:abcd:1::1
```

3. Configure OSPFv3 on both routers. R1 will only employ Area 0 but the loopbacks on R2 will be in Area 1.

```
R1(config)#ipv6 router ospf 1
*Mar  1 00:49:37.071: %OSPFv3-4-NORTRID: OSPFv3 process 1 could not
pick a router-id,
please configure manually
R1(config-rtr)#router-id 1.1.1.1
R1(config-rtr)#int f0/0
R1(config-if)#ipv6 ospf 1 area 0

R2(config)#ipv6 router ospf 3
R2(config-rtr)#router-id 2.2.2.2
R2(config-rtr)#int f0/0
R2(config-if)#ipv6 ospf 3 area 0
*Mar  1 00:53:38.419: %OSPFv3-5-ADJCHG: Process 3, Nbr 1.1.1.1 on
FastEthernet0/0 from LOADING to FULL, Loading Done
R2(config-if)#int lo0
R2(config-if)#ipv6 ospf 3 area 1
R2(config-if)#int lo1
R2(config-if)#ipv6 ospf 3 area 1
R2(config-if)#end
```

4. Issue some show commands to check our configurations. Note which router is designated and backup designated (DR/BDR). Remember that your commands need to include ipv6 in order to show the OSPFv3 outputs.

```
R1#show ipv6 ospf neighbor

Neighbor ID     Pri   State        Dead Time    Interface ID
Interface
2.2.2.2          1    FULL/BDR     00:00:33     4                Fa0/0

R1#show ipv6 ospf neighbor detail
 Neighbor 2.2.2.2
    In the area 0 via interface FastEthernet0/0
    Neighbor: interface-id 4, link-local address FE80::C007:9FF:FE41:0
    Neighbor priority is 1, State is FULL, 6 state changes
    DR is 1.1.1.1 BDR is 2.2.2.2
    [Output Truncated]

R1#show ipv6 route ospf
IPv6 Routing Table - 5 entries
Codes: C - Connected, L - Local, S - Static, R - RIP, B - BGP
       U - Per-user Static route, M - MIPv6
       I1 - ISIS L1, I2 - ISIS L2, IA - ISIS interarea, IS - ISIS
summary
       O - OSPF intra, OI - OSPF inter, OE1 - OSPF ext 1, OE2 - OSPF
ext 2
       ON1 - OSPF NSSA ext 1, ON2 - OSPF NSSA ext 2
       D - EIGRP, EX - EIGRP external
OI   3FFF:1234:ABCD:2::1/128 [110/10]
     via FE80::C007:9FF:FE41:0, FastEthernet0/0
OI   3FFF:1234:ABCD:3::1/128 [110/10]
     via FE80::C007:9FF:FE41:0, FastEthernet0/0
R1#
```

DAY 41

Review

DAY 41 TASKS

- Review theory and labs from the last two days
- Take today's exam on https://www.in60days.com/free/ccnain60days/
- Read the ICND2 cram guide
- Spend 15 minutes on the subnetting.org website

We've covered some tough and important topics over the last few days. Don't get too bogged down in the detail because CCNA level OSPF questions and labs should be pretty basic. Review the theory and highlight any important details.

Challenge 1—OSPF Lab

Topology

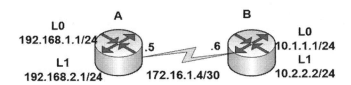

Instructions

Connect two routers together with a serial or crossover cable.

1. Add IP addresses to routers and loopback on Router A and B according to diagram.
2. Ping between Router A and B to test serial line (remember clock rates).
3. Configure OSPF on both routers.
4. Ensure you add all correct wildcard masks.
5. Double check the WAN wildcard mask and subnet. It ISN'T 172.16.1.0 0.0.0.3!!
6. Put all networks into area 0 including loopback networks.
7. Check the routing table has all networks.
8. Check the router ID for each router.
9. How would you change the router ID for each router?

Challenge 2—OSPFv3 Lab

Topology

2001:AAAA:BBBB:CCCC::/64

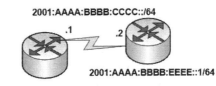

2001:AAAA:BBBB:EEEE::1/64

2001:AAAA:BBBB:DDDD::1/64

Instructions

Connect two routers together with serial or ethernet connections

1. Configure the IPv6 addresses above and loopback addresses.
2. Configure OSPFv3 on the two routers and check the routing tables.

Wide Area Networking Services

DAY 42 TASKS

- Read today's lesson notes and labs (below)
- Read the ICND2 cram guide
- Take today's exam at **https://www.in60days.com/free/ccnain60days/**
- Spend 15 minutes on the subnetting.org website

Cisco used to split WAN concepts between the ICND1 and ICND2 exams, with the latter focusing on HDLC and PPP protocols. Now it's all been lumped into the ICND2 syllabus. For this reason, we will tackle all the important WAN topics in this chapter.

Today you will learn about the following:

- WAN overview
- NBMA technologies
- WAN components
- WAN protocols
- WAN services
- VPN technologies
- MPLS
- Basic serial line configuration
- PPPoE
- PPP operations
- Troubleshooting PPP
- Configuring and verifying PPP and MLPPP
- Troubleshooting WAN connections

This lesson maps to the following CCNA syllabus requirements:

- 3.1 Configure and verify PPP and MLPPP on WAN interfaces using local authentication
- 3.2 Configure, verify, and troubleshoot PPPoE client-side interfaces using local authentication

- 3.5 Describe WAN access connectivity options
- 3.5.a MPLS
- 3.5.b MetroEthernet
- 3.5.c Broadband PPPoE
- 3.5.d Internet VPN (DMVPN, site-to-site VPN, client VPN)

WAN OVERVIEW

Wide Area Networks (WAN) span across large geographical distances in order to provide connectivity for various parts of the network infrastructure. Unlike the Local Area Network (LAN) environment, not all WAN components are owned by the specific enterprise they serve. Instead, WAN equipment or connectivity can be rented or leased from service providers.

Most service providers are well trained in order to make sure they can properly support not just the traditional data traffic but also voice and video services (which are more delay sensitive) over large geographical distances.

Another interesting thing about WANs is that, unlike LANs, there is typically some initial fixed cost and some periodic recurring fees for the services. With wide area networking, not only do you not own the connection and some of the equipment but you will also have to regularly pay fees to the service providers. This is one of the reasons why you should avoid over-provisioning (i.e., buy only the bandwidth you think you will use). This leads to the need for implementing effective Quality of Service mechanisms to avoid buying additional WAN bandwidth. The high costs are usually associated with the recurring fees that might appear in the case of over-provisioning the bandwidth.

WAN technology design requirements are typically derived from the following:

- Application type
- Application availability
- Application reliability
- Costs associated with a particular WAN technology
- Usage levels for the application

WAN Categories

An essential concept in WAN categorization is circuit-switched technology, the most relevant example of this technology being the Public Switched Telephone Network (PSTN). One of the technologies that fall into this category is ISDN. The way circuit-switched WAN connections function is by becoming established when needed and terminating when they are no longer required. Another example that reflects this circuit-switching behavior is the old-fashioned dial-up connection (dial-up modem analog access over the PSTN).

> **NOTE:** Not too long ago, dial-up technology was the only way to access Internet resources, offering an average usable bandwidth of around 40Kbps. Nowadays, this technology is almost extinct.

The opposite of the circuit-switched option is leased-line technology. This is a fully dedicated connection that is permanently up and is owned by the company. Examples of leased lines include Time Division Multiplexing (TDM)-based leased lines. These are usually very expensive because a single customer has full use of the connection.

Another popular category of WAN technology involves packet-switched networks. In a packet-switched infrastructure, shared bandwidth utilizes virtual circuits. The customer can create a virtual path (similar to a leased line) through the service provider infrastructure cloud. This virtual circuit has a dedicated bandwidth, even though technically this is not a real leased line. Frame Relay is an example of this type of technology.

Some legacy WAN technologies include X.25, which is the predecessor of Frame Relay. This technology is still present in some implementations but it is very rare (Frame Relay is also pretty rare nowadays).

Another WAN category you may have heard about is cell-switched technology. This is often included in packet-switched technologies, as they are very similar. A cell-switched technology example is ATM (Asynchronous Transfer Mode, which is also pretty rare nowadays). This operates by using fixed-size cells, instead of using packets (as used in Frame Relay). Cell-switched technologies form a shared bandwidth environment so that the service provider can guarantee customers a certain level of bandwidth through their infrastructure.

Broadband is another growing WAN category and this includes technologies such as the following:

- DSL
- Cable
- Wireless

Broadband has the capability of taking a connection, like the old-fashioned coaxial cable that carries TV signals, and figuring out how to use different aspects of that bandwidth. For example, by using multiplexing an additional data signal could be transmitted along with the original TV signal.

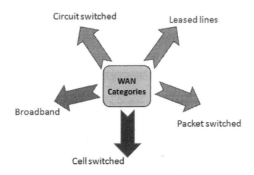

Figure 42.1—WAN Categories

As detailed in Figure 42.1 above, there are many options when discussing WAN categories and this is just a general introduction to them. All of these technologies can support the needs of modern networks that operate under the 20/80 design rule, meaning 80% of the network traffic uses some kind of WAN technology in order to access remote resources.

NBMA TECHNOLOGIES

A special technology that appears in wide area networking is Non-Broadcast Multi-Access (NBMA). This presents some challenges that are not present in traditional Broadcast networking. The need for NBMA arises when there is no native Broadcast support for a group of systems that want to communicate over the same network. Issues arise when the devices cannot natively send a packet destined for all the devices on the Multi-Access segment. Frame Relay, ATM, and ISDN are examples of technologies that are NBMA by default.

All of these technologies do not have any native ability to support Broadcasts. This prevents them from running routing protocols that use Broadcasts in their operation. Native Multicast support is also missing in Non-Broadcast networks. In the case of a routing protocol, all the nodes that participate must receive Multicast updates. One approach to this using an NBMA network is sending the Multicast or Broadcast packets as replicated Unicast packets. In this way, the Broadcast/Multicast frames are individually sent to every node in the topology. The tricky part in this scenario is that the device has to come up with a way to solve the Layer 3 to Layer 2 resolution. Particular packets have to be addressed for the specific machines that need to receive them.

Methodologies must exist for addressing this Layer 3 to Layer 2 resolution issue. The Layer 3 address is typically the IP address and the Layer 2 address usually varies, based on the technology used. In the case of Frame Relay, this will consist of the Data Link Connection Identifier (DLCI) number, so a way to resolve the DLCI to the IP address must be found.

In the case of Broadcast networks, Layer 3 resolution uses MAC addresses as the Layer 2 address and this has to be resolved to IPv4 addresses. This is accomplished with the Address Resolution Protocol (ARP). In a Broadcast-based network, the devices broadcast the requests by specifying the devices it wants to communicate with (typically learned via DNS) and asking for the MAC addresses specific to those devices. The reply is via Unicast and includes the requested MAC address.

In NBMA environments you still need to bind the Layer 3 address (IP address) to the Layer 2 address (DLCI). This can be done in an automated fashion using Inverse ARP. This is used to resolve the remote Layer 3 address to a Layer 2 address and is only used locally. Inverse ARP can be utilized in Frame Relay environments. The issue with Inverse ARP as the solution for the Layer 3 to Layer 2 resolution in an NBMA environment is that it is limited to directly connected devices. This creates issues in partial-mesh NBMA networks (where not all devices are directly connected).

Two types of NBMA interfaces exist—Multipoint and Point-to-Point, as illustrated in Figure 42.2 below. Multipoint interfaces require some kind of Layer 3 to Layer 2 resolution methodology. As its name implies, it can be the termination point of multiple Layer 2 circuits.

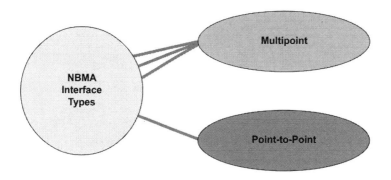

Figure 42.2—NBMA Interface Types

If Frame Relay is configured on the main physical interface of a device, that interface will be Multipoint by default. If a subinterface is created on a Frame Relay physical interface, the option of creating it as Multipoint exists. Layer 3 to Layer 2 resolution has to be configured for both the physical interfaces and for the subinterfaces. There are two options for doing this in Frame Relay:

- Inverse ARP
- Statically map

Layer 3 to Layer 2 resolution is not always an issue on NBMA interfaces because Point-to-Point WAN interfaces can be created. A Point-to-Point interface can only terminate a single Layer 2 circuit, so if the interface communicates with only one device, Layer 3 to Layer 2 resolution is not necessary. With only one circuit, there is only one Layer 2 address to communicate with. Layer 3 to Layer 2 resolution issues disappear when running a Frame Relay Point-to-Point sub interface type or an ATM Point-to-Point subinterface, for example.

WAN COMPONENTS

WAN requires a number of physical components to enable a connection. These will differ depending upon the type of connection you are using (e.g., ISDN, ADSL, Frame Relay, leased line, etc.) and other factors, such as backup connections and the number of incoming networks.

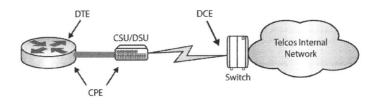

Figure 42.3—Basic WAN Components

Figure 42.3 above shows a basic serial connection going out to an ISP. As the customer, you are responsible for the Data Terminal Equipment (DTE), which is your router interface accepting the incoming link. You will also be responsible for the cable going to your Channel Service Unit/Data Service Unit (CSU/DSU), which converts your data into a format that your ISP can transport. The CSU/DSU is usually built into your router WAN interface card (WIC). CPE is the Customer Premise Equipment, which is your responsibility.

From this point on, your ISP or Telco is usually responsible for the connection. They lay the cables and provide switching stations, which transport the data across their network. The ISP owns the Data Communication Equipment (DCE), which is the end that provides the clocking, meaning the rate at which the data can pass on the line.

Common types of WAN connections include the following:

- Leased-line—a dedicated connection available 24/7
- Circuit-switching—set up when required
- Packet-switching—shared link/virtual circuit

The type of link you buy depends on your requirements and budget. If you can afford a dedicated line, you will have exclusive use of the bandwidth and security is less of an issue. A shared connection can mean a slower connection during peak times.

WAN PROTOCOLS

Common WAN protocols include PPP, HDLC, and Frame Relay. There are many others, of course, but you need to focus on those included in the CCNA syllabus.

Point-to-Point Protocol (PPP) can be used when you have a Cisco device connecting to a non-Cisco device. PPP also has the advantage of including authentication. It can be used over a number of connection types, including DSL, circuit-switched, and asynchronous/synchronous connections.

Cisco's High-Level Data Link Control (cHDLC) is its implementation of the open standard version of HDLC. HDLC requires DTE and DCE and is the default encapsulation type on Cisco routers (serial interfaces). Keepalives are sent from the DCE in order to check link status.

As already discussed, Frame Relay is a packet-switching technology which has become less popular in recent years, as DSL has become both more affordable and more readily available. It works at speeds from 56Kbps to 2Mbps and builds virtual circuits every time a connection is required. There is no security built into Frame Relay (but see Farai's comment below). Frame Relay will be covered in more detail later.

 FARAI SAYS—"Frame Relay commonly uses Permanent Virtual Circuits (PVCs), which are always present, although it can use Switched Virtual Circuits (SVCs), which are created on demand. A PVC is a type of Virtual Private Network (VPN). However, some people run PPP over Frame Relay (PPPoFR) to allow for PPP security for Frame Relay connections."

WAN SERVICES

Metro Ethernet

Metro Ethernet technologies involve the use of carrier Ethernet in Metropolitan Area Networks (MANs). Metro Ethernet can connect company LANs and individual end-users to a WAN or to the Internet. Companies often use Metro Ethernet to connect branch offices to an intranet.

A typical Metro Ethernet deployment uses a star or a mesh topology with interconnected network nodes using copper or fiber optic cables. Using the standard and widely deployed Ethernet technology in Metro Ethernet deployments offers a number of advantages, as opposed to using SONET/SDH or MPLS technologies:

- Less expensive
- Easier to implement
- Easier to manage
- Easy to connect customer equipment because it uses the standard Ethernet approach

A typical MAN can be structured under the access/aggregation/core standard design (a Cisco design model), as follows:

- Access Layer—usually at the customer's premises. This may include an office router or residential gateway
- Aggregation Layer—usually comprises microwave, DSL technologies, or Point-to-Point Ethernet links.
- Core Layer—may use MPLS to interconnect different MANs

Customer traffic separation is usually ensured in a MAN by using Ethernet VLAN tags that allow the differentiation of packets.

VSAT

Very Small Aperture Terminal (VSAT) technology is a telecommunication system based on wireless satellite technology. A VSAT deployment is made up of a small satellite earth station and a typical antenna, as shown in Figure 42.4 below:

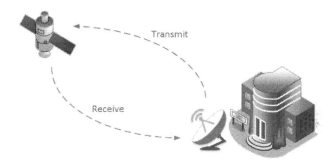

Figure 42.4—Satellite Communication

Typical VSAT components include the following:

- Master earth station
- Remote earth station
- Satellite

The master earth station is the network control center for the entire VSAT network. This is the place where the configuration, management, and monitoring of the entire network is done.

The remote earth station is the hardware installed at the customer premises and includes the following components:

- ODU (outdoor unit)
- IDU (indoor unit)
- IFL (inter-facility link)

The VSAT satellite orbits around the globe and receives and transmits signals from and to the earth stations.

VSAT networks can be configured in one of the following topologies:

- Star topology
- Mesh topology
- Star-mesh combination

Using satellite technology to ensure WAN connectivity is generally more expensive than using a traditional terrestrial network connection. The speeds offered by such connections can reach 5Mbps download and 1Mbps upload, which is usually enough for remote sites.

A significant disadvantage of using satellite connectivity is the increased traffic latency, which can reach up to 250 ms one way (antenna to satellite or satellite to antenna) due to the use of radio signals over a very long distance. This should be carefully analyzed when planning to install a satellite WAN connection because the increased latency could prevent sensible applications from functioning, while it has no impact on other applications.

Another challenge of using satellite connectivity is that the satellite dish has to have line of sight to the satellite. This means that you have to make use of high-frequency ranges (2 GHz), and any type of interference (e.g., natural phenomena like rain or storm clouds) may affect the connection throughput and availability.

T1/E1

Standards for T1 and E1 wide area networking have been around for a very long time. T1 stands for T-Carrier Level 1, which is a line that uses Time Division Multiplexing with digital signals associated with different channels based on time. T1 operates using 24 separate channels at a 1.544Mbps line rate, thus allocating 64Kbps per individual channel. You can use the 24 channels any way you want to, and you can even buy just a few channels from the service provider based on your needs. In general terms, consider a T1 connection as a trunk/bundle carrying 24 separate lines. T1 is a standard often used in the following geographical regions:

- North America
- Japan
- South Korea

E1 (E-Carrier Level 1) is a standard similar to T1 but it is used exclusively in Europe. The main difference between E1 and T1 is that E1 uses 32 channels instead of 24, also operating at 64kbps, thus offering a total line rate of 2.048Mbps. E1 functions based on Time Division Multiplexing, just like T1, so all other functionalities are common between the two standards.

T3/E3

T3 and E3 standards offer higher bandwidth than their T1 and E1 predecessors. T3 stands for T-Carrier Level 3 and is a type of connection usually based on coaxial cable and a BNC connector. This differs from T1, which is usually offered over twisted-pair media.

T3 connections are often referred to as DS3 connections, which is related to the data carried on the T3 line. T3 offers additional throughput because it uses the equivalent of 28 T1 circuits, meaning 672 T1 channels. This offers a total line rate of 44.736Mbps.

E3 connections are similar to those of T3, with the exception of being equivalent to 16 E1 circuits, meaning 512 E1 channels and a total line rate of 33.368Mbps.

T3/E3 connections are usually used in large data centers because they offer the ability to increase the total amount of throughput when needed.

ISDN

Integrated Services Digital Network (ISDN) is a technology that allows digital communication over a traditional analog phone line, so both voice and data can be digitally transmitted over the PSTN. ISDN never had the popularity that it was expected to have because it came along at a time when other alternative technologies were developed.

There are two flavors of ISDN:

- ISDN BRI (Basic Rate Interface)
- ISDN PRI (Primary Rate Interface)

The ISDN-speaking devices are called terminal emulation equipment and the devices can be categorized into native ISDN and non-native ISDN equipment. The native ISDN equipment is made up of devices that were built to be ISDN-ready and are called TE1 devices (Terminal Equipment 1). Non-native ISDN equipment is made up of TE2 devices. Non-native ISDN equipment can be integrated with native ISDN equipment by using special Terminal Adapters (TAs), meaning only TE2 devices require TA modules.

Moving towards the ISDN provider, you will find Network Termination 2 (NT2) devices and Network Termination 1 (NT1) devices. These are translation devices for media, transforming five-wire connections into two-wire connections (the local loop). The local loop is the user connection line and it is a two-wire link.

An interesting thing about the network termination devices is that in North America the customer is responsible for NT1 devices, while in other parts of the world this is the service provider's responsibility. Because of this issue, some Cisco routers provide built-in NT1 functionality and they will feature a visible "U" under the port number so that the user can quickly see this capability. The "U" notation comes from the ISDN reference points terminology that describes where you might have a problem in the ISDN infrastructure, as shown in Figure 42.5 below:

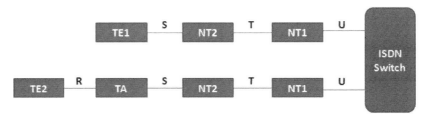

Figure 42.5—ISDN Reference Points

These reference points are important during the troubleshooting or maintaining process of an ISDN network. The ISDN switch is usually located at the service provider location. The different ISDN reference points are as follows:

- U reference point—between the ISDN switch and the NT1 device
- T reference point—between the NT2 and the NT1 devices
- S reference point—between terminals (TE1 or TA) and NT2 devices
- R reference point—between non-ISDN native devices and TAs

The ISDN Basic Rate Interface (BRI) connectivity contains two B (bearer) channels for carrying data and one D (delta) channel for signaling. The BRI connection is abbreviated as 2B+D to remind you about the number of channels each provides. Each of the bearer channels in ISDN will operate at a speed of 64Kbps. Multilink PPP can be configured on top of these interfaces to allow the user to reach a bandwidth of 128Kbps. This bandwidth is considered to be very low according to modern networks requirements.

The delta (D) channel in BRI ISDN is dedicated to 16Kbps for control traffic. There are also 48Kbps overall for framing control and other overhead in the ISDN environment, meaning the total ISDN bandwidth for BRI is 192Kbps (128Kbps from the B channels + 16Kbps from the D channel + 48Kbps overhead).

ISDN Primary Rate Interface (PRI) has 23 B channels and one D channel in the US and Japan. The bearer channels and the delta channels all support 64Kbps. If you include the overhead, the total PRI bandwidth is 1.544Mbps. In other parts of the world (i.e., Europe and Australia) the PRI connection contains 30 B channels and one D channel.

ISDN PRI connections are commonly used as connectivity from the PSTN to large phone systems (PBX). Each of the 23 or 30 B channels can be used as a single phone line, so the entire PRI connection can be considered a trunk that carries multiple lines. The main advantage of using a PRI connection instead of multiple individual lines is that it is easier to manage and it offers scalability.

The technologies described above are called Time Division Multiplexing (TDM) technologies. TDM refers to being able to combine multiple channels over a single overall transmission medium and using these different channels for voice, video, and data. Time division refers to splitting the connection into small windows of time for the various communication channels.

In a PSTN, you need to be able to transmit multiple calls along the same transmission medium, so TDM is used to achieve this goal. TDM actually started in the days of the telegraph and later on gained popularity with fax machines and other devices that use TDM technologies.

When you have leased lines (buying dedicated bandwidth), the circuits that are sold are measured in terms of bandwidth. A DS1 or T1 circuit in North America provides 24 time slots of 64Kbps each and a 9Kbps control time slot (for a total of 1.544Mbps, as mentioned earlier). TDM terminology is tightly connected with the leased-line purchasing process.

DSL

Digital Subscriber Line (DSL) is used as an alternative to ISDN for home users. There are a number of types of DSL connections, but the most important ones include the following:

- ADSL
- HDSL
- VDSL
- SDSL

Asymmetric Digital Subscriber Line (ADSL) is the most common form of DSL connection that functions over standard telephone lines. The reason it is called asymmetric is that it offers unequal download and upload throughput, with the download rate being higher than the upload rate. A standard ADSL connection usually offers a maximum of 24Mbps download throughput and a maximum of 3.5Mbps upload throughput over a distance of up to 3 km.

With ADSL the customer connects to a Digital Subscriber Line Access Multiplexer (DSLAM) located at the service provider. DSLAM is a DSL concentrator device that aggregates connections from multiple users.

NOTE: One of the issues with ADSL is the limited distance a subscriber can be from a DSLAM.

High Bitrate DSL (HDSL) and Very High Bitrate DSL (VDSL) are other DSL technologies used on a large scale that offer increased throughput when compared to ADSL. VDSL can operate at rates of up to 100Mbps.

Symmetric DSL (SDSL) offers the same download and upload throughput, but it was never standardized or used on a large scale.

Cable

Digital signals can also be received by home users over standard TV cable connections. Internet access can be provided over cable by using the Data Over Cable Service Interface Specification (DOCSIS) standard. This is usually a low-cost service, as the provider does not need to install a new infrastructure for the data services. The only upgrade to the existing network is the installation of a low-cost cable modem in the customer premises that usually offers RJ45 data connectivity for the user devices.

Data traffic transmission rates over cable technology can go up to 100Mbps, which is more than enough for home users and even small businesses.

NOTE: Besides TV and data signals, cable connection can also carry voice traffic.

Point-to-Point Protocol over Ethernet (PPPoE) is another technology that can be used in conjunction with cable. This can be used between the cable modem and the endpoint devices to add security to the cable modem infrastructure. This allows the user to log on and provide a username and a password that has to be authenticated in order for the cable service to be used. The credentials are carried across the Ethernet connection to the cable modem and beyond by using the PPP running over the Ethernet. We will cover PPPoE shortly.

Cellular Networks

Cellular networks are used in conjunction with mobile devices (e.g., cell phones, tablets, PDAs etc.) to send and receive data traffic with classic voice service. These networks cover large geographical areas by splitting them into cells. Antennas are strategically placed to ensure optimal coverage across these cells and seamless cell roaming for users going from one location to another. The traditional connectivity type is also called 2G and includes the following:

- GSM (Global System for Mobile Communications)
- CDMA (Code Division Multiple Access)

Depending upon the carrier you use and the country you live in, you might use a GSM or CDMA type of communication, although functionally they are often referred to as 2G networks. These networks were designed as analog connections using circuit switching and were not originally designed to send data. Because the data connections use a packet-switching technology, 2G connections offer limited data transmission support.

Newer connection types over cellular networks that allow full-featured packet switching and proper data transmission include the following:

- HSPA+ (High-Speed Packet Access)
- LTE (Long Term Evolution)

LTE and HSPA+ are standards created by the 3rd Generation Partnership Project (3GPP), which is a collaboration between a number of telecommunications companies that decided they needed a standardized way to send data on cellular networks.

HSPA+ is a standard based on CDMA that offers download rates up to 84Mbps and upload rates of up to 22Mbps. LTE is a standard based on GSM/EDGE that offers download rates up to 300Mbps and upload rates up to 75Mbps.

> **NOTE:** Each of these standards continues to develop, so the throughput rates might increase in the future.

GSM 3G (third generation) is a general term that describes networks with a capability of offering transmission rates of up to several Mbps. This can be achieved by increasing the channels' allocated bandwidth, along with using packet-switching technology.

GSM 4G (fourth generation) is the latest addition to the GSM portfolio and it is still under implementation in most countries. 4G offers transmission rates that exceed 100Mbps, which are suitable for high-speed broadband Internet access. GSM 4G is based exclusively on IP communication, as the spread spectrum radio technology used in 3G networks is replaced by ODFMA multi-carrier transmission that can assure high transmission rates.

VPN TECHNOLOGIES

VPN is a technology that overlays communications networks and gives them the security and manageability required by businesses. With VPN technology, you can set up secure relationships, automated connections, authorizations, and encryption, while still enjoying the low cost and availability of the Internet.

VPNs protect data while in transit across the Internet, or within a company's enclave. The VPN has many capabilities, but the primary functions include the following:

- Keep data confidential (encryption)
- Ensure the identities of two parties communicating (authentication)
- Safeguard the identities of communicating parties (tunneling)
- Ensure data is accurate and in its original form (non-repudiation)
- Guard against packets being sent over and over (replay prevention)

Even though the VPN concept implies security most of the time, unsecured VPNs also exist. Frame Relay is an example of this, as it provides private communications between two locations but it might not have any security features on top of it. Whether you should add security to the VPN connection depends upon the specific requirements for that connection.

VPN troubleshooting is difficult to manage because of the lack of visibility in the service provider infrastructure. The service provider is usually seen as a cloud that aggregates all the network locations' connections. When performing VPN troubleshooting, you should first make sure that the problem does not reside on your devices and only then should you contact your service provider.

There are many types of VPN technologies, including the following:

- Site-to-Site VPNs, or Intranet VPNs, for example Overlay VPNs (like Frame Relay) or Peer-to-Peer VPNs (like MPLS). You would use these when you want to connect different locations over the public infrastructure. When using a peer-to-peer infrastructure, you can seamlessly communicate between your sites without worrying about IP addressing overlap.
- Remote Access VPNs, for example Virtual Private Dialup Network (VPDN), which is a dial-up approach for the VPN that is usually done with security in mind.
- Extranet VPNs, when you want to connect to business partners or customer networks.

When you use VPNs, you are often tunneling traffic in order to send it over an infrastructure. One tunneling methodology for Layer 3 is called Generic Routing Encapsulation (GRE). GRE allows you to tunnel traffic but it does not provide security. In order to tunnel traffic and also provide security, you can use a technology called IP Security (IPSec). This is a mandatory implementation component of IPv6 but it is not a requirement for IPv4. IPSec is also used in conjunction with Authentication, Authorization, and Accounting (AAA) services, which allows tracking of user activity.

The main benefits of VPNs include the following:

- Scalability (you can continuously add more sites to the VPN)
- Flexibility (you can use very flexible technologies like MPLS)
- Cost (you can tunnel traffic through the Internet without much expense)

Client VPN
Surely you are aware of the Secure Sockets Layer (SSL) protocol simply through browsing the Internet. Anytime you have purchased something online, the Web address has started with https://, which is an indicator that you are leveraging SSL to ensure that your financial information is encrypted and secure.

SSL can also be used to create VPN sessions. For example, Cisco's AnyConnect software client can be installed on any operating system to allow users to establish a secure tunnel to a network. Once that tunnel is established, users can access network resources as if they were on the same network, meaning that they can view intranet pages, access email, or communicate using the internal Skype servers as if they were actually in the office. All of this information is encrypted over the Internet.

A client VPN SSL connection is typically established with a Cisco ASA firewall. When you are done working for the day, you would simply disconnect your VPN session.

DMVPN
Dynamic Multipoint VPN allows secure communication between sites without having to pass through a headquarters VPN server or router, which is the traditional method. A DMVPN saves costs and conserves bandwidth, and of course improves speed.

A hub-and-spoke topology is required for this connection type. The spoke will collect certain information about the destination spoke and then set up a direct VPN tunnel. Figure 42.6 below illustrates this connection type:

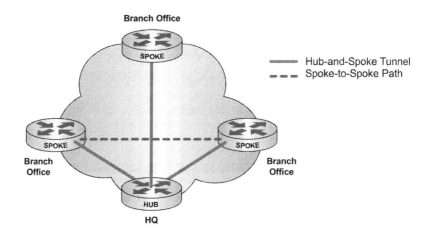

Figure 42.6—DMVPN in Action

MPLS

Multiprotocol Label Switching (MPLS) functions by appending a label to any type of packet. The packet is then forwarded through the network infrastructure based on this label value, instead of any Layer 3 information. The labeling of the packet provides very efficient forwarding and allows MPLS to work with a wide range of underlying technologies. By simply adding a label in the packet header, MPLS can be used in many Physical and Data Link Layer WAN implementations.

The MPLS label is positioned between the Layer 2 header and the Layer 3 header. By using MPLS, overhead is added only when the packet enters the service provider cloud. After entering the MPLS network, packet switching is done much faster than in traditional Layer 3 networks because it is based only on swapping the MPLS label, instead of stripping the entire Layer 3 header.

MPLS comes in two different flavors:

- Frame Mode MPLS
- Cell Mode MPLS

Frame Mode MPLS is the most popular MPLS type, and in this scenario the label is placed between the Layer 2 header and Layer 3 header (for this reason MPLS is often considered a Layer 2.5 technology). Cell Mode MPLS is used in ATM networks and uses fields in the ATM header that are used as the label.

MPLS-capable routers are also called Label Switched Routers (LSRs), and these routers come in two flavors:

- Edge LSR (PE routers)
- LSR (P routers)

PE routers are Provider Edge devices that take care of label distribution; they forward packets based on labels and they are responsible for label insertion and removal. P routers are Provider routers and their responsibility consists of label forwarding and efficient packet forwarding based on labels.

BASIC SERIAL LINE CONFIGURATION

If you don't want to change the default HDLC encapsulation, then, in order to set up your WAN connection, you need only to do the following:

1. Add an IP address to your interface
2. Bring the interface up (with the no shut command)
3. Ensure there is a clock rate on the DCE side

Here is the configuration if you have the DCE cable attached:

```
Router#config t
Router(config)#interface Serial0
Router(config-if)#ip address 192.168.1.1 255.255.255.0
Router(config-if)#clock rate 64000
Router(config-if)#no shutdown
Router(config-if)#^Z
Router#
```

PPPOE

Point-to-Point Protocol over Ethernet (PPPoE) is a network protocol used to encapsulate PPP frames inside Ethernet frames.

As customers deploy ADSL, they must support PPP-style authentication and authorization over a large installed base of legacy bridging customer premises equipment (CPE). PPPoE provides the ability to connect a network of hosts over a simple bridging access device to a remote access concentrator or aggregation concentrator. With this model, each host uses its own PPP stack, thus presenting the user with a familiar user interface. Access control, billing, and type of service can be done on a per-user, rather than a per-site, basis.

As specified in RFC 2516, PPPoE has two distinct stages: a discovery stage and a session stage. When a host initiates a PPPoE session, it must first perform discovery to identify which server can meet the client's request, and then identify the Ethernet MAC address of the peer and establish a PPPoE session ID. While PPP defines a peer-to-peer relationship, discovery is inherently a client-server relationship.

PPPoE Configuration

The following sections cover server (ISP premises) and client PPPoE configurations. I've included them because the CCNA syllabus now mandates that you know how to configure PPPoE!

Server Configuration

The first step in creating the PPPoE server configuration is to define a BBA (broadband aggregation) group which will manage the incoming connections. This BBA group must be associated to a virtual template:

```
Router(config)#bba-group pppoe GROUP
Router(config-bba-group)#virtual-template 1
```

The next step is to create a virtual template for the customer-facing interface. On the virtual template you need to configure an IP address and a pool of addresses from which clients are assigned a negotiated address:

```
Router(config)#interface virtual-template 1
Router(config-if)#ip address 10.10.10.1 255.255.255.0
Router(config-if)#peer default ip address pool POOL
```

The IP pool is defined in global configuration mode. This is similar to a DHCP pool configuration:

```
Router(config)#ip local pool POOL 10.10.10.2 10.10.10.254
```

The final step is to enable the PPPoE group on the customer-facing interface:

```
Router(config)#interface FastEthernet0/0
Router(config-if)#no ip address
Router(config-if)#pppoe enable group GROUP
Router(config-if)#no shutdown
```

Client Configuration

On the client side a dialer interface has to be created. This will manage the PPPoE connection. The dialer interface can be assigned a manual IP address or can be instructed to request one from the server (using the `ip address negotiated` command):

```
Router(config)#interface dialer1
Router(config-if)#dialer pool 1
Router(config-if)#encapsulation ppp
Router(config-if)#ip address negotiated
Router(config)#interface FastEthernet0/0
Router(config-if)#no ip address
Router(config-if)#pppoe-client dial-pool-number 1
Router(config-if)#no shutdown
```

Authentication

In order to secure the PPPoE connection, you can use two methods:

- PAP (Password Authentication Protocol)—insecure, sends the credentials (both username and password) in plain text
- CHAP (Challenge Handshake Authentication Protocol)—secure (clear text username and MD5 hashed password), the preferred method

PAP can be configured as follows:

```
Server(config)#username Client password Password
Server(config)#interface virtual-template 1
Server(config-if)#ppp authentication pap
Server(config-if)#ppp pap sent-username Server password Password

Client(config)#username Server password Password
Client(config)#interface dialer 1
Client(config-if)#ppp authentication pap
Client(config-if)#ppp pap sent-username Client password Password
```

CHAP can be configured as follows:

```
Server(config)#username Client password Password
Server(config)#interface virtual-template 1
Server(config-if)#ppp authentication chap

Client(config)#username Server password Password
Client(config)#interface dialer 1
Client(config-if)#ppp authentication chap
```

PPPoE Verification and Troubleshooting

The following message appears on the client console after the PPPoE session has successfully formed:

```
%DIALER-6-BIND: Interface Vi1 bound to profile Di1
%LINK-3-UPDOWN: Interface Virtual-Access1, changed state to up
%LINEPROTO-5-UPDOWN: Line protocol on Interface Virtual-Access1, changed
state to up
```

The following command can be used on the client router to verify the dialer interface obtained (negotiated) and the IP address from the PPPoE server:

```
Router#show ip interface brief
Interface                IP-Address      OK? Method Status
Protocol
Virtual-Access1          unassigned      YES unset  up/up
Dialer1                  10.10.10.2      YES IPCP   up/up
```

The following command can be used on the client router to show the PPPoE session status:

```
Router#show pppoe session
 1 client session

Uniq ID  PPPoE  RemMAC        Port       Source    VA           State
    SID  LocMAC                                    VA-st
N/A   16  ca00.4843.0008  Fa0/0      Di1       Vi1          UP
          ca01.4843.0008                                   UP
```

Useful troubleshooting commands for PPPoE connections are as follows:

```
Router#debug ppp ?
  authentication  CHAP and PAP authentication
  bap             BAP protocol transactions
  cbcp            Callback Control Protocol negotiation
  elog            PPP ELOGs
  error           Protocol errors and error statistics
  forwarding      PPP layer 2 forwarding
  mppe            MPPE Events
  multilink       Multilink activity
  negotiation     Protocol parameter negotiation
  packet          Low-level PPP packet dump
```

PPP OPERATIONS

PPP is considered an Internet-friendly protocol due to the following factors:

- It supports data compression
- Authentication is built in (PAP and CHAP)
- Network Layer address negotiation
- Error detection

You can use PPP over several connection types, including the following:

- DSL
- ISDN
- Synchronous and asynchronous links
- HSSI

PPP can be broken down into the following Layer 2 sub layers:

- NCP—establishes Network Layer protocols (serves the Network Layer)
- LCP—establishes, authenticates, and tests link quality (serves the Physical Layer)
- HDLC—encapsulates datagrams over the link

Knowing the above may well come in handy during your CCNA exam!

Configuring PPP

PPP is very easy to configure, as shown in Figure 42.7 and the following output below. You can also add authentication, which will be demonstrated in a moment.

Figure 42.7—PPP Connection

```
R1#conf t
R1(config)#interface s0
R1(config-if)#ip add 192.168.1.1 255.255.255.0
R1(config-if)#clock rate 64000
R1(config-if)#encapsulation ppp
R1(config-if)#no shut

R2#conf t
R2(config)#interface s0
R2(config-if)#ip add 192.168.1.2 255.255.255.0
R2(config-if)#encapsulation ppp
R2(config-if)#no shut
```

PPP Authentication

PPP has built-in authentication in the form of Password Authentication Protocol (PAP) or Challenge Handshake Authentication Protocol (CHAP). PAP sends the passwords over the link in clear text, which poses a security risk, whereas CHAP sends a hashed value using MD5 security. Here is a CHAP configuration:

Username – R2
Password – Cisco

Username – R1
Password – Cisco

Figure 42.8—PPP with CHAP

```
R1#conf t
R1(config)#username R2 password Cisco
R1(config)#interface s0
R1(config-if)#ip add 192.168.1.1 255.255.255.0
R1(config-if)#clock rate 64000
R1(config-if)#encapsulation ppp
R1(config-if)#ppp authentication chap
R1(config-if)#no shut

R2#conf t
R2(config)#username R1 password Cisco
R2(config)#interface s0
R2(config-if)#ip add 192.168.1.2 255.255.255.0
R2(config-if)#encapsulation ppp
R2(config-if)#ppp authentication chap
R2(config-if)#no shut
```

To configure PAP, you would replace the [chap] keyword in the configuration above with the [pap] keyword. You can also configure PPP to attempt authentication using CHAP, but if this isn't successful, attempt with PAP. This is known as PPP fallback and here is the command:

```
R2(config-if)#ppp authentication chap pap
```

TROUBLESHOOTING PPP

Issue a show interface serial 0/0 command, or the relevant interface number, to display the IP address, interface status, and the encapsulation type, as illustrated in the output below:

```
RouterA#show interface Serial0/0

Serial0 is up, line protocol is up
  Hardware is HD64570
  Internet address is 192.168.1.1/30
  MTU 1500 bytes, BW 1544 Kbit, DLY 20000 usec,
    reliability 255/255, txload 1/255, rxload 1/255
  Encapsulation PPP, loopback not set
  Keepalive set (10 sec)
```

If you are using CHAP, then check to ensure that the username matches that of the router you are calling, and bear in mind that the hostnames are case sensitive. You troubleshoot PPP session establishment with the commands debug ppp authentication and debug ppp negotiation.

CONFIGURING AND VERIFYING PPP AND MLPPP ON WAN INTERFACES USING LOCAL AUTHENTICATION

PPP has the capacity to run over multiple connections via Multilink PPP (MLPPP). You will often hear it referred to as Multilink when you are working in the field. We referred to link aggregation for LANs in the EtherChannel section, and this is another form but for WAN connections. MLPPP allows you to group a number of PPP connections into one logical connection; for example, if you had three 1 MB connections, you could group them into one 3 MB pipe.

Packets must be numbered when divided over the connections so they can be reassembled into the correct order upon arrival.

Figure 42.9 below demonstrates a scenario where MLPPP would prove useful. Without it, each physical connection would need its own IP address and you would have to manually configure load balancing. MLPPP allows you to group the physical connections into one logical connection.

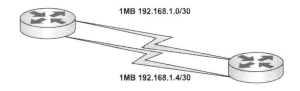

Figure 42.9—Connection Without MLPPP

In Figure 42.10 below, MLPPP is configured to make one logical 2 MB connection:

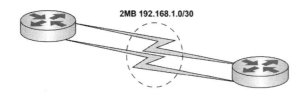

2MB 192.168.1.0/30

Figure 42.10—Connection Using MLPPP

Configuring MLPPP

Configuration for MLPPP is fairly straightforward. You need to put the relevant interfaces into a multilink group, set PPP authentication and encapsulation, and add an IP address to the multilink interface. Here is the configuration for R1:

```
R1(config)#username R2 password cisco
R1(config)#int s0/0
R1(config-if)#encap ppp
R1(config-if)#ppp multilink
R1(config-if)#ppp multilink group 1
R1(config-if)#ppp authentication chap
R1(config-if)#no shut
R1(config-if)#int s0/1
R1(config-if)#encap ppp
R1(config-if)#ppp multilink
R1(config-if)#ppp multilink group 1
R1(config-if)#ppp authen chap
R1(config-if)#no shut
R1(config-if)#interface multilink 1
R1(config-if)#encap ppp
R1(config-if)#ppp multilink group 1
R1(config-if)#ip address 192.168.1.1 255.255.255.0
R1(config-if)#no shut
```

When you have set the configuration for R2, the connection should come up. Verification commands include the following:

```
show interface multilink 1
show ppp multilink
show ip interface brief
```

TROUBLESHOOTING WAN CONNECTIONS

When trying to bring up a WAN connection (forgetting PPP and Frame Relay for the moment), you could use the OSI model:

Layer 1—Check the cable to ensure that it is attached correctly. Has the `no shut` command been applied? Is there a clock rate applied to the DCE side?

```
RouterA#show controllers serial 0
HD unit 0, idb = 0x1AE828, driver structure at 0x1B4BA0
buffer size 1524 HD unit 0, V.35 DTE cable
RouterA#show ip interface brief
Interface    IP-Address    OK? Method Status              Protocol
Serial0      11.0.0.1      YES unset  administratively down down
Ethernet0    10.0.0.1      YES unset  up                      up
```

Layer 2—Check to ensure that the correct encapsulation is applied to the interface. Ensure that the other side of the link has the same encapsulation type.

```
RouterB#show interface Serial0
Serial1 is down, line protocol is down
 Hardware is HD64570
 Internet address is 12.0.0.1/24
 MTU 1500 bytes, BW 1544 Kbit, DLY 1000 usec, rely 255/255, load 1/255
 Encapsulation HDLC, loopback not set, keepalive set (10 sec)
```

Layer 3—Is the IP address and subnet mask correct? Does the subnet mask match the other side?

```
RouterB#show interface Serial0
Serial1 is down, line protocol is down
 Hardware is HD64570
 Internet address is 12.0.0.1/24
 MTU 1500 bytes, BW 1544 Kbit, DLY 1000 usec, rely 255/255, load 1/255
 Encapsulation HDLC, loopback not set, keepalive set (10 sec)
```

Please complete today's exam at **https://www.in60days.com/free/ccnain60days/**

DAY 42 LABS

PPPoE

Configure PPPoE with CHAP authentication between two routers as per the information presented in this module:

Server configuration:
```
Router(config)#bba-group pppoe GROUP
Router(config-bba-group)#virtual-template 1
Router(config)#interface virtual-template 1
Router(config-if)#ip address 10.10.10.1 255.255.255.0
Router(config-if)#peer default ip address pool POOL
Router(config)#ip local pool POOL 10.10.10.2 10.10.10.254
Router(config)#interface FastEthernet0/0
Router(config-if)#no ip address
Router(config-if)#pppoe enable group GROUP
Router(config-if)#no shutdown
```

Client configuration:
```
Router(config)#interface dialer1
Router(config-if)#dialer pool 1
Router(config-if)#encapsulation ppp
Router(config-if)#ip address negotiated
Router(config)#interface FastEthernet0/0
Router(config-if)#no ip address
Router(config-if)#pppoe-client dial-pool-number 1
Router(config-if)#no shutdown
```

CHAP Authentication (server then client):
```
Router(config)#username Client password Password
Router(config)#interface virtual-template 1
Router(config-if)#ppp authentication chap

Router(config)#username Server password Password
Router(config)#interface dialer 1
Router(config-if)#ppp authentication chap
```

Verify the configuration:
```
Router#show pppoe session
 1 client session

Uniq ID  PPPoE  RemMAC        Port      Source   VA        State
         SID    LocMAC                           VA-st
N/A      16     ca00.4843.0008  Fa0/0     Di1      Vi1       UP
                ca01.4843.0008                              UP
```

HDLC

Topology

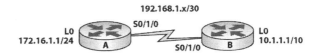

192.168.1.x/30

Purpose

Try your hand at WAN troubleshooting.

Walkthrough

No walkthrough for this lab. Configure the network above. Your WAN will work using HDLC automatically. Ping across the Serial link to ensure that it is working. Then, break the network in the following ways.

1. Change the encapsulation type on Router B to PPP (thus breaking the link at layer 2). Do this with the following configuration:

```
RouterB(config)#int Serial0/1/0
RouterB(config-if)#encapsulation ppp

%LINEPROTO-5-UPDOWN: Line protocol on Interface Serial0/1/0, changed
state to down
RouterB(config-if)#
```

2. Issue a `shut` command on the Serial interface on Router A. Then issue a `show ip interface brief` command. You should see your interface up/down.

3. Take the clock rate off your DCE interface side. Then issue the `show controllers serial x` command. It should tell you there is no clock rate configured.

4. Change the subnet mask on the Router B side to 255.255.255.0. You can see the subnet mask with a `show interface serial x` command. If that command isn't permitted in the exam, then issue a `show run` command.

5. Now fix all of the issues above. This is what you will have to do in the exam, and these are the most common issues. Please do test the commands you would enter if you were troubleshooting this issue to show you the IP address, encapsulation type, and clock rate.

Point-to-Point Protocol

Topology

10.0.0.0/30

S0/1/0

LO   A   S0/1/0   B   LO
172.20.1.1/24   192.168.1.1/26

Purpose

Learn how to configure PPP and CHAP.

Walkthrough

1. Configure IP addresses and hostnames as per the topology above.

2. Set the encapsulation on each side to PPP. Here is the command for Router A:

    ```
    RouterA(config)#interface s0/1/0
    RouterA(config-if)#encapsulation ppp
    ```

3. Set CHAP on each router. You will set the hostname of the opposite router and the password cisco.

    ```
    RouterA(config)#username RouterB password cisco
    RouterA(config)#interface s0/1/0
    RouterA(config-if)#ppp authentication chap
    RouterA(config-if)#exit

    RouterB(config)#username RouterA password cisco
    RouterB(config)#interface s0/1/0
    RouterB(config-if)#ppp authentication chap
    RouterB(config-if)#exit
    ```

4. Ping across the link to ensure it is up.

    ```
    RouterB#ping 10.0.0.1

    Type escape sequence to abort.
    Sending 5, 100-byte ICMP Echos to 10.0.0.1, timeout is 2 seconds:
    !!!!!
    Success rate is 100 percent (5/5), round-trip min/avg/max = 31/31/32
    ms

    RouterB#
    ```

5. Break the connection by changing the hostname on Router A to Router C. You will also want to turn on PPP debugs and shut/no shut the interface to open negotiation again. You will have to be quick to type undebug all. If you are at the interface prompt, then type do undebug all.

```
RouterA#conf t
Enter configuration commands, one per line.  End with CNTL/Z.
RouterA(config)#hostname RouterC
RouterC(config)#exit
RouterC#
RouterC#debug ppp neg
PPP protocol negotiation debugging is on
RouterC#debug ppp auth

RouterC#config t
RouterC(config)#int s0/1/0
RouterC(config-if)#shut

Serial0/1/0 LCP: State is Open
Serial0/1/0 PPP: Phase is AUTHENTICATING

Serial0/1/0 IPCP: O CONFREQ [Closed] id 1 len 10 ← Router won't
authenticate
RouterC(config-if)#do undebug all

RouterC#sh int s0/1/0
Serial0/1/0 is up, line protocol is down (disabled)
```

MLPPP

Topology

Purpose

Learn how to configure MLPPP using two serial links.

Walkthrough

1. Enable multilink on the two interfaces on R1. Repeat these commands on R2.

   ```
   R1(config)#int s0/0
   R1(config-if)#encapsulation ppp
   R1(config-if)#ppp multilink group 1
   R1(config-if)#no shut
   R1(config-if)#int s0/1
   R1(config-if)#encap ppp
   R1(config-if)#ppp multilink group 1
   R1(config-if)#no shut
   ```

2. Add CHAP authentication (optional step). On R2 you will change the username to R1.

   ```
   R1(config-if)#int s0/1
   R1(config-if)#ppp authentication chap
   ```

```
R1(config-if)#int s0/0
R1(config-if)#ppp authent chap
R1(config-if)#exit
R1(config)#username R2 password cisco
```

3.   Configure the Multilink interface and add an IP address. On R2 change the host to .2.

```
R1(config)#int multilink 1
R1(config-if)#encapsulation ppp
R1(config-if)#ppp multilink
R1(config-if)#ppp multilink group 1
R1(config-if)#ip add 192.168.1.1 255.255.255.0
R1(config-if)#no shut
```

4.   Issue some show commands to verify the connection. Feel free to try a ping also.

```
R2#show int multilink 1
Multilink1 is up, line protocol is up
  Hardware is multilink group interface
  Internet address is 192.168.1.2/24
  MTU 1500 bytes, BW 3088 Kbit/sec, DLY 100000 usec,
    reliability 255/255, txload 1/255, rxload 1/255
  Encapsulation PPP, LCP Open, multilink Open
[output truncated]

R2#show ppp multilink

Multilink1
  Bundle name: R1
  Remote Username: R1
  Remote Endpoint Discriminator: [1] R1
  Local Username: R2
  Local Endpoint Discriminator: [1] R2
  Bundle up for 00:01:20, total bandwidth 3088, load 1/255
  Receive buffer limit 24000 bytes, frag timeout 1000 ms
    0/0 fragments/bytes in reassembly list
    0 lost fragments, 1 reordered
    0/0 discarded fragments/bytes, 0 lost received
    0x2 received sequence, 0x2 sent sequence
  Member links: 2 active, 0 inactive (max not set, min not set)
    Se0/0, since 00:01:20
    Se0/1, since 00:01:16
No inactive multilink interfaces
R2#

R2#show ip int brief
Interface        IP-Address      OK? Method Status
Protocol
Fa0/0           unassigned      YES unset  administratively down down
S0/0            unassigned      YES unset  up                       up
Fa0/1           unassigned      YES unset  administratively down down
S0/1            unassigned      YES unset  up                       up
Multilink1      192.168.1.2     YES manual up                       up
```

Generic Routing Encapsulation

DAY 43 TASKS

- Read today's lesson notes (below)
- Review yesterday's lesson notes
- Complete today's lab
- Take today's exam
- Read the ICND2 cram guide
- Spend 15 minutes on the subnetting.org website

Generic Routing Encapsulation (GRE) is defined in RFC 2784, and was developed by Cisco Systems to encapsulate a number of network protocols over an IP point-to-point link. GRE provides the means to transport packets of another protocol, which is referred to as tunneling.

Today you will learn about the following:

- GRE tunnel connectivity
- Configuring GRE tunnels
- Troubleshooting GRE tunnels

This lesson maps to the following CCNA syllabus requirements:

- 3.3 Configure, verify, and troubleshoot GRE tunnel connectivity

GRE TUNNEL CONNECTIVITY

This topic is often grouped with a discussion about VPNs in study guides because it can be used with the Point-to-Point Tunneling Protocol (PPTP) to create a VPN, or with IPSec VPNs for secure transport of information. GRE traffic is insecure without additional security protocols.

Why would you want to tunnel a packet through a network? Here are just a few reasons:

- You might want to enable a routing protocol neighbor relationship between two routers, each of which are many hops away from one another.
- You might want to deploy a secure network leveraging the Internet by creating virtual circuits between your data center and remote offices.

GRE (as the name suggests) encapsulates, or wraps, the payload (headers and data) inside an outer packet compatible with GRE. The GRE tunnel endpoints then send the payload, de-encapsulating the GRE wrapper at the destination, as illustrated in Figure 43.1 below:

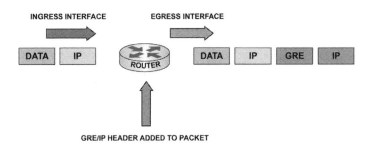

Figure 43.1—GRE Adds its Own Information to the Packet

The GRE packet format is illustrated in Figure 43.2 below:

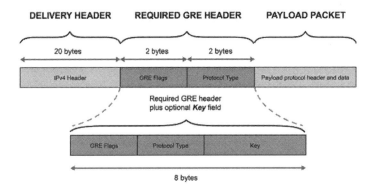

Figure 43.2—GRE Packet

CONFIGURING GRE TUNNELS

Configuring GRE tunnels is surprisingly easy. You simply need to designate a tunnel source IP and a tunnel destination IP. Once you know the two endpoints of the tunnel, you need to add either a routing protocol or static routes so that traffic can be routed correctly. Figure 43.3 below illustrates a simple GRE connection.

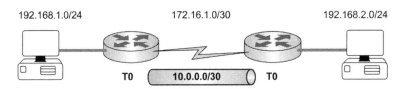

Figure 43.3—Simple GRE Connection

The configuration for the router on the left is shown below. You would need to make necessary adjustments to the router at the other end.

```
Router#show run
interface fast0/0
 ip address 192.168.1.1 255.255.255.0
!
interface Tunnel0
 ip address 10.0.0.1 255.255.255.252
 tunnel source Serial0/0
 tunnel destination 172.16.1.2
!
interface Serial0/0
ip address 172.16.1.1 255.255.255.252
!
ip route 192.168.2.0 255.255.255.0 10.0.0.2
[output truncated]
```

You can verify GRE with the show ip interface brief and show interfaces tunnel X commands. You can also issue a show ip route command.

```
R1#show ip int brief
Interface    IP-Address    OK? Method Status            Protocol
Fa0/0        192.168.1.1   YES manual up                up
Serial0/0    172.16.1.1    YES manual up                up
Tunnel0      10.0.0.1      YES manual up                up

R1#show interfaces tunnel 0
Tunnel0 is up, line protocol is up
  Hardware is Tunnel
  Internet address is 10.0.0.1/30
  MTU 1514 bytes, BW 9 Kbit/sec, DLY 500000 usec,
     reliability 255/255, txload 1/255, rxload 1/255
  Encapsulation TUNNEL, loopback not set
  Keepalive not set
  Tunnel source 172.16.1.1 (Serial0/0), destination 172.16.1.2
  Tunnel protocol/transport GRE/IP
[output truncated]
```

TROUBLESHOOTING GRE TUNNELS

GRE tunnels are relatively easy to program but are a bit more challenging to troubleshoot. The most common reason for a GRE tunnel issue is human error (i.e., a typo). This tends to affect novice engineers who mistype commands while looking down at the book and back at the console screen. It also affects experienced engineers who have configured the commands so many times that they go into autopilot mode and mix up commands from other technologies.

Keepalives are disabled by default on a GRE tunnel, so the tunnel interface will show up even if the remote side has gone down. You can enable keepalives on GRE tunnels; however, this may introduce other issues. Please refer to Cisco documentation regarding this issue.

With all of the IP addressing floating around in one's head (source, destination, tunnel), it's very easy to place the wrong IP in the wrong line of code. If you are having problems getting a tunnel up and running, it's best simply to go back to basics:

- Make sure that your tunnel destination IP is reachable via ping (or allowing your traffic via a firewall).
- Make sure that your tunnel source is a valid IP on your system and that the source interface is up/up.
- Make sure that you have an IP address assigned to each tunnel interface and that they are on the same subnet.
- Check that the default "deny any" ACL statement isn't blocking GRE (`permit gre any any`).
- Routes to the source and destination networks must be present in the routing table.

Referencing the lab above, here are some more outputs.

```
R1#ping 192.168.2.1
Type escape sequence to abort.
Sending 5, 100-byte ICMP Echos to 192.168.2.1, timeout is 2 seconds:
!!!!!
Success rate is 100 percent (5/5), round-trip min/avg/max = 1/30/72 ms
R1#traceroute 192.168.2.1
Type escape sequence to abort.
Tracing the route to 192.168.2.1

  1 10.0.0.2 4 msec *  12 msec
```

Please take today's exam at **https://www.in60days.com/free/ccnain60days/**

DAY 43 LAB

GRE

Topology

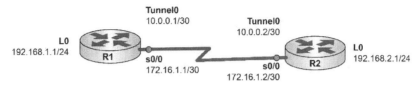

Purpose

Learn how to configure a GRE tunnel using two routers.

Walkthrough

1. Enable the indicated IP addresses on R1. Repeat these commands on R2 but change addresses to match the diagram.

```
R1(config)#int lo0
R1(config-if)#ip add
R1(config-if)#ip add 192.168.1.1 255.255.255.0
R1(config-if)#int s0/0
R1(config-if)#ip add 172.16.1.1 255.255.255.252
R1(config-if)#no shut
R1(config-if)#int tunnel 0
R1(config-if)#ip add 10.0.0.1 255.255.255.252
R1(config-if)#no shut
```

2. Add the GRE configuration creating the tunnel source and destination. You can choose from the interface IP address (serial) or interface name. Add the commands to R2 also but with the relevant changes.

```
R1(config-if)#tunnel source s0/0
R1(config-if)#tunnel destination 172.16.1.2
*Mar  1 00:19:26.031: %LINEPROTO-5-UPDOWN: Line protocol on Interface
Tunnel0, changed state to up
```

3. Confirm your configurations with some show commands.

```
R2#show ip interface brief
Interface    IP-Address  OK? Method Status                 Protocol
Fa0/0        unassigned  YES unset  administratively down  down
S0/0         172.16.1.2  YES manual up                       up
Fa0/1        unassigned  YES unset  administratively down  down
Loopback0    192.168.2.1 YES manual up                       up
Tunnel0      10.0.0.2    YES manual up                       up

R2#show int t0
Tunnel0 is up, line protocol is up
```

```
Hardware is Tunnel
Internet address is 10.0.0.2/30
MTU 1514 bytes, BW 9 Kbit/sec, DLY 500000 usec,
    reliability 255/255, txload 1/255, rxload 1/255
Encapsulation TUNNEL, loopback not set
Keepalive not set
Tunnel source 172.16.1.2 (Serial0/0), destination 172.16.1.1
Tunnel protocol/transport GRE/IP
   Key disabled, sequencing disabled
   Checksumming of packets disabled
Tunnel TTL 255
[Output Truncated]
```

4. Ping the remote loopback address. Note that it fails. Without a routing protocol or static route any routes not in the table will be dropped.

```
R2#ping 192.168.1.1

Type escape sequence to abort.
Sending 5, 100-byte ICMP Echos to 192.168.1.1, timeout is 2 seconds:
.....
Success rate is 0 percent (0/5)

R1(config)#ip route 192.168.2.0 255.255.255.0 10.0.0.2

R2(config)#ip route 192.168.1.0 255.255.255.0 10.0.0.1

R2#ping 192.168.1.1

Type escape sequence to abort.
Sending 5, 100-byte ICMP Echos to 192.168.1.1, timeout is 2 seconds:
!!!!!
Success rate is 100 percent (5/5), round-trip min/avg/max = 4/11/40 ms
R2#
```

eBGP

DAY 44 TASKS

- Review yesterdays lessons and labs
- Complete today's lab and theory
- Take today's exam
- Read the ICND2 cram guide (and the ICND1 cram guide, if taking the CCNA exam)
- Spend 15 minutes on the subnetting.org website

One of the biggest changes to the new CCNA syllabus is the introduction of the Border Gateway Protocol (BGP), which, until now, had been a CCNP and CCIE topic. Understanding BGP usually takes several weeks of study for experienced engineers, and any configurations usually have to be carefully planned weeks in advance as mistakes can cause havoc for Internet users.

Today you will learn about the following:

- eBGP
- eBGP configuration

This lesson maps to the following CCNA syllabus requirements:

- 3.6 Configure and verify single-homed branch connectivity using eBGP IPv4 (limited to peering and route advertisement using Network command only)

SINGLE-HOMED BRANCH EBGP CONNECTIVITY

For the CCNA exam, Cisco expects you to have a general understanding of what BGP does, how it works, and how to configure a simple eBGP connection between two routers. Advanced configurations and troubleshooting are outside the syllabus.

BGP was specifically designed to manage routing over the Internet. It replaced the Exterior Gateway Protocol (EGP) in the early 1990s. While routing protocols are usually concerned with routing within an autonomous system (AS), BGP deals with routing between AS numbers. These ASNs must be unique and are usually assigned by regional Internet registries—the available numbers range from 1 to 65565. We already know that an AS represents an entire network under the control of a certain company or ISP.

 DARIO SAYS—"Prior to January 2009, BGP ASNs that were allocated to companies were 2-byte numbers that ranged from 1 to 65535. Due to increased demand for autonomous system numbers, in January 2009, the IANA began to allocate 4-byte ASNs ranging from 65536 to 4294967295."

BGP speaking routers (speakers) form neighbor relationships with other BGP speakers. The neighbors are referred to as peers. The routers communicate using TCP port 179. Various specialized message types are used to initiate, maintain, and close sessions between peers. BGP tracks AS numbers rather than router hops, which could number in the hundreds (it's a path vector protocol).

BGP is used primarily to exchange Network Layer Reachability Information (NLRI) between routing domains or ASNs. The NLRI is composed of a prefix and a length. The prefix refers to the network address for that subnet, and the length specifies the number of network bits and is simply a network mask in CIDR notation. Some NLRI examples include 10.0.0.0/8 and 150.1.1.0/24.

As was stated earlier in this chapter, BGP provides NLRI connectivity between different routing domains (autonomous systems) or within the same routing domain. Therefore, when BGP is enabled, the BGP speaker must be configured with an ASN using the `router bgp [autonomous system number]` global configuration command.

While EIGRP also uses ASNs, there are some significant differences in the use of ASNs when implementing EIGRP and when implementing BGP. With EIGRP, routers establish a neighbor relationship only if they are part of the same autonomous system, although you should keep in mind that this is in addition to other EIGRP requirements, such as being in the same subnet, etc. With BGP, however, the peer relationship can be established between two BGP speakers in different autonomous systems, which is referred to as an external BGP (eBGP) relationship, or between BGP speakers within the same autonomous system, which is referred to as an internal (iBGP) relationship (see the section below).

Internal and External BGP

Figure 44.1 below illustrates the difference between the two varieties of BGP. Internal BGP is communication between routers within an AS. Once the communication leaves the AS destined for another, it becomes external BGP (eBGP).

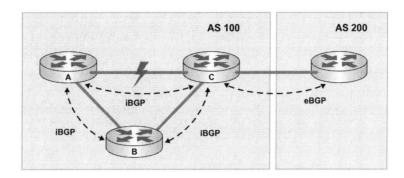

Figure 44.1—External Versus Internal BGP

For the sake of the ICND2 exam, Cisco wants you to be aware of how to deploy and support eBGP over a single circuit as you see in Figure 44.2 below. It's unlikely that you would have a single connection to your ISP if you were running BGP. This option is referred to as single-homing and it is covered in the CCNA syllabus in order to keep things simple. Figure 44.2 below illustrates a single-homed connection:

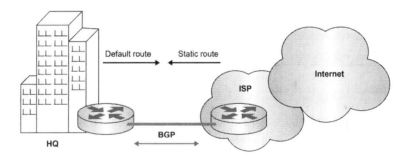

Figure 44.2—Single-homing

Here you can either send a default route to your ISP for your networks and receive a static route for customer networks, or announce your network to the ISP and use a default route received from your ISP. This type of connection is also referred to as a stub network.

Figure 44.3 below illustrates dual-homing. Here you have one router with two connections to the same ISP or two edge routers doing the same.

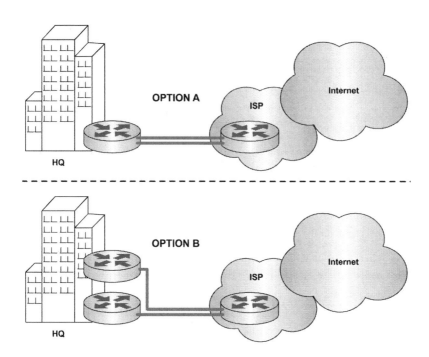

Figure 44.3—Dual-homing

In the example above, you would use either static routes or BGP.

Because there are over 600,000 BGP routes available on the Internet, you would usually route all BGP traffic to your ISP and let them deal with forwarding options. You could also choose to receive a partial Internet routing table from your ISP.

NLRI and Path Updates

We discussed NLRI briefly earlier. NLRI information is exchanged between BGP speakers (via TCP) using UPDATE messages. Figure 44.4 below is a packet capture of such a message:

```
⊟ Border Gateway Protocol              ⊟ Border Gateway Protocol
  ⊟ UPDATE Message                       ⊟ UPDATE Message
      Marker: 16 bytes                       Marker: 16 bytes
      Length: 55 bytes                       Length: 55 bytes
      Type: UPDATE Message (2)               Type: UPDATE Message (2)
      Unfeasible routes length: 0 bytes      Unfeasible routes length: 0 bytes
      Total path attribute length: 20 bytes  Total path attribute length: 20 bytes
    ⊞ Path attributes                      ⊟ Path attributes
    ⊞ Network layer reachability information: 12 bytes   ⊞ ORIGIN: IGP (4 bytes)
                                             ⊟ AS_PATH: 65100 65200 (9 bytes)
                                               ⊞ Flags: 0x40 (well-known, Transitive, Complete)
                                                 Type code: AS_PATH (2)
                                                 Length: 6 bytes
                                               ⊞ AS path: 65100 65200
                                             ⊞ NEXT_HOP: 1.1.1.1 (7 bytes)
                                           ⊟ Network layer reachability information: 12 bytes
                                             ⊟ 10.20.1.0/24
                                                 NLRI prefix length: 24
                                                 NLRI prefix: 10.20.1.0 (10.20.1.0)
                                             ⊞ 10.20.2.0/24
                                             ⊞ 10.20.3.0/24
```

Figure 44.4—BGP UPDATE message (Image ©http://blogbt.net)

The NLRI is composed of a length and a prefix. The length is the network mask represented in CIDR (e.g., /24), while the prefix is the network address (e.g., 10.20.2.0 and 10.20.3.0) and it lists a set of reachable destination networks.

BGP relies on routes passed from neighbors. The route update lists the ASN(s) the packet must pass through in order to reach a specific destination. Going back to Figure 44.4 above, you can see that the AS path is 65100 and 65200. The list of ASNs associated with the routes is called the AS_PATH. If the router sees its own ASN, the update is rejected because this indicates a loop.

Figure 44.5 below shows a simplified version of the NLRI received by R6 in AS 5 to reach R1 in AS 50:

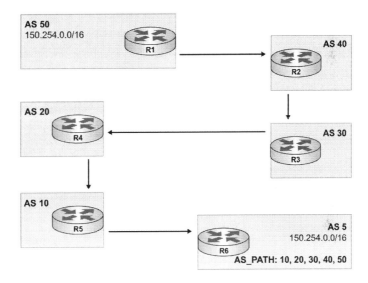

Figure 44.5—Sample NLRI Information

EBGP CONFIGURATION

As you can imagine, configuring BGP comes after careful planning and testing and is never something you would do on the fly. However, for the CCNA exam, Cisco expects you to know how to configure and verify eBGP. However, you aren't asked to perform any fine-tuning or troubleshooting.

We will use the topology in Figure 44.6 below. You can presume that the IP addresses have already been added because you already know how to do this step. The 10 network is a Loopback address to simplify the process.

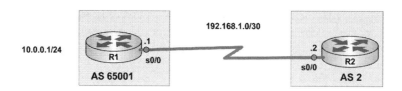

Figure 44.6—Simple BGP Topology

Let's go through the configuration for R1; you will easily be able to work out R2's configuration thereafter:

```
R1(config)#router bgp 65001
R1(config-router)#neighbor 192.168.1.2 remote-as 2
*Mar  1 00:17:07.567: %BGP-5-ADJCHANGE: neighbor 192.168.1.2 Up
```

You can verify your connection with the show tcp brief command, which won't work on Packet Tracer.

```
R1#show tcp brief
TCB        Local Address          Foreign Address          (state)
650D06B4   192.168.1.1.19120      192.168.1.2.179          ESTAB
```

You can see that the BGP session is in the Established (ESTAB) state, which is the one you want to see in fact, and it's using port 179. You can display a summary of the BGP neighbors with the show ip bgp summary command.

```
R1#show ip bgp summary
BGP router identifier 10.0.0.1, local AS number 65001
BGP table version is 1, main routing table version 1
Neighbor       V AS MsgRcvd MsgSent TblVer InQ OutQ Up/Down State/PfxRcd
192.168.1.2    4 2 10      10      1      0   0    00:07:18 0
```

Table 44.1 below illustrates the meaning of the various fields in the output.

Table 44.1—Fields in the Show ip bgp Summary Command

Field	Description
Neighbor	Specifies the IP address of the neighbor as specified in the neighbor configuration command
V	Specifies the BGP version; the default is 4
AS	Specifies the AS of the BGP neighbor
MsgRcvd	Specifies the number of messages received from the neighbor
MsgSent	Specifies the number of messages sent to the neighbor
TblVer	Specifies the last version of the BGP database that was sent to the neighbor
InQ	Specifies the number of messages queued to be processed from the neighbor
OutQ	Specifies the number of messages queued to be sent to the neighbor
Up/Down	Specifies the length of time that the BGP session has been in the Established state, or the current status if not in the Established state

State/ PfxRcd	Specifies the state of the BGP session and the number of prefixes that have been received from a neighbor or peer group. When the maximum number is reached, the string "PfxRcd" appears in the entry, the neighbor is shut down, and the connection is set to Idle. An (Admin) entry with Idle status indicates that the connection has been shut down using the neighbor shutdown command.

In addition to using the show ip bgp summary command, the show ip bgp neighbors command can be used to view detailed information for a specific neighbor or all configured neighbors. Keep in mind that this command produces a lot of output, which includes the neighbor address (as specified by the neighbor command), whether the neighbor is internal or external, the autonomous system the neighbor resides in, the BGP version, the neighbor RID, the state of the connection, and how long the connection has been up.

Additional information included in the output printed by this command includes the hold time and keepalive interval, the capabilities of the neighbor, the number of BGP messages sent and received, the number of prefixes sent and received, the default TTL of the BGP packets (this will be explained in the following section), and the local and remote ports used to establish the session. These fields are printed in bold in the following output:

```
R1#show ip bgp neighbors
BGP neighbor is 192.168.1.2,  remote AS 2, external link
  BGP version 4, remote router ID 192.168.1.2
  BGP state = Established, up for 00:20:59
  Last read 00:00:58, last write 00:00:58, hold time is 180, keepalive
interval is 60 seconds
  Neighbor capabilities:
    Route refresh: advertised and received(old & new)
    Address family IPv4 Unicast: advertised and received
  Message statistics:
    InQ depth is 0
    OutQ depth is 0
                         Sent          Rcvd
    Opens:                 1             1
    Notifications:         0             0
    Updates:               0             0
    Keepalives:           22            22
    Route Refresh:         0             0
    Total:                23            23
  Default minimum time between advertisement runs is 30 seconds

 For address family: IPv4 Unicast
  BGP table version 1, neighbor version 1/0
  Output queue size: 0
  Index 1, Offset 0, Mask 0x2
  1 update-group member
                         Sent          Rcvd
  Prefix activity:       ----          ----
    Prefixes Current:      0             0
    Prefixes Total:        0             0
    Implicit Withdraw:     0             0
```

```
Explicit Withdraw:              0           0
Used as bestpath:             n/a          0
Used as multipath:            n/a          0

                           Outbound    Inbound
Local Policy Denied Prefixes:  --------    -------
  Total:                           0          0
Number of NLRIs in the update sent: max 0, min 0

Connections established 1; dropped 0
Last reset never
Connection state is ESTAB, I/O status: 1, unread input bytes: 0
Connection is ECN Disabled, Minimum incoming TTL 0, Outgoing TTL 1
Local host: 192.168.1.1, Local port: 19120
Foreign host: 192.168.1.2, Foreign port: 179
[Output Truncated]
```

Because BGP is unique in that it uses TCP as the underlying protocol, the process of establishing a neighbor relationship is two-fold: the first phase is the establishment of the TCP session, and the second phase is the establishment of the BGP peer session. RFC 1771 includes a section on the BGP Finite State Machine (FSM). The FSM includes an overview of BGP operations by state. The six different states that BGP will go through before a neighbor relationship is established are as follows:

1. Idle state
2. Connect state
3. Active state
4. OpenSent state
5. OpenConfirm state
6. Established state

The first three states pertain to the establishment of the underlying TCP connection between the BGP speakers. The second three states pertain to the establishment of the actual BGP session. The show ip bgp summary or the show ip bgp neighbors commands can be used to view some, but not all, of these states in Cisco IOS software. Table 44.2 below illustrates the meaning of each of the states:

Table 44.2—BGP neighbor relationship states

BGP State	Event
Idle	The Idle state is the initial BGP state after BGP is enabled on a router, or when a router is reset. No BGP resources are allocated to the peer in this state. Additionally, when in this state, no incoming connections are allowed.
Connect	In this state, BGP waits for a TCP connection to be completed. If successful, the local router will send an OPEN message to the peer and the BGP state machine transitions to the OpenSent state.
Active	In the Active state, a TCP connection is initiated to establish a BGP neighbor relationship, also referred to as a BGP peer relationship.

OpenSent	After sending the OPEN message to the peer, BGP then transitions to the OpenSent state. In this state, the local router waits for a response to the sent OPEN message.
OpenConfirm	The OpenConfirm state is the penultimate state before the final state, the Established state, is reached. In this state, BGP waits for a KEEPALIVE or a NOTIFICATION message.
Established	The Established state is reached when the initial KEEPALIVE message is received while BGP is in the OpenConfirm state. This is the final state of a peer relationship, indicating a fully operational connection.

Advertising BGP Routes

The exam syllabus specifies that you need to understand the network command to advertise BGP routes. Before you use the command, it's important to note that your router will only advertise a network that already exists in the routing table (learned via OSPF, for example).

Using the topology above, we will add another command to advertise the Loopback network. The mask command isn't necessary if you are using classful addressing (i.e., the default mask), but we are using VLSM so you need to add it.

```
R1(config)#router bgp 65001
R1(config-router)#network 10.0.0.0 mask 255.255.255.0
R1(config-router)#^z
R1#show ip bgp
BGP table version is 2, local router ID is 10.0.0.1
Status codes: s suppressed, d damped, h history, * valid, > best,
              i - internal, r RIB - failure, S - Stale
Origin codes: i - IGP, e - EGP, ? - incomplete

   Network          Next Hop            Metric LocPrf Weight Path
*> 10.0.0.0/24      0.0.0.0             0             32768  i

R2#show ip bgp
BGP table version is 2, local router ID is 192.168.1.2
Status codes: s suppressed, d damped, h history, * valid, > best,
              i - internal, r RIB - failure, S - Stale
Origin codes: i - IGP, e - EGP, ? - incomplete

   Network          Next Hop            Metric LocPrf Weight Path
*> 10.0.0.0/24      192.168.1.1         0      0      65001  i
R2#
R2#show ip route bgp
     10.0.0.0/24 is subnetted, 1 subnets
B       10.0.0.0 [20/0] via 192.168.1.1, 00:14:16
```

Please take today's exam at https://www.in60days.com/free/ccnain60days/

DAY 44 LAB

eBGP

Topology

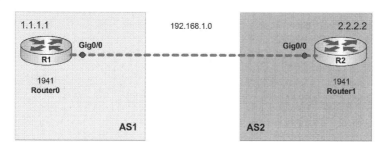

Purpose

Learn how to configure eBGP using routers.

Walkthrough

1. Enable the indicated IP addresses on R0. Repeat these commands on R1 but change addresses to match the diagram.

    ```
    R0(config)#int lo0
    R0(config-if)#ip add 1.1.1.1 255.255.255.0
    R0(config-if)#
    R0(config-if)#int g0/0
    R0(config-if)#ip add 192.168.1.1 255.255.255.0
    R0(config-if)#no shut
    ```

2. Configure BGP AS 1 on R0 and put the remote AS address in for R1. Swap the commands when you configure R1.

    ```
    R0(config)#router bgp 1
    R0(config-router)#neighbor 192.168.1.2 remote-as 2
    ```

3. Add the network commands. You can use the option of adding the subnet mask if you wish.

    ```
    R0(config-if)#router bgp 1
    R0(config-router)#network 1.1.1.0

    R1(config)#router bgp 2
    R1(config-router)#network 2.2.2.0 mask 255.255.255.0
    ```

4. Confirm your configurations with some show commands.

    ```
    R0#show ip bgp
    BGP table version is 2, local router ID is 1.1.1.1
    ```

```
Status codes: s suppressed, d damped, h history, * valid, > best, i
- internal,
r RIB-failure, S Stale
Origin codes: i - IGP, e - EGP, ? - incomplete

Network        Next Hop    Metric LocPrf    Weight Path
*> 2.2.2.0/24 192.168.1.2  0        0        0 2    i

R0#show ip bgp summary
BGP router identifier 1.1.1.1, local AS number 1
BGP table version is 2, main routing table version 6
1 network entries using 132 bytes of memory
1 path entries using 52 bytes of memory
1/1 BGP path/bestpath attribute entries using 184 bytes of memory
1 BGP AS-PATH entries using 24 bytes of memory
0 BGP route-map cache entries using 0 bytes of memory
0 BGP filter-list cache entries using 0 bytes of memory
Bitfield cache entries: current 1 (at peak 1) using 32 bytes of memory
BGP using 424 total bytes of memory
BGP activity 1/0 prefixes, 1/0 paths, scan interval 60 secs

Neighbor     V AS MsgRcvd MsgSent TblVer InQ OutQ Up/Down State/PfxRcd
192.168.1.2 4  2  8       7       2      0   0    00:05:41    4


R0#show ip bgp neighbors
BGP neighbor is 192.168.1.2,  remote AS 2, external link
  BGP version 4, remote router ID 2.2.2.2
  BGP state = Established, up for 00:08:25
  Last read 00:08:25, last write 00:08:25, hold time is 180, keepalive
interval is 60 seconds
  Neighbor capabilities:
    Route refresh: advertised and received(new)
    Address family IPv4 Unicast: advertised and received
  Message statistics:
    InQ depth is 0
    OutQ depth is 0
[output truncated]
```

5. Optionally. Check the current TCP session on the router. Note the BGP port of 179.

```
R0#show tcp brief
TCB        Local Address         Foreign Address        (state)
199CB440   192.168.1.1.179       192.168.1.2.1025       ESTABLISHED
R0#
```

Review

DAY 45 TASKS

- Review days 42-44 and redo the labs
- Take today's exam at https://www.in60days.com/free/ccnain60days/
- Read the ICND2 cram guide (and the ICND1 cram guide, if taking the CCNA exam)
- Complete today's challenge labs if you wish
- Spend 15 minutes on the subnetting.org website

Challenge 1—EIGRP with PPP Lab

Topology

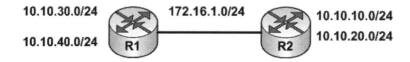

EIGRP 40

10.10.30.0/24   172.16.1.0/24   10.10.10.0/24

10.10.40.0/24   R1   R2   10.10.20.0/24

Instructions

Connect two routers together with a serial or crossover cable.

1. Add IP addresses to routers and loopback on Routers according to diagram
2. Ping between Router A and B to test serial line (remember clock rates)
3. Now set the serial lines to use PPP with CHAP (set usernames and passwords also)
4. Configure EIGRP 40 on all routers and add all networks
5. Fix the issue that prevents R2 pinging hosts on 10.10.30.0 and 10.10.40.0 and R1 from pinging the 10 addresses on R2.
6. Now change the routing so only 10.10.10.0 on R2 and 10.10.30.0 on R1 are advertised. Put the loopbacks using the other 10 networks into passive mode for EIGRP

Challenge 2—STP and VLANs Lab

Topology

VLAN 20

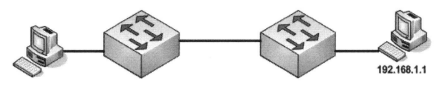

192.168.1.1

192.168.1.2

Instructions

Connect to the switch using a console connection. Connect a PC to each switch or connect the switch to the fast ethernet port on a router.

1. Add IP addresses to the PCs or router Ethernet interfaces
2. Create VLAN 20 on the switch
3. Set the ports the PCs connect to as access ports (default but do it anyway)
4. Put the two switch ports into VLAN 20
5. Check which switch is the root
6. Force the other switch to become the root
7. Hard set the switch ports to the PCs to 100mbps and full duplex
8. Wait 30 seconds and test a ping

Cloud Computing

DAY 46 TASKS

- Read today's theory
- Complete the labs from days 42-44
- Take today's exam
- Read the ICND2 cram guide (and the ICND1 cram guide, if taking the CCNA exam)
- Spend 15 minutes on the subnetting.org website

The world of IT is changing at a rapid pace. Two of the biggest changes and the most important developments is the creation of cloud computing and virtualization. Both represent huge changes in how organizations use and manage their infrastructure, and as network engineers, we need to understand the benefits and impact of these changes.

Today you will learn about the following:

- Cloud Computing
- Virtualization

This lesson maps to the following CCNA syllabus requirements:

- 4.2 Describe the effects of cloud resources on enterprise network architecture
- 4.2.a Traffic path to internal and external cloud services
- 4.2.b Virtual services
- 4.2.c Basic virtual network infrastructure

CLOUD COMPUTING

Cloud computing is a relatively new business model in the computing world. According to the official National Institute of Standards and Technology's (NIST) definition, *"cloud computing is a model for enabling ubiquitous, convenient, on-demand network access to a shared pool of configurable computing resources (e.g., networks, servers, storage, applications and services) that can be rapidly provisioned and released with minimal management effort or service provider interaction."*

Virtualization is the creation of a virtual (rather than actual) version of something, such as operating systems, servers, storage devices, or network resources. Using virtualization, we can achieve cloud computing. Virtualization shares hardware resources with different virtual machines or servers, while cloud computing employs virtualization and shares virtual servers with multiple users. Location is no longer a constraint.

In (public) cloud computing, ownership of physical servers resides with one organization and users are billed for their usage. The first official public cloud service was the e-mail service Hotmail, created by Sabeer Bhatia and Jack Smith and acquired by Microsoft in 1997. This allowed users to view, send, and receive e-mail on a remote platform without having to install an e-mail client on their PC.

Cloud computing very conveniently addresses two problem areas that we need to be aware of as network administrators—technical problems and business problems.

Technical problems include peak traffic loads, availability, redundancy, maintenance (e.g., patches), time between purchase and delivery, deployment planning and provisioning, and expertise and staff availability to install and configure. Business issues include cost (of course), time to market, ease of collaboration, and business continuity risks.

Cloud computing and virtualization allow a company to quickly create a virtual server or entire network infrastructure (including routers, firewalls, and switches), scale up or down, install services and software, test it all, and then close it down, paying only for what was used.

Cloud Models
You may have already heard these terms but may not understand what they specifically mean. Cloud computing can be employed as Software as a Service (SaaS), Platform as a Service (PaaS), or Infrastructure as a Service (IaaS).

SaaS is a type of cloud computing that provides answers to desktop needs for end-users, for example, Gmail from Google and Microsoft Office 365. PaaS enables developers to create and test software without investing in expensive hardware, for instance, Google App Engine. IaaS enables applications to run in the cloud instead of using their own infrastructure. Using IaaS, network administrators can build new servers and storage in a few minutes, for example, Amazon S3 storage.

Figure 46.1 below illustrates the visibility between these services in terms of visibility to the end-user:

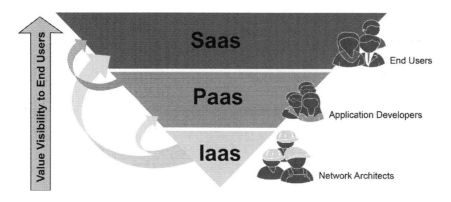

Figure 46.1—Cloud Services Visibility to End-users

The following are the cloud computing resources an organization can use:

- E-mail accounts
- Servers (virtual machines)
- Data storage
- Web sites
- Data backup

According to the NIST, cloud computing services consist of the attributes below:

- Elasticity
- On-demand
- Pooled computing resources at the provider's site
- Monitored and measured service usage
- Broad network access

Elasticity can add or remove cloud computing services or users at any time based on clients' business activity, and they pay for only what was used. Instead of having to physically install more RAM or hard disk space, users simply move a slider or enter a command. On-demand means that users can access the services from anywhere, at any time, and from any location. This increases the availability of cloud computing services. Pooled computing resources at the provider's site means that the cloud computing provider has to invest its money in proper hardware, configuration, and maintenance. The provider has to keep an eye on physical infrastructure usage as well.

Monitored and measured service usage refers to the fact that, mostly, cloud computing services will come with monthly subscription and usage fees. Cloud service providers will charge by usage of measured resources, like disk space and processing capability, with respect to time. Broad network access means that clients can access the services from any device (e.g., smartphone, tablet, laptop, or desktop computer) over the Internet.

Cloud Deployment Models

Based on the required usage and availability, cloud computing deployment models are classified into four groups. Which one you choose boils down to the needs of your organization, budget, and any regulations in place that your country may have for the storage and retrieval of personal or financial data (i.e., compliance).

Cloud computing may not fit the needs of every organization. A large data center will usually require its own resources as well as physical access for maintenance and troubleshooting. Organizations that must follow strict security protocols for physical and remote access to hardware may also not find cloud models useful (they could opt for a private cloud in this instance).

The four groups available are:

- Private cloud
- Community cloud
- Public cloud
- Hybrid cloud

Private cloud: In this type of model, organizations use their own hardware and software resources to achieve cloud services. This model mostly uses virtualization and operates entirely for the benefit of the organization.

Community cloud: This model consists of a pool of computer resources. These resources are available to different organizations with common needs. Clients can access the resources quickly and securely. In this model, clients are referred to as Tenants. Although clients are accessing the same computer resources, each client has his or her own computing environment with its own configuration and data. These details are stored securely.

Public cloud: This cloud model's services can be accessed by any Internet user. These computer resources are available to all public users. Examples of this cloud model are Gmail, Google Docs, and Hotmail. Currently, Amazon Web Services is the largest public cloud provider.

Hybrid cloud: This cloud model is a combination of both private and public clouds. Apart from the private cloud, users have no control of the hardware used or other networking components. They can, however, control which OS is installed on the server as well as the applications.

VIRTUALIZATION

Virtualization technology has been around for a long time in the computing world, but it has recently experienced a surge in server and desktop environments, in no small part due to its ability to scale out very large environments. Many virtual environments are made up of hundreds or thousands of devices and because of this, there are a large number of related networking concerns.

As network engineers, we need to understand how this technology works so we are in a position to contribute to meetings and give advice if required. If you wish to study virtualization further, then look into some of the market leaders, such as VMware and NetApp, that offer certifications.

Virtual Desktops and Servers

Virtualization allows you to take multiple physical devices and move them to a single physical device that is logically divided into smaller virtual domains (see Figure 46.2 below). In other words, it allows you to create a software environment that emulates the hardware that used to be there. The single device that will host all those virtual servers will have many resources available, in particular, the following:

- CPU capacity
- Memory
- Disk space
- Bandwidth

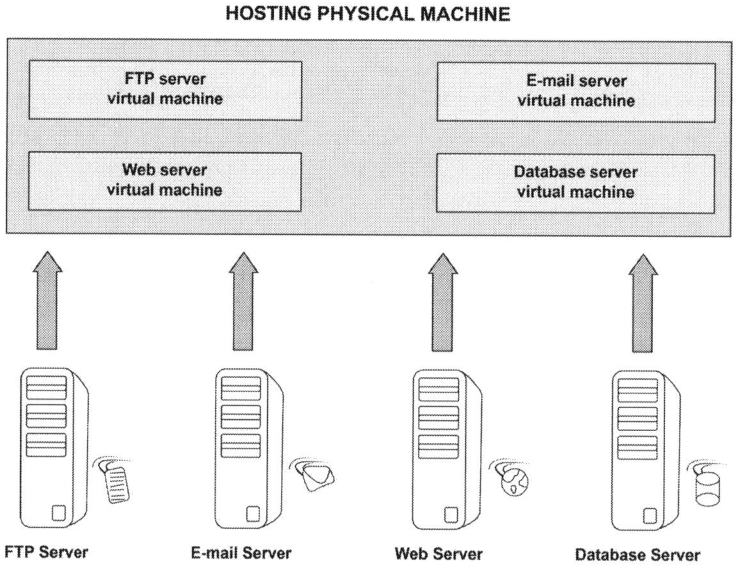

Figure 46.2—Network Virtualization

Virtualization involves having a single physical device on top of which you use virtualization software that is able to separate virtual machines inside the physical device. The virtualization software will allocate a certain amount of disk space, memory, and CPU capacity to each virtual machine (VM) defined inside. If you wanted to build a new server, you would just carve out a new section of the physical device to create another virtual operating system and allocate the necessary resources, making it act (and think) exactly as if it were a physical device (see Figure 46.3 below).

The software that makes this happen is called a virtual machine manager or a hypervisor (which is more than a supervisor). The hypervisor has the following responsibilities:

- Manages all the virtual systems
- Manages physical hardware resources
- Manages the VM relationships to the hardware components inside the physical server
- Bridges the virtual world to the physical world
- Maintains separation between virtual machines when you don't want them to communicate with each other

It's worth noting that the developers of hypervisor software must ensure that they have proper security features in place to restrict visibility and access between all VMs, even though they are sitting on the same physical device.

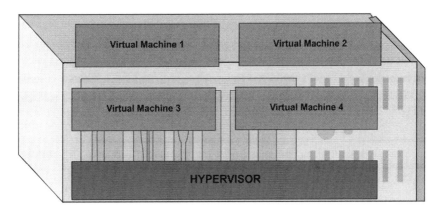

Figure 46.3—Virtualization Components and Hypervisor

There are two types of hypervisors:

- **Type 1—Bare metal machine managers:** With this type of virtual machine manager, you purchase a big server and simply load the VM software on the raw hardware. There is no underlying operating system involved and nothing else that you have to think about from an OS perspective. You simply load the hypervisor (e.g., VMware ESXi or Microsoft Hyper-V), which is the actual OS. This hypervisor type is often seen in very large enterprise server environments.
- **Type 2—Hypervisors that run on an existing OS:** This type of virtual machine manager runs on top of Windows/Linux/Mac OS hosts, and it is often used in desktop environments.

The hypervisor allows you to start all the virtual machines at one time, as well as to network between them by configuring how different systems can communicate across the network. This offers the system administrator a lot of power from both an OS and a networking perspective.

Regarding enterprise environments, it's not about users running their virtual systems and servers on Windows or Linux platforms; instead, it's about a bare metal installation. Because you will usually run tens or hundreds of servers on a single piece of hardware, that device needs to have a lot of resources allocated to it, including:

- Multicore CPU and multi-CPU sockets;
- Large memory capacities (usually above 128 GB, compared to 4 to 8 GB used in desktop environments); and
- Massive amounts of storage, either internal or network-attached storage (NAS).

These large resource requirements make sense because you are consolidating all the servers into a single physical machine. You used to have a data center that had hundreds of servers (physical devices) plugged in at the same time. Now you have taken them all away and moved them into a single physical device.

This server consolidation offers the following benefits:

- Saves a lot of room in the data center
- Increases flexibility on what you can do with the hardware
- Lowers costs on hardware, electricity, cooling, etc., both from a CAPEX (initial investment) and an OPEX (recurring operational and maintenance costs) perspective

Virtualization also affords a number of advantages from a management perspective:

- **Fast deployment:** You don't have to buy a new computer, load an operating system, plug it into the network, find a place in the rack for it, and do all the administrative tasks necessary with a physical server. Using virtualization, you can build an OS in a matter of minutes with the VM manager software, which includes an IP address and pre-built software that you might have configured as a template.
- **Managing the load across servers:** If one particular server is very busy during a particular time of year, you can allocate additional memory and disk space during that time. As other servers become utilized more often, you can allocate the resources in other directions. Unlike using a physical server, where you would normally have to unplug or upgrade the device memory, turn off the machine, and physically install memory chips, in a virtual environment you don't have to worry about these time-consuming tasks. If you need more disk space or memory, you can increase the virtual resources with just a few clicks from the hypervisor. Virtualization offers many advantages and this is the main reason virtual servers and networks have become so popular in modern data centers.

Virtual Switches
As with real servers, the virtual machines managed by the hypervisor need to communicate with each other and with the outside world to accomplish different tasks (e.g., an application server communicating with a database server). This leads to the concept of virtualizing networking devices, in addition to virtualizing desktops and servers as detailed in the previous section (see Figure 58 below).

Before moving to the virtual world, servers and desktops were connected to networks composed of enterprise switches, firewalls, routers, and other devices that offered necessary functionality and features, including redundancy features. Now that servers and desktops have moved to virtual worlds, network devices also have to migrate to the virtual environment to provide similar functionality. This is an important consideration when making the change from the physical world to the virtual world.

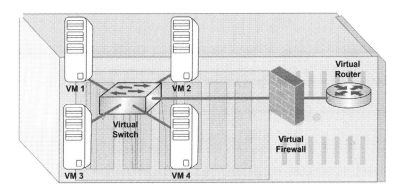

Figure 46.4—Virtualization of Network Devices

Network virtualization is almost as important as the actual server virtualization. When migrating from a physical to a virtual network infrastructure, a number of challenges must be taken into consideration:

- Integration with the outside world: how many NICs will the physical hosting machine have?
- How will the cumulative bandwidth from all the servers in the physical world be transposed to the virtual world and be accommodated with a limited number of Ethernet connections (sometimes just one)?
- Will the throughput offered by the physical server be enough to properly serve the virtualized servers running on the system?
- How will network redundancy be built into the virtual environment (multiple network connections into the VMs)?

The considerations presented above become very important in terms of uptime and availability, especially in large data centers that host critical business applications. Considering that network virtualization eliminates the need for a dedicated connection per server, everything should now be accomplished in software, including assigning IP addresses, VLANs, and other specific configurations. This can become even more difficult to manage because you cannot physically touch the network equipment or trace the cabling to and from the servers. All of these functionalities are fully accomplished using hypervisor software.

By virtualizing the Network Layer, you not only transfer all the functionality to the virtual world but also obtain extra features. Traditional switches don't have built-in functionalities like redundancy, load balancing, or QoS. These features can be easily implemented and configured in a virtual environment because everything is done in software, and the virtual system manufacturer might implement extra tweaks so you can manage certain applications to perform at a higher priority than others. For example, you can use integrated load balancing hypervisor functionality to balance the traffic between multiple VM Web servers.

Virtualizing network components offers two major advantages over using physical devices:

- Cost savings
- Centralized control

Many virtual systems also have some basic integrated security features, perhaps some firewall functionalities built right into the virtualization software. An important note is that third-party providers are starting to create virtual firewalls and Intrusion Prevention Systems (IPSs) that can be loaded into these virtual environments to provide exactly the same security posture in the virtual world as you had in the physical world.

> **NOTE:** Virtual network devices can be part of the hypervisor system or they can be dedicated virtual machines that can be loaded just like any other VM server.

Network as a Service

After virtualizing desktops, servers, and network devices, the next step is moving the entire network infrastructure into the cloud where it will operate as a Network as a Service. If things become too complicated within the network and you don't have the expertise to build and maintain it, you can outsource this process to another company and use it as a service, with all the required functionalities (usually by purchasing a subscription), and the network is now part of the cloud.

As virtualization software has become more popular, third-party providers have started to offer virtualization inside the cloud, with the customer not having anything at his facility. This implies that all the applications, platforms, and the network are moved into the cloud and all the IT functions of the company are virtualized so that everything is running in a completely separate facility. The network and everything associated with the management of the network then becomes invisible to the customer, who simply uses a single link that connects the local facility to the cloud without worrying about any network configuration aspects. In this case, everything is done separately because the network is running as a service at a third-party facility.

When offering NaaS in the cloud, any changes that occur within the network are invisible to the customer. The customer has a single connection to the cloud and does not care how the networking aspect works once the information is sent to the cloud, as the ISP is responsible for all of the virtualization services. This offers great flexibility in situations in which the ISP wants to take all the servers and move them into a data center that has much more capacity and availability. This is simply done by picking up the virtual system and deploying it almost immediately to a new physical location that may be geographically dispersed from the initial one, transparently and without the customer being affected in any way. Ultimately, the customer is not even interested in such details, as the main concern is that the service provided by the network and its applications are running as expected.

There might be many reasons why you would want to take your network and move it into the cloud, running it as a service. One situation might be that you have an important application that is used by thousands of people, which requires a lot of resources and bandwidth to operate. Instead of having all the networking and communication resources at your facility, including large network pipes and very expensive connections, you can simply put this into the cloud and have it managed by third-party providers. These service providers already have high-capacity connections to the Internet so you don't have to spend the money on the bandwidth and maintenance services of these connections.

Complete network virtualization offers another interesting advantage, which is commonly referred to as a "follow the sun" service. This is a concept that is based on the fact that servers can be relocated relatively quickly, and based on their geographical region, service providers can optimize resource utilization and response times (most of the traffic for certain applications is done during the day, which happens at different intervals across the globe).

Another advantage of network virtualization is the ease of expanding and contracting how many resources you are using. If your applications are used by millions of people on a particular day or time period (e.g., tax returns), you can easily allocate more bandwidth, disk space, or memory with just a few clicks and suddenly increase the application's capacity. When the busy period has passed and you don't need all the allocated resources, there is no need to pay for them, so you can decrease certain parameters (e.g., network throughput or CPU cycles) to a level that is more reasonable for what the application is doing, again, with just a few clicks.

If a customer uses NaaS and someday decides to move to a different location, it makes absolutely no difference how the applications will perform because they are hosted and managed by the service provider somewhere inside the cloud, which can be accessed from anywhere. Running NaaS inside the cloud provides a lot of functionality, which can be a perfect fit for certain business applications and services.

On-site versus Off-site Virtualization

Virtualization technology offers many choices regarding where you manage and maintain the virtualized environment. You might have everything on your premises or you might choose to install them at a different location, off-site.

In an on-site configuration, you own and manage the infrastructure within your premises. You are responsible for building and maintaining it, and if there are any issues associated with the hosting aspect, you are responsible for solving them. There are a number of advantages to hosting the virtualized environment on-site:

- You have control over what happens. If anything needs to be changed or moved, you have complete control over every modification on the hosting devices and connections.

- You also have control over possible resource upgrades on the devices, including memory, disk space, CPU capacity, and bandwidth.
- You have complete security over the entire infrastructure. You can install the equipment in a locked room and limit access to the physical servers, which is something that you usually don't have available if the virtual environment is hosted in a remote location (off-site).

There are also some disadvantages to the on-site approach:

- It is costlier than hosting the equipment at a third-party site because you have to purchase the servers, racks, connections, and the operating systems, and you have to make sure that you own a controlled environment. All of these aspects involve both CAPEX (initial expenses) and OPEX (recurring expenses) that you need to think about.
- You need a networking infrastructure that includes enterprise switches, routers, firewalls with redundancy, and security features built in.
- All of the factors above make the infrastructure hard to upgrade. You have to think about how much room is available in the racks, you have to purchase new equipment, and sometimes it is difficult to make rapid changes because there are a number of physical devices that offer limited performance.

In an off-site environment, everything is hosted in the cloud. You don't have to worry about where these particular systems are in the data center as they don't even exist at your facility. All the applications, servers, and operating systems are somewhere else and you don't necessarily care where that is. This brings the following main advantages:

- You don't have any kind of infrastructure costs: no servers, no cooling, or anything that requires an initial investment.
- The management and maintenance of all the infrastructure is handled by a third-party service provider, so you don't need a lot of staff to manage the devices and make sure that they are operating properly.
- The infrastructure can be located anywhere in the world (a single hosting location or multiple hosting locations).
- Many service providers offer huge-capacity virtual environments, so if you need more resources (e.g., disk space, memory, bandwidth, etc.), the ISP can provide this with minimum effort.

Hosting the infrastructure off-site also has some disadvantages:

- All of the customer data is stored at a different facility, with no physical access to it. In cases where the data is extremely sensitive, having your virtualized environment somewhere in the cloud may not be the best option.
- Off-site hosting has some associated contractual limitations. Usually, this involves signing a long-term contract with the service provider that offers limited flexibility for that duration. If the environment changes rapidly, you may need to modify some of the contractual terms to avoid different kinds of limitations.

Please complete today's exam at **https://www.in60days.com/free/ccnain60days/**

Hot Standby Router Protocol

DAY 47 TASKS

- Read today's notes and do the lab
- Take today's exam
- Review yesterdays notes
- Read the ICND2 cram guide (and the ICND1 cram guide, if taking the CCNA exam)
- Spend 15 minutes on the subnetting.org website

High Availability (HA) is an integral component when designing and implementing switched networks. HA is technology delivered in Cisco IOS software that enables network-wide resilience to increase IP network availability. All network segments must be resilient to recover quickly enough for faults to be transparent to users and network applications. First Hop Redundancy Protocols (FHRPs) provide redundancy in switched LAN environments.

Today you will learn about the following:

- Hot Standby Router Protocol
- Configuring HSRP

This lesson maps to the following ICND2 syllabus requirements:

- 4.1 Configure, verify, and troubleshoot basic HSRP
- 4.1.a Priority
- 4.1.b Preemption
- 4.1.c Version

HOT STANDBY ROUTER PROTOCOL

Hot Standby Router Protocol (HSRP) is a Cisco-proprietary First Hop Redundancy Protocol (FHRP). HSRP allows two physical gateways that are configured as part of the same HSRP group to share the same virtual gateway address. Network hosts residing on the same subnet as the gateways are configured with the virtual gateway IP address as their default gateway.

While operational, the primary gateway forwards packets destined to the virtual gateway IP address of the HSRP group. In the event that the primary gateway fails, the secondary gateway assumes the role of primary gateway and forwards all packets sent to the virtual gateway IP address. Figure 47.1 below illustrates the operation of HSRP in a network:

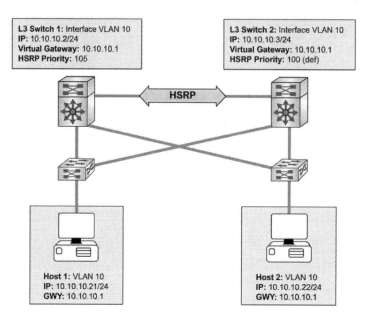

Figure 47.1—Hot Standby Router Protocol (HSRP) Operation

Referencing Figure 47.1, HSRP is configured between the Layer 3 (Distribution Layer) switches, providing gateway redundancy for VLAN 10. The IP address assigned to the Switch Virtual Interface (SVI) on Layer 3 Switch 1 is 10.10.10.2/24, and the IP address assigned to the SVI on Layer 3 Switch 2 is 10.10.10.3/24. Both switches are configured as part of the same HSRP group and share the IP address of the virtual gateway, which is 10.10.10.1.

Switch 1 has been configured with a priority of 105, while Switch 2 is using the default priority of 100. Because of the higher priority, Layer 3 Switch 1 is elected as the primary switch and Layer 3 Switch 2 is elected as the secondary switch. All hosts on VLAN 10 are configured with a default gateway address of 10.10.10.1. Based on this solution, Switch 1 will forward all packets sent to the 10.10.10.1 address. However, in the event that Switch 1 fails, then Switch 2 will assume this responsibility. This process is entirely transparent to the network hosts.

REAL-WORLD IMPLEMENTATION:

In production networks, when configuring FHRPs, it is considered good practice to ensure that the active (primary) gateway is also the Spanning Tree Root Bridge for the particular VLAN. Referencing the diagram in Figure 47.1, for example, Switch 1 would be configured as the Root Bridge for VLAN 10 in tandem with being the HSRP primary gateway for the same VLAN.

This results in a deterministic network and avoids suboptimal forwarding at Layer 2 or Layer 3. For example, if Switch 2 was the Root Bridge for VLAN 10, while Switch 1 was the primary gateway for VLAN 10, packets from the network hosts to the default gateway IP address would be forwarded as shown in Figure 47.2 below:

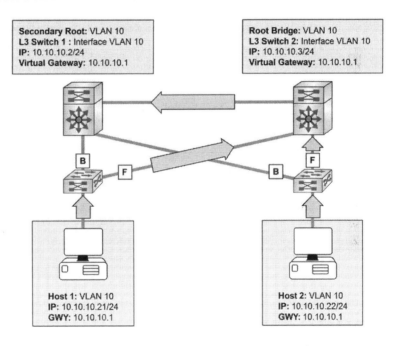

Figure 47.2—Synchronizing the STP Topology with HSRP

In the network above, packets from Host 1 to 10.10.10.1 are forwarded as follows:

1. The Access Layer switch receives a frame destined to the MAC address of the virtual gateway IP address from Host 1. This frame is received in VLAN 10 and the MAC address for the virtual gateway has been learned by the switch via its Root Port.
2. Because the Root Bridge for VLAN 10 is Switch 2, the uplink towards Switch 1 (the HSRP primary router) is placed into a Blocking state. The Access Layer switch forwards the frame via the uplink to Switch 2.
3. Switch 2 forwards the frame via the Designated Port connected to Switch 1. The same sub-optimal forwarding path is used for frames received from Host 2.

Currently, two versions of HSRP are supported in Cisco IOS software: versions 1 and 2. The similarities and differences between the versions will be described in the sections that follow.

HSRP Version 1

By default, when Hot Standby Router Protocol is enabled in Cisco IOS software, version 1 is enabled. HSRP version 1 restricts the number of configurable HSRP groups to 255. HSRP version 1 routers communicate by sending messages to Multicast group address 224.0.0.2 using UDP port 1985. This is shown in Figure 47.3 below:

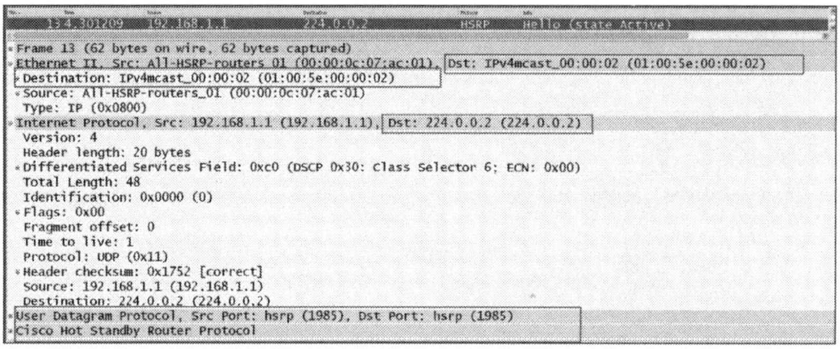

Figure 47.3—HSRP Version 1 Multicast Group Address

While going into detail on the HSRP packet format is beyond the scope of the CCNA exam requirements, Figure 47.4 below illustrates the information contained in the HSRP version 1 packet:

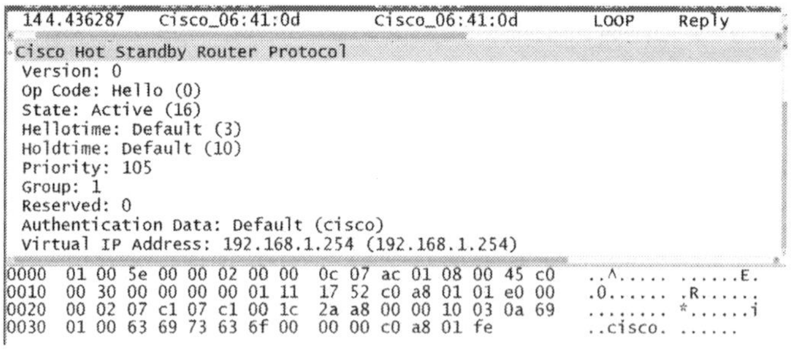

Figure 47.4—The HSRP Version 1 Packet Fields

In Figure 47.4, notice that the Version field shows a value of 0. This is the default value for this field when version 1 is enabled; however, remember that this implies HSRP version 1.

HSRP Version 2

HSRP version 2 uses the new Multicast address 224.0.0.102 to send Hello packets instead of the Multicast address of 224.0.0.2, which is used by version 1. The UDP port number, however, remains the same. This new address is also encoded in both the IP packet and the Ethernet frame, as shown below in Figure 47.5:

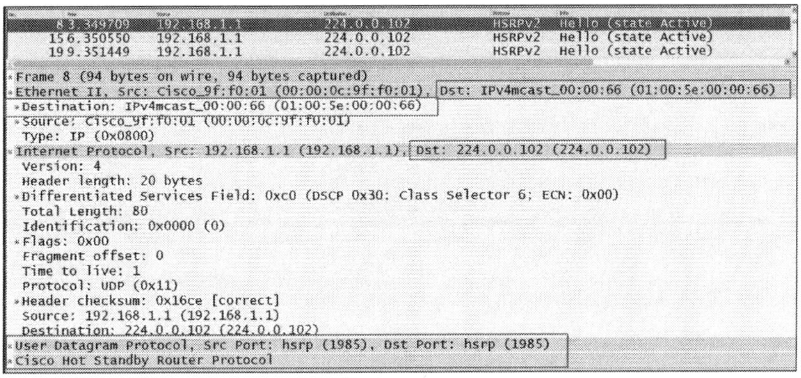

```
    8 3.349709    192.168.1.1         224.0.0.102          HSRPV2   Hello (state Active)
   156.350550    192.168.1.1         224.0.0.102          HSRPv2   Hello (state Active)
   199.351449    192.168.1.1         224.0.0.102          HSRPv2   Hello (state Active)
  Frame 8 (94 bytes on wire, 94 bytes captured)
  Ethernet II, Src: Cisco_9f:f0:01 (00:00:0c:9f:f0:01), Dst: IPv4mcast_00:00:66 (01:00:5e:00:00:66)
    Destination: IPv4mcast_00:00:66 (01:00:5e:00:00:66)
    Source: Cisco_9f:f0:01 (00:00:0c:9f:f0:01)
    Type: IP (0x0800)
  Internet Protocol, Src: 192.168.1.1 (192.168.1.1), Dst: 224.0.0.102 (224.0.0.102)
    Version: 4
    Header length: 20 bytes
    Differentiated Services Field: 0xc0 (DSCP 0x30: Class Selector 6; ECN: 0x00)
    Total Length: 80
    Identification: 0x0000 (0)
    Flags: 0x00
    Fragment offset: 0
    Time to live: 1
    Protocol: UDP (0x11)
    Header checksum: 0x16ce [correct]
    Source: 192.168.1.1 (192.168.1.1)
    Destination: 224.0.0.102 (224.0.0.102)
  User Datagram Protocol, Src Port: hsrp (1985), Dst Port: hsrp (1985)
  Cisco Hot Standby Router Protocol
```

Figure 47.5—HSRP Version 2 Multicast Group Address

While going into detail on the HSRP version 2 packet format is beyond the scope of the CCNA exam requirements, it is important to remember that HSRP version 2 does not use the same packet format as HSRP version 1.

The version 2 packet format uses a Type/Length/Value (TLV) format. HSRP version 2 packets received by an HSRP version 1 router will have the Type field mapped to the Version field by HSRP version 1 and will be subsequently ignored. Figure 47.6 illustrates the information contained in the HSRP version 2 packet:

```
   156.350550    192.168.1.1          224.0.0.102          HSRPV2   Hello (state Act
  Cisco Hot Standby Router Protocol
    Group State TLV: Type=1 Len=40
      Version: 2
      Op Code: Hello (0)
      State: Active (6)
      IP Ver.: IPv4 (4)
      Group: 1
      Identifier: Cisco_86:0a:20 (00:13:19:86:0a:20)
      Priority: 105
      Hellotime: Default (3000)
      Holdtime: Default (10000)
      Virtual IP Address: 192.168.1.254 (192.168.1.254)
    Text Authentication TLV: Type=3 Len=8
      Authentication Data: Default (cisco)
0000  01 00 5e 00 00 66 00 00  0c 9f f0 01 08 00 45 c0   ..^..f..  .....E.
0010  00 50 00 00 00 00 01 11  16 ce c0 a8 01 01 e0 00   .P......  ........
0020  00 66 07 c1 07 c1 00 3c  e1 4e 01 28 02 00 06 04   .f.....<  .N.(....
0030  00 01 00 13 19 86 0a 20  00 00 00 69 00 00 0b b8   .......   ...i....
0040  00 00 27 10 c0 a8 01 fe  01 02 00 00 00 00 00 00   ..'.....  ........
0050  00 00 00 00 03 08 63 69  73 63 6f 00 00 00         ......ci  sco...
```

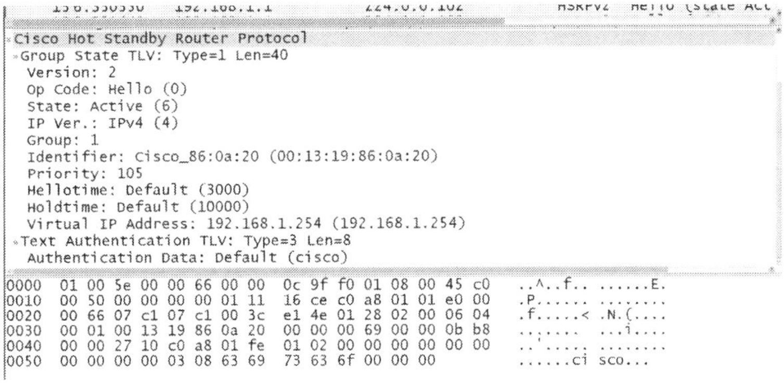

Figure 47.6—The HSRP Version 2 Packet Fields

HSRP Version 1 and Version 2 Comparison

HSRP version 2 includes enhancements to HSRP version 1. The version 2 enhancements and differences from version 1 will be described in this section.

Although HSRP version 1 advertises timer values, these values are always to the whole second, as it is not capable of advertising or learning millisecond timer values. Version 2 is capable of both advertising and learning millisecond timer values. Figures 47.7 and 47.8 below highlight the differences between the Timer fields for both HSRP version 1 and HSRP version 2, respectively:

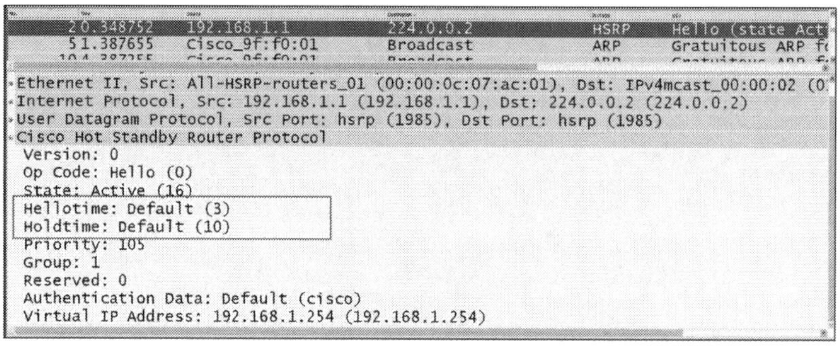

Figure 47.7—HSRP Version 1 Timer Fields

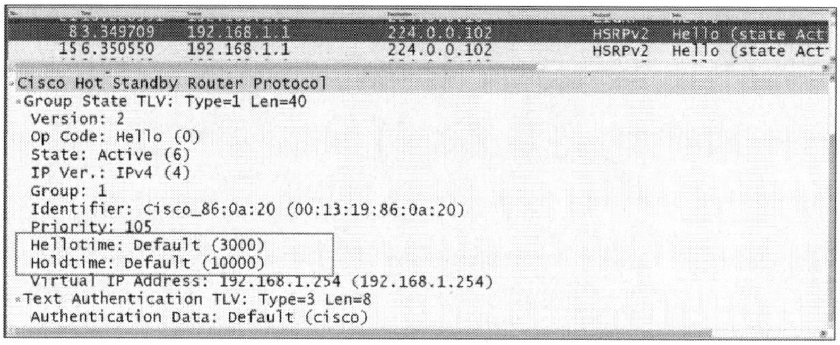

Figure 47.8—HSRP Version 2 Timer Fields

HSRP version 1 group numbers are restricted to the range of 0 to 255, whereas the version 2 group numbers have been extended from 0 to 4095. This difference will be illustrated in the HSRP configuration examples that will be provided later in this module.

Version 2 provides improved management and troubleshooting by including a 6-byte Identifier field that is populated with the physical router interface MAC address and is used to uniquely identify the source of HSRP active Hello messages. In version 1, these messages contain the virtual MAC address as the source MAC, which means it is not possible to determine which HSRP router actually sent the HSRP Hello message. Figure 47.9 below shows the Identifier field that is present in the version 2 packet but not in the HSRP version 1 packet:

```
    15 6.350550    192.168.1.1           224.0.0.102          HSRPv2  Hello (state Act
 Cisco Hot Standby Router Protocol
 Group State TLV: Type=1 Len=40
   Version: 2
   Op Code: Hello (0)
   State: Active (6)
   IP Ver.: IPv4 (4)
   Group: 1
   Identifier: Cisco_86:0a:20 (00:13:19:86:0a:20)
   Priority: 105
   Hellotime: Default (3000)
   Holdtime: Default (10000)
   Virtual IP Address: 192.168.1.254 (192.168.1.254)
 Text Authentication TLV: Type=3 Len=8
   Authentication Data: Default (cisco)
```

Figure 47.9—HSRP Version 2 Identifier Field

In HSRP version 1, the Layer 2 address that is used by the virtual IP address will be a virtual MAC address composed of 0000.0C07.AC*xx*, where "*xx*" is the HSRP group number in hexadecimal value and is based on the respective interface. HSRP version 2, however, uses a new MAC address range of 0000.0C9F.F000 to 0000.0C9F.FFFF for the virtual gateway IP address. These differences are illustrated below in Figure 47.10, which shows the version 1 virtual MAC address for HSRP Group 1, as well as in Figure 47.11, which shows the version 2 virtual MAC address, also for HSRP Group 1:

```
    8 3.349709    192.168.1.1          224.0.0.102          HSRPv2  Hello (state Active)
 Ethernet II, Src: All-HSRP-routers_01 (00:00:0c:07:ac:01), Dst: IPv4mcast_00:00:02 (01:00:5e:00:00:02)
 Destination: IPv4mcast_00:00:02 (01:00:5e:00:00:02)
   Address: IPv4mcast_00:00:02 (01:00:5e:00:00:02)
   .... ...1 .... .... .... .... = IG bit: Group address (multicast/broadcast)
   .... ..0. .... .... .... .... = LG bit: Globally unique address (factory default)
 Source: All-HSRP-routers_01 (00:00:0c:07:ac:01)
   Address: All-HSRP-routers_01 (00:00:0c:07:ac:01)
   .... ...0 .... .... .... .... = IG bit: Individual address (unicast)
   .... ..0. .... .... .... .... = LG bit: Globally unique address (factory default)
   Type: IP (0x0800)
 Internet Protocol, Src: 192.168.1.1 (192.168.1.1), Dst: 224.0.0.2 (224.0.0.2)
 User Datagram Protocol, Src Port: hsrp (1985), Dst Port: hsrp (1985)
 Cisco Hot Standby Router Protocol
   Version: 0
   Op Code: Hello (0)
   State: Active (16)
   Hellotime: Default (3)
   Holdtime: Default (10)
   Priority: 105
   Group: 1
   Reserved: 0
```

Figure 47.10—HSRP Version 1 Virtual MAC Address Format

```
    15 6.350550    192.168.1.1          224.0.0.102          HSRPv2  Hello (state Active)
 Ethernet II, Src: Cisco_9f:f0:01 (00:00:0c:9f:f0:01), Dst: IPv4mcast_00:00:66 (01:00:5e:00:00:66)
 Destination: IPv4mcast_00:00:66 (01:00:5e:00:00:66)
   Address: IPv4mcast_00:00:66 (01:00:5e:00:00:66)
   .... ...1 .... .... .... .... = IG bit: Group address (multicast/broadcast)
   .... ..0. .... .... .... .... = LG bit: Globally unique address (factory default)
 Source: Cisco_9f:f0:01 (00:00:0c:9f:f0:01)
   Address: Cisco_9f:f0:01 (00:00:0c:9f:f0:01)
   .... ...0 .... .... .... .... = IG bit: Individual address (unicast)
   .... ..0. .... .... .... .... = LG bit: Globally unique address (factory default)
   Type: IP (0x0800)
 Internet Protocol, Src: 192.168.1.1 (192.168.1.1), Dst: 224.0.0.102 (224.0.0.102)
 User Datagram Protocol, Src Port: hsrp (1985), Dst Port: hsrp (1985)
 Cisco Hot Standby Router Protocol
 Group State TLV: Type=1 Len=40
   Version: 2
   Op Code: Hello (0)
   State: Active (6)
   IP Ver.: IPv4 (4)
   Group: 1
   Identifier: Cisco_86:0a:20 (00:13:19:86:0a:20)
   Priority: 105
```

Figure 47.11—HSRP Version 2 Virtual MAC Address Format

HSRP Primary Gateway Election

HSRP primary gateway election can be influenced by adjusting the default HSRP priority of 100 to any value between 1 and 255. The router with the highest priority will be elected as the primary gateway for the HSRP group.

If two gateways are using the default priority values, or if the priority values on two gateways are manually configured as equal, the router with the highest IP address will be elected as the primary gateway. The HSRP priority value is carried in the HSRP frame, as is the current state of the router (e.g., primary or standby). Figure 34.12 below illustrates the Priority and State fields of a gateway configured with a non-default priority value of 105, which resulted in it being elected as the active gateway for the HSRP group:

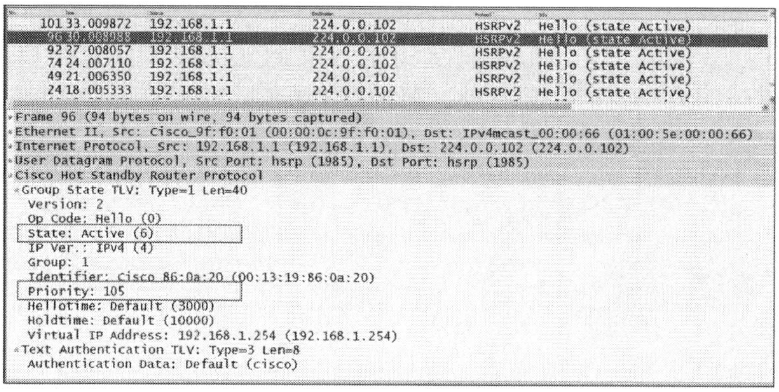

Figure 47.12—HSRP Priority and State Fields

HSRP Messages

HSRP routers exchange the following three types of messages:

- Hello messages
- Coup messages
- Resign messages

Hello messages are exchanged via Multicast and they tell the other gateway the HSRP state and priority values of the local router. Hello messages also include the Group ID, HSRP timer values, version, and authentication information. All of the messages shown in the previous screenshots are HSRP Hello messages.

HSRP Coup messages are sent when the current standby router wants to assume the role of active gateway for the HSRP group. This is similar to a coup d'état in real life.

HSRP Resign messages are sent by the active router when it is about to shut down or when a gateway that has a higher priority sends a Hello or Coup message. In other words, this message is sent when the active gateway concedes its role as primary gateway.

HSRP Preemption

If a gateway has been elected as the active gateway and another gateway that is part of the HSRP group is reconfigured with a higher priority value, the current active gateway retains the primary forwarding role. This is the default behavior of HSRP.

In order for a gateway with a higher priority to assume active gateway functionality when a primary gateway is already present for an HSRP group, the router must be configured for preemption. This allows the gateway to initiate a coup and assume the role of the active gateway for the HSRP group. HSRP preemption is illustrated in the configuration examples to follow.

NOTE: Preemption does not necessarily mean that the Spanning Tree topology changes also.

HSRP States

In a manner similar to Open Shortest Path First (OSPF), when HSRP is enabled on an interface, the gateway interface goes through the following series of states:

1. Disabled
2. Init
3. Listen
4. Speak
5. Standby
6. Active

NOTE: There are no set time values for these interface transitions.

In either the Disabled or the Init states, the gateway is not yet ready or is unable to participate in HSRP, possibly because the associated interface is not up.

The Listen state is applicable to the standby gateway. Only the standby gateway monitors Hello messages from the active gateway. If the standby gateway does not receive Hellos within 10 seconds, it assumes that the active gateway is down and takes on this role itself. If other gateways exist on the same segment, they also listen to Hellos and will be elected as the group active gateway if they have the next highest priority value or IP address.

During the Speak phase, the standby gateway exchanges messages with the active gateway. Upon completion of this phase, the primary gateway transitions to the Active state and the backup gateway transitions to the Standby state. The Standby state indicates that the gateway is ready to assume the role of active gateway if the primary gateway fails, and the Active state indicates that the gateway is ready to actively forward packets.

The following output shows the state transitions displayed in the `debug standby` command on a gateway for which HSRP has just been enabled:

```
R2#debug standby
HSRP debugging is on
R2#conf t
Configuring from terminal, memory, or network [terminal]?
Enter configuration commands, one per line.  End with CNTL/Z.
R2(config)#logging console
R2(config)#int f0/0
R2(config-if)#stand 1 ip 192.168.1.254
*Mar  1 01:21:55.471: HSRP: Fa0/0 API 192.168.1.254 is not an HSRP
address
*Mar  1 01:21:55.471: HSRP: Fa0/0 Grp 1 Disabled -> Init
*Mar  1 01:21:55.471: HSRP: Fa0/0 Grp 1 Redundancy "hsrp-Fa0/0-1" state
Disabled -> Init
*Mar  1 01:22:05.475: HSRP: Fa0/0 Interface up
[Truncated Output]

*Mar  1 01:22:06.477: HSRP: Fa0/0 Interface min delay expired
*Mar  1 01:22:06.477: HSRP: Fa0/0 Grp 1 Init: a/HSRP enabled
*Mar  1 01:22:06.477: HSRP: Fa0/0 Grp 1 Init -> Listen
*Mar  1 01:22:06.477: HSRP: Fa0/0 Redirect adv out, Passive, active 0
passive 1
[Truncated Output]

*Mar  1 01:22:16.477: HSRP: Fa0/0 Grp 1 Listen: d/Standby timer expired
(unknown)
*Mar  1 01:22:16.477: HSRP: Fa0/0 Grp 1 Listen -> Speak
[Truncated Output]

*Mar  1 01:22:26.478: HSRP: Fa0/0 Grp 1 Standby router is local
*Mar  1 01:22:26.478: HSRP: Fa0/0 Grp 1 Speak -> Standby
*Mar  1 01:22:26.478: %HSRP-5-STATECHANGE: FastEthernet0/0 Grp 1 state
Speak -> Standby
*Mar  1 01:22:26.478: HSRP: Fa0/0 Grp 1 Redundancy "hsrp-Fa0/0-1" state
Speak -> Standby
```

HSRP Addressing

Earlier in this module, you learned that in HSRP version 1, the Layer 2 address that is used by the virtual IP address will be a virtual MAC address composed of 0000.0C07.AC*xx*, where "*xx*" is the HSRP group number in hexadecimal value and is based on the respective interface. HSRP version 2, however, uses a new MAC address range of 0000.0C9F.F000 to 0000.0C9F.FFFF for the virtual gateway IP address.

In some cases, it may not be desirable to use these default address ranges. An example would be a situation where several HSRP groups were configured on a router interface connected to a switch port that was configured for port security. In such a case, the router would use a different MAC address for each HSRP group, the result being multiple MAC addresses that would all need to be accommodated in the port security configuration. This configuration would have to be modified each time an HSRP group was added to the interface; otherwise, a port security violation would occur.

To address this issue, Cisco IOS software allows administrators to configure HSRP to use the actual MAC address of the physical interface on which it is configured. The result is that a single MAC address is used by all groups (i.e., the MAC address of the active gateway is used) and the port security configuration need not be modified each time an HSRP group is configured between the routers connected to the switches. This is performed via the standby use-bia interface configuration command. The following output illustrates the show standby command, which shows a gateway interface that is configured with two different HSRP groups:

```
Gateway-1#show standby
FastEthernet0/0 - Group 1
  State is Active
    8 state changes, last state change 00:13:07
  Virtual IP address is 192.168.1.254
  Active virtual MAC address is 0000.0c07.ac01
    Local virtual MAC address is 0000.0c07.ac01 (v1 default)
  Hello time 3 sec, hold time 10 sec
    Next hello sent in 2.002 secs
  Preemption disabled
  Active router is local
  Standby router is 192.168.1.2, priority 100 (expires in 9.019 sec)
  Priority 105 (configured 105)
  IP redundancy name is "hsrp-Fa0/0-1" (default)
FastEthernet0/0 - Group 2
  State is Active
    2 state changes, last state change 00:09:45
  Virtual IP address is 172.16.1.254
  Active virtual MAC address is 0000.0c07.ac02
    Local virtual MAC address is 0000.0c07.ac02 (v1 default)
  Hello time 3 sec, hold time 10 sec
    Next hello sent in 2.423 secs
  Preemption disabled
  Active router is local
```

In the output above, based on the default HSRP version, the virtual MAC address for HSRP Group 1 is 0000.0c07.ac01, while that for HSRP Group 2 is 0000.0c07.ac02. This means that the switch port that this gateway is connected to learns three different addresses: the actual or burnt-in MAC address assigned to the actual physical FastEthernet0/0 interface, the virtual MAC address for HSRP Group 1, and the virtual MAC address for HSRP Group 2.

The following output illustrates how to configure HSRP to use the actual MAC address of the gateway interface as the virtual MAC address of the different HSRP groups:

```
Gateway-1#conf
Configuring from terminal, memory, or network [terminal]?
Enter configuration commands, one per line.  End with CNTL/Z.
Gateway-1(config)#int f0/0
Gateway-1(config-if)#standby use-bia
Gateway-1(config-if)#exit
```

Based on the configuration in the output above, the show standby command reflects the new MAC address for the HSRP group, as illustrated in the following output:

```
Gateway-1#show standby
FastEthernet0/0 - Group 1
  State is Active
    8 state changes, last state change 00:13:30
  Virtual IP address is 192.168.1.254
  Active virtual MAC address is 0013.1986.0a20
    Local virtual MAC address is 0013.1986.0a20 (bia)
  Hello time 3 sec, hold time 10 sec
    Next hello sent in 2.756 secs
  Preemption disabled
  Active router is local
  Standby router is 192.168.1.2, priority 100 (expires in 9.796 sec)
  Priority 105 (configured 105)
  IP redundancy name is "hsrp-Fa0/0-1" (default)
FastEthernet0/0 - Group 2
  State is Active
    2 state changes, last state change 00:10:09
  Virtual IP address is 172.16.1.254
  Active virtual MAC address is 0013.1986.0a20
    Local virtual MAC address is 0013.1986.0a20 (bia)
  Hello time 3 sec, hold time 10 sec
    Next hello sent in 0.188 secs
  Preemption disabled
  Active router is local
  Standby router is unknown
  Priority 105 (configured 105)
  IP redundancy name is "hsrp-Fa0/0-2" (default)
```

The MAC address used by both groups, 0013.1986.0a20, is the MAC address assigned to the physical gateway interface. This is illustrated in the following output:

```
Gateway-1#show interface FastEthernet0/0
FastEthernet0/0 is up, line protocol is up
  Hardware is AmdFE, address is 0013.1986.0a20 (bia 0013.1986.0a20)
  Internet address is 192.168.1.1/24
  MTU 1500 bytes, BW 100000 Kbit/sec, DLY 100 usec,
    reliability 255/255, txload 1/255, rxload 1/255
  Encapsulation ARPA, loopback not set

[Truncated Output]
```

NOTE: In addition to configuring HSRP to use the burnt-in address (BIA), administrators also have the option of statically specifying the MAC address that the virtual gateway should use via the standby [number] mac-address [mac] interface configuration command. This option is typically avoided, as it can result in duplicate MAC addresses in the switched network, which can cause severe network issues and possibly even an outage.

HSRP Plain Text Authentication

By default, HSRP messages are sent with the plain text key string "cisco" as a simple method to authenticate HSRP peers. If the key string in a message matches the key configured on an HSRP peer, the message is accepted. If not, HSRP ignores the unauthenticated message(s).

Plain text keys provide very little security because they can be "captured on the wire" using simple packet capture tools, such as Wireshark and Ethereal. Figure 47.13 below shows the default plain text authentication key used in HSRP messages:

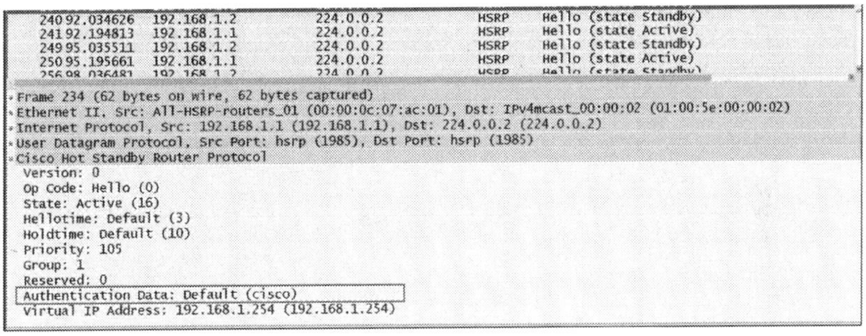

Figure 47.13—Viewing the Default HSRP Plain Text Key

Because plain text authentication provides very little security, Message Digest 5 (MD5) authentication, which is described in the following section, is the recommended authentication method for HSRP.

HSRP MD5 Authentication

This isn't a CCNA subject but it's included here for completeness and for those of you who will be applying these lessons in your job on a live network.

Message Digest 5 authentication provides greater security for HSRP than that provided by plain text authentication by generating an MD5 digest for the HSRP portion of the Multicast HSRP protocol packet. Using MD5 authentication allows each HSRP group member to use a secret key to generate a keyed MD5 hash that is part of the outgoing packet. A keyed hash of the incoming HSRP packet is generated and if the hash within the incoming packet does not match the MD5-generated hash, the packet is simply ignored by the receiving router.

The key for the MD5 hash can be either given directly in the configuration using a key string or supplied indirectly through a key chain. Both configuration options will be described in detail later in this module. When using plain-text or MD5 authentication, the gateway will reject HSRP packets if any of the following is true:

- The authentication schemes differ on the router and in the incoming packets
- The MD5 digests differ on the router and in the incoming packets
- The text authentication strings differ on the router and in the incoming packets

HSRP Interface Tracking

HSRP allows administrators to track the status of interfaces on the current active gateway so that when that interface fails, the gateway decrements its priority by a specified value, the default being 10, allowing another gateway to assume the role of active gateway for the HSRP group. This concept is illustrated below in Figure 47.14:

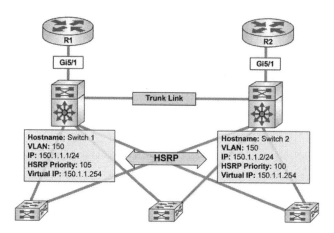

Figure 47.14—HSRP Interface Tracking

Referencing Figure 47.14, HSRP has been enabled on Switch 1 and Switch 2 for VLAN 150. Based on the current priority configuration, Switch 1, with a priority value of 105, has been elected as the primary switch for this VLAN. Both Switch 1 and Switch 2 are connected to two routers via their GigabitEthernet5/1 interfaces. It is assumed that these two routers peer with other external networks, such as the Internet.

Without HSRP interface tracking, if the GigabitEthernet5/1 interface between Switch 1 and R1 failed, Switch 1 would retain its primary gateway status. It would then have to forward any received packets destined for the Internet, for example, over to Switch 2 using the connection between itself and Switch 2. The packets would be forwarded out via R2 towards their intended destination. This results in a suboptimal traffic path within the network.

HSRP interface tracking allows the administrators to configure HSRP to track the status of an interface and decrement the active gateway priority by either a default value of 10 or a value specified by the administrators. Referencing Figure 47.14, if HSRP interface tracking was configured using the default values on Switch 1, allowing it to track the status of interface GigabitEthernet5/1, and that interface failed, Switch 1 would decrement its priority for the HSRP group by 10, resulting in a priority of 95.

Assuming that Switch 2 was configured to preempt, which is mandatory in this situation, it would realize that it had the higher priority (100 versus 95) and perform a coup, assuming the role of active gateway for this HSRP group.

REAL-WORLD IMPLEMENTATION:

In production networks, Cisco Catalyst switches also support Enhanced Object Tracking (EOT), which can be used with any FHRP (i.e., HSRP, VRRP, and GLBP). Enhanced Object Tracking allows administrators to configure the switch to track the following parameters:

- The IP routing state of an interface
- IP route reachability
- The threshold of IP route metrics
- IP SLA operations

FHRPs, such as HSRP, can be configured to track these enhanced objects, allowing for greater flexibility when implementing FHRP failover situations. For example, using EOT, the active HSRP router could be configured to decrement its priority value by a certain amount if a network or host route was not reachable (i.e., present in the routing table). EOT is beyond the scope of the CCNA exam requirements and will not be illustrated in the configuration examples.

HSRP Load Balancing

HSRP allows administrators to configure multiple HSRP groups on physical interfaces to allow for load balancing. By default, when HSRP is configured between two gateways, only one gateway actively forwards traffic for that group at any given time. This can result in wasted bandwidth for the standby gateway link. This is illustrated below in Figure 47.15:

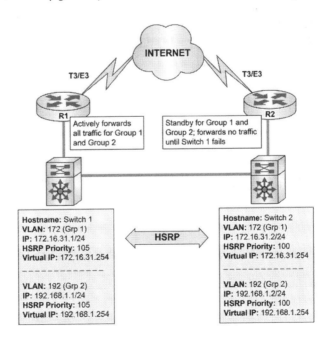

Figure 47.15—A Network without HSRP Load Balancing

In Figure 47.15, two HSRP groups are configured between Switch 1 and Switch 2. Switch 1 has been configured as the active (primary) gateway for both groups—based on the higher priority value. Switch 1 and Switch 2 are connected to R1 and R2, respectively. These routers are both connected to the Internet via T3/E3 dedicated lines. Because Switch 1 is the active gateway for both groups, it will forward traffic for both groups until it fails and Switch 2 will then assume the role of active (primary) gateway.

While this does satisfy the redundancy needs of the network, it also results in the expensive T3/E3 link on R2 remaining idle until Switch 2 becomes the active gateway and begins to forward traffic through it. Naturally, this represents a wasted amount of bandwidth.

By configuring multiple HSRP groups, each using a different active gateway, administrators can effectively prevent the unnecessary waste of resources and load balance between Switch 1 and Switch 2. This is illustrated below in Figure 47.16:

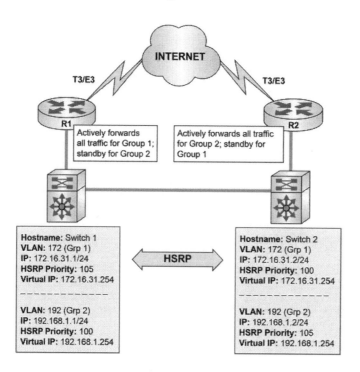

Figure 47.16—A Network Using HSRP for Load Balancing

By configuring Switch 1 as the active gateway for HSRP Group 1 and Switch 2 as the active gateway for HSRP Group 2, administrators can allow traffic from these two groups to be load balanced between Switch 1 and Switch 2, and ultimately across the two dedicated T3/E3 WAN connections. Each switch then backs up the other's group. For example, Switch 1 will assume the role of active gateway for Group 2 if Switch 2 fails, and vice versa.

REAL-WORLD IMPLEMENTATION:

In production networks, it is important to remember that creating multiple HSRP groups may result in increased gateway CPU utilization, as well as increased network utilization due to HSRP message exchanges. Cisco Catalyst switches, such as the Catalyst 4500 and 6500 series switches, support the implementation of HSRP client groups.

In the previous section, you learned that HSRP allows for the configuration of multiple groups on a single gateway interface. The primary issue with running many different HSRP groups on the gateway interface is that it increases CPU utilization on the gateway and may potentially also increase the amount of network traffic, given the 3-second Hello interval used by HSRP.

To address this potential issue, HSRP also allows for the configuration of client or slave groups. These are simply HSRP groups that are configured to follow a master HSRP group and that do not participate in the HSRP election. These client or slave groups follow the operation and HSRP status of the master group and, therefore, do not need to exchange periodic Hello packets themselves. This reduces CPU and network utilization when using multiple HSRP groups.

However, it should be noted that client groups send periodic messages in order to refresh their virtual MAC addresses in switches. The refresh message may be sent at a much lower frequency compared with the protocol election messages sent by the master group. While the configuration of client groups is beyond the scope of the CCNA exam requirements, the following output illustrates the configuration of two client groups, which are configured to follow master group HSRP Group 1, also named the SWITCH-HSRP group:

```
Gateway-1(config)#interface vlan100
Gateway-1(config-if)#ip address 192.168.1.1 255.255.255.0
Gateway-1(config-if)#ip address 172.16.31.1 255.255.255.0 secondary
Gateway-1(config-if)#ip address 10.100.10.1 255.255.255.0 secondary
Gateway-1(config-if)#standby 1 ip 192.168.1.254
Gateway-1(config-if)#standby 1 name SWITCH-HSRP
Gateway-1(config-if)#standby 2 ip 172.16.31.254
Gateway-1(config-if)#standby 2 follow SWITCH-HSRP
Gateway-1(config-if)#standby 3 ip 10.100.10.254
Gateway-1(config-if)#standby 3 follow SWITCH-HSRP
Gateway-1(config-if)#exit
```

In the configuration in the output above, Group 1 is configured as the master HSRP group and Groups 2 and 3 are configured as client or slave HSRP groups.

CONFIGURING HSRP

Configuring HSRP on the Gateway

The following steps are required to configure HSRP on the gateway:

1. Configure the correct IP address and mask for the gateway interface using the `ip address [address] [mask] [secondary]` interface configuration command.
2. Create an HSRP group on the gateway interface and assign the group the virtual IP address via the `standby [number] ip [virtual address][secondary]` interface configuration command. The `[secondary]` keyword specifies the IP address as a secondary gateway IP address for the specified group.
3. Optionally, assign the HSRP group a name using the `standby [number] name [name]` interface configuration command.
4. Optionally, if you want to control the election of the active gateway, configure the group priority via the `standby [number] priority [value]` interface configuration command.

The following HSRP configuration outputs in this section will be based on the network below in Figure 47.17:

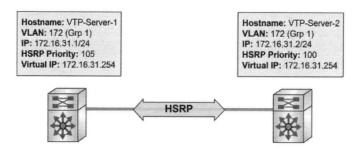

Hostname: VTP-Server-1
VLAN: 172 (Grp 1)
IP: 172.16.31.1/24
HSRP Priority: 105
Virtual IP: 172.16.31.254

Hostname: VTP-Server-2
VLAN: 172 (Grp 1)
IP: 172.16.31.2/24
HSRP Priority: 100
Virtual IP: 172.16.31.254

HSRP

Figure 47.17—HSRP Configuration Examples Topology

NOTE: It is assumed that the VLAN and trunking configuration between Switch-1 and Switch-2 is already in place and the switches are successfully able to ping each other across VLAN172. For brevity, this configuration output will be omitted from the configuration examples.

```
VTP-Server-1(config)#interface vlan172
VTP-Server-1(config-if)#ip address 172.16.31.1 255.255.255.0
VTP-Server-1(config-if)#standby 1 ip 172.16.31.254
VTP-Server-1(config-if)#standby 1 priority 105
VTP-Server-1(config-if)#exit
VTP-Server-2(config)#interface vlan172
VTP-Server-2(config-if)#ip address 172.16.31.2 255.255.255.0
VTP-Server-2(config-if)#standby 1 ip 172.16.31.254
VTP-Server-2(config-if)#exit
```

NOTE: No priority value is manually assigned for the HSRP configuration applied to Switch-2. By default, HSRP will use a priority value of 100, allowing Switch-1, with a priority value of 105, to win the election and to be elected the primary gateway for the HSRP group

Once implemented, HSRP configuration may be validated using the show standby [interface brief] command. The show standby brief command is shown in the following outputs:

```
VTP-Server-1#show standby brief
                    P indicates configured to preempt.
                    |
   Interface   Grp  Pri P State    Active  Standby        Virtual IP
   Vl172       1    105   Active   local   172.16.31.2    172.16.31.254

VTP-Server-2#show standby brief
                    P indicates configured to preempt.
                    |
   Interface   Grp  Pri P State    Active  Standby        Virtual IP
   Vl172       1    100   Standby  local   172.16.31.1    172.16.31.254
```

Based on this configuration, Switch-2 will become the active gateway for this group only if Switch-1 fails. Additionally, because preemption is not configured, when Switch-1 comes back online, it will not be able to assume forcefully the role of active gateway, even though it has a higher priority for the HSRP group than that being used on Switch-2.

Configuring HSRP Preemption

Preemption allows a gateway to assume forcefully the role of active gateway if it has a higher priority than the current active gateway. HSRP preemption is configured using the standby [number] preempt command. This configuration is illustrated on Switch-1 in the following output:

```
VTP-Server-1(config)#interface vlan172
VTP-Server-1(config-if)#standby 1 preempt
```

The show standby [interface [name]|brief] command is also used to verify that preemption has been configured on a gateway. This is illustrated by the "P" shown in the output of the show standby brief command below:

```
VTP-Server-1#show standby brief
                    P indicates configured to preempt.
                    |
   Interface   Grp  Pri P State    Active  Standby        Virtual IP
   Vl172       1    105 P Active   local   172.16.31.2    172.16.31.254
```

Based on this modification, if Switch-1 did fail and Switch-2 assumed the role of active gateway for VLAN 172, Switch-1 could forcibly reassume that role once it reinitializes. When configuring preemption, Cisco IOS software allows you to specify the duration the switch must wait before it preempts and forcibly reassumes the role of active gateway.

By default, this happens immediately. However, it may be adjusted using the `standby [number] preempt delay [minimum|reload|sync]` interface configuration command. The `[minimum]` keyword is used to specify the minimum amount of time to wait (seconds) before preemption. The following output shows how to configure the gateway to wait 30 seconds before preemption:

```
VTP-Server-1(config)#interface vlan172
VTP-Server-1(config-if)#standby 1 preempt delay minimum 30
```

This configuration may be validated using the `show standby [interface]` command. This is illustrated in the following output:

```
VTP-Server-1#show standby vlan172
Vlan172 - Group 1
  State is Active
    5 state changes, last state change 00:00:32
  Virtual IP address is 172.16.31.254
  Active virtual MAC address is 0000.0c07.ac01
    Local virtual MAC address is 0000.0c07.ac01 (v1 default)
  Hello time 3 sec, hold time 10 sec
    Next hello sent in 0.636 secs
  Preemption enabled, delay min 30 secs
  Active router is local
  Standby router is 172.16.31.2, priority 100 (expires in 8.629 sec)
  Priority 105 (configured 105)
  IP redundancy name is "hsrp-Vl172-1" (default)
```

The `[reload]` keyword is used to specify the amount of time the gateway should wait after it initializes following a reload. The `[sync]` keyword is used in conjunction with IP redundancy clients. This configuration is beyond the scope of the CCNA exam requirements but is very useful in production environments because it prevents an unnecessary change of roles in the case of a flapping interface that is being tracked, or similar activity.

Configuring HSRP Interface Tracking

HSRP interface tracking allows administrators to configure HSRP in order to track the state of interfaces and decrement the current priority value by the default value (10) or a preconfigured value, allowing another gateway to assume the role of primary gateway for the specified HSRP group.

In the following output, Switch-1 is configured to track the state of interface GigabitEthernet5/1, which is connected to an imaginary WAN router. In the event that the state of that interface transitions to "down," the gateway will decrement its priority value by 10 (which is the default):

```
VTP-Server-1(config)#interface vlan172
VTP-Server-1(config-if)#standby 1 track GigabitEthernet5/1
```

This configuration may be validated using the `show standby [interface]` command. This is illustrated in the following output:

```
VTP-Server-1#show standby vlan172
Vlan172 - Group 1
  State is Active
    5 state changes, last state change 00:33:22
  Virtual IP address is 172.16.31.254
  Active virtual MAC address is 0000.0c07.ac01
    Local virtual MAC address is 0000.0c07.ac01 (v1 default)
  Hello time 3 sec, hold time 10 sec
    Next hello sent in 1.085 secs
  Preemption enabled
  Active router is local
  Standby router is 172.16.31.2, priority 100 (expires in 7.616 sec)
  Priority 105 (configured 105)
  IP redundancy name is "hsrp-Vl172-1" (default)
  Priority tracking 1 interfaces or objects, 1 up:
  Interface or object          Decrement  State
  GigabitEthernet5/1              10       Up
```

To configure the gateway to decrement its priority value by 50, for example, the `standby [name] track [interface] [decrement value]` command can be issued, as shown in the following output:

```
VTP-Server-1(config)#interface vlan172
VTP-Server-1(config-if)#standby 1 track GigabitEthernet5/1 50
```

This configuration may be validated using the `show standby [interface]` command. This is illustrated in the following output:

```
VTP-Server-1#show standby vlan172
Vlan172 - Group 1
  State is Active
    5 state changes, last state change 00:33:22
  Virtual IP address is 172.16.31.254
  Active virtual MAC address is 0000.0c07.ac01
    Local virtual MAC address is 0000.0c07.ac01 (v1 default)
  Hello time 3 sec, hold time 10 sec
    Next hello sent in 1.085 secs
  Preemption enabled
  Active router is local
  Standby router is 172.16.31.2, priority 100 (expires in 7.616 sec)
  Priority 105 (configured 105)
  IP redundancy name is "hsrp-Vl172-1" (default)
  Priority tracking 1 interfaces or objects, 1 up:
  Interface or object          Decrement  State
  GigabitEthernet5/1              50       Up
```

Configuring the HSRP Version

As stated previously in this module, by default, when HSRP is enabled, version 1 is enabled. HSRP version 2 can be manually enabled using the `standby version [1|2]` interface configuration command. HSRP version 2 configuration is illustrated in the following output:

```
VTP-Server-1(config)#interface vlan172
VTP-Server-1(config-if)#standby version 2
```

This configuration may be validated using the `show standby [interface]` command. This is illustrated in the following output:

```
VTP-Server-1#show standby vlan172
Vlan172 - Group 1 (version 2)
  State is Active
    5 state changes, last state change 00:43:42
  Virtual IP address is 172.16.31.254
  Active virtual MAC address is 0000.0c9f.f001
    Local virtual MAC address is 0000.0c9f.f001 (v2 default)
  Hello time 3 sec, hold time 10 sec
    Next hello sent in 2.419 secs
  Preemption enabled
  Active router is local
  Standby router is 172.16.31.2, priority 100 (expires in 4.402 sec)
  Priority 105 (configured 105)
  IP redundancy name is "hsrp-Vl172-1" (default)
```

Enabling HSRP automatically changes the MAC address range used by HSRP from an address in the 0000.0C07.AC*xx* range to one in the 0000.0C9F.F000 to 0000.0C9F.FFFF range. It is therefore important to understand that this may cause some packet loss in a production network, as devices must learn the new MAC address of the gateway. Such changes are always recommended during a maintenance window or planned outage window.

Now please take today's exam at **https://www.in60days.com/free/ccnain60days/**

DAY 47 LAB

HSRP

Test the commands explained in this module, working on a scenario that includes two routers directly connected (i.e., Fa0/0 is connected to Fa0/0). Those routers should connect to a switch using, for example, ports Fa0/1. Connect a workstation on the switch.

- Configure a consistent IP addressing scheme on the two routers, for example, 192.168.0.1/24 and 192.168.0.2/24
- Configure HSRP 10 on the LAN-facing interfaces, using the 192.168.0.10 address
- Name the HSRP group as CCNA
- Control the election of the primary HSRP gateway using the `standby 10 priority 110` command
- Verify HSRP configuration using the `show standby [brief]` command
- Configure HSRP preemption on both routers
- Shut down Router 1 and see how Router 2 becomes primary
- Restart Router 1 and see how it becomes primary again due to preemption being enabled
- Configure the workstation with the IP address 192.168.0.100/24 and the gateway address 192.168.0.10; ping the gateway from the workstation
- Configure interface tracking: track an unused interface on the router using the `standby 10 track [int number]` command; cycle that interface through different states and see how the corresponding router priority changes based on the interface state
- Configure HSRP version 2 with the `standby version 2` command
- Adjust HSRP timers on both routers with the `standby 10 timers x y` command
- Configure MD5 HSRP authentication between the routers
- Debug HSRP using the `debug standby` command during a priority change on one of the routers and see how the second one is elected as the primary gateway

Quality of Service

DAY 48 TASKS

- Read today's notes
- Take today's exam
- Review yesterdays notes and lab
- Read the ICND2 cram guide (and the ICND1 cram guide, if taking the CCNA exam)
- Spend 15 minutes on the subnetting.org website

Quality of Service (QoS) is yet another new exam topic. It was previously in the Cisco CCNP RS exam but now it can be found in the Service Provider stream and the CCIE RS written exam. The Cisco QoS exam was retired in 2014.

Today you will learn about the following:

- Basic QoS concepts
- QoS models
- Catalyst ingress QoS mechanisms

This lesson maps to the following ICND2 syllabus requirements:

- 4.3 Describe basic QoS concepts
- 4.3.a Marking
- 4.3.b Device trust
- 4.3.c Prioritization
- 4.3.c. (i) Voice
- 4.3.c. (ii) Video
- 4.3.c. (iii) Data
- 4.3.d Shaping
- 4.3.e Policing
- 4.3.f Congestion management

BASIC QOS CONCEPTS

The principle behind QoS is fairly simple. Certain types of traffic in your network should be given a higher priority over others due to a business decision or because the traffic type doesn't tolerate delay very well, such as video conferencing or Voice over IP (VoIP). Modern networks support data, voice, and video traffic passing over a single transport infrastructure and so, for this reason, they are referred to as converged. However, it's up to you as the network administrator to configure your devices to make the most of these traffic types.

QoS lets you manage scarce bandwidth so you get the most out of what you have and provide predictable performance. It isn't a solution to a poorly designed, out-of-date, or poorly configured network, so ensure that you have taken care of cabling issues, high CPU utilization due to low specification routers or oversized routing tables, IOS bugs, and other issues before applying QoS, which is disabled by default (see below). You will usually have to interview key business stakeholders to determine which traffic gets priority.

Although bandwidth-intensive applications stretch network capabilities and resources, they also complement, add value, and enhance every business process.

Converged networks must provide secure, predictable, measurable, and sometimes guaranteed services. In order to ensure successful end-to-end business solutions, QoS is required to manage network resources. Most networks experience the following:

- Delay issues
- Bandwidth issues
- Jitter issues
- Packet loss issues

All packets in a network experience some kind of delay from the time the packet is first sent to when it arrives at its intended destination. This total delay, from start to finish, is referred to as latency. Packets or frames may experience several types of delay. While delving into the specifics of each type is beyond the scope of the CCNA exam requirements, some common causes of delay include the following:

- **Serialization delay:** the time it takes to send bits, one-at-a-time, across the wire
- **Queuing delay:** the delay experienced when packets wait for other packets to be sent
- **Forwarding delay:** the processing time from when a frame is sent and when the packet has been placed in the output queue

Generally speaking, bandwidth refers to the number of bits per second (bps) that are expected to be delivered successfully across some medium. Based on this definition, bandwidth is equal to the physical link speed or clock rate of the interface. In switching terms, however, the term bandwidth refers to the capacity of the switch fabric. Therefore, the bandwidth considerations for WAN connections, for example, are not necessarily the same as for LAN connections.

Jitter is the variation in delay between consecutive packets. Jitter is often referred to as variation delay. While such variations may be acceptable for applications and data traffic, they can severely impact isochronous traffic, such as digitized voice, which requires packets to be transmitted in a consistent, uniform manner.

Packet loss occurs when one or more packets traversing the network fail to reach their intended destination. This may occur for several reasons, such as bit errors or lack of space in queues, for example. While this does not generally affect connection-oriented protocols, such as TCP, packet loss can cause major issues for real-time traffic, such as voice and streaming video traffic.

In the default mode, it is important to know that all traffic, including real-time traffic such as voice, will be delivered on a best-effort basis, and all traffic will use a single queue on the switch. The different queues will be described later in this chapter. This default behavior is verified using the show mls qos command as shown in the following output:

```
Switch#show mls qos int g0/1
GigabitEthernet0/1
QoS is disabled. pass-through mode
[Output Truncated]
```

You can also enable it globally. Once enabled, the show mls qos command can be used to verify this configuration. The output of this configuration once QoS is enabled is illustrated as follows:

```
Switch#show mls qos
QoS is disabled
Switch#conf t
Switch(config)#mls qos
Switch(config)#end
Switch#show mls qos
QoS is enabled
QoS ip packet dscp rewrite is enabled
```

Note that these commands won't work on Packet Tracer and that some models will simply remove the QoS is disabled output to indicate that it is now in operation.

Traffic Types

Network traffic can be divided into three main types:

- Voice
- Video
- Data

Voice traffic creates flows with fixed data rates. Flows are isochronous (i.e., packets arrive at the same time or at equal intervals). Isochronous traffic doesn't tolerate delay very well, resulting in a choppy call or the call to be dropped entirely.

Video traffic can be interactive, such as a video conference, or non-interactive, such as watching a streaming video. Packet sizes vary but they are impacted by loss or delay.

Data traffic generally tolerates delay/packet loss well. Many applications simply resend lost packets. There is little to be gained by applying QoS in this instance.

QOS MODELS

QoS provides three broad delivery models to consider when designing and implementing a network infrastructure.

1. Best-effort delivery (default)
2. Integrated services
3. Differentiated services

Best-effort delivery provides no service guarantee. It scales well but it doesn't differentiate between voice, video, or data traffic. No QoS is applied in this instance. The type of delivery depends on the interface type and Layer 2 connection type (i.e., frame relay, PPP, Ethernet, etc.). Voice, video, and data traffic are all treated equally.

Integrated services (IntServ) was defined in RFC 1633, and is a set of extensions of the best-effort model. It applies a policy per flow of traffic and explicitly manages network resources to deliver end-to-end QoS. IntServ relies on the Resource Reservation Protocol (RSVP), which provides a setup mechanism to convey information to routers so they can provide the requested resources to the flows of traffic. This solution does not scale well at all due to the excessive cost of per-flow processing required.

Differentiated services (DiffServ) defines the concept of a service class. Each device handles the packet individually (on a per-hop basis). Layer 2 DiffServ uses Class of Service (CoS) bits encapsulated into an 802.1Q frame (in the VLAN field).

The IPv4 header actually contains an 8-bit Type of Service (ToS) field. Inside the packet header is a Differentiated Service Code Point (DSCP) field. It replaced the old IP Precedence field with the Differentiated Services (DS) field, which we will cover shortly. Figure 48.1 below demonstrates the IP Precedence field:

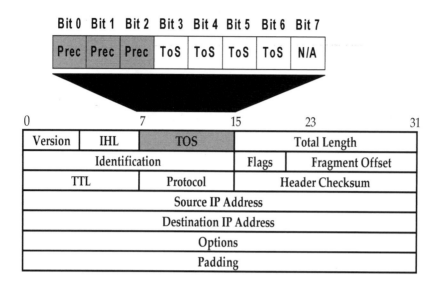

Figure 48.1—Type of Service IP Precedence Bits

Networks may use these settings to define the handling of the datagram during transport. This is typically performed using IP Precedence, which is contained in the first three bits of the ToS field. IP Precedence bits are illustrated above in Figure 48.1.

Figure 48.1 above illustrates the IPv4 packet header and highlights the 8-bit ToS field. The first three bits (bits 0 to 2) of this field are used for IP Precedence, which allows up to eight (2^3) IP Precedence values. The next four bits (bits 3 to 6) comprise the ToS field inside the ToS byte and they are used as flags for throughput, delay, reliability, and cost. These bits, however, are beyond the scope of the CCNA exam requirements. The last bit (bit 7) is unused.

The IP Precedence field values are used to imply a particular CoS. In essence, the higher the IP Precedence value (numerically), the more important the traffic. Table 48.1 below lists and describes the different IP Precedence values:

Table 48.1.—Type of Service IP Precedence values

IP Precedence Value	Bits	Description / Name
0	000 000	Routine
1	001 000	Priority
2	010 000	Immediate
3	011 000	Flash
4	100 000	Flash Override
5	101 000	Critical
6	110 000	Internetwork Control
7	111 000	Network Control

NOTE: The highest IP Precedence value that should be assigned to data traffic (e.g., voice packets) should always be 5. IP Precedence values 6 and 7 should never be assigned to user traffic, as these are used by the network to control traffic, such as routing protocol updates.

DiffServ defines a new DSCP field in the IP packet header by redefining the ToS byte and creating a replacement for the IP Precedence field with a new 6-bit field called the DS field. In addition, the last 2 bits of the ToS byte can now be used to perform flow control, and are referred to as Explicit Congestion Notification (ECN) bits. This is illustrated below in Figure 48.2:

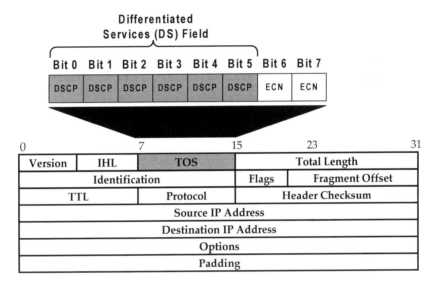

Figure 48.2—Type of Service Differentiated Services Code Point Bits

Figure 48.2 above illustrates the IPv4 packet header and highlights the 8-bit ToS field. The first six bits (bits 0 to 5) of this field are used for DSCP, which allows up to 64 (2^6) DSCP values. The decimal DSCP range is from 0 to 63. The next two bits are the ECN bits. Explicit Congestion Notification is beyond the scope of the CCNA exam requirements and will not be described in this chapter. The 64 DSCP values are backward compatible with IP Precedence values. This compatibility is based on the first three bits (bits 0 to 2), which both IP Precedence and DSCP share in common. Table 48.2 below shows how the decimal DSCP values are mapped to the IP Precedence values:

Table 48.2—Mapping decimal DSCP to IP Precedence values

IP Precedence Value	Decimal DSCP Value
0	0
1	8
2	16
3	24
4	32
5	40
6	48
7	56

NOTE: You are not expected to go into detail on how these values are derived. Instead, simply ensure that you are familiar with the decimal DSCP values that correspond to the IP Precedence values.

CATALYST INGRESS QOS MECHANISMS

Ingress QoS mechanisms are applied to frames and packets received by the switch in the inbound direction. The following Catalyst Switch ingress QoS mechanisms will be described in the following sections:

- Traffic classification
- Traffic policing
- Marking
- Congestion management and avoidance

NOTE: There is much more to QoS than we can fit into this small section, but we need to cover just enough for the purposes of the CCNA exam.

Traffic Classification

Classification is used to differentiate one stream of traffic from another so that different service levels can be applied to different streams of traffic. Frames can be classified based on the incoming CoS or DSCP values or even based on access control list (ACL) configuration. CoS classifies specific traffic (at Layer 2) by manipulating bits (in the frame header). CoS marks the traffic so that QoS can use this classification as a means to manipulate the traffic according to your policy. It is one way to identify traffic (along with ToS, ACLs, etc.) so that QoS knows what it is and how to manipulate it.

Frames contain CoS bits that are used to differentiate different classes of traffic. Classification in the Layer 3 header takes place in the ToS field. The QoS labels used in the Layer 3 IP header are IP Precedence and DSCP.

When the switch receives a frame or packet with an already existing QoS value, it must decide whether to trust the received QoS value. This is determined using the port trust setting. As stated earlier in this chapter, when QoS is enabled, by default, all switch interfaces are untrusted. Untrusted ports do not trust any of the QoS markings sent by the connected device and the switch will re-mark all inbound Ethernet frames to a CoS value of zero.

Port Trust

We already know that QoS is disabled by default (on switches). When enabled, all ports are untrusted in respect of QoS markings. Each port is given an equal CoS of zero by default.

```
Switch#conf t
Enter configuration commands, one per line.  End with CTRL/Z.
Switch(config)#mls qos
Switch(config)#end
Switch#show mls qos int f0/1
FastEthernet0/1
trust state: not trusted
trust mode: not trusted
COS override: dis
default COS: 0
```

Packets can arrive with QoS markings of trusted or untrusted, and trust is configured on the actual switchports. The trust domain stops at the port the host is connected to, as you can see in Figure 48.3 below:

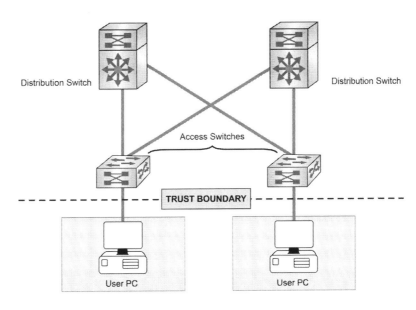

Figure 48.3—Trust Domain Stops at the Host Port

But it will include the voice VLAN as illustrated in Figure 48.4 below.

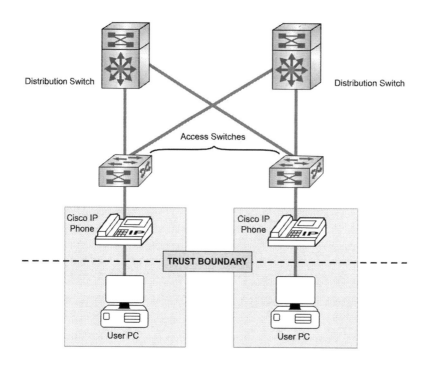

Figure 48.4—Trust Boundary with Cisco IP Phones

The trust configurations aren't relevant for the exam but when the configuration has been applied, the port is trusted.

```
Switch#show mls qos interface fastethernet0/1
FastEthernet0/1
trust state: trust cos
trust mode: trust cos
COS override: dis
default COS: 0
pass-through: none
trust device: cisco-phone
```

Traffic Shaping, Policing, and Marking

Traffic shapers and policers usually use the same method to identify traffic violations. The manner in which they respond to them differs though.

Shaping usually delays excess traffic by placing it into a buffer or queue for transmission when the data rate has returned to normal. Generic Traffic Shaping (GTS) and Class-based Traffic Shaping (CTS) both use a weighted fair queue to delay packets.

Policing is a process that is used to limit traffic to a prescribed rate. Policing is used to compare the ingress/egress traffic rate to a configured policer. The policer is configured with a rate and a burst. The rate defines the amount of traffic that is sent per given interval. When that specified amount has been sent, no more traffic is sent for that given interval. The burst defines the amount of traffic that can be held in readiness for being sent. Traffic in excess of the burst either can be dropped or have its priority setting reduced.

Traffic that conforms to the policing configuration is considered in-profile and will be forwarded, as configured, by the switch. However, traffic that does not conform to the policing configuration is considered out-of-profile, which either can be dropped or marked down (i.e., remarked with a lower QoS value).

Marking involves setting QoS bits inside the Layer 2 or Layer 3 headers, which allows the other internetwork devices to classify based on the marked values. Marking is typically used in conjunction with traffic policing. For example, if the traffic is in-profile, the switch will typically allow the packets to be passed through (i.e., it will not change or reset the QoS settings in the packets). However, if the traffic is out-of-profile, the switch may be configured to mark down this traffic with a lower QoS value. This concept is illustrated below in Figure 48.5:

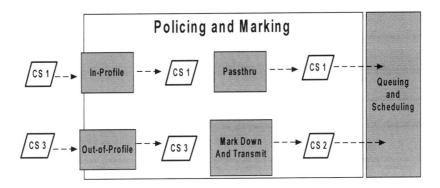

Figure 48.5—Understanding Policing and Marking

Figure 48.5 above shows two packets arriving at the policer. It is assumed that these packets have already been classified based on the port trust state configuration. The incoming packets are then compared against the configured policer rate. The packet with DSCP value CS 1 is in-profile (i.e., in conformance with the policing rate configuration). Based on the policing configuration, this packet is passed through the switch with the QoS setting unchanged.

The packet with DSCP CS 3 is out-of-profile (i.e., traffic is in excess of the burst configuration). This traffic either can be dropped or marked down. In Figure 63, assume that the policing configuration has been implemented so that this traffic is marked down and transmitted with the marked down DSCP value. The value is set to CS 2 and the packet is transmitted. The packet is then sent to the congestion management and avoidance mechanisms, which will determine the ingress queue in which to place the packet based on the QoS label.

Congestion Management and Avoidance

Congestion management and avoidance is comprised of the following three elements:

- Queuing
- Dropping
- Scheduling

Queuing is used to place packets into different software queues based on the QoS labels. After the traffic is classified and marked with QoS labels, it is assigned and placed into different queues based on those QoS labels.

> **NOTE:** Queuing is also spelled as queueing in some parts of the world. It means the same thing.

Catalyst Switches typically have two ingress queues, one of which either is a priority queue or can be configured as a priority queue. The ingress frames and packets received by the switch are placed in a queue based on the ingress (received) CoS value. Voice traffic, for example, that is received with CoS 5 or DSCP EF will be placed into the priority queue, while regular data traffic will be placed into the normal queue. This queuing concept is illustrated below in Figure 48.6:

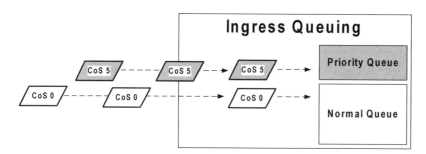

Figure 48.6—Catalyst Switch Ingress Queuing Operation

Once the packets have been placed into the appropriate queue based on their QoS values, dropping is used to manage queues. Dropping provides drop priorities for different classes of traffic. Queues have drop thresholds that are used to indicate which packets can be dropped once the queue has been filled beyond a certain threshold.

After ingress packets are placed into the queue, a congestion avoidance mechanism will use a CoS-to-threshold map to determine what frames are eligible to be dropped when a threshold is breached. This prevents the queues from filling up. The different congestion avoidance mechanisms that can be used are beyond the scope of the CCNA exam requirements and will not be described in this chapter.

Scheduling refers to how the queues are serviced or emptied. If a priority queue is configured, it only makes sense that this be serviced (emptied) before the normal queue. In other words, the packets in the priority queue should be sent before the packets in the normal queue. Catalyst Switches use Strict Round Robin (SRR) for ingress scheduling. However, going into any detail on SRR is beyond the scope of the CCNA exam requirements. SRR will not be described in any greater detail in this chapter. Figure 48.7 below illustrates the order of processing the ingress QoS mechanisms described in this section:

Ingress QoS Mechanisms

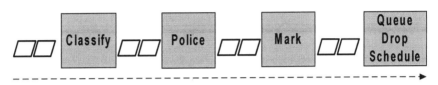

Figure 48.7—Ingress Quality of Service mechanisms

Referencing Figure 48.7 above, you can see that the packet or frame is classified, policed, and marked, and then it is sent to the ingress queue(s).

Egress QoS mechanisms are applied to frames and packets received by the switch in the outbound direction.

Now please take today's exam at **https://www.in60days.com/free/ccnain60days/**

Review

DAY 49 TASKS

- Review days 46-48 including labs
- Take today's exam at **https://www.in60days.com/free/ccnain60days/**
- Read the ICND2 cram guide (and the ICND1 cram guide, if taking the CCNA exam)
- Complete the below challenge lab (if you wish)
- Spend 15 minutes on the subnetting.org website

Challenge 1—HSRP Lab

Topology

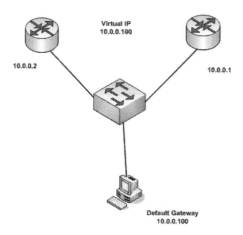

Instructions

Connect two routers together via a switch and a PC to the switch (or use Packet Tracer)

1. Do not add any configuration to the switch.
2. Configure IP addresses on all devices in the 10.0.0.0/8 network. Set an IP address on the PC.
3. Configure a HSRP group on the switch and give one of the routers a higher priority.
4. Configure preemption and a virtual IP of 10.0.0.100
5. Ping the virtual IP from the PC.
6. Now shut down the interface on the active router and check that the other router has become the primary gateway.

IPv6 Access Lists

DAY 50 TASKS

- Go through today's theory and lab
- Read the ICND2 cram guide (and the ICND1 cram guide, if taking the CCNA exam)
- Spend 15 minutes on the subnetting.org website

If you can configure and troubleshoot IPv4 ACLs, then IPv6 ACLs will be a cinch. There is a change to the command you use to apply it to a port or interface and, of course, you are using IPv6 addresses and networks with CIDR, but, after a few examples, you should feel confident.

Today you will learn about the following:

- Configuring IPv6 ACLs

This lesson maps to the following ICND2 syllabus requirements:

- 4.4 Configure, verify, and troubleshoot IPv4 and IPv6 access list for traffic filtering
- 4.4.a Standard
- 4.4.b Extended
- 4.4.c Named

CONFIGURING IPV6 ACCESS CONTROL LISTS

Hopefully, by now you are very familiar with IPv4 ACLs. If not, please go back and review it before you tackle IPv6 ACLs. I'm going to dispense with any information that is the same as that for IPv4 ACLs, making this section fairly short.

IPv6 ACLs must be named "standard" or "extended," as numbers are not used for IPv6 ACLs. If you have named IPv4 ACLs in place, then you must use a different name for your IPv6 ACLs. As stated, you will use CIDR notation for your IPv6 ACLs because a wildcard mask has no place in IPv6.

You can apply IPv6 ACLs to interfaces using the `ipv6 traffic-filter` command and to ports such as VTY lines or console ports using the `ipv6 access-class` command. Be careful to note that IPv6 ACL commands need to be prepended with `ipv6`. It's so easy to issue commands and show commands and get confused because (of course) IPv4 numbered ACLs don't require us to add ipv4 to the configurations, so we develop the habit of leaving the IP version off.

Both IPv4 and IPv6 ACLs can match hosts, networks, or source/destination addresses and be applied inbound or outbound to router interfaces. They can also match various Transport Layer protocols. IPv6 ACLs can also match information specific to the IPv6 header, including flow label and DSCP, for example. Options for IPv6 are shown in the following output:

```
R1(config-ipv6-acl)#permit ipv6 any any ?
  dest-option         Destination Option header (all types)
  dest-option-type    Destination Option header with type
  dscp                Match packets with given dscp value
  flow-label          Flow label
  fragments           Check non-initial fragments
  log                 Log matches against this entry
  log-input           Log matches against this entry, including input
  mobility            Mobility header (all types)
  mobility-type       Mobility header with type
  reflect             Create reflexive access list entry
  routing             Routing header (all types)
  routing-type        Routing header with type
  sequence            Sequence number for this entry
  time-range          Specify a time-range
  <cr>
```

You can see some of these options in the Wireshark capture of the IPv6 header in Figure 50.1 below. I recommend that you capture packets and examine them whenever possible so you can see the protocol in action for yourself.

```
▽ Internet Protocol Version 6, Src: fe80::c002:6ff:fee8:0 (fe80::c002:6ff:fee8
  ▷ 0110 .... = Version: 6
  ▽ .... 1110 0000 .... .... .... .... .... = Traffic class: 0x000000e0
      .... 1110 00.. .... .... .... .... .... = Differentiated Services Field:
      .... .... ..0. .... .... .... .... .... = ECN-Capable Transport (ECT): N
      .... .... ...0 .... .... .... .... .... = ECN-CE: Not set
      .... .... .... 0000 0000 0000 0000 0000 = Flowlabel: 0x00000000
    Payload length: 32
    Next header: ICMPv6 (58)
    Hop limit: 255
    Source: fe80::c002:6ff:fee8:0 (fe80::c002:6ff:fee8:0)
    Destination: ff02::1 (ff02::1)
    [Source GeoIP: Unknown]
```

Figure 50.1—Capture of an IPv6 Packet Header

IPv6 has some implicit permit and deny statements. You already know about the IPv4 implicit deny. IPv6 ACLs feature a deny ipv6 any any but also permit icmp any any nd-na (neighbor advertisements) and permit icmp any any nd-ns (neighbor solicitation). Without this, the core plug-and-play features of IPv6 wouldn't work.

If you are trying out IPv6 ACLs on a home lab, make sure that your platform and IOS release supports them. Many home users don't have access to the 15.X IOS track. Pre-12.0(23)S releases don't support IPv6 ACLs and 12.2(13)T supports standard IPv6 ACLs only. Let's look at a few examples of IPv6 ACLs.

Example 1

We will use Figure 50.2 below as a reference:

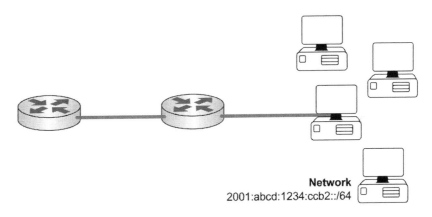

Network
2001:abcd:1234:ccb2::/64

Figure 50.2—IPv6 Example 1

You'll want to create an ACL to block the network shown on the right. Remember that you need to implicitly permit all other IPv6 traffic or it will be blocked. I'll use the ? syntax so that you can see the available options. Your options may differ depending on your platform and IOS (and if you are using Packet Tracer).

```
Router#conf t
Router(config)#ipv6 access-list ?
  WORD  User selected string identifying this access list
Router(config)#ipv6 access-list paul
Router(config-ipv6-acl)#deny ipv6 2001:abcd:1234:ccb2::/64 any
Router(config-ipv6-acl)#permit ?
  icmp  Internet Control Message Protocol
  ipv6  Any IPv6
  tcp   Transmission Control Protocol
  udp   User Datagram Protocol
Router(config-ipv6-acl)#permit ipv6 any any
Router(config-ipv6-acl)#int f0/0
Router(config-if)#ipv6 traffic-filter paul in
```

You can test it by pinging the router interface from any host on the network. Remove the ACL and it should work.

Example 2

This time you will create an ACL to block a particular host from accessing another host. Figure 50.3 below illustrates the topology. Test it by pinging from the blocked host and then a different host.

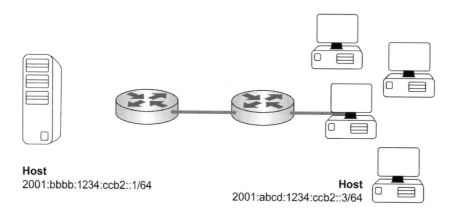

Host
2001:bbbb:1234:ccb2::1/64

Host
2001:abcd:1234:ccb2::3/64

Figure 50.3—Example 2 Topology

I've added the question mark to illustrate some of your options.

```
Router(config)#ipv6 access-list deny_host3
Router(config-ipv6-acl)#deny ipv6 host 2001:abcd:1234:ccb2::3 ?
  X:X:X:X::X/<0-128>  IPv6 destination prefix x:x::y/<z>
  any                 Any destination prefix
  host                A single destination host
Router(config-ipv6-acl)#deny ipv6 host 2001:abcd:1234:ccb2::3 host
2001:bbbb:1234:ccb2::2
Router(config-ipv6-acl)#permit ipv6 any any
Router(config-ipv6-acl)#int f0/0
Router(config-if)#ipv6 traffic-filter deny_host3 in
```

Example 3

The next example will permit Telnet traffic from one host to another. All other Telnet traffic will be denied. The topology is the same as that in Example 2. You can see how to test it out I'm sure.

```
Router(config)#ipv6 access-list permit_telnet
Router(config-ipv6-acl)#permit tcp host 2001:abcd:1234:ccb2::3 host
2001:bbbb:1234:ccb2::2 eq telnet
Router(config-ipv6-acl)#deny tcp any any eq telnet
Router(config-ipv6-acl)#permit ipv6 any any
Router(config-ipv6-acl)#int f0/0
Router(config-if)#ipv6 traffic-filter permit_telnet in
```

Example 4

Our last example will permit Telnet traffic from a host address to anywhere in the network by applying the ACL to the Telnet port (VTY lines). The topology is illustrated in Figure 50.4 below. Note that you have to change the command to apply it because you are using a port this time, not an interface.

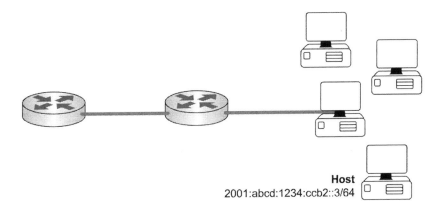

Figure 50.4—Example 4 topology

```
Router(config)#ipv6 access-list permit_telnet
Router(config-ipv6-acl)#permit ipv6 host 2001:abcd:1234:ccb2::3 any eq
telnet
Router(config-ipv6-acl)#deny tcp any any eq telnet
Router(config-ipv6-acl)#permit ipv6 any any
Router(config-if)#exit
Router(config)#line vty 0 15
Router(config-line)#ipv6 access-class permit_telnet in
```

The examples above were created just for you to try out the commands and syntax. We will cover configuration and verifying an IPv6 ACL in the lab. We have already covered troubleshooting access control lists in the ICND1 section. The same applies to IPv6.

Now take today's exam at **https://www.in60days.com/free/ccnain60days/**

DAY 50 LAB

IPv6 Access List

Topology

2001:aaaa:bbbb:cccc::/64

.1

R1
f0/0

.2

2001:aaaa:bbbb:dddd::/64

.1

R2
f0/0

Purpose

Learn how to configure IPv6 access lists.

Walkthrough

1. Enable IPv6 routing on both sides. Here is how to enable it on R1.

   ```
   R1(config)#ipv6 unicast-routing
   ```

2. Add the below IPv6 address to F0/0 on R1. For R2 add the .2 address and the .1 address for the loopback interface. Make sure you no shut the interfaces.

   ```
   R1(config)#int f0/0
   R1(config-if)#ipv6 address 2001:aaaa:bbbb:cccc::1/64
   R1(config-if)#no shut
   R2(config)#ipv6 unicast-routing
   R2(config)#int f0/0
   R2(config-if)#ipv6 address 2001:aaaa:bbbb:cccc::2/64
   R2(config-if)#no shut
   R2(config-if)#int lo0
   R2(config-if)#ipv6 address 2001:aaaa:bbbb:dddd::1/64
   ```

3. Ping from R2 to R1 or vice versa.

   ```
   R2#ping 2001:aaaa:bbbb:cccc::1

   Type escape sequence to abort.
   Sending 5, 100-byte ICMP Echos to 2001:AAAA:BBBB:CCCC::2, timeout is 2
   seconds:
   !!!!!
   Success rate is 100 percent (5/5), round-trip min/avg/max = 0/0/0 ms
   ```

4. Enable Telnet traffic for R1.

   ```
   R1(config-line)#password cisco
   R1(config-line)#login
   ```

5. Add an ACL to prevent telnet from the host on R2 loopback 0. All other Telnet traffic should be permitted. Apply it to the telnet lines (they are from 0-903 on GNS3).

   ```
   R1(config)#ipv6 access-list no_telnet
   ```

```
R1(config-ipv6-acl)#deny tcp host 2001:aaaa:bbbb:dddd::1 any eq telnet
R1(config-ipv6-acl)#permit tcp any any eq telnet
R1(config-ipv6-acl)#permit ipv6 any any
R1(config-ipv6-acl)#line vty 0 903
R1(config-line)#ipv6 access-class no_telnet in
R1(config-line)#exi
```

6. Test the ACL by telnetting from source loopback 0. It should be blocked. Telnet from the F0/0 should work. To quit a Telnet session hold down the Control-Shift-6 keys together and then press the X key.

```
R2#telnet 2001:aaaa:bbbb:cccc::1 /source-interface loopback 0
Trying 2001:AAAA:BBBB:CCCC::1 ...
% Connection timed out; remote host not responding

R2#telnet 2001:aaaa:bbbb:cccc::1
Trying 2001:AAAA:BBBB:CCCC::1 ... Open


User Access Verification

Password:
R1>enable
% No password set
```

7. Issue a show command for the ACL.

```
R1#show ipv6 access-list
IPv6 access list no_telnet
    deny tcp host 2001:AAAA:BBBB:DDDD::1 any eq telnet (1 match)
sequence 10
    permit tcp any any eq telnet (2 matches) sequence 20
    permit ipv6 any any sequence 30
```

NOTE: It's very important you make your own IPv6 ACLs up. Block various ports, networks and hosts. Try applying them on ports and interfaces.

Cisco APIC-EM Path Trace ACL Analysis Application

DAY 51 TASKS

- Complete today's lesson
- Review yesterdays lesson and lab
- Take today's exam
- Read the ICND2 cram guide (and the ICND1 cram guide, if taking the CCNA exam)
- Spend 15 minutes on the subnetting.org website

As you are probably already aware, Cisco is pushing very hard into the Software Defined Networking (SDN) market—and rightly so, because this is the future. APIC-EM (pronounced apick E.M.) is the acronym for Application Policy Infrastructure Controller Enterprise Module and it sits at the core of Cisco's Digital Network Architecture (DNA), which provides a simple user interface, allowing you to automate policy-based application profiles.

Today you will learn about the following:

- APIC-EM path trace tool

This lesson maps to the following ICND2 syllabus requirements:

- 4.5 Verify ACLs using the APIC-EM Path Trace ACL analysis tool

CISCO APIC-EM PATH TRACE TOOL

An entry in the new CCNA syllabus that raised a few eyebrows is "Verify ACLs using the APIC-EM Path Trace ACL analysis tool." If you check on the Cisco.com page for APIC, it explains that some of the features include:

- Rapid deployment of network devices
- Provides a programmable network
- Increase in productivity
- A great application experience

TechWise at Cisco.com covers APIC-EM from a business perspective if you want to learn more:

http://www.cisco.com/c/m/en_us/training-events/events-webinars/apic-em.html

The path trace ACL tool is just one of many under the APIC-EM umbrella. It can found at:

http://www.cisco.com/c/en/us/products/cloud-systems-management/application-policy-infrastructure-controller-enterprise-module/index.html

Or the shortened link:

http://bit.ly/1ijwyiK

You can access some of the APIC-EM tools by registering for free at the URL below:

https://developer.cisco.com/site/apic-em/

You can then reserve a session in the mini-lab (see Figure 51.1 below):

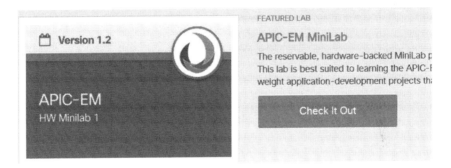

Figure 51.1—The APIC-EM MiniLab

Please read the instructions because you have to download VPN software, as well as reserve the session and obtain login details via e-mail.

The APIC-EM software runs on a server that allows you to discover the network topology (if CDP and SNMP is enabled). You can then enter a source and destination address, letting the application analyze where the traffic would flow.

Please take today's exam at https://www.in60days.com/free/ccnain60days/

IP SLA and Simple Network Managment Protocol

DAY 52 TASKS

- Read today's theory
- Complete today's lab
- Take today's exam
- Review yesterdays subject and any other subject and labs of your choice
- Read the ICND2 cram guide (and the ICND1 cram guide, if taking the CCNA exam)
- Spend 15 minutes on the subnetting.org website

The Simple Network Management Protocol (SNMP) is a widely used management protocol and defined set of standards for communications with devices connected to an IP network. SNMP provides a means to monitor and control network devices. Like Cisco IOS IP SLA operations (which allows customers to analyze IP service levels using active traffic monitoring for measuring network performance), SNMP can be used to collect statistics, monitor device performance, and provide a baseline of the network, and is one of the most commonly used network maintenance and monitoring tools.

Cisco IOS IP Service Level Agreement (SLA) allows you to monitor, analyze, and verify IP service levels for IP applications and services to increase productivity, lower operational costs, and reduce occurrences of network congestion or outages. IP SLA uses active traffic monitoring to measure network performance.

Today you will learn about the following:

- Cisco IOS IP SLA
- SNMP

This lesson maps to the following ICND2 syllabus requirements:

- 5.1 Configure and verify device-monitoring protocols
- 5.1.a SNMPv2
- 5.1.b SNMPv3
- 5.2 Troubleshoot network connectivity issues using ICMP echo-based IP SLA

CISCO IOS IP SERVICE LEVEL AGREEMENT

IP SLA was first integrated and introduced into Cisco IOS software as Response Time Reporter (RTR). Following some improvements, it was renamed Cisco Service Assurance Agent (SAA). In current IOS versions, the same tool is referred to as IP SLA.

IP SLA can measure and monitor network performance metrics such as jitter, latency (delay), and packet loss. IP SLA has evolved with advanced measurement features, such as application performance, MPLS awareness, and enhanced voice measurements. IP SLA uses active traffic monitoring, which is the generation of traffic in a continuous, reliable, and predictable manner, to measure network performance edge to edge over a network. Given this, IP SLA operations are based on active probes because synthetic network traffic is generated strictly for the purpose of measuring a network performance characteristic of the defined operation.

NOTE: A passive probe is one that captures actual network traffic flows for analysis. Examples would be a packet capture (e.g., Ethereal or Wireshark) and Cisco IOS NetFlow. Cisco IOS NetFlow has been dropped from the CCNA syllabus, so it will not be described in this guide.

IP SLA has several uses and advantages, including the following:

- IP SLA has visibility of the processing time on the device versus just the transit or on-the-wire time (passive probes), which gives a more granular and accurate measurement.
- IP SLA can differentiate among different measurements (e.g., UDP vs. ICMP or TCP statistics), so the measurement specifically reflects the current operation and not a generalized overview of the entire traffic.
- IP SLA can be used as a proactive tool since it allows traffic to be created in a controlled environment using different protocols and ports, which allows greater flexibility in terms of simulating future growth with expected traffic patterns or creating a baseline with existing benchmarks.
- IP SLA provides near-millisecond precision.
- IP SLA supports proactive notification using SNMP traps based on a defined threshold or trigger of another IP SLA operation.
- IP SLA allows for and provides historical data storage.
- IP SLA has comprehensive hardware support. Because it is integrated into Cisco IOS, it can be used on many different router and switch platforms, making this a cost-effective and scalable solution because it does not require dedicated probes.
- IP SLA can be used to monitor and measure Quality of Service (QoS) for Voice over IP (VoIP) and for video conferencing applications.
- From a business perspective, IP SLA provides Service Level Agreement monitoring, measurements, and verification.
- IP SLA can be used to perform a network health assessment.
- Because of its flexibility, IP SLA is a very powerful network troubleshooting tool.

IP SLA Components

The IP Service Level Agreement is comprised of the following two components:

1. Source
2. Target

The source, which is also sometimes referred to as the agent, is where IP SLA operations are defined. In other words, this is where the bulk of the configuration is implemented. Based on the configuration parameters, the source generates packets specific to the defined IP SLA operations, and analyzes the results and records them so they can be accessed through the command line interface (CLI) or using the Simple Network Management Protocol (SNMP).

A source router can be any Cisco router or switch that can support the IP SLA operation being configured. A particular source or agent can have multiple IP SLA tests running on many remote responders. In addition, a particular router or switch can be both an agent and a responder for different IP SLA configurations.

The IP SLA target depends on the type of IP SLA operation defined and may be a computer or an internetwork device, such as a router or a switch. For example, for IP SLA FTP or HTTP operations, the target would be an FTP or HTTP server. For Real-time Transport Protocol (RTP) and UDP jitter (VoIP), the target must be a Cisco device.

If the target is a Cisco device, the `ip sla responder` global configuration command must be configured on this device because both the source and the target participate in the performance measurement. The IP SLA responder has an added benefit of accuracy because it inserts in and out time stamps into the packet payload and therefore measures the CPU time spent.

The IP SLA responder (target) is a Cisco IOS software component that is configured to respond to IP SLA request packets. The IP SLA source establishes a connection with the target using control packets before the configured IP SLA operation begins.

Following the acknowledgment of the control packets, the source then sends the responder test packets. The responder inserts a timestamp when it receives a packet and factors out the destination processing time, and then adds timestamps to the sent packets. This allows for the calculation of unidirectional packet loss, latency, and jitter measurements with the kind of accuracy that is not possible using simple ping tests or other dedicated (passive) probe testing.

IP SLA Functional Areas

IP SLA operations can be broadly categorized into the following five functional areas:

1. Availability monitoring
2. Network monitoring
3. Application monitoring

4. Voice monitoring
5. Video monitoring

Availability monitoring can be used to monitor network-level availability and is performed primarily using ICMP and UDP packets. IP SLA availability monitoring operations will be described in detail in the following section.

Network monitoring is used to monitor Layer 2 operations, such as asynchronous transfer mode (ATM), frame relay, DLSw+, and Multiprotocol Label Switching (MPLS). ATM, frame relay, and DLSw+ are beyond the scope of the CCNA exam requirements. MPLS will be described later in this guide.

Application monitoring is used to monitor common network applications, which include HTTP, FTP, DHCP, and DNS. Voice monitoring is used to determine voice quality scores, Post Dial Delay (PDD), RTP, and gatekeeper registration delay. Video monitoring is used to monitor video traffic. No specific IP SLA tests for video monitoring exist; however, the UDP jitter operation can be used to simulate some video traffic.

IP SLA Availability Monitoring

IP SLA supports the following for availability monitoring:

- ICMP echo
- ICMP path echo
- ICMP jitter
- ICMP path jitter
- UDP echo
- UDP jitter

ICMP echo measures the end-to-end response time between a Cisco router or switch and any IP device by measuring the time between sending an ICMP echo request message to the destination and receiving an ICMP echo reply. This operation takes into account the processing time taken by the sender but cannot take into account any processing time in the target device. This is a good tool to measure availability but it does not give much indication of whether any underlying problems exist in the network or the destination host.

The ICMP path echo operation is different from the regular ICMP echo in that it first does a traceroute to discover the path from a source to the destination, and then measures the response time between the source router or switch and each of the intermittent hops in the path. It also has the option of using strict and loose source routing (LSR), which enables IP SLA to use a particular path instead of using the path discovered using Traceroute. This provides more detail on the IP addresses of the hops taken as well as any failures in the intermediate path.

The ICMP jitter operation is very similar to ICMP echo, but it also provides latency, jitter, and packet loss in addition to the round-trip measurement. Jitter, also known as IP Packet Delay Variation (IPDV), is a measurement of delay variation.

The ICMP path jitter operation is very similar to the ICMP path echo operation, but it also includes jitter operation statistics, such as latency, jitter, and packet loss on a per-hop basis. The operation first discovers the path using Traceroute, and then it sends an ICMP echo message to determine the response time, jitter, and packet loss for each of the hops.

The UDP echo operation is more useful than the ICMP echo operation because the target understands UDP echo packets; therefore, this operation accounts for the processing time taken by the target system, or responder, to generate a more accurate measurement.

The IP SLA UDP jitter operation was primarily designed to determine IP network suitability for traffic applications, such as VoIP, video over IP, or real-time conferencing. This is the only IP SLA operation that supports microsecond precision, which makes it ideal for monitoring voice, video, and other highly sensitive applications. One-way jitter accuracy depends on clock synchronization between the source and its destination. It is therefore recommended that Network Time Protocol (NTP) be used in conjunction with this for accuracy because The UDP jitter packets generated have sequencing information as well as timestamps for both the sending and receiving sides. IP SLA UDP jitter operations are capable of measuring the following:

- Per-direction jitter (source to destination and destination to source)
- Per-direction packet loss
- Per-direction delay (one-way delay)
- Round-trip delay (average round-trip time)
- Out-of-sequence and corrupted packets

Configuring Cisco IOS IP SLA Operations

IP SLA operations are configured in global configuration mode. The configuration of the IP SLA feature depends on the software version running on the router.

In Cisco IOS software versions 12.3(14)T, 12.4, 12.4(2)T, and 12.2(33)SXH, IP SLA is configured using the `ip sla monitor [operation number]` global configuration command. In Cisco IOS 12.4(4)T and later, IP SLA is configured using the `ip sla [operation number]` global configuration command.

The `operation number` keyword used in all three variations of IP SLA configuration is an integer between 1 and 2147483647. This allows for the configuration of multiple IP SLA operations on the same device. Following IP SLA configuration in global configuration mode, the router transitions to the `IP SLA monitor` command.

In Cisco IOS software versions 12.3(14)T, 12.4, 12.4(2)T, and 12.2(33)SXH, the IP SLA operation is configured using the `type IP SLA monitor` command. Given that the most commonly used operation is to send ICMP echo packets, this would be configured using the `type echo protocol ipIcmpEcho [hostname | address] [source-ipaddr <address> | hostname]` IP SLA monitor command.

In Cisco IOS 12.4T and later, the `icmp-echo [hostname | address] [source-ip <address>`
`| hostname | source-interface <name>]` `IP SLA monitor` command is used to configure
the same ICMP echo operation.

Three additional parameters that are commonly specified when configuring the IP SLA
ICMP echo operation are time out, frequency, and threshold. The timeout parameter is used
to specify the amount of time the Cisco IOS IP SLA's operation waits for a response from
its request packet. This value is specified in milliseconds. The default timeout value varies
depending on the type of IP SLA operation you are configuring.

The frequency parameter is specified in seconds and is used to specify the rate at which a
specified Cisco IOS IP SLA operation is sent into the network. For example, if you specify
a frequency of 10 when using the ICMP echo operation, ping packets will be sent every 10
seconds.

The threshold parameter sets the rising threshold used to generate a reaction event and stores
the history information for the Cisco IOS IP SLA operation. The threshold is specified in
milliseconds and the default is 5000 ms. The threshold parameter commonly used in advanced
IP SLA implementations will not be included in the configuration examples in this chapter.

After configuring the IP SLA operation and specifying additional parameters, the operation
can then be enabled using the `ip sla monitor schedule [operation number]` command
in global configuration mode. While this command can be used with several parameters,
parameters typically used when configuring IP SLA for use with the Reliable Static Routing
Backup Using Object Tracking include the `life` keyword and the `start-time` keyword.

The `life` keyword is used to specify the length of time to execute the operation, and it can be
specified in either seconds (up to 2147483647) or infinitely using the `forever` keyword. The
`start-time` keyword is used to specify when the operation should begin. The most common
implementation is to use the `now` keyword to begin the operation immediately. However, the
operation can be configured to start at a specified time, after a specified amount of time, or
on a specific date at a specific time, for example.

> **NOTE:** After configuring and starting IP SLA operations, the results of the operations
> are then stored on the source device in the Cisco RTTMON MIB. This MIB can also
> be used to configure IP SLA operations using SNMP set commands. No explicit
> configuration is required to begin storing data in the Cisco RTTMOM MIB. You are
> not required to go into any further detail on either the Cisco RTTMON MIB or SNMP
> configuration for the current CCNA exam.

SIMPLE NETWORK MANAGEMENT PROTOCOL

SNMP is an Application Layer (Layer 7) protocol, using UDP ports 161 and 162, that facilitates the exchange of management information between network devices. An SNMP-managed network consists of a management system, agents, and managed devices. The management system executes monitoring applications and controls managed devices. It also executes most of the management processes and provides the bulk of memory resources used for network management. A network might be managed by one or more management systems.

An SNMP agent resides on each managed device and translates local management information data, such as performance information or event and error information caught in software traps, into a readable form for the management system. SNMP agents use get-requests that transport data to the network management software. SNMP agents capture data from Management Information Bases (MIBs), which are device parameter and network data repositories, or from error or change traps.

A managed element, such as a router, a switch, a computer, or a firewall, is accessed via the SNMP agent. Managed devices collect and store management information, making it available through SNMP to other management systems having the same protocol compatibility. Figure 52.1 below illustrates the interaction of the three primary components of an SNMP-managed network:

Figure 52.1—SNMP Network Component Interaction

Referencing Figure 52.1, R1 is the SNMP-managed device. Logically residing on the device is the SNMP agent. The SNMP agent translates local management information data, stored in the management database of the managed device, into a readable form for the management system, which is also referred to as the Network Management Station (NMS).

When using SNMP, managed devices are monitored and controlled using three common SNMP commands: read, write, and trap. The read command is used by an NMS to monitor managed devices. This is performed by the NMS examining different variables that are maintained by managed devices. The write command is used by an NMS to control managed devices. Using this command, the NMS can change the values of variables stored within managed devices. Finally, the SNMP trap command is used by managed devices to report events to the NMS. Devices can be configured to send SNMP traps or informs to an NMS. The traps and informs that are sent are dependent on the version of Cisco IOS software running on the device, as well as the platform.

SNMP traps are simply messages that alert the SNMP manager of a condition on the network. An example of an SNMP trap could include an interface transitioning from an up state to a down state. The primary issue with SNMP traps is that they are unacknowledged. This means that the sending device is incapable of determining whether the trap was received by the NMS.

SNMP informs are SNMP traps that include a confirmation of receipt from the SNMP manager. These messages can be used to indicate failed authentication attempts, or the loss of a connection to a neighbor router, for example. If the manager does not receive an inform request, then it does not send a response. If the sender never receives a response, then the inform request can be sent again. Thus, informs are more likely to reach their intended destination.

While informs are more reliable than traps, the downside is that they consume more resources on both the router and in the network. Unlike a trap, which is discarded as soon as it is sent, an inform request must be held in memory until a response is received or the request times out. In addition, traps are sent only once, while an inform may be resent several times if a response is not received from the SNMP server (NMS).

Figure 52.2 below illustrates the communication between the SNMP manager and the SNMP agent for sending traps and informs:

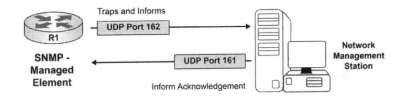

Figure 52.2—UDP Ports Used by the NMS and the SNMP-Managed Element

The three versions of SNMP are versions 1, 2, and 3. Version 1, or SNMPv1, is the initial implementation of the SNMP protocol. SNMPv1 operates over protocols such as User Datagram Protocol (UDP), Internet Protocol (IP), and the OSI Connectionless Network Service (CLNS). SNMPv1 is widely used and is the de facto network-management protocol used within the Internet community.

SNMPv2 revises SNMPv1 and includes improvements in the areas of performance, security, confidentiality, and manager-to-manager communications. SNMPv2 also defines two new operations: GetBulk and Inform. The GetBulk operation is used to retrieve large blocks of data efficiently. The Inform operation allows one NMS to send trap information to another NMS and then to receive a response. In SNMPv2, if the agent responding to GetBulk operations cannot provide values for all the variables in a list, then it provides partial results.

SNMPv3 provides the following three additional security services that are not available in previous versions of SNMP: message integrity, authentication, and encryption. SNMPv3 uses message integrity to ensure that a packet has not been tampered with in-transit. SNMPv3 also utilizes authentication, which is used to determine whether the message is from a valid source. Finally, SNMPv3 provides encryption, which is used to scramble the contents of a packet to prevent it from being seen by unauthorized sources.

In Cisco IOS software, the `snmp-server host [hostname | address]` command is used to specify the hostname or IP address of the NMS to which the local device will send traps or informs. To allow the NMS to poll the local device, SNMPv1 and SNMPv2c require that a community string be specified for either read-only or read-write access using the `snmp-server community <name> [ro | rw]` global configuration command.

SNMPv3 does not use the same community-based form of security but instead uses user and group security. The following configuration example illustrates how to configure the local device with two community strings, one for read-only access and the other for read-write access. In addition, the local device is also configured to send SNMP traps for Cisco IOS IP SLA operations and syslog to 1.1.1.1 using the read-only community string:

```
R2#config t
Enter configuration commands, one per line.  End with CNTL/Z.
R2(config)#snmp-server community unsafe RO
R2(config)#snmp-server community safe RW
R2(config)#snmp-server host 1.1.1.1 traps readonlypassword rtr syslog
```

Figure 52.3 below illustrates a sample report for device resource utilization and availability based on SNMP polling using ManageEngine OpManager network monitoring software:

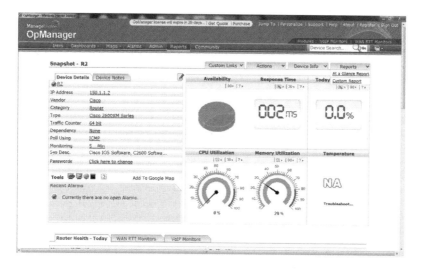

Figure 52.3—Sample SNMP Report on Device Resource Utilization

Please take today's exam at https://www.in60days.com/free/ccnain60days/

Switched Port Analyzer and AAA

DAY 53 TASKS

- Complete today's lesson
- Review yesterdays lesson and any subject and labs of your choice
- Read the ICND2 cram guide (and the ICND1 cram guide, if taking the CCNA exam)
- Spend 15 minutes on the subnetting.org website

SPAN is one of several products which allows you capture packets as they traverse the wire so they can be analyzed. This is most useful when you are troubleshooting complex or obscure problems. It has been in use for many years but only now has been added to the exam syllabus.

Authentication, authorization, and accounting, referred to as AAA (triple-A), provide the framework that controls and monitors network access. This has always been a feature of the CCNA exam syllabus however, it is now tested in more detail.

Today you will learn about the following:

- SPAN
- AAA

This lesson maps to the following ICND2 syllabus requirements:

- 5.3 Use local SPAN to troubleshoot and resolve problems
- 5.4 Describe device management using AAA with TACACS+ and RADIUS

MONITORING AND CAPTURING PACKETS USING SPAN

While there are many products available that can be used to view captured packets on the wire, the CCNA certification exam only asks for an understanding of how to redirect this captured information from Cisco switches to the appropriate application using the local Switched Port Analyzer (SPAN).

Cisco IOS software supports different packet capture mechanisms, depending on whether the device is a router or a switch. On Cisco IOS software-switching routers, such as the Cisco 1800, 2800, and 3800 Series Routers running IOS 12.4T or 15.X, the Route IP Traffic Export (RITE) tool allows network administrators to configure the router to export IP packets received on multiple simultaneous WAN or LAN interfaces to a single LAN or VLAN interface, to which a protocol analyzer or monitoring application is connected. The RITE feature can also allow you to configure the router to capture IP packets in a buffer within the router, and then to dump the packets into a specified memory device.

On Cisco IOS-distributed router platforms, such as the Cisco 7600 Series Routers, as well as on Cisco IOS Catalyst Switches, the SPAN feature is used to capture packets instead. There are three variations of SPAN, which include the local SPAN feature, Remote SPAN (RSPAN), and Encapsulated RSPAN (ERSPAN). Only local SPAN is mentioned in the exam syllabus.

The local SPAN feature, commonly referred to as SPAN, copies traffic from one or more CPUs, one or more ports, one or more EtherChannels, or one or more VLANs and sends the copied traffic to one or more destinations for analysis by a network analyzer, such as a Switch Probe device or other Remote Monitoring (RMON) probe. Traffic can also be sent to the processor for packet capture by the Mini Protocol Analyzer. A typical SPAN scenario is illustrated in Figure 53.1 below:

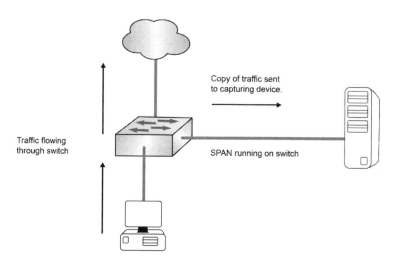

Figure 53.1—SPAN Operating on a Layer 2 Switch

While SPAN does not affect the switching of traffic on sources, it is important to remember that the SPAN-generated copies of traffic compete with user traffic for switch resources. Local SPAN sessions are comprised of an association of source ports and source VLANs with one or more destinations. Each local SPAN session can have either ports or VLANs as sources, but not both. Local SPAN sessions are configured on a single switch. When configuring SPAN, the following restrictions apply when specifying ports as the source:

- The port can be any port type, such as EtherChannel, FastEthernet, or GigabitEthernet.
- The same local port can be monitored in multiple SPAN sessions.
- The local SPAN source port cannot be configured as a destination port.
- Each source port can be configured with a direction (ingress, egress, or both) to monitor.
- Source ports can be in the same or different VLANs.

When configuring a VLAN as the SPAN source, the following restrictions apply:

- On a given port, only traffic on the monitored VLAN is sent to the destination port.
- All active ports in the source VLAN are included as source ports.
- Destination ports that belong to the source VLAN are excluded from the source list.
- Removed or added ports in a VLAN are removed or added to the session.
- You can monitor only Ethernet VLANs.
- You cannot use filtered VLANs in the same local SPAN session with VLAN sources.

Finally, the following restrictions apply to the SPAN destination ports:

- The destination port must reside on the same physical single switch as the source port.
- The destination port can be any Ethernet physical port.
- The destination port can participate in only one SPAN session at a time.
- The destination port cannot be a source port.
- The destination port cannot be an EtherChannel group.
- If the destination port resides in an EtherChannel group, it is removed from the group.
- The destination port will not transmit traffic unless learning is enabled.
- The destination port line protocol will show a state of up/down (monitoring) by design.
- If ingress forwarding is enabled, the destination port forwards traffic at Layer 2.
- A destination port does not participate in Spanning Tree while the SPAN session is active.
- When it is a destination port, it does not participate in any of the Layer 2 protocols.
- If the port belongs to a source VLAN, then it is excluded from the source and is not monitored.
- The port cannot be configured with port security.

In Cisco IOS Catalyst Switches, the local SPAN source is configured using the `monitor session <session_number> source [[single_interface | interface_list | interface_range | mixed_interface_list | single_vlan | vlan_list | vlan_range | mixed_vlan_list] [rx | tx | both]]` command in global configuration mode. Keep in mind that the options available will vary depending on the switch platform.

The local SPAN destination is configured using the `monitor session <session_number> destination [single_interface | interface_list | interface_range | mixed_interface_list]` command in global configuration mode.

The following configuration example illustrates how to configure local SPAN on the switch to copy inbound and outbound traffic on FastEthernet0/1 and send this traffic to interface FastEthernet0/2. It is assumed that a monitoring device is connected to the FastEthernet0/2 interface:

```
Sw1#configure terminal
Enter configuration commands, one per line.  End with CTRL/Z.
Sw1(config)#monitor session 1 source interface Fa0/1 both
Sw1(config)#monitor session 1 destination interface Fa0/2
Sw1(config)#end
```

Following this implementation, use the `show monitor session [<session | all] detail` command to verify the local SPAN configuration:

```
Sw1#show monitor session 1
Session 1
---------
Type              : Local Session
Source Ports      :
Both              : Fa0/1
Destination Ports : Fa0/2
     Encapsulation : Native
          Ingress : Disabled
```

The `detail` keyword can be appended to view detailed information as follows:

```
Sw1#show monitor session 1 detail
Session 1
---------
Type              : Local Session
Source Ports      :
     RX Only      : None
     TX Only      : None
     Both         : Fa0/1
Source VLANs      :
     RX Only      : None
     TX Only      : None
     Both         : None
Source RSPAN VLAN : None
Destination Ports : Fa0/2
     Encapsulation: Native
          Ingress: Disabled
Reflector Port    : None
Filter VLANs      : None
Dest RSPAN VLAN   : None
```

Unlike local SPAN, Remote SPAN (RSPAN) supports source ports and VLANs, as well as destinations on different switches, allowing you to perform remote monitoring of multiple switches across your network. RSPAN does this by using a Layer 2 VLAN to carry SPAN traffic between switches. RSPAN configuration is therefore comprised of an RSPAN source session, an RSPAN destination session, and an RSPAN VLAN. RSPAN source and destination sessions can also be configured on different switches.

AUTHENTICATION, AUTHORIZATION, AND ACCOUNTING

As identity security and access management become more complex, networks and network resources require safeguarding from unauthorized access. The AAA framework addresses this need.

AAA Overview

Authentication is used to validate identity (i.e., who the user is); authorization is used to determine what that particular user can do (i.e., the services available to the user); and accounting is used for audit trails (i.e., what that user did).

AAA provides a flexible, modular solution for controlling access to the network. It provides the primary framework through which access control is set up on a network device, such as a router, switch, or firewall. In such devices, AAA services can be used to control administrative access, such as via Telnet and Console login, which is referred to as character mode access. In addition, AAA can also be used to manage network access, such as via dial-up or Virtual Private Network (VPN) clients, which is referred to as packet mode access. The primary advantages of using AAA are as follows:

- Standard authentication methods
- Scalability
- Greater flexibility and control
- Multiple backup systems

AAA uses standard authentication methods, which include Remote Authentication Dial-In User Service (RADIUS), Terminal Access Controller Access Control System Plus (TACACS+), and Kerberos. TACACS+ and AAA authentication methods will be described in detail later in this chapter, while Kerberos isn't in the exam syllabus currently.

AAA scales to networks of all sizes. Multiple security servers can be implemented, allowing access control to be added easily. This allows AAA to scale from small networks with very few devices to very large networks that may contain hundreds of devices.

In addition to scalability, AAA provides great flexibility and control. For example, in small networks, AAA services can be administered by local databases that are stored on network devices instead of using a security server. Username and password credentials can be stored on the local database of the device and referenced by the AAA services. AAA services can also be configured for per-user, per-group, or per-service control.

AAA allows devices to point to multiple security servers, often referred to as server groups. User, device, and services information can be replicated between multiple servers, which provides redundancy in large networks.

The AAA Model

The AAA framework uses a set of three independent security functions in a modular format to offer secure access control. The AAA model is used to control access to network devices (authentication), enforce policies (authorization), and audit usage (accounting). AAA uses RADIUS, TACACS+, and Kerberos as authentication protocols to administer the AAA security functions. Using the AAA engine, network devices establish communication with the security server(s) using these protocols. The three independent security functions that offer secure access control and are provided by AAA are as follows:

- Authentication
- Authorization
- Accounting

Authentication

Authentication is used to validate user identity before allowing access to network resources. It occurs when a client passes the appropriate credentials to a security server for validation. This validation is based on verifying user credentials, which can be any of the following:

- Something the user knows, which is referred to as authentication by knowledge. This method verifies identity by something known only to the user, such as a username and password, for example.
- Something the user possesses, which is referred to as authentication by possession. This method verifies identity by something possessed only by the user. Examples of this type of authentication include ATM cards or tokens (such as RSA Secure ID tokens).
- Something the user is, which is referred to as user characteristics or biometrics. This is the strongest authentication method because it avoids the problems that are associated with other authentication methods, for example, the password being cracked or the ATM card being stolen. Examples of biometrics include fingerprints, face recognition, and DNA.

Once the security server has received the credentials, it will respond with a pass (accept) or fail (deny) message. Authentication also offers additional services, such as challenge and response, messaging support, and even encryption, depending on the security protocol implemented.

Authorization

Authorization provides the capability to enforce policies for network resources after the user has been successfully authenticated. In other words, authorization is used to determine the actions a user, group, system, or server is allowed to perform. Attribute-value (AV) pairs— which will be described in the next section—that define user rights are associated with the user to determine the specific rights of the user.

Clients query the AAA server to determine what actions a user is authorized to perform, and the server provides AV pairs that define user authorization. The client is then responsible for enforcing user access control based on those AV pairs.

Accounting

Accounting provides the means to capture resource utilization by collecting and sending information that can be used for billing, auditing, and reporting to the security server. This information can include user identities (who logged in), session start and stop times, the command(s) executed, and traffic information such as bytes or packets transmitted.

Accounting records are also made up of accounting AV pairs. Accounting methods must be defined through AAA. The client then sends the accounting records, with the relevant AV pairs, to the AAA server for storage.

Now that you are familiar with the three independent security functions within the AAA framework, it is important to understand what their correlation is, as follows:

1. **Authentication is valid without authorization**. This means that you can enable and authenticate users without enabling and authorizing those same users.
2. **Authentication is valid without accounting**. This means that you can enable and authenticate users without enabling accounting for the actions performed by those users.
3. **Authorization is not valid without authentication**. This means that you must authenticate users before you can authorize them. You cannot authorize anyone who has not been authenticated.
4. **Accounting is not valid without authentication**. This means that you must authenticate users before you enable accounting for them. You do not need to enable authorization because authentication is valid without authorization.

AAA Operation

In order for AAA to work, the Network Access Server (NAS), which is any device—such as a router, switch, or firewall—must be able to access security information for a specific user before providing AAA services. This information may be stored locally (i.e., on the NAS itself) or remotely (i.e., on a RADUIS, TACACS+, or Kerberos server).

Although both methods are valid, it is important to keep in mind that the local user database supports only a limited number of Cisco-specific security AVs, but server-based AAA provides more capabilities and security information is stored on the server, not the network device. An AV pair is simply a secured network object comprised of an attribute, such as a username or password, and a value for that particular attribute.

To reinforce the concept of AV pairs, Figure 53.2 illustrates their use in AAA services when the security information is stored locally on the NAS:

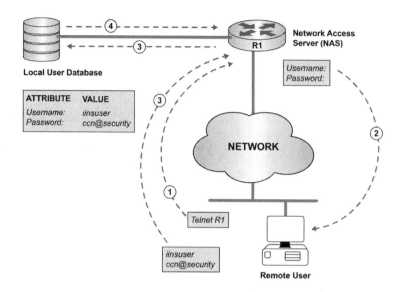

Figure 53.2—AV Pairs on the NAS

Based on Figure 53.2 above, in step 1, the remote user attempts to connect to R1 (NAS) via Telnet. Assuming that the NAS has been configured for AAA services, using its local database for authentication, the NAS presents the remote user with the username and password prompt as illustrated in step 2.

The remote user then enters his or her credentials, providing the username iinsuser (which is the attribute) and password ccn@security (which is the value for that attribute) as illustrated in step 3. The NAS then checks the information against its local database as shown in Table 53.1 below:

Table 53.1—NAS checks user credentials against its local database

Attribute	Value
Username	iinsuser
Password	ccn@security

Assuming that the NAS has been configured with the `username iinsuser secret ccn@ security` command in global configuration mode, each AV is on file and the AV pair is found. The request is accepted and a pass message is returned (as illustrated in step 4), which enables the connection from the remote user to be made. The same logic would apply if AAA services were authenticating against a remote server, such as TACACS+ or RADIUS, for example.

Taking this example a step further, this time depicting the use of an external AAA server, Figure 53.3 below illustrates the use of AV pairs for authorization:

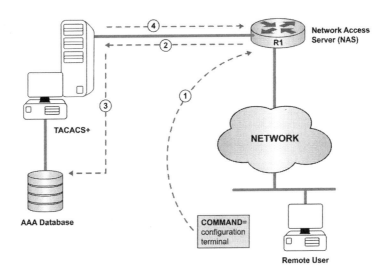

Figure 53.3—AV Pairs for Authorization

In Figure 53.3 above, assume that the remote user has been successfully authenticated. Once logged in to R1 (NAS), the remote user attempts to issue the `configure terminal` command as illustrated in step 1. The NAS has been configured to use AAA services for authorization, and so the request is sent to the TACACS+ server as illustrated in step 2. The TACACS+ server then checks the following information against its local database as shown in Table 53.2 below:

Table 53.2—TACACS+ server checks authorization information against its local database

Attribute	Value
command	configure terminal

In step 3, the server finds that the attribute and value are on file, and an AV pair is found. The request is accepted and the `configure terminal` command is successfully authorized on R1 as illustrated in step 4. The remote user successfully enters configuration mode. Again, the same concept would be applicable if authorization was being performed using the local database.

Unlike authentication and authorization, there is no search for AV pairs in any kind of database for accounting. Instead, information is simply received with AV pairs and is stored in the database. Accounting is illustrated in Figure 53.4 below:

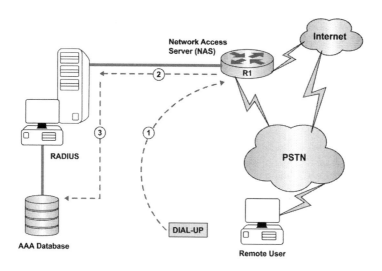

Figure 53.4—Accounting in Action

Based on Figure 54.4 above, in step 1, the remote user dials into the NAS for access to the network resources and services. Assume that R1 belongs to an ISP providing its customers with Internet service via dial-up modems. Also assume that the remote user has authenticated successfully and is authorized to use this service. The NAS has been configured for accounting so that the ISP can bill customers based on usage, etc. Based on this, in step 2, the NAS sends the following accounting AV pair information to the AAA server:

Table 53.3—Accounting AV pair information

Attribute	Value
start time	02:30:00
stop time	04:30:00
elapsed time	02:00:00
packets sent	1234567
packets received	9876543

The AAA server simply receives this information and performs no AV pair searches. Instead, the information is stored in the local database, as illustrated in step 3, where it can later be retrieved and the remote user billed for the amount of time spent on the ISP network. Now that you have an understanding of AAA and how it works, we will move along and learn about the two main security server protocols: RADIUS and TACACS+.

RADIUS

RADIUS is a client/server protocol that is used to secure networks against intruders. RADIUS was created by Livingston Enterprises but is now defined in RFC 2138 and RFC 2139. The

RADIUS protocol authentication and accounting services are documented separately in RFC 2865 and RFC 2866, respectively. These two RFCs replaced RFC 2138 and RFC 2139.

A RADIUS server is a device that has the RADIUS daemon or application installed. Unlike TACACS+, which will be described in detail in the following section, RADIUS is an open-standard protocol that is distributed in C source code format. This allows for interoperability and flexibility between RADIUS-based products from different vendors; however, as will be explained later in this chapter, this is also one of the main problems with using RADIUS.

RADIUS Authentication and Authorization

RADIUS uses UDP as the Transport Layer protocol for communication between the client and the server, using UDP port 1812 for authentication and authorization and UDP port 1813 for accounting. However, it should be noted that earlier deployments of RADIUS used UDP port 1645 for authentication and authorization and UDP port 1646 for accounting. Because RADIUS uses UDP as a transport protocol, there is no offer of guaranteed delivery of RADIUS packets. Therefore, any issues related to server availability, the retransmission of packets, and timeouts, for example, are handled by RADIUS-enabled devices.

RADIUS communication is triggered by a user login that consists of a query. Figure 53.5 below illustrates the sequence of messages that are exchanged:

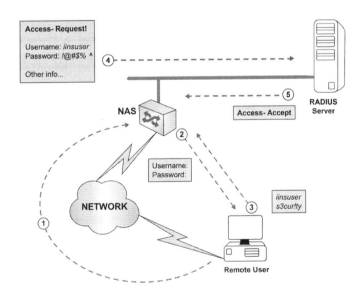

Figure 53.5—RADIUS Message Sequence

Following Figure 53.5 above, in step 1, the remote user dials into the NAS. The NAS proceeds to ask the remote user for a username and password as illustrated in step 2. The user then proceeds to input his or her assigned, valid credentials, which are the username iinsuser and the password s3cur!ty. This process is illustrated in step 3.

This received username and encrypted password, as well as the NAS IP address and NAS port information, is sent as an Access-Request packet from the NAS to the RADIUS server as illustrated in step 4. The Access-Request packet will also contain other information on the type of session that the user wants to initiate. For example, if the query is presented in character mode (e.g., Telnet), the packet will include Service-Type=Shell; however, if the packet is presented in PPP mode, for example, it will include Service-Type=Framed-User, as well as Framed-Type=PPP.

When the RADIUS server receives the Access-Request packet from the NAS, the first thing it will check is the shared secret key for the client that is sending the request. This step is performed to ensure that only authorized clients are able to communicate with the server. In the event that the shared secret key is not configured or is incorrect, the server will silently discard the Access-Request packet without sending back a response.

However, if the username is found in the database and the password is validated, the server will return an Access-Accept response back to the client as illustrated in step 5. The Access-Accept response carries a list of AV pairs that describe the parameters to be used for this session. In addition to the standard set of attributes, RADIUS also specifies the vendor-specific attribute (Attribute 26) that allows vendors to support their own extended attributes, which may be specifically tailored to their particular application and are not for general use.

TACACS+

Unlike RADIUS, which is an open-standard protocol, TACACS+ is a Cisco-proprietary protocol that is used in the AAA framework to provide centralized authentication of users who are attempting to gain access to network resources.

There are several notable differences between TACACS+ and RADIUS. One of the most notable differences is that TACACS+ uses TCP as a Transport Layer protocol, using TCP port 49. In addition, TACACS+ separates the three AAA architectures, unlike RADIUS, which groups authentication and authorization together and separates accounting. TACACS+ also encrypts the data between the user and the server, unlike RADUIS, which encrypts only the password. Finally, TACACS+ supports multiple protocols, such as IP, IPX, AppleTalk, and X.25, whereas RADIUS has limited protocol support.

TACACS+ Authentication

TACACS+ authentication is typically initiated when a user attempts an ASCII login by authenticating to a server running the TACACS+ daemon. The TACACS+ authentication phase uses three distinct packet types, as follows:

1. START packets, which are used initially when the user attempts to connect
2. REPLY or RESPONSE packets, which are sent by the AAA server during authentication
3. CONTINUE packets, which are used by AAA clients to return username and password information to the TACACS+ server

The TACACS+ authentication communication process is illustrated in Figure 53.6 below:

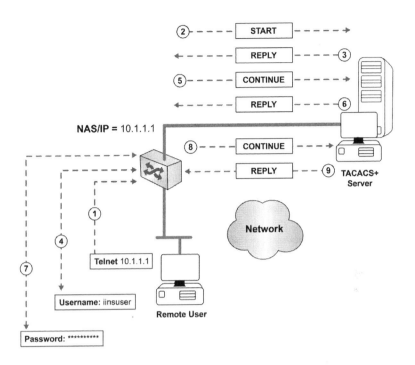

Figure 53.6—TACACS+ Authentication Process

In Figure 53.6 above, in step 1, the remote user initiates a connection to the NAS, which is configured for AAA services using TACACS+.

The NAS then contacts the TACACS+ server (START packet) to get a username prompt as illustrated in step 2. The TACACS+ server responds (REPLY packet) with the username prompt, illustrated in step 3, and this is then displayed to the user in step 4.

The user types in his or her username, also illustrated in step 4, and the NAS sends this information (CONTINUE packet) to the TACACS+ server as illustrated in step 5.

The TACACS+ server receives the username and checks its local or external database for the username. The name is found and the TACACS+ server sends a request for a password (REPLY packet) as illustrated in step 6. The NAS relays this information to the remote user, who inputs the password as illustrated in step 7.

The NAS relays the password (CONTINUE packet) to the TACACS+ server, in step 8, and the TACACS+ server checks its local and external database for the correct password. The TACACS+ server responds, as illustrated in step 9, with the result (REPLY packet), which could be any number of messages (this is outside the scope of the exam syllabus).

You would globally enable AAA services using the `aaa new-model` command in global configuration mode. Other configuration commands are outside the syllabus.

Now please take today's exam at **https://www.in60days.com/free/ccnain60days/**

Network Programmability

DAY 54 TASKS

- Read today's lesson
- Review yesterdays lesson
- Review any other theory and labs you wish
- Take today's exam
- Read the ICND2 cram guide (and the ICND1 cram guide, if taking the CCNA exam)
- Spend 15 minutes on the subnetting.org website

Today is a super easy day so make the best of it and include reviews of any weak areas.

Cisco and its many competitors are plowing time, money, and resources into a new networking paradigm commonly referred to as Software Defined Networking (SDN). As with most developments, it has been created to address a gap in the market. The primary goal of SDN is to move control of data flow on networks from hardware to software.

Today you will learn about the following:

- Software defined networking

This lesson maps to the following ICND2 syllabus requirements:

- 5.5 Describe network programmability in enterprise network architecture
- 5.5.a Function of a controller
- 5.5.b Separation of control plane and data plane
- 5.5.c Northbound and southbound APIs

SOFTWARE DEFINED NETWORKING

Traditional networks are non-homogeneous (i.e., not "composed of parts or elements that are all of the same kind"; dictionary.com). You have different network devices running various operating systems, each processing frames and packets in a way that matches that particular technology or protocol. Larger networks require specialist teams for security, collaboration, data, etc. Changes in the way data flows in the network would have to be carried out by the team that manages the devices on those devices.

SDN aims to disassociate the decisions about traffic flow from the systems that forward the network traffic. Network managers (using SDN) are now able to manage and control network behavior dynamically using open interfaces and application programming interfaces (APIs). In a nutshell, its aim is to move configuration and control of the network from hardware to software control.

The OpenFlow protocol was traditionally associated with SDN; however, vendors such as Cisco Systems have developed their own solutions (such as Evolved Programmable Network).

Planes of Operation

It's worth mentioning how planes of operation on Cisco devices are separated so you can separate the functions they perform. Generally, devices process traffic transiting through them and this process takes place on the data plane; this is also referred to as the forwarding plane, which switches traffic through the router. The devices can be managed remotely by network management software (via SNMP) in the management plane. Protocols at the management plane include Telnet, SSH, and FTP.

The control plane is considered to be the brains of the router. It handles routing protocols, routing tables, and neighbor device discovery. It also exchanges protocol information with other network devices and maintains sessions.

The planes of operation are illustrated in Figure 54.1 below:

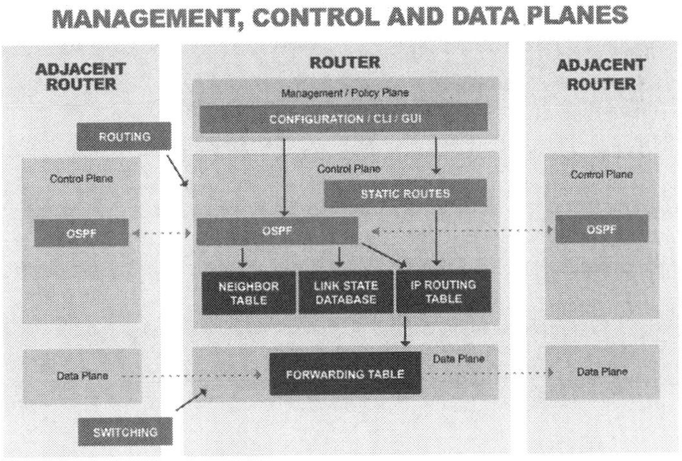

Figure 54.1—Device Planes of Operation

SDN Operation

The goal of SDN is to separate the control plane from the forwarding plane, enabling the control plane to become programmable and the infrastructure to be accessible by applications and network services. There are a number of competing architectures but they all aim to move control plane logic to computer-resources-managed network administrators. To this end, they all feature APIs and SDN controllers.

The controllers are now the brains of the network. They allow network administrators to decide how underlying devices, including routers and switches, forward packets. SDN controllers give a centralized picture of the network, giving the administrators the information they need.

Southbound APIs relay information to routers and switches. OpenFlow was the first to market and was the originator of the southbound API. Cisco offers the Application Centric Infrastructure (see Figure 54.2 below). Devices sit below the controller and the API allows data exchange. The southbound interface allows the controller and the network device to communicate. There are different types of controllers, each with different capabilities. Here are three you should be aware of:

- OpenFlow (from the ONF; https://www.opennetworking.org)
- OpFlex (from Cisco; used with ACI)
- CLI (Telnet/SSH) and SNMP (from Cisco; used with APIC-EM)

Northbound APIs are used by SDN to communicate with applications and business logic. The northbound interface opens the controller, allowing data and functions access by programs.

The entire process is illustrated in Figure 54.2 below:

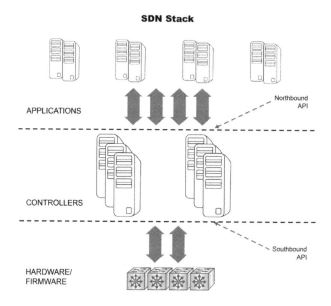

Figure 54.2—APIs as Used by SDN

The CCNA Cloud certification covers SDN concepts if you want to go into more detail.

Now please take today's exam at https://www.in60days.com/free/ccnain60days/

Review

DAY 55 TASKS

- Review yesterdays lesson
- Review days 35-37 and redo the labs
- Take today's exam at **https://www.in60days.com/free/ccnain60days/**
- Write out the ICND2 cram guide (and the ICND1 cram guide, if taking the CCNA exam) from memory
- Spend 15 minutes on the subnetting.org website

We have a full five days to review several important subjects. We'll be giving the highest priority to the topics most likely to crop up in the exam in the form of labs and questions so EIGRP and OSPF will be high on the list and cloud computing lower because you are likely to see one or no questions on this subject.

Challenge 1—3 Router OSPF Lab

Topology

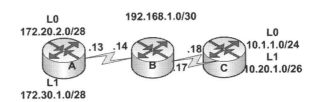

Instructions

Connect three routers together with a serial or crossover cable.

1. Add IP addresses to routers and loopback on Router A B and C according to diagram
2. Ping between Router A and B and B to C to test serial line (remember clock rates)
3. Now set the serial lines to use PPP with CHAP (set usernames and passwords also)
4. Configure OSPF on all routers. Put one loopback either end in a non-zero area
5. Check the routing tables and make sure you include both the 192.168.1.x networks
6. Ensure you can ping all networks from either end

Now redo the lab creating your own IPv6 subnets.

Challenge 2—IPv6 Named ACL Lab

Topology

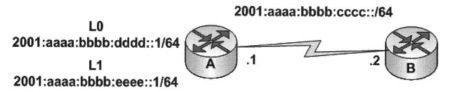

Instructions

Connect two routers together with a serial or crossover cable.

1. Add IP addresses to routers and loopback on Router A according to diagram.
2. Add an IPv6 static route on Router B to send all traffic back to Router A.
3. Ping between Router A and B to test the serial line (remember clock rates).
4. Create a local username and password for the routers.
5. Permit connections to the telnet (vty) lines on the Router A and login local.
6. Create an IPv6 ACL on Router A it should block all telnet traffic from Router B (network or serial IP address) unless it is destined for 2001:aaaa:bbbb:eeee::1/64
7. Apply the ACL to the serial interface on RouterA.
8. Test by telnetting to the serial and other loopback addresses.
9. Issue a show `ip ipv6 access-list`.

Challenge 3—EIGRPv6 Lab

Topology

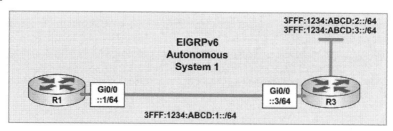

Instructions

Connect two routers together with a serial or crossover cable.

1. Add IP addresses to routers and loopbacks on Router 3 according to diagram
2. Ensure you can ping across from R1 to R3
3. Configure EIGRPv6 as per the diagram with two loopbacks on R3 in area 1.
4. Check the routing table on R1 for the EIGRP routes
5. Configure PPP encapsulation between R1 and R3 and add CHAP (with usernames and passwords)

Review

DAY 56 TASKS

- Complete the challenge labs below
- Review the days 39-40
- Take today's exam at **https://www.in60days.com/free/ccnain60days/**
- Write out the ICND2 cram guide (and the ICND1 cram guide, if taking the CCNA exam) from memory
- Spend 15 minutes on the subnetting.org website

Challenge 1—STP Root Lab

Topology

Instructions

Connect two switches together with a crossover cable (or use Packet Tracer)

1. Create a trunk link between the switches
2. Create VLANs 10 and 20 on both switches
3. Ensure Switch A is the STP root for VLAN 10. Do not use the `priority` command
4. Ensure Switch B is the STP root for VLAN 20. Do not use the `root primary` command

Challenge 2—OSPFv3

Topology

2001:aaaa:bbbb:cccc::/64

.1   .2   **2001:aaaa:bbbb:dddd::1/64**

Instructions

Connect two routers together with a serial or crossover cable.

1. Add IPv6 addresses to routers and loopback on Router B according to diagram.
2. Set enable secret password cisco on Router A and enable password on Router B.
3. Ping between Router A and B to test serial line (remember clock rates).
4. Configure OSPFv3 on both Routers.
5. Check the IPv6 routing table on Router A and ensure the network on Loopback 0 of Router B can be seen.
6. Check which link-local address Router A is receiving the route from.

Challenge 3—InterVLAN SVI Lab

Topology

Instructions

Connect to the switch using a console connection. Connect two PCs to the switch Ethernet interface. Set VLAN2 as 172.16.0.0/16 and VLAN3 as 192.168.1.0/24. You will need a layer 3 switch so use PT if you don't have one to hand.

1. Configure two VLANs on the switch and put each PC in one of the VLANs. Set default gateways as necessary.
2. Add correct IP addresses and gateways to the PCs.
3. Set two SVIs on the switch, one per VLAN and match the subnet to the correct PC.
4. Enable ip routing on the switch.
5. Ping one PC to the other.

Review

DAY 57 TASKS

- Complete the challenge labs below
- Review days 42-44 and redo all labs for these days
- Take today's exam at **https://www.in60days.com/free/ccnain60days/**
- Write out the ICND2 cram guide (and the ICND1 cram guide, if taking the CCNA exam) from memory
- Spend 15 minutes on the subnetting.org website

Challenge 1—OSPFv3 Lab

Topology

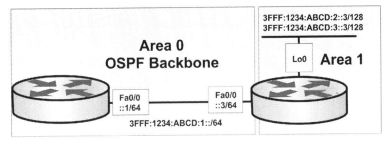

Instructions

Connect two routers together with a serial or crossover cable.

1. Add IP addresses to routers and loopbacks on Router 3 according to diagram
2. Ensure you can ping across from R1 to R3
3. Configure OSPFv3 as per the diagram with two loopbacks on R3 in area 1.
4. Check the routing table on R1 for the OSPF routes

Challenge 2—STP and OSPF

Topology

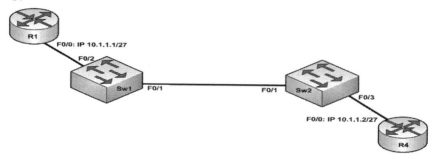

Instructions

Connect two switches together with a crossover cable (or use Packet Tracer)

1. Configure Sw1 and Sw2 to support extended range VLANs. Both switches should be in the VTP domain CISCO with a VTP password of HOWTONETWORK. In addition to that, both switches should only send VTP version 2 updates
2. Configure the following VLANs on Sw1 and Sw2 VLAN4010, 4020, 4030, 4040
3. Assign port Fa0/2 on Sw1 and Fa0/3 on Sw2 to VLAN 4040. These ports should be configured to transition immediately to a Spanning Tree forwarding state. Ports Fa0/1 on Sw1 and Sw2 should be configured a trunk link; however, this trunk link must only allow the VLANs configured on the switches.
4. Configure IP addresses as specified in the topology on routers R1 and R4. Verify these routers can ping each other.
5. Configure Sw1 to be the Root Bridge for VLANs 4010 and 4030 with a priority of 4096. Configure Sw2 to be the root bridge for VLANs 4020 and 4040 using the built-in Cisco macro. Verify the Root Bridge states using the correct Spanning Tree commands.
6. Configure OSPF Area 0 between R1 and R4 on the 10.1.1.0/27 subnet. Ensure that an OSPF adjacency forms and a DR and BDR is elected on the subnet. Verify your configuration with the appropriate OSPF commands.

Review

DAY 58 TASKS

- Complete the challenge labs below
- Review days 46-48 and redo all labs for these days
- Take today's exam at **https://www.in60days.com/free/ccnain60days/**
- Write out the ICND2 cram guide (and the ICND1 cram guide, if taking the CCNA exam) from memory
- Spend 15 minutes on the subnetting.org website

Challenge 1—OSPF Multi Area Lab

Topology

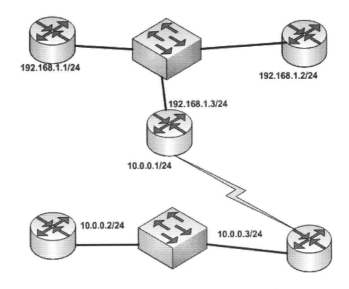

Instructions

Connect the routers and switches together as above

1. Configure the IP addresses on all the routers and test pings between routes on the same subnets
2. Configure OSPF on all routers and put them all into area 0
3. Add loopback addresses to routers in the 192 network to force a router of your choice to become DR for the segment
4. Add an OSPF priority to a router in the 10 segment to force it to become DR
5. Use show commands to check your configurations worked

Challenge 2—OSPFv3 Lab

Topology

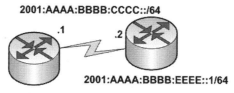

2001:AAAA:BBBB:CCCC::/64

.1   .2

2001:AAAA:BBBB:EEEE::1/64

2001:AAAA:BBBB:DDDD::1/64

Instructions

Connect two routers together with serial or ethernet connections

1. Configure the IPv6 addresses above and loopback addresses.
2. Configure OSPFv3 on the two routers and check the routing tables.

Challenge 3—IPv6 ACL

Topology

Instructions

Connect to a router with a console cable and Ethernet cable.

1. Configure an IPv6 address on the PC and the router in the same subnet.
2. Add a telnet username and password to the router and test by telnetting in.
3. Create an ACL to block the IPv6 host address.
4. Test telnet again.

Review

DAY 59 TASKS

- Complete the challenge labs below
- Review days 50-54 and redo all IPv6 ACL labs
- Take today's exam at **https://www.in60days.com/free/ccnain60days/**
- Write out the ICND2 cram guide (and the ICND1 cram guide, if taking the CCNA exam) from memory
- Spend 15 minutes on the subnetting.org website

Challenge 1—InterVLAN Routing SVI

Topology

Instructions

Connect to the switch using a console connection. Connect two PCs to the switch Ethernet interface. Set VLAN2 as 172.16.0.0/16 and VLAN3 as 192.168.1.0/24.

1. Configure two VLANs on the switch and put each PC in one of the VLANs. Set default gateways as necessary.
2. Add correct IP addresses and gateways to the PCs.
3. Set two SVIs on the switch, one per VLAN and match the subnet to the correct PC.
4. Enable ip routing on the switch.
5. Ping one PC to the other.

DAY 60

Review

DAY 60 TASKS

Exam day for you (or tomorrow).

Nothing else I can teach you or recommend. You know your weak areas, so good luck.

When you pass the exam, please drop me a line at howtonetwork@gmail.com, along with a photo of you holding your CCNA certificate.

Bonus Labs

In order to save space I've moved all the bonus challenge labs to
https://www.in60days.com/free/ccnain60days/

Made in the USA
Columbia, SC
08 July 2018